Lonely Planet Publications
Melbourne | Oakland | London | Paris

D1466644

Steve Fallon

Paris

The Top Five

1 Notre Dame
Rose windows, medieval statuary, and gargoyles (p91)

2 Champs-Élysées
Bustling and best seen from the top of the Arc de Triomphe (p117)

3 Eiffel Tower
More Parisian than Paris itself (p114)

4 The Louvre
The world's richest art depository (p80)

5 Montmartre
Paris of story, song and myth (p126)

Contents

Introducing Paris	5
City Life	7
Arts	21
Architecture	33
Food & Drink	43
History	59
Quarters & Arrondissements	73
Walking Tours	137
Eating	149
Entertainment	205
Sports, Health & Fitness	243
Shopping	251
Fashion	269
Sleeping	279
Excursions	305
Directory	331
Language	355
Index	369
Map Section	379

Published by Lonely Planet Publications Pty Ltd
ABN 36 005 607 983

Australia Head Office, Locked Bag 1, Footscray,
Victoria 3011, ☎ 03 8379 8000, fax 03 8379 8111,
talk2us@lonelyplanet.com.au

USA 150 Linden St, Oakland, CA 94607,
☎ 510 893 8555, toll free 800 275 8555,
fax 510 893 8572, info@lonelyplanet.com

UK 72–82 Rosebery Ave, Clerkenwell, London, EC1R 4RW,
☎ 020 7841 9000, fax 020 7841 9001, go@lonelyplanet.
co.uk

France 1 rue du Dahomey, 75011 Paris,
☎ 01 55 25 33 00, fax 01 55 25 33 01,
bip@lonelyplanet.fr, www.lonelyplanet.fr

The Author

STEVE FALLON

Born in Boston, Massachusetts, Steve can't remember a time when he was not obsessed with travel, other cultures and languages. As a teenager he worked an assortment of jobs to finance trips to Europe and South America, and graduated from Georgetown University with a Bachelor of Science in modern languages, completing a year-long degree course at the Sorbonne as part of the course. The following year he taught English at the University of Silesia near Katowice, Poland. After he had worked for several years for one of the Gannett newspapers and obtained a master's degree in journalism, his fascination with the 'new' Asia took him to Hong Kong, where he lived and worked for 13 years for a variety of publications and was editor of *Business Traveller* magazine. In 1987 he put journalism on hold when he opened Wanderlust Books, Asia's only travel bookshop.

Steve lived in Budapest for 2½ years before moving to London in 1994, from where he travels to Paris as often as he can. He has contributed to or written more than two dozen Lonely Planet titles, including *France* and *World Food: France*.

PHOTOGRAPHER

JONATHAN SMITH

Raised in the Scottish Highlands, Jonathan Smith graduated from St Andrews University in 1994 with a Master of Arts in German. Unsure of what to do with his life, he took a flight to Vilnius and spent the next four years travelling around the former USSR. Having tried everything from language teaching to translating Lithuanian cookery books into English, Jon resolved to seek his fortune as a freelance travel photographer. A fan of candid photography, Jon was in his element exploring Parisian café society, in the footsteps of his photographic idol Henri Cartier-Bresson. The assignment also allowed him to indulge his penchant for freshly baked *pain au chocolat*.

Jon's byline has appeared in over 50 Lonely Planet titles, notably *Edinburgh*, *Stockholm*, *Moscow* and *St Petersburg*.

Introducing Paris

Coiffed, buffed and looking like €1 million, Paris is at once a beautiful woman and a sexy guy. Well informed, eloquent and oh-so-romantic, the City of Light is a philosopher, a poet, a crooner to bring you to your knees. Sitting before a stylish table laid with unimagined treats, Paris is a *bon vivant*, a banquet, a wine of impeccable vintage. Paris is all these and more because Paris always has been and always will be a million different things to a million different people.

It is not hyperbole to say that Paris is the most beautiful, the most romantic city in the world. A lot of people who have come before you have not hesitated to say so, in prose or poetry or song. Indeed, Paris has just about exhausted the superlatives that can be reasonably applied to any city. Notre Dame, the Eiffel Tower, the av des Champs-Élysées – at sunrise, at sunset, at night, in the sun, in the rain – have all been painted, sung about and described, as have the Seine and the subtle (and not-so-subtle) differences between the Left and Right Banks. What artists, singers and writers have rarely been able to capture, though, is the sheer magic of strolling along the city's broad avenues, which lead from impressive public buildings and museums to parks, gardens and esplanades.

Paris probably has more landmarks familiar to people who've never visited the place than any other city in the world. So first-time visitors often arrive in the French capital with all sorts of expectations: grand vistas, of intellectuals discussing weighty matters in cafés, romance along the Seine, sexy cabaret revues, rude people who don't (or won't) speak English. You'll find all those things, no doubt. But another approach is to set aside your preconceptions of Paris and explore the city's avenues and backstreets as if the tip of the Eiffel Tower and the spire of Notre Dame weren't about to pop into view at any moment.

Paris is no longer the living museum or Gallic theme park it may have seemed a generation ago. Today it's a welcoming, fun and cosmopolitan city to visit. By all means do the sights and visit the museums – they're part of the Paris package. But then jump on the metro or a bus and get off at a place you've never heard of, wander through a neighbourhood where French mixes easily with Arabic, Bengali or Vietnamese, poke your head into little shops, invite yourself to play *basket* (basketball) in a park or just lounge on a café terrace with a glass of wine and watch Paris pass by.

Parisians believe they have savoir-faire and, indeed, you'll find Paris a feast for the senses. It's a city to look at, with wide boulevards, monuments, works of art and magical lights. It's a city to taste: cheese, chocolate, wine, *charcuterie* (cold meats), bread. It's a city to hear, whether you like opera, jazz or world music, or you just like the sound of metro cars whooshing by on their rubber wheels. It's a city to smell: perfume boutiques, cafés with fresh coffee and croissants, chestnuts roasting on charcoal in winter. It's a city to feel: the wind in your face as you cycle along the Seine, the *frisson* of fear and pleasure as you peer out from the top of the Eiffel Tower or the Grande Arche de la Défense. Above all, it's a city to discover. Read *Paris* – it's designed to whet your appetite and to guide you when you arrive. But remember: it's a guidebook not a handbook. Leave it in your hotel from time to time, and find your own Paris.

You will soon discover that Paris is enchanting almost everywhere, at any time, even 'in the summer, when it sizzles' and 'in the winter, when it drizzles' as Cole Porter put it in 'I Love Paris'. And, like a good meal, it excites, it satisfies, the memory lingers. In *A Moveable Feast*, a book of recollections of Paris in the 1920s, the American novelist Ernest Hemingway wrote: 'If you are lucky enough to have lived in Paris as a young man, then wherever you go for the rest of your life, it stays with you, for Paris is a moveable feast.' Those of us who took Hemingway's advice in our salad days could not agree more. We're still dining out on the memories. And so will you.

STEVE'S TOP PARIS DAY

After a tiptop Paris night, a tiptoe Paris day might be more in order, but let's (unreasonably) assume that I wake up bright-eyed and bushy-tailed in my friend's *belle époque* apartment near Place de la République on a Sunday morning. To market, to market – in this case my favourite Marché Bastille to stock up on anchovy fillets, *trompettes de la mort* (a type of mushroom) and other essentials. After, I'll wend my way through medieval Marais, stopping for a *grand crème* (coffee with cream) and a *pain au chocolat* (chocolate brioche) at Ma Bourgogne in the scrumptious place des Vosges. The landmark bridge Pont de Sully leads to my favourite island, Île St-Louis, but once I reach the Île de la Cité, I'll eschew Notre Dame in favour of the smaller, more delicate Ste-Chapelle. Before lunch (somewhere on the rue Montorgueil) I'll window-shop at the boutiques of rue Étienne Marcel or have another look at the antique clothes for sale in the Galerie de Montpensier (it's Sunday!). Though close, the Louvre is just too daunting for a postprandial visit; instead I'll rent a bike from Fat Tire Bike Tours and play chicken with the traffic in the middle of place de l'Étoile, where motorists *entering* the roundabout have right of way. If I feel culturally peckish, I'll make my way to the Musée Auguste Rodin and have a kip under *The Kiss*. As far as I'm concerned, any corner café works for an *apéro* (sundowner), but since I'm having dinner at Juan et Juanita in Ménilmontant, I head for L'Autre Café. They've just got to have a bottle of Pastis 51 with my name on it.

Essential Paris

Centre Pompidou (p83)

Cimetière du Père Lachaise (p123)

Marais (p86)

Musée National du Moyen Age (p94)

Parc de la Villette (p128)

City Life

Paris Today	8
City Calendar	**9**
January & February	9
March & April	10
April & May	10
June & July	10
September	11
October	11
December	11
Culture	**11**
Identity	11
Lifestyle	13
Sport	16
Media	16
Language	17
Economy & Costs	**18**
Government & Politics	**18**
National Government	18
Local Government	19
Environment	**19**
The Land	19
Green Paris	19
Urban Planning & Development	20

City Life

PARIS TODAY

The architecture both old and new, the spruce parks and squares, the timeless Seine, the café life and Parisians' *joie de vivre* – not to mention their dress sense – all combine to make Paris a monumental, handsome and endlessly fascinating place in which to live and to visit. A centre of culture, art and gastronomy it may be, but – like all large cities – Paris is not without its share of problems, some of them uniquely French or even Parisian. Take industrial actions, for example. Is this the Britain of the 1970s? Just a few months in 2003 saw Régie Autonome des Transports Parisians (RATP) public transport workers, teachers, doctors, hospital employees and people involved in the arts all walk off their jobs.

And then there was the strange fall and then rise of the chief resident of the Palais de l'Élysée and the trickle-down effect it had on the City of Light. Early in 2003 President Jacques Chirac vetoed, to widespread praise at home, France's involvement in a US-led UN resolution authorising military action against Iraq. This was the same man who had been overwhelmingly (but grudgingly) returned to office in May 2002 when political parties united to exclude right-wing Front National Jean-Marie Le Pen. The rallying cry at the time was 'Vote for the crook, not the fascists'. In a *tour de force* worthy of the theatre, Chirac went from being a tried and convicted crook in many people's minds to a national saviour who had raised France's stature at home and abroad. Problem was, the Americans (who make up 20% of tourist numbers in Paris) didn't see it that way and stayed away in droves. In fact, 30% fewer visited the city throughout the year.

Paris is divided over a number of issues that are also confronting the nation. Interior Minister Nicolas Sarkozy's get-tough approach to crime and his increase in the budget by almost €10 billion to fight even the minor stuff like loitering and prostitution has been welcomed by some and denounced by others, who see immigrants and the poor as the most likely targets. In arguably the most controversial and divisive issue the city and the nation have faced in decades, legislators voted 494 to 36 in February 2004 to ban Muslim

People eating outdoors, Rue Mouffetard (p168)

Hot Conversation Topics

- Food – Good food, bad food, fast food, *les bonnes addresses* (good restaurants)
- Interior Minister Sarkozy – Too far or not far enough?
- Muslim headscarves – Is wearing one really 'an act of intimidation, provocation, proselytising or propaganda'?
- Property prices – How high is the sky and is Ménilmontant the next Marais?
- US, Iraq & the war – Pro, con, anti-American, anti-anti-American
- Sex – This is Paris, after all

headscarves and other religious apparel (including Jewish skullcaps and large Christian crosses) in public schools despite protests that the measure infringes on religious freedom.

And then there are the ongoing Paris problems of litter – notably cigarette butts and dog droppings (see p20) – and the in-your-face billboards in the metro and elsewhere, featuring half-naked women being used to sell cars and watches, that are routinely defaced by *les antipublicistes* (those against advertising). Heroes to some, vandals to others, along with food, wine and women (or men), they'll keep Paris talking. And talking. And talking.

CITY CALENDAR

As the old song says, Paris is lovely in springtime – though winter-like relapses and heavy rains are not uncommon in the otherwise beautiful month of April. The best months are probably May and June – but early, before the hordes descend. Autumn is also pleasant – some people say the best times to come here are in September and October – but of course the days are getting shorter. In winter Paris has all sorts of cultural events going on, while in summer the weather is warm – sometimes sizzling; in August 2003 temperatures exceeded 35°C for more than a week and hundreds of people died from complications resulting from the heat. In any case, in August Parisians flee for the beaches to the west and south and many restaurateurs and café owners lock up and leave town too. It's true that you will find considerably more places open in August than even a decade ago but it still can feel like a ghost town in certain districts.

Innumerable cultural and sporting events take place in Paris throughout the year; weekly details appear in *Pariscope* and *L'Officiel des Spectacles* (see p206). You can also find them listed month by month under the heading '*Évènements*' (Events) on the tourist office's website (www.paris-touristoffice.com).

The following abbreviated list gives you a taste of what to expect through the year. To ensure that your trip does not coincide with a public holiday, when *everything* will be shut, see p343. See also p19 for an explanation of the city's addresses and arrondissements.

JANUARY & FEBRUARY

LA GRANDE PARADE DE PARIS
www.parisparade.com
The city's New Year's Day parade originated in Montmartre but may take place in different venues (eg along the Grands Boulevards) depending on the year. Check the website for details.

LOUIS XVI COMMEMORATIVE MASS
☎ 01 44 32 18 00
On the Sunday closest to 21 January, royalists and right-wingers attend a mass at the Chapelle Expiatoire (square Louis XVI, 8e; metro St-Augustin) marking the execution of King Louis XVI in 1793.

CHINESE NEW YEAR
www.paris.fr
Dragon parades and other festivities are held late January/early February in Chinatown, the 13e area between av d'Ivry and av de Choisy (metro Porte de Choisy or Tolbiac), with an abridged version along rue Au Maire, 3e.

SALON INTERNATIONAL DE L'AGRICULTURE
www.salon-agriculture.com
A 10-day international agricultural fair with lots to eat and drink, including dishes and wine from all over France, is held at the Parc des Expositions at Porte de Versailles in the 15e (metro Porte de Versailles) from late February to early March.

MARCH & APRIL
JUMPING INTERNATIONAL DE PARIS
www.bercy.fr in French
Annual showjumping tournament featuring the world's most celebrated jumpers at the Palais Omnisports de Paris-Bercy in the 12e (metro Bercy) in early March.

BANLIEUES BLEUES
www.banlieuesbleues.org
'Suburban Blues' jazz and blues festival (with world, soul, funk, and rhythm and blues thrown in for good measure) are held in March and April in St-Denis and heaps of other Paris suburbs, attracting big-name talent.

FESTIVAL DU FILM DE PARIS
www.festivaldufilmdeparis.com in French
More than 80 international films, some previewing, are screened over 10 days from late March to early April at the Cinéma Gaumont Marignan (Map pp383-5; ☎ 01 42 89 12 74; 27 av des Champs-Élysées, 8e; metro Franklin D Roosevelt).

APRIL & MAY
MARATHON INTERNATIONAL DE PARIS
www.parismarathon.com
The Paris International Marathon, held in early April, starts on place de la Concorde, 1er, and finishes on av Foch, in the 16e. The **Semi-Marathon de Paris** is a half-marathon held in March (see the above website for details).

FOIRE DU TRÔNE
www.foiredutrone.com in French
This is a huge funfair (350 attractions) held on the pelouse de Reuilly of the Bois de Vincennes (metro Porte Dorée) for eight weeks during April and May.

FOIRE DE PARIS
www.comexpo-paris.com
This huge modern-living fair, including crafts, gadgets of all types, and food and wine, is held in early May at the Parc des Expositions at Porte de Versailles in the 15e (metro Porte de Versailles).

ATELIERS D'ARTISTES DE BELLEVILLE-LES PORTES OUVERTES
www.ateliers-artistes-belleville.org in French
Some 200 painters, sculptors and other artists in Belleville (metro Belleville) in the 10e open their studio doors to some 50,000 visitors over four days in mid-May.

INTERNATIONAUX DE FRANCE DE TENNIS
www.frenchopen.org
The glitzy French Open tennis tournament takes place from late May to early June at Stade Roland Garros (metro Porte d'Auteuil) at the southern edge of the Bois de Boulogne in the 16e.

JUNE & JULY
FÊTE DE LA MUSIQUE
www.fetedelamusique.culture.fr
A national music festival welcoming in summer that caters to a great diversity of tastes (jazz, reggae, classical etc) and features staged and impromptu live performances all over the city. Held on 21 June.

GAY PRIDE MARCH
www.gaypride.fr in French
This colourful, Saturday afternoon parade through the Marais to Bastille celebrates Gay Pride Day, with various bars and clubs sponsoring floats, and participants in some pretty outrageous costumes. Held in late June.

PARIS JAZZ FESTIVAL
www.parcfloraldeparis.com
Free jazz concerts every Saturday and Sunday afternoon in June and July in the Parc Floral (metro Château de Vincennes).

LA COURSE DES GARÇONS ET SERVEUSES DE CAFÉ
☎ 01 42 96 60 75
A Sunday afternoon 8km foot race starting and finishing at the Hôtel de Ville (metro Hôtel de Ville) in the 4e, with some 500 waiters and waitresses balancing a glass and a bottle on a small tray. Spilling or breaking anything results in disqualification. Held in mid-June/early July.

LA GOUTTE D'OR EN FÊTE
www.gouttedorenfete.org
World-music festival (raï, reggae, rap and so on) at square Léon, 18e (metro Barbès Rochechouart or Château Rouge). Held in late June/early July.

Top Five Unusual Events

- **Fête des Vendanges à Montmartre** Lots of noise for a bunch of sour grapes
- **Gay Pride March** Feathers and beads and participants in and out of same
- **La Course des Garçons et Serveuses de Café** The fastest service you'll ever see in or out of Paris
- **Louis XVI Commemorative Mass** Sob-fest for aristocrats, pretenders and hangers-on
- **Paris Plage** The next best thing to the seaside along France's smallest beach

BASTILLE DAY (14 JULY)

Paris is *the* place to be on France's national day. Late on the night of the 13th, *bals des sapeurs-pompiers* (dances sponsored by Paris' fire-fighters, who are considered sex symbols in France) are held at fire stations around the city. At 10am on the 14th there's a military and fire-brigade parade along av des Champs-Élysées, accompanied by a fly-past of fighter aircraft and helicopters. In the evening, a huge display of *feux d'artifice* (fireworks) is held at around 11pm on the Champ de Mars, 7e.

TOUR DE FRANCE

www.letour.fr

The last stage of this prestigious cycling event finishes with a race up av des Champs-Élysées on the 3rd or 4th Sunday of July.

PARIS PLAGE

www.paris.fr

'Paris Beach', one of the most unique and successful city recreational events in the world, sees 3km of embankment from the quai Henri IV (metro Sully Morland) in the 4e to the quai des Tuileries (metro Tuileries) in the 1er transformed from mid-July to mid-August into three sand and pebble beaches with sun beds, umbrellas, atomisers and plastic palm trees.

SEPTEMBER

JAZZ À LA VILLETTE

www.cite-musique.fr

Super 10-day jazz festival with sessions in Parc de la Villette, at the Cité de la Musique and in surrounding bars in early September.

FESTIVAL D'AUTOMNE

www.festival-automne.com in French

'Autumn Festival' of arts has painting, music, dance and theatre at venues throughout the city from mid-September to December.

OCTOBER

FÊTE DES VENDANGES À MONTMARTRE

☎ 01 46 06 00 32

Harvesting of grapes in early October from Le Clos du Montmartre (cnr rue St-Vincent & rue des Saules, 18e), a small vineyard in Montmartre, with costumes, speeches and a parade.

FOIRE INTERNATIONALE D'ART CONTEMPORAIN

www.fiac-online.com in French

Huge contemporary art fair held in late October with some 160 galleries represented held at the Parc des Expositions at Porte de Versailles in the 15e (metro Porte de Versailles).

DECEMBER

CHRISTMAS EVE MASS

Celebrated at midnight on Christmas Eve at many Paris churches, including Notre Dame, but get there by 11pm to find a place.

NEW YEAR'S EVE

Blvd St-Michel (5e), place de la Bastille (11e), the Eiffel Tower (7e) and especially av des Champs-Élysées (8e) are the places to be.

CULTURE

IDENTITY

The population of central Paris is 2.15 million, while the greater metropolitan area – in effect, the Île de France – has 10.95 million inhabitants, or just over 18.5% of France's total population. The largest arrondissement (district), the 15e, is the most populous, with 225,360 people while the 1er, the third-smallest district, is the least populous, with just 16,800 people. Large working-class arrondissements such as the 11e and the 20e are growing rapidly.

France has had waves of immigration, particularly from its former colonies (see p146) for centuries. The number of official immigrants in central Paris is just under 375,000 or

Places of Worship

The following places offer services in English. For a more comprehensive list of churches and other places of worship, check the **Pages Jaunes** (yellow pages; www.pagesjaunes.fr).

Adath Shalom Synagogue (Map pp389-91; ☎ 01 45 67 97 96; www.adathshalom.org; 8 rue George Bernard Shaw, 15e; metro Dupleix) Conservative Jewish.

American Cathedral in Paris (Map pp383-5; ☎ 01 53 23 84 00; www.us.net/amcathedral -paris; 23 av George V, 8e; metro George V) Anglican/Episcopal.

American Church in Paris (Map pp389-91; ☎ 01 40 62 05 00; www.acparis.org; 65 quai d'Orsay, 7e; metro Pont de l'Alma or Invalides) Nondenominational Protestant.

Mosquée de Paris (Map pp392-5; ☎ 01 45 35 97 33; www.mosquee-de-paris.org in French; 39 rue Geoffroy St-Hilaire, 5e; metro Censier Daubenton or Place Monge) Muslim; see p97.

St Joseph's Catholic Church (Map pp383-5; ☎ 01 42 27 28 56; www.stjoeparis.org; 50 av Hoche, 8e; metro Charles de Gaulle-Étoile) Roman Catholic.

Sri Manikar Vinayakar Alayam Temple (Map pp386-8; ☎ 01 40 34 21 89; 72 rue Philippe de Girard, 18e; metro La Chapelle or Marx Dormoy) Hindu.

17% of the city's population; the figure would be much higher if the number of those living clandestinely was known.

Some of the 375,000 immigrants includes Algerians, the largest ethnic group with a population of just under 50,000. The second most significant (though less visible) group is the Portuguese (42,500) followed by Moroccans (28,650) and Tunisians (24,500). The largest Asian assembly is made up of ethnic Chinese with a population of 17,300. The largest group from sub-Saharan Africa is that from Mali (10,300).

Immigrants from Algeria, Morocco and Tunisia, all French colonies until the 1950s and 1960s, have been settling and working in France since the beginning of the 20th century, especially in the districts of Belleville in the 19e and 20e and La Goutte d'Or in the 18e. French-born North Africans are often called *beurs*, which is a nonpejorative term and is used frequently by the media and second-generation North Africans themselves.

The majority of black Africans in Paris hail from Mali as well as from Senegal, the Côte d'Ivoire, Cameroon, Mauritania, Congo, Guinea, Togo and Benin. Among the first immigrants were Senegalese soldiers who had fought for the French during WWI. They moved into the 18e, which remains the heart of African Paris. Students and intellectuals arrived from Africa in the 1940s and 1950s, and immigration was actively promoted during this time to boost France's workforce.

Many of the ethnic Chinese in Paris hail from the former French colonies of Indochina. Large waves of Asians arrived in France at the end of the Indochinese war in 1954, to escape the Khmer Rouge and Pathet Lao regimes in Cambodia and Laos in the 1970s, and as a result of the exodus of the Vietnamese boat people that continued well into the 1980s. The events in Tiananmen Square in 1989 prompted the flight of many Chinese. But Chinese immigration is nothing new; Chinese from Zhejiang province have been settling in Paris since the 1920s, mainly in the 3e, 13e, 19e and 20e arrondissements.

Immigrants from India, Pakistan, Bangladesh and Sri Lanka, as well as from the former French colonies of Madagascar and Mauritius and the overseas *département* (department or, loosely, county) of Réunion, often appear to share a common culture, but each group is quite distinct and has its own network in Paris. Many immigrants from this region tend to work in and around the 10e; others commute from the suburbs.

Jews have come to live and work in Paris since the Middle Ages, and today Ashkenazi Jews (from Germany and Eastern Europe) tend to live in the Marais while Sephardic Jews (of Spanish, Portuguese and North African descent) live in Belleville. In the latter, so-called 'Tunes' have managed to recreate something of the 1950s Tunisia they left behind. Other Jews work around rue du Sentier, 2e, the heart of Paris' rag trade.

The Portuguese presence in Paris dates back to the late 19th century. Political refugees were fleeing Portugal up until 1974, but the majority of Portuguese living in greater Paris are workers who helped build the new suburbs. Turks and Kurds started arriving in the late 1960s and number some 45,000 in the greater Paris region. They, too, commonly live in the suburbs and commute into the city.

Paris has long been a haven for intellectuals in search of freedom of expression. Many of the Paris-based Greeks arrived during the dictatorship of the colonels (1967–74); exiles from South America settled in the city for similar reasons. Many of the 4300-odd Lebanese immigrants fled the civil war that began there in 1975.

Russians have emigrated to Paris throughout the 20th century. Immigration from Poland and other Eastern and central European countries has also figured largely. In inner Paris there are now some 10,500 immigrants from the former Yugoslavia.

Though Paris may at times appear to be multiracial heaven, racism does exist here, and what may appear to be exotic to the outsider (an elderly Maghrebi man selling salted nuts in the metro) is simply a tough struggle for survival for those who cannot find employment. The incidence of racist acts of violence have been high in recent years, particularly in Paris' crowded suburbs. In the workplace, young people of non-French origin often face discrimination. This is widespread.

In recent years there has been racist agitation by right-wing parties and extremist groups against the country's nonwhite immigrant communities, especially Muslims from North Africa. Many North Africans complain of discrimination by employers and the police. In 1993 the French government changed its immigration laws to make it harder for immigrants to get French citizenship or bring their families into the country.

More than half of all French people identify themselves as Roman Catholic but, although most have been baptised, very few ever attend church or receive the sacraments. In fact, church attendance in Paris has fallen to about 10% (against 15% in the rest of France). The Catholic Church in France is generally very progressive and ecumenically minded. Cardinal Jean-Marie Lustiger, archbishop of Paris since 1981, was born in Paris to Jewish immigrants from Poland in 1926. He converted to Catholicism at the age of 14. France's Protestants, who were severely persecuted during much of the 16th and 17th centuries, make up only about 2% of the population (about 1.2 million). They are largely concentrated in Alsace, the Jura, the southeastern part of the Massif Central, along the Atlantic coast and in Paris.

Between five and six million French citizens and residents – 8% to 10% of the population – are nominally Muslim, and they now make up the country's second-largest religious group. The vast majority are immigrants (or their offspring) who arrived from North Africa starting in the 1950s. The Jewish community in France, which now numbers some 650,000 – the largest in Europe – or just over 1% of the population, increased dramatically in the 1960s as a result of immigration from Algeria, Tunisia and Morocco.

LIFESTYLE

As long as there has been a Paris, visitors have complained that its citizens can be bitchy, arrogant, full of attitude and as prickly as hedgehogs. If you do encounter some irritability, remember that the more tourists a city attracts – and Paris, as the first- or second-most

Top Five Books about Parisians & the French

- *The French*, Theodore Zeldin (1992) – highly acclaimed and useful overview of French passions, peculiarities and perspectives.
- *Sixty Million Frenchmen Can't Be Wrong*, Jean-Benoit Nadeau & Julie Barlow (2003) – Paris-based Canadian journalist couple explains the essence of what it means to be French and how they got to be the way they are.
- *An Englishman in Paris: L'Écation Continentale*, Michael Sadler (2003) – rollicking, very funny (mis)adventures of self-proclaimed Francophile teacher in the City of Light with a preface from Peter Mayle.
- *The Last Time I Saw Paris*, Elliot Paul (1993) – classic work by an American expat looks back on the working-class Paris of the interwar years in a series of interwoven episodes.
- *Paris to the Moon*, Adam Gopnik (2001) – two dozen essays on Paris, Parisians and everyday life by respected *New Yorker* contributor.

Food: The Great Ice-Breaker

Nothing breaks the ice like food at a French gathering – or so we discovered one weekend in spring when we'd zipped across the Channel on the Eurostar for a quick visit to friends in Paris.

We'd arrived at the Gare du Nord late, eating an indifferent meal with our hostess at a trendy restaurant done up in carnival chic, gossiping and catching up, and downing more than just a few *verres* (glasses) in the process. We were rolling by the time we got back to her place to throw ourselves in our beds but looked forward to a bit of marketing the next day and a quiet Saturday night in.

We were on our third *café noir* (black coffee) late the next morning and contemplating our purchases at the nearby market when the telephone rang. 'That was my sister,' our hostess said. 'I'd completely forgot. It's her boyfriend's surprise birthday party tonight. We're going to have to go to Pontoise.'

Pontoise... Wasn't that deep in the north country? A land of igloos and Eskimos, snowshoes and the Klondike? It sounded a rather harsh place and we feared nosebleed.

The party started off a bit, well, slowly. Picture the scene: a large sitting room with chairs lined up against the walls and two groups at either end – all the men in one corner, all the women in the other. What was this? A church dance in the Australian outback?

The party-thrower, sister of our hostess, began to set the dishes out on the buffet tables – *charcuterie* (cold cooked meats) and cheese, salads and a range of tarts and gateaux not seen since Marie-Antoinette told us all to eat that cake. The room went still, the two groups eyed one another, and slowly moved forward to begin that evergreen communal rite called *bouffer* (gobbling).

And like a groundswell the whispering began among the ranks. 'Have you tried the *tomates glacées* (glazed tomatoes)?' asked a woman of her companion. 'They're stuffed with *purée de haricots verts* (green bean puree)!' Another was quizzing the baker: 'Now where did you get the cherries for the *clafoutis* (an upside-down custard and cherry tart)? Are they from Auxerre (a town in Burgundy famous for its cherries)? So very sweet...' Behind us an elderly gentleman regaled us with tales of days and dishes of times past. 'I just adore les *grands vins* (great vintages)...' he mused.

We had reached Pontoise for sure, but we had arrived in *la belle France* (lovely France).

popular destination in Europe (depending on who is doing the counting), gets more than its fair share – the less patience locals tend to have for them. At the same time, there are certain peculiarities about Parisians that do make them both frustrating and endearing to outsiders. Though it is difficult – and dangerous – to generalise about a city of just under 11 million people, we're going to give it a go anyway.

Like all French people, Parisians have a very strong sense of national identity based on their history, language, culture and pursuit of the finer things in life. But not only do a large number of Parisians believe that they live in the most civilised country in the world, they are also convinced that they are in the most civilised city in that country. Once you accept that fact, you're halfway to understanding in what high esteem most Parisians hold themselves.

However, surprising as it sounds, Parisians tend to be somewhat shy with strangers but will readily help if approached in a friendly manner and with a word or two of even imperfect French. Etiquette is extremely important here and to be *correct* – a catch-all word that can mean everything from acting properly to being honest – is all-important. To do (or *not* to do, as the case may be) certain things is considered extremely boorish. It is not rocket science, but there are pitfalls for the uninitiated.

In Paris, one does not commonly smile at a passer-by or acknowledge a stranger's existence; this is considered unnecessary – even silly. However, if there is a 'relationship' involved – even one as simple as buyer and seller – you should greet people. When greeting one another, people who know each other exchange *bises* (kisses on the cheek). Close male friends and relations always did this in the south of France, but it is becoming increasingly common nowadays among younger and educated 21st-century Parisians who don't give a hoot that older males consider it *pédérastique* (queer). The usual ritual is one glancing peck on each cheek, but some people go for three or even four kisses. People who don't kiss each other will almost always shake hands when meeting up. People always stand up when meeting one another for the first time, including women with women.

An important distinction is made in French between *tu* and *vous*, which both mean 'you'. *Tu* is only used when addressing people you know well, children or animals. When addressing an adult who is not a personal friend, *vous* should be used until the person invites you to use *tu*. In general, younger people insist less on this distinction and they may use *tu* from the beginning of an acquaintance.

In general people tend to meet outside when they socialise. Invitations to a private home are infrequent and if you do get one consider it a compliment and a privilege as a foreigner. Along with the address, be sure to get the entry code to the street door of the apartment building (see p78), and bring some sort of gift, such as a good bottle of wine (French and not a cheap *vin de table*). Flowers are always a good idea, but *chrysanthèmes* (chrysanthemums) are only brought to cemeteries and *œillets* (carnations) are said to bring bad luck. Flowers are usually presented in odd-numbered bunches (eg seven not a half-dozen and 11 not a dozen and certainly not 13). It is impossible to overdress for a Parisian soiree (evening out). Both women and men take tremendous care of how they groom and dress themselves; 'smart casual' is always the safest way to go.

After what might seem a cool start, warmed up no doubt when food and drink is served (see p14), a meal with French friends will be fuelled by chat, badinage (light-hearted banter) and gesticulation. Parisians are great conversationalists and love debating everything from the best restaurant in the *quartier* (quarter) to subjects of great intellectual import. Like most French people, they are competitive and will try to win you over to their side (or at least way of thinking). And they can't stand being bored; you will know when they are. Use humour – Parisians can be among the funniest people anywhere – but charm is always preferential to mere jokes.

Education is everything here and there is a great emphasis on learning and logical thought. Unlike in what the French call *le monde Anglo-Saxon* (the English-speaking world), in France certificates and diplomas take precedence over experience. Where you went and what grades you received at the end of your course is all-important.

The French education system has long been highly centralised. Its high standards have produced great intellectuals and almost universal literacy, but equal opportunities are still not available to people of all classes. Most children attend a primary school and then the *lycée* (secondary school), with some 73% of students sitting the matriculation exam called the Baccalauréat (or *bac*). Education is compulsory until the age of 16.

The largest university, of which there are 77 in France, is the University of Paris system, which was decentralised and split into 13 autonomous universities after the violent student protests of 1968 (see p71), one of which is the prestigious Sorbonne. About one-third of all tertiary students in France study in Paris.

Some of the most able and ambitious young people do not attend the overcrowded universities, however. About 5% of students are enrolled in the country's 140 prestigious *grandes écoles*, institutions offering training in such fields as business management, engineering and the applied sciences. Students do not pay tuition and even receive salaries but they must work as civil servants after graduation – for up to 10 years in some cases. An overwhelming proportion of students come from highly educated, well-to-do families and end up in top positions in the public sector, the traditionally less prestigious private sector and politics. Thus education produces a meritocratic elite who all recognise and know one another.

Any number of topics is deemed acceptable for discussion and/or debate at a Parisian table – politics, religion, films, sports, even sex – though some subjects are generally avoided among people who are close friends or meeting for the first time. Obvious ones are money (especially salaries) and age but family, considered a very private affair here, is generally off limits in the early stages. For detailed information on how to conduct yourself *à table* see p46. A polite way of getting rid of guests, by the way, is to serve them all a glass of orange juice – a sign recognised by most that it's time to say *bonne nuit* (good night). The idea is that the vitamin C will dilute the alcohol for those staggering home.

The following are examples of other topics and situations where a Parisian's reaction may differ from yours. When buying fruit, vegetables or flowers anywhere except at supermarkets, do not touch the produce or blossoms unless invited to do so. Indicate to the shopkeeper what you want and they will choose for you. This is produce after all, something near and dear to every French person.

How Much?

Copy of Le Monde €1.20 (€2 weekend edition)

Pop music CD €15

Pint of Kronenbourg From €6 (€3 at happy hour)

Entry to the Louvre €7.50 (adult)

Cinema ticket €6.50 to €9 (adult)

An hour's car parking From €1.50 (street), €2.60 (garage)

Cup of coffee at a café bar From €1

Average seat at the Opéra Bastille €40

The French are generally more relaxed about relations between men and women – and about sex – than many English-speaking visitors might be accustomed to. Marital fidelity is not quite the precious stone it is in Anglo-Saxon countries, as we all know from those old B&W French films. Most people here are genuinely bemused by the American 'political correctness' of the past 20 years and the fuss made over sex scandals involving politicians. Touching, kissing and flirting are a generally accepted part of daily relationships, even at work.

By their very nature French people do not take seriously laws they consider stupid or intrusive; whether others feel the same is another matter. Laws banning smoking in public places in Paris do exist, but no one pays much attention to them. Diners will often light up in the nonsmoking sections of restaurants (which is usually no more than 70cm away from the smoking section, in any case) and the waiter will happily bring them an ashtray if asked. Parisians smoke between courses both at home and when dining out.

SPORT

Parisians love spectator sports and in addition to such international sports as football, rugby and tennis, they're mad for cycling and horse racing and showjumping. Depending on what time of year you visit, you can catch all types of matches and events (see p244).

Le foot (football), by far the most popular sport here, acquired an even larger following after the national team won the 1998 World Cup at home, beating the reigning champions and tournament favourite, Brazil, in a one-sided final 3–0. Footballer Zinedine Zidane was immediately catapulted to the status of national hero, the first Frenchman of North African origin to reach such dizzying heights. France went on to win the 2000 European Championships, defeating Italy in the final in spectacular style, but everything went pear-shaped in the first round of the 2002 World Cup when Senegal beat France 1–0, and again in the quarter-finals of the 2004 European championships when Greece, the eventual winners, beat France by the same score.

Rugby has a strong following in the southwest of France with the favourite teams being Toulouse, Montauban and St-Godens though it has gained tremendously in popularity in Paris recently following the repeat successes of its own team, Stade Français CASG, on the field. (Some say it is the team's too-hot-to-handle calendar that has increased their, er, exposure among hitherto nonfans.)

The big sporting event in Paris in late May/early June is the French Open, the second of the four Grand Slam tournaments, at the Stade Roland Garros in the Bois de Boulogne. The following month tens of thousands of spectators gather along the av des Champs-Élysées to watch the final stage of the prestigious Tour de France cycling race.

Gambling on various sporting events, including horseracing (see p245) is also popular.

MEDIA

The main national daily newspapers are *Le Figaro* (centre-right; aimed at professionals, businesspeople and the bourgeoisie), *Le Monde* (centre-left; popular with professionals and intellectuals), *France Soir* (right-wing; working and middle-class), *Libération* (left-wing; popular with students and intellectuals) and *L'Humanité* (communist; working-class and intellectuals). The capital's own daily is *Le Parisien* (centre; middle-class) and is easy to read if you have basic French. *L'Équipe* is a daily devoted exclusively to sport.

News weeklies with commentary include the left-leaning, comprehensive *Le Nouvel Observateur* and the more conservative *L'Express*. For investigative journalism blended with satire, pick up *Le Canard Enchaîné* (assuming your French is of a certain level). *Paris Match* is a gossipy, picture-heavy weekly with a penchant for royalty.

Public radio is grouped under the umbrella of Radio France, which broadcasts via a network of 53 radio stations, of which five are national: France Inter, France-Culture, France-Musique (which broadcasts over 1000 concerts each year), Radio Bleue for over-50s listeners and France Info, a 24-hour news station that broadcasts headlines in French every few minutes. In Paris, France Info is at 105.5 MHz FM.

Among the private radio networks, RTL is the leading general-interest station with over eight million listeners. The droves of FM pop-music stations include Fun Radio, Skyrock and Nostalgie, most of which follow the breakfast-time format with phone-ins and wisecracking DJs. Hard-core clubbers turn the dial to Radio Nova at 101.5 MHz FM for the latest on the nightclub scene.

Radio France Internationale (RFI) has been France's voice abroad since 1931 and broadcasts in 17 languages (including English); in Paris the frequency is 738 kHz AM.

Reading, Jardin du Palais Royal (p83)

By law, at least 40% of musical variety broadcasts must consist of songs in French and stations can be fined if they don't comply. This helps explain why so many English-language hits are re-recorded in French – not always very successfully.

Half of France's six major national TV channels are public: France 2 and France 3 are general-interest stations designed to complement each other: the former focuses on news, entertainment and education, while the latter broadcasts regional programmes and news. La Cinquième targets a daytime audience with a diet of cartoons, game shows and documentaries; at 7pm it becomes Arte, a highbrow cultural channel.

The major private stations are Canal+, TF1 and M6. Canal+ is a pay channel that shows lots of films, both foreign and French – which isn't surprising, as it's the chief sponsor of the French cinema industry. In the private sector, TF1 focuses on news, sport and variety programmes and, with about one-third of viewers, is the most popular station in France. M6 lures a youngish audience with its menu of drama, music and news programmes. There are also 25 or so French cable stations.

LANGUAGE

Respect for the French language is one of the most important aspects of claiming French nationality and the concept of *la francophonie*, linking the common interests where French is spoken, is supported by both the government and the people. Modern French developed from the *langue d'oïl*, a group of dialects spoken north of the River Loire that grew out of the vernacular Latin used during the late Gallo-Roman period. The *langue d'oïl* – particularly the *francien* dialect spoken in the Île de France around today's Paris – eventually displaced the *langue d'oc*, the dialects spoken in the south of the country.

Standard French is taught and spoken in schools but its various accents and subdialects are an important source of identity in certain regions. In addition, some traditional languages belonging to peoples long since subjected to French rule have been preserved. These include Flemish in the far north, Alsatian in Alsace, Breton (a Celtic tongue related to Cornish and Welsh) in Brittany, Basque (a language unrelated to any other) in the Pays Basque,

Catalan (the official language of nearby Andorra and the Spanish autonomous region of Catalonia) in Roussillon, Provençal in Provence and Corsican on the island of Corsica.

French was *the* international language of culture and diplomacy until WWI, and the French are sensitive to its decline in importance and the hegemony of English. It is impossible to separate a French person from his or her language and it is one of the things they love most about their own culture. Your best bet is always to approach people politely in French, even if the only words you know are '*Pardon, parlez-vous anglais?*' (Excuse me, do you speak English?).

For more on what to say and how to say it *en français*, see p355. Lonely Planet also publishes the more comprehensive *French phrasebook*.

ECONOMY & COSTS

In Paris proper, some 334,000 firms employ a total of 1.6 million people. Not surprisingly only 0.2% of Parisians are involved in agriculture or the fishing industry and 3% are in administration and teaching. The rest are employed by the construction (11.7%), commerce (19.7%) and service industries (65.4%). About 20% of all economic activity in France takes place in the Paris region. Because of the centralised bureaucracy, the capital accounts for 40% of the nation's white-collar jobs. Tourism produces 12% of the country's GDP.

To the surprise of many outsiders, the French *dirigiste* (interventionist) model of state ownership is still alive and well. More than 50% of GDP is spent by the government, which employs one in every four French workers despite a series of heavyweight privatisations during the 1990s. The 'family silver' – including Air France, France Telecom and Aerospatiale – has been partly sold off, but many other mammoth concerns, such as the car-maker Renault, remain government-controlled.

Pragmatism had something to do with the socialist-dominated coalition going back on its word in the late 1990s and opting for privatisation, as it helped to top up the state coffers. After the overtaxed, free-spending 1980s, the next decade brought sluggish growth and high unemployment as France curbed its deficit spending to qualify for inclusion in the European Monetary Union (EMU). The effort paid off at first but predictions have been less optimistic in recent years, with annual growth at just over 1% and unemployment hovering at just under 10%. Inflation increased to 2.5% following the introduction of the euro.

France is one of the world's most industrialised nations, with some 40% of the workforce employed in the industrial sector. About half of the economy's earnings come from industrial production. However, there is poor coordination between academic research and the companies that might turn good ideas into products, and the country has fewer large corporations – an important source of private capital and investment in research and development – than other industrialised nations of similar size.

France can lay claim to being the largest agricultural producer and exporter in the EU, with significant production of wheat, barley, maize (corn) and cheese. The country is largely self-sufficient in food, except for certain tropical products such as bananas and coffee.

GOVERNMENT & POLITICS

For an update on who's in charge at national and local levels of government, see p72.

NATIONAL GOVERNMENT

France is a republic with a written constitution. As the capital city, Paris is home to almost all the national offices of state, including, of course, the Parlement (French Parliament), which is divided into two houses: the Assemblée Nationale (National Assembly) and Sénat (Senate). The 577 deputies of the National Assembly are directly elected in single-member constituencies for five-year terms. The 321 members of the rather powerless Senate, who serve for nine years, are indirectly elected. The president of France is directly elected for a term now lasting five years (reduced from seven years in 2000) and can stand for re-election.

Executive power is shared by the president and the Council of Ministers, whose members (including the prime minister) are appointed by the president but are responsible to parliament. The president serves as commander-in-chief of the armed forces and theoretically makes all major policy decisions.

LOCAL GOVERNMENT

Paris is run by the *maire* (mayor), who is elected by the 163 members of the Conseil de Paris (Council of Paris), who are elected for six-year terms. The mayor has 18 *adjoints* (deputy mayors), whose offices are in the Hôtel de Ville (City Hall).

The first mayor of Paris to be elected with real powers was Jacques Chirac in 1977; from 1871 until that year, the mayor was nominated by the government as the capital was considered a dangerous and revolutionary hotbed. After the 1995 election of Chirac as national president, the Council of Paris elected Jean Tiberi as mayor, a man who was very close to the president and from the same party. In May 2001, Bertrand Delanoë, a socialist with support from the Green Party, became Paris' – and a European capital's – first openly gay mayor. The mayor has many powers, but they do not include control of the police, which is handled by the Préfet de Police (Chief of Police), part of the Ministère de l'Intérieur (Ministry of the Interior).

Paris is a *département* as well as a city and the mayor is the head of both. The city is divided into 20 arrondissements and each has its own *maire d'arrondissement* (mayor of the arrondissement) and *conseil d'arrondissement* (council of the arrondissement), who are also elected for six-year terms. They have very limited powers, principally administering local cultural, sporting and social activities and the like.

ENVIRONMENT

THE LAND

The city of Paris – the capital of both France and the historic Île de France region – measures approximately 9.5km (north to south) by 11km (west to east), not including the Bois de Boulogne and the Bois de Vincennes; its total area is 105 sq km. Within central Paris – which Parisians call *intra-muros* (Latin for 'within the walls') – the Right Bank is north of the Seine, while the Left Bank is south of the river.

Paris is a relatively easy city to negotiate. The ring road, known as the Périphérique – Périphe for short – makes an irregularly shaped oval containing the entire central area. The Seine cuts an arc across the oval, and the terrain is so flat that the 126m-high Butte de Montmartre (Montmartre Hill) to the north really stands out.

Central Paris divided neatly in two by the Seine, with the arrondissements spiralling clockwise from the centre in a logical fashion. City addresses always include the number of the arrondissement, as streets with the same name exist in different districts. In this book, arrondissement numbers are given after the street address using the usual French notation: 1er for *premier* (1st), 2e for *deuxième* (2nd), 3e for *troisième* (3rd) and so on. On some signs or commercial maps, you will see the variations 2ème, 3ème etc.

There is almost always a metro station within 500m of wherever you want to go in Paris, so all offices, museums, hotels, restaurants and so on included in this book have the nearest metro station given immediately after the contact details. Metro stations generally have a *plan du quartier* (map of the neighbourhood) on the wall near the exits.

GREEN PARIS

For a densely populated urban centre inhabited for more than two millennia, Paris is a surprisingly healthy and clean city. Thanks mainly to Baron Haussmann (see p34), who radically reshaped the city in the second half of the 19th century, a small army of street sweepers brush litter into the gutters from where it is then hosed into sewers, and a city ordinance requires residents to have the façades of their buildings cleaned every 10 years.

Cathedral for the Birds

Birdwatchers estimate that about 40 pairs of kestrels (*Falco tinnunculus*; also known as a sparrow hawks in the USA, windhovers in the UK and faucons crécerelles in France) currently nest in Paris, preferring tall old structures like the towers of Notre Dame. Four or five pairs of kestrels regularly breed in niches and cavities high up in the cathedral, and once a year (usually late June), local ornithologists set up a public kestrel-watching station behind the cathedral, with telescopes and even a camera transmitting close-up pictures of one of the kestrels' nesting sites. The birds form their partnerships in February, eggs are laid in April, the kestrel chicks hatch in May and are ready to depart by early July. In late June, birdwatchers may spot the adult kestrels returning to their young with a tasty mouse or sparrow. Unfortunately, Paris' pigeons – those dirty flying rats – are too large for a kestrel chick to handle.

These days, despite the city's excellent public transport system, Haussmann's wide boulevards are usually choked with traffic, and air pollution is undoubtedly the city's major environmental hazard. But things are improving on that score; the city leadership, which came to power in coalition with the Green Party, has restricted traffic on some roads at certain times and created lanes only for buses, taxis and bicycles.

At first glance Paris does not appear to have much parkland but see p82 and look again. In virtually every park in Paris, regardless of the size, you'll see a signboard illustrating and explaining the trees, flowers and other plants of the city, and most are rich in birdlife, including magpies, jays, blue and great tits, and even woodpeckers. In winter, seagulls are sometimes seen on the Seine, and a few hardy ducks also brave the river's often swift-flowing waters. Believe it or not, there are actually crayfish in the city's newly cleaned canals.

If you want to keep Paris at least as clean as it is now, leave your car at home and resist the temptation to rent one unless you're touring around the Île de France (see p305). Instead, bring or rent a bike (see p246), enjoy the city on foot (Paris is an eminently walkable city) and/or use the public transport system – it's cheap and extremely efficient. For further tips on how you can reduce your impact on the environment, contact **Les Amis de la Nature** (☎ 01 42 85 29 84; www.amisnature-pariscentre.org in French; 18 rue Victor Massé, 9e) or the **World Wildlife Fund France** (☎ 01 55 25 84 67; www.wwf.fr in French; 188 rue de la Roquette, 11e). In theory Parisians can be fined over €150 for littering but we've never seen (or heard of) anyone ever having to pay up. Don't be nonplussed if you see locals drop paper wrappings or other detritus along the side of the pavement, however; the gutters in every quarter of Paris are washed and swept out daily and Parisians are encouraged to use them if litter bins are not available.

The Paris municipality spends €11 million each year to keep the city's pavements relatively free of dog dirt, and the technology it employs – most notably the distinctive *moto-crottes* (motorised pooper-scooters) – is undeniably impressive. But it would seem that repeated campaigns to get people to clean up after their pooches, owned by 160,000 households in Paris, have been less than a howling success, with only an estimated 60% of dog owners doing so. Until Parisians – and their beloved canines – change their ways, the word on the street remains the same: watch your step. Some 200,000 dogs produce 16 tonnes of dog dirt a day and 650 accidents each year are caused by *la pollution canine*.

URBAN PLANNING & DEVELOPMENT

The very fabric of Paris could be ripped apart and restitched over the next decade if the current mayor, a big fan of the vertical city like his counterpart in London, has his way. For a full look at what may or may not happen see p40.

Arts

Literature	22
Philosophy	25
Visual Arts	28
Painting	28
Sculpture	29
Music	30
Cinema	31
Dance	32
Theatre	32

Arts

Paris is a bottomless cup when it comes to the arts. There are philharmonic orchestras, ballet and opera troupes, theatre companies and copious numbers of cinemas – both cineplexes and studio theatres – from which to choose. And its museums are among the richest in the world, with artwork representing the best of every historical period and school from the Romans to postmodernism. Generous government funds allow local venues to attract top international performers, and the number of international arts festivals hosted here seems to grow each year.

LITERATURE

Paris does not figure largely in the history of early medieval French literature, though the misadventures of Pierre Abélard and Héloïse (p26), the daughter of Canon Fulbert, took place here as did their mutual correspondence, which ended only with their deaths.

François Villon, considered the finest poet of the late Middle Ages in any language, received the equivalent of a master of arts degree from the Sorbonne before he turned 20 years. Involved in a series of brawls, robberies and generally illegal escapades, 'Master Villon' (as he became known) was sentenced to be hanged in 1462 for stabbing a lawyer, but the sentence was commuted to banishment from Paris for 10 years and he disappeared from Paris. As well as a long police record, Villon left behind a body of poems charged with a highly personal lyricism, among them the *Ballade des Pendus* (Ballad of the Hanged Men), in which he writes his own epitaph, and the *Ballade des Femmes du Temps Jadis*, which was translated by the English poet and painter Dante Gabriel Rossetti as the 'Ballad of Dead Ladies'.

The great landmarks of French Renaissance literature are the works of Rabelais, La Pléiade and Montaigne. The exuberant narratives of François Rabelais, one-time monk, blend coarse humour with erudition in a vast oeuvre that seems to include every kind of person, occupation and jargon to be found in mid-16th-century France. Rabelais had friends in high places

Galerie Vivienne (p145)

in Paris, including Archbishop Jean du Bellay, whom he accompanied to Rome on two occasions. But some of Rabelais' friends and associates fell afoul with the clergy, including his publisher Étienne Dolet. After being convicted of heresy and blasphemy in 1546, Dolet was hanged and then burned at place Maubert in the 5e arrondissement.

During the 17th century François de Malherbe, court poet under Henri IV, brought a new rigour to the treatment of rhythm in literature. One of his better-known works is his sycophantic *Ode* (1600) to Marie de Médici. Transported by the perfection of Malherbe's verses, Jean de La Fontaine went on to write his charming *Fables* in the manner of Aesop – though he fell afoul of the Académie Française in the process. The mood of classical tragedy permeates *La Princesse de Clèves* by Marie de La Fayette, which is widely regarded as the precursor of the modern psychological novel.

The literature of the 18th century is dominated by philosophers, among them

The Hunchback of Notre Dame

The story of the Hunchback of Notre Dame as told by Victor Hugo in his romantic novel *Notre Dame de Paris* (1831) – and not some silly musical or Disney cartoon version with happy endings – goes something like this. It's 15th-century Paris during the reign of King Louis XI. A gypsy dancer called Esmeralda is in love with Captain Phoebus, but the evil and jealous archdeacon, Claude Frollo, besotted by Esmeralda, denounces her as a witch. The deformed bell-ringer Quasimodo is devoted to Esmeralda and saves her (for a while) when she seeks protection from the mob in the belfry of Notre Dame. We won't give the ending away, but suffice to say that everyone comes to a tragic end – including Captain Phoebus, who marries someone else.

So is *Notre Dame de Paris*, which is not based on historical fact, just a good story or a commentary on the times? Hugo began the book during the reign of the unpopular and reactionary Charles X who had abolished freedom of the press and dissolved parliament. The ascent of Louis-Philippe, a bourgeois king with liberal leanings, in the July Revolution of 1830 took place shortly before the book was published. The novel can thus be seen as a condemnation of absolutism (ie of Charles X) and of a society that allows the likes of Frollo and Phoebus to heap scorn and misery on marginalised characters, such as Esmeralda and Quasimodo.

Hugo's evocation of the colourful and intense life of the medieval city is seen by some as a plea for the preservation of Gothic Paris and its decaying architecture. Indeed, the condition of Notre Dame in the early 19th century was so bad that artists, politicians and writers, including Hugo, beseeched Louis-Philippe to rectify the situation. Hugo was appointed to the new Commission for Monuments and the Arts, on which he sat for 10 years. In 1845 the Gothic revivalist architect Eugène Viollet-le-Duc began his renovation of Notre Dame, during which he added, among other things, the steeple and the gargoyles. The work continued for almost two decades.

Voltaire and Jean-Jacques Rousseau. Voltaire's political writings, in which it is argued that society is fundamentally opposed to nature, were to have a profound and lasting influence on the century, and he is buried in the Panthéon. Rousseau's sensitivity to landscape and its moods anticipates romanticism, and the insistence on his own singularity in *Les Confessions* makes it the first modern autobiography. He, too, is buried in the Panthéon.

The 19th century brought Victor Hugo, as much acclaimed for his poetry as for his novels, who lived on the place des Vosges before fleeing to the Channel Islands during the Second Empire. *Les Misérables* (1862) describes life among the poor and marginalised of Paris during the first half of the 19th century; the flight of the central character, Jean Valjean, through the sewers of the capital is memorable, as are Hugo's descriptions (all 20 pages of them). *Notre Dame de Paris* (The Hunchback of Notre Dame), published just over 30 years earlier, made Hugo the key figure of French romanticism (see above).

Other outstanding 19th-century novelists include Stendhal, Honoré de Balzac, Amandine Aurore Lucie Dupin (better known as George Sand) and, of course, Alexandre Dumas, who wrote the swashbuckling adventures *Le Compte de Monte Cristo* (The Count of Monte Cristo) and *Les Trois Mousquetaires* (The Three Musketeers). The latter tells the story of d'Artagnan (based on the historical personage Charles de Baatz d'Artagnan, 1623–73), who arrives in Paris as a young Gascon determined to become one of Louis XIII's guardsmen.

In 1857 two landmarks of French literature appeared: *Madame Bovary* by Gustave Flaubert and *Les Fleurs du Mal* by Charles Baudelaire. Both writers were tried for the supposed immorality of their works. Flaubert won his case, and his novel was distributed without censorship. Baudelaire, who moonlighted as a translator in Paris (he introduced the works of the American writer Edgar Allan Poe to Europe in editions that have since become French classics), was obliged to cut several poems from his work, and he died an early and painful death, practically unknown. Flaubert's second-most popular novel, *L'Éducation Sentimentale* (Sentimental Education), presents a vivid picture of life among Parisian dilettantes, intellectuals and revolutionaries during the decline and fall of Louis-Philippe's monarchy and the February Revolution of 1848.

The aim of Émile Zola, who came to Paris with his close friend Paul Cézanne in 1858, was to convert novel-writing from an art to a science by the application of experimentation. His theory may seem naive, but his work influenced most significant French writers of the late 19th century and is reflected in much 20th-century fiction as well. *Nana* tells the decadent tale of a young woman who resorts to prostitution to survive the Paris of the Second Empire.

Paul Verlaine and Stéphane Mallarmé created the symbolist movement, which strove to express states of mind rather than simply detail daily reality. Arthur Rimbaud, apart from crowding an extraordinary amount of rugged, exotic travel into his 37 years and having a tempestuous homosexual relationship with Verlaine in Paris, produced two enduring pieces of work: *Illuminations* and *Une Saison en Enfer* (A Season in Hell). Rimbaud quit writing and left Europe for Africa in 1874. Verlaine died at 39 rue Descartes in the 5e in 1896.

Marcel Proust dominated the early 20th century with his giant seven-volume novel *À la Recherche du Temps Perdu* (Remembrance of Things Past), which is largely autobiographical and explores in evocative detail the true meaning of past experience recovered from the unconscious by 'involuntary memory'. In 1907 Proust moved from the family home near av des Champs-Élysées to the apartment on blvd Haussmann famous for the cork-lined bedroom (on display at the Musée Carnavalet in the Marais) from which he almost never stirred. André Gide found his voice in the celebration of homosexual sensuality and, later, left-wing politics. *Les Faux-Monnayeurs* (The Counterfeiters) exposes the hypocrisy and self-deception with which people try to avoid sincerity.

André Breton led the group of French surrealists and wrote its three manifestos, although the first use of the word 'surrealist' is attributed to the poet Guillaume Apollinaire, a fellow traveller. As a poet, Breton was overshadowed by Paul Éluard and Louis Aragon, whose most famous surrealist novel was *Le Paysan de Paris*. Colette enjoyed tweaking the nose of conventionally moral readers with titillating novels that detailed the amorous exploits of such heroines as the schoolgirl Claudine. One of her most interesting works, *Paris de Ma Fenêtre* (Paris from My Window), concerned the German occupation of Paris. Her view, by the way, was from 9 rue de Beaujolais in the 1er, overlooking the Jardin du Palais Royal.

After WWII existentialism developed as a significant literary movement around Jean-Paul Sartre (see p27), Simone de Beauvoir and Albert Camus, who worked and conversed in the cafés around the Église St-Germain des Prés. All three stressed the importance of the writer's political engagement. *L'Âge de Raison* (The Age of Reason), the first volume of Sartre's trilogy *Les Chemins de la Liberté* (The Roads to Freedom), is a superb Parisian novel; the subsequent volumes recall Paris immediately before and during WWII. De Beauvoir, author of the ground-breaking study *Le Deuxième Sexe* (The Second Sex), had a profound influence on feminist thinking.

In the late 1950s some younger novelists began to look for new ways of organising narrative. The so-called *nouveau roman* (new novel) refers to the works of Nathalie Sarraute, Alain Robbe-Grillet, Boris Vian, Julien Gracq, Michel Butor and others. These writers never formed a close-knit group, however, and their experiments took them in divergent directions. Today the *nouveau roman* is very much out of favour in France.

Mention must also be made of *Histoire d'O*, the highly erotic sadomasochistic novel written by Dominique Aury under a pseudonym in 1954. It sold more copies than any other contemporary French novel outside France.

In 1980 Marguerite Yourcenar, best known for her memorable historical novels such as *Mémoires d'Hadrien* (Hadrian's Memoirs), became the first woman to be elected to the Académie Française (French Academy).

Marguerite Duras came to the notice of a larger public when she won the prestigious Prix Goncourt for her novel *L'Amant* (The Lover) in 1984. She also wrote the screenplay of *Hiroshima Mon Amour*, described by one critic as part *nouveau roman*, part Mills & Boon.

Literary Awards

The most highly respected and coveted literary award in France is the Prix Goncourt, awarded annually since 1903 to the best volume of imaginative work in prose published during that year. In the event of a tie, novels are to be given preference over collections of short stories or sketches. The winner is selected by the 10-strong Académie Goncourt each year at the Drouant restaurant in the 2e arrondissement. Though the prize comes with a purse of less than €10, it guarantees much media attention and soaring sales.

A dozen different French writers and poets have been awarded the Nobel Prize for Literature since its inception in 1901, including such celebrated names as Anatole France (1921), André Gide (1947) and Jean-Paul Sartre (1964; refused) as well as less well-known Robert Martin du Gard (1937) and St-John Perse (1960).

Paris in Print

- *The Autobiography of Alice B Toklas,* Gertrude Stein (1933) – autobiographical account of the author's years in Paris written through the eyes and ears of her secretary and long-term lover, with much on their salon at 27 rue de Fleurus near the Luxembourg Gardens and her friendship with Matisse, Picasso, Braque, Hemingway and others.
- *Birds of America,* Mary McCarthy (1971) – philosophical novel about a young man and his over-indulgent mother who makes his way to Paris.
- *Le Divorce,* Diane Johnson (1997) – expatriate society and French manners through the eyes of a young American woman in 1990s Paris, embroiled in her sister's divorce.
- *Down and Out in Paris and London,* George Orwell (1940) – intriguing account of a time spent working as a *plongeur* (dishwasher) in Paris and living with tramps in both cities in the early 1930s.
- *Giovanni's Room,* James Baldwin (1956) – poignant account of a young American in Paris who falls in love with an Italian bartender, and his struggle with his sexuality.
- *The Hunchback of Notre Dame,* Victor Hugo (1831) – medieval romance and tragedy that revolves around the life of the celebrated cathedral in Paris.
- *The Life of Samuel Johnson,* James Boswell (1791) – milestone biography of Johnson includes account of travels to France and Paris in the autumn of 1775.
- *A Moveable Feast,* Ernest Hemingway (1961) – celebrated American novelist's humorous and sometimes bitchy reminiscences on bohemian life in Paris in the late 1920s.
- *Satori in Paris,* Jack Kerouac (1966) – entertaining (eg the scene in the Montparnasse gangster bar) but at times intensely irritating account of American beat writer's last trip to France.
- *Scarlet Pimpernel,* Baroness Orczy (1905) – adventure story set during the French Revolution in which the foppish young English protagonist turns out to be the daring rescuer of aristocrats in distress.
- *Shakespeare and Company,* Sylvia Beach (1960) – recollections of the proprietor of Paris' most famous literary bookshop between the wars.
- *A Tale of Two Cities,* Charles Dickens (1859) – Paris and London are the settings for the greatest novel ever written about the French Revolution.
- *Tropic of Cancer* & *Quiet Days in Clichy,* Henry Miller – steamy novels set in Paris, which were published in France in the 1930s but banned under obscenity laws in the UK and USA until the 1960s.

Philippe Sollers was one of the editors of *Tel Quel,* a highbrow, then left-wing, Paris-based review that was very influential in the 1960s and early 1970s. His 1960's novels were highly experimental, but with *Femmes* (Women) he returned to a conventional narrative style.

Another editor of *Tel Quel* was Julia Kristeva, best known for her theoretical writings on literature and psychoanalysis. In recent years she has turned her hand to fiction, and *Les Samuraï,* a fictionalised account of the heady days of *Tel Quel,* is an interesting document on the life of the Paris intelligentsia. Roland Barthes and Michel Foucault are other authors and philosophers associated with this period.

More accessible authors who enjoy a wide following include Françoise Sagan, Patrick Modiano, Yann Queffélec, Pascal Quignard and Denis Tillinac. Nicole de Buron is a very popular mainstream humour writer whose books – *Docteur, Puis-Je Vous Voir avant Six Mois*? (Doctor, Can I See You within Six Months?), *Chéri, Tu M'écoutes?* (My Dear, You Hear Me?) – sell in the hundreds of thousands. The *roman policier* (detective novel) has always been a great favourite with the French, and among its greatest exponents has been Belgian-born Georges Simenon, author of the Inspector Maigret novels. *Maigret at the Crossroads* portrays Montmartre at its sleaziest and seediest best.

PHILOSOPHY

France may be one of the few countries in the world to require its secondary-school students to demonstrate a solid mastery of philosophical concepts before pursuing an academic career. Forced to expostulate upon such brain ticklers as 'Can demands for justice be separated from demands for liberty?' or 'Do passions prevent us from doing our duty?' in order to receive a Baccalauréat (school-leaving certificate), many people here develop a lifelong passion for philosophical discourse. Most French towns of any size have at least one bar or

Star-Crossed Lovers

He was a handsome 39-year-old philosopher and logician who had gained a reputation for controversial ideas. She was the beautiful teenage niece of a priest at Notre Dame. And like Bogart and Bergman in *Casablanca*, they didn't even end up with Paris.

In 1118 the wandering scholar Pierre Abélard (1079–1142) went to Paris, having clashed with yet another theologian in the provinces. There he was employed by one Canon Fulbert of Notre Dame to tutor his niece Héloïse (1101–64). One thing led to another and a son called Astrolabe was born. Abélard did the gentlemanly thing and married his sweetheart, but when Fulbert found out about it he was outraged. The canon had Abélard castrated and sent Héloïse packing to a nunnery. Abélard took monastic vows at the abbey in St-Denis, and continued his studies and controversial writings. Héloïse, meanwhile, was made abbess of the convent.

All the while, however, the star-crossed lovers continued to correspond: he sending tender advice on how to run the abbey and she writing passionate, poetic letters to her lost lover. The two were reunited only in death; in 1817 their remains were disinterred and brought to Cimetière du Père Lachaise (p123), where they lie together beneath a neogothic tombstone.

café that will sponsor a regular 'café philo' in which anyone may contribute their ideas on a particular philosophical question; in Paris the most popular is the Café des Phares (p209).

Left Bank philosophers Bernard-Henri Levy, Jean-François Revel, André Glucksmann and the late Marc Sautet, who founded the Café des Phares and died in 1998 at the age of 51, have achieved a level of celebrity normally reserved for film stars. Even politicians are expected to show a philosophical bent. Prime Minister Chirac has opined that 'Poetry is a necessity for daily living', and in 2003 Foreign Minister Dominique de Villepin quietly published *Éloge des Voleurs de Feu* (Elegy to the Fire Thieves), an 824-page critique and homage to such 'Promethean rebels' as Villon and Rimbaud (p24) in French poetry. It was his third work in as many years.

René Descartes, who lived in the first half of the 17th century, was the founder of modern philosophy and one of the greatest thinkers since Aristotle. After making important contributions to analytical geometry and algebra, Descartes sought to establish certainty from a position of absolute doubt. Descartes' famed phrase 'Cogito, ergo sum' (I think, therefore I exist) is the basis of modern philosophical thought. His method and systems of thought came to be known as Cartesianism. In positing that there is an external reality that can be grasped through reason, Descartes rendered possible the development of modern science.

Blaise Pascal, a contemporary of Descartes, was also a mathematician, but addressed the absurdity of the human predicament in a manner that foreshadowed the existentialists. Pascal's central concern was in reconciling his religious devotion – he was a convert to Jansenist Catholicism and ended his days at Port Royal, an abbey near Versailles – with his scientific background. Thus, in *Pensées* (Thoughts) he put forth 'Pascal's Razor', which stated that the most logical approach is to believe in God. If God does not exist, one has lost nothing; if God does exist one has assured a favourable afterlife.

As one of the major thinkers of the Age of Enlightenment in the 18th century, Jean-Jacques Rousseau addressed the relationship of the individual to society. His 1762 work *Le Contrat Social* (The Social Contract) laid the foundations for modern democracy by arguing that sovereignty resides with the people who express their will through majority vote. Liberty is an inalienable 'natural' right that cannot be traded in exchange for civil peace.

In the late 19th century Henri Bergson abandoned reason as a tool towards discovering the truth, arguing that direct intuition is deeper than intellect. He developed the concept of *élan vital* (creative impulse), a spirit of energy and life that moves all living things, as the heart of evolution – not Darwin's theory of natural selection. His thoughts about the subjective experience of time greatly influenced his brother-in-law, Marcel Proust, and his long work *A la Recherche du Temps Perdu* (Remembrance of Things Past; p24).

The 20th century's most famous French thinker was Jean-Paul Sartre, the quintessential Parisian intellectual who was born in Paris on 21 June 1905 and died there on 15 April 1980. For most people he embodied an obscure idea known as existentialism. It's one of the great 'isms' of popular culture, but even philosophers have trouble explaining what existentialism really means (p27). The word derives from Sartre's statement, 'Existence takes priority over essence', meaning that man must create himself because there is no eternal 'natural self' or 'meaning of life'. Realising that there is no meaning of life provokes 'existential dread' and 'alienation'.

A woman must also create herself, according to philosopher Simone de Beauvoir, who applied existentialist concepts to the predicament of women. There is no essential 'female' or 'male' nature, she opined in her seminal work *Le Deuxième Sexe* (The Second Sex) published in 1949. According to Beauvoir, women's status as the perpetual 'other' relegates them to remaining 'objects' of the subjective male gaze.

Both Sartre and de Beauvoir were strong advocates of communism until 1956 and the Soviet invasion of Hungary. Disillusionment with communism and with the political engagement implied by existentialism led a new generation towards the new social science called structuralism. Coined by the anthropologist Claude Levi-Strauss, who died in 2004 at the age of 95, structuralists believe that sociological, psychological and linguistic structures shape individuals. Individuals do not shape themselves as the existentialists believe. Beginning as a scientific method for studying differences between cultures, structuralism soon came to imply a rejection of all the universal ideas – reason, progress, democracy – that had held sway since the Age of Enlightenment.

As a poststructuralist, Michel Foucault rejected the idea that it was possible to step outside the 'discursive practices' that claim to reveal knowledge and arrive at an ultimate truth. The search for knowledge cannot be separated from the power relationships that lie at the heart of every social and political relationship.

Jacques Derrida, first published in the influential *Tel Quel* (p25) in the 1960s and now director of the École des Hautes Études en Science Sociales in Paris, introduced the concept of deconstructionism, which holds that outside language there is nothing to which we can refer directly, since all language is indicative only of itself (*il n'y a pas de hors texte*). Thus knowledge outside of language is literally unthinkable; it is not a natural reflection of the world. Each text allows for multiple interpretations making it impossible to find certainty in textual analysis. Deconstructionism thus posed an obvious paradox: how can one use language to claim that language is meaningless?

In recent years French philosophers have turned back to political commitment and moral philosophy. Bernard-Henri Levy was an outspoken critic of the war in Bosnia and made several films on the subject in the 1990s. André Glucksmann's *Ouest contre Ouest* (West against West), published in 2003, looks at the Iraq war and the paradox that both those groups for and against the war claimed to be inspired by the same principles.

Existence vs Essence

Jean-Paul Sartre never used the term existentialism in his early defining works, but it came to represent a body of thought that he, in part, inherited from the German philosopher Edmund Husserl. It was also adopted by a Parisian café clique of writers, dramatists and intellectuals (which included his lifelong companion Simone de Beauvoir), and even painters and musicians. Sartre's intellectual influences were the German philosophers, in particular Martin Heidegger and Friedrich Nietzsche, and he was also influenced by the Dane Søren Kierkegaard.

Sartre was an atheist, and the 'loss of God' was a phrase he used often. In the 1930s he wrote a series of analyses of human self-awareness that culminated in his most important philosophical work, *L'Être et le Néant* (Being and Nothingness; 1943). The central idea of this long and complex book is to distinguish between objective things and human consciousness, and to assert that consciousness is a 'non-thing'. Consciousness is made real by taking a point of view on things, on 'being'. He claimed that we are 'condemned to be free' and that even in indecision we choose not to choose, thus making freedom inescapable.

For all its lofty language and convoluted philosophical argument, *Being and Nothingness* is a treatise on a fairly simple way of life that embraces one's own autonomy and seeks to maximise one's choices (or one's awareness of choice). Many read Sartre's message as a positive one, but for him this heightened human awareness was characterised by emptiness, boredom and negativity.

The many literary works, essays, plays and political writings of Sartre were charged with his philosophical ideas. In 1938 his first published novel, *La Nausée* (Nausea), introduced many themes common in his later philosophical works. *Huis Clos* (No Exit; 1944), his most popular play, is an allegorical and unnerving story about three people who find themselves in a room together with no way out. This work includes Sartre's famous words 'Hell is other people'.

VISUAL ARTS
PAINTING

Voltaire wrote that French painting began with Nicolas Poussin, a 17th-century baroque painter who frequently set scenes from classical mythology and the Bible in ordered landscapes bathed in golden light.

In the 18th century Jean-Baptiste Chardin brought the humbler domesticity of the Dutch masters to French art. In 1785 the public reacted with enthusiasm to two large paintings with clear republican messages: *The Oath of the Horatii* and *Brutus Condemning His Son* by Jacques Louis David. David became one of the leaders of the French Revolution, and a virtual dictator in matters of art, where he advocated a precise, severe classicism. He was made official state painter by Napoleon, glorifying him as general, first consul and then emperor, and is best remembered for his painting of Marat lying dead in his bath.

Jean-Auguste-Dominique Ingres, David's most gifted pupil in Paris, continued in the neoclassical tradition. The historical pictures to which he devoted most of his life (*Oedipus and the Sphinx*) are now generally regarded as inferior to his portraits.

The gripping *Raft of the Medusa* by Théodore Géricault is on the threshold of romanticism; if Géricault had not died at a young age – he was 33 – he would probably have become a leader of the movement, along with his friend Eugène Delacroix. Delacroix's most famous picture, perhaps, is *Liberty Leading the People*, which commemorates the July Revolution of 1830 (p67).

The members of the Barbizon School brought about a parallel transformation of landscape painting. The school derived its name from a village near the Forêt de Fontainebleau (p313), where Camille Corot and Jean-François Millet, among others, gathered to paint in the open air. Corot is best known for his landscapes; Millet took many of his subjects from peasant life (*The Gleaners*) and had a great influence on Van Gogh.

Millet anticipated the realist programme of Gustave Courbet, a prominent member of the Paris Commune (he was accused of and imprisoned for destroying the Vendôme Column), whose paintings show the drudgery of manual labour and dignity of ordinary life (*Funeral at Ornans*, *The Angelus*).

Édouard Manet used realism to depict the life of the Parisian middle classes, yet he included in his pictures numerous references to the old masters. Both his *Déjeuner sur l'Herbe* and *Olympia* were considered scandalous, largely because they broke with the traditional treatment of their subject matter.

Impressionism, initially a term of derision, was taken from the title of an 1874 experimental painting by Claude Monet, *Impression: Soleil Levant* (Impression: Sunrise). Monet was the leading figure of the school, which counted among its members Alfred Sisley, Camille Pissarro, Berthe Morisot and Pierre-Auguste Renoir. The impressionists' main aim was to capture the effects of fleeting light, painting almost universally *en plein air*, and light came to dominate the content of their painting.

Edgar Degas was a fellow traveller, but he favoured his studio to the open air, preferring to paint at the racecourse (*At the Races*) and in ballet studios (*The Dance Class*). Henri de Toulouse-Lautrec was a great admirer of Degas, but chose subjects one or two notches below: people in the bistros, brothels and music halls of Montmartre (eg *Au Moulin Rouge*). He is best known for his posters and lithographs, in which the distortion of the figures is both satirical and decorative.

Paul Cézanne is celebrated for his still-lifes and landscapes depicting the south of France, though he spent many years in Paris after breaking with the impressionists. The name of Paul Gauguin immediately conjures up his studies of Tahitian and Breton women. Both painters are usually referred to as postimpressionists, something of a catch-all term for the diverse styles that flowed from impressionism.

In the late 19th century Gauguin worked for a time in Arles in Provence with the Dutch-born Vincent Van Gogh, who spent most of his painting life in France (p327).

A brilliant, innovative artist, Van Gogh produced haunting self-portraits and landscapes in which colour assumes an expressive and emotive quality. His later technique paralleled pointillism, developed by Georges Seurat, who applied paint in small dots or uniform brush strokes of unmixed colour, producing fine mosaics of warm and cool tones. Henri Rousseau was a contemporary of the postimpressionists but his 'naive' art was totally unaffected by them. His dream-like pictures of the Paris suburbs and of jungle and desert scenes have had a lasting influence on 20th-century art.

Gustave Moreau was a member of the symbolist school. His eerie treatment of mythological subjects can be seen in his old studio, which is now the Musée Gustave Moreau (p128) in the 9e. Fauvism took its name from the slur of a critic who compared the exhibitors at the 1905 Salon d'Automne (Autumn Salon) with *fauves* (beasts) because of their radical use of intensely bright colours. Among these 'beastly' painters were Henri Matisse, André Derain and Maurice de Vlaminck.

Cubism was effectively launched in 1907 by the Spanish prodigy Pablo Picasso with his *Les Demoiselles d'Avignon*. Cubism, as developed by Picasso, Georges Braque and Juan Gris, deconstructed the subject into a system of intersecting planes and presented various aspects simultaneously.

In the 1920s and 1930s the École de Paris (School of Paris) was formed by a group of expressionists, mostly foreign born, including Amedeo Modigliani from Italy, the Japanese Foujita and the Russian Marc Chagall, whose works combine fantasy and folklore.

Dada, both a literary and artistic movement of revolt, started in Zürich in 1915. In Paris, one of the key Dadaists was Marcel Duchamp, whose *Mona Lisa* adorned with moustache and goatee epitomises the spirit of the movement. Surrealism, an offshoot of Dada, flourished between the wars. Drawing on the theories of Freud, it attempted to reunite the conscious and unconscious realms, to permeate everyday life with fantasies and dreams. Among the most important proponents of this style in Paris were Chagall, as well as René Magritte, André Masson, Max Ernst, André Breton and Piet Mondrian. The most influential, however, was the Spanish-born artist Salvador Dalí, who arrived in the French capital in 1929 and painted some of his most seminal works (eg *Sleep, Paranoia*) while residing here.

WWII ended Paris' role as the world's artistic capital. Many artists left France, and though some returned after the war, the city never regained its old magnetism, with New York and then London picking up the baton. A few postwar Parisian artists are noteworthy, however, including Nicolas de Staël, Jean Fautrier and Bernard Buffet.

Top Five Art Museums

- Musée d'Art Moderne de la Ville de Paris (p116)
- Musée du Louvre (p80)
- Musée Gustave Moreau (p128)
- Musée d'Orsay (p111)
- Musée Rodin (p111)

SCULPTURE

By the 14th century sculpture was increasingly commissioned for the tombs of the nobility. In Renaissance Paris, Pierre Bontemps decorated the beautiful tomb of François I at the Basilique St-Denis (p135), and Jean Goujon created the Fontaine des Innocents in central Paris. The baroque style is exemplified by Guillaume Coustou's *Horses of Marly* at the entrance to the av des Champs-Élysées.

In the 19th century, memorial statues in public places came to replace sculpted tombs. One of the best artists in the new mode was François Rude, who sculpted the Maréchal Ney statue, *Maréchal under Napoleon*, outside the Closerie des Lilas and the relief on the Arc de Triomphe. Another sculptor was Jean-Baptiste Carpeaux, who began as a romantic, but whose work – such as *The Dance* on the Palais Garnier and his fountain in the Jardin du Luxembourg – look back to the warmth and gaiety of the baroque era. At the end of the 19th century Auguste Rodin's work overcame the conflict between neoclassicism and romanticism; his sumptuous bronze and marble figures of men and women did much to revitalise sculpture as an expressive medium. One of Rodin's most gifted pupils was Camille Claudel, whose work can be seen along with that of Rodin in the Musée Rodin (p111).

Braque and Picasso experimented with sculpture, and in the spirit of Dada, Marcel Duchamp exhibited 'found objects', one of which was a urinal, which he mounted, signed and titled *Fountain*.

One of the most influential sculptors to emerge before WWII was the Romanian-born (but Paris-based) sculptor Constantin Brancusi, whose work can be seen in the Atelier Brancusi outside the Centre Pompidou (p83). After the war César Baldaccini – known as César to the world – used iron and scrap metal to create his imaginary insects and animals, later graduating to pliable plastics. Among his best-known works are the *Centaur* statue (p95) in the 6e and the statuette handed to actors at the Césars, French cinema's equivalent to the Oscars. Two sculptors who lived and worked most of their adult lives in Paris and each have a museum devoted to their life and work are Ossip Zadkine (p107) and Antoine Bourdelle (p109).

MUSIC

In the 17th and 18th centuries French baroque music influenced much of Europe's musical output. Composers François Couperin and Jean Philippe Rameau were two major players during this period.

France produced and cultivated a number of musical luminaries in the 19th century. Among these were Hector Berlioz, Charles Gounod, César Franck, Camille Saint-Saëns and Georges Bizet. Berlioz was the founder of modern orchestration, while Franck's organ compositions sparked a musical renaissance in France that would go on to produce such greats as Gabriel Fauré, and the impressionists Claude Debussy and Maurice Ravel.

More recent classical composers include Olivier Messiaen, the chief organist at the Église de la Trinité in the 9e for decades, who combined modern, almost mystical music with natural sounds such as birdsong until his death in 1992 at the age of 84, and his student, the radical Pierre Boulez, who includes computer-generated sound in his compositions.

Jazz hit Paris in the 1920s with a bang and has remained popular ever since. France's contribution to the world of jazz has been great, including the violinist Stéphane Grapelli and the legendary three-fingered Roma guitarist Django Reinhardt.

The most popular form of indigenous music is the *chanson française*, with a tradition going back to the troubadours of the Middle Ages. 'French songs' have always emphasised lyrics over music and rhythm, which may explain the enormous success of rap in France today. The chanson tradition was revived from the 1930s onwards by such singers as Édith Piaf and Charles Trenet. In the 1950s singers such as Georges Brassens, Léo Ferré, Claude Nougaro, Jacques Brel and Barbara became national stars; a big revival is taking place now called *La Nouvelle Chanson Française*. Among the most exciting performers of this genre are Vincent Delerm, Bénabar, Thomas Fersen, Sanseverino, Jeanne Cherhal, Dominique A and a group called Les Têtes Raides.

Top Five CDs

- *Absolute Raï* – four-disk set featuring la crème de la crème of *raï* (type of Algerian popular music) artistes, including Cheb Khaled and Cheb Mami.
- *Anthologie Serge Gainsbourg* – three-CD anthology includes the metro man's most famous tracks, including 'Le Poinçonneur des Lilas' and 'Je t'aime…Moi Non Plus' sung with Brigitte Bardot.
- *Édith Piaf: 30e Anniversaire* – released to mark the 30th year of the belle of Belleville's death, this double CD contains some 44 classic Piaf songs – from 'La Vie en Rose' and 'Hymne à l'Amour' to 'Amants de Paris'.
- *Négresses Vertes: Le Grand Déballage* – twenty-track 'best-of' compilation from the band that took *sono mondiale* (world music), added some local sounds and put it on the streets of Paris; includes 'La Valse', 'Zobi La Mouche' and the incomparable 'I Love Paris' (complete with zee Frensh ac-sanz).
- *Olivier Messiaen: Turangalila Symphonie* – the great organist-composer's weird but wonderful 10-movement symphony conducted by Antoni Wit and delivered by the Polish National Radio Symphony.

France was among the first countries to 'discover' *sono mondiale* (world music). You'll hear everything from Algerian *raï* (type of Algerian popular music) to North African music (Khaled, Cheb Mami, Racid Taha) and Senegalese *mbalax* (Youssou N'Dour) to West Indian *zouk* (Kassav, Zouk Machine), and Cuban salsa and Brazilian music blaring from radios and at clubs. Magic System from Côte d'Ivoire has helped popularise *zouglou* (a kind of West African rap and dance music) with its album Premier Gaou, and Congolese Koffi Olomide still packs the halls. A truly world band is the Afro-Cuban Africando, whose members hailed from West Africa, Cuba, Puerto Rico (via New York) and Vietnam.

Today's popular music has come a long way since the *yéyé* (imitative rock) of the 1960s sung by Johnny Halliday. In recent years a distinctly urban and highly exportable Parisian sound has developed, often mixing computer-enhanced Chicago blues and Detroit techno with 1960s lounge music, vintage tracks from the likes of Serge Gainsbourg and, yes, even *yéyé*. For reviews of music venues around Paris, see p229.

CINEMA

Parisians go to the cinema on average once a week and take films – especially French films (of which 25 are released each year) – very seriously. In general they prefer to watch foreign films in their original language with French subtitles.

France's place in film history was firmly ensured when the Lumière brothers invented 'moving pictures' and organised the world's first paying public film-screening – a series of two-minute reels – in Paris' Grand Café on the blvd des Capucines in December 1895.

In the 1920s and 1930s avant-garde directors, such as René Clair, Marcel Carné and the intensely productive Jean Renoir, son of the artist, searched for new forms and subjects.

In the late 1950s a large group of young directors arrived on the scene with a new genre, the *nouvelle vague* (new wave). This group included Jean-Luc Godard, François Truffaut, Claude Chabrol, Eric Rohmer, Jacques Rivette, Louis Malle and Alain Resnais. This disparate group of directors believed in the primacy of the film maker, giving rise to the term *film d'auteur* (loosely, 'art house film').

Many films followed, among them Alain Resnais' *Hiroshima Mon Amour* and *L'Année Dernière à Marienbad* (Last Year at Marienbad), and Luis Buñuel's *Belle de Jour*. François Truffaut's *Les Quatre Cents Coups* (The 400 Blows) was partly based on his own rebellious adolescence. Jean-Luc Godard made such films as *À Bout de Souffle* (Breathless), *Alphaville* and *Pierrot le Fou*, which showed even less concern for sequence and narrative. The new wave continued until the 1970s, by which stage it had lost its experimental edge.

Of the directors of the 1950s and 1960s not part of this school, one of the most notable was Jacques Tati, who made many comic films based around the charming, bumbling figure of Monsieur Hulot and his struggles to adapt to the modern age. Probably the best example is *Les Vacances de M Hulot* (Mr Hulot's Holiday).

The most successful directors of the 1980s and 1990s included Jean-Jacques Beineix, who made *Diva* and *Betty Blue*, Jean-Luc Besson, who made *Subway* and *The Big Blue*, and Léos Carax (*Boy Meets Girl*).

Light social comedies, such as *Trois Hommes et un Couffin* (Three Men and a Cradle) by Coline Serreau and *La Vie Est un Long Fleuve Tranquille* (Life is a Long Quiet River) by Étienne Chatiliez, have been among the biggest hits in France in recent years. A French hit in the international market recently has been Jean-Pierre Jeunet's *Le Fabuleux Destin d'Amélie Poulain* (Amelie), nominated for five Oscars in 2002 and winner of none.

Matthieu Kassovitz's award-winning *La Haine*, apparently inspired by *Meanstreets*, *Taxi Driver* and *Do the Right Thing*, examines the prejudice and violence among young French-born Algerians. Alain Resnais' *On Connaît la Chanson*, based on the life of the late British TV playwright Dennis Potter, received international acclaim and six Césars in 1997.

Other well-regarded directors today include Bertrand Blier (*Trop Belle pour Toi*; Too Beautiful for You), Cédric Klapisch (*Un Air de Famille*; Family Relations), German-born Dominik Moll (*Harry, un Ami qui Vous Veut du Bien*; With a Friend like Harry), Agnès Jaoul (*Le Gout des Autres*; The Taste of Others), Yves Lavandier (*Oui, mais...*; Yes, but...) and Catherine Breillat (*À Ma Sœur*; Fat Girl).

Top Five Paris Films

- *À Bout de Souffle* (*Breathless*; France, 1959) – Jean-Luc Godard's first feature is a carefree, fast-paced B&W celebration of Paris – from av des Champs-Élysées to the cafés of the Left Bank. Technically it challenged gangster movie conventions with the inspired new technique of jump-cutting (ie cutting a scene within the same camera setup).
- *Le Fabuleux Destin d'Amélie Poulain* (*Amelie*; France, 2001) – one of the most popular French films internationally in years, Jean-Pierre Jeunet's feel-good story of a winsome young Parisian do-gooder named Amélie takes viewers on a technicolour tour of Pigalle, Notre Dame, train stations and, above all, Montmartre.
- *Last Tango in Paris* (USA, 1972) – in Bernardo Bertolucci's classic, Marlon Brando gives the performance of his career portraying a grief-stricken American in Paris trying to find salvation in anonymous, sadomasochistic sex.
- *La Haine* (*Hate*; France, 1995) – Matthieu Kassovitz's incendiary B&W film examines the racism, social repression and violence among Parisian *beurs*, young French-born Algerians.
- *Boy Meets Girl* (France, 1984) – this moody B&W film from Léos Carax – his first feature – creates a kind of Parisian purgatory of souls lost in the eternal night.

DANCE

Ballet as we know it today originated in Italy but was brought to France in the late 16th century by Catherine de Médici. The first *ballet comique de la reine* (dramatic ballet) was performed at an aristocratic wedding at the court in Paris in 1581. It combined music, dance and poetic recitations (usually in praise of the monarchy), and was performed by male courtiers with women of the court forming the *corps de ballet*. Louis XIV so enjoyed the spectacles that he danced many leading roles himself at Versailles. In 1661 he founded the Académie Royale de Danse (Royal Dance Academy), from which modern ballet developed.

By the end of the 18th century, choreographers such as Jean-Georges Noverre had become more important than musicians, poets and the dancers themselves. In the early 19th century romantic ballets, such as *Giselle* and *Les Sylphides*, were better attended than the opera. Between 1945 and 1955 Roland Petit created such innovative ballets as *Turangalila*, with music composed by Olivier Messiaen, and *Le Jeune Homme et la Mort*. Maurice Béjart shocked the public with his *Symphonie pour un Homme Seul*, which was danced in black in 1955, *Le Sacre du Printemps* and *Le Marteau sans Maître*, with music by Pierre Boulez.

Today French dance seems to be moving in a new, more personal direction with performers such as Caroline Marcadé, Maguy Martin, Laurent Hilaire and Aurélie Dupont, and choreographers such as Odile Duboc, Jean-Claude Gallotta and Jean-François Duroure.

For more information and reviews on dance performances, see p242.

THEATRE

France' first important dramatist was Alexandre Hardy, who appeared in Paris in 1597 and published almost three-dozen plays over a relatively short period. Though few of his plays have withstood the test of time, Hardy was an innovator who helped bridge the gap between the French theatre of the Middle Ages and Renaissance and that of the 17th century.

During the golden age of French drama the most popular playwright was Molière, who (like William Shakespeare) started his career as an actor. Plays such as *Tartuffe*, a satire on the corruption of the aristocracy, won him the enmity of both the state and the church and a ban, but are now staples of the classical repertoire. The playwrights Pierre Corneille and Jean Racine, in contrast, drew their subjects from history and classical mythology. Racine's *Phèdre*, for instance, taken from Euripides, is a story of incest and suicide among the descendants of the Greek gods, while Corneille's tragedy *Horace* is derived from Livy.

Theatre in France didn't really come into its own again until the postwar period of the 20th century with the arrival of two foreigners, both proponents of the so-called Theatre of the Absurd who wrote in French. Works by Irish-born Samuel Beckett, such as *En Attendant Godot* (Waiting for Godot; 1952), are bleak and point to the meaninglessness of life but are also richly humorous. The plays of Eugène Ionesco – eg *La Cantatrice Chauve* (The Bald Soprano; 1948) – are equally dark, satirical and ultimately compassionate.

Architecture

Gallo-Roman   35

Merovingian & Carolingian   35

Romanesque   35

Gothic   36
Rayonnant Gothic   36
Flamboyant Gothic   37

Renaissance   37
Early Renaissance   37
Mannerism   37

Baroque   37
Rococo   38

Neoclassicism   38

Art Nouveau   39

Modern   39

Contemporary   40

Architecture

Parisians traditionally have not been as intransigent as, say, Londoners, in accepting changes to their cityscape nor as unshocked by the new as New Yorkers seem to be. But then Paris never had as great a fire as London did (1666), which offered architects a *tabula rasa* on which to redesign and build a modern city, or the green field that was New York in the late 18th century.

It took disease, clogged streets, an antiquated sewage system, a lack of open spaces and one Baron Georges-Eugène Haussmann to move Paris from the Middle Ages into a modern age, and few town planners anywhere in the world have had as great an impact on the city of their birth as Haussmann (1809–91) did on his. As prefect of the Seine *département* under Napoleon III between 1853 and 1870, Haussmann and his staff of engineers and architects completely rebuilt huge swathes of the capital. He's best known (and most bitterly attacked) for having demolished much of medieval Paris, replacing the chaotic narrow streets – easy to barricade in an uprising – with the handsome, arrow-straight thoroughfares for which the city is now celebrated. The 12 avenues leading out from the Arc de Triomphe, for example, were his work, as were many of the city's loveliest parks, including the Parc des Buttes-Chaumont (19e), Parc Montsouris (14e) and large areas of the Bois de Boulogne (16e) and Bois de Vincennes (12e).

The transformation was not as easy as it might seem from a distance of one and a half centuries. Parisians endured years of 'flying dust, noise, and falling plaster and beams', as one contemporary observer wrote; entire areas (for example, the labyrinth-like Île de la Cité) of the city were razed and hundreds of thousands of (mostly poor) people displaced. Even worse – or better, depending on your outlook – it brought to a head the *vieux* Paris versus *nouveau* Paris debate in which the writer Victor Hugo played a key role (see p23) and which continues to this day (see p40).

At first glance, much of the architecture of Paris may appear to be the same – six- or seven-storey apartment blocks in the style of the Deuxième Empire (Second Empire; 1852–70) lining grand boulevards and interspersed with leafy squares. That is in effect exactly what Haussmann had in mind when he oversaw the construction of a new city in

Arc de Triomphe du Carrousel (p82)

the middle of the 19th century. But Paris is a treasure trove of architectural styles: from Roman arenas and Gothic cathedrals to postmodernist cubes and glass pyramids that not only look great but serve a function.

GALLO-ROMAN

Classical architecture is characterised both by its elegance and its grandeur. The Romans' use and adaptation of the classical Greek orders, Doric, Ionic and Corinthian, influenced Western architecture for millennia. The Romans were the first to use bricks and cement to build vaults, arches and domes. The emphasis was on impressive public buildings, aqueducts, triumphal arches, temples, fortifications, marketplaces, amphitheatres and bathhouses, some examples of which can be found in Paris. The Romans also established regular street grids.

From the mid-1st century BC, the Romans turned a small Gallic settlement of wattle and daub huts on the Île de la Cité into a provincial capital called Lutetia (Lutèce in French). A temple to Jupiter was erected on the site where the **Cathédrale de Notre Dame de Paris** (p91) now stands, and the Roman town spread to the south bank, with rue St-Jacques as the main north–south axis. A forum stood at the corner of today's rue Soufflot, near the Panthéon and the Jardin du Luxembourg.

Traces of Roman Paris can be seen in the residential foundations and dwellings in the **Crypte Archéologique** (p92) under the square in front of Notre Dame; in the partially reconstructed **Arènes de Lutèce** (p95); and in the *frigidarium* (cooling room) and other remains of Roman baths dating from around AD 200 at the **Musée National du Moyen Age** (p94).

The Musée National du Moyen Age also contains the so-called **Pillier des Nautes** (Boatsmen's Pillar), one of the most valuable legacies of the Gallo-Roman period. It is a 2.5m-high monument dedicated to Jupiter and was erected by the boatmen's guild during the reign of Tiberius (AD 14–37) on the Île de la Cité. What makes it so important is that is it lined with bas-reliefs of both Roman (eg Jupiter, Venus, Mercury, Mars) and Gallic (eg Esus, Cernunnos, Smertrios) deities, suggesting that while the Gauls had submitted to Roman authority, part of their ancient Celtic culture survived alongside as late as the 1st century AD. The boat remains the symbol of Paris and the city's Latin motto is *'Fluctuat Nec Mergitur'* (Tosses but Does Not Sink).

MEROVINGIAN & CAROLINGIAN

Although quite a few churches were built in Paris during the Merovingian and Carolingian periods (5th to 10th centuries), very little of them remain.

After the Merovingian ruler Clovis I made Paris his seat in the early 6th century, he established an abbey dedicated to Sts Peter and Paul on the south bank of the Seine. All that remains of this once great abbey (later named in honour of Paris' patron, Sainte Geneviève, and demolished in 1802) is the **Tour Clovis** (p141), a heavily restored Romanesque tower within the grounds of the prestigious Lycée Henri IV just east of the Panthéon.

Clovis' son and successor, Childeric II, founded the Abbey of St-Germain des Prés; the Merovingian kings were buried here during the 6th and 7th centuries, but their tombs disappeared during the French Revolution. The dynasty's most productive ruler, Dagobert, established an abbey at St-Denis north of Paris, which would soon become the richest and most important monastery in France. Archaeological excavations in the crypt of the 12th-century **Basilique St-Denis** (p135) have uncovered extensive tombs from both the Merovingian and Carolingian periods. The oldest of these dates from around AD 570.

ROMANESQUE

A religious revival in the 11th century led to the construction of a large number of *roman* (Romanesque) churches, so called because their architects adopted many architectural elements (for example, vaulting) from Gallo-Roman buildings still standing at the time.

Romanesque buildings typically have round arches, heavy walls, few windows that let in very little light, and a lack of ornamentation that borders on the austere. Chateaux built during this era tended to be massive, heavily fortified structures that afforded few luxuries to their inhabitants.

No civic buildings or churches in Paris are entirely Romanesque in style, but a few have important representative elements. The **Église St-Germain des Prés** (p97), built in the 11th century on the site of the Merovingian ruler Childeric's 6th-century abbey, has been altered many times over the centuries, but the Romanesque bell tower over the west entrance has changed little since 1000. There are also some decorated capitals (the upper part of the supporting columns) in the nave dating from this time. The choir and apse of the **Église St-Nicholas des Champs** (Map pp386-8), just south of the Musée des Arts et Métiers, are Romanesque dating from about 1130 as is the truncated bell tower. The **Église St-Germain L'Auxerrois** (p82) was built in a mixture of Gothic and Renaissance styles between the 13th and 16th centuries on a site used for Christian worship since about AD 500. But the square belfry that rises from next to the south transept arm is Romanesque in style.

The choir and ambulatory of the **Basilique de St-Denis** (p135) have features illustrating the transition from Romanesque to Gothic while the magnificent 13th-century **Cathédrale Notre Dame** at Chartres (see p322) is crowned by two soaring spires – one Romanesque and the other Gothic. The west entrance to the cathedral, known as the **Portail Royal** (Royal Portal), is adorned with statues whose features are elongated in the Romanesque style. The other main Romanesque feature of the cathedral at Chartres is the **Clocher Vieux** (Old Bell Tower), which was begun in the 1140s. At 105m, it is the tallest Romanesque steeple still standing. Also in Chartres is the empty shell of the **Collégiale St-André**, a Romanesque collegiate church dating from the 12th century.

GOTHIC

The Gothic style originated in the mid-12th century in northern France, where great wealth attracted the finest architects, engineers and artisans. Gothic structures are characterised by ribbed vaults carved with great precision, pointed arches, slender verticals, chapels (often built or endowed by the wealth or by guilds), galleries and arcades along the nave and chancel, refined decoration and large stained-glass windows. If you look closely at certain Gothic buildings, however, you'll notice minor asymmetrical elements. These elements were introduced to avoid monotony, in accordance with standard Gothic practice.

The first Gothic building was the **Basilique de St-Denis** (p135), which combined various late Romanesque elements to create a new kind of structural support in which each arch counteracted and complemented the next. Begun in around 1135, the basilica served as a model for many other 12th-century French cathedrals, including Notre Dame de Paris and the one at Chartres. Gothic technology and the width and height it made possible subsequently spread to the rest of Western Europe.

Cathedrals built in the early Gothic style, which lasted until about 1230, were majestic but lacked the lightness and airiness of later works. Since the stained-glass windows could not support the roof, thick stone buttresses were placed between them. It was soon discovered that reducing the bulk of the buttresses and adding outer piers to carry the thrust created a lighter building without compromising structural integrity.

This discovery gave rise to flying buttresses, which helped lift the Gothic style to its greatest achievements between 1230 and 1300. During this period, when French architecture dominated the European scene for the first time, High Gothic masterpieces such as the seminal cathedral at Chartres were decorated with ornate tracery (the delicate stone ribwork on stained-glass windows) and huge, colourful rose windows.

RAYONNANT GOTHIC

In the 14th century, the Rayonnant (Radiant) Gothic style – named after the radiating tracery of the rose windows – developed, with interiors becoming even lighter thanks to broader windows and more translucent stained glass. One of the most influential Rayonnant buildings was the **Ste-Chapelle** (p92), whose stained glass forms a curtain of glazing.

The two transept façades of the **Cathédrale de Notre Dame de Paris** (p91)and the vaulted **Salle des Gens d'Armes** (Cavalrymen's Hall) in the **Conciergerie** (p92), the largest surviving medieval hall in Europe, are other fine examples of the Rayonnant Gothic style.

FLAMBOYANT GOTHIC

By the 15th century, decorative extravagance led to Flamboyant Gothic, so named because the wavy stone carving made the towers appear to be blazing or flaming (*flamboyant*). Beautifully lacy examples of Flamboyant architecture include the **Clocher Neuf** at Chartres' **Cathédrale Notre Dame** (p322), the **Église St-Séverin** and the **Tour St-Jacques** (p86), a 52m tower which is all that remains of the Église St-Jacques la Boucherie from the early 16th century. Inside the **Église St-Eustache** (p85), there's some exceptional Flamboyant Gothic archwork holding up the ceiling of the chancel. Several *hôtels particuliers* (private mansions) were also built in this style, including the **Hôtel de Cluny**, now the **Musée National du Moyen Age** (p94) and the **Hôtel de Sens** (p138).

RENAISSANCE

The Renaissance, which began in Italy in the early 15th century, set out to realise a 're-birth' of classical Greek and Roman culture. It had its first impact on France at the end of the 15th century, when Charles VIII began a series of invasions of Italy, returning with some new ideas. The French Renaissance is usually divided into two periods: early Renaissance and Mannerism.

EARLY RENAISSANCE

During the first period, a variety of classical components and decorative motifs (columns, tunnel vaults, round arches, domes etc) were blended with the rich decoration of Flamboyant Gothic. The Early Renaissance style of architecture is best exemplified in Paris by the **Église de St-Eustache** (p85) on the Right Bank and **Église St-Étienne du Mont** (p94) on the Left Bank.

MANNERISM

Mannerism began around 1530, when François I (who'd been so deeply impressed by what he'd seen in Italy that he brought Leonardo da Vinci back with him in 1516) hired Italian architects and artists – many of them disciples of Michelangelo or Raphael – to design and decorate his new **Château de Fontainebleau** (p313). Over the following decades, French architects who had studied in Italy took over from their Italian colleagues. In 1546 Pierre Lescot designed the richly decorated southwestern corner of the **Cour Carrée** of the **Louvre** (p80). The **Petit Château** at the **Château de Chantilly** (p318) was built about a decade later. The Marais remains the best area for spotting reminders of the Renaissance in Paris proper, with some fine *hôtels particuliers* from this era such as the **Hôtel Carnavalet** (p88) and **Hôtel Lamoignan**.

Because French Renaissance architecture was very much the province of the aristocracy and designed by imported artists, the middle classes – resentful French artisans among them – remained loyal to the indigenous Gothic style, and Gothic churches continued to be built in Paris throughout the 1500s. The Mannerist style lasted until the early 17th century.

BAROQUE

During the baroque period, which lasted from the tail end of the 16th to the late 18th centuries, painting, sculpture and classical architecture were integrated to create structures and interiors of great subtlety, refinement and elegance. With the advent of the baroque, architecture became more pictorial, with the painted ceilings in churches illustrating the Passion of Christ and infinity to the faithful, and palaces invoking the power and order

Five Controversial Buildings

The following are the five structures (one of which was never erected) that have sparked the most controversy in Paris over the years.

- **Eiffel Tower** (p114)
- **Grande Pyramide** (p80)
- **Opéra Bastille** (p90)
- **Tour Montparnasse** (p108)
- **Tour sans Fin** (p134)

of the state. Baroque architecture in Paris bears little resemblance to that in the capital cities of Catholic central and southern Europe. Here, as in the Protestant countries of northern Europe, baroque architecture was meant to appeal to the intellect – not the senses. As a result it was more geometric, formal and precise.

Salomon de Brosse, who designed Paris' **Palais du Luxembourg** (p107) in 1615, set the stage for two of France's most prominent early baroque architects: François Mansart, designer of the **Église Notre Dame du Val-de-Grâce** (p231), and his young rival Louis Le Vau, the architect of the **Château de Vaux-le-Vicomte** (p317), which served as a model for Louis XIV's palace at Versailles. Baroque elements are particularly evident in the lavish interiors of the **Château de Versailles** (p308), such as the **Galerie des Glaces** (Hall of Mirrors). Jules Hardouin-Mansart, Le Vau's successor at Versailles, also designed the landmark **Église du Dôme** (p112), considered the finest church built in France during the 17th century.

Other fine examples of French baroque are the **Église St-Louis en l'Île** (p93), built between 1656 and 1725; the **Chapelle de la Sorbonne** (p94); the **Palais Royal** (p83); and the 17th-century **Hôtel de Sully** (p88), with its inner courtyard decorated with allegorical figures. The **Cathédrale St-Louis** in **Versailles** (p311) fuses elements of baroque and neoclassicism.

ROCOCO

Rococo, a derivation of late baroque, was popular during the Enlightenment (1700–80). The word comes from the French *rocaille* for 'loose pebbles' which, together with shells, were used to decorate inside walls and other surfaces. In Paris, rococo was confined almost exclusively to the interiors of private residences and had a minimal impact on churches and civic façades, which continued to follow the conventional rules of baroque classicism. Rococo interiors, such as the oval rooms of the **Archives Nationales** (p89), were lighter, smoother and airier than their baroque predecessors and favoured pastels over vivid colours.

NEOCLASSICISM

Neoclassical architecture, which emerged in about 1740 and remained popular in Paris until well into the 19th century, had its roots in the renewed interest in classical forms. Although it was in part a reaction against baroque and rococo, with their emphasis on decoration and illusion, neoclassicism was more profoundly a search for order, reason and serenity through the adoption of the forms and conventions of Graeco-Roman antiquity: columns, simple geometric forms and traditional ornamentation.

Among the earliest examples of this style in Paris are the Italianate façade of the **Église St-Sulpice** (p107), designed in 1733 by Giovanni Servandoni, which took inspiration from Christopher Wren's Cathedral of St Paul in London, and the **Petit Trianon** at **Versailles** (p308), designed by Jacques-Ange Gabriel for Louis XV in 1761. The domed building housing the **Institut de France** (p98) is a masterpiece of early French neoclassical architecture, but France's greatest neoclassical architect of the 18th century was Jacques-Germain Soufflot, who designed the **Panthéon** (p94).

Neoclassicism really came into its own, however, under Napoleon, who used it extensively for monumental architecture intended to embody the grandeur of imperial France and its capital. Well-known Paris sights designed (though not necessarily completed) under the First Empire (1804–14) include the **Arc de Triomphe** (p117); the **Arc de Triomphe du Carrousel** (p82); the **Église de la Madeleine** (p119); the **Pont des Arts**; the **Bourse de Commerce** (p85); and the **Assemblée Nationale** in the **Palais Bourbon** (p111).

Neoclassicism remained very much in vogue in Paris, though in slightly different forms, until late into the 19th century, spilling even into the 20th century in some cases; eg the **Palais de Chaillot** (p114), which was built for the World Exhibition of 1937. Two architects associated with Paris' École des Beaux-Arts, the most important centre of architectural education in Europe in the 19th century, who best exemplify this late period of classicism are Jacques-Ignace Hittorff, who designed the **Gare du Nord** (p121) in 1861 and Louis Duc, responsible for the **Palais de Justice** (p92). The work of both men influenced a generation of architects, including Henri Deglane and Victor Laloux, who designed the **Grand Palais** (p118) and the **Gare d'Orsay**, now the **Musée d'Orsay** (p111) for the World Exhibition in 1889, held to commemorate the centenary of the French Revolution. The **Eiffel Tower** (p114), which at first faced massive opposition from Paris' artistic and literary elite, was also opened for the 1889 World Exhibition. Two years previously the dramatist Alexandre Dumas *fils* (the son rather than the father of the same name) and the short-story writer Guy de Maupassant signed a petition protesting the construction of a 'gigantic black factory chimney'; when the tower was complete Maupassant frequented the restaurant at its base, claiming it was the only place where he couldn't see the monstrosity.

The climax of 19th-century classicism in Paris, however, is thought to be the **Palais Garnier** (p121), designed by Charles Garnier to house the opera and to showcase the splendour of Napoleon III's France. It was one of the crowning glories of the urban redevelopment plans of Baron Haussmann.

ART NOUVEAU

Gothic Revival, a style of architecture popular between the late 18th and late 19th centuries, never caught on in Paris as it did in London and New York; much of that style was confined to restorations by architect Eugène Emmanuel Viollet-le-Duc at **Ste-Chapelle** (p92) **Notre Dame** (p91) and the **Église St-Germain L'Auxerrois** (p82). However, Art Nouveau, which emerged in Europe and the USA in the second half of the 19th century under various names (Jugendstil, Sezessionstil, Stile Liberty) caught on quickly in Paris and its influence lasted until about 1910.

Art Nouveau was characterised by sinuous curves and flowing, asymmetrical forms reminiscent of tendrilous vines, water lilies, the patterns on insect wings and the flowering boughs of trees. Influenced by the arrival of *objets d'art* from Japan, its French name came from a Paris gallery that featured works in the 'new art' style.

Art Nouveau had a profound impact on all of the applied arts, including interior design, glass work, wrought-iron work, furniture making and graphics. Art Nouveau combined a variety of materials – including iron, brick, glass and ceramics – in ways never seen before. Paris is still graced by Hector Guimard's **Art Nouveau metro entrances** (p84). There are some fine Art Nouveau interiors in the **Musée d'Orsay** (p111), an Art Nouveau glass roof over the **Grand Palais** (p118) and, on rue Pavée in the Marais, a **synagogue** designed by Guimard (p89). The city's three main department stores – **Le Bon Marché** (p261), **Galeries Lafayette** (p265) and **La Samaritaine** (p254) – also have elements of this style throughout their interiors.

MODERN

France's best known 20th-century architect, Charles-Édouard Jeanneret (better known as Le Corbusier), was born in Switzerland but settled in Paris in 1917 at the age of 30. A radical modernist, he tried to adapt buildings to their functions in industrialised society without ignoring the human element. Not everyone thinks he was particularly successful in his endeavours, however.

Most of Le Corbusier's work was done outside Paris though he did design several private residences and the **Pavillon Suisse**, a dormitory for Swiss students at the **Cité Universaire** in the southeastern 14e bordering the Périphérique. Perhaps most interesting – and frightening – is Le Corbusier's plans for Paris that never left the drawing board. Called Projet Voisin (Neighbour Project), they envisaged a wide boulevard linking the Gare Montparnasse with the Seine and lined with skyscrapers. The project would have required bulldozing much of the Latin Quarter.

Until 1968 French architects were still being trained almost exclusively at the conformist École de Beaux-Arts, which certainly shows in most of the early structures erected in the skyscraper district of **La Défense** (p133) and among such buildings as the Unesco building, erected in 1958 southwest of the École Militaire in the 7e, and the unspeakable, 210m-tall **Tour Montparnasse** (p108), whose architects should have been frogmarched to the place de la Concorde and guillotined.

CONTEMPORARY

France owes many of its most attractive and successful contemporary buildings in Paris to the vanity of its presidents. For centuries France's leaders have sought to immortalise themselves by erecting huge, public edifices – known as *grands projets* – in the capital, and the recent past has been no different. The late President Georges Pompidou commissioned the once reviled but now beloved **Centre Beaubourg** (Renzo Piano & Richard Rogers, 1977), later renamed the **Centre Pompidou** (p83), in which the architects – in order to keep the exhibition halls as spacious and uncluttered as possible – put the building's insides outside.

Pompidou's successor, Valéry Giscard d'Estaing, was instrumental in transforming the derelict Gare d'Orsay train station into the glorious **Musée d'Orsay** (p111), a design carried out by the Italian architect Gaeltana Aulenti in 1986. But François Mitterrand, with his decided preference for the modern, surpassed them both with a dozen or so monumental projects in Paris.

Since the early 1980s, Paris has seen the construction of such structures as IM Pei's controversial **Grande Pyramide** (p80), a glass pyramid (1993) that serves as the main entrance

The Great Divide

Though differing greatly in terms of size, outlook and historical development, Paris and London share a number of parallels in modern architecture and town planning. The erection of the unattractive and unpopular **Tour Montparnasse** in Paris (1973) and the **NatWest Tower** (1980; now Tower 42) in London precluded further development in the central part of both cities; in Paris, developers moved westward to **La Défense** and in London, eastward to the **Docklands**. Both areas failed to attract investors – or lessors for that matter – throughout the 1980s and almost went belly-up before catching their respective breaths in the 1990s.

At present Paris and London have populist (and popular) mayors – the socialist Bertrand Delanoë and the born-again Labourite Ken Livingstone – who are very much in favour of seeing their cities grow upward. And both cities have had strict regulations controlling just how high buildings could go. In London they are the infamous St Paul's Heights, which have restricted the growth of anything that exceeds (or obscures) the dome of Christopher Wren's work. In 1967 stringent town-planning regulations in Paris, which had been on the books since Haussmann's day, were eased and buildings were allowed to 'soar' to 36m though they had to be set back from the road so as not to block the light. But this change allowed the erection of high-rise buildings, which broke up the continuity of many streets. A decade later new restrictions required that buildings again be aligned along the road and that their height be in proportion to the width of the street. In some central areas that means buildings cannot go higher than 18m.

And that's where the parallels end. While Livingstone has been able to bend the rules and convince city administrators to allow the erection of such structures as Norman's Foster's **Swiss Re building** (nicknamed the 'erotic gherkin' for its unconventional shape), in the heart of London, and Renzo Piano's 66-storey **London Bridge Tower** (called the 'Shard of Glass' tower and Europe's tallest structure at 310m), at London Bridge, Delanoë has had to be content with developing areas on the edge of the city, such as the mixed-use **ZAC Paris Rive Gauche project**, the massive redevelopment of the old industrial quarter along the Seine in the 13e arrondissement with the central av de France and the stunning new **MK2 Bibliothèque cinema** (see p239) as its current showcases.

Building Inspiration

For the most part skyscrapers and other tall buildings are restricted to La Défense, but that doesn't mean other parts of Paris are bereft of interesting and inspired new buildings. Here is a list of some personal favourites:

1er arrondissment – Marché de St-Honoré (Map pp383-5; place du Marché St-Honoré; metro Tuileries or Opéra) This monumental glass hall (Ricardo Bofill, 1996) of offices and shops replaces an unsightly parking garage (now underground) and evokes the wonderful covered *passages couverts* (covered shopping arcades) that begin a short distance to the northeast (see p144).

7e arrondissement – Musée du Quai Branly (Map pp389-91; quai Branly; metro Pont de l'Alma) Jean Nouvel's as yet unveiled glass-and-wooden structure, which will combine the collection of the now defunct Musée National des Arts d'Afrique et d'Océanie in the Bois de Vincennes and some items from the Musée de l'Homme (see p114), takes advantage of its experimental garden designed by Gilles Clément and is virtually transparent from the street. It is scheduled to open to the public in late 2005.

9e arrondissement – Drouot Auction House (p265) We like this zany structure (Jean-Jacques Fernier & André Biro, 1980), a rebuild of the mid-19th-century Hôtel Drouot, for its oh-so-70s retro design and the way the architect describes it: 'a Surrealist reinterpretation of Haussmann architecture'. Go look (and then go figure).

10e arrondissement – Crèche (Map pp386-8; 8ter rue des Récollets; metro Gare de l'Est) This day nursery (Marc Younan, 2002) of wood and resin in the garden of the Couvent des Récollets looks like a jumbled pile of coloured building blocks. A central glass atrium functions as a 'village square'.

12e arrondissement – Direction de l'Action Sociale Building (Map pp392-5; 94-96 quai de la Rapée; metro Quai de la Rapée) The headquarters of Social Action (Aymeric Zublena, 1991) is unabashed in proclaiming the power of the state, with an enormous central square within and vast glass-and-metal gates. When the gates are closed the square turns into an antechamber worthy of a palace.

Cinémathèque (Map p401; place Leonard Bernstein; metro Bercy) The former American Centre (Frank Gehry, 1994), from the incomparable American architect of the Guggenheim Museum in Bilbao, is a fascinating building of creamy stone that looks from some angles as though it is falling in on itself. It will eventually house the **Maison du Cinéma** and the archives of the **Bibliothèque du Film**.

14e arrondissement – Fondation Cartier d'Art Contemporain (Map pp389-91; 261 blvd Raspail; metro Raspail) As with his Musée du Quai Branly (see earlier in this list), Master Nouvel set to 'conceal' the Cartier Foundation for Contemporary Arts when he designed it in 1993. In some ways the structure (lots of glass and what looks like scaffolding) appears both incomplete and invisible at once.

19e arrondissement – Les Orgues de Flandre (Map pp386-8; 67-107 av de Flandre & 14-24 rue Archereau; metro Riquet) As zany a structure as you'll find anywhere, these two enormous housing estates opposite one another are known as 'The Organs of Flanders' due to their resemblance to that musical instrument and their street address. Storeys are stacked at oblique angles and the structures appear to be swaying, though they are firmly anchored at the end of a small park just south of blvd Périphérique.

to the hitherto sacrosanct (and untouchable) Louvre and an architectural cause célèbre in the late 1980s; the city's second opera house, the tile-clad **Opéra Bastille** (p80) designed by Carlos Ott (1989); the Danish architect Johann-Otto von Sprekelsen's monumental **Grande Arche de la Défense** (p134), which opened in 1989; the delightful **Conservatoire de Paris** of the Cité de la Musique, which was designed by Christian de Portzamparc (1990 & 1994) and serves as a sort of gateway from the city to the whimsical **Parc de la Villette** (p128), with its wonderful museums, concert venues and other attractions; Patrick Berger's twinned **Grandes Serres**, or 'Great Greenhouses', at the main entrance to the **Parc André Citroën** (p82) built in 1992; the **Ministry of Finance** (p124) designed by Paul Chemetov and Borja Huidobro in 1990, with its striking 'pier' overhanging the Seine in Bercy; and the four glass towers of Dominique Perrault's **Bibliothèque Nationale de France** (p125), which opened in 1995.

One of the most beautiful and successful of the late-20th-century modern buildings in Paris is the **Institut du Monde Arabe** (p96), a highly praised structure that opened in 1987 and successfully mixes modern and traditional Arab and Western elements. It was designed by Jean Nouvel, France's leading and arguably most talented architect.

Grande Arche de la Défense (p134), La Défense

Not everything new, different and/or monumental that has appeared in the past two decades has been a government undertaking, however. The vast majority of the buildings in **La Défense** (p133), Paris' skyscraper district on the Seine to the west of the city centre, are privately owned and house some 1500 companies, including the head offices of more than a dozen of France's top corporations. Unfortunately, most of the skyscrapers here are impersonal and forgettable 'lipstick tubes' and 'upended shoeboxes' with the exception of the twin-towered **Cœur Défense** (p133) designed by Jean-Paul Viguier (2001) and, diagonally opposite, the elongated oval-shaped **Tour EDF** (Cobb & Pei, 2001), which appears to undulate in the breeze that forever whips across place de la Défense. It's a triumphal solution to a relatively small space and as attractive a stainless steel and glass skyscraper as you'll find anywhere.

Those wanting to learn more about Paris' contemporary architecture should visit the **Pavillon de l'Arsenal** (Map pp396-9; ☎ 01 42 76 33 97; www.pavillon-arsenal.com; 21 blvd Morland, 4e; metro Sully Morland; admission free; ☼ 10.30am-6.30pm Tue-Sat, 11am-7pm Sun), which is the city's town-planning and architectural centre and has both a permanent collection called 'Paris: The Making of a City' and rotating exhibits.

Food & Drink

History	44
Culture	**45**
Etiquette	46
How Parisians Eat	46
Staples & Specialities	**47**
Staples	47
Regional Specialities	49
Drinks	**51**
Alcoholic Drinks	51
Nonalcoholic Drinks	53
Celebrating with Food	**54**
Where to Eat & Drink	**55**
Auberge	55
Bar	55
Bistro	55
Brasseries	55
Buffet	55
Café	55
Cafetéria	56
Creperie	56
Restaurant	56
Restaurant Libre-Service	57
Restaurant Rapide	57
Restaurant Universitaire	57
Salon de thé	57
Self-Catering	57
Vegetarians & Vegans	58
Children	58
Quick Eats	58

Food & Drink

The world has three essential cuisines, the Hungarians like to say: Chinese, French and our own. They're right on the first two counts. In the East, no other style of cooking comes close to that of the Chinese for freshness of ingredients, natural flavours and refined, often complex, cooking methods. The same can be said for French cuisine, the West's most important and seminal style of cooking.

The word 'cuisine', of course, is French in origin (the English 'cooking style' just cannot handle all the nuances), while 'French' conjures up a sophisticated, cultured people who know their arts – including gastronomy. While there is only some truth to that notion, eating well is still of prime importance to most people here, and they continue to spend an inordinate amount of time thinking about, talking about and consuming food. As one well-fed *bon vivant* friend in the capital once told us: 'The French think mainly about two things – their two main meals. Everything else is in parentheses'. And it starts at a very young age. That same friend once offered to take a colleague's nine-year-old son along with her on a business trip to London. 'I would love to visit Londres,' said the young boy when she invited him, 'but I understand that one does not eat very well there.'

Lonely Planet's *World Food: France* will take you on a culinary tour of Paris and the Île de France as well as the rest of the country.

HISTORY

Up to the Middle Ages, dining – at least for the wealthier classes and the court in Paris – essentially meant sitting around a large table, sawing off hunks of meat with small knives. Even by the time the first French-language cookbook was published by Charles V's head chef, Guillaume Tirel (or Taillevent) in about 1375, menus consisted almost entirely of 'soups' (actually sodden pieces of bread, or sops, boiled in a thickened stock) and meat and poultry heavy with the taste of herbs and spices, including new ones, such as ginger, cinnamon and cloves, first introduced into Spain by the Moors. The book's very title, *Le Viander de Taillevent*, would suggest a carnivorous diet; at that time *viande* (meat) simply meant 'food'.

The 16th century was something of a watershed for French cuisine. When Catherine de Médici, future consort to François' son, Henri II, arrived in Paris in 1533, she brought with her a team of Florentine chefs and pastry cooks adept in the subtleties of Italian Renaissance cooking. They introduced such delicacies as aspics, truffles, *quenelles* (dumplings), artichokes, macaroons and puddings to the French court. Catherine's cousin Marie de Médici brought even more chefs to Paris when she married Henry IV in 1600. The French cooks, increasingly aware of their rising social status, took the Italians' recipes and sophisticated cooking styles on board, and the rest – to the eternal gratitude of epicures everywhere – is history.

France and its capital enjoyed an era of order and prosperity in the 17th century under the rule of Henri IV (1589–1610), who is famously credited with having wished all of his subjects to have a *poule au pot* (chicken in the pot) every Sunday. Later in the century the sweet tooth of Louis XIV (1643–1715) launched the custom of eating desserts, once reserved for feast days and other celebrations, at the end of a meal.

The most decisive influence on French cuisine at this time, however, was the work of chef François-Pierre de la Varenne, who learned his trade in Marie de Médici's kitchens. La Varenne's cookbook, *Le Cuisinier françois* (1652), was a gastronomic landmark for many reasons. It was the first to give instructions for preparing vegetables; it introduced soups in the modern sense, with the 'soup' being more important than the sops it contained; and it discarded bread and breadcrumbs as thickening agents in favour of *roux*, a much more versatile mixture of flour and fat. Most importantly, La Varenne downplayed the use of spices, preferring to serve meat in its natural juices sharpened with vinegar or lemon juice.

The 18th century, the Grand Siècle (Great Century) of reason, brought little enlightenment to the French menu apart from dishes and sauces named after *grands seigneurs* (great lords) and royalty by their sycophantic chefs. This was the century when newfangled foodstuffs from the New World – the tomato, corn, bean, red pepper and especially the potato so integral today in French cuisine – gained currency, when the fork became a standard part of the table setting, and when the first restaurant as we know it today opened (p167). Most important was the new trend to serve dishes in a logical order rather than heaping them in a pyramid on the table all at the same time.

During the French Revolution and the Reign of Terror that followed, the ovens in the kitchens of the great aristocratic households went cold, and their chefs were driven in tumbrels to the guillotine. But a new avenue soon opened to those who managed to escape execution: employment in the kitchens of the hundreds of restaurants opening to the public in Paris. This development would put the country's most talented chefs in charge of both safeguarding and developing *la cuisine française*.

The first and most important of these chefs was Marie-Antoine Carême (1784–1833), who became personal chef to such luminaries as French statesman Talleyrand, England's Prince Regent and Russia's Tsar Alexander I. But to most English speakers, the name Georges-August Escoffier (1846–1935) is more synonymous with *haute cuisine* (high cuisine). Escoffier, nicknamed 'the king of chefs and the chef of kings', was a reformer who simplified or discarded decorations and garnishes, shortened menus and streamlined food preparation in kitchens, having taken his cue from Prosper Montagné, one of the great French chefs of all time and author of *Larousse Gastronomique*, the seminal encyclopaedia of French gastronomy.

The most important development in French gastronomy in the 20th century was the arrival of so-called *nouvelle cuisine* (new cuisine) a reaction against the *grande cuisine* of Escoffier. The low-fat *nouvelle cuisine* eliminated many sauces in favour of stock reductions, prepared dishes in such a way as to emphasise the inherent textures and colours of the ingredients, and served them artistically on large plates. Nouvelle cuisine made a big splash at home and abroad in the diet-conscious 1970s and '80s, when it was also know as *cuisine minceur* (lean cuisine), and its proponents, including chefs Paul Bocuse, Jean and Pierre Troisgros, and Michel Guérard, became the new saints of the grazing faithful from Paris to Perth.

CULTURE

When it comes to food, Paris has everything and nothing. As the culinary centre of the most aggressively gastronomic country in the world, it has more 'generic French', regional and ethnic restaurants, fine food shops and markets than any other place in the country. But *la cuisine parisienne* (Parisian cuisine) is a poor relation of that extended family known as *la cuisine des provinces* (provincial cuisine). That's because those greedy country cousins have consumed most of what was once on Paris' own plate. Today very few dishes are associated with the capital.

Since the time of the French Revolution and the advent of the restaurant (p167), the cuisines of the capital and the surrounding Île de France have been basically indistinguishable from the cooking of France in general. Dishes associated with the regions are few – *vol-au-vent*, the 'flight in the wind' that is a light pastry shell filled with chicken or fish in a creamy sauce; *potage Saint Germain*, a thick green pea soup; *gâteau paris-brest*, a ring-shaped cake filled with *praline* (butter cream) and topped with flaked almonds and icing sugar; and the humble onion soup and pig's trotters described so intimately in Ernest Hemingway's *The Sun Also Rises*. Deep-frying potatoes (ie *frites*) and other dishes has always been a Parisian speciality here as well.

At the same time, a lot of dishes have been created in Paris that seem to have flown the coop and settle elsewhere. The 'Breton' *homard à l'américaine*, lobster chunks simmered in white wine and tomatoes, was created in Paris. *Sole normande*, a dish of sole caught off the Norman coast cooked with shrimps in a white cream sauce, was first made in the Île de France. Even *crepes Suzette*, those thin pancakes served with liberal doses of orange-flavoured brandy and usually associated with Brittany, were first served in Paris with Grand Marnier made at Neauphle-le-Château, just southwest of Paris.

ETIQUETTE

It's not easy to cause offence at a French table, and manners have more to do with common sense than learned behaviour as they do at home. Still, there are subtle differences in the way French people handle themselves while eating that are worth pointing out. Attitudes are more relaxed in a private home than in a top-class restaurant, of course, but even those distinctions are becoming somewhat blurred.

A French table will be set for all courses at restaurants (not always at home), with two forks, two knives and a large spoon for soup or dessert. When diners finish each course, they cross their knife and fork (not lay them side by side) face down on the plate to be cleared away. If there's only one knife and fork at your setting, you should place the cutlery back on the table after each course.

At a dinner party courses may not be served in the order that you are accustomed; salad may follow the main course and cheese always precedes dessert (p46). A separate plate for bread may or may not be provided. If it is missing, rest the slice on the edge of the main plate or on the tablecloth itself. It is quite acceptable – in fact, encouraged – to sop up sauces and juices with bread.

You will not be expected to know the intricacies of cutting different types of cheese (p48), but at least try to remember two cardinal rules: never cut off the tip of pie-shaped soft cheeses (eg Brie, Camembert) and cut cheeses whose middle is the best part (eg the blues) in such a way as to take your fair share of the crust.

If there are wine glasses of varying sizes at each place setting, the larger one (or ones) will be for red wine (and water), the smaller one for white wine. If in doubt, just follow the lead. In general it's better to wait for the host to pour the wine rather than helping yourself, but this depends on your relationship and the tone of the evening. Serving the wine at home and tasting it in restaurants have traditionally been male tasks, but these days many women will happily pour and more enlightened *sommeliers* (wine waiters) will ask which one of a male/female couple would prefer to try the wine.

HOW PARISIANS EAT

French people do not eat in the clatter-clutter style of the Chinese or with the exuberance and sheer gusto of, say, the Italians. A meal is an artistic and sensual delight to most people here, something to be savoured and enjoyed with a certain amount of style and savoir-vivre.

Breakfast

What the French call *petit déjeuner* is the least impressive and memorable meal of the day in Paris. The whole idea is not to fill up – *petit déjeuner* means 'little lunch' and the real *déjeuner* (lunch) is just around the corner!

In the Continental style, people here traditionally start the day with a bread roll or a bit of baguette left over from the night before eaten with butter and jam and followed by a *cafe au lait* (coffee with lots of hot milk), a small black coffee or even a hot chocolate. Some people also eat cereal, toast, fruit and even yogurt in the morning – something they never did before. City dwellers will often eschew breakfast at home altogether, opting for a quick coffee and a sweet roll at a train station concession or at their desk in the office.

First Things First

The order in which courses are served at a traditional French meal – be it lunch starting at around 1pm or dinner at about 8.30pm – is as follows:

Apéritif (aperitif) A predinner drink

Hors-d'œuvre Appetisers – cold and/or warm snacks taken before the start of the meal

Entrée First course, starter

Plat principal Main course

Salade (salad) Usually a relatively simple green salad with dressing

Fromage Cheese

Dessert Dessert!

Fruit Sometimes served in place of dessert

Cafe (coffee) Almost always drunk black

Digestif (digestive) An after-dinner drink

Contrary to what many foreigners think, Parisians do not eat croissants every day but usually reserve these for a treat at the weekend, when they may also choose *brioches* (small roll or cake sometimes flavoured with nuts, currants or candied fruits), *pains au chocolat* (chocolate-filled brioche) or other *viennoiserie* (baked goods).

Lunch & Dinner

Many Parisians still consider *le déjeuner* (lunch) to be the main meal of the day. Restaurants generally serve it between noon and 2.30pm to 3pm and *dîner* (dinner or supper) from 7.30pm to sometime between 10pm and midnight. Very few restaurants are open between lunch and dinner, with the exception of brasseries, cafés and fast-food places (p55). The vast majority of restaurants close on Sunday in Paris and in August, when most Parisians flee for the beaches or the mountains, many restaurateurs lock up and leave town along with their clients.

As the pace of life is as hectic here as it is elsewhere in the industrialised world nowadays, the two-hour midday meal has become increasingly rare, at least on weekdays. Dinners, however, are still turned into elaborate affairs whenever time and finances permit. A fully fledged, traditional French meal at home is an awesome event, often comprising six distinct *plats* (courses). They are always served with wine – red, white or rosé (or a combination of two or all three), depending on what you're eating. A meal in a restaurant almost never consists of more than three courses: the *entrée* (starter or first course), the *plat principal* (main course) and dessert.

STAPLES & SPECIALITIES

Every nation or culture has its own staples dictated by climate, geography and tradition. French cuisine has long stood apart for its great use of a variety of foods – beef, lamb, pork, poultry, fish and shellfish, cereals, vegetables and legumes – but its staple 'trinity' is bread, cheese and *charcuterie* (cured smoked or processed meat products). And as for regional and national specialities, well, *tout est possible* (the sky's the limit).

STAPLES

Bread

Nothing is more French than *pain* (bread). More than 80% of all French people eat it at every meal, and it comes in infinite varieties. One smallish bakery we happened to pass listed no fewer than 28 types.

All bakeries have *baguettes* (and the somewhat similar *flûtes*), which are long and thin and weigh 250g, and wider loaves of what are simply called *pains*. A *pain*, which weighs 400g, is softer on the inside and has a less crispy crust than a baguette. Both types are at their best if eaten within four hours of baking; if you're not very hungry, ask for a half a loaf: a *demi baguette* or a *demi pain*. A *ficelle* is a thinner, crustier 200g version of a baguette – not unlike a very thick breadstick, really.

Bread has experienced a renaissance here in recent years, and most bakeries also carry heavier, more expensive breads made with all sorts of grains and cereals; you will also find loaves studded with nuts, raisins or herbs. These heavier breads keep much longer than baguettes and standard white-flour breads.

Bread is baked at various times during the day, so it's available fresh as early as 6am and also in the afternoon. Most bakeries close for one day a week, but the days are staggered so that a town or neighbourhood is never left without a place to buy a loaf (except, perhaps, on Sunday afternoon).

Cheese

France has nearly 500 varieties of *fromage* (cheese) produced at farms, dairies, mountain huts, monasteries and factories. They're made of either cow's, goat's or ewe's milk, which can be raw, pasteurised or *petit-lait* ('little milk', the whey left over after the milk fats and solids has been curdled with rennet, an enzyme derived from the stomach of a calf or young goat).

Fromagerie Barthelemy (p261)

A Platter of Cheeses

The choice on offer at a *fromagerie* (cheese shop) can be overwhelming, but *fromagers* (cheese merchants) always allow you to sample before you buy, and are usually very generous with their advice and guidance. The following list divides French cheeses into five main groups as they are usually divided in a *fromagerie* and recommends several types to try.

Fromage à pâte demi-dure 'Semi-hard cheese' denotes uncooked, pressed cheese. Among the finest are Tomme de Savoie made from either raw or pasteurised cow's milk; Cantal, a cow's-milk cheese from Auvergne that tastes something like cheddar; Saint Nectaire, a strong-smelling pressed cheese that has a strong and complex taste; and Ossau-Iraty, a ewe's milk cheese made in the Basque Country.

Fromage à pâte dure 'Hard cheese' in France is always cooked and pressed. Among the most popular are: Beaufort, a grainy cow's milk cheese with a slightly fruity taste from Rhône-Alpes; Comté, a cheese made with raw cow's milk in Franche-Comté; Emmental, a cow's milk cheese made all over France; and Mimolette, an Edam-like bright orange cheese from Lille that can be aged for up to 36 months.

Fromage à pâte molle 'Soft cheese' is moulded or rind-washed. Camembert de Normandie, a classic moulded cheese that for many is synonymous with 'French cheese', and the refined Brie de Meaux are both made from raw cow's milk; Munster from Alsace and the strong Époisses de Bourgogne are rind-washed, fine textured cheeses.

Fromage à pâte persillée 'Veined' or 'blue cheese' is so called because the veins often resemble *persille* (parsley). Roquefort is a ewe's-milk veined cheese that is to many the king of French cheese. Fourme d'Ambert is a very mild cow's milk cheese from Rhône-Alpes. Bleu du Haut Jura (also called Bleu de Gex) is a mild blue-veined mountain cheese.

Fromage de chèvre 'Goat's milk cheese' is usually creamy and both sweet and a little salty when fresh, but hardens and gets much saltier as it matures. Among the best are: Sainte Maure de Touraine, a creamy, mild cheese from the Loire region; Crottin de Chavignol, a classic though saltier variety from Burgundy; Cabécou de Rocamadour from Midi-Pyrénées, often served warm with salad or marinated in oil and rosemary; and Saint Marcellin, a soft white cheese from Lyon.

When cutting cheese at the table, remember that a small circular cheese like a Camembert is cut in slices like a pie. If a larger cheese (eg Brie) has been bought already sliced, cut from the tip to the rind; cutting off the top is considered rude. Slice cheeses whose middle is the best part (eg the blue or veined cheeses) in such a way as to take your fair share of the rind. A flat piece of semi-hard cheese like Emmental is usually just cut horizontally in hunks.

Wine and cheese are a match made in heaven. It's a matter of taste, but in general, strong, pungent cheeses require a young, full-bodied red or a sweet wine, while soft cheeses with a refined flavour call for more quality and age in the wine. Some classic pairings include: Alsatian Gewürztraminer and Munster; Côtes du Rhone red and Roquefort; Côte d'Or (Burgundy) red with Brie or Camembert; and mature Bordeaux with Emmental or Gruyère.

Charcuterie

Traditionally *charcuterie* is made only from pork, though a number of other meats – from beef and veal to chicken and goose – are now used in making sausages, blood puddings, hams, and other cured and salted meats. *Pâtés*, *terrines* and *rillettes* are essentially *charcuterie* and are prepared in many different ways.

The difference between a pâté and a terrine is academic: a pâté is removed from its container and sliced before it is served or sold, while a terrine is sliced from the container itself. *Rillettes,* on the other hand, is potted meat (pork, goose, duck or rabbit) or even fish that is not ground, chopped or sliced but shredded with two forks, seasoned, mixed with fat and spread cold like pâté over bread or toast.

While every region in France produces standard *charcuterie* favourites as well as its own specialities, Alsace, Lyon and the Auvergne produce the best sausages, and Périgord and the north of France some of the most popular pâtés.

REGIONAL SPECIALITIES

There are all sorts of reasons for the amazing variety of France's regional cuisine. Climatic and geographical factors have been particularly important: the hot south tends to favour olive oil, garlic and tomatoes, while the cooler, pastoral northern regions prefer cream and butter. Coastal areas specialise in mussels, oysters and saltwater fish, while those near lakes and rivers make full use of the freshwater fish available.

Diverse though it is, French cuisine is typified by certain regions, most notably Normandy, Burgundy, Périgord, Lyon and, to a lesser extent, Alsace, Provence and the Loire region. The first four cuisines can be found in restaurants throughout Paris, while Alsatian *choucroute* (sauerkraut with sausage and other prepared meats) is the dish of choice at the

---

Charcuterie on Show

The following list outlines the basic types of *charcuterie* you'll encounter at a *charcuterie* or *charcuterie-traiteur* (delicatessen/caterer)

Andouille Large smoked tripe (chitterling) sausage cooked and ready to eat (usually cold) when bought

Andouillette Soft raw sausage made from the pig's small intestines that is grilled and eaten with onions and potatoes

Boudin blanc Smooth white sausage made from poultry, veal, pork or even rabbit, which is cooked and can be served with, say, haricot beans or apples

Boudin noir Blood sausage or pudding made with pig's blood, onions and spices, and usually eaten hot with stewed apples and potatoes

Fromage de tête Brawn or head cheese

Jambon Ham; smoked or salt-cured pork made from a pig's hindquarters

Saucisse Usually a small fresh sausage that is boiled or grilled before eating

Saucisson Usually a large salami eaten cold

Saucisson sec Air-dried salami

capital's many brasseries. *La cuisine provençale* can be somewhat elusive in Paris, though many seafood restaurants claim to do an authentic *bouillabaisse* (fish soup). Cuisine of the Loire region has made more contributions to what can generically be called French food than any other.

Normandy

Cream, apples and seafood are the three essentials of Norman cuisine. Specialities include *moules à la crème normande* (mussels in cream sauce with a dash of cider) and *canard á la rouennaise* ('Rouen-style duck'; duck stuffed with its liver and served with a red wine sauce), preferably interrupted by a *trou normand* (literally 'Norman hole'; a glass of Calvados) to allow room for more courses.

Burgundy

The 'trinity' of the Burgundy kitchen is beef, red wine and mustard. *Bœuf bourguignon* (beef marinated and cooked in young red wine with mushrooms, onions, carrots and bacon) combines the first two; Dijon, the Burgundian capital, has been synonymous with mustard for centuries.

Périgord

This region is famous for its truffles and its poultry, especially the ducks and geese whose fattened livers are turned into *pâté de foie gras* (duck or goose liver pâté), which is sometimes flavoured with cognac and truffles. Regional meat dishes described as *à la périgourdine* usually come with a rich brown sauce made with foie gras and truffles. *Confit de canard* and *confit d'oie* are duck or goose joints cooked very slowly in their own fat. The preserved fowl is then left to stand for some months before being eaten. This style of cooking is also called 'southwest cuisine'.

Lyon

Many people consider France's third-largest city to be France's *temple de gastronomie* (gastronomic temple), and Paris has many Lyonnaise restaurants. Typical *charcuteries* are *saucisson de Lyon*, which feature in Lyons' trademark dish, *saucisson aux pommes* (sausage with potatoes). Another speciality is the *quenelle*, a poached dumpling made of freshwater fish (usually pike) and served with a *sauce Nantua*, a sauce made with cream and a paste made from freshwater crayfish.

Alsace

The Alsatian table is top-heavy with meat; a classic dish of the region is *choucroute alsacienne* (or *choucroute garnie*), sauerkraut flavoured with juniper berries and served hot with sausages, bacon, pork and/or ham knuckle. But the region is also celebrated for its vineyards and fruit orchards. You should drink chilled Riesling or Alsatian Pinot Noir with *choucroute* – not beer – and follow it with a *tarte alsacienne*, a scrumptious custard tart made with local fruits like *mirabelle* (sweet-as-sugar yellow plums), *quetsches* (a variety of purple plum) or cherries.

Provence

The Roman legacy of olives, wheat and wine remain the triumvirate of *la cuisine provençale*, and many dishes are prepared with olive oil and generous amounts of garlic. Provence's most famous dish is *bouillabaisse*, a chowder made with at least three kinds of fresh fish, cooked for 10 minutes or so in broth with onions, tomatoes, saffron and various herbs, and eaten as a main course with toasted bread and *rouille*, a spicy mayonnaise of olive oil, garlic and chilli peppers.

Loire Region

The cuisine of the Loire, refined in the kitchens of the region's chateaux from the 16th century onwards, ultimately became the cuisine of France as a whole; *rillettes*, *coq au vin*, basic *beurre blanc* sauce and *tarte Tatin*, a caramelised upside-down apple pie, are all specialities from this area. The Loire region is also known for the misnamed *champignons de Paris*, mushrooms raised in the quarries from where stones for the chateaux were mined, and *pruneaux de Tours*, prunes dried from luscious Damson plums and used in poultry, pork or veal dishes.

DRINKS

ALCOHOLIC DRINKS

Although alcohol consumption has dropped by one-third in less than two decades, France still ranks 6th in the world in the boozing stakes behind Luxembourg, Romania, Portugal, Ireland and the Czech Republic. The average French person consumes 10.5L of pure alcohol a year, compared to 8.4L in the UK and 6.7L in the USA. In 1979 that figure stood at 16L.

Wine & Champagne

Grapes and the art of winemaking were introduced to Gaul by the Romans. In the Middle Ages important vineyards developed around monasteries as the monks needed wine to celebrate Mass. Large-scale wine production later moved closer to the ports (eg Bordeaux) from where it could be exported.

In the middle of the 19th century phylloxera aphids were accidentally brought to Europe from the USA. The pests ate through the roots of Europe's grapevines, destroying some 10,000 sq km of vineyards in France alone. European wine production appeared to be doomed until root stocks resistant to phylloxera were brought from California and original cuttings grafted onto them.

Winemaking is a complicated chemical process, but ultimately the taste and quality of the wine depend on four key factors: the type(s) or blend of grape, the climate, the soil, and the art of the *vigneron* (winemaker).

Some viticulturists have honed their skills and techniques to such a degree that their wine is known as a *grand cru* (literally 'great growth'). If this wine has been produced in a year of optimum climatic conditions, it becomes a *millésime* (vintage) wine. *Grands crus* are aged first in small oak barrels and then in bottles, sometimes for 20 years or more, before they develop their full taste and aroma. These are the memorable (and pricey) bottles that wine experts talk about with such passion.

There are dozens of wine-producing regions throughout France, but the seven principal regions are Alsace, Bordeaux, Burgundy, Champagne, Languedoc-Roussillon, the Loire Valley and the Rhône. Areas such as Burgundy comprise many well-known districts, including Chablis, Beaujolais and Mâcon, while Bordeaux encompasses Médoc, St-Émilion and Sauternes – to name just a few of its many subregions.

With the exception of Alsatian ones, wines in France are named after the location of the vineyard rather than the grape varietal.

Food & Drink – Drinks

ALSACE

Alsace has been producing wine since about AD 300. These days, the region produces almost exclusively white wines – mostly varieties produced nowhere else in France – that are known for their clean, fresh taste and compatibility with the often heavy local cuisine. The vineyards closest to Strasbourg produce light red wines from Pinot Noir that are similar to rosé. This wine is best served chilled.

Alsace's four most important varietal wines are Riesling, known for its subtlety; the more pungent and highly regarded Gewürztraminer; the robust, high-alcohol Pinot Gris; and Muscat d'Alsace, which is not as sweet as that made with Muscat grapes grown further south.

BORDEAUX

Bordeaux has been synonymous with full-bodied red wine since the time of the Romans. Britons, who call them clarets, have had a taste for the red wines of Bordeaux since the mid-12th century when King Henry II, who controlled the region through marriage, tried to gain the favour of the locals by granting them tax-free trade status with England. Thus began a roaring business in wine exporting that continues to this day.

The reds of Bordeaux, which produces more fine wine than any other region in the world, are often described as well balanced, a quality achieved by blending several grape varieties. The grapes predominantly used are Merlot, Cabernet Sauvignon and Cabernet Franc. Bordeaux's foremost wine-growing areas are Médoc, Pomerol, St-Émilion and Graves; the sweet whites of the Sauternes area are the world's finest dessert wines.

BURGUNDY

Burgundy has produced wines since the time of the Celts, but developed its reputation during the reign of Charlemagne, when monks first began to produce wine here.

Burgundy's red wines are produced with Pinot Noir grapes; the best vintages need 10 to 20 years to age. White wine is made from the Chardonnay grape. The five main wine-growing areas of Burgundy are Chablis, Côte d'Or, Côte Chalonnais, Mâcon and Beaujolais, which alone produces 13 different types of light Gamay-based red wine.

CHAMPAGNE

Champagne is made from the red Pinot Noir, the black Pinot Meunier or the white Chardonnay grape. Each vine is vigorously pruned and trained to produce a small quantity of high-quality grapes. Indeed, to maintain exclusivity (and price), the amount of Champagne that can be produced each year is limited to between 160 and 220 million bottles, most of which is consumed in France and the UK.

The process of making Champagne – carried out by innumerable *maisons* (houses) – is a long, complex one. There are two fermentation processes, the first in casks and the second after the wine has been bottled and had sugar and yeast added.

During the two months that the bottles are aged in cellars kept at 12°C, the wine turns effervescent. The sediment that forms in the bottle is removed by *remuage*, a painstakingly slow process in which each bottle – stored horizontally – is rotated slightly every day for weeks until the sludge works its way to the cork. Next comes *dégorgement*: the neck of the bottle is frozen, creating a blob of solidified Champagne and sediment, which is then removed.

At this stage, the Champagne's sweetness is determined by adding varying amounts of syrup dissolved in old Champagne. Then the bottles of young Champagne are laid in a cellar and aged for between two and five years (sometimes longer), depending on the *cuvée* (vintage).

If the final product is labelled *brut*, it is extra dry, with only 1.5% sugar content. *Extra-sec* means it's very dry (but not as dry as *brut*), *sec* is dry and *demi-sec* is slightly sweet. The sweetest Champagne is labelled *doux*.

Some of the most famous Champagne houses are Dom Pérignon, Möet et Chandon, Veuve Cliquot, Mercier, Mumm, Krugg, Laurent-Perrier, Piper-Heidsieck and Taittinger.

LANGUEDOC

This region is the country's most important wine-growing area, with up to 40% of France's wine – mainly cheap red *vin de table* (table wine) produced here. About 300,000 hectares of the region is 'under vine', which represents one-third of France's total.

In addition to the well-known Fitou label, the area's other quality wines are Coteaux du Languedoc, Faugères, Corbières and Minervois. The region also produces about 70% of France's *vin de pays*, 'country wine' from a particular named village or region, most of which is labelled Vin de Pays d'Oc.

LOIRE REGION

The vineyards of the fertile Loire Valley are small and winemakers are used to selling directly to Parisians who take day trips to buy their favourite wines. The Loire's 75,000 hectares of vineyards rank the region as the third-largest area in France for the production of quality wines. Although sunny, the climate is moist and not all grape varieties thrive here.

The most common grapes are the Muscadet, Cabernet Franc and Chenin Blanc varieties. Wines tend to be light and delicate. The most celebrated areas are Pouilly-Fumé, Vouvray, Sancerre, Bourgueil, Chinon and Saumur.

RHÔNE REGION

The Rhône region is divided up into northern and southern areas. The different soil, climate, topography and grapes used means there is a dramatic difference in the wines produced by each area.

Set on steep hills beside the river, the northern vineyards make red wines exclusively from the ruby-red Syrah grape; the aromatic Viognier grape is the most popular for white wines. The south is better known for the quantity rather than quality of the wine it produces. The Grenache grape, which ages well when blended, is used in the reds, while the whites use the Ugni Blanc grape.

Aperitifs & Digestifs

Meals here are often preceded by an appetite-stirring *apéritif,* such as *kir* (white wine sweetened with cassis or blackcurrant syrup), *kir royale* (Champagne with cassis) or *pineau* (cognac and grape juice). *Pastis,* a 90-proof, anise-flavoured alcoholic drink that turns cloudy when you add water, is especially popular at cafés.

After-dinner drinks are often ordered along with coffee. France's most famous brandies are Cognac and Armagnac, both of which are made from grapes in the regions of those names. *Eaux de vie,* literally 'waters of life', can be made with grape skins and the pulp left over after being pressed for wine (Marc de Champagne, Marc de Bourgogne), apples (Calvados), pears (Poire William), as well as plums (*eau de vie de prune*) and raspberries (*eau de vie de framboise*).

Beer & Cider

The *bière à la pression* (draft beer) served by the *demi* (about 33mL) in bars and cafés across Paris is usually one of the national brands, such as Kronenbourg, 33 or Pelforth, and totally forgettable. Alsace, with its close cultural ties to Germany, produces some excellent local beers (eg Bière de Scharrach, Schutz Jubilator and Fischer, a hoppy brew from Scilligheim), and northern France, close to Belgium and the Netherlands, has its own great beers, including Saint Sylvestre Trois Monts, Colvert, Terken Brune and Brasserie Jeanne d'Arc's Grain d'Orge made from barley.

Cidre (apple cider) is made in many parts of France, including Savoy, Picardy and the Basque Country, but its real home is Normandy and Brittany.

NONALCOHOLIC DRINKS

The most popular nonalcoholic beverages consumed in Paris are coffee and mineral water, with fruit juices, squashes, soft drinks and tea trailing behind.

Water & Mineral Water

All tap water in Paris is safe to drink, so there is no need to buy bottled water. Parisians don't agree, however, and less than 1% of the water consumed by a typical Parisian household each day is actually drunk. Tap water that is not drinkable (eg at most public fountains and on trains) will usually have a sign reading *'eau non potable'*.

If you prefer tap water rather than some pricey bottled water, make sure you ask for *de l'eau* (some water), *une carafe d'eau* (a jug of water) or *de l'eau du robinet* (tap water). Otherwise you'll most likely get bottled *eau de source* (spring water) or *eau minérale* (mineral water), which comes *plate* (flat or still) or *gazeuse* (fizzy or sparkling).

Coffee

The most ubiquitous form of coffee in Paris is espresso, made by forcing steam through ground coffee beans. A small espresso, served without milk, is called *un café noir, un express* or simply *un café*. You can also ask for a *grand* (large) version.

Café crème is espresso with steamed milk or cream. *Café au lait* is lots of hot milk with a little coffee served in a large cup or, sometimes, a bowl. A small *café crème* is a *petit crème*. A *noisette* (literally 'hazelnut') is an espresso with just a dash of milk. Decaffeinated coffee is *café décafeiné*.

Tea & Hot Chocolate

The French have never taken to *thé* (tea) the way the British have, and there's a slightly snobbish and Anglophile association attached to it here. Even worse, many people consider it somewhat medicinal and drink *thé noir* (black tea) only when they are feeling unwell.

Tea is usually served *nature* (plain) or *au citron* (with lemon) and never with milk. *Tisanes* (herbal teas) are widely available.

Chocolat chaud (hot chocolate), available at most cafés, varies greatly and can be excellent or verging on the undrinkable.

Squashes & Soft Drinks

All the international brands of soft drinks are available in Paris, as well as many overly sweet, fizzy local ones, such as Orangina and the 7 UP-like Pschitt.

One popular and inexpensive café drink is *sirop* (fruit syrup or cordial) served *à l'eau* (mixed with water), with soda or with a carbonated mineral water like Perrier – basically a squash. A *citron pressé* is a glass of iced water (either flat or carbonated) with freshly squeezed lemon juice and sugar. The French are not particularly fond of drinking very cold things, so you'll probably have to ask for ice cubes *(des glaçons)*.

CELEBRATING WITH FOOD

Food itself makes French people celebrate and, hey, any excuse for a party. There are birthdays and engagements and weddings and christenings and, like everywhere, special holidays.

One tradition that is very much alive is called the *jour des rois*, which falls on 6 January and marks the feast of the Épiphanie (Epiphany), when the Three Wise Men called on the Infant Jesus. A *galette des rois* (kings' cake), a puff pastry with frangipane cream, a little dried *fève* bean (or plastic or silver figurine) and topped with a gold paper crown that goes on sale in patisseries throughout Paris after the new year, is placed on the table. The youngest person in the room goes to the table and calls out which member of the party should get each slice. The person who gets the bean is named king or queen, dons the crown and chooses his or her consort. This tradition is popular not just at home among families but also at offices and dinner parties.

At Chandeleur (Candlemas, marking the Feast of the Purification of the Virgin Mary) on 2 February, family and friends gather together in their kitchens to make *crepes de la Chandeleur* (sweet pancakes).

Pâques (Easter) is marked here as elsewhere with *œufs au chocolat* (chocolate eggs) filled with candy fish and chickens, and there is always an egg hunt for the kids. The traditional meal at Easter lunch is *agneau* (lamb) or *jambon de Pâques*, which – like hot-cross buns in Britain – seems to be available throughout the year nowadays.

After the *dinde aux marrons* (turkey stuffed with chestnuts) eaten at lunch on Noël (Christmas), a *bûche de Noël*, a 'log' of chocolate and cream or ice cream, is served.

WHERE TO EAT & DRINK

There's a vast number of eateries in Paris where you can get breakfast or brunch (p158), a full lunch or dinner, and a snack between meals. Most have defined roles, though some definitions are becoming a bit blurred.

AUBERGE

In the provinces, an *auberge* (inn), which may also appear as an *auberge de campagne* or *auberge du terroir* (country inn), is just that: a restaurant serving traditional country fare attached to a rural inn or small hotel. If you see the word attached to an eatery in Paris, they're just being cute.

BAR

A *bar* or *bar américain* (cocktail bar) is an establishment dedicated to elbow-bending and rarely serves food beyond pre-made sandwiches or snacks. A *bar à vins* is a 'wine bar', which may or may not (usually the former) serve full meals at lunch and dinner. A *bar à huîtres* is an 'oyster bar'.

BISTRO

A *bistro* (often spelled *bistrot*) is not clearly defined in Paris. It can be simply a pub or bar serving snacks and light pub meals, or a fully fledged restaurant.

BRASSERIES

Unlike the vast majority of restaurants in Paris, brasseries – which can look very much like cafés – serve full meals, drinks and coffee from morning till late at night. The dishes served almost always include *choucroute* and sausages because the brasserie, which actually means 'brewery' in French, originated in Alsace. Most Parisians go to a brasserie as much for the lively atmosphere and the convenience as for the food.

BUFFET

A *buffet* (or *buvette*) is a kiosk usually found at train stations and airports selling drinks, filled baguettes and snacks.

CAFÉ

Cafés are an important focal point for social life in Paris, and sitting in a café to read, write, talk with friends or just daydream is an integral part of many French people's day-to-day existence. Many people see café-sitting – like shopping at outdoor markets – as a way of keeping in touch with their neighbourhood and maximising their chances of running into friends and acquaintances.

The main focus here, of course, is coffee (p54), and only basic food is available in most cafés. Common options include a baguette filled with Camembert or pâté with *cornichons*, a *croque-monsieur* (grilled ham and cheese sandwich) or a *croque-madame* (a croque-monsieur topped with a fried egg).

Three factors determine how much you'll pay in a café: where the café is situated, where you are sitting within the café, and what time of day it is. Progressively more expensive tariffs apply at the *comptoir* or *zinc* (counter), in the *salle* (inside seating area) and on the *terrasse* (pavement terrace), the best vantage point from which to see and be seen. Some of the cheapest soft drinks may be available only at the bar. A café on a grand boulevard, such as blvd du Montparnasse or the av des Champs-Élysées, will charge considerably more than a place that fronts a quiet side street. The price of drinks goes up at night (usually after 8pm).

All in all it comes down to this: you are paying for your espresso or mineral water as much as for the right to occupy an attractive and visible bit of ground. Ordering a cup of coffee (or anything else) earns you the right to sit there for as long as you like. Rarely, if ever, will you feel pressured to order something else.

You usually run a tab at a café and pay the *addition* (bill or check) right before you leave. If your waiter is going off duty, you may be asked to pay up at the end of his or her shift, however.

CAFETÉRIA

Paris has several chains of cafétérias (cafeteria restaurants), including Flunch, that offer a decent selection of dishes that you can see before ordering, a factor that can make life easier if you're travelling with kids.

CREPERIE

Creperies (sometimes seen as *galetteries*) specialise in crepes, ultra-thin pancakes cooked on a flat surface and then folded or rolled over a filling. Sometimes the word *crepe* is used to refer only to sweet crepes made with *farine de froment* (wheat flour), whereas a savoury crepe, more accurately a *galette*, is made with *farine de sarrasin* (buckwheat flour), and filled with cheese, mushrooms and the like. You'll find a preponderance of *creperies* near the Gare de Lyon.

RESTAURANT

The *restaurant*, the French word for 'restorative', comes in many guises and price ranges in Paris – from ultra-budget *restaurants universitaires* (canteens or refectories) to three-star Michelin *restaurants gastronomiques* (gourmet restaurants).

An important distinction between a brasserie and a restaurant is that while the former serves food throughout the day, a restaurant is usually open only for lunch and dinner (p150). Almost all restaurants close for at least 1½ days (ie a full day and either one lunch or one dinner period) each week and this schedule will be posted on the front door. Chain restaurants are usually open throughout the day, seven days a week.

Restaurants also always have a *carte* (menu) posted outside, so you can decide before going in whether the selection and prices are to your liking. Most offer at least one fixed-price, multi-course meal known in French as a *menu, menu à prix fixe* or *menu du jour* (daily menu). A *menu* (not to be confused with a *carte*) almost always costs much less than ordering à la carte.

When you order a *menu*, you usually get to choose an entrée, such as salad, pâté or soup; a main dish (several meat, poultry or fish dishes, including the *plat du jour*, or 'the daily special', are generally on offer); and one or more final courses (usually cheese or dessert). In some places, you may also be able to order a *formule*, which usually has fewer choices but allows you to pick two of three courses – an entrée and a main course, or a main course and a dessert.

Boissons (drinks), including wine, cost extra unless the menu says *boisson comprise* (drink included), in which case you may get a beer or a glass of mineral water. If the *menu* has *vin compris* (wine included), you'll probably be served a 25mL *pichet* (jug) of wine. The waiter will always ask if you would like coffee to end the meal, but this will almost always cost extra.

Restaurant meals in Paris are almost always served with bread, which is rarely accompanied by butter. If you run out of bread in your basket, don't be afraid to ask the waiter for more (*'Pourrais-je avoir encore du pain, s'il vous plaît'*).

RESTAURANT LIBRE-SERVICE

A *restaurant libre-service* is a self-service restaurant similar to a cafetéria.

RESTAURANT RAPIDE

A *restaurant rapide* is a fast-food restaurant, be it imported (McDonald's, Pizza Hut and KFC, with branches all over Paris) or home-grown, like Quick.

RESTAURANT UNIVERSITAIRE

The University of Paris system has some 17 *restaurants universitaires* (canteens or refectories) subsidised by the Ministry of Education and operated by the Centre Régional des Œuvres Universitaires et Scolaires, better known as CROUS (p152). They serve very cheap meals (typically under €5) and are open to nonstudents.

SALON DE THÉ

A *salon de thé* (tearoom) is a trendy and somewhat pricey establishment that usually offers quiches, salads, cakes, tarts, pies and pastries, in addition to black and herbal teas.

SELF-CATERING

French food retailing is organised in such a way that most people buy a good part of their food from a series of small neighbourhood shops, each with its own speciality, though like everywhere more and more people are relying on supermarkets, hypermarkets and ready-made food. At first, having to go to four shops and stand in four queues to fill the fridge (or assemble a picnic) may seem rather a waste of time, but the whole ritual is an important part of the way many French people live their daily lives.

Since each *commerçant* (shopkeeper) specialises in purveying only one type of food, he or she can almost always provide all sorts of useful tips: which round of Camembert is ripe, which wine will complement a certain food, which type of pot to cook *coq au vin* in and so on. In any case, most products for sale at *charcuteries* (delicatessens), patisseries and *traiteurs* or *charcuteries-traiteurs* (delicatessens/caterers) are clearly marked and labelled. We often ask ourselves why that is so if French on the whole are such experts in things gastronomic. Perhaps they just need a reminder of the abundance and the great choice available to them most of the time.

As these stores are geared to people buying small quantities of fresh food each day, it's perfectly acceptable to purchase only meal-size amounts: a few *tranches* (slices) of meat to make a sandwich, perhaps, or a *petit bout* (small hunk) of sausage. You can also request just enough for *une/deux personne(s)* (one/two persons). If you want a bit more, ask for *encore un petit peu*, and if you are being given too much, say '*C'est trop*'.

Fresh bread is baked and sold at *boulangeries*; mouth-watering pastries are available at patisseries; a *fromagerie* can supply you with cheese that is *fait* (ripe) to the exact degree that you request; a *charcuterie* offers sliced meat, pâtés and so on; and fresh fruit and vegetables are sold at *épiceries* (greengrocers), supermarkets and open-air markets.

A *boucherie* is a general butcher, but for specialised poultry you have to go to a *marchand de volaille*. A *boucherie chevaline*, easily identifiable by the gilded horse's head above the entrance, sells horse meat, which some people prefer to beef or mutton. Fresh fish and seafood are available from a *poissonnerie*.

Paris' neighbourhood food markets offer the freshest and best quality fruit, vegetables, cheese, prepared salads and so on at the lowest prices. For details see the boxed text p152. Note that many food shops are closed on Sunday afternoon and all day Monday. For reviews of self-catering options in Paris, see p153.

VEGETARIANS & VEGANS

Vegetarians and vegans make up a small minority in a society where *viande* (meat) once also meant 'food', and they are not particularly well catered for; specialist vegetarian restaurants are few and far between. In fact, the vegetarian establishments that do exist in Paris often look more like laid-back cafés than restaurants. On the bright side, more and more restaurants are offering vegetarian choices on their set menus and *produits biologiques* (organic products) are all the rage nowadays, even among carnivores. Other options include *saladeries*, casual restaurants that serve a long list of *salades composées* (mixed salads).

CHILDREN

It is sometimes said here that France treats its children as adults until they reach puberty – at which time they revert to being children again. You'll see a fair few *petits hommes* (little men) and *petites dames* (little ladies) dining decorously on the town with their parents, and quite a few Parisian restaurants offer a *menu enfant* (children's set menu), usually available for children under 12. Some restaurants have high chairs and baby seats and offer features of interest for parents with children, including an enclosed area or terrace allowing games. Cafétérias are a good place to bring kids if you just want to feed and water them fast and cheaply.

QUICK EATS

Though Parisians may *grignoter entre les repas* (snack or eat between meals), they do not seem to relish street food; hot dogs stands and noodle carts are just not for them. You may encounter a crepe maker on a busy (and touristed) street corner in Bastille, Marais or the Latin Quarter, or someone selling roasted *châtaignes* (chestnuts) in the autumn, but generally people will duck into a café for *un truc à grignoter* (something to nibble on) or a patisserie for a slice of something sweet to be eaten on the trot. Food shop window displays in Paris, among the most attractive and tempting in the world, certainly have something to do with this; patisseries, *traiteurs* (caterers/delicatessens selling prepared dishes) and *confiseries* (sweet shops or candy stores) arrange their wares in such a way as to pull in the crowds. And they succeed every time.

History

The Recent Past	**60**
From the Beginning	**60**
The Gauls & the Romans	60
The Merovingians & Carolingians	61
The Middle Ages	61
The Renaissance	62
The Reformation	63
Louis XIV & the Ancien Régime	64
The French Revolution & the First Republic	65
Napoleon & the First Empire	66
The Restoration & the Second Republic	67
From the Second Republic to the Second Empire	67
The Third Republic & the Belle Époque	68
WWI & the Interwar Years	69
WWII & the Occupation	69
The Fourth Republic	70
The Fifth Republic	70
1969 to the Present	72

History

THE RECENT PAST

With some 10.952 million inhabitants, the greater metropolitan area of Paris is home to more than 18.5% of France's total population. Paris is what urban planners call a hypertrophic city – the enlarged 'head' of a nation-state's 'body'. The next biggest city (Marseilles) is barely a 10th of its size. As the capital city, it is the administrative, business and cultural centre. As the French say: '*Quand Paris éternue, la France s'enrhume*' (When Paris sneezes, France catches cold). Virtually everything of importance in the republic starts, finishes or is currently taking place in Paris. This hasn't, of course, happened overnight and while the cafés of Montmartre, the cobbled back streets of the Marais and the placid Seine may have some visitors believing that the city has been here forever, that's hardly the case.

FROM THE BEGINNING

THE GAULS & THE ROMANS

The early history of the Celts is murky, but it is thought that they originated somewhere in the eastern part of central Europe around the 2nd millennium BC and began to migrate across the continent, arriving in France sometime in the 7th century BC. In the 3rd century a group of Celtic Gauls called the Parisii (believed to mean 'boat men') set up a few wattle-and-daub huts on what is now the Île de la Cité and engaged in fishing and trading.

Centuries of conflict between the Gauls and Rome ended in 52 BC, when Julius Caesar's legions crushed a Celtic revolt led by Vercingétorix and took control of the territory. The settlement on the Seine prospered as the Roman town of Lutetia (from the Latin for 'mid-water dwelling'), counting some 10,000 inhabitants by the 3rd century AD.

Rose window, Ste-Chapelle (p92)

TIMELINE	3rd century BC	52 BC	AD 253
	Celtic Gauls called Parisii arrive in what is now Paris	Roman legions crush Celtic Gauls and establish the town of Lutetia	Lutetia razed by the Franks at the start of the Great Migrations

The Great Migrations, beginning around the middle of the 3rd century AD with raids by the Franks and then the Alemanii from the east, left the settlement on the south bank scorched and pillaged, and its inhabitants fled to the Île de la Cité, which was subsequently fortified with stone walls. Christianity had been introduced early in the previous century, and the first church, probably made of wood, was built in the western part of the island.

THE MEROVINGIANS & CAROLINGIANS

The Romans occupied what would become known as Paris (after its first settlers) from AD 212 to the late 5th century when a second wave of Franks and other Germanic groups under Merovius from the north and northeast overran the territory. Merovius' grandson, Clovis I, converted to Christianity, making Paris his seat in 508. Childeric II, Clovis' son and successor, founded the Abbey of St-Germain des Prés in 558, and the dynasty's most productive ruler, Dagobert, established an abbey at St-Denis, which soon became the richest, most important monastery in France and was, for a time, the final resting place of its kings.

The militaristic rulers of the Carolingian dynasty, beginning with Charles Martel (688–741), were almost permanently away fighting wars in the east, and Paris languished, controlled mostly by the counts of Paris. When Charles Martel's grandson, Charlemagne (768–814), moved his capital to Aix-la-Chapelle (today's Aachen in Germany), Paris' fate was sealed. Basically a group of separate villages with its centre on the island, Paris was badly defended throughout the second half of the 9th century and suffered a succession of raids by the 'Norsemen', or Vikings.

THE MIDDLE AGES

The counts of Paris, whose powers had increased as the Carolingians feuded among themselves, elected one of their own, Hugh Capet, as king at Senlis (see p321) in 987. He made Paris the royal seat. Under Capetian rule, which would last for the next 800 years, Paris prospered as a centre of politics, commerce, trade, religion and culture. By the time Hugh Capet had assumed the throne, the Norsemen (or Normans, descendants of the Vikings) were in control of northern and western French territory. In 1066 they mounted a successful invasion of England, the so-called Norman Conquest, from their base in today's Normandy. This would lead to almost 300 years of conflict between the Normans and the Capetians.

Paris' strategic riverside position ensured its importance throughout the Middle Ages, although settlement remained centred on the Île de la Cité, with the *rive gauche* (left bank) given over to fields and vineyards; the Marais area on the *rive droite* (right bank) was a waterlogged 'marsh' as its French name implies. The first guilds were established in the 11th century, and rapidly grew in importance; in the mid–12th century the ship merchants' guild bought the principal river port, by today's Hôtel de Ville (city hall), from the crown.

This was a time of frenetic building activity in Paris. Abbot Suger, both confessor and minister to several Capetian kings, was one of the powerhouses of this period, and in 1136 he commissioned the basilica at St-Denis (see p135). Less than 30 years later, work started on the cathedral of Notre Dame, the greatest creation of medieval Paris, under Maurice de Sully, the bishop of Paris. At the same time Philippe-Auguste (ruled 1180–1223) expanded the city wall, adding 25 gates and hundreds of protective towers.

The swampy Marais was drained and settlement moved to the north (or right) bank of the Seine, which would become the mercantile centre, especially around place de Grève (today's place de l'Hôtel de Ville). The food markets at Les Halles first came into existence around 1110, the beautiful Ste-Chapelle on the Île de la Cité was consecrated in 1248 and the Louvre began its existence as a riverside fortress in the 13th century. In a bid to do something about the city's horrible traffic congestion and stinking excrement (the population numbered

422	508	845–85	987
Sainte Geneviève, patroness of Paris, is born at Nanterre	Merovingian King Clovis I makes Paris his capital	Paris repeatedly raided by Vikings	Capetian dynasty begins under Hugh Capet

about 200,000 by the year 1200), Philippe-Auguste paved some of Paris' streets for the first time since the Roman occupation, using metre-square sandstone blocks.

Meanwhile, the area south of the Seine – today's Left Bank – was developing as the centre of European learning and erudition, particularly in the area known as the Latin Quarter, where students and their teachers communicated in that language. The ill-fated lovers Abélard and Héloïse (see p26) wrote their treatises on philosophy and the finest poetry and Thomas Aquinas taught at the new University of Paris (founded under papal protection in about 1215), and some 30 other colleges were established, including the Sorbonne, founded in 1253 by Robert de Sorbon, confessor to Louis IX.

In 1337 some three centuries of hostility between the Capetians and the Anglo-Normans degenerated into the Hundred Years' War, which would be fought on and off until 1453. The Black Death (1348–49) killed about a third of Paris' population (an estimated 80,000 souls) but only briefly interrupted the fighting. Paris would not see its population reach 200,000 again until the beginning of the 16th century.

The Hundred Years' War and the plague, along with the development of free, independent cities elsewhere in Europe, brought political tension and open insurrection to Paris. In 1356, the provost of the merchants, a wealthy draper named Étienne Marcel, allied himself with peasants revolting against the dauphin (the future Charles V) and seized Paris in a bid to limit the power of the throne and secure a city charter. But the dauphin's supporters recaptured it within two years, and Marcel and his followers were executed at place de Grève. Charles then had a new city wall built on the right bank.

After the French forces were defeated by the English at Agincourt in 1415, Paris was once again embroiled in revolt. The dukes of Burgundy, allied with the English, occupied the capital in 1420. Two years later John Plantagenet, duke of Bedford, was installed as regent of France for England's Henry VI, then an infant. Henry was crowned king of France at Notre Dame less than 10 years later, but Paris was almost continously under siege from the French for much of that time.

In 1429 a 17-year-old peasant girl known to history as Jeanne d'Arc (Joan of Arc) persuaded the French pretender Charles VII that she'd received a divine mission from God to expel the English from France and bring about Charles' coronation. She rallied French troops and defeated the English at Patay, north of Orléans, and Charles was crowned at Reims. But Joan of Arc failed to take Paris. In 1430 she was captured by the Burgundians and sold to the English. She was convicted of witchcraft and heresy by a tribunal of French ecclesiastics and burned at the stake two years later at Rouen. Charles VII returned to Paris in 1437 ending 16 years of occupation, but the English were not entirely driven from French territory (with the exception of Calais) until 1453. The occupation had left Paris a disaster zone. Conditions improved while the restored monarchy moved to consolidate its power under Louis XI (ruled 1461–83), in whose reign the city's first printing press was installed at the Sorbonne (1463). Churches were rehabilitated or built in the Flamboyant Gothic style and a number of *hôtels particuliers* (private mansions) such as the Hôtel de Cluny and the Hôtel de Sens – now the Bibliothèque Forney (see p138) – were erected.

THE RENAISSANCE

The culture of the Italian Renaissance (French for 'rebirth') arrived in full swing in France in the early 16th century, during the reign of François I (1515–47), partly because of a series of indecisive French military operations in Italy. For the first time, the French aristocracy was exposed to Renaissance ideas of scientific and geographical scholarship and discovery as well as the value of secular over religious life.

Writers such as Rabelais, Marot and Ronsard were influential at this time, as were the architectural disciples of Michelangelo and Raphael. Evidence of this architectural influence

1066	1136	1163	1253
Normans conquer and occupy England	Abbot Suger commissions the basilica at St-Denis	Construction of Notre Dame Cathedral begins	La Sorbonne founded

can be seen in François I's chateau at Fontainebleau (p313) and the Petit Château at Chantilly (p318). In the city itself, a prime example of the period is the Pont Neuf, literally 'new bridge', which is in fact the oldest bridge in Paris. This new architecture was meant to reflect the splendour of the monarchy, which was fast moving towards absolutism, and of Paris as the capital of a powerful centralised state. But all this grandeur and show of strength was not enough to stem the tide of Protestantism that was flowing into France.

THE REFORMATION

By the 1530s the position of the Protestant Reformation sweeping across Europe had been strengthened in France by the ideas of John Calvin, a Frenchman exiled to Geneva. The edict of January 1562, which afforded the Protestants certain rights, was met by violent opposition from ultra-Catholic nobles whose fidelity to their faith was mixed with a desire to strengthen their power bases in the provinces. Paris remained very much a Catholic stronghold, and executions by burning at the stake (some 40 took place between 1547 and 1550, for example) in place de Grève continued apace up to the outbreak of religious civil war.

The Wars of Religion (1562–98) essentially involved three groups: the Huguenots (French Protestants supported by the English), the Catholic League and the Catholic king. The fighting severely weakened the position of the monarchy and brought the kingdom of France close to disintegration. The most grievous massacre took place in Paris on 23–24 August 1572, when some 3000 Huguenots who had come to Paris to celebrate the wedding of the Protestant Henri of Navarre (the future Henri IV) were slaughtered in what is now called the St Bartholomew's Day Massacre. On 7 May 1588, on the 'Day of the Barricades', the Catholic League rose up against Henri III and forced him to flee the Louvre; he was assassinated the following year.

Henri III was succeeded by Henri IV (ruled 1589–1610), who inaugurated the Bourbon dynasty. In 1598 he promulgated the Edict of Nantes, which guaranteed the Huguenots religious freedom and many civil and political rights as well, but this was not universally accepted. Catholic Paris refused to allow its new Protestant king entry into the city, and a siege of the capital continued for almost five years. Only when Henri embraced Catholicism at St-Denis – 'Paris vaut bien une messe' (Paris is well worth a Mass), he is reputed to have said upon taking Communion there – did the capital welcome him.

Henri consolidated the monarchy's power and began to rebuild Paris (the population of which was by now about 400,000) after more than 30 years of fighting. The magnificent place Royale (today's place des Vosges in the Marais) and place Dauphine at the western end of the Île de la Cité are prime examples of the new era of town planning. But Henri's rule ended as abruptly and violently as that of his predecessor. In 1610 he was assassinated by a Catholic fanatic when his coach got stuck in traffic along rue de la Ferronnerie in the Marais.

At nine years of age, Henri IV's son, the future Louis XIII, was too young to assume the throne, so his mother, Marie de Médici, was named regent. She set about building the

Italian Takeaway

The 16th century was something of a watershed for French cuisine. When Catherine de Médici, future consort to the son of François I, Henri II, arrived in Paris in 1533, she brought with her a team of Florentine *maître queux* (master chefs) and pasty cooks adept in the subtleties of Italian Renaissance cooking. They introduced such delicacies as aspics, truffles, *quenelles* (dumplings), artichokes, macaroons and puddings to the French court. Catherine's cousin, Marie de Médici, imported even more chefs into France when she married Henry IV in 1600. The French cooks, increasingly aware of their rising social status, took the Italians' recipes and sophisticated cooking styles on board, and the rest – to the eternal gratitude of epicures everywhere – is history.

1337–1453	1356	1429	1532–64
Hundred Years' War between France and England	Peasants' revolt led by Étienne Marcel fails	French forces under Joan of Arc defeat the English near Orléans	Rabelais publishes the humanistic satires *Gargantua and Panagruel*, during the reign of the enlightened king François I

magnificent Palais du Luxembourg and its enormous gardens for herself just outside the city wall. Louis XIII ascended the throne in 1617 but throughout most of his undistinguished reign he remained under the control of his ruthless chief minister, Cardinal Richelieu. Richelieu is best known for his untiring efforts to establish an all-powerful monarchy in France, opening the door to the absolutism of Louis XIV, and French supremacy in Europe, which would see France fighting Holland, Austria and England almost continuously. Under Louis XIII's reign, a number of palaces and churches were commissioned, including the Palais Royal and the Église Notre Dame du Val-de-Grâce.

LOUIS XIV & THE ANCIEN RÉGIME

Le Roi Soleil (literally 'the Sun King') ascended the throne in 1643 at the tender age of five. His mother, Anne of Austria, was appointed regent and Cardinal Mazarin, a protégé of Richelieu, was named chief minister. One of the decisive events of Louis XIV's early reign was the War of the Fronde (1648–53), a rebellion by the bourgeoisie and some of the nobility who were opposed to taxation and the increasing power of the monarchy. The revolt forced the royal court to flee Paris for a time.

When Mazarin died in 1661, Louis XIV assumed absolute power until his own death in the year 1715. Throughout his long reign, characterised by 'glitter and gloom' as one historian has put it, Louis sought to project the power of the French monarchy – bolstered by claims of divine right – both at home and abroad. He involved France in a long series of costly, almost continuous wars with Holland, Austria and England, which gained France territory but terrified its neighbours and nearly bankrupted the treasury. State taxation to fill the coffers caused widespread poverty and vagrancy in Paris, which was by then a city of almost 600,000 people.

But Louis – whose widely quoted line 'L'État, c'est moi' (I am the State) is often taken out of historical context – was able to quash the ambitious, feuding aristocracy and create

Column detail, place Vendôme (p83)

1572	1589	1615	1634
Thousands of Protestants killed	Henry IV, the first Bourbon king, ascends the throne	The Palais du Luxembourg and its gardens built for Marie de Médici	Cardinal Richelieu founds the Académie Française, the first and best known of France's five academies of arts and sciences

the first truly centralised French state, elements of which can still be seen in France today. While he did pour huge sums of money into building his extravagant palace at Versailles, by doing so he was able to sidestep the endless intrigues of the capital. And by turning his nobles into courtiers, Louis forced them to compete with one another for royal favour, reducing them to ineffectual sycophants. Although he hated Paris (due largely to his experiences during the War of the Fronde), Louis commissioned the fine place des Victoires, place Vendôme, the Hôtel des Invalides and the colonnaded Cour Carrée at the Louvre.

Louis mercilessly persecuted his Protestant subjects, who he considered a threat to the unity of the State and thus his power. In 1685 he revoked the Edict of Nantes, which had guaranteed the Huguenots freedom of conscience.

It was Louis XIV who said '*Après moi, le déluge*' (After me, the flood); in hindsight his words were more than prophetic. His grandson and successor, Louis XV (ruled 1715–74), was an oafish, incompetent buffoon, and grew to be universally despised. However, Louis XV's regent, Philippe of Orléans, did move the court from Versailles back to Paris; in the Age of Enlightenment, the French capital had become, in effect, the centre of Europe.

As the 18th century progressed, new economic and social circumstances rendered the *ancien régime* (old order) dangerously out of step with the needs of the country and its capital. The regime was further weakened by the anti-establishment and anticlerical ideas of the Enlightenment, whose leading lights included Voltaire, Rousseau and Diderot. But entrenched vested interests, a cumbersome power structure and royal lassitude prevented change from starting until the 1770s, by which time the monarchy's moment had passed.

The Seven Years' War (1756–63) was one of a series of ruinous military engagements pursued by Louis XV. It led to the loss of France's flourishing colonies in Canada, the West Indies and India. It was in part to avenge these losses that Louis XVI sided with the colonists in the American War of Independence (1775–83). But the Seven Years' War cost France a fortune and, more disastrously for the monarchy, it helped to disseminate at home the radical democratic ideas that were thrust upon the world stage by the American Revolution.

THE FRENCH REVOLUTION & THE FIRST REPUBLIC

By the late 1780s, the indecisive Louis XVI (ruled 1774–93) and his dominating queen, Marie-Antoinette, had managed to alienate virtually every segment of society – from the enlightened bourgeoisie to conservatives – and the king became increasingly isolated as unrest and dissatisfaction reached boiling point. When he tried to neutralise the power of the more reform-minded delegates at a meeting of the États-Généraux (States-General) at the Jeu de Paume in Versailles from May to June 1789 (see p311), the masses took to the streets of Paris. On 14 July, a mob raided the armoury at the Hôtel des Invalides for rifles and then stormed the prison at Bastille – the ultimate symbol of the despotic *ancien régime*. The French Revolution had begun.

At first, the Revolution was in the hands of moderate republicans called the Girondins. France was declared a constitutional monarchy and various reforms were introduced, including the adoption of the 'Déclaration des Droits de l'Homme and du Citoyen' (Declaration of the Rights of Man and Citizen), the document setting forth the principles of the Revolution in a preamble and 17 articles and modelled after the American Declaration of Independence. But as the masses armed themselves against the external threat to the new government posed by Austria, Prussia and the exiled French nobles, patriotism and nationalism mixed with radical fervour and then popularised and radicalised the Revolution. It was not long before the Girondins lost out to the extremist Jacobins, led by Robespierre, Danton and Marat, who abolished the monarchy and declared the First Republic in September 1792 after Louis XVI proved unreliable as a constitutional monarch. The Assemblée Nationale (National Assembly) was replaced by an elected Revolutionary Convention.

1672	1682	14 July 1789	1793
Le Journal de la Ville de Paris, the city's first daily newspaper, appears	Louis XIV moves his court to Versailles	French Revolution begins with the storming of the Bastille	Louis XVI and Marie-Antoinette executed

Red-Letter Days

Along with standardising France's – and, later, most of the world's – standard of weights and measures with the metric system, the Revolutionary government adopted a new, 'more rational' calendar from which all 'superstitious' associations (eg saints' days and mythology) were removed. Year 1 began on 22 September 1792, the day the republic was proclaimed. The names of the 12 months – Vendémaire, Brumaire, Frimaire, Nivôse, Pluviôse, Ventôse, Germinal, Floréal, Prairial, Messidor, Thermidor and Fructidor – were chosen according to the seasons. The autumn months, for instance, were Vendémaire, derived from *vendange* (grape harvest or vintage); Brumaire, derived from *brume* (mist or fog); and Frimaire, derived from *frimas* (frost). In turn, each month was divided into three 10-day weeks called *décades*, the last day of which was a rest day. The five remaining days of the year were used to celebrate Virtue, Genius, Labour, Opinion and Rewards. While the republican calendar worked well in theory, it caused no end of confusion for France in its communication and trade abroad as the months and days kept on changing in relation to those of the Gregorian calendar. The old system was restored in France by Napoleon in 1806.

In January 1793 Louis XVI, who had tried to flee the country with his family but only got as far as Varennes, was tried as 'Louis Capet' (as all kings since Hugh Capet were declared to have ruled illegally), convicted of 'conspiring against the liberty of the nation' and guillotined at place de la Révolution, today's place de la Concorde. His consort, Marie-Antoinette, was executed in October of the same year.

In March 1793 the Jacobins set up the notorious Committee of Public Safety to deal with national defence and to apprehend and try 'traitors'. This body virtually had dictatorial control over the city and the country during the so-called Reign of Terror (September 1793 to July 1794), which saw most religious freedoms revoked, churches desecrated and closed, and cathedrals turned into 'Temples of Reason'. Paris during the Reign of Terror was not unlike Moscow under Joseph Stalin.

The Jacobin propagandist Marat was assassinated in his bathtub by the Girondin Charlotte Corday in July 1793 and by autumn, the Reign of Terror was in full swing; by mid-1794 some 2500 people had been beheaded in Paris and more than 14,500 executed elsewhere in France. Finally, the Revolution turned on itself, 'devouring its own children' in the words of the Jacobin Louis Antoine Léon de Saint-Just, an intimate of Robespierre. Robespierre sent Danton to the guillotine; Saint-Just and Robespierre eventually met the same fate.

After the Reign of Terror faded, a five-man delegation of moderate republicans led by Paul Barras, who had ordered the arrests of Robespierre and Saint-Just, set itself up to rule the republic as the Directoire (Directory). On 5 October 1795 (or 13 Vendémaire in year 6, see p65), a group of royalist *jeunesse dorée* (gilded youth) bent on overthrowing the Directory was intercepted in front of the Église St-Roch on rue St-Honoré by loyalist forces led by a young Corsican general named Napoleon Bonaparte, who fired into the crowd. For this 'whiff of grapeshot', Napoleon was put in command of French forces in Italy, where he was particularly successful in the campaign against Austria. His victories soon turned him into an independent political force.

NAPOLEON & THE FIRST EMPIRE

The post-revolutionary government led by the five-man Directory was far from stable, and when Napoleon returned to Paris in 1799 he found a chaotic republic in which few citizens had any faith. In November, when it appeared that the Jacobins were again on the ascendancy in the legislature, Napoleon tricked the delegates into leaving Paris for St-Cloud to the southwest 'for their own protection', overthrew the discredited Directory and assumed power himself.

1799	1804	1815	1830
Napoleon Bonaparte seizes control of government in a coup d'état	Napoleon crowned 'Emperor of the French' at Notre Dame	Napoleon defeated by the British at Waterloo	Charles X overthrown in July Revolution

At first, Napoleon took the title of First Consul. In 1802 a referendum declared him 'Consul for Life' and his birthday became a national holiday. By December 1804, when he had himself crowned 'Emperor of the French' by Pope Pius VII at Notre Dame, the scope and nature of Napoleon's ambitions were obvious to all. But to consolidate and legitimise his authority, Napoleon needed more victories on the battlefield. So began a seemingly endless series of wars and victories by which France came to control most of Europe.

Napoleon invaded Russia in 1812 to do away with his last major rival on the Continent, the tsar. Although his Grande Armée captured Moscow, it was wiped out by the brutal Russian winter. Prussia and Napoleon's other adversaries quickly recovered from their earlier defeats, and less than two years after the fiasco in Russia the allied armies entered Paris. Napoleon abdicated and left France for the island of Elba off the coast of Italy.

At the Congress of Vienna (1814–15), the allies restored the House of Bourbon to the French throne, installing Louis XVI's brother as Louis XVIII (Louis XVI's second son, Charles, had been declared Louis XVII by monarchists in exile but died in 1795). But in March 1815 Napoleon escaped from Elba, landed in southern France and gathered a large army as he marched towards Paris. His so-called Hundred Days back in power ended, however, when his forces were defeated by the British under the Duke of Wellington at Waterloo in Belgium. Napoleon was exiled to the remote South Atlantic island of St Helena, where he died in 1821.

Although reactionary in some ways – he re-established slavery in France's colonies, for example – Napoleon instituted a number of important reforms, including a reorganisation of the judicial system; the promulgation of a new legal code, the Code Napoléon (or civil code), which forms the basis of the French legal system to this day; and a new educational system. More importantly, he preserved the essence of the changes brought about by the Revolution. Napoleon is therefore remembered by many French people as the nation's greatest hero.

Few of Napoleon's grand architectural plans for Paris were completed, but the Arc de Triomphe, the Arc de Triomphe du Carrousel, La Madeleine, the Pont des Arts, rue de Rivoli and the Canal St-Martin all date from this period.

THE RESTORATION & THE SECOND REPUBLIC

The reign of 'the gouty old gentleman' Louis XVIII (1814–24) was dominated by the struggle among extreme monarchists who wanted a return to the *ancien régime*, liberals who saw the changes wrought by the Revolution as irreversible and the radicals of the working-class neighbourhoods of Paris. His successor, the reactionary Charles X (ruled 1824–30), handled this struggle with great incompetence and was overthrown in the so-called July Revolution of 1830 when a motley group of revolutionaries seized the Hôtel de Ville.

Louis-Philippe (ruled 1830–48), an ostensibly constitutional monarch of bourgeois sympathies and tastes, was then chosen by parliament to head what became known as the July Monarchy. He was in turn overthrown in the February Revolution of 1848, and the Second Republic was established.

FROM THE SECOND REPUBLIC TO THE SECOND EMPIRE

In presidential elections held in 1848, Napoleon's inept nephew Louis Napoleon Bonaparte was overwhelmingly elected. Legislative deadlock caused Louis Napoleon to lead a coup d'état in 1851, after which he was proclaimed Emperor Napoleon III (Bonaparte had conferred the title Napoleon II on his son upon his abdication in 1814 but the latter never ruled) and moved into the Palais des Tuileries, which would be destroyed during the Paris Commune 20 years later.

1848	1852–70	1855	1870–71
Second Republic established	Second Empire under Napoleon III	First of five *Expositions Universelles* opens in Paris	Prussia defeats France; Communards seize power in Paris

The Second Empire lasted from 1852 until 1870. During this period, France enjoyed significant economic growth, and Paris was transformed under Baron Georges-Eugène Haussmann (see p68). The city's first department stores were also built at this time – the now defunct La Ville de Paris in 1834 followed by Le Bon Marché in 1852 – as were the *passages couverts*, Paris' delightful covered shopping arcades (see p144).

Napoleon III – like his uncle before him – embroiled France in a number of costly conflicts, including the disastrous Crimean War (1854–56). In 1870 Otto von Bismarck goaded Napoleon III into declaring war on Prussia. Within months the thoroughly unprepared French army was defeated and the emperor taken prisoner. When news of the debacle reached Paris, the masses took to the streets and demanded that a republic be declared.

THE THIRD REPUBLIC & THE BELLE ÉPOQUE

The Third Republic began as a provisional government of national defence in September 1870. The Prussians were, at the time, advancing on Paris and would subsequently lay siege to the capital, forcing starving Parisians to bake bread laced with sawdust and consume most of the animals in the Ménagerie at the Jardin des Plantes. In January 1871 the government negotiated an armistice with the Prussians, who demanded that National Assembly elections be held immediately. The republicans, who had called on the nation to continue to resist the Prussians and were overwhelmingly supported by Parisians, lost to the monarchists, who had campaigned on a peace platform.

As expected, the monarchist-controlled assembly ratified the Treaty of Frankfurt (1871). However, when ordinary Parisians heard of its harsh terms – a huge war indemnity, cession of the provinces of Alsace and Lorraine and the occupation of Paris by 30,000 Prussian troops – they revolted against the government.

Following the withdrawal of Prussian troops on 18 March 1871, an insurrectionary government, known to history as the Paris Commune, was established and its supporters, the Communards, seized control of the capital; the legitimate government had fled to Versailles. In late May, the government launched an offensive on the Commune known as La Semaine Sanglante (Bloody Week) in which several thousand rebels were killed. After a mop-up of the Parc des Buttes-Chaumont, the last of the Communard insurgents, cornered by government forces in the Cimetière du Père Lachaise, fought a hopeless, all-night battle among the tombstones. In the morning, the 147 survivors were lined up against the Mur des Fédérés (Wall of the Federalists), shot, and buried where they fell in a mass grave. A further 20,000 or so Communards, mostly working class, were rounded up throughout the city and summarily executed.

Karl Marx interpreted the Communard insurrection as the first great proletarian uprising against the bourgeoisie, and socialists came to see its victims as martyrs of the class struggle. Among the buildings destroyed in the fighting were the original Hôtel de Ville, the Palais des Tuileries and the Cours des Comptes (site of the present-day Musée d'Orsay).

Despite this disastrous start, the Third Republic ushered in the glittering *belle époque* (literally 'beautiful age'), with Art Nouveau architecture, a whole field of artistic 'isms' from impressionism onwards and advances in science and engineering, including the construction of the first metro line, which opened in 1900. *Expositions universelles* (world exhibitions) were held in Paris in 1889 (showcasing the then maligned Eiffel Tower) and again in 1900 in the purpose-built Petit Palais. The Paris of nightclubs and artistic cafés made its first appearance around this time.

But France was obsessed with a desire for revenge after its defeat by Germany, and jingoistic nationalism, scandals and accusations were the order of the day. The most serious moral and political crisis of the Third Republic, however, was the infamous 'Dreyfus Affair', which began in 1894 when a Jewish army captain named Alfred Dreyfus was accused of

1889	1894	1905	1914
Eiffel Tower completed for *Exposition Universelle*	Army Captain Alfred Dreyfus accused of spying for Germany	Legal separation of Church and State in France	France enters WWI

betraying military secrets to Germany, court-martialled and sentenced to life imprisonment on Devil's Island, a penal colony off the northern coast of South America. Leftists and liberals, including the novelist Émile Zola, succeeded in having the case reopened – despite bitter opposition from the army command, right-wing politicians and many Catholic groups – and Dreyfus was vindicated in 1900. When he died in 1935 Dreyfus was laid to rest in the Cimitière de Montparnasse. The Dreyfus affair discredited both the army and the Catholic Church in France. The result was more rigorous civilian control of the military and, in 1905, the legal separation of Church and State.

WWI & THE INTERWAR YEARS

Central to France's entry into WWI was the desire to regain the provinces of Alsace and Lorraine, lost to Germany in 1871. Indeed, Raymond Poincaré, president of the Third Republic from 1913 to 1920 and later prime minister, was a native of Lorraine and a firm supporter of war with Germany. But when the heir to the Austrian throne, Archduke Franz Ferdinand, was assassinated by Serbian nationalists at Sarajevo on 28 June 1914, precipitating what would erupt into a global war, Germany jumped the gun. Within a month, it had declared war on Russia *and* France.

By early September German troops had reached the River Marne, just 15km east of Paris, and the government was moved to Bordeaux. But Marshal Joffre's troops, transported to the front by Parisian taxis, brought about the 'Miracle of the Marne', and Paris was safe within a month. In November 1918 the armistice was finally signed in a railway carriage in a clearing of the Forêt de Compiègne, 82km northeast of Paris.

The defeat of Austria-Hungary and Germany in WWI, which regained Alsace and Lorraine for France, was achieved at an unimaginable human cost. Of the eight million French men who were called to arms, 1.3 million were killed and almost one million crippled. In other words, two of every 10 Frenchmen aged between 20 and 45 years of age were killed in WWI. At the Battle of Verdun (1916) alone, the French, led by Général Philippe Pétain, and the Germans each lost about 400,000 men.

The 1920s and 1930s saw Paris as a centre of the avant-garde, with artists pushing into new fields of cubism and surrealism, Le Corbusier rewriting the textbook for architecture, foreign writers such as Ernest Hemingway and James Joyce drawn by the city's liberal atmosphere, and nightlife setting a reputation for everything from jazz clubs to the cancan.

France's efforts to promote a separatist movement in the Rhineland and its occupation of the Ruhr in 1923 to enforce German reparations payments proved disastrous. But it did lead to almost a decade of accommodation and compromise with Germany over border guarantees and Germany's admission to the League of Nations. The naming of Adolf Hitler as German chancellor in 1933, however, would put an end to all that.

WWII & THE OCCUPATION

During most of the 1930s, the French, like the British, had done their best to appease Hitler but, two days after the German invasion of Poland on 1 September 1939, Britain and France declared war on Germany. For the first nine months Parisians joked about le drôle de guerre – the 'funny war' in which nothing happened. But the battle for France began in early May 1940 and by 14 June France had capitulated and Paris was occupied; almost half the population of just under five million fled the city by car, on bicycle or on foot. The British expeditionary force sent to help the French barely managed to avoid capture by retreating to Dunkirk and crossing the English Channel in small boats. The Maginot Line, a supposedly impregnable wall of fortifications along the Franco-German border, had proved useless – the German armoured divisions simply outflanked it by going through Belgium.

1918	1922	1940	25 Aug 1944
Armistice ending WWI signed near Paris	Sylvia Beach of the Shakespeare & Company bookshop publishes James Joyce's *Ulysses*	Germans occupy Paris	Allied forces liberate Paris

The Germans divided France into a zone under direct German rule (along the western coast and the north, including Paris) and a puppet state based in the spa town of Vichy, led by Pétain, the ageing WWI hero of the Battle of Verdun. Both Pétain's collaborationist government, whose leaders and supporters assumed that the Nazis were Europe's new masters and had to be accommodated, and French police forces in German-occupied areas (including Paris) helped the Nazis round up French Jews and others for deportation to concentration and extermination camps in Germany and Poland.

After the fall of Paris, General Charles de Gaulle, France's undersecretary of war, fled to London. In a radio broadcast on 18 June 1940, he appealed to French patriots to continue resisting the Germans. He set up a French government-in-exile and established the Forces Françaises Libres (Free French Forces), a military force dedicated to fighting the Germans.

The underground movement known as the Résistance (Resistance), whose active members never amounted to more than about 5% of the population (the other 95% were either collaborators, such as the film stars Maurice Chevalier and Arletty, and the designer Coco Chanel, or did nothing whatsoever), engaged in such activities as sabotaging railways, collecting intelligence for the Allies, helping Allied airmen who had been shot down and publishing anti-German leaflets. Paris was the centre for the activities of the Resistance.

The liberation of France began with the Allied landings in Normandy on D-day (*Jour J* in French): 6 June 1944. On 15 August Allied forces also landed in southern France. After a brief insurrection by the Resistance, Paris was liberated on 25 August by an Allied force spearheaded by Free French units led by General Leclerc, who were sent in ahead of the Americans so that the French led by de Gaulle would have the honour of liberating the capital the following day. Hitler, who visited Paris in June 1940 and loved it, ordered that the city be torched toward the end of the war. It was an order that, fortunately, had not been obeyed.

THE FOURTH REPUBLIC

Charles de Gaulle returned to Paris and set up a provisional government, but in January 1946 he resigned as president, wrongly believing that the move would provoke a popular outcry for his return. A few months later, a new constitution was approved by referendum. The Fourth Republic was a period that saw unstable coalition cabinets follow one another with bewildering speed (on average, one every six months), and economic recovery, helped immeasurably by massive American aid. The war to reassert French colonial control over Indochina ended with the disastrous French defeat at Dien Bien Phu in 1954. France also tried to suppress an uprising by Arab nationalists in Algeria, where over one million French settlers lived.

THE FIFTH REPUBLIC

The Fourth Republic came to an end in 1958, when extreme right-wingers, furious at what they saw as defeatism rather than tough action in dealing with the uprising in Algeria, began conspiring to overthrow the government. De Gaulle was brought back to power to prevent a military coup and possible civil war. He soon drafted a new constitution that gave considerable powers to the president at the expense of the National Assembly.

The Fifth Republic, which continues to this day, was rocked in 1961 by an attempted coup staged in Algiers by a group of right-wing military officers. When it failed, the Organisation de l'Armée Secrète (OAS; a group of French settlers and sympathisers opposed to Algerian independence) turned to terrorism, trying several times to assassinate de Gaulle and nearly succeeding in August 1962 in the Parisian suburb of Petit Clamart. The book and film *The Day of the Jackal* portrayed a fictional OAS attempt on de Gaulle's life.

1945	1949	1954	1958
WWII ends	Simone de Beauvoir publishes *Le Deuxième Sexe* (The Second Sex)	French forces defeated at Dien Bien Phu in Vietnam	De Gaulle returns to power and forms the Fifth Republic

Top Five Books on Paris' History

- *Cross Channel*, Julien Barnes (1997) – a witty collection of key moments in shared Anglo-French history – from Joan of Arc to a trip via Eurostar from London to Paris – by one of Britain's most talented novelists.
- *Is Paris Burning?* Larry Collins & Dominique Lapierre (1965) – a tense and very intelligent reportage of the last days of the Nazi occupation of Paris.
- *The Seven Ages of Paris*, Alistair Horne (2002) – this superb, very idiosyncratic 'biography' of Paris divides the city's history into seven ages – from the 13th-century reign of Philippe-Auguste to the period from the occupation to de Gaulle's retirement in 1969.
- *The Sun King*, Nancy Mitford (1995) – this excellent work on Louis XIV and the country he ruled from Versailles looks not so much at international politics or wars but at the court intrigue and how Versailles came about.
- *A Traveller's History of Paris*, Robert Cole (1999) – at just over 300 pages, this book is hardly the most in-depth treatment of Parisian history but as an introductory text it's easy to read and at times witty.

In 1962 de Gaulle negotiated an end to the war in Algeria. Some 750,000 *pied-noir* (literally 'black feet' – as Algerian-born French people are known in France) flooded into France and the capital. Meanwhile, almost all of the other French colonies and protectorates in Africa had demanded and achieved independence. Shrewdly, the French government began a program of economic and military aid to its former colonies to bolster France's waning importance internationally and create a bloc of French-speaking nations in the Third World.

Paris retained its position as a creative and intellectual centre, particularly in philosophy and film making, and the 1960s saw large parts of the Marais beautifully restored. But the loss of the colonies, the surge in immigration and economic difficulties, including an increase in unemployment, weakened de Gaulle's government.

In March 1968 a large demonstration in Paris against the war in Vietnam was led by student Daniel 'Danny the Red' Cohn-Bendit, now the leader of the French Green Party and European Member of Parliament. This gave impetus to the student movement and protests were staged throughout the spring. A seemingly insignificant incident in May, in which police broke up yet another in a long series of demonstrations by students of the University of Paris, sparked a violent reaction on the streets of the capital; students occupied the Sorbonne and barricades were erected in the Latin Quarter. Workers joined in the protests and some six million people across France participated in a general strike that virtually paralysed both the country and the city. It was a period of much creativity and new ideas with slogans appearing everywhere such as *'L'Imagination au Pouvoir'* (Put Imagination in Power) and *'Sous les Pavés, la Plage'* (Under the Cobblestones, the Beach), a reference to Parisians' favoured material for building barricades and what they could expect to find beneath them.

The alliance between workers and students couldn't last long. While the former wanted to reap greater benefits from the consumer market, the latter wanted to destroy it (and were called 'fascist *provocateurs*' and 'mindless anarchists' by the French Communist leadership). De Gaulle took advantage of this division and appealed to people's fear of anarchy – if not civil war. Just as Paris and the rest of France seemed on the brink of revolution and an overthrow of the Fifth Republic appeared imminent, 100,000 Gaullists demonstrated on the av des Champs-Élysées in support of the government and stability was restored. The government made a number of immediate changes, including the decentralisation of the higher education system, and reforms (eg lowering the voting age to 18, a new abortion law and workers' self-management) continued through the 1970s.

1968	1977	1992	1992
Student-led riots lead to de Gaulle's resignation the following year	Controversial Centre Pompidou opens	Disneyland Paris (then EuroDisney) opens at Marne-la-Valée	IM Pei's Grande Pyramide at the Louvre and Opéra Bastille open

1969 TO THE PRESENT

In 1969 de Gaulle resigned and was succeeded by the Gaullist leader Georges Pompidou, who was in turn replaced by Valéry Giscard d'Estaing in 1974. François Mitterrand, long-time head of the Partie Socialiste (PS), was elected president in 1981 and, as the business community had feared, immediately set out to nationalise privately owned banks, large industrial groups and various other parts of the economy, increasing the state-owned share of industrial production from 15% to more than 30%. However, during the mid-1980s Mitterrand followed a generally moderate economic policy and in 1988, aged 69, he was re-elected for a second seven-year term.

In the 1986 parliamentary elections, the right-wing opposition led by Jacques Chirac, mayor of Paris since 1977, received a majority in the National Assembly; for the next two years Mitterrand was forced to work with a prime minister and cabinet from the opposition, an unprecedented arrangement known as *cohabitation*.

In the May 1995 presidential elections Chirac had a comfortable victory (the ailing Mitterrand, who would die in January 1996, decided not to run again). In his first few months in office Chirac received high marks for his direct words and actions in matters relating to the EU and the war raging in Bosnia. His cabinet choices, including the selection of 'whiz kid' foreign minister Alain Juppé as prime minister, were well received. But Chirac's decision to resume nuclear testing on the French Polynesian island of Mururoa and a nearby atoll was met with outrage both in France and abroad. On the home front, Chirac's moves to restrict welfare payments (a move designed to bring France closer to meeting the criteria for European Monetary Union; EMU) led to the largest protests since 1968. For three weeks in late 1995 Paris was crippled by public-sector strikes, battering the economy.

In 1997 Chirac took a big gamble and called an early parliamentary election for June. The move backfired. Chirac remained president but his party, the Rassemblement Pour la République (RPR; Rally for the Republic) lost support and a coalition of Socialists, Communists and Greens came to power. Lionel Jospin, a former minister of education in the Mitterrand government (who, most notably, promised the French people a shorter working week for the same pay), became prime minister. France had once again entered into a period of *cohabitation* – with Chirac on the other side this time around.

For the most part, Jospin and his government continued to enjoy the electorate's approval, thanks largely to a recovery in economic growth and the introduction of a 35-hour working week, which created thousands of (primarily part-time) jobs. But this period of *cohabitation*, the longest lasting government in the history of the Fifth Republic, would end in May 2002.

Chirac and Jospin were neck-to-neck as voters went to the polls for the first round of voting in the May 2002 elections. But, due to extremely low turnout, Jean-Marie Le Pen, leader of the right-wing Front National, garnered nearly 17% of the vote against Jospin's 16%, knocking the latter out of the race; Chirac received about 20%. Fearing the advent of an extremist government under Le Pen, political parties across the spectrum united behind Chirac and a record number of voters turned up at the polls in the second round, handing Chirac 82% of the vote. Chirac appointed Jean-Pierre Raffarin, a popular regional politician, as prime minister.

During the election campaign, President Chirac's team made pledges to lower taxes with declining revenues from a sluggish economy, and there have been widespread calls to reduce government spending, allow more flexibility in the implementation of the 35-hour work week and improve the business climate by further privatisation and liberalisation.

In May 2001, Bertrand Delanoë, a socialist with support from the Green Party, became Paris' – and a European capital's – first openly gay mayor. He continues to enjoy widespread popularity, particularly for his efforts to make Paris more liveable by promoting bicycles and buses and to create a more approachable and responsible city administration.

1994	1998	2001	2002
Eurostar trains link London's Waterloo station with the Gare du Nord in Paris	Arc de Triomphe eternal flame extinguished by urinating Mexican soccer fan	Socialist Bertrand Delanoë becomes Paris' – and a European capital's – first openly gay mayor	President Chirac overwhelmingly defeats Front National leader Jean-Marie Le Pen to win second term

Itineraries 75
Organised Tours 76
Louvre & Les Halles 79
Marais & Bastille 86
The Islands 91
Latin Quarter & Jardin
des Plantes 93
St-Germain, Odéon &
Luxembourg 97
Montparnasse 108
Faubourg St-Germain &
Invalides 110
Eiffel Tower Area &
16e Arrondissement 113
Étoile & Champs-Élysées 117
Concorde & Madeleine 118
Clichy & Gare St-Lazare 119
Opéra & Grands Boulevards 120
Gare du Nord, Gare de
l'Est & République 121
Ménilmontant & Belleville 123
Gare de Lyon, Nation
& Bercy 124
13e Arrondissement &
Chinatown 125
15e Arrondissement 126
Montmartre & Pigalle 126
La Villette 128
Outside the Walls: Beyond
Central Paris 130

Quarters &
Arrondissements

Quarters & Arrondissements

Paris – at least the central bit that Parisians call *intra-muros* (Latin for 'within the walls') – is a compact, easily negotiated city. Some 20 arrondissements (city districts) spiral clockwise more or less from the centre and are important locators; their numbers are always included in the addresses given on business cards, flyers, the Internet and in this guide.

Unlike numbered districts or postcodes in many other cities, Paris' arrondissements do have distinct personalities: the 1er has plenty of sights but few residents, the 5e is studenty, the 7e full of ministries and embassies, the 10e has traditionally been working class but is becoming a relatively cheap and trendy district in which to live, and the 16e is a bastion of the very well-heeled. But such profiles are always so cut-and-dried, and the lay of the land becomes much clearer to visitors when they see the city as composed of about two-dozen named *quartiers* (quarters) and arrondissements.

This guide starts in the heart of the Right Bank, in the area around the **Louvre** and **Les Halles**, which largely takes in the 1er but also part of the 2e and the westernmost edge of the 4e. Next come the **Marais** (4e and 3e) and the contiguous **Bastille** district (11e) to the east and southeast.

The two islands in the Seine – the **Île de la Cité** and the **Île St-Louis** – are neither fish nor fowl when it comes to the question of Right or Left Bank but they do belong to an arrondissement. Most of the former is in the 1er and all of the latter is in the 4e.

We encounter the Left Bank for the first time in the **Latin Quarter**, traditional centre of learning in Paris, and the leafy **Jardin des Plantes** to the east (both 5e). The 6e, to the west and southwest, is both a frenetic district of sights, shops, galleries and cafés (**St-Germain** and **Odéon**) and a tranquil park and residential neighbourhood (**Luxembourg**). To the south is **Montparnasse**

Mural on building, Gare du Nord

(14e), once the centre of nightlife in Paris and now best known for its massive train station and unsightly landmark, the **Tour Montparnasse**. The **Faubourg St-Germain** and **Invalides** (7e) to the north are both important for their sights but also as the locations of many branches of government, including the **Assemblée Nationale**, embassies and cultural centres. To the west is the **Eiffel Tower** and, across the Seine on the Right Bank, the posh **16e arrondissement**, a district of broad, tree-lined avenues, grand apartment blocks and small but exquisite museums.

To the east and still on the Right Bank is the 8e, which includes what to many are the quintessential Parisian areas and sights: **Étoile**, with its landmark **Arc de Triomphe**, and the wide boulevard known as the **Champs-Élysées**. At the end of this grand avenue is **Concorde** and to the north of that **Madeleine**, two very important – and very different – *places* (squares). Above the 8e is the schizophrenic 17e, with its beautiful, Haussmann-era buildings beyond the **Gare St-Lazare** and the working-class neighbourhoods of **Clichy**. To the east is the 9e, where you'll find the city's original **Opéra** and most of the **Grands Boulevards**.

The 10e, boasting both the **Gare du Nord** and the **Gare de l'Est**, is the city's rail hub. It also has some wonderful residential districts around the **Canal St-Martin**. **République** gets a toehold in to the south but most of this enormous and chaotic square is in the 3e. To the south is the *branché* (trendy) district of **Ménilmontant**, awash in alternative bars, cafés and restaurants in the northern 11e, and to the east, the solidly working-class neighbourhood of **Belleville** (20e), where Édith Piaf was born, socialism once thrived and Paris' first immigrants from North Africa settled.

The 12e contains three very different districts: the **Gare de Lyon** to the northwest, the large square called **Nation** to the east and, to the south, the redeveloped area of **Bercy**, its old wine warehouses having been turned into a Disneyland-like wining and dining theme park. Across the Seine is the **13e arrondissement**, home to the grandiose **Bibliothèque Nationale de France François Mitterrand** and **Chinatown**, and currently the scene of one of the largest, most important civil-engineering projects in the history of Paris redevelopment. The **15e arrondissement**, the most populous but arguably least interesting district to tourists, is to the west.

To the north in the 18e is **Montmartre**, the Paris of myth and films, but not of history, and **Pigalle**, the naughty red-light district that looks positively tame when compared with its equivalents in London or New York. **La Villette**, with its lovely park, canal, and cutting-edge museums and other attractions in the far-flung 19e arrondissement in the northeast, is the last district of major importance *intra-muros*. 'Outside the walls', however, are at least four areas of particular interest to visitors: the **Bois de Vincennes** and **Bois de Boulogne**, Paris' green lungs and recreational centres to the east and the west; **La Défense**, the futuristic business and residential district at the end of metro line No 1 to the west of Étoile; and **St-Denis**, to the north on metro line No 13, where France's kings were laid to rest for well over a millennium and where there is an important 12th-century cathedral, the Basilique de St-Denis.

In this chapter, the Transport boxed texts provide a quick reference for the location of metro and train stations, tram and bus stops and ferry piers in each district. For more detailed information on how to get to, from and around Paris, see p332.

ITINERARIES

If you want a general overview of Paris before striking out on your own, take one of the tours described later in this chapter (p76). At least you'll be sure to see what the French call *les incontournables* (the unmissables) even on a very brief visit. The 'jump-on/jump-off' bus tours are particularly useful for this purpose though the Batobus (p334) is another option if you're visiting Paris any time between late March and October.

Failing that, you can always go up to look down. Paris is a very flat city and the views are excellent from the Eiffel Tower, the Centre Pompidou, Sacré Cœur, La Samaritaine department store, the Tour Montparnasse, Parc de Belleville and the Grande Arche de la Défense. The highest point in Paris, by the way, is the elevated Télégraphe metro station on line No 11.

Opening times and prices for Paris' museums and sites can vary, and closing times for parks, in particular, may vary according to the season. In this chapter, we have indicated seasonal opening and closing times with a span; so '9am-5.30pm to 9.30pm' indicates that the sight in question may close any time between 5.30pm and 9.30pm, according to the time of year.

One Day

Those with just one day in Paris – what *were* you thinking? – should definitely join a morning tour and then concentrate on the most Parisian of sights and attractions: **Notre Dame** (p91), the **Louvre** (p80), the **Eiffel Tower** (p114) and the **Arc de Triomphe** (p117). In the late afternoon have a coffee or a pastis on the **av des Champs-Élysées** (p118) and then make your way to **Montmartre** (p186) for dinner.

Two Days

If you have two days to spare in the City of Light, you could also take in such sights as the **Musée d'Orsay'** (p111), **Ste-Chapelle** (p92), **Conciergerie** (p92), **Musée National du Moyen Age** (p94) and/or the **Musée Rodin** (p111). Have brunch on the **place des Vosges** (p87) and enjoy a night of mirth and gaiety in the **Marais** (p240).

Three Days

With another day to look around the city, you should consider a **cruise** (p77) along the Seine or the Canal St-Martin and visit some place further afield – the **Cimetière du Père Lachaise** (p123), say, or the **Parc de la Villette** (p128). Take in a concert, opera or ballet at the **Palais Garnier** (p241) or **Opéra Bastille** (p241) or a play at the **Comédie Française** (p239), and go on a bar and club crawl in **Ménilmontant** (p226).

One Week

If you have one week here you can see many of the major sights listed in this chapter, visit places 'outside the walls' such as **La Défense** (p133) and **St-Denis** (p135), and leave Paris for a day or two on an **excursion** (p305): Vaux-le-Vicomte can be easily combined with Fontainebleau, Senlis with Chantilly and, if you travel hard and fast, Chartres with Versailles.

ORGANISED TOURS

If you can't be bothered making your own way around Paris or don't have the time, consider a tour by helicopter, bus, boat or bicycle or on foot. There's no reason to feel sheepish or embarrassed about taking a guided tour – even one of those super-touristy ones in eight languages. They are an excellent way to learn the lay of the land in a new place, and even guidebook writers have been known to join them from time to time. Most useful, though, are the buses and other conveyances that allow you to disembark when you want and board the next one that suits you. They usually offer little or no commentary aside from calling out the stop names but offer the most freedom to do what you want.

Couch potatoes will head for **Paris Story** (Map pp383–5; ☎ 01 42 66 62 06; www.paris story.com; 11bis rue Scribe, 9e; metro Auber or Opéra; adult €8, family €21, student & under 18 €5, under 6 free; ☾ 9am-7pm, tours hourly), a 50-minute audiovisual romp through Paris' 2000-year history, with headset commentary in 13 different languages.

AIR

BALLON EUTELSAT

☎ 01 44 26 20 00; www.aeroparis.com; Parc André Citroën, 2 rue de la Montagne de la Fage, 15e; metro Balard; Mon-Fri adult/child 12-17 yrs/child 3-11 yrs €10/9/5, Sat & Sun €12/10/6, under 3 free; ☾ 9am-5.30pm to 9.30pm (seasonal)

The Eutelsat Balloon run by Aeroparis in Parc André Citroën (Map pp389–91) will take you 150m off the ground and provide fabulous views of Paris and the Seine but do not ex-pect to get very far; the helium-filled balloon remains firmly tethered to the ground. The balloon does not take on passengers in windy conditions. Be sure to call in advance.

PARIS HÉLICOPTÈRE

☎ 01 48 35 90 44; www.paris-helicoptere.com; €122; ☾ 9am-6pm Sun

This outfit based at the Aéroport du Bourget, north of Paris, offers 80km circular flights over Paris every Sunday, lasting 25 minutes. Book 10 days in advance. You can reach Le Bourget by RER line B3 or B5 or by RATP bus No 350 from Gare du Nord, Gare de l'Est or Porte de la Chapelle, or bus No 152 from Porte de la Villette (stop: Musée de l'Air et de l'Espace).

BICYCLE

FAT TIRE BIKE TOURS Map pp389-91
☎ 01 56 58 10 54; www.fattirebiketoursparis.com; 24 rue Edgar Faure, 15e; metro La Motte-Picquet Grenelle; ⌚ office 9am-7pm

An English-speaking company that gets rave reviews from readers, Fat Tire Bike Tours (formerly Mike's Bike Tours) offers day tours of the city (adult/student €24/22; four hours), starting at 11am in March and April and September to November, and at 11am and 3.30pm from May to August. Night bicycle tours (adult/student €28/26) depart at 7pm on Sunday, Tuesday and Thursday in March and November and at 7pm daily from April to October.

Participants can meet at the Fat Tire Bike Tours office, where you can store bags, log on to the Internet and get tourist information, but tours actually depart from av Gustave Eiffel, 7e, just opposite the Eiffel Tower's South Pillar at the start of the Champ de Mars. All costs include the bicycle and, if necessary, raingear.

The same company runs **Paris Segway Tours** (www.parissegwaytours.com) which, though not on bicycles, involve two-wheeled, electric-powered conveyances. Segway tours (€70), which follow the same routes as the bike tours and last four to five hours, depart at 10.30am daily March to November and at 6.30pm daily, April to October. You must book in advance.

GEPETTO & VÉLOS Map pp392-5
☎ 01 43 54 19 95; www.gepetto-et-velos.com in French; 59 rue du Cardinal Lemoine, 5e; metro Cardinal Lemoine; ⌚ 9am-1pm & 2-7.30pm Tue-Sat, 9am-1pm & 2-7pm Sun

Bike tours cost €30, including guide, bicycle and insurance. There is a **5e arrondissement branch** (⌚ 01 43 37 16 17; 46 rue Daubenton, 5e; metro Censier Daubenton; ⌚ 9am-1pm & 2-7.30pm Mon-Sat), which is open on Monday.

MAISON ROUE LIBRE Map pp396-9
☎ 08 10 44 15 34; www.rouelibre.fr; Forum des Halles, 1 passage Mondétour, 1er; metro Les Halles; ⌚ 9am-7pm mid-Jan–mid-Dec

This RATP-sponsored outfit has city tours lasting 1½ hours (adult/child under 12 €21/14). There are also tours further afield (full-/half-day adult €29/25, child under 12 €22/15).

PARIS À VÉLO, C'EST SYMPA!
Map pp392-5
☎ 01 48 87 60 01; www.parisvelosympa.com in French; 37 blvd Bourdon, 4e; metro Bastille; ⌚ 9.30am-1pm & 2-6.30pm Mon-Fri, 9am-7pm Sat & Sun Apr-Oct

Three-hour tours are adult/12-25 years/under 12 €30/26/16. From November to March, closing time is at 6pm daily.

BOAT

Be it on *la ligne de vie de Paris* ('the lifeline of Paris' as the Seine is called) or the rejuvenated canals to the northeast, a boat cruise is the most relaxing way to watch the city glide by.

Canal Cruises

CANAUXRAMA Maps pp386-8 & pp392-5
☎ 01 42 39 15 00; www.canauxrama.com; Bassin de la Villette, 13 quai de la Loire, 19e; Mon-Fri adult €13, senior & student €11, child 6-12 yrs €8, under 6 free, admission after noon Sat & Sun €13; ⌚ Mar-Nov

Barges travel between Port de Plaisance de Paris-Arsenal, 12e, opposite 50 blvd de la Bastille, and the Parc de la Villette, 19e, along charming Canal St-Martin and Canal de l'Ourcq. Departs around 9.45am and 2.45pm from Bassin de la Villette, and 9.45am and 2.30pm from Port de Plaisance de Paris-Arsenal.

PARIS CANAL CROISIÈRES Map pp386-8
☎ 01 42 40 96 97; Bassin de la Villette, 19-21 quai de la Loire, 19e; adult €16, senior & 12-25 yrs €12, child 4-11 yrs €9

This outfit has daily three-hour cruises from quai Anatole France (7e), just northwest of the Musée d'Orsay (Map pp389–91), leaving at 9.30am and departing from Parc de la Villette for the return trip at 2.30pm.

River Cruises

BATEAUX PARISIENS Map pp389-91
☎ 01 44 11 33 44; www.bateauxparisiens.com; Port de la Bourdonnais, 7e; metro Pont de l'Alma; adult/child 3-12 yrs €9/4.10; ⌚ every ½hr 10am-11pm Apr-Oct, hourly 10am-1pm & 5-8pm, every ½hr 1-5pm & 8-10pm Nov-Mar

From its base northwest of the Eiffel Tower Bateaux Parisiens runs one-hour river circuits with recorded commentary in a dozen different languages.

BATEAUX MOUCHES Map pp383-5

☎ 01 42 25 96 10; www.bateauxmouches.com; Port de la Conférence, 8e; metro Alma Marceau; adult €7, senior & child 4-12 yrs €4, under 4 free; ⏰ every ½hr 10am-8pm, every 20 min 8-11pm mid-Mar–mid-Nov

On the Right Bank just east of Pont de l'Alma, the most famous river-boat company in Paris runs 1000-seat tour boats, the biggest on the Seine. Cruises (one hour) run at 11am, 2.30pm, 4pm, 6pm and 9pm mid-November to mid-March, with additional winter cruises, depending on demand. Commentary is in several languages.

MARINA DE BERCY Map p401

☎ 01 43 43 40 30; www.marinadebercy.com; Port de Bercy, 12e; metro Cour St-Émilion

This outfit offers lunch cruises at 12.15pm (€49) and dinner cruises at 6.15pm (€57) and 9pm (€84). They last about two hours and a menu for children under 12 (€39) is available at lunch and dinner.

VEDETTES DU PONT NEUF Map pp396-9

☎ 01 46 33 98 38; www.pontneuf.net; square du Vert Galant, 1er; metro Pont Neuf; adult/child 4-12 yrs to 8pm €9/4.50, after 8pm €10/5; ⏰ every 30-45 min 10.30am-noon & 1.30-8pm, every ½hr 9-10.30pm Mar-Oct

Vedettes du Pont Neuf, whose home dock is at the far western tip of the Île de la Cité (1er), has one-hour boat excursions year round. From November to February there are 12 departures from 10.30am to 10pm Monday to Friday; 19 departures until 10.30pm on weekends.

BUS
BALABUS

RATP ☎ 08 92 68 77 14 in French, 08 92 68 41 14 in English; www.ratp.fr in French; €1.30 or 1 metro/bus ticket; ⏰ phones 6am-9pm daily, tours 12.30-8pm Sun Apr-Sep

In season this RATP bus designed for tourists follows a 50-minute route from Gare de Lyon to La Défense, passing many of central Paris' most famous sights.

CITYRAMA Map pp383-5

☎ 01 44 55 61 00; www.cityrama.fr; 4 place des Pyramides, 1er; metro Tuileries; €24; ⏰ tours 11am, noon, 2pm & 3pm Apr-Oct, 10am & 2pm Nov-Mar

Located just opposite the western end of the Louvre, Cityrama runs two-hour tours of the city, accompanied by taped commentaries in 12 or so languages, between two and four times a day year round.

L'OPEN TOUR Map pp383-5

☎ 01 42 66 56 56; www.paris-opentour.com; 13 rue Auber, 9e; metro Havre Caumartin or Opéra; adult/child 4-11 yrs 1 day €25/12, 2 consecutive days €28/12

L'Open Tour runs open-deck buses along four circuits (central Paris, 2¼ hours; Montmartre–Grands Boulevards, 1¼ hours; Bastille–Bercy, one hour; and Montparnasse–St-Germain, one hour) daily year round. You can jump on and off at more than 50 stops. On the 'Grand Tour' of central Paris, with some 20 stops on both sides of the river between Notre Dame and the Eiffel Tower, buses depart every 10 to 15 minutes from 9.30am to 6pm April to October and every 25 to 30 minutes from 9.30am to 4.30pm November to March. Paris Visite cardholders pay €21 for a day.

WALKING

If your French is up to scratch, the sky's the limit on specialised and themed walking tours available in Paris. Both *Pariscope* and *Officiel des Spectacles* (p206) list a number of themed walks (usually €8.50) each week under the heading 'Conférences'. They are

Urban Orienteering

In Paris, when a building is put up in a location where they've run out of consecutive street numbers, a new address is formed by fusing the number of an adjacent building with the notation *bis* (twice), *ter* (thrice) or, very rarely, *quater* (four times). Therefore, the street numbers 17bis and 89ter are the equivalent of 17a and 89b in English.

The street doors of most apartment buildings in Paris can be opened only if someone has given you the entry code, which is changed periodically; the days of the concierges, who would vet every caller before allowing them in, are well and truly over. In some buildings the entry-code device is deactivated during the day but to get in (or out) you still have to push a button (usually marked *porte*) to release the electric catch.

The doors of many apartments are unmarked: the occupants' names are nowhere in sight and there isn't even an apartment number. To know which door to knock on, you'll usually be given cryptic instructions, such as *cinquième étage, premier à gauche* (5th floor, first on the left) or *troisième étage, droite droite* (3rd floor, turn right twice).

In France (and in this book), the 1st floor is the floor above the *rez-de-chaussée* (ground floor).

almost always informative and entertaining, particularly those run by **Paris aux Cents Visages** (☎ 01 44 67 92 33) and **Paris Passé, Présent** (☎ 01 42 58 95 99).

PARIS WALKING TOURS
☎ 01 48 09 21 40; www.paris-walks.com; adult/student under 25/10-18 yrs €10/7/5
This has tours in English of several different districts, including Montmartre at 10.30am on Sunday and Wednesday (leaving from metro Abbesses; Map p400) and the Marais at 10.30am on Tuesday and Saturday and 2.30pm on Sunday (departing from metro St-Paul; Map pp396–9). There are other tours focusing on people and themes, eg Hemingway, impressionism, Thomas Jefferson, and the French Revolution.

LOUVRE & LES HALLES
Drinking p208; Eating p155; Shopping p253; Sleeping p284

The fascinating and complex **1er arrondissement** contains some of the most important sights for visitors to Paris. And while there are some who frown on the area's wild side, it remains a place where history and culture embrace on the banks of the Seine.

Sculptures merge with trees, grassy lawns, flowers, pools and fountains, while casual strollers lose themselves in the lovely promenade stretching from the gardens of the Tuileries to the square courtyard of the Louvre. A few metres away, under the arcades of the rue de Rivoli, the pace quickens with bustling shops and chaotic traffic. Parallel to rue de Rivoli, rue St-Honoré runs from place Vendôme to the Halles, leaving in its wake the Comédie Française and the manicured gardens of the Palais Royal. Opulent, affected, but anxious to please, this street combines classic style with new trends, and tasteful colours and pure lines with a quiet atmosphere.

The Forum des Halles and rue St-Denis seem miles away but are already visible, soliciting unwary passers-by with bright lights and jostling crowds. The mostly pedestrian zone between the Centre Pompidou and the Forum des Halles, with rue Étienne Marcel to the north and rue de Rivoli to the south, is filled with people day and night, just as it was for the 850-odd years when part of it served as Paris' main marketplace *(halles)*.

Tourists, Musée du Louvre (p80)

The Bourse (Stock Exchange) is the financial heart of the **2e arrondissement** to the north, the Sentier district the centre of its rag trade and the Opéra its ode to music and dance. From rue de la Paix, where glittering jewellery shops display their wares, to blvd Poissonnière and blvd de Bonne Nouvelle, where stalls and fast-food outlets advertise with garish neon signs, this arrondissement is a real hotchpotch.

Banks and insurance agencies have head offices in solid, elegant 19th-century buildings here, and business and finance types in smart suits abound. The surrounds and atmosphere change as soon as you hit rue d'Aboukir or rue du Sentier. Retail and wholesale outlets and clothing workshops buzz with the sound of haggling.

This arrondissement is a busy place during the week, its neighbourhoods divided by a thin line; you only need cross the street to find yourself in an area characterised by a completely different look, feel and rhythm. On weekends, most of the hustle and bustle is in the areas around rue Étienne Marcel.

Eiffel Tower

Transcport

Bus Louvre (rue de Rivoli) for No 27 over Pont St-Michel, up blvd St-Michel to Jardin du Luxembourg, rue Monge & rue Claude Bernard (for rue Mouffetard) and Place d'Italie; rue de Rivoli (near Louvre Rivoli metro) for No 69 to Invalides, Champ de Mars (Eiffel Tower) and for No 72 to Place de la Concorde, Grand Palais, Alma Marceau, Bois de Boulogne and Porte de St-Cloud; Châtelet for No 38 to blvd St-Michel and Jardin du Luxembourg, for No 47 to Place Monge (rue Mouffetard), Place d'Italie and 13e (Chinatown), for No 67 to Pigalle and for No 85 to Barbès and Porte de Clignancourt and Porte de St-Ouen flea markets

Metro & RER Bourse, Châtelet, Châtelet-Les Halles, Concorde, Étienne Marcel, Les Halles, Louvre-Rivoli, Palais Royal-Musée du Louvre, Pont Neuf, Rambuteau, Tuileries

Boat Musée du Louvre Batobus stop (Map pp396–9; quai du Louvre)

MUSÉE DU LOUVRE Map pp396-9
☎ 01 40 20 53 17, 01 40 20 51 51; www.louvre.fr; metro Palais Royal-Musée du Louvre; permanent collections/permanent collections & temporary exhibits €7.50/11.50, after 3pm Mon & Wed, Thu-Sat & all day Sun €5/9.50, permanent collections only under 18 yrs free, 1st Sun of the month free; ☺ 9am-9.45pm Mon & Wed, 9am-6pm Thu-Sun

The vast Palais du Louvre was constructed as a fortress by Philippe-Auguste in the early 13th century and rebuilt in the mid-16th century for use as a royal residence. The Revolutionary Convention turned it into a national museum in 1793.

The paintings, sculptures and artefacts on display in the Louvre Museum have been assembled by French governments over the past five centuries. Among them are works of art and artisanship from all over Europe and collections of Assyrian, Etruscan, Greek, Coptic and Islamic art and antiquities. The Louvre's *raison d'être* is to present Western art from the Middle Ages to about the year 1848 (at which point the Musée d'Orsay takes over) as well as the works of ancient civilisations that formed the starting point for Western art, but in recent years it has acquired, and begun to exhibit, other important collections as well.

When the museum opened in the late 18th century it contained 2500 paintings; today some 30,000 are on display. The 'Grand Louvre' project inaugurated by the late President Mitterrand in 1989 doubled the museum's exhibition space, and new and renovated galleries have opened in recent years devoted to *objets d'art* such as Sèvres porcelain and the crown jewels of Louis XV (Sully Wing, 1st floor), as well as primitive art collected from Africa, Asia, Australasia and the Americas (Denon Wing, ground floor). The latter actually belongs to the new Musée du Quai Branly (p41) and will be moved in time for its opening in late 2005.

The Louvre may be the most actively avoided museum in the world. Daunted by the richness and sheer size of the place (the side facing the Seine is some 700m long and it is said that it would take nine months to see every piece of art here), both local people and visitors often find the prospect of an afternoon at a smaller museum far more inviting. Eventually, most people do their duty and come, but many leave overwhelmed, unfulfilled, exhausted and frustrated at having got lost on their way to Da Vinci's *La Joconde*, better known as *Mona Lisa* (Denon Wing, 1st floor, Rm 13). Since it takes several serious visits to get anything more than a brief glimpse of the works on offer, your best bet – after checking out a few you really want to see – is to choose a particular period or section of the Louvre and pretend that the rest is in another museum somewhere across town.

The most famous works from antiquity include the *Seated Scribe* (Sully Wing, 1st floor), the *Code of Hammurabi* (Richelieu Wing, ground floor) and that armless duo, the *Venus de Milo* (Sully Wing, ground floor) and the *Winged Victory of Samothrace* (Denon Wing, 1st floor). From the Renaissance, don't miss Michelangelo's *The Dying Slave* (Denon Wing, ground floor) and works by Raphael, Botticelli and Titian (Denon Wing, 1st floor). French masterpieces of the 19th century (Sully Wing, 2nd floor) include Ingres' *The Turkish Bath*, Géricault's *The Raft of the Medusa* and works by Corot, Delacroix and Fragonard.

The main entrance and ticket windows in the Cour Napoléon are covered by the 21m-high **Grande Pyramide**, a glass pyramid designed by the Chinese-born American architect IM Pei. You can avoid the queues outside the pyramid or at the Porte des Lions entrance by entering the Louvre complex via the Carrousel du Louvre entrance (Map pp392–5), at 99 rue de Rivoli, or by following the 'Louvre' exit from the Palais Royal-Musée du Louvre metro station. Those in the know buy their tickets in advance by ringing ☎ 08 92 69 70 73, from the billeteries (ticket offices) of Fnac (p207) or Virgin Megastores (p207), or from any of the major department stores (p252) for an extra €1, and walk straight in without queuing. Tickets are valid for the whole day, so you can come and go as you please. If planning to visit during one of the two weekly *nocturnes* (night sessions), remember that on Wednesday virtually the entire museum remains open after 6pm but on Monday evening there's only a *circuit court* (short tour) of selected galleries.

The Louvre is divided into four sections: the Sully, Denon and Richelieu Wings and the Hall Napoléon. **Sully** creates the four sides of the Cour Carrée (literally 'square courtyard') at the eastern end of the complex. **Denon** stretches along the Seine to the south; **Richelieu** is the northern wing along rue de Rivoli.

The split-level public area under the Grande Pyramide is known as the **Hall Napoléon** (✥ 9am-10pm Thu-Mon). The hall has an exhibit on the history of the Louvre, a bookshop, a restaurant, a café, auditoriums for concerts, lectures and films, and **CyberLouvre** (✥ 10am-6.45pm Wed-Mon), an Internet salon with monitors that allow virtual-reality access to some 20,000 works of art. The centrepiece of the **Carrousel du Louvre shopping centre** (☎ 01 40 20 67 30; ✥ 8.30am-11pm), which runs underground from the pyramid to the **Arc de Triomphe du Carrousel** (p82), is an **inverted glass pyramid** *(pyramide inversée)*, also created by Pei.

Free English-language maps (titled *Louvre Plan/Information*) of the complex can be obtained from the information desk in the centre of the Hall Napoléon. Excellent publications to guide you if you are doing the Louvre on your own are *Destination Louvre: A Guided Tour* (€7.50), *Louvre: The Visit* (€7.90) and *The Louvre: Key Art Works* (€15). All are available from the museum bookshop.

English-language guided **tours** (☎ 01 40 20 52 63) lasting 1½ hours depart from the area under the Grande Pyramide, marked 'Acceuil des Groupes' (Groups Welcome), at 11am, 2pm and 3pm Monday to Saturday. Tickets cost €6, 13 to 18 years €3.50, under 12 free, in addition to the cost of admission. Groups are

Top Five

- Centre Pompidou (p83)
- Église St-Eustache (p85)
- Jardin des Tuileries (p82)
- Musée de la Publicité (right)
- Musée du Louvre (opposite)

Museum Closing Times

The vast majority of museums in Paris close on Monday though more than a dozen (including the Louvre, the Centre Pompidou and Musée Picasso) are closed on Tuesday instead. It is also important to remember that all museums and monuments in Paris shut their doors or gates between 30 minutes and an hour before their actual closing times, which are the ones listed in this chapter. Therefore if we say a museum or monument closes at 6pm, for example, don't count on getting in much later than 5pm.

limited to 30 people, so it's a good idea to sign up at least 30 minutes before departure time.

Audioguide tours in six languages and lasting 1½ hours can be rented for €5 under the pyramid at the entrance to each wing until 4.30pm.

OTHER PALAIS DU LOUVRE MUSEUMS

The Palais du Louvre contains three other museums run by the **Union Centrale des Arts Décoratifs** (UCAD; ☎ 01 44 55 57 50; www.ucad.fr; 107 rue de Rivoli, 1er; metro Palais Royal-Musée du Louvre; adult/18-25 yrs €6/4.50, under 18 free; ✥ 11am-6pm Tue-Fri, 10am-6pm Sat & Sun), in the Rohan Wing of the Louvre, which were revamped or created under the Grand Louvre project. Admission includes entry to all three museums.

The **Musée des Arts Décoratifs** (Applied Arts Museum) on the 3rd floor displays furniture, jewellery and such *objets d'art* as ceramics and glassware from the Middle Ages and the Renaissance through the Art Nouveau and Art Deco periods to Modern and Contemporary in five departments. Some departments may be closed over the next several years as the museum undergoes extensive renovations.

The **Musée de la Publicité** (Advertising Museum), which shares the 3rd floor, has some 100,000 posters dating as far back as the 13th century, and innumerable promotional materials touting everything from 19th-century elixirs and early radio advertisements to Air France and electronic publicity. Only certain items are on exhibit at any one time.

The **Musée de la Mode et du Textile** (Museum of Fashion & Textiles) on the 1st and 2nd floors has some 16,000 costumes dating from the 16th century till today. These are warehoused and only displayed during unusual themed exhibitions.

Keep on the Grass

Though upwards of 90,000 trees (mostly plane trees and horse chestnuts) line the avenues and boulevards of Paris, the city can often feel excessively built-up. You don't have to escape to the **Bois de Boulogne** (Map pp380–2) in the 16e or the **Bois de Vincennes** (Map pp380–2) in the 12e, the city's 'green lungs' to the west and southeast, respectively, to get a bit of grass under your feet and a leafy canopy over your head, however; there are over 400 parks to choose from – some not much bigger than a beach blanket, others the size of a small village.

The **Jardin du Luxembourg** (Map pp392–5) in the 6e and the **Jardin des Tuileries** (Map pp383–5 and pp389–91) in the 1er, while small, formal affairs, offer the illusion of regimented countryside. **Parc des Buttes-Chaumont** (Map pp386–8) in the 19e and the **Parc de Monceau** (Map pp383–5) in the 8e, on the other hand, are fully fledged open green spaces.

Over the past decade or so, the city government has spent a small fortune transforming vacant lots and derelict industrial land into new parks. Some of the better ones are **Parc de Bercy** (Map p401) and the unique **Promenade Plantée** (Map pp392–5), the 'planted walkway' above the Viaduc des Arts, both in the 12e; the **Jardin de l'Atlantique** (Map pp389–91), behind the Gare Montparnasse, and **Parc André Citroën** (Maps pp380–2 and pp389–91) on the banks of the Seine, both in the 15e; **Parc de la Villette** (Map pp380–2), 19e; and **Parc de Belleville** (Map pp386–8), 20e.

In general, Parisian lawns are meant to be looked at and admired for their green lushness – not sat upon and enjoyed and the ones at the Tuileries are no exception. Keep an eye open for signs advising *Pelouse Interdite* (Keep off the Grass). But in many places this has changed in recent years, with such signs being removed and replaced with *Pelouse Autorisée*, meaning you're permitted to sit, eat, play and walk on the grass in certain areas.

ÉGLISE ST-GERMAIN L'AUXERROIS

Map pp396-9

place du Louvre, 1er; metro Louvre-Rivoli or Pont Neuf; 8am-8pm

Built between the 13th and 16th centuries in a mixture of Gothic and Renaissance styles, this once royal parish church stands on a site, at the eastern end of the Louvre, that has been used for Christian worship since about AD 500. After being mutilated in the 18th century by churchmen intent on 'modernisation', and damaged during the Revolution, the church was restored by the Gothic Revivalist architect Eugène Viollet-le-Duc in the mid-19th century. It boasts some fine stained glass.

JARDIN DES TUILERIES

Maps pp383-5 & pp389-91

metro Tuileries or Concorde; 7am-7.30pm late Sep–late-Mar, 7am-9pm late Mar–late Sep

The formal, 28-hectare Tuileries Garden, which begins just west of the Jardin du Carrousel, was laid out in its present form, more or less, in the mid-17th century by André Le Nôtre, who also created the gardens at Vaux-le-Vicomte (p317) and Versailles (p308). The Tuileries soon became the most fashionable spot in Paris for parading about in one's finery; today it is a favourite of joggers.

The **Voie Triomphale** (Triumphal Way), also called the Axe Historique (Historic Axis), the western continuation of the Tuileries' east-west axis, follows the av des Champs-Élysées to the Arc de Triomphe and, ultimately, to the Grande Arche in the skyscraper district of La Défense (p133).

ARC DE TRIOMPHE DU CARROUSEL

Map pp396-9

place du Carrousel, 1er; metro Palais Royal-Musée du Louvre

Built by Napoleon to celebrate his battlefield successes of 1805, this triumphal arch, which is set in the Jardin du Carrousel at the eastern end of the Jardin des Tuileries, was once crowned by the *Horses of St Mark's*, 'borrowed' from Venice by Napoleon but returned after his defeat at Waterloo in 1815. The quadriga (a two-wheeled chariot drawn by four horses) on the top, added in 1828, celebrates the return of the Bourbons to the French throne after Napoleon's downfall. The sides of the arch are adorned with depictions of Napoleonic victories and eight pink marble columns, atop each of which stands a soldier of the emperor's Grande Armée.

ORANGERIE Map pp383-5

01 42 97 48 16; www.rmn.fr; place de la Concorde, 1er; metro Concorde

The Musée de l'Orangerie (Orangerie Museum) in the southwestern corner of the Jardin des Tuileries is, with the Jeu de Paume, all that remains of the once palatial Palais des Tuileries, which was razed during the Paris Commune (p68) in 1871. It exhibits important impressionist works, including a series of Monet's exquisite *Decorations des Nymphéas* (Water Lilies) and paintings by Cézanne, Matisse, Picasso, Renoir, Sisley, Soutine and Utrillo. Undergoing extensive renovations at the time of writing, the museum will reopen at the end of 2004.

JEU DE PAUME Map pp383-5

☎ 01 47 03 12 52; 1 place de la Concorde, 1er; metro Concorde; adult €6, senior, student & 13-18 yrs €4.50; ☽ noon-9.30pm Tue, noon-7pm Wed-Fri, 10am-7pm Sat & Sun

The Galerie Nationale du Jeu de Paume (Jeu de Paume National Gallery) is housed in an erstwhile *jeu de paume* (real, or royal, tennis court), built in 1861 during the reign of Napoleon III, in the northwestern corner of the Jardin des Tuileries. Once the home of a good part of France's national collection of impressionist art, which is now housed across the Seine in the Musée d'Orsay (p111), the two-storey Jeu de Paume now stages innovative exhibitions of contemporary art.

PLACE VENDÔME Map pp383-5
metro Tuileries or Opéra

This octagonal *place*, and the arcaded and colonnaded buildings around it, were built between 1687 and 1721. In March 1796, Napoleon married Josephine, Viscountess Beauharnais, in the building that's at No 3. Today, the buildings around the square house the posh Hôtel Ritz Paris (p291) and some of the city's most fashionable boutiques. The **Ministry of Justice** (Map pp383–5) has been at Nos 11 to 13 since 1815.

In the centre, the 43.5m-tall **Colonne Vendôme** (Vendôme Column) consists of a stone core wrapped in a 160m-long bronze spiral that's made from 1250 Austrian and Russian cannons captured by Napoleon two centuries ago at the Battle of Austerlitz in 1805. The bas-reliefs on the spiral celebrate Napoleon's victories between 1805 and 1807. The statue on top, originally thought to be of Charlemagne, depicts Napoleon as a Roman emperor.

PALAIS ROYAL Map pp396-9
place du Palais Royal, 1er; metro Palais Royal-Musée du Louvre

The Royal Palace, which accommodated a young Louis XIV for a time in the 1640s, lies to the north of place du Palais Royal and the Louvre. Construction was begun in the 17th century by Cardinal Richelieu, though most of the present neoclassical complex dates from the latter part of the 18th century. It now contains the governmental **Conseil d'État** (State Council) and is closed to the public.

The colonnaded building facing place André Malraux is the **Comédie Française** (p239), founded in 1680 and the world's oldest national theatre.

Just north of the palace is the **Jardin du Palais Royal** (Maps pp386–8 & pp396-9; ☽ 7.30am-8.30pm Oct-Mar, 7.30am-10.15pm Apr & May, 7.30am-11pm Jun-Aug, 7.30am-9.30pm Sep), a lovely park surrounded by two arcades (p144). Nowadays **Galerie de Valois** on the eastern side shelters designer fashion shops, art galleries and jewellers, though Guillaumot Graveur, an engraver's at Nos 151 to 154, has been trading here since 1785. **Galerie de Montpensier** on the western side has a few old shops remaining, selling things like colourful Légion d'Honneur-style medals (shop No 6–8) and lead toy soldiers (shop No 14–15). **Le Grand Véfour** (p157), one of Paris' oldest and most illustrious restaurants, is at the northern end of the park. At the southern end there's a controversial **sculpture** of black-and-white striped columns of various heights by Daniel Buren placed here in 1986. Don't miss the zany Palais Royal-Musée du Louvre **metro entrance** on the place du Palais Royal (see p84).

CABINET DES MONNAIES, MÉDAILLES ET ANTIQUES Map pp386-8

☎ 01 53 79 53 79; www.bnf.fr; 58 rue de Richelieu, 2e; metro Bourse; adult/senior & student €5/4; ☽ 1-5pm Tue-Sat, noon-6pm Sun

Housed in the original home of the Bibliothèque Nationale de France before it moved to its swanky headquarters in the 13e arrondissement in 1995 is this enormous hoard of coins, medals and tokens numbering more than 500,000. There's also an important collection of antiques, including items confiscated during the French Revolution from Ste-Chapelle and the abbey at St-Denis, including the 7th-century Dagobert's Throne, on which French kings were once crowned.

CENTRE POMPIDOU Map pp396-9

☎ 01 44 78 12 33; www.centrepompidou.fr; place Georges Pompidou, 4e; metro Rambuteau

The Centre National d'Art et de Culture Georges Pompidou (Georges Pompidou National Centre of Art & Culture) is the most successful such centre in the world. A €85 million renovation

Art in the Metro

Art is not just in the museums and galleries of Paris, it's all around you – even in metro stations. Few underground railway systems are as convenient as, as reasonably priced or, at the better stations, more elegant than the Paris one. Some 175 metro stations were given a face-lift to mark the centenary of the system in 2000, with their lighting improved, permanent decorations spruced up and/or rearranged, and new ones added. The following list is just a sample of the most interesting stations from an artistic perspective. The specific platform is mentioned for those stations served by more than one line.

Abbesses (Map p400; line No 12) The noodle-like pale-green metalwork and glass canopy of the station entrance is one of the finest examples of the work of Hector Guimard (1867–1942), the best-known French Art Nouveau architect, whose signature style once graced most metro stations.

Arts et Métiers (Map pp386–8; line No 11 platform) The copper panelling, portholes and mechanisms of this station recall Jules Verne, Captain Nemo and the nearby Musée des Arts et Métiers.

Bastille (Map pp392–5; line No 5 platform) A large ceramic fresco features scenes taken from newspaper engravings published during the Revolution.

Bibliothèque (Map p401; line No 14) This enormous station – all screens, steel and glass, and the terminus of the high-speed Météor line that opened in 1998 – resembles a high-tech cathedral.

Bonne Nouvelle (Map pp386–8; platforms on line Nos 8 & 9) The theme here is cinema.

Carrefour Pleyel (line No 13) This station just south of St-Denis (p135) and named in honour of composer and piano-maker Ignace Joseph Pleyel (1757–1831) has been reconfigured as a 'contemporary musical instrument', with the rumble of the trains the 'music' and, no doubt, commuters the 'picks'.

Champs-Élysées Clemenceau (Map pp383–5; transfer corridor between line Nos 1 & 13) The elegant frescoes in blue, enamelled faïence recall Portuguese *azulejos* tiles and so they should: they were installed as part of a cultural exchange between Paris and Lisbon.

Cluny-La Sorbonne (Map pp396–9; line No 10 platform) A large ceramic mosaic replicates the signatures of intellectuals, artists and scientists from the Latin Quarter, through history.

Concorde (Map pp383–5; line No 12 platform) On the walls of the station, what look like children's building blocks in white and blue ceramic are 45,000 tiles that spell out the text of the *Déclaration des Droits de l'Homme et du Citoyen* (Declaration of the Rights of Man and of the Citizen), the document setting forth the principles of the French Revolution.

Louvre-Rivoli (Map pp396–9; line No 1 platform & corridor) Statues, bas-reliefs and photographs offer a small taste of what to expect at the Musée du Louvre above ground.

Palais Royal-Musée du Louvre (Map pp396–9) The unusual modern entrance on the place du Palais Royal (a kind of back-to-the-future look at the Guimard entrances), designed by young artist Jean-Michel Othoniel, is made up of 800 red, blue, amber and violet glass balls and resembles a crown.

Parmentier (Map pp386–8; line No 3) The theme in this station is agricultural crops, particularly the potato since is was the station's namesake, Antoine-Auguste Parmentier (1737–1817), who brought the potato into fashion in France. Today, any dish with the word Parmentier has potatoes in it: *potage Parmentier* (a thick potato soup), *hachis Parmentier* (minced meat cooked with potatoes) etc.

Pont Neuf (Map pp396–9; line No 7) With the old mint and the Musée de la Monnaie de Paris just above, the focus here is on coins: obsolete francs and all-too-current euros.

completed at the start of the new millennium, which expanded exhibition space and created a new cinema, CD and video centre, dance and theatre venues and a chichi restaurant, has made it even more popular.

Of course, the Centre Pompidou, also known as the Centre Beaubourg, has amazed and delighted visitors since it was inaugurated in 1977, not just for its outstanding collection of modern art but for its radical architectural statement (p40). But it all began to look somewhat *démodé* by the late 1990s, hence the refit.

The **Forum du Centre Pompidou** (admission free; ☉ 11am-10pm Wed-Mon), the open space at ground level, has temporary exhibits and information desks. The 4th and 5th floors of the centre exhibit about a fraction of the 50,000-plus works of the **Musée National d'Art Moderne**

(MNAM; National Museum of Modern Art; adult €7, senior & 18-25 yrs €5, under 18 free, 1st Sun of the month free; ☽ 11am-9pm Wed-Mon), France's national collection of art dating from 1905 onward, and including the work of the Surrealists and Cubists, as well as pop art and contemporary works.

The huge (free) **Bibliothèque Publique d'Information** (BPI; ☎ 01 44 78 12 33; www.bpi.fr in French; ☽ noon-10pm Mon & Wed-Fri, 11am-10pm Sat & Sun) takes up the 3rd, 2nd and part of the 1st floors. The 6th floor has three galleries for **temporary exhibitions** (adult/senior & 18-25 yrs usually €7/5) and a trendy Costes restaurant called Georges with panoramic views of Paris. There are **cinemas** (adult/senior & 18-25 yrs usually €5/3) and other entertainment venues on the 1st floor and in the basement.

Place Georges Pompidou, west of the centre, and the nearby pedestrian streets attract buskers, musicians, jugglers and mime artists, and can be as much fun as the centre itself. South of the centre on place Igor Stravinsky, the fanciful **mechanical fountains** (Map pp396–9) of skeletons, dragons, treble clefs and a big pair of ruby-red lips, created by Jean Tinguely and Niki de St-Phalle, are a positive delight.

The **Atelier Brancusi** (Map pp396-9; place Georges Pompidou; ☽ 2-6pm Wed-Mon), to the west of the main building, contains almost 140 examples of the work of Romanian-born sculptor Constantin Brancusi (1876–1957) as well as drawings, paintings and glass photographic plates. A MNAM ticket allows entry.

The **Défenseur du Temps** (Defender of Time; Map pp396-9; 8 rue Bernard de Clairvaux; ☽ 9am-10pm), a mechanical clock (1979) whose protagonist does battle on the hour with the elements (air, water and earth in the form of a phoenix, crab and dragon), is a block north of the Centre Pompidou just off rue Brantôme (3e), in a development known as Quartier de l'Horloge. Particularly lively combat takes place at noon, 6pm and 10pm when our hero is attacked by all three 'villains'.

FORUM DES HALLES Map pp396-9

☎ 01 44 76 96 56; 1 rue Pierre Lescaut, 1er; metro Les Halles or Châtelet Les Halles

Les Halles, the city's main wholesale food market, occupied the area just south of the Église St-Eustache from the early 12th century until 1969, when it was moved to the southern suburb of Rungis near Orly. In its place, this unspeakable underground shopping centre was constructed in the glass-and-chrome style of the early 1970s.

Inside the Forum des Halles is the **Pavillon des Arts** (☎ 01 42 33 82 50; 101 rue Rambuteau, 1er; adult €5.50, senior & student €4, 14-26 yrs €2.50, under 14 free; ☽ 11.30am-6.30pm Tue-Sun), with temporary exhibits, and a popular rooftop **park**. In the warmer months, street musicians, fire-eaters and other performers display their talents here, especially at **place du Jean Bellay**, which is adorned by a multitiered Renaissance fountain, the **Fontaine des Innocents** (1549). It is named after the Cimetière des Innocents, a cemetery on this site from which two million skeletons were disinterred after the Revolution, and transferred to the Catacombes (p110), south of the Cimetière du Montparnasse in the 14e. A block south of the fountain is **rue de la Ferronnerie**, where erstwhile Huguenot Henri IV was assassinated in 1610, while passing house No 11 in his carriage, by a Catholic fanatic named François Ravaillac.

ÉGLISE ST-EUSTACHE Map pp396-9

☎ 01 42 36 31 05; www.st-eustache.org in French; 2 impasse St-Eustache, 1er; metro Les Halles; ☽ 9am-7.30pm

This majestic church, one of the most beautiful in Paris, is just north of the gardens next to the Forum des Halles. Constructed between 1532 and 1640, St-Eustache is primarily Gothic, though a neoclassical façade was added on the western side in the mid-18th century. Inside, there are some exceptional Flamboyant Gothic arches holding up the ceiling of the chancel, though most of the ornamentation is Renaissance and classical. Above the western entrance, the gargantuan organ with 101 stops and 8000 pipes is used for concerts (long a tradition here), and at Sunday Mass (11am and 6pm), when a chorus sings.

BOURSE DE COMMERCE Map pp396-9

☎ 01 55 65 55 65; 2 rue de Viarmes, 1er; metro Les Halles; admission free; ☽ 9am-6pm Mon-Fri

At one time the city's grain market, the Trade Exchange was capped with a copper dome in 1813. The murals showing French trade and industry through the ages were painted in 1889 and restored in 1998.

TOUR JEAN SANS PEUR Map pp386-8

☎ 01 40 26 20 28; www.tourjeansanspeur.com in French; 20 rue Étienne Marcel, 2e; metro Étienne Marcel; adult €5, student & 7-18 yrs €3; ☽ 1.30-6pm Wed, Sat & Sun, school holidays 1.30-6pm Tue-Sun

The Gothic, 29m-high John the Fearless Tower was built by the duke of Bourgogne as part of a splendid mansion in the early 15th century so he could hide at the very top, safe from his enemies. You can climb to the top, too.

LA SAMARITAINE ROOFTOP
TERRACE Map pp396-9
☎ 01 40 41 20 20; www.lasamaritaine.com; 19 rue de la Monnaie, 1er; metro Pont Neuf; 🕥 9.30am-7pm Mon-Wed & Fri, till 10pm Thu, till 8pm Sat

For an amazing 360° panoramic view of central Paris, head for the roof of this department store's main building. A lift will take you to the 9th floor; you then walk two flights up to

the lookout on the 11th floor. Be advised that at the time of research the terrace was closed for security reasons.

TOUR ST-JACQUES Map pp396-9
place du Châtelet, 4e; metro Châtelet

The Flamboyant Gothic, 52m-high St James Tower is all that remains of the Église St-Jacques la Boucherie, which was built by the powerful butchers' guild in 1523 and demolished by the Directory in 1797. The tower is topped by a weather station and it is not open to the public.

MARAIS & BASTILLE

Drinking p208; Eating p159; Shopping p254; Sleeping p285

The Marais, the area of the Right Bank directly north of Île St-Louis, was exactly what its name implies – 'marsh' or 'swamp' – until the 13th century, when it was put to agricultural use. In the early 17th century, Henri IV built the place Royale (today's place des Vosges), turning the area into Paris' most fashionable residential district and attracting wealthy aristocrats who then erected their own luxurious private mansions and less expensive *pavillons* (smaller houses).

When the aristocracy moved out of Paris to Versailles and Faubourg St-Germain during the late 17th and the 18th centuries, the Marais and its town houses passed into the hands of ordinary Parisians. The 110-hectare area was given a major face-lift in the late 1960s and early '70s.

Centuries of history are inscribed on the façades and pediments of the **4e arrondissement** and in the narrow streets, alleys, porches and courtyards; today the Marais is one of the few neighbourhoods of Paris that still has most of its pre-Revolution architecture. These include

the house at 3 rue Volta (Map pp386–8) in the 3e, parts of which date back to 1292; the one at 51 rue de Montmorency (Map pp396–9) in the 3e dating back to 1407 and the half-timbered 16th-century building at 11 and 13 rue François Miron (Map pp396–9) in the 4e.

Though the Marais has become a much desired address in recent years, it remains home to a long-established Jewish community and is the centre of Paris' gay life. At night the short walk from Beaubourg to the place des Vosges is intoxicating. The historic Jewish quarter – the so-called Pletzel – starts in rue des Rosiers then continues along rue Ste-Croix de la Bretonnerie to rue du Temple; you'll also find a lot of gay and lesbian bars and restaurants in this area. Re-entering the urban bustle as rue St-Antoine becomes rue de Rivoli, the small, dark streets of the Marais seem like a distant memory. But you only have to cross the street at rue St-Paul or rue du Pont Louis-Philippe to experience something of the bourgeois and bohemian tranquillity of the Marais of the past.

The **3e arrondissement** contains a small corner of the Marais that has managed to remain friendly and picturesque. Noisy during the week, calm and languid on weekends, the opulent renovations of its period homes and the dictates of fashion haven't yet destroyed its soul. Rue du Temple and rue de Turenne move to the rhythm of clothing workshops, artisans and wholesalers. The tempo picks up along rue de Turbigo, rue Réaumur and blvd de Sébastopol, and is perfectly offset by the place de la République. Business calls at all hours and the blvd du Temple, blvd des Filles du Calvaire and blvd Beaumarchais barely manage to contain the hive of activity. Properties on rue des Archives, rue Charlot, rue de Saintonge and rue de Bretagne require neither artifice nor restoration to reveal their lovely bas-reliefs, balustrades, courtyards and stairways. Suddenly, the tempo takes on an elegant nonchalance. The Musée Picasso and the Musée Carnavalet appear, and the Archives Nationales makes its presence felt. The rue de Rambuteau and rue des Francs-Bourgeois are also part of the gay life of the Marais.

After years as a run-down immigrant neighbourhood notorious for its high crime rate, the Bastille area has undergone a fair degree of gentrification, largely due to the opening of the Opéra Bastille back in 1989. The courtyards and alleyways of the **11e arrondissement** used to belong to artisans and labourers. When you went into a building or entered a cul-de-sac off rue du Faubourg St-Antoine, rue de Charonne or rue de la Roquette, you'd find workshops, factories and warehouses: cabinet makers, joiners, gilders, dressmakers, lace makers; a whole range of crafts, each with its characteristic activities and sounds. Today most of that's gone, replaced with artists, lofts, bohemia. But the old spirit lives on in some hidden parts of the 11e, and the areas to the east of place de la Bastille in particular retain their lively atmosphere and ethnicity.

HÔTEL DE VILLE Map pp396-9

☎ 08 20 00 75 75; www.paris.fr; place de l'Hôtel de Ville, 4e; metro Hôtel de Ville

After having been gutted during the Paris Commune of 1871, Paris' city hall was rebuilt in the neo-Renaissance style from 1874 to 1882. The ornate façade is decorated with 108 statues of noteworthy Parisians. There's a **Salon d'Accueil** (Reception Hall; 29 rue de Rivoli, 4e; 🕑 9.30am-6pm to 7pm Mon-Sat), which dispenses copious amounts of information and brochures, and is used for temporary exhibitions.

The Hôtel de Ville faces majestic **place de l'Hôtel de Ville**, used since the Middle Ages to stage many of Paris' celebrations, rebellions, book-burnings and public executions. Known as place de Grève (Strand Square) until 1830, it was in centuries past a favourite gathering place of the unemployed, which is why a strike is, to this day, called *une grève* in French.

Transport

Bus rue des Francs Bourgeois for No 29 to Bastille & Gare de Lyon; rue de Rivoli for No 76 through the 11e via rue de Charonne to 20e and Porte de Bagnolet

Metro Arts et Métiers, Bastille, Chemin Vert, Hôtel de Ville, Pont Marie, Rambuteau, St-Paul

Boat Hôtel de Ville Batobus stop (quai de l'Hôtel de Ville); Canauxrama pier at Port de Plaisance de Paris-Arsenal (12e) south of place de la Bastille for canal boat to Bassin de la Villette (13 quai de la Loire)

PLACE DES VOSGES Map pp392-5

metro St-Paul or Bastille

Place des Vosges (4e), inaugurated in 1612 as place Royale, is an ensemble of 36 symmetrical houses with ground-floor arcades, steep slate roofs and large dormer windows arranged around a large square. Only the earliest houses were built of brick; to save time, the rest were given timber frames and faced with plaster, which was later painted to resemble brick.

The author Victor Hugo lived at the square's Hôtel de Rohan-Guéménée from 1832 to 1848, moving here a year after the publication of *Notre Dame de Paris* (The Hunchback of Notre Dame). The **Maison de Victor Hugo** (Victor Hugo House; ☎ 01 42 72 10 16; www.paris.fr /musees/maison_de_victor_hugo; permanent collections admission free, temporary exhibits adult €5.50, senior & student €4, 14-25 yrs €2.50, under 14 free; 10am-6pm Tue-Sun) is now a municipal museum devoted to the life and times of the celebrated novelist and poet, with an impressive collection of his personal drawings, portraits and furniture.

HÔTEL DE SULLY Map pp396-9
62 rue St-Antoine, 4e; metro St-Paul

This aristocratic mansion dating from the early 17th century was given a major face-lift in 1973. Today it houses both the headquarters of the **Centre des Monuments Nationaux** (Monum; ☎ 01 44 61 20 00; www.monum.fr; 9am-12.45pm & 2-6pm Mon-Thu, 9am-12.45pm & 2-5pm Fri), the body responsible for many of France's historical monuments (with lots of brochures and information available), as well as the **Mission du Patrimoine Photographique** (☎ 01 42 74 47 75; www.patrimoine-photo.org; adult/ child €4/2.50; 10am-6.30pm Tue-Sun), which has excellent rotating photographic exhibits. The Hôtel de Sully bookshop (p256) is very good, and the two Renaissance-style courtyards (p140) alone are worth the trip.

MUSÉE CARNAVALET Map pp396-9
☎ 01 44 59 58 58; www.paris.fr/musees/musee _carnavalet in French; 23 rue de Sévigné, 3e; metro St-Paul or Chemin Vert; permanent collections admission free, temporary exhibits adult €5.50, senior & student €4, 14-25 yrs €2.50, under 14 free; 10am-6pm Tue-Sun

This museum, subtitled Musée de l'Histoire de Paris (Paris History Museum), is housed in two *hôtels particuliers* (private mansions): the mid-16th-century, Renaissance-style Hôtel Carnavalet, home to the 17th-century writer Madame de Sévigné from 1677 to 1696, and the Hôtel Le Peletier de St-Fargeau, which dates from the late 17th century.

The artefacts on display in the museum's sublime rooms chart the history of Paris from

Top Five
- **Maison Européenne de la Photographie** (p90)
- **Musée Carnavalet** (left)
- **Musée Picasso** (below)
- **Place des Vosges** (p87)
- **Pletzel** (p89)

the Gallo-Roman period, in the museum's **Orangerie** section, to the 20th century. Some of the nation's most important documents, paintings and other objects from the French Revolution are here (rooms 101 to 113), as is Fouquet's stunning Art Nouveau jewellery shop from the rue Royale (room 142) and Marcel Proust's cork-lined bedroom from his apartment on blvd Haussmann (room 147), where he wrote most of the 7350-page *À la Recherche du Temps Perdu*.

MUSÉE PICASSO Map pp396-9
☎ 01 42 71 25 21; 5 rue de Thorigny, 3e; metro St-Paul or Chemin Vert; adult/18-25 yrs €6.70/5.20 Wed-Sat & Mon, admission for all €5.20 Sun, 1st Sun of the month free; 9.30am-6pm Wed-Mon Apr-Sep, 9.30am-5.30pm Wed-Mon Oct-Mar

The Picasso Museum, housed in the mid-17th-century Hôtel Salé, forms one of Paris' best-loved art collections. It includes more than 3500 of the *grand maître's* engravings, paintings, ceramic works, drawings and sculptures, which the heirs of Pablo Picasso (1881–1973) donated to the French government in lieu of inheritance taxes. You can also see part of Picasso's personal art collection, which includes works by Braque, Cézanne, Matisse, Modigliani and Degas.

MUSÉE COGNACQ-JAY Map pp396-9
☎ 01 40 27 07 21; www.paris.fr/musees/cognacq_jay in French; 8 rue Elzévir, 3e; metro St-Paul or Chemin Vert; permanent collections admission free, temporary exhibits adult €4.60, senior & student €3, 14-25 yrs €2.30, under 14 free; 10am-6pm Tue-Sun

This museum in the Hôtel de Donon brings together oil paintings, pastels, sculpture, *objets d'art* jewellery, porcelain and furniture from the 18th century. The objects on display, assembled by Ernest Cognacq (1839–1928), founder of La Samaritaine department store, give a pretty good idea of upper-class tastes during the Age of Enlightenment.

ARCHIVES NATIONALES Map pp396-9

☎ 01 40 27 60 96; www.archivesnationales.culture
.gouv.fr; 60 rue des Francs Bourgeois, 3e; metro
Rambuteau

France's National Archives are housed in the
Soubise wing of the impressive, early-18th-
century Hôtel de Rohan-Soubise, which also
contains the **Musée de l'Histoire de France** (Museum of French History; ☎ 01 40 27 60 96;
87 rue Vieille du Temple, 3e; metro Rambuteau or St-Paul; adult €3, 18-25 yrs & seniors
€2.30, under 18 free, 1st Sun of the month free;
🕑 10am-12.30pm & 2-5.30pm Mon & Wed-
Fri, 2-5.30pm Sat & Sun), which has been
undergoing ambitious renovations for some
time but opens up part of its collection year
round. Here you'll find documents dating from
the Middle Ages, antique furniture and 18th-
century paintings. The ceiling and walls of the
interior are extravagantly painted and gilded
in the rococo style.

MUSÉE DE LA CHASSE ET DE LA
NATURE Map pp396-9

☎ 01 53 01 92 40; Hôtel Guénégaud, 60 rue des
Archives, 3e; metro Rambuteau or Hôtel de Ville; adult
€4.60, senior & student €2.30; 🕑 11am-6pm Tue-Sun

The Hunting and Nature Museum may sound
like an absolute oxymoron to the politically
correct, but in France, where hunting is a very
big deal, to show your love for nature is to
go out and shoot something. The delightful
Hôtel Guénégaud, dating from 1651, is positively crammed with weapons, paintings, *objets d'art* related to hunting and, of course, lots
and lots of trophies – heads of dead animals –
adorning the walls.

PLETZL Map pp396-9

metro St-Paul

When renovation of the Marais (4e) began
in the late 1960s, the area around **rue des Rosiers** and **rue des Écouffes** – traditionally known
as the Pletzl and home to a poor but vibrant
Jewish community – was pretty run-down.
Now trendy and expensive boutiques sit side-
by-side with Jewish bookshops and *cacher*
(kosher) grocery shops, butchers' shops, restaurants and felafel takeaway joints. The area
is very quiet on the Sabbath (sundown Friday
to sundown Saturday).

The Art Nouveau **Guimard synagogue** (Map
pp396-9; 10 rue Pavée, 4e) was designed by
Hector Guimard in 1913, designer of the famous metro entrances (p84). The interior is
closed to the public.

MUSÉE D'ART ET D'HISTOIRE DU
JUDAÏSME Map pp396-9

☎ 01 53 01 86 60; www.mahj.org; 71 rue du Temple,
3e; metro Rambuteau; adult €6.10, student & 18-25 yrs
€3.80, under 18 free; 🕑 11am-6pm Mon-Fri,
10am-6pm Sun

The Museum of the Art & History of Judaism
is in the sumptuous 17th-century Hôtel de St-
Aignan. The museum was formed by combining the crafts, paintings and ritual objects from
Eastern Europe and North Africa of the Musée
d'Art Juif (Jewish Art Museum) in Montmartre
with medieval Jewish artefacts from the Musée
National du Moyen Age (p94).

The museum traces the evolution of Jewish communities from the Middle Ages to the
present, with particular emphasis on the history of the Jews in France. Highlights include
documents relating to the Dreyfus Affair
(p68) and works by Chagall, Modigliani and
Soutine. Expect a gamut of security measures
and searches. The admission fee includes an
audioguide.

MUSÉE DE LA POUPÉE Map pp396-9

☎ 01 42 72 73 11; www.museedelapoupeeparis
.com; Impasse Berthaud, 3e; metro Rambuteau; adult
€6, senior & student €4, under 18 €3; 🕑 10am-6pm
Tue-Sun

Frightening to some – all those beady eyes
staring out at you – the Doll Museum is more
for adults than for children, with some 500
of the lifeless creatures dating back to 1800
arranged in scenes representing Paris through
the centuries. There are also temporary exhibitions (think Barbie and Cindy) as well as a
'hospital' for antique dolls.

MÉMORIAL DU MARTYR JUIF
INCONNU Map pp396-9

☎ 01 42 77 44 72; 37 rue de Turenne, 3e; metro
St-Paul; admission €2.30; 🕑 10am-1pm & 2-5.30pm
Mon-Thu, 10am-1pm & 2-5pm Fri

Established in 1956, the Memorial to the Unknown Jewish Martyr has a permanent collection and temporary exhibits relating to the
Holocaust and the German occupation of
parts of France and Paris during WWII. The
actual memorial to the victims of the Holocaust is in the original building on allée des
Justes, 4e (metro St-Paul), which has been
under renovation for some four years now. It
is planned that the exhibits and archives will
return there at some future date. A plaque on
the wall of the building opposite recalls that

as many as 500 of the 11,000 Jewish children deported by the Germans between 1942 and 1944 lived in the 4e.

As at the Musée d'Art et d'Histoire du Juda-ïsme, be prepared for heightened security on entry.

MAISON EUROPÉENNE DE LA PHOTOGRAPHIE Map pp396-9

☎ 01 44 78 75 00; www.mep-fr.org in French; 5-7 rue de Fourcy, 4e; metro St-Paul or Pont Marie; adult €5, senior & 9-25 yrs €2.50, under 9 free, free 5-8pm Wed; ☺ 11am-8pm Wed-Sun

The European House of Photography, housed in the rather overwrought Hôtel Hénault de Cantorbe dating from the early 18th century, has cutting-edge temporary exhibits (usually retrospectives on single photographers), as well as an enormous permanent collection on the history of photography and its connections with France.

MUSÉE DE LA CURIOSITÉ ET DE LA MAGIE Map pp396-9

☎ 01 42 72 13 26; www.museedelamagie.com in French; 11 rue St-Paul, 4e; metro St-Paul; adult/child 3-12 yrs €7/5; ☺ 2-7pm Wed, Sat & Sun, school holidays 2-7pm Wed-Sun

The Museum of Curiosity & Magic in the 16th-century *caves* (cellars) of the house of the Marquis de Sade examines the ancient arts of magic, optical illusion and sleight of hand, with regular magic shows (last one at 6pm) included. But the displays – optical illusions and wind-up toys – and very basic magic tricks do not justify the very high admission fee. Audioguides are an extra €3.

MUSÉE DES ARTS ET MÉTIERS Map pp386-8

☎ 01 53 01 82 00; www.arts-et-metiers.net in French; 60 rue de Réaumur, 3e; metro Arts et Métiers; adult/student €6.50/4.50, under 18 free; ☺ 10am-6pm Tue & Wed, Fri-Sun, 10am-9.30pm Thu

The Arts & Crafts Museum, the oldest museum of science and technology in Europe, is a must for anyone with an interest in how things work. Housed in the 18th-century priory of St-Martin des Champs, some 80,000 instruments, machines and working models from the 18th to 20th centuries are displayed across three floors. Taking pride of place is Foucault's original pendulum, which he introduced to the world in 1855 with the words 'Come and see the world turn'.

PLACE DE LA BASTILLE Map pp392-5

metro Bastille

The Bastille, built during the 14th century as a fortified royal residence, is the most famous monument in Paris that no longer exists; the notorious prison – the quintessential symbol of monarchical despotism – was demolished shortly after a mob stormed it on 14 July 1789 and freed a total of just seven prisoners.

The site where it once stood, place de la Bastille (11e and 12e), is now a very busy traffic roundabout.

In the centre of place de la Bastille is the 52m-high **Colonne de Juillet** (July Column), whose shaft of greenish bronze is topped by a gilded and winged figure of Liberty. It was erected in 1833 as a memorial to those killed in the street battles that accompanied the July Revolution of 1830 – they are buried in vaults under the column – and was later consecrated as a memorial to the victims of the February Revolution of 1848 (p67).

OPÉRA BASTILLE Map pp392-5

☎ 08 92 89 90 90, 01 44 61 59 65; www.opera-de -paris.fr in French; 2-6 place de la Bastille, 12e; metro Bastille

Paris' giant 'second' opera house, designed by the Canadian Carlos Ott, was inaugurated on 14 July 1989, the 200th anniversary of the storming of the Bastille. There are 1¼-hour **guided tours** (☎ 01 40 01 19 70; adult €10, senior & student €8, under 19 €5) of the building, which usually depart at 1pm and 5pm Monday to Saturday. Tickets go on sale 15 minutes before departure at window No 4 of the **box office** (130 rue de Lyon, 12e; ☺ 11am-6.30pm Mon-Sat).

ÉGLISE NOTRE DAME DE L'ESPÉRANCE Map pp392-5

☎ 01 40 21 49 39; 47 rue de la Roquette, 11e; metro Bastille; ☺ 8am-6.30pm

If you're in the area (or feeling a bit guilty about the night before) head for the wonderful Church of Our Lady of Hope designed by Bruno Legrand. Startling both for its modern design and size (it stands 20m tall and is 11m wide), the interior is filled with all sorts of interesting elements and features, including Nicolas Alquin's *Croix d'Espérance* (Cross of Hope) made of three pieces of 18th-century oak and three gold squares representing the Trinity, and calligrapher Franck Lalou's fragments of the Gospel etched onto glass behind the altar.

THE ISLANDS

Drinking p220; Eating p167; Shopping p258; Sleeping p289

The site of the first settlement in Paris around the 3rd century BC, and later the centre of the Roman town of Lutèce (p60), the Île de la Cité (Map pp396–9), most of which lies in the **4e arrondissement** though its western tip is in the **1er arrondissement**, remained the centre of royal and ecclesiastical power even after the city spread to both banks of the Seine during the Middle Ages. The buildings on the middle part

of the island were demolished and rebuilt during Baron Haussmann's great urban renewal scheme of the late 19th century (p34).

The smaller of the Seine's two islands, Île St-Louis (Map pp396–9), is just downstream from the Île de la Cité and entirely in the **4e arrondissement**.

Transport

Bus Île de la Cité for No 47 through the Marais to Gare de l'Est, No 21 to Opéra & Gare St-Lazare; Île St Louis for No 67 to Jardin des Plantes, Mosquée de Paris & Place d'Italie; No 87 through Latin Quarter to Place St-Sulpice, Sèvres Babylone, École Militaire & Champ de Mars

Metro & RER Cité, Pont Marie, Pont Neuf, St-Michel Notre Dame, Sully Morland

Boat Notre Dame Batobus stop (quai Montebello)

ÎLE DE LA CITÉ

CATHÉDRALE DE NOTRE DAME DE PARIS Map pp396-9

☎ 01 42 34 56 10; place du Parvis Notre Dame, 4e; metro Cité; ⏱ 8am-6.45pm Mon-Fri, 8am-7.45pm Sat & Sun

The Cathedral of Our Lady of Paris is the true heart of Paris; in fact, distances from Paris to every part of metropolitan France are measured from **place du Parvis Notre Dame**, the square in front of Notre Dame. A bronze star, set in the pavement across the street from the cathedral's main entrance, marks the exact location of *point zéro des routes de France* (point zero of French roads).

Notre Dame is not only a masterpiece of French Gothic architecture but has also been the focus of Catholic Paris for seven centuries. In recent years its western façade has had a thorough cleaning, which makes it even more attractive and inspiring.

Built on a site occupied by earlier churches – and, a millennium before that, a Gallo-Roman temple – it was begun in 1163 and largely completed by the middle of the 14th century.

The architect Eugène Emmanuel Viollet-le-Duc carried out extensive renovations in the 19th century. The interior is 130m long, 48m wide and 35m high and can accommodate more than 6000 worshippers.

Notre Dame is known for its sublime balance, though if you look closely you'll see all sorts of minor asymmetrical elements introduced to avoid monotony, in accordance with standard Gothic practice. These include the slightly different shapes of each of the three main **portals**, whose statues were once brightly coloured to make them more effective as a *Biblia pauperum* – a 'Bible of the poor' to help the illiterate understand the Old Testament stories, the Passion of the Christ and the lives of the saints. One of the best views of Notre Dame is from Square Jean XXIII, the lovely little park behind the cathedral, where you can view the mass of ornate **flying buttresses** that encircle the chancel and support its walls and roof.

Inside, exceptional features include three spectacular **rose windows**, the most renowned of which is the 10m-wide one over the western façade above the 7800-pipe organ, and the window on the northern side of the transept, which has remained virtually unchanged since the 13th century. The central choir with its carved wooden stalls and statues representing the Passion of the Christ is also noteworthy. There are free **guided tours** (⏱ noon Wed & Thu, 2.30pm Sat) of the cathedral, in English.

The **trésor** (treasury; adult/student/child 3-12 yrs €2.50/2/1; ⏱ 9.30am-6pm Mon-Sat, 1.30-5.30pm Sun) in the southeastern transept contains artwork, liturgical objects, church plate and relics, some of them of questionable origin. Among these is the **Ste-Couronne**, the 'Holy Crown', which is purportedly the wreath of thorns placed on Jesus' head before he was crucified and was brought here in the mid-13th century. It is exhibited at 4.45pm on each Friday of Lent and on the first Friday of the month during the rest of the year.

The entrance to **Tours de Notre Dame** (Towers of Notre Dame; ☎ 01 53 10 07 00; www.monum .fr; rue du Cloître Notre Dame; adult €6.10, student & 18-25 yrs €4.10, under 18 free, admission free 1st Sun of the month Oct-Mar; ☾ 9.30am-7.30pm daily Apr-Jun & Sep, 9.30am-7.30pm Mon-Fri, 9am-9pm Sat & Sun Jul & Aug, 10am-5.30pm daily Oct-Mar) is from the **North Tower**, which is to the right and round the corner as you walk out of the cathedral's main doorway. Climb the 387 spiralling steps to the top of the **western façade**, where you'll find yourself face-to-face with the cathedral's most frightening gargoyles, the 13-tonne bell **Emmanuel** (all the cathedral's bells are named) in the South Tower, and a spectacular view of Paris.

CRYPTE ARCHÉOLOGIQUE Map pp396-9

☎ 01 55 42 50 10; 1 place du Parvis Notre Dame, 4e; metro Cité; adult €3.30, senior & student €2.20, 14-25 yrs €1.60, under 14 free, admission free 10am-1pm Sun; ☾ 10am-6pm Tue-Sun Apr-Oct, 10am-5pm Tue-Sun Nov-Mar

The Archaeological Crypt under the square in front of the Notre Dame displays *in situ* the remains of structures built on this site from the Gallo-Roman period to the early 19th century.

MUSÉE DE NOTRE DAME DE PARIS
Map pp396-9

☎ 01 43 25 42 92; 10 rue du Cloître Notre Dame, 4e; adult/student/child 3-12 yrs €2.50/1.50/1.20; ☾ 2.30-6pm Wed, Sat & Sun

The small Museum of Notre Dame traces the cathedral's history and life on the Île de la Cité from Gallo-Roman times to today, via scale models, contemporary paintings, engravings and lithographs. An interesting document in the collection is a petition signed by Victor Hugo, the artist Ingres and others that sparked the campaign to restore the cathedral (p23).

STE-CHAPELLE Map pp396-9

☎ 01 53 40 60 97; www.monum.fr; 4 blvd du Palais, 1er; metro Cité; adult/18-25 yrs €6.10/4.10, under 18 free; ☾ 9.30am-6pm Mar-Oct, 9am-5pm Nov-Feb

The Holy Chapel, the most exquisite of Paris' Gothic monuments, is tucked away within the walls of the **Palais de Justice** (Law Courts). The 'walls' of the **upper chapel** are sheer curtains of richly coloured and finely detailed **stained glass**, which bathe the chapel in an extraordinary light

on a sunny day. Built in just under three years (compared with nearly 200 for Notre Dame), Ste-Chapelle was consecrated in 1248. The chapel was conceived by Louis IX to house his personal collection of holy relics (now kept in the treasury at Notre Dame). A joint ticket with the Conciergerie (below) costs adult/18-25 yrs €10.40/7.40. Admission is free on the first Sunday of the month from October to March.

CONCIERGERIE Map pp396-9

☎ 01 53 40 60 97; www.monum.fr; 2 blvd du Palais, 1er; metro Cité; adult/18-25 yrs €7.50/5.50, under 18 free; ☾ 9.30am-6pm Mar-Oct, 9am-5pm Nov-Feb

The Conciergerie, built in the 14th century for the concierge of the Palais de la Cité, was the main prison during the Reign of Terror.

Alleged enemies of the Revolution were incarcerated here prior to appearing before the Revolutionary Tribunal in the Palais de Justice next door. Among the 2700 prisoners held in the *cachots* (dungeons) here before being sent in tumbrels to the guillotine were Queen Marie-Antoinette and, as the Revolution began to turn on its own, the radicals Danton and Robespierre.

The Gothic **Salle des Gens d'Armes** (Cavalrymen's Hall) dates from the 14th century and is a fine example of the Rayonnant Gothic style. It is the largest surviving medieval hall in Europe. The **Tour de l'Horloge** (Map pp396-9; cnr blvd du Palais & quai de l'Horloge), built in 1353, has held a public clock aloft since 1370.

A joint ticket with Ste-Chapelle (left) costs adult/18-25 yrs €10.40/7.40. Admission is free for everyone on the first Sunday of the month from October to March.

MARCHÉ AUX FLEURS Map pp396-9
place Louis Lépin, 4e; metro Cité; ☾ 8am-7.30pm Mon-Sat

The Île de la Cité's flower market, surprisingly the oldest in Paris, has been at this square just north of the Préfecture de Police since 1808. On Sunday, it is transformed into the **marché aux oiseaux** (bird market; ☾ 8am-7.30pm).

MÉMORIAL DES MARTYRS DE LA DÉPORTATION Map pp396-9
Square de l'Île de France, 4e; metro St-Michel Notre Dame

The Memorial to the Victims of Deportation, erected in 1962 on the southeastern tip of the Île de la Cité, is a haunting monument to the 200,000 French people – including 76,000 Jews – who were killed in Nazi concentration camps during WWII. A single barred 'window' separates the bleak, rough concrete courtyard from the waters of the Seine.

The **Tomb of the Unknown Deportee** is flanked by 200,000 bits of back-lit glass, and the walls are etched with inscriptions from celebrated writers and poets.

PONT NEUF Map pp396-9
metro Pont Neuf
The white-stone spans of Paris' oldest bridge, ironically called 'New Bridge', have linked the western end of the Île de la Cité with both banks of the Seine since 1607. Its seven arches, decorated with humorous and grotesque figures of barbers, dentists, pickpockets, loiterers and the like are best viewed from the river.

ÎLE ST-LOUIS
In the early 17th century, when Île St-Louis was actually two uninhabited islets called Île Notre Dame (Our Lady Isle) and Île aux Vaches (Cows Island), a building contractor and two financiers worked out a deal with Louis XIII to create one island out of the two and build two stone bridges to the mainland. In exchange they would receive the right to subdivide and sell the newly created real estate.

This they did with great success, and by 1664 the entire island was covered with fine houses.

Today, the island's 17th-century, grey-stone houses and the small-town shops that line the streets and quays impart a village-like, provincial calm.

The central thoroughfare, rue St-Louis en l'Île, is home to a number of upmarket art galleries, boutiques and the French Baroque **Église St-Louis en l'Île** (Map pp396-9; ☎ 01 46 34 11 60; 19bis rue St-Louis en l'Île, 4e; metro Pont Marie; ☺ 9am-noon & 3-7pm Tue-Sun) built between 1656 and 1725.

LATIN QUARTER & JARDIN DES PLANTES
Drinking p221; Eating p168; Shopping p258; Sleeping p290

Eiffel Tower

Known as the Quartier Latin (Maps pp392–5 and pp396–9), because here students and professors communicated in Latin until the Revolution, the **5e arrondissement** has been the centre of Parisian higher education since the Middle Ages. It still has a large population of students and academics affiliated with the Sorbonne (now part of the University of Paris system), the Collège de France, the École Normale Supérieure and other institutions of higher learning. Bookshops and libraries, cafés and restaurants are like annexes to these venerable institutions and are packed at all times.

People linger on the terraces spilling out over place St-Michel or place de la Sorbonne. In rue de la Harpe, rue Mouffetard, rue de la Huchette or place de la Contrescarpe, restaurant windows display set menus appealing to customers' cravings for Mediterranean or Asian food. Movie buffs flock to rue des Écoles to see classics while activists and sympathisers come together under the same banner at the Mutualité, chanting slogans and fighting the good fight.

The Institut du Monde Arabe offers a glimpse of another world and the lush Jardin des Plantes, with its tropical greenhouses and Musée National d'Histoire Naturelle, opens new horizons in a bucolic, romantic setting.

Transport

Bus Panthéon for No 89 to Jardin des Plantes and 13e (Bibliothèque National François Mitterrand); blvd St-Michel for No 38 to Centre Pompidou, Gare de l'Est & Gare du Nord; rue Gay Lussac for No 27 to Île de la Cité, Opéra and Gare St-Lazare

Metro & RER Cardinal Lemoine, Censier Daubenton, Cluny-La Sorbonne, Gare d'Austerlitz, Jussieu, Luxembourg, Maubert Mutualité, Place Monge, St-Michel

Boat Jardin des Plantes Batobus stop (quai St-Bernard)

Train Gare d'Austerlitz

Top Five

- **Église St-Étienne du Mont** (right)
- **Grande Galerie de l'Évolution** (Musée Nationale d'Histoire Naturelle; p96)
- **Institut du Monde Arabe** (p96)
- **Mosquée de Paris** (p97)
- **Musée National du Moyen Age** (below)

MUSÉE NATIONAL DU MOYEN AGE
Map pp396-9

☎ 01 53 73 78 16, 01 53 73 78 00; www.musee-moyenage.fr in French; Thermes de Cluny, 6 place Paul Painlevé, 5e; metro Cluny-La Sorbonne or St-Michel; adult €5.50, senior, student & 18-25 yrs €4, under 18 free, 1st Sun of the month free; 🕒 9.15am-5.45pm Wed-Mon

The National Museum of the Middle Ages, sometimes called the Musée de Cluny, is housed in two structures: the *frigidarium* (cooling room) and other remains of Gallo-Roman baths dating from around AD 200, and the late-15th-century **Hôtel de Cluny**, considered the finest example of medieval civil architecture extant in Paris. The spectacular displays include statuary, illuminated manuscripts, arms, furnishings and objects made of gold, ivory and enamel. A sublime series of late-15th-century tapestries from the southern Netherlands, *La Dame à la Licorne* (The Lady with the Unicorn), hangs in circular room 13 on the 1st floor. Five of them are devoted to the senses and the sixth is the enigmatic *À Mon Seul Désir* (To My Sole Desire), a reflection on vanity. A medieval garden east of the museum, including the **Jardin Céleste** (Heavenly Garden) and the **Jardin d'Amour** (Garden of Love) are planted with flowers, herbs and shrubs that appear in masterpieces hanging throughout the museum. The **Forêt de la Licorne** (Unicorn Forest) based on the illustrations in the tapestries lie to the north of the museum.

SORBONNE Map pp392-5

12 rue de la Sorbonne, 5e; metro Luxembourg or Cluny-La Sorbonne

Paris' renowned university, the Sorbonne was founded in 1253 by Robert de Sorbon, confessor of Louis IX, as a college for 16 impoverished theology students. Today, the Sorbonne's main complex, bounded by rue de la Sorbonne, rue des Écoles, rue St-Jacques and rue Cujas, and other buildings in the vicinity house most of the 13 autonomous universities created when the University of Paris was reorganised after the student protests of 1968.

Place de la Sorbonne links blvd St-Michel and the **Chapelle de la Sorbonne** (Map pp392–5), the university's gold-domed church built between 1635 and 1642. The remains of Cardinal Richelieu (1585–1642) lie here.

PANTHÉON Map pp392-5

☎ 01 44 32 18 00; www.monum.fr; place du Panthéon, 5e; metro Luxembourg; adult €7, 18-25 yrs €4.50, under 18 free, 1st Sun of the month Oct-Mar free; 🕒 9.30am-6.30pm Apr-Sep, 10am-6.15pm Oct-Mar

The domed landmark was commissioned around 1750 as an abbey church dedicated to Ste-Geneviève, but due to financial and structural problems it wasn't completed until 1789 – not a good year for church openings in Paris. The Constituent Assembly converted it into a secular mausoleum for the *grands hommes de l'époque de la liberté française* (great men of the era of French liberty) two years later.

The Panthéon is a superb example of 18th-century neoclassicism but its ornate marble interior is gloomy. The 80-odd permanent residents of the crypt include Voltaire, Jean-Jacques Rousseau, Louis Braille, Victor Hugo, Émile Zola and Jean Moulin. Personages removed for reburial elsewhere after a re-evaluation of their greatness include Mirabeau and Marat. The first woman to be interred in the Panthéon was the two-time Nobel Prize-winner Marie Curie (1867–1934), who was reburied here (along with her husband Pierre) in 1995.

CENTRE DE LA MER Map pp392-5

☎ 01 44 32 10 70; www.oceano.org in French; Institut Océanographique; 195 rue St-Jacques, 5e; metro Luxembourg; adult €4.60, senior & student €3, child 3-12 yrs €2; 🕒 10am-12.30pm & 1.30-5.30pm Tue-Fri, 10am-5.30pm Sat & Sun

France has a long history of success in the field of oceanography (just think of Jacques Cousteau) and the Sea Centre cruises through that science, as well as marine biology, through temporary exhibitions, aquariums, scale models and audiovisuals. It's educational, and also a great deal of fun.

ÉGLISE ST-ÉTIENNE DU MONT
Map pp392-5

☎ 01 43 54 11 79; place de l'Abbé Basset, 5e; metro Cardinal Lemoine; 🕒 noon-7.30pm Mon, 8am-7.30pm Tue-Fri, 8am-noon & 2-7.30pm Sat, 9am-noon & 2-7.30pm Sun

The lovely Church of Mount St-Stephen, built between 1492 and 1655, contains Paris' only surviving **rood screen** (1535) separating the chancel from the nave; all the others were removed during the late Renaissance because they prevented the faithful assembled in the nave from seeing the priest celebrate Mass. In the southeastern corner of the nave is a highly decorated **reliquary** containing the finger of Ste-Geneviève, the patron saint of Paris. Also of interest is the carved **wooden pulpit** of 1650, held aloft by a figure of Samson, and the 16th- and 17th-century **stained glass**. Just inside the entrance, a plaque in the floor marks the spot where a defrocked priest stabbed an archbishop to death in 1857.

MUSÉE DE LA PRÉFECTURE DE POLICE Map pp396-9

☎ 01 44 41 52 50; 4 rue de la Montaigne Ste-Geneviève, 5e; metro Maubert Mutualité; admission free; 🕑 9am-5pm Mon-Fri, 10am-5pm Sat

The Police Headquarters Museum is a low-tech museum of documents, photos, uniforms and weapons used in crimes, but some of the items, including Louis XVI's court summons and, in effect, his death sentence, are fascinating. Look for the anti-Nazi posters and other propaganda confiscated during the WWII German occupation, and the bundle of orders for the detainment of Jewish citizens of Paris.

ARÈNES DE LUTÈCE Map pp392-5

49 rue Monge, 5e; metro Place Monge; admission free; 🕑 9am-5.30 to 9.30pm Apr-Oct, 8am-5.30 to 9.30pm Nov-Mar

The Roman amphitheatre called Lutetia Arena, dating from the 2nd century, could once seat around 10,000 people for gladiatorial combats and other events. Discovered in 1869 and heavily reconstructed in 1917, it is now used by neighbourhood youths playing football and *boules*.

MUSÉE DE L'ASSISTANCE PUBLIQUE-HÔPITAUX DE PARIS Map pp396-9

☎ 01 40 27 50 05; Hôtel de Miramion, 47 quai de la Tournelle, 5e; metro Maubert Mutualité; adult €4, senior & student €2; 🕑 10am-6pm Tue-Sun

A museum devoted to the history of hospitals in Paris doesn't sound like a crowd-pleaser but

---

Immortal Remains

Paris loves to immortalise people from its past with statues and monuments. Père Lachaise, Montmartre and Montparnasse cemeteries are bursting with wonderfully evocative likenesses of heroes and villains, poets and philosophers, and revolutionaries and autocrats, and there's a resident stone or bronze celebrity in even the tiniest park or square. The following is a selection of the larger-than-life characters you might bump into on your way around Paris.

St-Denis, patron saint of France (also known as Dionysius of Paris), introduced Christianity to Paris and was beheaded by the Romans for his pains. You can see him carrying his unfortunate head under his arm on the carved western portal of Notre Dame Cathedral (Map pp396–9).

Ste-Geneviève, patroness of Paris born at Nanterre in 422, turned Attila the Hun away from Paris in AD 451. Now she stands, ghostly pale and turning her back on the city, high above the Pont de la Tournelle (Map pp396–9), just south of Île St Louis in the 5e.

Plucky **Jeanne d'Arc** (Joan of Arc) tried unsuccessfully to wrest Paris from the English almost a millennium later; her gilded likeness now stands in place des Pyramides next to 192 rue de Rivoli (Map pp383–5).

Henri IV, known as the Vert Galant ('jolly rogue' or 'dirty old man', depending on your perspective), sits astride his white stallion on the Pont Neuf (Map pp396–9) in the 1er, exactly as he did when he inaugurated the 'New Bridge' in 1607.

Charlemagne, emperor of the Francs, rides his steed under the trees in front of Notre Dame (Map pp396–9), while a poor imitation of the Sun King, **Louis XIV**, prances in place des Victoires (Map pp386–8) in the 2e.

Georges Danton, a leader of the Revolution and later one of its victims sent to the guillotine, stands with his head very much intact near the site of his house at carrefour de l'Odéon (Map pp396–9) in the 6e.

Napoleon, horseless and in Roman garb, stands atop the column in place Vendôme (Map pp383–5) in the 1er. The latest addition is a 3.6m-tall bronze of **General Charles de Gaulle** in full military regalia at the bottom of av des Champs-Élysées (Map pp383–5) ready to march down to the Arc de Triomphe in a liberated Paris on 26 August 1944.

But it's not just people who are immortalised. An illuminated bronze replica of New York's **Statue of Liberty** faces the Big Apple from an artificial island in the Seine (Map pp389–91). And have a look at the impressive **Centaur** statue in the centre of Carrefour de la Croix Rouge (Map pp389–91) in the 6e, which was sculpted by César Baldaccini. Impossible to miss, the statue of the mythological half-horse, half-man has disproportionate gonads the size of grapefruits. Now that's what we call larger than life.

some of the items on display – paintings, sculptures, drawings, medical instruments etc – are fascinating and very evocative of their times. The lovely Hôtel Miramion, dating from the 17th century and the city's central pharmacy until the mid-1970s, is a positive delight.

INSTITUT DU MONDE ARABE
Map pp392-5

☎ 01 40 51 38 38; www.imarabe.org; 1 rue des Fossés St-Bernard, 5e; metro Cardinal Lemoine or Jussieu

The Institute of the Arab World, established to promote cultural contacts between the Islamic and Western worlds, is housed in Jean Nouvel's stunning building that successfully mixes modern and traditional Arab and Western elements (p41). The **museum** (adult €4, senior, student & 18-25 yrs €3, under 18 free; 🕑 10am-6pm Tue-Fri, 10am-7pm Sat & Sun), spread over three floors and entered via the 7th floor, displays 9th- to 19th-century art and artisanship from all over the Islamic world, as well as instruments from astronomy and other fields of scientific endeavour in which Arab technology once led the world. Temporary exhibitions usually cost between €7 and €9 for adults and €5 and €7 for the reduced tariff. Audioguides are €4.50.

The most unique feature of this building is its thousands of *mouche-arabies* (photo-electrically sensitive apertures built into the glass walls), inspired by the traditional latticed wooden windows found throughout the Arab world that let you see out without being seen. These apertures also regulate the amount of light and heat that reaches the interior of the building.

JARDIN DES PLANTES
Map pp392-5

☎ 01 40 79 30 00; 57 rue Cuvier, 5e; metro Gare d'Austerlitz, Censier Daubenton or Jussieu; 🕑 7.30am-5.30pm to 8pm (seasonal)

Paris' 24-hectare botanical garden was founded in 1626 as a medicinal herb garden for Louis XIII. Here you'll find the Eden-like **Jardin d'Hiver** (Winter Garden; adult €2.30, senior & 16-25 yrs €1.50; 🕑 1-5pm Mon & Wed-Fri, 1-6pm Sat & Sun Apr-Sep, 1-5pm Wed-Sun Oct-Mar), which are also called the **Serres Tropicales** (Tropical Greenhouses); the **Jardin Alpin** (Alpine Garden; admission free; 🕑 8-11am & 1.30-5pm Mon-Fri Apr-Sep), with 2000 mountainous plants; and the gardens of the **École de Botanique** (admission free; 🕑 8-11am & 1.30-5pm Mon-Fri), which is where students of the School of Botany 'practice'.

The rather pitiful **Ménagerie du Jardin des Plantes** (☎ 01 40 79 37 94; 57 rue Cuvier & 3 quai St-Bernard, 5e; metro Jussieu or Gare d'Austerlitz; adult €6, senior, student & 4-15 yrs €3.50; 🕑 9am-6pm Mon-Sat, 9am-6.30pm Sun Apr-Sep, 9am-5pm Mon-Sat, 9am-5.30pm Sun Oct-Mar), a medium-sized (5.5-hectare) zoo in the northern section of the garden, was founded in 1794. During the Prussian siege of Paris in 1870, most of the animals were eaten by starving Parisians. The **Microzoo** (🕑 10am-noon & 2-5.15pm Apr-Sep, 10am-noon & 1.30-4.45pm Oct-Mar), included in the admission fee, is open to those over 11 years of age.

MUSÉE NATIONAL D'HISTOIRE NATURELLE
Map pp392-5

☎ 01 40 79 30 00; www.mnhn.fr in French; 57 rue Cuvier, 5e; metro Censier Daubenton or Gare d'Austerlitz

The National Museum of Natural History, created by a decree of the Revolutionary Convention in 1793, was the site of important scientific research in the 19th century. It is housed in four different buildings along the southern edge of the Jardin des Plantes.

The **Grande Galerie de l'Évolution** (Great Gallery of Evolution; 36 rue Geoffroy St-Hilaire, 5e; adult €7, senior & 16-25 yrs €5; 🕑 10am-6pm Wed-Mon) has some imaginative exhibits on evolution and humanity's effect on the global ecosystem, spread over four floors and 6000 sq metres of space. The **Salle des Espèces Menacées et des Espèces Disparues** (Hall of Threatened and Extinct Species) on level 2 displays extremely rare specimens of endangered and extinct species while the **Salle de Découverte** (Room of Discovery) on level 1 houses interactive exhibits for kids. There's a guided tour in English (€5) at 3pm on Saturday, but it depends on demand.

The **Galerie de Minéralogie, de Géologie et de Paléobotanie** (36 rue Geoffroy St-Hilaire; adult €5, senior & 16-25 yrs €3; 🕑 10am-5pm Wed-Mon Oct-Mar, 10am-5pm Mon-Fri, 10am-6pm Sat & Sun Apr-Oct), which covers mineralogy, geology and palaeobotany (fossilised plants), has an amazing exhibit of giant natural crystals and a basement display of jewellery and other objects made from minerals. The **Galerie de Botanique** (10-18 rue Buffon, 5e), the Botany Gallery to the east, is used for temporary exhibits. The **Galerie d'Anatomie Comparée et de Paléontologie** (2 rue Buffon; adult €5, senior & 16-25 yrs €3; 🕑 10am-5pm Wed-Mon Oct-Mar, 10am-5pm Mon-Fri, 10am-6pm Sat & Sun Apr-Sep) has displays on comparative anatomy and palaeontology (the study of fossils).

MOSQUÉE DE PARIS Map pp392-5

☎ 01 45 35 97 33; www.mosquee-de-paris.org; 39 rue Geoffroy St-Hilaire, 5e; metro Censier Daubenton or Place Monge; adult €2.30, senior & 7-25 yrs €1.50; 🕑 9am-noon & 2-6pm Sat-Thu
Paris' central mosque with its striking 26m-high minaret was built in 1926 in the ornate Moorish style popular at the time. Visitors must remove their shoes at the entrance to the prayer hall and must be modestly dressed. The complex includes a North African-style **salon de thé** (tearoom) and **restaurant** (p169) and a **hammam** (p249), a traditional Turkish bath open to men and women on different days.

ST-GERMAIN, ODÉON & LUXEMBOURG

Drinking p222; Eating p181; Shopping p260; Sleeping p294

Centuries ago, the Église St-Germain des Prés and its affili-ated abbey owned most of today's 6e and 7e. The neighbour-hood around the church began to develop in the late 17th century, and these days the **6e arrondissement** is celebrated for its heterogeneity. Cafés such as Les Deux Magots (p223) and Café de Flore (p222) were once favourite hang-outs of postwar Left Bank intellectuals, but bohemia and jazz have deserted its streets and basements. Today artists and writers, students and jour-nalists, actors and musicians cross paths in the shadow of the École Nationale Supérieure des Beaux Arts, the Académie Française and the Odéon-Théâtre de l'Europe. The arrival of the fashion industry many years ago changed the general tenor of the districts. Since then, cloth-ing and footwear shops exist alongside bookshops, art galleries, publishing houses, antique dealers and interior design boutiques; but while *haute couture* and *prêt-à-porter* make flirta-tious neighbours, each sector keeps for the most part to itself. Cinemas still advertise their multiple screenings, making no distinction between new films and old, small works and big extravaganzas. The statue of Danton at the carrefour de l'Odéon is a favourite meeting spot, with groups flocking to this landmark before invading the area's cafés, bars and restaurants. In the nearby rue de Seine, market stalls still groan under the weight of fresh fruit and vegetables, a reminder that village life here survives despite the passing fashions.

Transport

Bus blvd St-Germain for No 86 to Odéon, Pont Sully (Île St-Louis), Bastille, Ledru Rollin (Marché d'Aligre), place de la Nation & zoo; rue de Rennes for No 96 to place Châtelet, Hôtel de Ville, St-Paul (Marais), rue Oberkampf & rue de Ménilmontant

Metro & RER Luxembourg, Mabillon, Odéon, Pont Neuf, Port Royal, St-Germain des Prés, St-Sulpice

Boat St-Germain des Prés Batobus stop (quai Malaquais)

ÉGLISE ST-GERMAIN DES PRÉS

Map pp396-9

☎ 01 43 25 41 71, 01 55 42 81 33; 3 place St-Germain des Prés, 6e; metro St-Germain des Prés; 🕑 8am-7pm Mon-Sat, 9am-8pm Sun
The Romanesque church of St Germanus of the Fields, the oldest church extant in Paris, was built in the 11th century on the site of a 6th-century abbey and was the dominant church in Paris until the advent of Notre Dame. It has been altered many times since, but the **Chapelle de St-Symphorien**, to the right as you enter, was part of the original abbey and is the final resting place of St Germanus (AD 496–576), the first bishop of Paris. The Merovingian kings were buried here during the 6th and 7th centuries, but their tombs disappeared during the Revolution. Columns in the **chancel** were taken from the Merovingian abbey. The **bell tower** over the western entrance has changed little since AD 990, although the spire dates only from the 19th century.

MUSÉE DE L'HISTOIRE DE LA MÉDECINE Map pp396-9

☎ 01 40 46 16 93; www.bium.univ-paris5.fr in French; Université René Descartes, 12 rue de l'École de Médecine, 6e; metro Odéon; adult €3.50, senior & student €2.50; 🕑 2-5.30pm Mon-Wed, Fri & Sat
This gruesome house of horrors looks at the history of medicine starting in ancient Europe

Circling the Squares

Postcard views of Paris often focus on pretty little squares, flanked with café tables where happy imbibers quaff wine or sip coffee in the spring sunshine. And these really do exist throughout the city. A perfect example is **place du Marché Ste-Catherine** (Map pp392–5), in the Marais district, 4e. **Place des Vosges** (Map pp392–5) is only a few minutes' stroll away if you want a more formal version of a *place parisienne*. And while you're in the Marais, search out the intricate courtyards of the **Village St-Paul** (Map pp396–9), just off rue St-Paul.

On the Left Bank, **place de la Contrescarpe** (Map pp392–5) in the 5e is a lively and picturesque little square surrounded by cafés and bars. Once upon a time this area was just outside the city walls, and there are chunks of medieval city wall still standing off rue du Cardinal Lemoine and rue Clovis. Over in the 6e, what is now called **rue de Furstemberg** (Map pp396–9) takes on a special life on summer evenings, when magnolias scent the air and buskers serenade lovers under the old-fashioned street lamp. It will always be lovely little place de Furstemberg as far as we're concerned.

and continuing on to medieval Europe. Primitive scalpels, leeches for 'bleeding', skulls with holes drilled into them – this place is not for the squeamish though teenage boys will find it entertaining and, no doubt, enlightening.

MUSÉE NATIONAL EUGÈNE DELACROIX Map pp396-9

☎ 01 44 41 86 50; www.musee-delacroix.fr in French; 6 rue de Furstemberg, 6e; metro Mabillon or St-Germain des Prés; adult €4, senior & student €2.60, under 18 free, 1st Sun of the month free; ⏱ 9.30am-5pm Wed-Mon)

The Eugène Delacroix Museum, in a courtyard just off a delightfully leafy square, was the Romantic artist's home and studio at the time of his death in 1863 and contains many of his oils, watercolours, pastels and drawings. If you want to see his major works, such as Liberty Leading the People, visit the Louvre (p80) or the Musée d'Orsay (p111); here you'll find many of his more intimate works (eg *An Unmade Bed*, 1828) and his paintings of Morocco.

INSTITUT DE FRANCE Map pp396-9

☎ 01 44 41 44 41; www.institut-de-france.fr; 23 quai de Conti, 6e; metro Mabillon or Pont Neuf

The French Institute, created in 1795, brought together five of France's academies of arts and sciences. The most famous of these is the **Académie Française** (French Academy), founded in 1635 by Cardinal Richelieu. Its 40 members, the Immortels (Immortals), have the Herculean (some say impossible) task of safeguarding the purity of the French language. The other academies are the Académie des Inscriptions et Belles-lettres, the Académie des Sciences, the Académie des Beaux-arts, and the Académie des Sciences Morales et Politiques.

The domed building housing the institute, across the Seine from the Louvre's eastern end,

dates from the mid-17th century. It's a masterpiece of French neoclassical architecture. There are usually tours (adult/under 25 €9/6) at 10.30am and 3pm on the first Saturday of the month and occasionally on Sunday. Check *Pariscope* or *L'Officiel des Spectacles* (p206) under 'Conférences' or ring the institute for details.

In the same building is the **Bibliothèque Mazarine** (Mazarine Library; ☎ 01 44 41 44 06; www.bibliotheque-mazarine.fr; ⏱ 10am-6pm Mon-Fri), founded in 1643 and the oldest public library in France. You can visit the bust-lined, late-17th-century reading room or consult the library's collection of 500,000 volumes, using a free two-day admission pass obtained by leaving your ID at the office to the left of the entrance. Annual membership to borrow books costs €15; a *carnet* of 10 visits costs €7.50.

MUSÉE DE LA MONNAIE DE PARIS Map pp396-9

☎ 01 40 46 55 35; www.monnaiedeparis.fr; 11 quai de Conti, 6e; metro Pont Neuf; admission €4, with audioguide €8, under 18 free, 1st Sun of the month free; ⏱ 11am-5.30pm Tue-Fri, noon-5.30pm Sat & Sun

The Parisian Mint Museum traces the history of French coinage from antiquity to the present, and displays presses and other minting equipment. There are some excellent audiovisual and other displays, which help to bring to life this otherwise niche subject.

The **Hôtel de la Monnaie**, which houses the museum, became the royal mint during the 18th century and is still used by the Ministry of Finance to produce commemorative medals and coins, as well as official weights and measures. One-hour tours of the *ateliers* (workshops) leave at 2.15pm on Wednesday and Friday (€3 in addition to the admission fee).

(Continued on page 107)

Quarters & Arrondissements – St-Germain, Odéon & Luxembourg

1 *Seine riverboat (p77)*
2 *Cyclists, roller-bladers and pedestrians, banks of the Seine* 3 *Pont Neuf (p93)*

1 Posters, the Louvre (p80)
2 Musée Picasso (p88)
3 Galerie Vivienne (p145)

1 Graffiti on market truck, Belleville (p123) *2* Stained glass, Église St-Germain L'Auxerrois (p82) *3* Centre Pompidou (p83)

1 Sculpture of an archer, Musée d'Orsay (p111)
2 Musée de la Monnaie de Paris (p98) 3 'The Thinker', Musée Rodin (p111)

1 Sculpture, Musée National
d'Histoire Naturelle (p96)
2 Sign, Musée National
Eugène Delacroix (p98)
3 Musée de l'Histoire de
France (p89)

1 *Basilique du Sacré Cœur (p127)* **2** *Tour Jean Sans Peur (p85)* **3** *Place des Vosges (p87)*

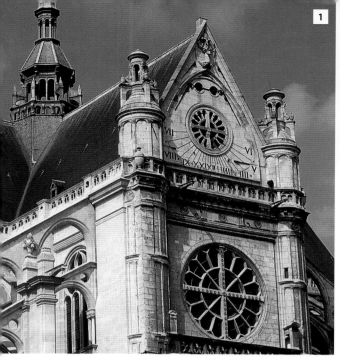

1 *Église St-Eustache (p85)*
2 *Eiffel Tower (p114)* **3** *Notre Dame (p91)*

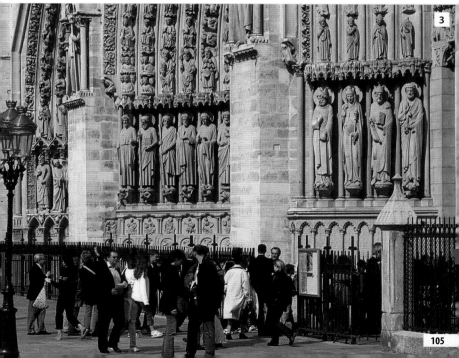

1 Arc de Triomphe du Carrousel (p82) 2 Window Montmartre 3 Skyscrapers and detail of the Grand Arche, La Défense (p133)

(Continued from page 98)

JARDIN DU LUXEMBOURG Map pp392-5
metro Luxembourg; 🕐 7.30am-sunset Apr-Oct, 8am-sunset Nov-Mar

When the weather is warm Parisians of all ages flock to the formal terraces and chestnut groves of the 23-hectare Luxembourg Garden to read, relax and sunbathe. In the southern part of the garden you'll find urban **orchards** and the honey-producing **Rucher du Luxembourg** (Luxembourg Apiary; Map pp389–91).

Palais du Luxembourg (Luxembourg Palace; rue de Vaugirard, 6e), at the northern end of the garden, was built in the 1620s for Marie de Médicis, Henri IV's consort, to assuage her longing for the Pitti Palace in Florence, where she spent her childhood. The palace has housed the **Sénat** (Senate), the upper house of the French parliament, since 1958. There are tours of the interior (🕿 reservations 01 44 61 20 89; adult/under 25 €9/6) at 10am on the first Sunday of each month, but you must book by the preceding Wednesday. The palace gardens, the main draw, are strewn with **sculptures**, including likenesses (real and imagined) of the queens of France. East of the palace is the Italianate **Fontaine des Médicis**, a long, ornate fish pond built around 1630.

The **Musée du Luxembourg** (Luxembourg Museum; 🕿 01 42 34 25 95; 19 rue de Vaugirard, 6e; metro Luxembourg; 🕐 11am-7pm Tue-Thu, 11am-10.30pm Fri-Mon) opened at the end of the 19th century in the orangery of the Palais du Luxembourg as an exhibition space for artists still living. It now hosts very prestigious temporary art exhibitions (eg Botticelli). Admission can cost up to €9 (students & 13-26 yrs €6, 8-12 yrs €4), but it depends on the exhibit.

Luxembourg Garden offers all the delights of a Parisian childhood a century ago and is one of the best places in Paris to take kids. At the octagonal **Grand Bassin**, model sailboats can be rented (from €3.50) from 2pm until sometime between 4.30pm (in winter) and 7pm (in spring and summer) on Wednesday, Saturday and Sunday (daily during school holidays).

About 200m southwest of the pond, the pint-sized **Théâtre du Luxembourg** (🕿 01 43 26 46 47) puts on marionette shows, whose antics can be enjoyed even if you don't understand French. There are performances (€3.90) at 3.15pm on Wednesday, Saturday and Sunday, with an additional one at 11am on Saturday and Sunday. They're staged daily during the school holidays.

Top Five for Children
- Bois de Boulogne (p131)
- Bois de Vincennes (p130)
- Jardin du Luxembourg (p82)
- La Villette (p129)
- Palais de la Découverte (p118)

Next to the Théâtre du Luxembourg, is the modern **playground** (adult/child €1.50/2.40). One half of it is for kids aged up to seven, the other half is for children aged seven to 12.

ÉGLISE ST-SULPICE Map pp396-9
🕿 01 46 33 21 78, 01 44 07 29 57; place St-Sulpice, 6e; metro St-Sulpice; 🕐 8am-7pm

The Church of St Sulpicius, lined with small side chapels inside, was built between 1646 and 1780 on the site of earlier churches dedicated to the eponymous 6th-century archbishop of Bourges. The Italianate façade, designed by a Florentine architect, has two rows of superimposed columns and is topped by two towers. The neoclassical décor of the vast interior is influenced by the Counter-Reformation.

The frescoes in the **Chapelle des Sts-Anges** (Chapel of the Holy Angels), first to the right as you enter, depict Jacob wrestling with the angel and Michael the Archangel doing battle with Satan and were painted by Eugène Delacroix between 1855 and 1861. The monumental **organ loft** dates from 1781. The 10.30am Mass on Sunday is accompanied by organ music.

Place St-Sulpice is adorned by a very energetic fountain, **Fontaine des Quatre Évêques** (Fountain of the Four Bishops) dating from 1844. Nearby streets are known for their couture houses (p270).

MUSÉE-ATELIER ZADKINE Map pp389-91
🕿 01 55 42 77 20; 100bis rue d'Assas, 6e; metro Port Royal or Vavin; permanent collections admission free, temporary exhibits adult €4, senior & student €3, 14-25 yrs €2, under 14 free; 🕐 10am-6pm Tue-Sun

This museum is devoted to the life and work of Russian Cubist sculptor Ossip Zadkine (1890–1967), who arrived in Paris in 1908, and lived and worked in this cottage in a lovely courtyard opposite the Jardin du Luxembourg for almost 40 years. Though his work is little known outside France, Zadkine produced an enormous catalogue of work in wood, clay, stone and bronze.

MONTPARNASSE

Drinking p223; Eating p183; Sleeping p296

After WWI, writers, poets and artists of the avant-garde abandoned Montmartre and crossed the Seine, shifting the centre of Paris' artistic ferment to the area around blvd du Montparnasse. Chagall, Modigliani, Léger, Soutine, Miró, Kandinsky, Picasso, Stravinsky, Hemingway, Ezra Pound and Cocteau, as well as such political exiles as Lenin and Trotsky, all used to hang out here, talking endlessly in the cafés and restaurants for which the quarter became famous. Montparnasse remained a creative centre until the mid-1930s. Today, especially since the construction of the Gare Montparnasse complex, there is little to remind visitors of the area's bohemian past except those now touristy restaurants and cafés.

Although the Latin Quarter crowd considers the area hopelessly nondescript, blvd du Montparnasse (on the southern border of the 6e) and its many fashionable restaurants, cafés and cinemas attract large numbers of people in the evening. In fact, the **14e arrondissement**, which is where the lion's share of the district falls, has a lot to offer: delightful Parc Montsouris; the Cimetière du Montparnasse, final resting place of such luminaries as Sartre and Serge Gainsbourg; posh place de la Catalogne; and place Denfert Rochereau, gateway to the Catacombes (p110). To the south the extraordinary Cité Universitaire, a lush oasis reserved for students, acts as a buffer between Parc Montsouris and the Périphérique. The somewhat cold elegance of rue Froidevaux, which runs along the southern border of the Cimetière du Montparnasse, stands in sharp contrast to the neon signs and nightlife of the rue de la Gaîté. Pedestrians have the run of rue Daguerre, whose market, shops and bars attract friendly hordes on the weekends. Less flamboyant than the Latin Quarter, less hip than Bastille and less audacious than Bercy, the unpretentious 14e arrondissement has perhaps struck a better balance than most.

Transport

Bus Gare Montparnasse for No 91 to Gare d'Austerlitz, Gare de Lyon & Bastille, for No 92 to place de l'Étoile, for No 94 to Sèvres Babylone (Le Bon Marché); blvd du Montparnasse for No 82 to Invalides & Eiffel Tower, rue de Rennes & Concorde; rue de Rennes for No 95 to St-Germain des Prés, Quai Voltaire, Louvre, Palais Royal, Opéra & Lamarck-Caulaincourt (Montmartre)

Metro Denfert Rochereau, Duroc, Edgar Quinet, Falguière, Montparnasse Bienvenüe, Pasteur, Raspail, St-Placide

Train Gare Montparnasse

GARE MONTPARNASSE Map pp389-91

Place Raoul Dautry, 14e; metro Montparnasse Bienvenüe
This sprawling train station has several unusual attractions on – of all places – its rooftop. The unique **Jardin de l'Atlantique** (Atlantic Garden; place des Cinq Martyrs du Lycée Buffon, 15e; metro Montparnasse Bienvenüe), whose 3.5 hectares of landscaped terraces veil the top of the station, offers a bit of greenery and tranquillity in the heart of a very busy district. Don't miss the futuristic **Observatoire Météorologique** 'sculpture', which measures precipitation, temperature and wind speed.

Next to the garden the small **Musée Jean Moulin** (☎ 01 40 64 39 44; www.paris.fr/musees /memorial/index.html in French; 23 allée de la 2e DB, 15e; permanent collections admission free, temporary exhibits adult/14-25 yrs €4/2, senior & student €3, under 14 free; ☽ 10am-6pm Tue-Sun) is devoted to the WWII German occupation of Paris, with the focus on the Resistance and its leader, Jean Moulin (1899–1943). The attached **Mémorial du Maréchal Leclerc de Hauteclocque et de la Libération de Paris** shows a panoramic film on the eponymous general (1902–47) who led the Free French units during the war and the city's liberation in 1944.

TOUR MONTPARNASSE Map pp389-91

☎ 01 45 38 52 56; www.tourmontparnasse56.com; rue de l'Arrivée, 15e; metro Montparnasse Bienvenüe; admission 56th/59th floor adult €7/8, senior & student €6/6.80, under 14 €4.50/5.50; ☽ 9.30am-11.30pm Apr-Sep, 9.30am-10.30pm Sun-Thu, 9.30am-11pm Fri & Sat Oct-Mar

The 210m-high Montparnasse Tower, built in 1974 with steel and smoked glass (p40), affords spectacular views over the city and is just about the best place to be since it is one of the few spots in Paris where you can't see this startlingly ugly oversized lipstick tube. A lift takes you up to the 56th-floor indoor observatory, with an exhibition centre and a video about Paris. You can combine the lift trip with a hike up the stairs to the open-air terrace on the 59th floor.

MUSÉE DU MONTPARNASSE
Map pp389-91

☎ 01 42 22 91 96; 21 av du Maine, 15e; metro Montparnasse Bienvenüe; adult €5, senior & student €4, under 12 free; ⏰ 12.30-7pm Tue-Sun
Housed in the erstwhile studio of Russian Cubist artist Marie Vassilieff (1884–1957), the Museum of Montparnasse does not have a permanent collection but recalls the great role Montparnasse played during various artistic periods of the 20th century through temporary exhibitions.

MUSÉE BOURDELLE Map pp389-91

☎ 01 49 54 73 73; www.paris.fr/musees/bourdelle in French; 18 rue Antoine Bourdelle, 15e; metro Falguière; permanent collections admission free; temporary exhibits adult/14-25 yrs €4.60/2.30, senior & student €3, under 14 free; ⏰ 10am-6pm Tue-Sun
The Bourdelle Museum, due north of Gare Montparnasse, contains monumental bronzes in the very house and workshop where the sculptor Antoine Bourdelle (1861–1929), a pupil of Rodin, lived and worked. The three sculpture gardens, one of which faces rue Antoine Bourdelle, are particularly lovely and impart a flavour of the Montparnasse of the *belle époque* and post-WWI periods.

FONDATION DUBUFFET Map pp389-91

☎ 01 47 34 12 63; 137 rue de Sèvres, 6e; metro Duroc; admission €4; ⏰ 2-6pm Mon-Fri
Situated in a lovely 19th-century *hôtel particulier*, the foundation houses and administers the collection of Jean Dubuffet (1901–85), chief of the Art Brut school, a term he himself coined

Top Five

- **Catacombes** (p110)
- **Cimetière de Montparnasse** (right)
- **Fondation Dubuffet** (above)
- **Musée Pasteur** (right)
- **Tour Montparnasse** (view from top only; p108)

to describe all works of artistic expression not officially recognised. Much of his work is incredibly modern and expressive.

MUSÉE ERNEST HÉBERT Map pp389-91

☎ 01 42 22 23 82; www.rmn.fr; 85 rue du Cherche Midi, 6e; metro St-Placide; adult €3, senior & student €2.30; ⏰ 12.30-6pm Mon & Wed-Fri, 2-6pm Sat & Sun
The eponymous portrait painter Ernest Hébert (1817–1908) did likenesses of society people of the Second Empire and *belle époque* and was thus not short of a sou or two. Come here for the artist's wonderful 18th-century townhouse and its baubles – not his saccharine, almost cloying portraits.

MUSÉE DE LA POSTE Map pp389-91

☎ 01 42 79 24 24; 34 blvd de Vaugirard, 15e; metro Montparnasse Bienvenüe; adult €4.50, senior, student & 13-18 yrs €3, under 13 free; ⏰ 10am-6pm Mon-Sat
The Postal Museum, a few hundred metres southwest of Tour Montparnasse, has some pretty impressive exhibits illustrating the history of the French postal service – a matter of importance in a highly centralised state like France. The exhibition rooms, dispersed over several floors, showcase the original designs of French stamps, antique postal and telecommunications equipment and models of postal conveyances. An audioguide costs €1.

MUSÉE PASTEUR Map pp389-91

☎ 01 45 68 82 83; www.pasteur.fr; Institut Pasteur, 25 rue du Docteur Roux, 15e; metro Pasteur; adult €2.30, senior & student €1.30; ⏰ 2-5.30pm Mon-Fri
Housed in the apartment where the famous chemist and bacteriologist spent the last seven years of his life (1888–95), a tour of this museum takes you through Pasteur's private rooms, a hall with such odds and ends as gifts presented to him by heads of state and drawings he did as a young man and the crypt where the remains of the great savant lie.

CIMETIÈRE DU MONTPARNASSE
Map pp389-91

blvd Edgar Quinet & rue Froidevaux, 14e; metro Edgar Quinet or Raspail; ⏰ 8am-6pm Mon-Fri, 8.30am-6pm Sat, 9am-6pm Sun mid-Mar–early Nov, to 5.30pm early Nov–mid-Mar
Montparnasse Cemetery received its first 'lodger' in 1824. It contains the tombs of such illustrious personages as Charles Baudelaire, Guy de Maupassant, Samuel Beckett, Constantin Brancusi, Chaim Soutine, Man Ray, André

Citroën, Alfred Dreyfus, Jean Seberg, Simone de Beauvoir, Jean-Paul Sartre and the crooner Serge Gainsbourg, whose grave in division No 1 just off av Transversale is a pilgrimage site for fans who place metro tickets atop his tombstone, a reference to *Le Poinçonneur des Lilas*, one of his more famous songs.

Maps showing the location of the tombs are available free from the **conservation office** (☎ 01 44 10 86 50; 3 blvd Edgar Quinet, 14e) at the main entrance. Guided tours (€6/3) depart at 2.30pm on different days of the week. Ring ☎ 01 40 71 75 60 for information.

CATACOMBES Map pp380-2

☎ 01 43 22 47 63; www.paris.fr/musees/musee_carna valet in French; 1 place Denfert Rochereau, 14e; metro Denfert Rochereau; adult/14-25 yrs €5/2.60, senior & student €3.30, under 14 free; ☼ 10am-5pm Tue-Sun
In 1785 it was decided to solve the hygiene and aesthetic problems posed by Paris' over-flowing cemeteries by exhuming the bones and storing them in the tunnels of three disused quarries. One ossuary created in 1810 is now known as the Catacombs and is without a doubt the most macabre place in Paris. After descending 20m (130 steps) from street level, visitors follow 1.6km of underground corridors in which the bones and skulls of millions of Parisians are neatly stacked along the walls. During WWII, these tunnels were used as a headquarters by the Resistance; so-called *cataphiles* looking for cheap thrills are often caught roaming the tunnels at night (there's a fine of €60).

The route through the Catacombes begins at a small, dark green *belle époque*–style building in the centre of place Denfert Rochereau. The exit is on rue Remy Dumoncel (metro Mouton Duvernet), 700m southwest of place Denfert Rochereau, where a guard will check your bag for 'borrowed' bones.

FAUBOURG ST-GERMAIN & INVALIDES

Drinking p224; Eating p184; Shopping p261; Sleeping p297

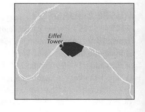

The **7e arrondissment** has the reputation of being rather staid. At first glance, its formal beauty and conventional manners give an impression of restraint and distance. But this world of elaborate ironwork, flashing gold leaf and hewn stone has an extravagance all of its own.

Faubourg St-Germain, the area between the Musée d'Orsay and, 1km south, rue de Babylone, was Paris' most fashionable neighbourhood in the 18th century. Some of the most interesting mansions, many of which now serve as embassies, cultural centres and government ministries, are along three streets running east to west: rue de Lille, rue de Grenelle and rue de Varenne. Hôtel Matignon at 57 rue de Varenne has been the official residence of the French prime minister since the start of the Fifth Republic (1958).

Watching over the district and the city, the Eiffel Tower dominates the Paris skyline. At its feet, the Seine flows in a gracious curve and the smooth lawns of the Champ

Église du Dôme (p113)

de Mars stretch away. Somehow it always feels like Sunday in the alleys of this park, with its sweeping prospects and precise design. To the east, the well-to-do and sleepy rue de l'Université and rue St-Dominique make their calm way down to the blvd St-Germain, leaving behind the bright dome of Les Invalides. The National Assembly is over by the river as is the celebrated Musée d'Orsay, housed in the cavernous shell of an old railway station and displaying the patrimony's rich collection of impressionist art. The Musée du Quai Branly (p41) will be the feather in the cap of the 7e arrondissement when it opens in late 2005.

Transcport

Bus Quai d'Orsay for No 63 to St-Germain, Odéon, Gare d'Austerlitz & Gare de Lyon, for No 83 to Grand Palais, Rond Point des Champs Élysées & rue du Faubourg St-Honoré; Musée d'Orsay for No 73 to Jardin des Tuileries, place de la Concorde, av des Champs-Élysées & La Défense

Metro & RER Assemblée Nationale, École Militaire, Invalides, Musée d'Orsay, Rue du Bac, Solférino, La Tour Maubourg

Boat Musée d'Orsay Batobus stop (quai de Solférino); Paris Canal Croisières pier at quai Anatole France (7e) near the Musée d'Orsay for canal boat to stop Bassin de la Villette (19-21 quai de la Loire)

MUSÉE D'ORSAY Map pp389-91

☎ 01 40 49 48 84; www.musee-orsay.fr; 1 rue de la Légion d'Honneur, 7e; metro Musée d'Orsay or Solférino; adult €7 (€5 Sun), senior & 18-25 yrs €5, under 18 free, 1st Sun of the month free; ☼ 9am-6pm Tue, Wed, Fri & Sat, 9am-9.45pm Thu, 9am-6pm Sun late Jun–Sep, 10am-6pm Tue, Wed, Fri & Sat, 10am-9.45pm Thu, 9am-6pm Sun Oct–late Jun

The Musée d'Orsay, in a former train station (1900) facing the Seine from quai Anatole France, displays France's national collection of paintings, sculptures, *objets d'art* and other works produced between the 1840s and 1914, including the fruits of the impressionist, post-impressionist and Art Nouveau movements; the Musée National d'Art Moderne at the Centre Pompidou (p83) then picks up the torch.

Many visitors head straight to the upper level (lit by a skylight) to see the famous impressionist paintings by Monet, Renoir, Pissarro, Sisley, Degas and Manet and the postimpressionist works by Van Gogh, Cézanne, Seurat and Matisse, but there's also a great deal to see on the ground floor, including some early works by Manet, Monet, Renoir and Pissarro. The middle level has some magnificent Art Nouveau rooms.

English-language tours (information ☎ 01 40 49 48 48; tour €6/4.50 plus admission fee), lasting 1½ hours, include 'Masterpieces of the Musée d'Orsay', departing at 11.30am Tuesday to Saturday, with an additional one at 4pm on Thursday from February to August; and an in-depth tour focusing on the impressionists at 2.30pm on Tuesday and 4pm on Thursday at least once a month. The 1½-hour audioguide tour (€5), available in six languages, points

out 80 major works. Be aware that tickets are valid all day so you can leave and re-enter the museum as you please.

ASSEMBLÉE NATIONALE Map pp389-91

☎ 01 40 63 60 00; www.assemblee-nat.fr; 33 quai d'Orsay & 126 rue de l'Université, 7e; metro Assemblée Nationale or Invalides

The National Assembly, the lower house of the French parliament, meets in the 18th-century Palais Bourbon fronting the Seine. There are usually free guided tours in French (10am, 2pm and 3pm on Saturday). Join the queue early with your passport. Next door is the Second Empire–style **Ministère des Affaires Étrangères** (Ministry of Foreign Affairs; ☎ 01 44 54 19 49; 37 quai d'Orsay), built between 1845 and 1855 and often referred to as the 'Quai d'Orsay'.

MUSÉE RODIN Map pp389-91

☎ 01 44 18 61 10; www.musee-rodin.fr; 77 rue de Varenne, 7e; metro Varenne; adult €5 (€3 Sun), senior & 18-25 yrs €3, under 18 free, 1st Sun of the month free, garden only €1; ☼ 9.30am-5.45pm Apr-Sep, 9.30am-4.45pm Oct-Mar

The Rodin Museum, many visitors' favourite in Paris, is also one of the most relaxing spots in the city, with a lovely garden full of sculptures and shade trees in which to rest and contemplate the *Thinker*. Rooms on two floors of the 18th-century Hôtel Biron display extraordinarily vital bronze and marble sculptures by Rodin, including casts of some of his most celebrated works: the *Hand of God*, the *Burghers of Calais*, *Cathedral*, that perennial crowd-pleaser the *Thinker* and the sublime, the incomparable, the romance-hewn-in-marble the *Kiss*. There are also some 15 works by Camille Claudel (1864–1943), sister to the writer Paul and Rodin's mistress. An excellent audioguide (€3) is the perfect accompaniment to your visit.

MUSÉE MAILLOL-FONDATION DIANA VIERNY Map pp389-91

☎ 01 42 22 59 58; www.museemaillol.com; 59-61 rue de Grenelle, 7e; metro Rue du Bac; adult €8, student & 16-25 yrs €6, under 16 free; ☼ 11am-6pm Wed-Mon

This splendid small museum focuses on the work of the sculptor Aristide Maillol (1861–1944) and also includes works by Matisse, Gauguin, Kandinsky, Cézanne and Picasso from the private collection of Dina Vierny (1915), who was Maillol's principal model for 10 years from the age of 15. The museum is located in the stunning 18th-century Hôtel Bouchardon.

It's a Free-For-All

The permanent collections at about a dozen of the 15 *musées municipaux*, 'city museums' run by the Mairie de Paris, are now open to one and all for free. Remember, however, this does not apply to temporary or special exhibitions, which always incur a separate admission fee.

City museums taking part in the scheme include the following:

Maison de Balzac (p115)

Maison de Victor Hugo (p88)

Musée-Atelier Zadkine (p107)

Musée Bourdelle (p109)

Musée Carnavalet (p88)

Musée Cernuschi (p120)

Musée Cognacq-Jay (p88)

Musée d'Art Moderne de la Ville de Paris (p116)

Musée de la Vie Romantique (p128)

Musée des Beaux-Arts de la Ville de Paris (p117) In the Petit Palais.

Musée Jean Moulin & Mémorial du Maréchal Leclerc de Hauteclocque et de la Libération de Paris (p108)

At the same time, the *musées nationaux* (national museums) in Paris have a reduced rate for those aged over 60 and between 18 and 25 and sometimes for everyone else on one day or part of a day (eg Sunday morning) per week. They are always free for those under 18 years of age and for everyone on the first Sunday of each month. Again, this does not include temporary exhibitions, for which you will have to pay separately.

The following national museums are always free for those under 18 and, on the first Sunday of each month, to everyone else as well:

Arc de Triomphe (p117) October to March only.

Conciergerie (p92) October to March only.

Galeries Nationales du Grand Palais (p118)

Musée de l'Histoire de France (p89) In the Archives Nationales.

Musée d'Orsay (p111)

Musée du Louvre (p80)

Musée Guimet des Arts Asiatiques (p116)

Musée National d'Art Moderne (p84) In the Centre Pompidou.

Musée National des Arts et Traditions Populaires (p132)

Musée National du Moyen Age (Musée de Cluny; p94)

Musée National Eugène Delacroix (p98)

Musée National Gustave Moreau (p128)

Musée Picasso (p88)

Musée Rodin (p111)

Palais de Tokyo (p116)

Panthéon (p94) October to March only.

Ste-Chapelle (p92)

Tours de Notre Dame (p92) October to March only.

ESPLANADE & HÔTEL DES INVALIDES Map pp389–91
metro Invalides, Varenne or La Tour Maubourg

A 500m-long expanse of lawn called the **Esplanade des Invalides** separates Faubourg St-Germain from the Eiffel Tower area. At the southern end of the esplanade, laid out between 1704 and 1720, is the final resting place of the man many French people consider to be the nation's greatest hero.

The **Hôtel des Invalides** was built in the 1670s by Louis XIV to provide housing for 4000 *invalides* (disabled war veterans). On 14 July 1789, a mob forced its way into the building and, after fierce fighting, seized 28,000 rifles before heading on to the prison at Bastille and revolution. North of the Hôtel des Invalides' main courtyard, the so-called **Cour d'Honneur**, is the **Musée de l'Armée** (Army Museum; ☎ 01 44 42 37 72; www.invalides.org; 129 rue de Grenelle, 7e; adult €7, senior, student & 18-25 yrs €5.50, under 18 free; ☉ 10am-6pm Apr-Sep, 10am-5pm Oct-Mar, closed 1st Mon of the month), which holds the nation's largest collection on

the history of the French military. To the south are the **Église St-Louis des Invalides**, once used by soldiers, and the **Église du Dôme**, with its sparkling dome (1677–1735) and considered to be one of the finest religious edifices erected under Louis XIV. It received the remains of Napoleon in 1840. The very extravagant **Tombeau de Napoléon 1er** (Napoleon's Tomb; ☉ 10am-6pm Apr-Sep, 10am-5pm Oct-Mar, closed 1st Mon of the month), in the centre of the church, consists of six coffins that fit into one another like a Russian *matryoshka* doll. Admission to the Army Museum allows entry to all the other sights in the Hôtel des Invalides.

EIFFEL TOWER AREA & 16E ARRONDISSEMENT

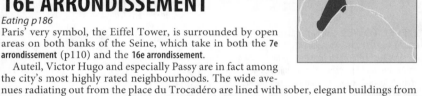

Eating p186

Paris' very symbol, the Eiffel Tower, is surrounded by open areas on both banks of the Seine, which take in both the **7e arrondissement** (p110) and the **16e arrondissement**.

Auteil, Victor Hugo and especially Passy are in fact among the city's most highly rated neighbourhoods. The wide avenues radiating out from the place du Trocadéro are lined with sober, elegant buildings from the Haussmann era. Luxury boutiques abound, frequented by posh customers who desert the area come nightfall. It's here, on the banks of the Seine, that the architectural curiosity known as the 'Maison Ronde' – the Maison de Radio France – was constructed. Just north, the Maison de Balzac keeps alive the memory of the illustrious author of *Le Père Goriot*. Further north, the ultra-bourgeois av Foch thumbs its nose at the restless av de la Grande Armée, teeming with motorbike fanatics. The 16e arrondissement also hosts football meets at the Parc des Princes and, as summer approaches, the thud of tennis balls on asphalt can be heard at Stade Roland Garros. There are some fabulous cultural institutions here, including the Musée d'Art Moderne, the Musée de la Marine, the Musée de l'Homme and the beautiful Musée Guimet as well as lots and lots of smaller and lesser known museums on such diverse subjects as wine, radio, counterfeiting and the pen.

Eiffel Tower (p114).

Transport

Bus Quai Branly for No 82 to Trocadéro (Palais de Chaillot), Porte Maillot, Palais des Congrès & Neuilly; Champ de Mars for No 42 to av Montaigne, Madeleine, Opéra (blvd Haussmann) & Gare du Nord & for No 69 to Invalides, Musée d'Orsay, Louvre, Châtelet, Marais, Bastille & Gambetta; Trocadéro for No 22 to place de l'Étoile, Grands Boulevards, Gare St-Lazare & Opéra

Metro & RER Alma-Marceau, Bir Hakeim, Champ de Mars-Tour Eiffel, École Militaire, Iéna, Kennedy Radio France, Passy, Pont de l'Alma, Porte Dauphine, Trocadéro, Victor Hugo

Boat Eiffel Tower Batobus stop (Port de la Bourdonnais)

EIFFEL TOWER Map pp389-91

☎ 01 44 11 23 23; www.tour-eiffel.fr; metro Champ de Mars-Tour Eiffel or Bir Hakeim; ☽ lifts 9.30am-11pm Sep–mid-Jun, 9am-midnight mid-Jun–Aug; stairs 9.30am-6.30pm Sep–mid-Jun, 9am-midnight mid-Jun–Aug

La Tour Eiffel faced massive opposition from Paris' artistic and literary elite (p39) when it was built for the 1889 Exposition Universelle (World Fair), marking the centenary of the Revolution.

The 'metal asparagus', as some Parisians snidely called it, was almost torn down in 1909 but was spared because it proved an ideal platform for the transmitting antennas needed for the newfangled science of radiotelegraphy. It welcomed two million visitors the first year it opened and three times that number make their way to the top each year, now.

The Eiffel Tower, named after its designer, Gustave Eiffel, is 324m high, including the television antenna at the tip. This figure can vary by as much as 15cm, however, as the tower's 10,000 tonnes of iron, held together by 2.5 million rivets, expand in warm weather and contract when it's cold.

Three levels are open to the public. The lifts (in the west and north pillars), which follow a curved trajectory, cost €4 to the 1st platform (57m above the ground), €7.30 to the 2nd (115m) and €10.40 to the 3rd (276m). Children aged three to 11 pay €2.20, €4 or €5.70, respectively; there are no youth or student discounts and children under three years are free. Avoid the lift queues by taking the stairs (€3.50) in the south pillar to the 1st and 2nd platforms.

PARC DU CHAMP DE MARS Map pp389-91
metro Champ de Mars-Tour Eiffel or École Militaire

Running southeast from the Eiffel Tower, the grassy 'Field of Mars' (named after Mars, the Roman god of war) was originally used as a parade ground for the cadets of the 18th-century **École Militaire** (Military Academy), the vast, French-classical building (1772) at the southeastern end of the park, which counts no less than Napoleon among its graduates.

On 14 July 1790 the Fête de la Fédération (Federation Festival) was held on the Champ de Mars to celebrate the first anniversary of the storming of the Bastille. Four years later it was the location of the Fête de l'Être-Suprême (Festival of the Supreme Being), at which Robespierre presided over a ceremony that established a revolutionary state religion.

The **Marionettes du Champ de Mars** (☎ 01 48 56 01 44; metro École Militaire) stage puppet shows (€2.80) in a covered and heated *salle* (hall) in the park at 3.15pm and 4.15pm on Wednesday, Saturday and Sunday.

PALAIS DE CHAILLOT Map pp389-91
metro Trocadéro

The two curved, colonnaded wings of the Palais de Chaillot, built for the 1937 World Exhibition held in Paris, and the terrace in between them afford an exceptional panorama of the Jardins du Trocadéro, the Seine and the Eiffel Tower.

At the far eastern tip of the Palais de Chaillot is the main branch of the **Cinémathèque Française** (p238). In its western wing there are two interesting museums. The **Musée de l'Homme** (Museum of Mankind; ☎ 01 44 05 72 72; www .mnhn.fr in French; 17 place du Trocadéro, 16e; adult/child 4-16 yrs €7/3, senior & student €5; ☽ 9.45am-5.15pm Wed-Mon) contains an excellent display on population growth linked with UN databases as well as anthropological and ethnographical exhibits from Africa and Europe (1st floor) and the Americas, the Pacific and the Arctic (2nd floor).

The **Musée de la Marine** (Maritime Museum; ☎ 01 53 65 69 53; www.musee-marine.fr in French; 17 place du Trocadéro; adult €7, senior & student €5.40, under 18 free; ☽ 10am-6pm Wed-Mon) focuses on France's naval adventures from the 17th century until today and boasts one of the world's finest collections of model ships.

JARDINS DU TROCADÉRO Map pp389-91

metro Trocadéro
The Trocadero Gardens, whose fountains and statue garden are grandly illuminated at night, are in the posh 16e, accessible across Pont d'Iéna from the Eiffel Tower. They are named after a Spanish stronghold near Cádiz captured by the French in 1823.

MAISON DE BALZAC Map pp389-91

☎ 01 55 74 41 80; www.paris.fr/musees/balzac in French; 47 rue Raynouard, 16e; metro Passy or Kennedy Radio France; permanent collections admission free, temporary exhibits adult/14-25 yrs €5.50/2.50, senior & student €4, under 14 free; ☾ 10am-6pm Tue-Sun
Balzac's House, about 800m southwest of the Jardins du Trocadéro, is the Passy spa house where the realist novelist Honoré de Balzac (1799–1850) lived and worked (editing the entire *La Comédie Humaine* and writing various books) from 1840 to 1847. There's lots of memorabilia, letters, prints and portraits; this place is decidedly for dyed-in-the-wool Balzac fans only.

MUSÉE DU VIN Map pp389-91

☎ 01 45 25 63 26; www.museeduvinparis.com; 5 square Charles Dickens, 16e; metro Passy; admission €6.50; ☾ 10am-6pm Tue-Sun
The not-so-comprehensive Wine Museum introduces visitors to the fine art of viticulture with mock-ups and displays of tools. Admission includes a wine tasting at the end of the visit, and entry is free if you have lunch at the restaurant attached to the museum.

MUSÉE DE RADIO FRANCE Map pp389-91

☎ 01 56 40 15 16; www.radiofrance.fr/chaines/radio -france/musee in French; 116 av du Président Kennedy, 16e; metro Kennedy Radio France; adult €5, senior & student €3; ☾ 10.30-11.30am & 2.30-4pm
Housed in a curious circular building (1963) fronting the Seine, this museum with the very abbreviated opening hours traces the history of France's most audible mouthpiece radio,

from the transmitter used to establish radio transmission between the Eiffel Tower and the Panthéon in 1898 to Internet broadcasting. Some exhibits focus on TV.

MUSÉE-ATELIER HENRI BOUCHARD

Map pp380-2
☎ 01 46 47 63 46; www.musee-bouchard.com; 25 rue de l'Yvette, 16e; metro Jasmin; adult €4, senior & student €2.50; ☾ 2-7pm Wed & Sat
The workshop of the sculptor Henri Bouchard (1875–1960), who produced some 1300 works in his prolific career, is a jumble sale of sculptures, sketches and tools, and an interesting place to visit to get a feel of how the 16e once was – artsy and creative. The museum is run by the sculptor's son and daughter-in-law.

MUSÉE DU STYLO ET DE L'ÉCRITURE

Map pp380-2
☎ 06 07 94 13 21; 3 rue Guy de Maupassant, 16e; metro Avenue Henri Martin; adult €2, senior & student €1; ☾ 2-6pm Sun
The Museum of the Pen and of Penmanship has the most important collection of writing utensils in the world, with pens dating back to the early 18th century, as well as paper and calligraphy. It can be visited on other days if you phone and book in advance.

MUSÉE DAPPER Map pp383-5

☎ 01 44 00 01 50; www.dapper.com.fr in French; 35 rue Paul Valéry, 16e; metro Victor Hugo; adult €5, senior & student €2.50, under 16 free, last Wed of the month free; ☾ 11am-7pm Wed-Sun
This museum of Sub-Saharan African art collected and exhibited by the nonprofit Dapper Foundation in a 16th-century *hôtel particulier* stages two major exhibitions each year. The collection is mostly of carved wooden figurines and masks, which famously influenced the work of Picasso, Braque and Man Ray.

MUSÉE DU CRISTAL BACCARAT

Map pp383-5
☎ 01 40 22 11 33; www.baccarat.fr; 11 place des États-Unis, 16e; metro Boissière or Kléber; admission €7; ☾ 10am-7pm Mon, Wed, Sat & Sun
That's gratitude for you… For decades the glittering Baccarat Crystal Museum displayed its 1000 stunning pieces of crystal, many of them custom-made for princes and dictators of desperately poor ex-colonies, at the CIAT (Centre International des Arts de la Table) building, a fine example of Napoleon III–era industrial

Top Five

- Musée des Égouts de Paris (p116)
- Eiffel Tower (opposite)
- Musée de l'Homme (opposite)
- Musée Guimet des Arts Asiatiques (p116)
- Palais de Tokyo (p115)

architecture in the gritty but gracious 10e arrondissement. And then the Noailles stately home became available in the uppity 16e, interior designer Philippe Starck was called in and the museum was at home precisely where you'd expect it to be. Shame, rue de Paradis (Paradise St) will never be the same.

MUSÉE GUIMET DES ARTS ASIATIQUES Map pp383-5

☎ 01 56 52 53 00; www.museeguimet.fr; 6 place d'Iéna; metro Iéna; permanent collections adult €5.50 (€4 Sun), student, senior & 18-25 yrs €4, under 18 free, 1st Sun of the month free; ☺ 10am-6pm Wed-Mon

The Guimet Museum of Asiatic Arts is France's foremost repository for Asian art and has sculptures, paintings, *objets d'art* and religious articles from Afghanistan, India, Nepal, Pakistan, Tibet, Cambodia, China, Japan and Korea. The core of the collection – Buddhist paintings and sculptures brought to Paris in 1876 by collector Émile Guimet – is housed in the annexe called the **Galeries du Panthéon Bouddhique du Japon et de la Chine** (Buddhist Pantheon Galleries of Japan & China; ☎ 01 47 23 61 65; 19 av d'Iéna; metro Iéna), in the scrumptious Hôtel Heidelbach a short distance to the north. Don't miss the wonderful Japanese garden here.

MUSÉE GALLIERA DE LA MODE DE LA VILLE DE PARIS Map pp383-5

☎ 01 56 52 86 00; www.paris.fr/musees/musee_galliera; 10 av Pierre 1er de Serbie; metro Iéna; adult/13-25 yrs €7/3.50, student & senior €5.50, under 13 free; ☺ 10am-6pm Tue-Sun

The Fashion Museum of the city of Paris, housed in the 19th-century Palais Galliera, warehouses some 100,000 outfits and accessories from the 18th century to the present day and exhibits them – and items borrowed from abroad – in tremendously successful temporary exhibitions. The sumptuous Italianate building and gardens are worth a visit in themselves.

MUSÉE D'ART MODERNE DE LA VILLE DE PARIS Map pp383-5

☎ 01 53 67 40 00; www.paris.fr/musees/mamvp in French; 11 av du Président Wilson; metro Iéna; permanent collections admission free, temporary exhibits adult/14-25 yrs €4.60/2.30, senior & student €3, under 14 free; ☺ 10am-5.30pm Tue-Fri, 10am-6.45pm Sat & Sun

The Modern Art Museum of the City of Paris, established in 1961 and housed in what was the Electricity Pavilion during the 1937 Exposition Universelle, displays works representative of just about every major artistic movement of the 20th century: Fauvism, cubism, Dadaism, surrealism, the School of Paris, expressionism, abstractionism and so on. Artists with works on display include Matisse, Picasso, Braque, Soutine, Modigliani and Chagall.

PALAIS DE TOKYO Map pp383-5

☎ 01 47 23 38 86; www.palaisdetokyo.com; 13 av Président Wilson; adult €6, senior, student & 18-26 yrs €4, under 18 free, 1st Sun of the month free; ☺ noon-midnight Tue-Sun

The Tokyo Palace, in yet another 1937 World Exhibition building next door to the Musée d'Art Moderne de la Ville de Paris, opened in 2002 as a 'Site de Création Contemporain' (site for contemporary arts). Translation: it has no permanent collection and plans no exhibitions of a single artist or theme but will showcase ephemeral artwork, installations and performances. It's an event-driven rather than a static museum.

FLAME OF LIBERTY MEMORIAL
Map pp383-5
metro Alma-Marceau

Due east of the Palais de Tokyo, over the border to the 8e, is place de l'Alma. On 31 August 1997 in the underpass parallel to the Seine, Diana, Princess of Wales, was killed in a car accident, with her companion, Dodi Fayed, and their chauffeur, Henri Paul. The bronze Flame of Liberty to the east, a replica of the one topping the torch of the Statue of Liberty, was placed here by Paris-based US firms in 1987 on the centenary of the *International Herald Tribune* newspaper as a symbol of friendship between France and the USA. It became something of a memorial to Diana and was decorated with flowers, photographs, graffiti and personal notes for almost five years. It was renovated and cleaned in 2002 and, this being the age of short memories, there are few reminders of the tragedy that happened so close by.

MUSÉE DES ÉGOUTS DE PARIS
Map pp389-91

☎ 01 53 68 27 81; place de la Résistance, 7e; metro Pont de l'Alma; adult €3.80, student & 5-16 yrs €3.05, under 5 free; ☺ 11am-6pm Sat-Wed May-Sep, 11am-5pm Sat-Wed Oct-Apr

The Paris Sewers Museum is a working museum whose entrance, a rectangular maintenance hole topped with a kiosk, is across the street from 93 quai d'Orsay, 7e. Raw sewage flows beneath your feet as you walk through 480m of odoriferous tunnels, passing artefacts illustrating the development of Paris' waste-water disposal system. It'll take your breath away, it will. The sewers keep regular hours except, God forbid, when rain threatens to flood the tunnels.

ÉTOILE & CHAMPS-ÉLYSÉES

Eating p186; Shopping p262; Sleeping p297

The **8e arrondissement** was born under a lucky star. Its avenues radiate from place de l'Étoile – officially place Charles de Gaulle – bathing in the glow of fame. First among them is the av des Champs-Élysées. From the Arc de Triomphe to the place de la Concorde, this broad boulevard rules supreme. On New Year's Eve and after major sporting victories there's always a party on the Champs. Like a splendid, regal hostess,

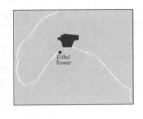
Eiffel Tower

the avenue receives its guests, makes them mingle and moves them along. And the guests keep coming. Just a short walk away, the av Montaigne haughtily displays its designer wares. Motorboats are moored by the pont de l'Alma. And members of the jet-set go shopping in the av George V and the rue du Faubourg St-Honoré. Here fashion, art and luxury hotels go hand in hand. Only the finest are on display, as in the neighbourhood's theatres and museums, such as the Grand Palais.

Transport

Bus av des Champs-Élysées for No 73 to La Défense (west) & Musée d'Orsay (east), for No 42 to Grands Boulevards, Opéra & Gare du Nord

Metro Champs-Élysées Clemenceau, Charles de Gaulle-Étoile, Franklin D Roosevelt, George V

Boat Champs-Élysées Batobus stop (Port des Champs-Élysées)

ARC DE TRIOMPHE Map pp383-5

☎ 01 55 37 73 77, 01 44 95 02 10; www.monum.fr; metro Charles de Gaulle-Étoile; viewing platform adult/18-25 yrs €7/4.50, under 18 free, 1st Sun of the month free; ☯ 9.30am-11pm Apr-Sep, 10am-10.30pm Oct-Mar

The Triumphal Arch is 2km northwest of place de la Concorde in the middle of place Charles de Gaulle (or place de l'Étoile), the world's largest traffic roundabout and the meeting point of 12 avenues (and three arrondissements). It was commissioned in 1806 by Napoleon to commemorate his imperial victories but remained unfinished when he started losing – first battles and then whole wars. It was finally completed in 1836. Among the armies to march triumphantly through the Arc de Triomphe were the Germans in 1871, the Allies in 1919, the Germans again in 1940 and the Allies in 1944. Since 1920, the body of an Unknown Soldier from WWI taken from Ver-

dun in the Lorraine has lain beneath the arch, his fate and that of countless others like him commemorated by a **memorial flame** rekindled each evening around 6.30pm. In July 1998 a drunken Mexican football fan celebrating France's victory over Brazil in the World Cup (p16) urinated on the flame and extinguished it. He was arrested and charged with public drunkenness and offending the dead.

The most famous of the four high-relief panels is to the right, facing the arch from the av des Champs-Élysées side. Entitled *Départ des Volontaires de 1792* (Departure of the Volunteers of 1792) and also known as *La Marseillaise* (France's national anthem), it is the work of François Rude. Higher up, a frieze running around the whole monument depicts hundreds of figures, each one 2m high.

From the viewing platform on top of the arch (284 steps and well worth the climb) you can see the 12 avenues – many of them named after Napoleonic victories and illustrious generals – radiating toward every part of Paris. Av de la Grande Armée heads northwest to the skyscraper district of **La Défense** (p133), where the **Grande Arche**, a hollow cube 110m on each side, defines the western end of the Grand Axe (the Louvre-Arc de Triomphe axis). Tickets to the viewing platform of the Arc de Triomphe are sold in the underground passageway that surfaces on the even-numbered side of av des Champs-Élysées. It is the only *sane* way to get to the base of the arch and is *not* linked to nearby metro tunnels. Driving around the roundabout – where motorists already on it have right of way – is Paris' ultimate driving challenge, especially during rush hour.

AV DES CHAMPS-ÉLYSÉES Map pp383-5
metro Charles de Gaulle-Étoile, George V, Franklin D Roosevelt or Champs-Élysées Clemenceau

Av des Champs-Élysées, (the name refers to the 'Elysian Fields' where happy souls dwelt after death according to Greek myth), links place de la Concorde with the Arc de Triomphe. The avenue has symbolised the style and *joie de vivre* of Paris since the mid-19th century and remains a popular tourist destination.

Some 400m north of av des Champs-Élysées is rue du Faubourg St-Honoré (8e), the western extension of rue St-Honoré. It has renowned couture houses, jewellers, antique shops (p263) and the 18th-century **Palais de l'Élysée** (cnr rue du Faubourg St-Honoré & av de Marigny, 8e; metro Champs-Élysées Clemenceau), the official residence of the French president.

GRAND PALAIS Map pp383-5
☎ 01 44 13 17 17; www.rmn.fr; 3 av du Général Eisenhower, 8e; metro Champs-Élysées Clemenceau; with/without booking adult €10/9; student, senior & everyone on Mon €8/7, under 18 free, 1st Sun of the month free; ☻ without booking 1-8pm Thu-Mon, 1-10pm Wed; with booking 10am-8pm Thu-Mon, 10am-10pm Wed

The 'Great Palace', erected for the 1900 Exposition Universelle, houses the **Galeries Nationales du Grand Palais** beneath its huge Art Nouveau glass roof. Special exhibitions, among the biggest the city stages, last three or four months.

PETIT PALAIS Map pp383-5
☎ 01 42 65 12 73, 01 44 51 19 31; www.paris.fr /musees/petit_palais/index.html in French; av Winston Churchill, 8e; metro Champs-Élysées Clemenceau

The 'Little Palace', also built for the 1900 fair, is home to the **Musée des Beaux-Arts de la Ville de Paris**, the Paris municipality's Museum of Fine Arts, with medieval and Renaissance *objets d'art*, tapestries, drawings and 19th-century French painting and sculpture. It was closed at the time of research; expected to reopen in 2005.

PALAIS DE LA DÉCOUVERTE
Map pp383-5

☎ 01 56 43 20 21; www.palais-decouverte.fr in French; av Franklin D Roosevelt, 8e; metro Champs-Élysées Clemenceau; adult €6, senior, student & 5-18 yrs €3.90, under 5 free; ☻ 9.30am-6pm Tue-Sat, 10am-7pm Sun

The Palace of Discovery, inaugurated during the 1937 Exposition Universelle and thus the world's first interactive museum, is a fascinating science museum with interactive exhibits on astronomy, biology, medicine, chemistry, mathematics, computer science, physics and earth sciences. The **planetarium** (admission €3.50 extra) usually has four shows a day in French; ring or consult the website for current schedules.

CONCORDE & MADELEINE
Drinking p224; Shopping p263

The cobblestone expanses of 18th-century place de la Concorde are sandwiched between the Jardin des Tuileries and the parks at the eastern end of av des Champs-Élysées. Delightful place de la Madeleine is to the north. Both are in the **8e arrondissement**.

Transport

Bus place de la Concorde & place de la Madeleine for No 24 to quai du Louvre, Pont Neuf, blvd St-Michel, quai St Bernard & Bercy, for No 84 for Musée d'Orsay, blvd St-Germain, Jardin du Luxembourg & Panthéon

Metro Concorde, Madeleine

Boat Champs-Élysées Batobus stop (Port des Champs-Élysées)

PLACE DE LA CONCORDE Map pp383-5
Place de la Concorde was laid out between 1755 and 1775. The 3300-year-old pink granite **obelisk** with the gilded top in the centre of the square was given to France in 1831 by Muhammad Ali, viceroy and pasha of Egypt. Weighing 230 tonnes and towering 23m over the cobblestones, it once stood in the Temple of Ramses at Thebes (modern-day Luxor). The eight **female statues** adorning the four corners of the square represent France's largest cities.

In 1793, Louis XVI's head was lopped off by a guillotine set up in the northwest corner of the square near the statue representing the city of Brest. During the next two years, another guillotine – this one near the entrance to the Jardin des Tuileries – was used to behead 1343 more people, including Marie-Antoinette and, six months later, the Revolutionary leader Danton. Shortly thereafter, Robespierre lost his head here, too. The square was given its present name after the Reign of Terror had come to an end in the hope that it would be a place of peace and harmony.

The two imposing buildings on the north side of Place de la Concorde are the **Hôtel de la Marine**, headquarters of the French Navy, and the **Hôtel de Crillon** (p291), one of Paris' most luxurious and exclusive hotels. In 1778, the treaty by which France recognised the independence of the new USA was signed in the Hôtel de Crillon by Louis XVI and Benjamin Franklin.

PLACE DE LA MADELEINE Map pp383-5

Ringed by a plethora of fine-food and gourmet shops, the place de la Madeline is named after the 19th-century neoclassical church in its centre, the **Église de la Madeleine** (Church of St Mary Magdalene; ☎ 01 44 51 69 00; rue Royale, 8e; metro Madeleine; ☼ 7.30am-7pm Mon-Sat, 7.30am-1.30pm & 3.30-7pm Sun), which is 350m north of place de la Concorde along rue Royale. Constructed in the style of a Greek temple, La Madeleine was consecrated in 1845 after almost a century of design changes and construction delays. It is surrounded by 52 Corinthian columns standing 20m tall, and the marble and gilt interior is topped by three sky-lit cupolas. You can hear the massive organ being played at Mass on Saturday at 6pm and on Sunday at 11am and 6pm.

The **monumental staircase** on the south side affords one of the city's most quintessential Parisian panoramas: down rue Royale to place de la Concorde (and the obelisk) and on across the Seine to the Assemblée Nationale. The gold dome of the Invalides appears in the background, a bit to the right of the Assemblée Nationale.

Paris' cheapest *belle époque* attraction is the **public toilet** on the east side of La Madeleine, which dates from 1905. There has been a **flower market** (☼ 8am-7.30pm Mon-Sat) on the east side of the church since 1832.

CLICHY & GARE ST-LAZARE

Drinking p224; Eating p188; Sleeping p298

This area stretches from the elegant residential districts of the *haute bourgeoisie* that surround 8.25-hectare Parc de Monceau (metro Monceau) in the 8e eastward to the Gare St-Lazare and then north to Clichy and the **17e arrondissement**.

The 17e suffers from acute schizophrenia. Its southern neighbourhoods – with their beautiful, Haussmann-era buildings – seem like an extension of the 8e and 16e arrondis-

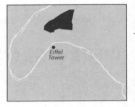

Eiffel Tower

sements, while its northern neighbourhoods assert their working-class, anarchistic identity. The wide av de Wagram, av des Ternes and av de Villiers have both a residential and commercial vocation and boast some of the capital's most famous shops and restaurants. A maze of small streets with a pronounced working-class character stretches out around the av de Clichy, a pocket of old Paris that has survived without becoming ossified.

Transport

Bus place de Clichy for No 68 to Opéra, Musée d'Orsay, rue du Bac, St-Germain & blvd du Montparnasse; Gare St-Lazare for No 21 to Opéra, Latin Quarter, Jardin du Luxembourg & Cité Universitaire

Metro Malesherbes, Monceau, Place de Clichy Rome, St-Lazare, Villiers

Train Gare St-Lazare

MUSÉE JACQUEMART-ANDRÉ

Map pp383-5

☎ 01 45 62 11 59; www.musee-jacquemart-andre .com; 158 blvd Haussmann, 8e; metro Miromesnil; adult/family €8.50/26.50, student & 7-17 yrs €6.50, under 7 free; ☼ 10am-6pm Tue-Sun, 10am-10pm Mon

The Jacquemart-André Museum, founded by collector Édouard André and his portraitist wife Nélie Jacquemart, is in an opulent mid-19th century residence. It contains furniture, tapestries and enamels but is most noted for its paintings by Rembrandt and Van Dyck and

Italian Renaissance works by Bernini, Botticelli, Carpaccio, Donatello, Mantegna, Tintoretto, Titian and Uccello. The museum is often compared to the Frick Collection in New York. The relatively high price of admission includes an audioguide. Don't miss the Jardin d'Hiver (Winter Garden), with its marble statuary, tropical plants and double-helix marble staircase.

MUSÉE NISSIM DE CAMONDO
Map pp383-5

☎ 01 53 89 06 40; www.ucad.fr; 63 rue de Monceau, 8e; metro Monceau or Villiers; adult €4.60, 18-25 yrs €3.10, under 18 free; 🕒 10am-5pm Wed-Sun

The Nissim de Camondo Museum, housed in a sumptuous mansion modelled on the Petit Trianon at Versailles (p308), displays 18th-century furniture, wood panelling, tapestries, porcelain and other *objets d'art* collected by Count Moïse de Camondo, a Jewish banker who settled in Paris from Constantinople in the late 19th century. He bequeathed the mansion and his collection to the state on the proviso that it would be a museum named in memory of his son Nissim, a pilot killed in 1917 during WWI.

MUSÉE CERNUSCHI Map pp383-5

☎ 01 45 63 50 75; www.paris.fr/musees/cernuschi; 7 av Vélasquez, 8e; metro Villiers; permanent collection admission free; 🕒 10am-6pm Tue-Sun

The Cernuschi Museum, closed for renovations at the time of writing, will reopen in late 2004. It houses a collection of ancient Chinese art (funerary statues, bronzes, ceramics) and works from Japan assembled during a 1871–3 world tour by the banker and philanthropist Henri Cernuschi (1820–96), who settled here from Milan before the unification of Italy.

MUSÉE JEAN-JACQUES HENNER
Map pp383-5

☎ 01 47 63 42 73; www.rmn.fr; 43 av de Villiers, 17e; metro Malesherbes; admission free; 🕒 10am-noon & 2-5pm Tue-Sun

This museum pays homage to the Alsatian *belle époque* painter Jean-Jacques Henner (1829–1905) who specialised in portraits and female nudes with red hair.

CHAPELLE EXPIATOIRE Map pp383-5

☎ 01 44 32 18 00; square Louis XVI, opp 29 rue Pasquier, 8e; metro St-Augustin; admission €2.50, under 18 free; 🕒 1-5pm Thu-Sat

The austere, neoclassical Atonement Chapel sits atop the section of a cemetery where Louis XVI, Marie-Antoinette and many other victims of the Reign of Terror were buried after their executions in 1793. It was erected by Louis' brother, the restored Bourbon king Louis XVIII, in 1815.

OPÉRA & GRANDS BOULEVARDS

Drinking p225; Eating p189; Shopping p265; Sleeping p298

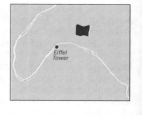

Place de l'Opéra, site of Paris' world-famous opera house, abuts the Grands Boulevards, the eight contiguous 'Grands Boulevards' (Madeleine, Capucines, Italiens, Montmartre, Poissonnière, Bonne Nouvelle, St-Denis and St-Martin) that stretch from elegant place de la Madeleine (Map pp383–5) in the 8e eastwards to the less-than-desirable place de la République (Map pp386–8) in the 3e, a distance of just under 3km. The Grands Boulevards were laid out in the 17th century on the site of obsolete city walls and served as a centre of café and theatre life in the 18th and 19th centuries, reaching the height of fashion during the *belle époque*. North of the western end of the Grands Boulevards is blvd Haussmann (8e and 9e), the heart of the commercial and banking district and known for some of Paris' most famous department stores, including Galeries Lafayette and Le Printemps (p265).

Place de l'Opéra and the lion's share of the Grands Boulevards are in the 9e arrondissement, a somewhat misleading district where the smart set and the riff-raff, the foodies and the gluttons all rub shoulders. It's not in the least uncommon to find wildly different establishments just across the road or round the corner from one other. Leaving the Opéra or Drouot auction house in the southern part of the arrondissement, you can wander and window shop on the boulevards. Department stores and little boutiques jostle for space on blvd Haussmann and blvd des Capucines. On rue de Provence, rue Richer and rue du Faubourg-Montmartre, fast-food outlets and restaurants are crammed into every bit of space, and you'll hear a babel of languages.

PALAIS GARNIER Map pp383-5

☎ 08 92 89 90 90, tours ☎ 01 40 01 22 63; place de l'Opéra, 9e; metro Opéra; tour €10; ☽ 10.30am & noon late Jul–early Sep)

This renowned opera house was designed in 1860 by Charles Garnier to showcase the splendour of Napoleon III's France. Unfortunately, by the time it was completed 15 years later, the Second Empire was a distant memory (p68) and Napoleon III was six feet under. Still it is one of the most impressive monuments erected in Paris during the 19th century and today stages operas, ballets and classical-music concerts (p241). In summer it can be visited on English-language guided tours.

The Palais Garnier houses the **Musée de l'Opéra** (☎ 01 47 42 07 02, 01 40 01 22 63; www.opera-de-paris.fr in French; adult €6, senior, student & 10-26 yrs €3, under 10 free; ☽ 10am-5pm Sep-Jun, 10am-6pm Jul & Aug), which contains a lot of documentation (it also functions as an important research library) and some memorabilia. More interestingly, admission to the museum includes a visit to the opera house itself as long as there's not a daytime rehearsal or performance going on.

MUSÉE DU PARFUM FRAGONARD

Map pp383-5

☎ 01 47 42 04 56; www.fragonard.com; 9 rue Scribe, 2e; metro Opéra; admission free; ☽ 9am-5.30pm Mon-Sat, 9.30am-4.30pm Sun Apr-Oct, 9am-5.30pm Mon-Sat Nov-Mar

The Fragonard Perfume Museum is a fragrant collection opposite the Palais Garnier, which traces the history of scent and perfume-making from ancient Egypt (those mummies wouldn't have smelled very nice undoused) to today's designer brands. A short distance to the south in the old Théâtre des Capucines is the **museum annexe** (Map pp383-5; ☎ 01 42 60 37 14; 39 blvd

Transport

Bus Opéra for No 20 to République, Bastille & Gare de Lyon, for No 22 to Charles de Gaulle, place de l'Étoile & Trocadéro, and for No 29 to place des Victoires, Marais & Bastille,

Metro Cadet, Grands Boulevards, Opéra

des Capucines, 2e; metro Opéra), which concentrates on bottling (for example, crystal flasks from Bohemia), packaging and marketing the heady stuff.

MUSÉE GRÉVIN Map pp386-8

☎ 01 47 70 85 05; www.grevin.com; 10 blvd Montmartre, 9e; metro Grands Boulevards; adult/student/6-14 yrs €16/13.80/9; ☽ 10am-6.30pm Mon-Fri, 10am-7pm Sat & Sun

This recently renovated waxworks museum inside the passage Jouffroy boasts 250 wax figures that look more like caricatures than characters, but where else do you get to see Marilyn Monroe and Charles de Gaulle face to face or the real death masks of French Revolutionary leaders? The admission fee is positively outrageous and just keeps growing.

MUSÉE INTERNATIONALE DE LA FRANC-MAÇONNERIE Map pp386-8

☎ 01 45 23 20 92; 16 rue Cadet, 9e; metro Cadet; admission €2; ☽ 2-6pm Tue-Sat

This museum housed in the colossal and quite impressive Grande Orient de France building provides a brief introduction to the secretive world of freemasonry, which grew out of medieval stone masons' guilds of the 16th century.

GARE DU NORD, GARE DE L'EST & RÉPUBLIQUE

Drinking p225; Eating p191; Shopping p266; Sleeping p299

Two sorts of foot traffic give the **10e arrondissement** its distinctive feel. The canal banks draw leisurely strollers, while travellers part and are reunited on the platforms of the Gare du Nord and Gare de l'Est. Each arrival and departure announced over the loudspeakers produces a burst of frenetic

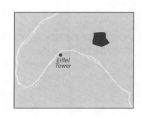

Eiffel Tower

activity. Outside, the cafés and brasseries do a brisk trade, catering to travellers and locals. Nearby, the blvd de Magenta rushes like a swollen river, the noisy, impatient crowd spreading through the adjoining streets and pouring out onto the place de la République.

The buzzy working-class area around blvd de Strasbourg and rue du Faubourg St-Denis, especially south of blvd de Magenta, is home to large communities of Indians, Bangladeshis, Pakistanis, West Indians, Africans, Turks and Kurds. Strolling through passage Brady (p193) is almost like stepping into a back alley in Mumbai or Dhaka.

Canal St-Martin, especially the quai de Jemmapes and the quai de Valmy with their rows of plane and chestnut trees, seems a world away. Barges appear, pass silently, then vanish behind a lock. Little iron bridges and walkways span the still water. Run-down until recently, the canal is getting spruced up and bistros too are now getting into the act.

Transport

Bus Gare de l'Est for No 30 to Barbès, Pigalle, Place Clichy, Parc Monceau, place des Ternes, place de l'Étoile & Trocadéro, for No 31 to Barbès, Château Rouge, 18e arrondissement Mairie, Batignolles & place de l'Étoile, for No 32 to Rond Point des Champs-Élysées, av des Champs-Élysées & Passy, for No 39 to Palais Royal, St-Germain, rue de Sèvres & Porte de Versailles, for No 47 to Centre Pompidou & Châtelet

Metro & RER Château d'Eau, Gare de l'Est, Gare du Nord, République, Strasbourg St-Denis

Train Gare de l'Est, Gare du Nord

CANAL ST-MARTIN Map pp386-8
metro République, Jaurès, Jacques Bonsergent
The tranquil, 4.5km-long St-Martin Canal, which has undergone a major renovation and clean-up recently, links the 10e with Parc de la Villette (Map pp380–2) in the 19e via the Bassin de la Villette and Canal de l'Ourcq and the canal makes its famous dogleg turn in this arrondissement. Its shaded towpaths are a wonderful place for a romantic stroll or a bike ride and take you past nine locks, metal bridges and ordinary Parisian neighbourhoods. Parts of the waterway – built between 1806 and 1825 to link the Seine with the 108km-long Canal de l'Ourcq – are higher than the surrounding land. The best way to see the canal is from a canal barge (p77).

PORTE ST-DENIS & PORTE ST-MARTIN Map pp386-8
cnr rue du Faubourg St-Denis & blvd St-Denis, 10e;
metro Strasbourg St-Denis
Porte St-Denis a 24m-high triumphal arch, was built in 1673 to commemorate Louis XIV's campaign along the Rhine. On the northern side, carvings represent the fall of Maastricht in the same year.

Two blocks east is a similar arch, the 17m-high Porte St-Martin at the corner of rue du Faubourg St-Martin and blvd St-Denis. It was erected two years later to commemorate the capture of Besançon and the Franche-Comté region by Louis XIV's armies.

MUSÉE DE L'ÉVANTAIL Map pp386-8
☎ 01 42 08 90 20; 2 blvd de Strasbourg, 10e; metro Strasbourg St-Denis; adult/senior/student €5/3.50/2.50; ☻ permanent collection 2-6pm Mon-Wed, temporary exhibitions 2-6pm Mon-Fri
Big fans of this museum, we always find it impossible to walk by without checking in on our favourite fans – screen, folding and *brisé* (the kind with overlapping struts). Around 900 fans are on display, dating as far back as the mid-18th century. The small museum is housed in what was once a well-known fan manufactory and its original showroom, dating from 1893, is sublime.

Street performer, Canal St-Martin

MÉNILMONTANT & BELLEVILLE

Drinking p226; Eating p194; Sleeping p301

A solidly working-class *quartier* with little to recommend it until just a few years ago, Ménilmontant, which shares the 11e arrondissement with Bastille (p86), now boasts a surfeit of restaurants, bars and clubs to rival those of the Marais. On the other hand, the inner-city 'village' of Belleville, centred on blvd de Belleville in the 20e to the east, remains for the most part unpretentious and working-class and is home to

large numbers of immigrants, especially Muslims and Jews from North Africa and Vietnamese and ethnic Chinese from Indochina (p147). The **20e arrondissement** has retained its working-class character. The city centre is far away, the Eiffel Tower but a beacon on the horizon; this Paris is rough and rebellious, friendly and alive. The multicultural tone of rue de Belleville and rue de Ménilmontant is amplified by blvd de Belleville, blvd de Ménilmontant and blvd de Charonne. The air is filled with the aroma of coriander, saffron and cumin, and the exotic sounds of languages from faraway lands. A colourful, abundant market spills out over the footpaths of blvd de Belleville.

Transport

Bus rue de Ménilmontant for No 96 to rue Oberkampf, St-Paul, Hôtel de Ville, blvd St-Michel, Odéon & rue de Rennes; rue des Pyrénées for No 26 to Parc des Buttes Chaumont, Gare du Nord & Gare St-Lazare

Metro Belleville, Couronnes, Ménilmontant, Oberkampf

PARC DE BELLEVILLE Map pp386–8
metro Couronnes

This lovely park, which opened in 1992 a few blocks east of blvd de Belleville, occupies a hill almost 200m above sea level amid 4.5 hectares of greenery. It offers superb views of the city. The **Maison de l'Air** (☎ 01 43 28 47 63; 27 rue Piat, 20e; metro Pyrénées; adult €2, senior & student €1; ☺ 1.30-5.30pm Tue-Sat, 1.30-6.30pm Sun Apr-Sep, 1.30-5pm Tue-Sun Oct-Mar) stages temporary exhibitions related to ecology and the environment.

MUSÉE ÉDITH PIAF Map pp386–8
☎ 01 43 55 52 72; 5 rue Crespin du Gast, 11e; metro Ménilmontant; admission free; ☺ by appointment 1-6pm Mon-Thu

Some 1.5km from the birthplace of the iconic chanteuse (1915–63) and even closer to her final resting place in the Cimetière du Père Lachaise, the small Édith Piaf museum follows the life and career of the 'urchin sparrow' (p234) through memorabilia, recordings and video.

MUSÉE DU FUMEUR Map pp392–5
☎ 01 46 59 05 51; 7 rue Pache, 11e; metro Voltaire; admission free; ☺ 11.30am-7.30pm Tue-Sat, 12.30-7.30pm Sun

The Smoking Museum traces the history of one of man's greatest vices: the smoking of tobacco and other substances of various strengths and weaknesses. Hard-core butt-fiends will feel vindicated, though the museum takes an impartial stance.

CIMETIÈRE DU PÈRE LACHAISE
Map pp380–2
☎ 01 55 25 82 10; metro Philippe Auguste, Gambetta or Père Lachaise; ☺ 8am-6pm Mon-Fri, 8.30am-6pm Sat, 9am-6pm Sun mid-Mar–early Nov

The world's most visited cemetery, Père Lachaise (named after the confessor of Louis XIV) opened its one-way doors in 1804. Its 70,000 ornate, even ostentatious, tombs of the rich and/or famous form a verdant sculpture garden. Among the one million people buried here are Chopin, Molière, Apollinaire, Oscar Wilde, Balzac, Proust, Gertrude Stein, Colette, Simone Signoret, Pissarro, Seurat, Modigliani, Sarah Bernhardt, Yves Montand, Delacroix, Édith Piaf, Isadora Duncan and even those immortal 12th-century lovers, Abélard and Héloïse (p26). One particularly frequented grave is that of 1960s rock star **Jim Morrison**, who died in an apartment at 17-19 rue Beautreillis (4e; Map pp396–9) in the Marais in 1971 and is buried in Division 6.

On 27 May 1871, the last of the Communard insurgents, cornered by government forces, fought a hopeless, all-night battle among the tombstones. In the morning, the 147 survivors were lined up against the **Mur des Fédérés** (Wall of the Federalists), shot, and buried where they fell in a mass grave.

Père Lachaise has four entrances, two of which are on blvd de Ménilmontant. Maps indicating the location of noteworthy graves are posted around the cemetery including one by the **conservation office** (16 rue du Repos, 20e)

on the western side of the cemetery. Better yet, newsstands and flower kiosks in the area, especially those by the metro stations, sell the primitive but useful *Plan Illustré du Père Lachaise* (Illustrated Map of Père Lachaise) for €2. Two-hour **English-language tours** (☎ 01 40 71 75 60; adult/under 25 €9/6) leave from the main entrance near the conservation office usually at 3pm on Saturday from June to September.

GARE DE LYON, NATION & BERCY

Drinking p227; Eating p197; Shopping p267; Sleeping p302

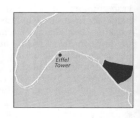

The southern part of the 12e arrondissement, which borders on the Bois de Vincennes, is fairly well-to-do, and at the weekend hordes of cyclists and soccer players head for the woods. But walkers can also clear away the cobwebs with a stroll along the Promenade Plantée, a green footpath along the av Daumesnil viaduct. At the foot of the arches, shops, art galleries and cafés have opened up one by one. On the other side of the Gare de Lyon, you can take a break in the very pretty parc de Bercy, where an orchard, a vegetable patch and a garden have replaced the old wine market.

Long cut off from the rest of the city by railway tracks and the Seine but now joined to the Left Bank by the driverless Météor metro line (no 14) and Pont Charles de Gaulle (1996), Bercy has some of Paris' most important new buildings, including the octagonal Palais Omnisports de Paris-Bercy (Map p401), designed to serve as both an indoor sports arena and a venue for concerts, ballet and theatre, and the giant Ministry of Finance (Map pp392–5). The development of Bercy Village (Map p401), a row of former wine warehouses dating from 1877 that now house bars and restaurants, and the arrival of river barges fitted out with more glitzy eateries and music clubs has turned the 12e into a seriously happening district.

Transport

Bus Gare de Lyon for No 65 to Bastille, République, Gare de l'Est. Gare du Nord (via rue du Faubourg St-Denis); place de la Nation for No 86 to Ledru Rollin (Marché d'Aligre), Bastille, Pont Sully (Île St-Louis) & Odéon; Bercy (rue de Bercy) for No 24 to quai St Bernard, blvd St-Michel, Pont Neuf, quai du Louvre, place de la Madeleine & place de la Concorde

Metro & RER Bercy, Cour St-Émilion, Daumesnil, Gare de Lyon, Nation

Train Gare de Lyon

and artisans; if you need your Gobelins tapestry restored, the bottom of an antique saucepan re-coppered or a gilded frame made good again, this is the place for you. The top of the viaduct forms a leafy, 4km-long promenade called the **Promenade Plantée** (☻ 8am-5.30pm to 6.30pm Mon-Fri, 9am-5.30pm to 6.30pm Sat & Sun Oct–mid-Apr, 8am-7pm to 9.30pm Mon-Fri, 9am-7pm to 9.30pm Sat & Sun mid-Apr–Sep), which offers excellent views of the surrounding area. Don't miss the spectacular Art Deco **police station** (85 av Daumesnil, 12e), opposite rue de Rambouillet, which is topped with a dozen huge marble torsos.

VIADUC DES ARTS Map pp392-5
metro Gare de Lyon or Daumesnil

The arches beneath this disused railway viaduct southeast of place de la Bastille along av Daumesnil, which was taken out of service in 1969, are now a showcase for trendy designers

PARC DE BERCY Map p401
41 rue Paul Belmondo, 12e; metro Bercy or Cour St-Émilion; ☻ **8am-5.30pm to 9.30pm Mon-Fri, 9am-5.30pm to 9.30pm Sat & Sun**

This park, which links the Palais Omnisports with Bercy Village, is a particularly attractive 14-

hectare public garden. On an island in the centre of one of its large ponds is the **Maison du Lac de Parc de Bercy** (☎ 01 53 46 19 34; ☽ 10am-6pm Apr-Sep, 11am-5pm Oct-Mar), with temporary exhibitions.

The **Maison du Jardinage** (☎ 01 53 46 19 19; ☽ 1.30-5.30pm Tue-Fri, 1.30-6.30pm Sat & Sun Apr-Sep; 1.30-5.30pm Tue-Sun Mar & Oct, 1.30-5pm Tue-Sat Nov-Feb) in the centre of the park takes a close look at gardening and the environment.

MUSÉE DES ARTS FORAINS Map p401

☎ 01 43 40 16 22; www.pavillons-de-bercy.com in French; Les Pavillons de Bercy, 53 av des Terroirs de France, 12e; metro Cour St-Émilion; adult €5, senior & student €4; ☽ by appointment

The Museum of the Fairground Arts in trendy Bercy Village, housed in an old *chai* (wine warehouse), is a wonderful collection of old amusements from 19th-century funfairs – carrousels, organs, stalls etc. Most of the items still work and are pure works of art.

13E ARRONDISSEMENT & CHINATOWN

Drinking p228; Eating p199; Sleeping p302

The **13e arrondissement** begins a few blocks south of the Jardin des Plantes in the 5e and is undergoing a true renaissance following the opening of the Bibliothèque Nationale de France François Mitterrand, the arrival of the high-speed Météor metro line and the start of the massive ZAC Paris Rive Gauche redevelopment project (p40). The stylishness of the neighbouring 5e extends to the av des Gobelins, while further south, between av d'Italie and av de Choisy, the succession of Asian restaurants, stalls and shops in the capital's version of Chinatown (Map p401) gives passers-by the illusion of having imperceptibly changed continents. This place is proud of its history. A working-class district if ever there was one, it's home to both a place Nationale and a blvd Auguste Blanqui, a pairing propitious to the reconciliation between anarchism and patriotism. At the butte aux Cailles, the jewel in this arrondissement's crown, people still sing revolutionary songs from the time of the Paris Commune.

Transport

Bus Bibliothèque Nationale de France François Mitterrand for No 62 through 13e along rue Tolbiac to rue d'Alésia (14e) & rue de la Convention (15e); porte d'Italie for No 47 to place d'Italie, rue Monge, quai St Michel, Hôtel de Ville & Gare de l'Est; place d'Italie for No 67 to Mosquée de Paris, Jardin des Plantes, Île de St-Louis, Hôtel de Ville & Pigalle

Metro & RER Bibliothèque François Mitterrand, Porte de Choisy, Porte d'Italie, Place d'Italie

BIBLIOTHÈQUE NATIONALE DE FRANCE Map p401

☎ 01 53 79 53 79; www.bnf.fr; 11 quai François Mauriac, 13e; metro Bibliothèque; admission 2 days/year €4.50/46; ☽ 10am-8pm Tue-Sat, noon-7pm Sun

Across the Seine from Bercy are the four glass towers of the late President François Mitterrand's controversial €2 billion National Library of France, conceived as a 'wonder of the modern world' and opened in 1998. No expense was spared to carry out a plan that many said defied logic. While books and historical documents were shelved in the sunny, 23-storey and 79m-high towers (shaped like half-open books), patrons sat in artificially lit basement halls built around a 'forest courtyard' of 140 50-year-old pines, trucked in from the countryside. The towers have since been fitted with a complex (and expensive) shutter system and the basement is prone to flooding from the Seine. The national library contains around 12 million tomes stored on some 420km of shelves and can hold 2000 readers and 2000 researchers.

MANUFACTURE DES GOBELINS

Map pp380-2

☎ 01 44 08 52 00; 42 av des Gobelins, 13e; metro Les Gobelins; adult/8-25 yrs €8/6, under 8 free; ☽ guided tour 2pm & 2.45pm Tue-Thu

The Gobelins Factory has been weaving *haute lisse* (high-relief) tapestries on specialised looms since the 18th century along with Beauvais-style *basse lisse* (low-relief) ones and Savonnerie rugs.

15E ARRONDISSEMENT

Eating p200; Sleeping p302

After the war, entire battalions of steelworkers were drawn into the orbit of the **15e arrondissement** (Map pp389-91), clocking in every morning at the Citroën factory or one of the neighbourhood's numerous aeronautical companies. Over the years, the area has become more gentrified and residential. Av de la Motte-Picquet, blvd Pasteur and av Félix Faure are peaceful places – too peaceful for some tastes. For Unesco, the area seemed just right and, not far away, the republic's future officers converge on the

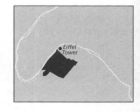

majestic École Militaire. But the 15e offers much more than bourgeois homes and institutions. Parisians flock to the shops and restaurants that line rue de la Convention, rue de Vaugirard, rue St-Charles and rue du Commerce. On the quays, the towers of the Centre Beaugrenelle have long since abandoned their monopoly on futurism to the stylish, functional buildings occupied by television stations Canal Plus and France Télévision, and Parisians with their heart in the country can enjoy the parc André-Citroën, one of the capital's most beautiful open spaces.

Transport

Bus blvd de Grenelle for No 80 to Alma-Marceau, av Montaigne, av Matignon, Gare St-Lazare, Place Clichy and Lamarck Caulaincourt; rue de Vaugirard for No 89 to Jardin du Luxembourg, Panthéon, Jardin des Plantes, Gare d'Austerliz and Bibliothèque Nationale de France François Mitterrand

Metro Commerce, Convention, Duroc, La Motte-Picquet Grenelle, Vaugirard

MONTMARTRE & PIGALLE

Drinking p228; Eating p202; Shopping p267; Sleeping p302

During the late 19th and early 20th centuries the bohemian lifestyle of Montmartre in the 18e attracted a number of important writers and artists, many of whom lived at a studio called Bateau Lavoir at 11bis place Émile Goudeau between 1892 and 1930. Picasso worked from here between 1908 and 1912 during his so-called Blue Period.

Although the activity shifted to Montparnasse after WWI, the **18e arrondissement** thrives on crowds and a strong sense of community. Its old-fashioned village atmosphere is lovingly preserved without being dolled up. When you've got Montmartre and Sacré Coeur, what more do you need? Cascading steps, streets with old cobblestones, small houses with wooden shutters in narrow, quiet lanes… The charm of the Butte de Montmartre (Montmartre Hill) is eternal. Rue Caulaincourt and rue Junot flaunt their bourgeois credentials, while the streets around the square Willette, place des Abbesses and rue Lepic become steeper and narrower, the inhabitants younger and hipper. The northern part of the **9e arrondissement** has a rough and ready charm. The lights of the Moulin Rouge dominate blvd de Clichy and only a few blocks southeast is lively, neon-lit place Pigalle, one of Paris' two main sex districts (the other, which is *much* more low-rent, is along rue St-Denis, 1er). Pigalle is more than just a sleazy red-light district: the area around blvd de Clichy between the Pigalle and Blanche metro stations is lined with erotica shops and striptease parlours, but there are also plenty of trendy nightspots, clubs and cabarets. On place Gustave Toudouze (Map pp386–8) the shops, cafés and restaurants are a colourful feast for the eye. Between Pigalle and the church of the Trinity, the Nouvelles Athènes (New Athens) district with its beautiful Greco-Roman architecture has a singular elegance. This little corner of Paris, full of grand houses and private gardens, has long been favoured by artists.

The easiest way to reach Montmartre is via the RATP's sleek funicular (p338). Montmartrobus, a bus run by the RATP, makes a circuitous route from place Pigalle through Montmartre to the 18e Mairie on place Jules Joffrin. Detailed maps are posted at bus stops.

Transport

Bus No 85 bus from Mairie du 18, stop Muller for Montmartre/Sacre Coeur (10- to 15-minute walk), Palais Royal, Châtelet; place Pigalle for Montmartobus through Montmartre to 18e Mairie on place Jules Joffrin

Metro Abbesses, Anvers, Blanche, Lamarck Caulaincourt, Pigalle

Train The Petit Train de Montmartre (☎ 01 42 62 24 00; adult/child 3-12 yrs €5/3), a touristic 'train' with commentary, runs through Montmartre every 30 minutes or so from 10am or 10.30am to between 5.30pm and 9pm daily

BASILIQUE DU SACRÉ CŒUR Map p400
☎ 01 53 41 89 00; www.sacre-coeur-montmartre .com; place du Parvis du Sacré Cœur, 18e; metro Anvers; ◷ 6am-11pm

Sacred Heart Basilica, perched at the very top of Butte de Montmartre, was built from contributions pledged by Parisian Catholics as an act of contrition after the humiliating Franco-Prussian War of 1870–1. Construction began in 1873, but the basilica was not consecrated until 1919. In a sense atonement here has never stopped; a perpetual prayer 'cycle' that began at the consecration of the basilica continues till this day.

Some 234 spiralling steps lead you to the basilica's **dome** (admission €5; ◷ 9am-7pm Apr-Sep, 9am-6pm Oct-Mar), which affords one of Paris' most spectacular panoramas; they say you can see for 30km on a clear day. The chapel-lined **crypt**, which can be visited in conjunction with the dome and keeps the same hours, is huge but not very interesting.

PLACE DU TERTRE Map p400
metro Abbesses

Half a block west of **Église St-Pierre de Montmartre**, which once formed part of a 12th-century Benedictine abbey, is what was once the main square of the village of Montmartre. These days it's filled with cafés, restaurants, portrait artists and tourists and is always animated. Look for the **Moulin de la Galette** and **Moulin Radet**, two old-style windmills to the west on rue Lepic.

ESPACE SALVADOR DALÍ Map p400
☎ 01 42 64 40 10; www.dali-espacemontmartre .com; 11 rue Poulbot, 18e; metro Abbesses; adult/senior

€7/6, student & 8-16 yrs €5, under 8 free; ◷ 10am-6.30pm Sep-Jun, 10am-9pm Jul & Aug

Some 330 works by Salvador Dalí (1904–89), the flamboyant Catalan surrealist printmaker, painter, sculptor and self-promoter, are on display at this surrealist-style museum just west of place du Tertre. The collection includes Dalí's strange sculptures (most in reproduction), lithographs, many of his illustrations and furniture (including the famous 'lips' sofa). There's a guided tour in English at 10.30am every 1st and 3rd Sunday of the month.

MUSÉE DE MONTMARTRE Map p400
☎ 01 46 06 61 11; www.museedemontmartre.com; 12-14 rue Cortot, 18e; metro Lamarck Caulaincourt; adult €4.50, senior, student & 10-25 yrs €3, under 10 free; ◷ 10am-12.30pm & 1.30-6pm Tue-Sun

The Montmartre Museum displays paintings, lithographs and documents mostly relating to the area's rebellious and bohemian/artistic past in a 17th-century manor house, the oldest structure in the quarter. It also stages exhibitions of artists still living in the *quartier*.

Just behind the museum to the northwest is **Le Close du Montmartre** (cnr rue St-Vincent & rue des Saules, 18e), a small vineyard dating from 1933 whose 2000 vines produce an average 850 bottles of wine each October (p11). Samples of the wine are sold in the museum bookshop.

MUSÉE D'ART NAÏF MAX FOURNY
Map p400
☎ 01 42 58 72 89; www.hallesaintpierre.org; 2 rue Ronsard, 18e; metro Anvers; adult €6, student, senior & 4-16 yrs €4.50; ◷ 10am-6pm

Founded in 1986, the Max Fourny Museum of Naive Art is housed in Halle St-Pierre, across from square Willette and the base of the funicular. The dozen or so paintings in the permanent collection represent both the primitive and Art Brut (p109) and were gathered from around the world. The museum stages some three temporary exhibitions a year.

Top Five

- **Basilique du Sacré Cœur** (left)
- **Espace Salvador Dalí** (left)
- **Musée de la Vie Romantique** (p128)
- **Musée de l'Érotisme** (p128)
- **Place du Tertre** (left)

CIMETIÈRE DE MONTMARTRE Map p400

☎ 01 43 87 64 24; metro Place de Clichy;
🕙 8am-6pm Mon-Fri, 8.30am-6pm Sat, 9am-6pm Sun mid-Mar–early Nov, to 5.30pm early Nov–mid-Mar

Established in 1798, Montmartre Cemetery is perhaps the most celebrated necropolis in Paris after Père Lachaise. It contains the graves of Zola, Alexandre Dumas the younger, Stendhal, Jacques Offenbach, Degas, François Truffaut and Vaslav Nijinsky – among others. The entrance closest to the Butte de Montmartre is at the end of av Rachel, just off blvd de Clichy or down the stairs from 10 rue Caulaincourt.

MUSÉE DE L'ÉROTISME Map p400

☎ 01 42 58 28 73; 72 blvd de Clichy, 18e; metro Blanche; adult/student €7/5; 🕙 10am-2am

The Museum of Erotic Art tries to put some 2000 titillating statuary, stimulating sexual aids and fetishist items from days gone by on a loftier plane, with antique and modern erotic art from four continents spread over seven floors. But most of the punters know why they are here. Still, some of the techniques are, well, breathtaking and instructive.

MUSÉE NATIONAL GUSTAVE MOREAU Map pp386-8

☎ 01 48 74 38 50; www.musee-moreau.fr; 14 rue de La Rochefoucauld, 9e; metro Trinité; adult €4, senior, student & 18-25 yrs €2.60, under 18 free, 1st Sun of the month free; 🕙 10am-12.45pm & 2-5.15pm Wed-Mon

The National Gustave Moreau Museum, about 500m southwest of place Pigalle, is dedicated to the eponymous symbolist painter's work. Housed in what was once Moreau's studio, the two-storey museum is crammed with 4800 of his paintings, drawings and sketches. Some of Moreau's paintings are fantastic – in both senses of the word. We particularly like *La Licorne* (The Unicorn), inspired by *La Dame à la Licorne* (The Lady with the Unicorn) cycle of tapestries in the Musée National du Moyen Age (p94).

MUSÉE DE LA VIE ROMANTIQUE Map pp383-5

☎ 01 55 31 95 67; www.paris.fr/musees/vie_romantique; 16 rue Chaptal, 9e; metro Pigalle; permanent collection admission free, temporary exhibitions adult/under 18 €7/3.50, senior & student €5.50;
🕙 10am-6pm Tue-Sun

In the centre of the district once known as 'New Athens' (due to all the writers and scholars who once lived here), the Museum of the Romantic Life in the lovely Hôtel Scheffer-Renan is devoted to the life and work of the Baronne Aurore Dupkin (1804–76), better known to the world as George Sand, and her intellectual circle of friends.

LA VILLETTE

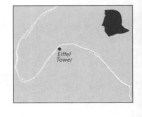

The Buttes Chaumont, the Canal de l'Ourcq and the Parc de la Villette, with its wonderful museums and other attractions, create the winning trifecta of the **19e arrondissement**. Combining the traditional with the innovative, the old-fashioned with the contemporary, this area makes a virtue of its contradictions. It may not have the beauty of central Paris but is nonetheless full of delightful surprises. An aimless stroll finds narrow streets lined with small houses. The Parc des Buttes Chaumont, with its strange rocky promontory, attracts local inhabitants at dawn. The quays along the Canal de l'Ourcq have been transformed over the past few years and are now one of the area's main attractions. Most important is the Parc de la Villette, whose erstwhile abattoirs have made way for a cultural centre (Cité de la Musique, exhibitions, open-air cinema, games for children, the Zénith concert hall) and a burgeoning Cité des Sciences et de l'Industrie.

PARC DE LA VILLETTE Map pp380-2

☎ 01 04 03 75 75, 01 40 03 75 03; www.villette.com; metro Porte de la Villette or Porte de Pantin

This whimsical, 35-hectare park in the city's far northeastern corner, which opened in 1993, stretches from the Cité des Sciences et de l'Industrie (metro Porte de la Villette) southwards to the Cité de la Musique (metro Porte de Pantin). Split into two sections by the Canal de l'Ourcq, the park is enlivened by shaded walkways, imaginative street furniture, a series of themed gardens and fanciful, bright-red pavilions known as *folies*. It is the largest open green space in central Paris and has been called 'the prototype of the urban park of the 21st century'.

Transport

Bus Porte de la Villette for No 75 to Buttes Chaumont, Canal St-Martin, République, Centre Pompidou, Marais, Hôtel de Ville & Châtelet

Metro Botzaris, Buttes-Chaumont, Porte de Pantin, Porte de la Villette

Boat Canauxrama Bassin de la Villette stop (13 quai de la Loire) for canal boat to Port de Plaisance de Paris-Arsenal (12e) south of place de la Bastille & Paris Canal Croisières stop (19-21 quai de la Loire) for boat to quai Anatole France (7e) near the Musée d'Orsay

For kids, there are 10 themed playgrounds, including the **Jardin des Îles** (Garden of Islands), **Jardin des Bambous** (Bamboo Gardens) and **Jardin des Miroirs** (Mirror Gardens). The best are the **Jardin du Dragon**, with an enormous dragon slide between the Géode and the nearest bridge, and the **Jardin des Vents et des Dunes** (Wind & Dunes Garden), which is across Galerie de la Villette (the covered walkway) from the **Grande Halle**, a wonderful old abattoir of wrought iron and glass now used for concerts, theatre performances, expos and conventions.

CITÉ DES SCIENCES ET DE L'INDUSTRIE Map pp380-2

☎ 01 40 05 80 00, reservations ☎ 08 92 69 70 72; www.cite-sciences.fr; 30 av Corentin Cariou, 19e; metro Porte de la Villette; ☻ 10am-6pm Tue-Sat, 10am-7pm Sun

The enormous City of Science and Industry, at the northern end of Parc de la Villette, has all sorts of high-tech exhibits.

Free attractions include **Cyber-base Internet centre** (level 1; ☻ noon-7.30pm Tue, noon-6.30pm Wed-Sun); **Médiathèque** (levels 0 & -1; ☻ noon-7.45pm Tue, noon-6.45pm Wed-Sun), multimedia exhibits dealing with childhood, the history of science and health; **Cité des Métiers** (level -1; ☻ 10am-6pm Tue-Fri, noon-6pm Sat), with information about trades, professions and employment; and the small **Aquarium** (level -2; ☻ 10am-6pm Tue-Sat, 10am-7pm Sun).

A free (and very useful) map/brochure in English called the *Keys to the Cité* is available from the circular information counter at the main entrance to the complex. If you really want more detail, buy a copy of the 80-page *Guide to the Permanent Exhibitions* (€3) at reception. An audioguide costs €4.

The huge, rather confusingly laid-out **Explora** (levels 1 & 2; adult/7-25 yrs €7.50/5.50, under 7 free) exhibitions look at everything from train technology and space to biology and sound. Tickets are valid for a full day and allow you to enter and exit up to four times.

The **Planétarium** (level 1; admission €3, child 3-7 yrs free; ☻ 11am-5pm Tue-Sun) has six shows a day on the hour (except at 1pm) on a screen measuring 1000 sq metres. Children under three are not admitted.

The highlight of the Cité des Sciences et de l'Industrie is the brilliant **Cité des Enfants** (Children's Village; level 0), whose imaginative hands-on demonstrations of basic scientific principles are in three sections: one for three- to five-year-olds, and two for five- to 12-year-olds. In the first, kids can explore, among other things, the conduct of water (waterproof ponchos provided). The second allows children to build toy houses with industrial robots, and stage news broadcasts in a TV studio. The third, Électricité, is a special electricity exhibition devoted to the five-to-12 age group.

Visits to Cité des Enfants lasting 1½ hours begin four times a day: at 9.45am, 11.30am, 1.30pm and 3.30pm on Tuesday, Thursday and Friday and at 10.30am, 12.30pm, 2.30pm and 4.30pm on Wednesday, Saturday and Sunday. Each child (€5) must be accompanied by an adult (maximum two per family). During school holidays, book two or three days in advance by phone or via the Internet.

The **Cinaxe** (☎ 08 92 68 45 40, 01 42 09 85 83; admission €5.20, if holding any other ticket to the Cité des Sciences €4.80; ☻ screenings 11am-1pm & 2-5pm Tue-Sun), a cinema with hydraulic seating for 60 people, moves in synchronisation with the action on the screen. It's across the walkway from the southwestern side of the Cité des Sciences. Shows begin every 15 minutes.

The **Géode** (☎ 08 92 68 45 40, 01 40 05 79 99; www.lageode.fr; 26 av Corentin Cariou, 19e; adult €8.75, senior & 3-25 yrs €6.75 except 3-5.30pm Sun, double feature €11; ☻ 10.30am-9.30pm Tue-Sat, 10.30am-7.30pm Sun) is a 36m-high sphere whose mirror-like surface of thousands of polished, stainless-steel triangles has made it one of Paris' architectural calling-cards. Inside, high-resolution, 70mm 45-minute films – on virtual reality, special effects, nature etc – are projected onto a 180° screen that gives a sense of being surrounded by the action. There is a special double feature at 6.30pm. Headsets that pick up an English soundtrack are available for no extra charge.

The **Argonaut** (admission €3, child under 7 free; 10.30am-5.30pm Tue-Fri, 11am-6.30pm Sat & Sun), a French Navy submarine commissioned in 1957 and dry-docked in the park, is just southeast of the Géode. Get to it from level 0 of the Cité des Sciences et de l'Industrie.

CITÉ DE LA MUSIQUE Map pp380-2
☎ 01 44 84 44 84; www.cite-musique.fr; 221 av Jean Jaurès, 19e; metro Porte de Pantin

The City of Music, on the southern edge of Parc de la Villette, is a striking triangular-shaped concert hall whose brief is to bring non-elitist music from around the world to Paris' multi-ethnic masses. For information on concerts and other musical events, see p232. Next door to the Cité de la Musique is the prestigious **Conservatoire National Supérieur de Musique et de Danse** (National Higher Conservatory of Music & Dance; ☎ 01 40 40 45 45; 209 av Jean Jaurès, 19e; metro Porte de Pantin), with concerts and dance performances throughout the year.

The **Musée de la Musique** (Music Museum; ☎ 01 44 84 44 84; adult €6.10, senior, student & 18-25 yrs €4.80, under 18 free; noon-6pm Tue-Sat, 10am-6pm Sun) in the Cité de la Musique displays some 900 rare musical instruments (from a collection of 4500 warehoused); you can hear many of them being played through the earphones included in the admission cost. In the museum, the **Centre d'Informations Musicales** (Centre for Musical Information; noon-6pm Tue-Sun) can answer your music questions via the Internet; it has terminals with about 500 music-related sites.

PARC DES BUTTES-CHAUMONT
Map pp386-8
rue Manin & rue Botzaris, 19e; metro Buttes-Chaumont or Botzaris; 7am-9.15pm Oct-Apr, 7am-10.15pm May-Sep

Encircled by tall apartment blocks, the 25-hectare Buttes-Chaumont Park is the closest thing in Paris to Manhattan's Central Park. The park's forested slopes hide grottoes and artificial waterfalls, and the lake is dominated by a temple-topped island linked to the mainland by two footbridges. Once a quarry and rubbish tip, the park was given its present form by Baron Haussmann in the 1860s.

OUTSIDE THE WALLS: BEYOND CENTRAL PARIS

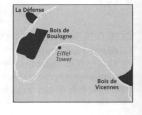

Eating p204; Shopping p267; Sleeping p304

Worth a visit are several places just 'outside the walls' of central Paris. To the southeast and the southwest are the 'lungs' of Paris, the Bois de Vincennes and the Bois de Boulogne, both important recreational areas. The modern cityscape of La Défense, a mere 20 minutes away at the end of metro line No 1 or RER line A, is so different from the rest of centuries-old Paris that it's worth a visit to put it all in perspective. To the north on metro line 13 is St-Denis, France's royal resting place and site of an impressive medieval basilica. And at Le Bourget, Paris' original airport (actually aerodrome) before the advent of Orly and Roissy Charles de Gaulle is the Musée de l'Air et de l'Espace, the oldest and most complete aeronautics museum in the world.

BOIS DE VICENNES & SURROUNDS
BOIS DE VINCENNES Map pp380-2
blvd Poniatowski, 12e; metro Porte de Charenton or Porte Dorée

The Vincennes Wood (995 hectares) is in the southeastern corner of the city; most of it just outside the blvd Périphérique. The **Parc Floral de Paris** (Paris Floral Park; ☎ 08 20 00 75 75; www .parcfloraldeparis.com; esplanade du Château de Vincennes & route de la Pyramide, 12e; metro Château de Vincennes; adult/child 7-18 yrs €15/3; 9.30am-6.30pm Tue-Sun Apr-Sep, to 5.30pm Tue-Sun Oct-Mar) is south of the Château de Vincennes, and amusements for kids include the **Bibliothèque-Ludothèque Nature** (Nature Library & Puppetry; admission €1; 1.30-5.30pm Tue-Sat, to 6.30pm Sun Apr-Sep, to 5.30pm Tue-Sun Oct-Mar) and a lovely **Jardin des Papillons** (Butterfly Garden). The **Jardin Tropical** (Tropical Garden; ☎ 01 40 71 75 60; av de la Belle Gabrielle; metro Nogent-sur-Marne),

Transport

Bus Château de Vincennes for No 46 to rue du Faubourg St-Antoine, place Voltaire, av Parmentier, Gare de l'Est & Gare du Nord, for No 56 to place de la Nation, place de la République, Gare de l'Est, Barbès & Porte de Clignancourt

Metro Château de Vincennes, Porte de Charenton, Porte Dorée

a vestige of the 1907 Exposition Coloniale, is at the park's eastern edge.

Every year a huge amusement park known as the **Foire du Trône** (p10) installs itself on the Pélouse de Reuilly for eight weeks in April and May at the Bois de Vincennes. The 15-hectare **Parc Zoologique de Paris** (Paris Zoological Park; ☎ 01 44 75 20 14; www.mnhn.fr in French; 53 av de St-Maurice, 12e; metro Porte Dorée; adult €8, senior, student & 4-16 yrs €5, under 4 free; ⏰ 9am-6pm Mon-Sat, to 6.30pm Sun Apr-Sep, to 5pm Mon-Sat, to 5.30pm Sun Oct-Mar), just east of Lac Daumesnil, was established in 1934. It has some 1200 animals.

CHÂTEAU DE VINCENNES Map pp380-2
☎ 01 48 08 31 20; www.monum.fr; av de Paris, 12e; metro Château de Vincennes; ⏰ 10am-noon & 1-6pm May-Aug, 10am-noon & 1-5pm Sep-Apr

At the northern edge of the wood, the Palace of Vincennes is a *bona fide* royal chateau with massive fortifications and a moat. Louis XIV spent his honeymoon at the mid-17th-century **Pavillon du Roi**, the westernmost of the two royal pavilions flanking the **Cour Royale** (Royal Courtyard). The 52m-high **dungeon**, completed in 1369, was used as a prison during the 17th and 18th centuries. You can walk round the grounds for free, but the only way to see the Gothic **Chapelle Royale** (Royal Chapel), built between the 14th and 16th centuries, is to take a guided tour (in French; information booklet in English). Long-tour tickets are €6.10 for seniors and students, €4.10 for ages 18 to 25; short tours €4.60 and €3.10 (under 18 free). There are an average of five long and short tours each daily from April to September. Ring ahead for exact times.

AQUARIUM TROPICAL Map pp380-2
☎ 01 44 74 85 01; www.musee-afriqueoceanie.fr in French; Palais de la Porte Dorée, 293 av Daumesnil, 12e; metro Porte Dorée; adult/family €4/5, senior & student €2.60; ⏰ 10am-5.15pm Wed-Mon

The Tropical Aquarium at the edge of the Bois de Vincennes is Paris' most ambitious, with fish and other sea creatures from around the world in tanks spread throughout a dozen rooms.

CITÉ DE L'ARCHITECTURE ET DU PATRIMOINE Map pp380-2
☎ 01 58 51 52 00; Palais de la Porte Dorée, 293 av Daumesnil, 12e; metro Porte Dorée; admission free; 10am-6pm Wed-Mon

The City of Architecture and Patrimony was supposed to be relocated in the refurbished Palais de Chaillot by now but continues to share space with the Aquarium Tropical. The museum traces Paris' architecture through the centuries and helps to put in perspective just how and why the city grew as it did.

Top Five

- **Basilique de St-Denis** (p135)
- **Château de Vincennes** (p131)
- **Grande Arche de la Défense** (p134)
- **Musée de la Contrefaçon** (p132)
- **Stade de France** (p136)

BOIS DE BOULOGNE & SURROUNDS

BOIS DE BOULOGNE Map pp380-2
blvd Maillot, 16e; metro Porte Maillot

The 845-hectare Boulogne Wood on the western edge of the city owes its informal layout to Baron Haussmann, who was inspired by London's Hyde Park. Renovation of the Bois de Boulogne, which includes some 125 hectares of forested land, was recently completed after it suffered severe storm damage in late 1999.

The enclosed **Parc de Bagatelle**, in the northwestern corner, is renowned for its beautiful gardens surrounding the 1775-built **Château de Bagatelle** (☎ 01 40 67 97 00; route de Sèvres à Neuilly, 16e; metro Pont de Neuilly; admission €3; ⏰ 9am-6pm Apr-Sep, 10am-5pm Oct-Mar). There are areas dedicated to irises (which bloom in May), roses (June to October) and water lilies (August). The **Pré Catalan** (Catalan Meadow) to the southeast includes the **Jardin Shakespeare** (⏰ 8.30am-7pm) in which plants, flowers and trees mentioned in Shakespeare's plays are cultivated.

Located at the southeastern end of the Bois de Boulogne is the **Jardin des Serres d'Auteuil**

Transport

Bus Porte d'Auteuil for No 32 through the 16e arrondissement to av des Champs-Élysées, av Matignon, Trinité & Gare de l'Est; Porte Maillot for No 73 to place de l'Étoile, av des Champs-Élysées, place de la Concorde & Musée d'Orsay

Metro av Foch, Pont de Neuilly, Porte d'Auteuil, Porte Dauphine, Porte Maillot

(☎ 01 40 71 75 23; av de la Porte d'Auteuil, 16e; metro Porte d'Auteuil; adult/6-18 yrs €1.50/1, under 6 free; ☎ 10am-6pm Apr-Sep, 10am-5pm Oct-Mar), a garden with impressive conservatories that opened in 1898.

The 20-hectare **Jardin d'Acclimatation** (☎ 01 40 67 90 82; av du Mahatma Gandhi; metro Les Sablons; adult/4-18 yrs €2.50/1.25, under 4 free; ☎ 10am-6pm), a kids-oriented amusement park whose name is another word for 'zoo' in French, includes the high-tech **Exploradôme** (☎ 01 53 64 90 40; www.exploradome.com in French; adult/4-18 yrs €4.50/3), a tented structure devoted to science and the media.

The **Musée National des Arts et Traditions Populaires** (National Museum of Popular Arts & Traditions; ☎ 01 44 17 60 00; 6 av du Mahatma Gandhi, 16e; metro Les Sablons; adult €3.85, senior, student & 18-25 yrs €2.60, under 18 free, 1st Sun of the month free; ☎ 9.30am-5.15pm Wed-Mon), just outside the Jardin d'Acclimatation but still within the Boulogne Wood, has displays of the life of peasants and craftspeople in rural France before and during the Industrial Revolution. It is outdated and not particularly interesting. The southern part of the wood take in two horse-racing tracks, the **Hippodrome de Longchamp** for flat races and the **Hippodrome d'Auteuil** for steeplechases (p245) as well as the **Stade Roland Garros**, home of the French Open tennis tournament (p245). Also here is the **Tenniseum-Musée de Roland Garros** (☎ 01 47 43 48 48; www.roland garros.com; 2 av Gordon Bennett, 16e; metro Porte d'Auteuil; adult/under 18/family €7/4/15, with stadium visit €15/10/30; ☎ 10am-6pm Tue-Sun), the world's most extravagant tennis museum, tracing the sport's 500-year history through paintings, sculptures and posters. Visitors to the museum can watch some 200 hours of play from 1897 till today, including all the men's singles matches since 1990 and interviews with all the key players.

Rowing boats (☎ 01 42 88 04 69; per hr €8.50; ☎ noon-6pm Mon-Fri, 10am-7pm Sat & Sun mid-Apr–mid-Oct) can be hired at **Lac Inférieur** (metro av Henri Martin), the largest of the wood's lakes and ponds. **Paris Cycles** (☎ 01 47 47 76 50; 30 min/1hr/half-day/day €3.80/5/10/12; ☎ 10am-sunset mid-Apr–mid-Oct, 10am-sunset Wed, Sat & Sun mid-Oct–mid-Apr) hires out bicycles at two locations in the Bois de Boulogne: on av du Mahatma Gandhi (metro Les Sablons), across from the Porte Sablons entrance to the Jardin d'Acclimatation amusement park, and near the Pavillon Royal (metro av Foch) at the northern end of Lac Inférieur.

MUSÉE MARMOTTAN-MONET
Map pp380-2

☎ 01 42 24 07 02, 01 44 96 50 33; www.marmottan .com; 2 rue Louis Boilly, 16e; metro La Muette; adult/ 8-25 yrs €6.50/4, under 8 free; ☎ 10am-6pm Tue-Sun
The Marmottan-Monet Museum, which is two blocks east of the Bois de Boulogne and between Porte de la Muette and Porte de Passy, has the world's largest collection of works by the impressionist painter Claude Monet (1840–1926) – some 100 chefs d'œuvre as well as paintings by Gauguin, Sisley, Pissarro, Renoir, Degas, Manet and Morisot.

MUSÉE DE LA CONTREFAÇON
Map pp383-5

☎ 01 56 26 14 00; www.museedelacontrefacon.com; 16 rue de la Faisanderie, 16e; metro Porte Dauphine; admission €2.50, child under 12 free; ☎ 2-5.30pm Tue-Sun
This fascinating museum east of Porte Dauphine is the real thing, dedicated to the not-so-fine art of counterfeiting. Apparently nothing is sacred to the manufacturers of the ersatz: banknotes, liqueurs, design clothing, even Barbie dolls. What makes this museum, established by the Union des Fabricants (Manufacturers' Union) so interesting is that it displays the real against the fake and lets you spot the difference. Most of the time it's as plain as the nose (the real one) on your face.

MUSÉE D'ENNERY Map pp383-5
☎ 01 45 53 57 96; www.rmn.fr; 59 av Foch, 16e; metro Porte Dauphine
This museum of Asian art and artefacts displayed in a Second Empire mansion is named after Clemence d'Ennery, wife of a 19th-century playwright, who amassed 7000 objects from China and Japan – somewhat blindly at first. Closed for renovation at the time of research, the museum should reopen in 2005.

LA DÉFENSE

When development of 750-hectare La Défense, Paris' skyscraper district on the Seine to the west of the 17e arrondissement, began in the late 1950s, it was one of the world's most ambitious civil-engineering projects. Its first major structure was the vaulted, largely triangular-shaped **Centre des Nouvelles Industries et Technologies** (CNIT; Centre for New Industries & Technologies), a giant 'pregnant oyster' inaugurated in 1958 and extensively rebuilt 30 years later. But after the economic crisis of the mid-1970s, office space in La Défense became hard to sell or lease. Buildings stood empty and further development of the area all but ceased.

Things picked up, and today La Défense counts more than 100 buildings, the tallest of which is the 187m-tall **Total Fina Elf Coupole** (1985). Among the most attractive is the 161m twin-towered, aptly named **Cœur Défense** (Défense Heart; see p42), more or less in the centre, which replaced the monstrous Esso building from the 1960s. The towers stand over a light-filled atrium big enough to contain the nave of Notre Dame. Now the head offices of 14 of France's 20 largest corporations are housed here, and a total of 1500 companies of all sizes employ some 150,000 people. Some 35,000 people live here and in the contiguous Park District.

La Défense is easy enough to explore on foot but there's also the **Petit Train de la Défense** (La Défense Little Train), which covers all the major sights in a 6km, 40-minute loop starting at the foot of the Grande Arche.

LA DÉFENSE		0 _____ 200 m 0 _____ 0.1 miles
SIGHTS & ACTIVITIES (pp133-4)	Petit Train de la Défense Stop.........9 A3	Le Petit Bofinger...................15 A3
Bassin Agam.................................1 B3	Sources d'Europe..................(see 5)	
Calder Stabile..............................2 B3	Technip Building....................10 B2	**SHOPPING** (pp251-78)
CNIT...3 B3	Total Fina Elf Coupole.........11 B3	Les Quatre Temps
Cœur Défense..............................4 C3	Tour EDF................................12 B3	Shopping Centre...........16 B3
Grande Arche de la Défense.......5 A3	Église Notre Dame de la Pentecôte...13 B3	
La Défense de Paris Monument...6 B3		**INFORMATION**
Miró Sculpture.............................7 B3	**EATING** (p204)	CIC...17 B3
Musée de la Défense...............(see 18)	Bistro Romain.......................14 A3	Espace Info-Défense...........18 B3
Patinoire du Parvis de la Défense...8 B3	Brasserie du Toit de la Grande Arche...(see 5)	Post Office.............................19 B3

Transport

Bus No 73 from Musée d'Orsay, place de la Concorde or place Charles de Gaulle

Metro Line No 1 to La Défense Grande Arche (terminus)

RER Line A (station: La Défense Grande Arche); if you take the faster RER, remember that La Défense is in zone three and you must pay a supplement (€1.95) if you are carrying a travel pass for zones 1 and 2 only

Train Petit Train de la Défense (☎ 01 42 62 24 00; adult/child 3-10 yrs €5/3, under 3 free; ⊗ 11am-5pm Mar-Jul & Sep, 11am-6pm Aug)

MUSÉE DE LA DÉFENSE Map p133

☎ 01 47 74 84 24; www.ladefense.fr in French; 15 place de la Défense; admission free; ⊗ 9.30am-5.30pm Mon-Fri Oct-Mar, 10am-6pm Apr-Sep

La Défense Museum below the **Espace Info-Défense** (p351) traces the development of La Défense via drawings, architectural plans and scale models. Especially interesting are the projects that were never built: the 750m-tall Tour Tourisme TV (1961); Hungarian-born artist Nicholas Schöffer's unspeakable Tour Lumière Cybernetque (1965), a 'Cybernetic Light Tower' that, at 324m, would stand at the same height as the Eiffel Tower; and the horrendous Tour sans Fin, a 'Never-Ending Tower' that would be 425m, yet be only 39m in diameter.

GRANDE ARCHE DE LA DÉFENSE
Map p133

☎ 01 49 07 27 27; www.grandearche.com; 1 parvis de la Défense; adult €7.50, child under 12 & student €6, family €16-22; ⊗ 10am-6.30pm

La Défense's biggest drawcard is the remarkable, cube-like **Grande Arche** (Great Arch). Designed by Danish architect Johan-Otto von Spreckelsen and housing government and business offices, it is made of white Carrara marble, grey granite and glass and measures 110m exactly along each side. Inaugurated on 14 July 1989, it marks the western end of the 8km-long **Axe Historique** (Historic Axis), begun in 1640 by André Le Nôtre of Versailles fame and stretching from the Louvre's glass pyramid through the Jardin des Tuileries and along av des Champs-Élysées to the Arc de Triomphe, Porte Maillot and finally La Défense's Esplanade du Général de Gaulle. The structure

symbolises a window open to the world and is slightly out of alignment with the Axe Historique – on purpose. Lifts will whisk you up to the 35th floor of the arch, but (frankly) neither the views from the rooftop nor the temporary exhibitions justify the ticket price.

GARDENS & MONUMENTS Map p133
Le Parvis, place de la Défense & Esplanade du Général de Gaulle

The Parvis, place de la Défense and Esplanade du Général de Gaulle, which form a pleasant, 1km walkway, have been turned into a **garden of contemporary art**. The 60-odd monumental sculptures and murals here, and west of the Grande Arche in the **Quartier du Parc** (Park District) and **Jardins de l'Arche**, a 2km-long extension of the Axe Historique, include colourful and imaginative works by Calder, Miró, Agam and Torricini. In the southeastern corner of place de la Défense (opposite the Info-Défense office) is an older **La Défense de Paris monument** honouring the defence of Paris during the Franco-Prussian War of 1870–1 (see below). Behind is **Bassin Agam**, a pool with colourful mosaics and fountains; *ballets muets* take place between noon and 2pm and 5pm and 6pm on weekdays, 3pm to 6pm at the weekend. Musical water displays are at 1pm on Wednesday and 4pm at the weekend.

ÉGLISE NOTRE DAME DE LA PENTECÔTE Map p133

☎ 01 47 75 83 25, 1 place de la Défense; ⊗ 8am-6.30pm Mon-Fri, 2.30-6.30pm Sat & Sun

If the hub and the bub and the crowds of 'suits' get you down, head for the futuristic Our Lady of the Pentecost Catholic Church next to the CNIT building that opened in 2001. The interior is sublime; check out the flame-shaped pulpit, the image of the Virgin Mary that looks uncannily like the Buddha and the individual chairs that unfold to create benches.

ST-DENIS

For 1200 years St-Denis was the burial place of the kings of France; today it is a quiet suburb just north of Paris' 18e arrondissement. The ornate **royal tombs**, adorned with some truly remarkable statuary, and **Basilique de St-Denis** that contains them (the world's first major Gothic structure) are worth a visit and the town is easily accessible by metro in 20 minutes or so. St-Denis' more recent claim to fame is the **Stade de France** just south of the Canal de St-Denis, the futuristic stadium where France beat Brazil to win the World Cup in July 1998. St-Denis is easily negotiable on foot but the **Petit Train de St-Denis** (St-Denis Little Train) takes in the town's key sights in a loop lasting about 40 minutes.

BASILIQUE DE ST-DENIS Map below

☎ 01 48 09 83 54; www.monum.fr; 1 rue de la Légion d'Honneur; basilica admission free, tombs adult €6.10, senior, student & 18-25 yrs €4.10, under 18 free;
🕑 10am-6.15pm Mon-Sat, noon-6.15pm Sun Apr-Sep, to 5.15pm Oct-Mar

St-Denis Basilica was the burial place for all but a handful of France's kings and queens from Dagobert I (ruled 629–39) to Louis XVIII (ruled 1814–24); constituting one of Europe's most important collections of funerary sculpture. The single-towered basilica, begun around 1135, was the first major structure to be built in the Gothic style, serving as a model for other 12th-century French cathedrals including the one at Chartres (p322). Features illustrating the transition from Romanesque to Gothic can be seen in the **choir** and **ambulatory**, which are adorned with a number of 12th-

Transport

Metro Line No 13 to Basilique de St-Denis station for the basilica and tourist office, to St-Denis-Porte de Paris station for the Musée d'Art et d'Histoire and the Stade de France (make sure to board a train heading for St-Denis Université, not for Gabriel Péri/Asnières-Gennevilliers, as the line splits at La Fourche station)

RER Line B (station: La Plaine-Stade de France) for the State de France

Tram Line T1 – one of only two tramways in Paris that links Bobigny Pablo Picasso metro station, the terminus of line No 5, with Basilique de St-Denis station

Train Petit Train de St-Denis (☎ 01 42 62 24 00; adult/child 3-10 yrs €5/3; 🕑 11am-5pm Mar-Jul & Sep, 11am-6pm Aug)

century **stained-glass windows**. The **narthex** (the portico running along the western end of the basilica) also dates from this period. The nave and transept were built in the 13th century.

During the Revolution and the Reign of Terror, the basilica was devastated; human remains from the royal tombs were dumped into two big pits outside the church. The mausoleums were put into storage in Paris, however, and survived. They were brought back in 1816, and the royal bones were reburied in the crypt a year later. Restoration of the structure was begun under Napoleon, but most of the work was carried out by the Gothic Revivalist architect Eugène Viollet-le-Duc from 1858 until his death in 1879. The **tombs** in the

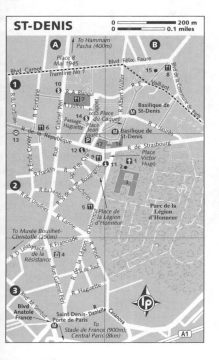

ST-DENIS

0 ——— 200 m
0 ——— 0.1 miles

SIGHTS & ACTIVITIES	(pp134–6)
Basilique de St-Denis...1 B2	
Crypt Entrance...2 B2	
Maison d'Éducation de la Légion d'Honneur.................3 B2	
Musée d'Art et d'Histoire..4 A3	

EATING 🍴	(p204)
Au Petit Breton...5 A2	
Franprix...6 A1	
Halle du Marché...7 A1	
Le Café de l'Orient..8 B1	
Les Arts...9 A2	

INFORMATION	
Banque Populaire Nord de Paris....................................10 A1	
Le Kiosk..11 B2	
Office de Tourisme de St-Denis Plaine..........................12 A2	
Post Office..13 A1	
Société Générale Basilique...14 A1	

OTHER	
Chemin des Poulies...15 B1	
Hôtel de Ville (Modern Annexe)...................................16 B2	
Hôtel de Ville...17 A2	

crypt are decorated with life-sized figures of the deceased. Those built before the Renaissance are adorned with *gisants* (recumbent figures). Those made after 1285 were carved from death masks and are thus fairly, well, lifelike; the 14 figures commissioned under Louis IX (St Louis; ruled 1214–70) are depictions of how earlier rulers might have looked. The oldest tombs (from around 1230) are those of Clovis I (died 511) and his son Childebert I (died 558). Just south of the basilica is the former royal abbey and now the **Maison d'Éducation de la Légion d'Honneur**, a school for 500 pupils.

Self-paced 1¼-hour tours of the Basilique on CD-ROM headsets cost €4 (€5.50 for two sharing), available at the crypt ticket kiosk.

MUSÉE D'ART ET D'HISTOIRE Map p135
☎ 01 42 43 05 10; 22bis rue Gabriel Péri; adult €4, student & senior €2, under 16 free; ☽ 10am-5.30pm Mon, Wed & Fri, 10am-8pm Thu, 2-6.30pm Sat & Sun

To the southwest of the basilica is the Museum of Art & History, housed in a restored Carmelite convent founded in 1625 and later presided over by Louise de France, the youngest daughter of Louis XV. Displays include reconstructions of the Carmelites' cells, an 18th-century apothecary section and, in the archaeology section, items found during excavations around St-Denis. There's a section on modern art, with a collection of work by local boy, the surrealist artist Paul Éluard (1895–1952) as well as politically charged posters, cartoons, lithographs and paintings from the 1871 Paris Commune.

MUSÉE BOUILHET-CHRISTOFLE
Map p135
☎ 01 49 22 40 40; 112 rue Ambroise Croizat; adult €5, senior & student €3, under 16 free; ☽ 9.30am-5.30pm Mon-Fri

About 250m to the southwest and just over the Seine is the ivy-covered Bouilhet-Christofle Museum, with some 2000 pieces of silverware created by the same family concern from its founding in 1830 to the present day. The silversmiths' skills seemed to have reached their apogee in the 1920s and '30s when they turned out some exquisite Art Deco pieces.

STADE DE FRANCE Map p135
☎ 08 92 70 09 00; www.stadefrance.com; rue Francis de Pressensé, ZAC du Cornillon Nord, 93216 St-Denis la Plaine; adult/student/child 6-11 yrs €10/8.50/7;

☽ tours on the hour in French 10am-5pm year-round, in English 10.20am & 2.30pm Jun-Aug

The 80,000-seat Stadium of France just south of central St-Denis and in full view from rue Gabriel Péri was built for the 1998 football World Cup, which France won by miraculously defeating Brazil 3-0. The futuristic and quite beautiful structure, with a roof the size of place de la Concorde, is used for football and rugby matches, major gymnastic events and big-ticket music concerts. It can be visited on guided tours from Porte H (Gate H).

LE BOURGET
The northeastern suburb of Le Bourget served as the principal airfield for WWI pilots from 1915 and was where Charles Lindbergh landed in 1927 after completing his solo crossing of the Atlantic. The airport building erected in 1937 now contains an important museum devoted to air travel and space exploration.

Transport

Bus No 350 from Gare du Nord, Gare de l'Est or Porte de la Chapelle or bus No 152 from Porte de la Villette (stop: Musée de l'Air et de l'Espace)

Metro Line No 7 to Porte de la Villette or La Courneuve and then bus No 152

RER Line B3 or B5 (station: Le Bourget)

MUSÉE DE L'AIR ET DE L'ESPACE
Map pp380-2
☎ 01 49 92 70 62; www.mae.org in French; adult €7, student & senior €5, under 18 free, planetarium €2; ☽ 10am-5pm Tue-Sun Nov-Apr, 10am-6pm May-Oct

The oldest aeronautics museum in the world, the Air and Space Museum (1919) contains some 150 military and civilian aircraft, dozens of rockets and spacecraft, as well as other displays that chart the history of flight from the hot air balloon to the exploration of space. Along with the **Aérogare** and **Hall de l'Espace** there's also a **Hall Concorde**, with a prototype of the now disused aircraft, and a **planetarium** with 45-minute shows.

Walking Tours

Marais Medieval Meanderings   138
Left Bank Bookworming   141
Right Bank Time Passages   144
Parisian World Tour   146

Walking Tours

Paris is best seen on foot and the four thematic walks outlined in this chapter are designed to help you appreciate Paris' rich heritage (architectural, artistic and ethnic) on both the Left and Right Banks. The first takes you to the Marais, where the finest Renaissance residences are located. The second explores the Left Bank and the hikes and haunts of important 20th-century literary figures. The third walk concentrates on the Right Bank's sumptuous, covered shopping arcades dating from the 19th century. The fourth takes you though the heart of *Paris Mondial* (literally 'World Paris') on a walk that will have you visiting Africa, Asia and the Middle East in a few hours.

The times given to complete each walk are not exact as they depend on your own pace and the number of stops you make along the way.

MARAIS MEDIEVAL MEANDERINGS

Monks and the Knights Templar settled in the Marais (largely in the 4e but also spilling into the 3e) as early as the 13th century, which explains the religious nature of many of its street names (eg rue du Temple, rue des Blancs Manteaux). But it wasn't until Henri IV began construction of place Royale (today's place des Vosges) in the early 17th century that the aristocracy began building the *hôtels particuliers* (private mansions) and *pavillons* (somewhat less-grand houses) so characteristic of the district. These golden and cream-coloured brick buildings are among the most beautiful Renaissance structures in the city and, because so many were built at more or less the same time, the Marais enjoys an architectural harmony unknown elsewhere in Paris.

The golden age of the Marais' *hôtels particuliers* was the 17th century, though construction continued into the first half of the 18th. The removal of the royal court – lock, stock and satin slipper – to Versailles in 1692 sounded the death knell for the Marais, and the mansions passed into the hands of commoners, who used them as warehouses, markets and shops. The quarter was given a major face-lift in the late 1960s and early 1970s, and today many of the *hôtels particuliers* house government offices, libraries and museums.

> **Walk Facts**
> **Start** Metro St-Paul
> **End** Hôtel de Sully
> **Distance** 2km
> **Duration** One hour
> **Transport** Metro St-Paul; bus No 67 to Hôtel de Ville or Châtelet
> **Fuel Stop** Ma Bourgogne

Begin the tour at St-Paul metro station on rue François Miron facing rue de Rivoli. Walk south on narrow rue du Prévôt to rue Charlemagne, once called rue des Prestres (Street of the Priests). To the right (west) on the corner of rue des Nonnains d'Hyères at 7 rue de Jouy stands the majestic **Hôtel d'Aumont 1**, built around 1650 for a financier and one of the most beautiful *hôtels particuliers* in the Marais. It now contains offices of the Tribunal Administratif, the body that deals with – *sacré bleu!* – internal disputes in the bloated and litigious French civil service. Opposite Hôtel d'Aumont, at the corner of rue de Jouy and rue de Fourcy, is a wonderful **17th-century relief of a winemaker 2**.

Continue south along rue des Nonnains d'Hyères past the Hôtel d'Aumont's geometrical gardens and turn left (east) onto rue de l'Hôtel de Ville. On the left at 1 rue du Figuier is **Hôtel de Sens 3**, the oldest private mansion in the Marais. Begun around 1475, it was built as the Paris digs for the powerful archbishops of Sens, under whose authority Paris fell at the time. When Paris was made an archbishopric, Hôtel de Sens was rented out to coach drivers, fruit sellers, a hatter and even a jam-maker. It was heavily restored in mock Gothic style (complete with turrets) in 1911; today it houses the **Bibliothèque Forney** (Forney Library); ☎ 01 42 78 14 60; ☯ 1.30-8pm Tue-Fri, 10am-8.30pm Sat).

Continue east along rue de l'Ave Maria and then go north along rue des Jardins de St-Paul. The truncated and crumbling twin towers across the football pitch on the left are all that remain of **Philippe-Auguste's enceinte 4**, a fortified medieval wall built around 1190 and once guarded by 39 towers. They are now part of the prestigious Lycée Charlemagne. To the right along rue des Jardins de St-Paul are the entrances to **Village St-Paul 5**, a courtyard of antique and crafts sellers.

Cross over rue Charlemagne and duck into rue Eginhard, a street with a tiny courtyard and a grated well built during the reign of Louis XIII. The street doglegs into rue St-Paul; at the corner above 23 rue Neuve St-Pierre housing a bed-linen shop are the remains of the medieval **Église St-Paul 6**. Tiny passage St-Paul (covered arcade) leads to the side entrance of the **Église St-Louis-St-Paul 7** (🕐 8am-8pm Mon-Sat, 9am-9pm Sun), a Jesuit church completed in 1641 during the Counter-Reformation.

Rue St-Paul debouches into rue St-Antoine. Turn left, passing the front entrance of Église St-Louis-St-Paul at No 99, cross over rue de Rivoli and head north up rue Malher. A **former boulangerie-pâtisserie 8** at No 13 (now a clothes shop) has fine old shop signs advertising *pains de seigle et gruau* (rye and wheaten breads), *gateaux secs* (biscuits) and *chaussons de pommes* (apple turnovers). Head west on rue des Rosiers and a short distance south on rue Pavée to No 10 and the Art Nouveau **Guimard synagogue 9** (p89). Continue north on rue Pavée (Paved Street), the first cobbled road in Paris. At No 24 stands **Hôtel Lamoignon 10**,

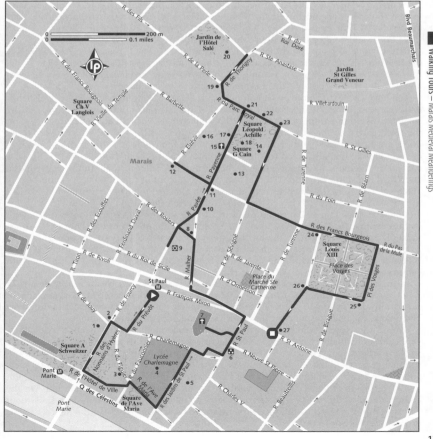

built between 1585 and 1612 for Diane de France (1538–1619), duchess of Angoulême and legitimised daughter of Henri II. It is a fine example of late-Renaissance architecture; note the Corinthian capitals and, above the main gate, the cherubs holding the symbolic mirror (truth) and snake (prudence). It now houses the **Bibliothèque Historique de la Ville de Paris** (☎ 01 44 59 29 40; ☻ 9.30am-6pm Mon-Sat).

The initials 'SC' at the corner of rue Pavée and rue des Francs Bourgeois mark the site of the medieval **priory of Ste-Catherine 11**; to the west, at 31 rue des Francs Bourgeois, is **Hôtel d'Albret 12**, among the last of the great *hôtels particuliers* (1740) to be built. Return to the crossroads and walk north along rue Payenne. The building immediately on the right at No 2 is the back of the mid-16th-century, Renaissance-style **Hôtel Carnavalet 13** built between 1548 and 1654 and home to the letter-writer Madame de Sévigné (1626–96). Further north is the **Hôtel Le Peletier de St-Fargeau 14**, which dates from the late 17th century. Both now form the Musée Carnavalet (p88).

From the grille just past the **Chapelle de l'Humanité 15**, a Revolutionary-era 'temple of reason' at 5 rue Payenne (the quote on the façade reads: 'Love as the principal, order as the base, progress as the goal'), you can see the rear of **Hôtel Donon 16** at 8 rue Elzévir, built in 1598 and now the Musée Cognacq-Jay (p88). At 11 rue Payenne is the lovely **Hôtel de Marle 17**, built in the late 16th century and now the Swedish Cultural Institute.

Opposite is a pretty green space called **square George Cain 18** with the remains of what was once the Hôtel de Ville. Have a look at the relief of Judgement Day and the one-handed clock on the tympanum (the façade beneath the roof) on the southern side. From the square walk a short distance northwest to two spectacular 17th-century *hôtels particuliers*: **Hôtel de Libéral Bruant 19** at 1 rue de la Perle and **Hôtel Aubert de Fontenay 20** at rue de Thorigny, whose three floors and vaulted cellars house the wonderful Musée Picasso (p88).

Retrace your steps to rue du Parc Royal. Heading east you'll pass three hôtels (**Hôtel de Croisille 21** at No 12, **Hôtel de Vigny 22** at No 10 and pink-brick **Hôtel Duret de Chevry 23** at No 8, the loveliest of the trio) before turning south down rue de Sévigné. All of these date from about 1620 and now do civic duty as archives and historical libraries.

You have already seen the two hôtels on rue de Sévigné from the back – Hôtel Le Peletier de St-Fargeau at No 29 and Hôtel Carnavalet at No 23. Take a moment to check out the spaghetti-like monogram of the former's original owner, Michel Le Peletier de Souzy, on the front gate, and the exterior courtyard of the latter, with its wonderful reliefs. To the north are Roman gods and goddesses, to the south the elements, and to the west reliefs of the four seasons attributed to the Renaissance sculptor Jean Goujon (1510–68), who created the Fontaine des Innocents near the Forum des Halles in 1549. In the centre of the courtyard is a statue of Louis XIII that was placed in front of the Hôtel de Ville on 14 July 1689 – a century to the day before an armed mob attacked the Bastille prison and sparked the revolution that would change the course of history. Little did they know...

Follow rue des Francs Bourgeois eastwards to the sublime place des Vosges (p87), with its four symmetrical fountains and an 1829 copy of a mounted statue of Louis XIII, originally placed here in 1639. In the northwestern corner at No 19 is **Ma Bourgogne 24** (p165), a delightful place for a meal, a snack or just a drink. In the southeastern corner at No 6 is **Hôtel de Rohan-Guéménée 25**, home to Victor Hugo for 16 years in the first half of the 19th century and now the Maison de Victor Hugo (p88).

In the southwestern corner of place des Vosges is the **back entrance 26** to **Hôtel de Sully 27** (p88), a restored aristocratic mansion at 62 rue St-Antoine built in 1624, now housing an exhibition space, a bookshop (p256) and, appropriately enough, the Centre des Monuments Nationaux, the body responsible for France's national historical monuments.

Behind the Hôtel de Sully are two beautifully decorated late-Renaissance-style courtyards, both of which are festooned with allegorical reliefs of the seasons and the elements. In the northern courtyard look to the southern side for spring (flowers and birds) and summer (wheat); in the southern courtyard turn to the northern side for autumn (grapes) and winter, with a symbol representing both the end of the year and the end of life. On the western side of the second courtyard are air on the left and fire on the right. On the eastern side look for earth on the left and water on the right. St-Paul metro station is about 250m west of the Hôtel de Sully's main entrance or catch bus No 67 to the metro stations of Hôtel de Ville or Châtelet.

LEFT BANK BOOKWORMING

Writers have found their way to Paris ever since that 16th-century hedonist François Rabelais forsook his monastic vows and hightailed it to the capital. The 1920s saw the greatest influx of outsiders, particularly Americans. Many assume it was Paris' reputation for liberal thought and relaxed morals that attracted the likes of Ernest Hemingway, F Scott Fitzgerald, Ezra Pound and so on, but that's just part of the story. Paris was cheap, particularly the Left Bank, and in France, unlike in Prohibition-era America, you could drink alcohol to your heart's (or liver's) content.

Begin your tour at the Cardinal Lemoine metro station, where rue du Cardinal Lemoine meets rue Monge (5e). Walk southwest along rue du Cardinal Lemoine, peering down the **passageway 1** at No 71, which is now closed to the public. The Irish writer James Joyce (1882–1941) lived in the courtyard flat at the back marked 'E' when he first arrived in Paris in 1921, and it was here

Walk Facts

Start Metro Cardinal Lemoine
End Dingo Bar
Distance 7km
Duration Three hours
Transport Metro Port Royal, Vavin or Cardinal Lemoine
Fuel Stop Les Deux Magots; Café de Flore

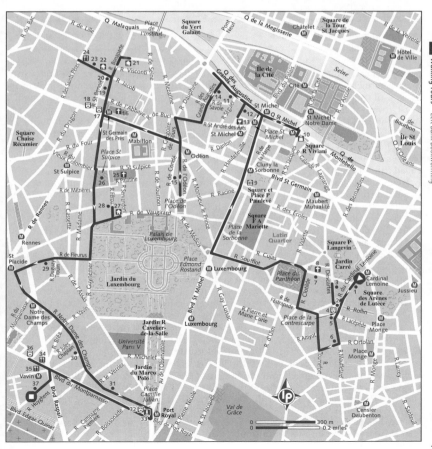

Directing traffic, near Notre Dame

that he finished editing *Ulysses*. Further south at **74 Cardinal Lemoine 2** is the 3rd-floor apartment where Ernest Hemingway (1899–1961) lived with his first wife Hadley from January 1922 until August 1923. The flat figures prominently in his book of memoirs, *A Moveable Feast*, from which the quotation on the wall plaque (in French) is taken: 'This is how Paris was in the early days when we were very poor and very happy'. Just below the flat was the Bal au Printemps, a popular *bal musette* (dancing club), which served as the model for the one where Jake Barnes met Brett Ashley in Hemingway's *The Sun Also Rises*. It is now a bookshop called **Les Alizées** (The Trade Winds; ☎ 01 43 25 20 03; ✆ 10am-10pm) with a gallery called Salon Hemingway.

Hemingway lived on rue du Cardinal Lemoine, but he actually wrote in a top-floor garret of a hotel round the corner at **39 rue Descartes 3**, the very hotel where the poet Paul Verlaine (1844–96) had died less than three decades before. The plaque on what is now a restaurant incorrectly states that Hemingway lived here from 1921 to 1925.

Rue Descartes runs south into place de la Contrescarpe, now a well scrubbed square with Judas trees and a fountain, but once a 'cesspool' (or so Hemingway said), especially the **Café des Amateurs 4** at No 2–4, which is today the flashy Café Delmas (p221). The **Nègre Joyeux 5** at No 12, which sports a large painted-glass mural of a jolly black servant and his white master, was another popular music club at the time.

Rue Mouffetard (from *mofette*, meaning 'skunk') runs south of place de la Contrescarpe. Turn west (right) at the first street on the right (pedestrian rue du Pot de Fer); in 1928 one Eric Blair – better known to the world as George Orwell (1903–50) – stayed in a cheap and dirty boarding house at 6 rue du Pot de Fer called the **Hôtel des Trois Moineaux 6** (Hotel of the Three Sparrows) while working as a dishwasher. He wrote all about it and the street, which he called 'rue du Coq d'Or', in *Down and Out in Paris and London*.

Turn north (right) on rue Tournefort (the street where much of Balzac's novel *Père Goriot* takes place) and go left into rue de l'Estrapade. The large building on the right is the prestigious Lycée Henri IV; the tower in the northern part of the school is the 13th-century (but heavily restored) **Tour Clovis 7**, all that remains of an abbey founded by Clovis I.

From here follow Hemingway's own directions provided in *A Moveable Feast* as he made his way to a favourite café in the Place St-Michel. Walk along rue Clotilde, past the ancient **Église St-Étienne-du-Mont 8** (p94) and through large and windy place du Panthéon. Walk west along rue Soufflot and turn right onto the blvd St-Michel and follow it past **Hôtel de Cluny 9**, now the Musée National du Moyen Age (p94). The cafés on place St-Michel were taken over by tourists decades ago and **Shakespeare & Company 10** (p260) round the corner at 37 rue de la Bûcherie has nothing to do with the real bookshop of that name frequented by Hemingway, but that comes later in the tour. Follow the Seine west along quai des Grands Augustins. Hemingway used to buy books from the **bouquinists 11** (second-hand booksellers), some of whom still line the embankment. At No 9 of tiny rue Gît le Cœur to the south is the **Relais Hôtel du Vieux Paris 12**, a favourite of the poet Allen Ginsberg (1926–97) and Beat writer Jack Kerouac (1922–69) in the 1950s. There's an unsubstantiated story that when Truman Capote first read Kerouac's stream-of-consciousness *On the Road* he exclaimed: 'That's not writing – it's typewriting!' Ginsberg and Kerouac drank just down the road in a bar called **Le Gentilhomme 13** at 28 rue St-André des Arts. It's now a large Irish pub called Corcoran's.

Pablo Picasso (1881–1973) had his studio at **7 rue des Grands Augustins 14**, which runs south from quai des Grands Augustins. Picasso stayed here from 1936 to 1955 and completed his masterpiece *Guernica* here in 1937 – exactly a century after Balzac's *Le Chef d'Œuvre Inconnu* (The Unknown Masterpiece), set in this *hôtel particulier*, was published.

Walk south to rue St-André des Arts, follow it westwards and then turn south on rue de l'Ancienne Comédie. At No 12 rue de l'Odéon, the continuation of rue de L'Ancienne Comédie over blvd St-Germain, stood the original **Shakespeare & Company 15** bookshop, where founder/owner Sylvia Beach (1887–1962) lent books to Hemingway, and edited, retyped and published *Ulysses* for Joyce in 1922. The bookshop was closed during the occupation when Beach refused to sell her last copy of Joyce's *Finnegan's Wake* to a Nazi officer.

Return to blvd St-Germain and walk westwards to the 11th-century **Église St-Germain des Prés 16** (p97). Just opposite is **Les Deux Magots 17** (p223) and beyond it **Café de Flore 18** (p222), favourite hang-outs of post-war Left Bank intellectuals such as Jean-Paul Sartre (1905–80) and Simone de Beauvoir (1908–86) and good places to stop for a snack or a drink.

From place St-Germain des Prés (half of which is now called place Sartre–Beauvoir) walk north along rue Bonaparte. In spring 1930 Henry Miller (1891–1980) stayed in a 5th-floor mansard room in the **Hôtel St-Germain des Prés 19** at No 36 and later wrote about the experience in *Letters to Emil* (1989). A few doors down at No 30 is the **Bistrot Le Pré aux Clercs 20**, another Hemingway hang-out. Continue further north on rue Bonaparte and turn east (right) onto rue des Beaux-Arts. Walk to No 13 and you'll reach what is now **L'Hôtel 21**, the former Hôtel d'Alsace, where Oscar Wilde (born 1854) died of meningitis in 1900, but not before proclaiming, in his typical style, that he and the wallpaper of his room were 'fighting a duel to the death'. The Argentinean writer Jorge Luis Borges (1899–1986) also stayed in the same hotel many times in the late 1970s and early '80s.

Rue Jacob, which runs perpendicular to rue Bonaparte, has literary associations from the sublime to the ridiculous. At No 44, the **Hôtel d'Angleterre 22** (p295) is where Hemingway spent his first night in Paris (room No 14, 20 December 1921). A few doors down at No 56, the former **Hôtel d'York 23** is of great historic, if not literary, significance – this is where David Hartley, George III's representative, met with Benjamin Franklin, John Adams and John Hay on 3 September 1783 to sign the treaty recognising American independence.

At the corner of rue Jacob and rue des Sts-Pères is a nondescript café called **Le Comptoir des Sts-Pères 24**, which under normal circumstances you would not glance at twice. But this was the fashionable restaurant Michaud's, where Hemingway stood outside watching Joyce and his family dine and, later, when he was on the inside looking out, where a memorable event may or may not have taken place. According to Hemingway's *A Moveable Feast*, F Scott Fitzgerald (1896–1940), concerned about not being able to sexually satisfy his wife, Zelda, asked Hemingway to inspect him in the café's toilet. 'It is not basically a question of the size in repose...' Hemingway advised him, in what is surely the greatest example of the 'big lie' in American literary history. Sadly, the old Art Deco-style loo has been removed in recent years and when we told the owner that he had thrown a footnote of American literature on the scrap heap and explained why, he looked incredulous. *'Je ne le crois pas'* (I don't believe it), he said with Gallic self-assurance. *'C'est pas vrai,'* (It's not true).

Return to rue Bonaparte and follow it south this time past **Église St-Sulpice 25** and the **Fontaine des Quatre Évêques 26** (p107). It eventually leads to the northwestern corner of the Jardin du Luxembourg and rue de Vaugirard. This is the area to where Hemingway and many other members of the so-called 'lost generation' moved after slumming it for a few years in the Latin Quarter. William Faulkner (1897–1962) spent a few months at 42 rue de Vaugirard in what is now the posh **Hôtel Luxembourg Parc 27** (p29) in 1925. Hemingway lived his last few years in Paris in a rather grand flat at **6 rue Férou 28**, within easy striking (the operative word, as they had fallen out by then) distance of **27 rue de Fleurus 29**, where the American novelist Gertrude Stein (1874–1946) first lived with her brother Leo and then her life-long companion, Alice B Toklas for 35 years. Stein entertained such luminaries as Matisse, Picasso, Braque, Gauguin, Pound and of course the young Hemingway and Hadley, who were treated as though they were 'very good, well-mannered and promising children'. It's odd to think that this splendid *belle époque* block was less than 10 years old when Stein first moved in 1903. Pound (1885–1972) lived not far away at **70bis rue Notre Dame des Champs 30** in a flat filled with Japanese paintings and with packing crates as furniture, as did Katherine Anne Porter (1890–1980) in the same flat in 1934. Hemingway's first apartment in this part of town was above a sawmill at **113 rue Notre Dames des Champs 31**, now part of the École Alsacienne. Further to the east is **La Closerie des Lilas 32** (p223) on blvd du Montparnasse, where Hemingway often met John Dos Passos or just sat alone, contemplating the **Maréchal Ney statue 33** in front.

Port Royal metro station, where you might end the tour, is just opposite La Closerie des Lilas. But west of here and clustered around place Pablo Picasso and Vavin metro station is a triad of café-restaurants that have hosted more literary luminaries than any others in the world: **La Rotonde 34**, **Le Dôme 35** (p184) and, as Jake Barnes puts it in *The Sun Also Rises*, 'that new dive, the **Select' 36** (p224). But just off blvd Raspail at 10 rue Delambre is the former **Dingo Bar 37**, now an ordinary Italian restaurant called the Auberge de Venise. It was here that Hemingway, the ambitious, middle-class kid from the Midwest, and Fitzgerald, the well-heeled, dissolute Princeton graduate, met for the first time, became friends (of sorts) and went on to change the face of American literature. For one of us, at least, the erstwhile Dingo is a church.

RIGHT BANK TIME PASSAGES

Stepping into the *passages couverts* (covered shopping arcades) or *galeries* (galleries) of the Right Bank is the simplest way to get a feel for early 19th century Paris. These arcades emerged during a period of relative peace and prosperity under the restored House of Bourbon (after the fall of Napoleon) and the rapid growth of the new industrial classes. In a city without sewers, pavements or sheltered walkways, these arcades let shoppers stroll from boutique to boutique protected from the elements and the filth and noise of the streets.

The *passages* quickly became some of Paris' top attractions – provincials made them their first port of call to kit themselves out for the capital – and by the mid-19th century Paris counted some 150 of these sumptuously decorated temples to Mammon. As well as shopping, visitors could dine and drink, play billiards, bathe (all the *passages* had public baths), attend the theatre and, at night (the *passages* were open 24 hours in those days), engage in activities of a carnal nature; the arcades were notorious for attracting prostitutes after dark and there were rooms available on the 1st floor.

The demise of the *passages* came about for a number of reasons, but the most important was the opening of the first of the capital's department stores, Le Bon Marché,

Walk Facts

Start Metro Louvre-Rivoli
End Corner rue du Faubourg Montmartre and rue Richer
Distance 3km
Duration Two hours
Transport Metro Louvre-Rivoli and Le Peletier
Fuel Stop Café du Théâtre

in 1852. Today only 18 arcades remain – mostly in the 1er, 2e and 9e – in various states of repair. They are among the best places to get an idea of how Parisians and their tastes have changed over the years, with traditional millinery and cane shops mixing happily with post-modern designer fashion, and hand-worked printing presses sitting next to Internet cafés. And if you really wanted to you could spend your entire time in Paris under the glass roofs

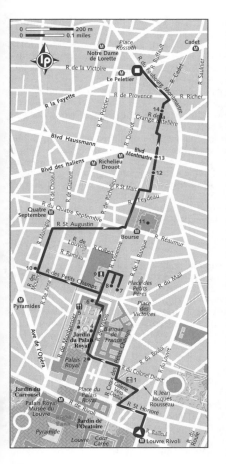

of the *passages*; they still contain everything you need – from restaurants, bars and theatres to hotels and, of course, shops.

Begin the walk at the Louvre-Rivoli metro station (1er) on rue de Rivoli; go north along rue du Louvre, turn left (west) onto rue St-Honoré and then right (north) again on rue Jean-Jacques Rousseau. The entrance to the **Galerie Véro Dodat 1**, built in 1823 by two well-heeled *charcutiers* (butchers), is at No 19. The arcade retains its 19th-century skylights, ceiling murals, Corinthian columns, tiled floor, gas globe fittings and shop fronts, among the most interesting of which include the *papeterie-imprimerie* (stationer-printer's) at No 2–4, in place since 1848; the Luthier music store with guitars, violins and ukuleles at No 17; the Capia shop with antique dolls and gramophones at No 23; and the Marini France stained-glass workshop at No 28.

The gallery's western exit leads onto rue Croix des Petits Champs. Head north to the corner with rue du Colonel Driant – the massive building ahead of you is the headquarters of the Banque de France – and turn left (west) and walk to rue de Valois. At No 5 is one of the entrances to the **Galeries du Palais Royal 2**. Strictly speaking, these galleries are not *passages* as they are arcaded rather than covered, but since they date from 1786 they are considered to be the prototypes of what was to come. The Café de Foy, from where the revolution sparked on a warm July day just three years after the galleries opened, once stood on the western side at what is today's **Galerie de Montpensier 3**. Charlotte Corday, Jean-Paul Marat's assassin, once worked in a shop in the **Galerie de Valois 4**. Galerie de Montpensier has more traditional shops, such as Abacqueville at No 6–8 with medals and ribbons, Les Drapeaux de France at 14–5 with tin soldiers and Didier Ludot (p253) at No 19–20 and No 23–24 with exquisite antique clothes. The **Café du Théâtre 5** at No 67 is a decent place to stop for something to eat or drink.

Galerie de Valois is more upmarket, with posh galleries and designer shops such as an outlet of Hong Kong-based boutique, Joyce. Other shops worth a peak include Le Prince Jardinier gardening shop at No 114–121, the FC autograph shop at 149 and the *graveur héraldiste* (coat of arms engraver) Guillemot, truly a niche concern that prints family coats-of-arms at No 153.

The tiny arcade that doglegs from the north of the Galeries du Palais Royal into rue de Beaujolais is **passage du Perron 6**; the writer Colette (1873–1954) lived the last years of her life in a flat above here (9 rue de Beaujolais), from which she wrote her *Paris de Ma Fenêtre* (Paris from My Window), her description of the German occupation of Paris. Diagonally opposite from where you emerge at 4 rue des Petits Champs are the entrances to two of the most stunningly restored *passages* in Paris. **Galerie Vivienne 7**, built in 1823 and decorated with bas-reliefs of snakes (signifying prudence), anchors (hope) and beehives (industry) and floor mosaics, was and still is one of the poshest of the *passages*. As you enter, look to the stairwell to the left at No 13 with its false marble walls; François Eugène Vidocq

(1775–1857), master burglar *and* the chief of detectives in Paris in the early 19th century, lived upstairs. Some shops to check out are Legrand Fille et Fils, which sells wine and wine-related paraphernalia, at No 7–11; Wolff et Descourtis and its silk scarves at No 18; L'Atelir Emilio Robbo, one of the most beautiful flower shops in Paris, at No 29–33; the Librairie Ancienne & Moderne at No 45–46, which Colette frequented; and designer Jean-Paul Gaultier's first boutique (main entrance: 6 rue Vivienne, 2e).

The major draw of the inter-connecting **Galerie Colbert 8**, built in 1826 and undergoing renovations at the time of research, is its huge glass dome and rotunda, which served as a car workshop and garage as recently as the early 1980s. Check out the bizarre fresco above the rue des Petits Champs exit; it's completely disproportional.

Emerge onto rue Vivienne and head south – passing the original home of the Bibliothèque Nationale (p125) before it moved to Bercy with its curiously leaning **statue of Sartre 9** in the courtyard – to rue des Petits Champs and turn right (west). At No 40 is the entrance to **passage Choiseul 10**. Passage Choiseul (1828), some 45m long and containing 80 shops, is more ordinary than many of the other *passages* covered here but is rapidly raising its profile. Discount clothing and shoe shops (Nos 7–9 and 43), Greek and Asian fast-food shops (for example, Nos 44 and 59) and second-hand bookshops are getting fewer and fewer. Passage Choiseul has a long literary pedigree: Paul Verlaine (1844–96) drank absinthe here and Céline (1894–1961) grew up in his mother's shop at No 62. Check out the Théâtre des Bouffes Parisiens, where comedies are performed, at No 61 (main theatre around the corner at 4 rue Monsigny, 2e).

Leave passage Choiseul at 23 rue St-Augustin and walk eastwards to where it meets rue du Quatre Septembre. The building across the square is the **Bourse du Commerce 11**, built in 1826. Head north and walk up rue Vivienne, and then east (right) along rue St-Marc. The entrance to the maze-like **passage des Panoramas 12** is at 10 rue St-Marc.

Built in 1800, Passage des Panoramas is the oldest covered arcade in Paris and the first to be lit by gas (1817). It was expanded in 1834 with the addition of four other interconnecting *passages*: Feydeau, Montmartre, St-Marc and Variétés. It's a bit faded around the edges, but keep an eye open for Jean-Paul Belmondo's Théâtre des Variétés at No 17, the erstwhile vaudeville Théâtre d'Offenbach, from where spectators would come out to shop during the interval and the engraver Mercier at No 8 and the engraver Stern at No 47. Exit at 11 blvd Montmartre. Directly across the road, at No 10–12, is the entrance to **passage Jouffroy 13**.

Passage Jouffroy, the last major *passage* to open in Paris (1846), but the first to use metal and glass in its skylights and to have central heating, remains a personal favourite; no other *passage* offers so much or feels so alive. There are two hotels here, including the Hôtel Chopin (p298) as well as the Musée Grévin (p121) of wax figures. There are also some wonderful boutiques, including the bookshops Librairie du Passage (Nos 48 and 62) and Paul Vulin (No 50); M&G Segas (No 34), where Toulouse Lautrec bought his walking sticks; the rococo Thomas Boog (No 36), where everything seems to be made of or depict shells; and Brésilophile (No 40) filled with colourful rocks and minerals.

Leave passage Jouffroy at 9 rue de la Grange Batelière, cross the road to No 6, and enter **passage Verdeau 14**, the last and most modest of this stretch of covered arcades. Verdeau wasn't particularly successful because of its 'end-of-the-line' location. Still, there's lots to explore here: Le Cabinet des Curieux (No 12) with weird and curious objects; daguerreotypes at Photo Verdeau (No 14); and vintage Tintin and comic books at Roland Buret (No 6).

The northern exit from passage Verdeau will leave you on the corner of rue du Faubourg Montmartre and rue Richer. Walk north along the former and turn left (west) on rue La Fayette – you'll soon reach Le Peletier metro station.

PARISIAN WORLD TOUR

And you thought it was all berets, baguettes and bistros... To be sure Paris is and will always be *français* (french) – the *couturiers* (designers) will continue to spin their glad rags, the *boulangeries* (bakeries) will churn out those long, crispy loaves and the terrace cafés will remain the places from which to watch the world go by. But it's a much more international world nowadays, and Paris *mondial* (literally 'world Paris'), a diverse, dynamic, multicultural city, vibrates to its rhythms.

France ruled a considerable part of the world until as recently as the middle of the 20th century, and today its population includes a large number of immigrants and their descendants from its former colonies and protectorates in Africa, Indochina, the Middle East, India, the Caribbean and the South Pacific. At the same time, France has continued to accept significant numbers of exiles and refugees. Most of these immigrants have settled in specific areas of the capital, especially Belleville in the 19e and 20e, rue du Faubourg St Denis in the 10e and La Goutte d'Or and Château Rouge in the 18e. A stroll through these quarters will have you touring the globe without even boarding an aeroplane.

Walk Facts
Start Metro Pyrénées
End Rue Dejean
Distance 8km
Duration 3½ hours
Transport Metro Château Rouge and Pyrénées
Fuel Stop Passage Brady

Begin the walk at the Pyrénées metro stop in Belleville, a district where Jewish kosher and Muslim halal butchers share the same streets with cavernous Chinese eating establishments, their windows festooned with dripping *cha siu* (roast pork). Walk west on rue de Belleville past the **birthplace of Édith Piaf 1** (see the boxed text, p234) at No 72 and turn left (south) onto rue Piat, which you will be forgiven for thinking says 'Piaf'. Rue Piat will bring you to the Parc de Belleville (p123) which, at 200m above sea level, offers wonderful views of what is a very flat city. Descend the steps at the end of rue du Transvaal that lead to the **Maison de l'Air 2** (p123) nature centre exhibition space and follow the path to rue de Pali Kao and on to blvd de Belleville.

Blvd de Belleville is like a microcosm of Paris *mondial* and on market mornings (see the boxed text, p152), you might think you've been transported to the Mediterranean, Africa or even Asia. Watch the elegant, turbaned African women in technicolour boubous brush past frenzied young Asians with mobile phones glued to their ears, and more relaxed Orthodox

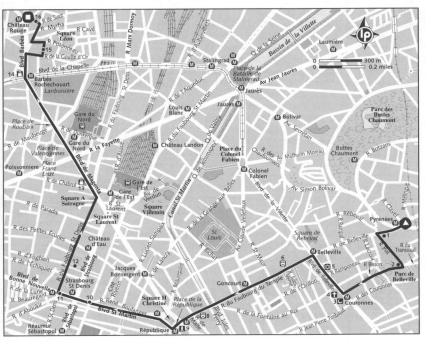

Jews wearing yarmulkes alongside North Africans in jellabas on their way to the mosque. At No 39 is the **Mosquée Abou-Bakr 3** just a few doors down from the modern **Église Notre Dame Réconciliatrice 4** at the corner of rue de la Fontaine au Roi. About 100m up on the right-hand – or Tunisian – side of blvd de Belleville is the **Synagogue Michkan-Taachov 5** at No 110. In nearby rue Ramponeau you'll encounter a Jewish shop call La Maison du Taleth at No 10 with religious tomes and articles and a kosher butcher Boucherie Zlassi at No 7.

Walk north up blvd de Belleville and turn left (west) at the top and continue down rue du Faubourg du Temple (11e). The walk along rue du Faubourg du Temple to place de la République is a long one and you can take the metro for a couple of stops. But in doing so you'd miss the vibrancy and assorted sights: **La Java 6** (p232) at No 105, where Piaf once warbled, and the **Épicerie Asie, Antilles, Afrique 7** at No 88 that sells goods from three worlds.

Once you've cross the placid Canal St-Martin and walked past the decrepit entrances to the popular clubs **La Favela Chic** (p235) and **Gibus 8** (p235), the enormous place de la République, where many political rallies and demonstrations in Paris start, end or are taking place and its **statue of the Republic 9** (erected in 1883) pop into view. Make your way to the square's northwest corner and follow blvd St-Martin past the **Porte St-Martin 10** and the **Porte St-Denis 11** (p122). Turn right (north) and follow rue du Faubourg St-Denis, the main artery linking Tamil Nadu with Turkey. **Passage Brady 12** (p193) at No 46, built in 1828 and once housing 100 tiny boutiques, is now a warren of Indian, Pakistani and Bangladeshi cafés and restaurants and the perfect spot for a break and some refuelling. Alternatively you might pop into a Turkish *çay salonu* (tea house) or *döner ve yemek salon*, which offer kebabs, *pide* (Turkish pizza, for lack of a better term) and *lahmacun* (thin pitta bread topped with minced meat, tomatoes, onions and fresh parsley) for a cheap and tasty snack.

Those wanting to check out the latest in Black beauty preparations or have tresses added at one of the Afro-Caribbean hairdressers should detour at rue du Château d'Eau.

A few blocks up, the grocers betray their British colonial past: Horlicks, Bird's custard, Glenrych pilchards, HP sauce and Tetley tea bags rub shoulders with naan and *dosas* mixes in the well-stocked shopfronts of Wembley Bazaar, Asia Cash & Carry and their competitors just off rue du Faubourg St Denis in rue Jarry. The names of nearby streets and *passages* – rue de Paradis, rue de la Fidelité, passage du Désir – suggest that this was once a red-light district.

When the Gare de l'Est comes into view turn left onto blvd de Magenta and carry on north past the 19th-century **Marché St-Quentin 13** (see the boxed text, p153) and the Gare du Nord. The big pink sign announcing the **Tati department store 14** (p267) marks the start of La Goute d'Or, the north African quarter called the 'Golden Drop' after a white wine produced here in the 19th century. The district is contiguous with African Château Rouge and outside the metro station you'll most likely be presented with the calling cards of various *médiums* (mediums) or *voyants* (fortune tellers) promising to effect the return of your estranged spouse, unrequited lover or misplaced fortune.

From the Barbés Rochechouart metro stop walk north up blvd Barbés past numerous goldsmiths and fast-food shops and turn east into rue de la Goutte d'Or, a great souk of a street selling everything from gaudy tea glasses and pointy-toed leather *babouches* (slippers) to belly dancers' costumes. From every direction the sounds of *raï* (a fusion of Algerian folk music and rock) fill the air.

Cut up **Villa Poissonnière 15**, a cobbled street that looks straight out of the 19th-century daguerreotype, and turn left and then right onto rue des Poissoniers, 'Street of Fishermen' that is anything but: here you're more likely to find halal butchers offering special deals on sheep heads and 5kg packets of chicken.

Rue Myrha on your left is the frontier between Central and West Africa and the Maghreb; *raï* music quickly gives way to Cameroonian *bikutsi* (a fusion of ancestral rhythms and fast electric guitars) and Senegalese *mbalax* (Senegalese drum music). After crossing over rue Myrha, turn left (west) into **rue Dejean 16** where an open-air market is held from 8am to 1pm and 3.30pm to 7.30pm Tuesday to Saturday and 8am to 1pm on Sunday. Here you *will* find fish and lots of it, especially fresh *capitaine* (Nile perch) and *thiof* from Senegal, alongside stalls selling fiery Caribbean Scotch Bonnet chillies, plantains and the ever-popular *dasheen* (taro). It's everything you'd need, in fact, to succeed in the art of Afro-Caribbean cuisine.

The Château Rouge metro station is a few steps to the southwest.

Louvre & Les Halles   155
Marais & Bastille   159
The Islands   167
Latin Quarter & Jardin des
Plantes   168
St-Germain, Odéon &
Luxembourg   181
Montparnasse   183
Faubourg St-Germain &
Invalides   184
Eiffel Tower Area &
16e Arrondissement   186
Étoile & Champs-Élysées   186
Clichy & Gare St-Lazare   188
Opéra & Grands Boulevards   189
Gare du Nord, Gare de
l'Est & République   191
Ménilmontant & Belleville   194
Gare de Lyon, Nation &
Bercy   197
13e Arrondissement &
Chinatown   199
15e Arrondissement   200
Montmartre & Pigalle   202
Outside the Walls:
Beyond Central Paris   204

Eating

Eating

As the culinary centre of the most aggressively gastronomic country in the world, Paris has more 'generic French', regional and ethnic restaurants, fine food shops and markets (see the boxed text p152) than any other place in France. Generally speaking, *la cuisine parisienne* (Parisian cuisine) is a poor relation of that extended family known as *la cuisine des provinces* (provincial cuisine) and today very few dishes are associated with the capital as such. Still, the surfeit of other cuisines available in Paris will have you spoiled for choice and begging for more.

Opening Hours

Restaurants generally open from noon to 2.30pm or 3pm for lunch and 7.30pm to between 10pm and midnight. Only brasseries serve full meals continuously throughout the day (usually from 11am to noon to as late as 1am). National and local laws require that restaurants close one and a half days a week and that employees work no more than 35 hours a week. That means most eateries will be shut tight for a full day and (usually) an afternoon. Be advised that the vast majority of restaurants in Paris close on Sunday – there's a distressing tendency for many to shut down the entire weekend. Supermarkets are generally open from between 8.30am and 9am till 8pm Monday to Saturday with very few open Sunday (9am to 12.30pm or 1pm). Only opening hours that differ from usual hours are given.

How Much?

When it comes to eating out in Paris, the question 'How much?' is like asking 'How long is a piece of string'? It all depends... Three-course dinner *menus* can be had for as little as €10 at budget places and one-plate *plats du jour* (daily specials) at lunch are even cheaper. On the other hand three courses for lunch at **Le Grand Véfour** (p157) overlooking the Jardin du Palais Royal will set you back €75 and dinner more than three times that amount.

In general, however, you should be able to enjoy a substantial sit-down lunch for €15 at a medium-priced restaurant and an excellent three-course dinner with wine for under €30. Cheap eats are under €10.

Generally, higher-priced *menus* are available at lunch and dinner. Lower-priced good-value *menus* that are available at lunch only or dinner only are noted as such throughout the chapter.

Booking Tables

It is always advisable to book in advance at mid-range restaurants and mandatory at top-end ones. If you do arrive at a restaurant without a reservation, you will be treated more seriously if you state the number of *couverts* (covers) required (*'Avez-vous deux couverts?'*) upon entry rather than the number of places.

La Maison Rose (p203)

Con Fusion: Don't Food Us

In this ever-globalising world, it was, as they say, inevitable. In 1999 a French journalist combined the English words 'food' and 'feeling' and came up not with 'fooling' but with 'fooding'. Apparently he used it to describe the art of appreciating not only the contents on your plate but also what's going on around you – ambience, décor, scene. Before long it was *the* word in the mouths of *branché* (trendy) Parisians and within a year an annual Fooding Festival in December was established. The popular entertainment weekly *Nova* even relaunched their annual food guide as *Guide Fooding*.

But what on God's green earth is it all about really? The funny (perhaps predictable) thing is that no-one seems to know. The *foodeur* (ie he/she who 'foods') frequents places as different as Spoon, Food & Wine (p188), the chichi Georges at the Pompidou Centre, Man Ray (p187) and Favela Chic (p235). It would seem, then, that 'food' is not really a big part of 'fooding'; after all, the truly trendy Parisians are much more concerned with appearance than taste. So paying through the nose for mediocre food in a really trendy spot has got to be better than eating a superb meal somewhere that is uncool, right? Indeed, just ask any Londoner.

Paying & Tipping

With the exception of *cafétérias* (cafeterias), *restaurants libre-service* (self-service restaurants) and the like, most eateries in Paris take credit cards (p347) though there is usually a €15 minimum charge. A hand-held machine used to verify your credit card and payment is brought to the table, where the transaction takes place. Always check your bill before paying; small 'mistakes' do happen from time to time in Paris.

Many French people traditionally seemed to feel that 'going Dutch' (ie splitting the bill) at restaurants was an uncivilised custom, and in general the person who did the inviting would pay for the meal. That may still happen but nowadays close friends and colleagues will usually share the cost equally. They will never calculate it down to the last euro and cent, however, the way some Americans and most Germans and Austrians seem to do in groups.

French law requires that restaurant and café bills include the service charge, which is usually between 12% and 15%. But a word of warning is in order... *Service compris* (service included, often abbreviated as s.c. at the bottom of the bill) means that the service charge is built into the price of each dish; *service non-compris* (service not included) or *service en sus* (service in addition) means that the service charge is calculated after the food and/or drink you've consumed has been added up. In either case you pay only the total of the bill so a *pourboire* (tip) on top of that is neither necessary nor expected in most cases. However, many Parisians will leave a few coins on the table in a restaurant, unless the service was particularly bad. They rarely tip in cafés and bars when they've just had a coffee or a drink, however.

Cheap Eats

Along with the less-expensive places listed under specific quarters and arrondissements below, French chain and university restaurants offer excellent value for those counting their centimes.

FAST-FOOD & CHAIN RESTAURANTS

The American fast-food chains have busy branches all over Paris as does the local hamburger chain Quick. In addition, a number of restaurants have outlets around Paris with standard menus. They are definitely a cut above fast-food outlets and can be good value in areas such as the av des Champs-Élysées, where restaurants tend to be overpriced or bad value (or both).

BISTRO ROMAIN

starters €4.70-9.50, pasta €9.90-13.40, mains €8.90-17.50, menus €10.95 (lunch), €14.90 & €22.70; 11.30am-1am

This ever popular bistro-restaurant chain, which has some 16 branches in Paris proper and another 10 in the *banlieues* (suburbs) around the city, is surprisingly an upmarket place for its price category, and service is always pleasant and efficient. It's been part of the Flo group of restaurants and brasseries since the year 2000. The **Champs-Élysées Bistro Romain** (Map pp383-5; ☎ 01 43 59 93 31; 122 av des Champs-Élysées, 8e; metro George V), one of three along the city's most famous thoroughfare, is a stone's throw form Place Charles de Gaulle and the Arc de Triomphe.

BUFFALO GRILL

mains €8-15, menus from €8; 🕒 **usually 11am-11pm Sun-Thu, 11am-midnight Fri & Sat**

This is a successful chain that took over the old Batifol restaurants. Buffalo Grill has some 10 branches in Paris, including the **Gare du Nord Buffalo Grill** (Map pp386-8; ☎ 01 40 16 47 81; 9 blvd de Denain, 10e; metro Gare du Nord). Not surprisingly, the emphasis here is on grills and steak – everything from T-bone (€16) to ostrich (€13.50).

HIPPOPOTAMUS

starters €3.90-8.50, mains €9.80-17.50, menus € 9.9-22.90; 🕒 **usually 11.45am-12.30am Sun-Thu, 11.45am-1am Fri & Sat**

This chain, which has 10 branches in Paris proper, specialises in solid, steak-based meals and is also part of the Flo stable. Four of the outlets stay open to 5am daily, including the **Opéra Hippopotamus** (Map pp386-8; ☎ 01 47 42 75 70; 1 blvd des Capucines, 2e; metro Opéra).

LÉON DE BRUXELLES

starters €3.80-6, mains 9.50-15, menus €9.90-13.60; 🕒 **11.45am-11pm**

Here the focus is on one thing and one thing only: *moules* (mussels). Meal-size bowls of the meaty bivalves, served with chips and bread, start at under €10 and are exceptionally good value, especially at lunch. There are 13 Léons in Paris, including the **Les Halles Léon de Bruxelles** (Map pp396-9; ☎ 01 42 36 18 50; 120 rue Rambuteau, 1er; metro Châtelet-Les Halles).

UNIVERSITY CANTEENS

Stodgy but filling cafeteria food is available in copious quantities at Paris' 17 *restaurants universitaires* (student restaurants) and 20 cafés run by the universities.

CENTRE RÉGIONAL DES ŒUVRES UNIVERSITAIRES ET SCOLAIRES

CROUS; ☎ **01 40 51 55 55; www.crous-paris.fr in French**

Tickets for three-course meals at the restaurants are €2.60 for students with a French uni-

---

To Market, to Market...

There is no better way to feel part of Paris than to engage in that most Parisian of pastimes: shopping at a street *marché alimentaire* (food market). Forsake that morning at the Louvre; instead, grab a basket and load up with fresh provisions.

The city's *marchés découverts* (open-air markets) – some five dozen of which pop up in public squares around the city two or three times a week – are usually open from about 7am or 8am to 1pm or 2pm, depending on the time of year. The 19 *marchés couverts* (covered markets) keep more regular hours: 8am to 1pm and 3.30pm or 4pm to 7pm or 7.30pm from Tuesday to Saturday and till lunch time on Sunday. Completing the picture are numerous independent *rues commerçantes*, pedestrian streets where the shops set up outdoor stalls. To find out when there's a market near your hotel or hostel, ask the staff or anyone who lives in the neighbourhood.

The following is a list of Paris markets rated according to the variety of their produce, their ethnicity and the neighbourhood. They are *la crème de la crème*.

Av du Prèsident Wilson (Map pp383-5; av du Président Wilson east of place d'Iéna, 16e; metro Iéna or Alma Marceau; 🕒 9am-1.30pm Wed & Sat) This upscale market attracts a well-heeled crowd from the 16e arrondissement.

Blvd de Grenelle (Map pp389-91; blvd de Grenelle between rue de Lourmel & rue du Commerce, 15e; metro La Motte-Picquet Grenelle; 🕒 7am-1pm Wed & Sun) Arranged below an elevated railway and surrounded by stately Haussmann boulevards and Art Nouveau apartment blocks, the Grenelle market attracts a posh clientele.

Marché aux Enfants Rouges (Map pp396-9; 39 rue de Bretagne, 3e; metro Temple or Arts et Métiers; 🕒 8am-1pm & 4-7.30pm Tue-Sat, 8am-1pm Sun) This recently reopened covered market south of place de la République has both ethnic (Italian, North African etc) stalls as well as French ones.

Marché d'Aligre (Map pp392-5; place d'Aligre, 12e; metro Ledru Rollin; 🕒 8am-1pm & 4-7.30pm Tue-Sat, 8am-1pm Sun) This covered market remains a colourful Arab and North African enclave a stone's throw from the Bastille.

Marché Bastille (Map pp392-5; blvd Richard Lenoir, 11e; metro Bastille; 🕒 7am or 8am-1pm Tue & Sun) Stretching as far north as the Richard Lenoir metro station, this is arguably the best roving street market in Paris.

Marché Batignolles-Clichy (Map pp383-5; blvd des Batignolles between rue des Batignolles & rue Puteaux, 17e; metro Place de Clichy or Rome; 🕒 9am-1.30pm Sat) This is one of the several *marchés biologiques* (organic markets) in Paris that are becoming increasingly popular.

versity or college ID card, €4.50 with an ISIC or youth card and €5 for guests. CROUS restaurants (usually called 'restos U') have variable hours that change according to university holiday schedules and weekend rotational agreements; check the schedule posted outside any of the following or the CROUS website for current times. Branches include **Assas** (Map pp389-91; ☎ 01 44 41 58 01; 92 rue d'Assas, 6e; metro Port Royal or Notre Dame des Champs; ☾lunch 11am-2.30pm Mon-Fri), **Bullier** (Map pp392-5; ☎ 01 40 51 37 85; 39 av Georges Bernanos, 5e; metro Port Royal; ☾lunch 11.30am-2pm, dinner 6.15-8pm), **Censier** (Map pp392-5; ☎ 01 45 35 41 24; 31 rue Geoffroy St-Hilaire, 5e; metro Censier Daubenton or Jussieu; ☾lunch 11am-2.30pm Mon-Fri), **Châtelet** (Map pp392-5; ☎ 01 43 31 51 66; 10 rue Jean Calvin, 5e; metro Censier Daubenton; ☾lunch 11.30am-2pm, dinner 6.30-8pm Mon-Fri), **Mabillon** (Map pp396-9; ☎ 01 43 25 66 23; 3 rue Mabillon, 6e; metro Mabillon; ☾lunch 11.30am-2pm, dinner 6-8pm) and **Mazet** (Map pp396-9; 5 rue André Mazet, 6e; metro Odéon; ☾lunch 11.30am-2pm Mon-Fri).

Self-Catering

There is a wide variety of self-catering options available from small neighbourhood stores specialising in just one product to large supermarkets and Paris' great open-air markets.

LOUVRE & LES HALLES

There are a number of supermarkets along av de l'Opéra and rue de Richelieu, as well as around Forum des Halles, including a large one in the basement of **Monoprix** (Map pp386-8; 21 av de l'Opéra, 2e; ☾9am-9.50pm Mon-Fri, 9am-8.50pm Sat). Other supermarkets include: **Ed l'Épicier** (Map pp396-9; 80 rue de Rivoli, 4e; ☾9am-8pm Mon-Sat); **Franprix** (Map pp396-9; 35 rue Berger, 1er; ☾8.30am-7.50pm Mon-Sat); **Franprix Châtelet branch** (Map pp396-9; 16 rue Bertin Poirée, 1er; metro Châtelet; ☾9am-8pm Mon-Sat).

Marché Belleville (Map pp386-8; blvd de Belleville between rue Jean-Pierre Timbaud & rue du Faubourg du Temple, 11e & 20e; metro Belleville or Couronne; ☾7am or 8am-1pm Tue & Fri) This market offers a fascinating (and easy) entry into the large, vibrant ethnic communities of the *quartiers de l'est* (eastern neighbourhoods), home to African, Middle Eastern and Asian immigrants as well as artists and students.

Marche Poncelet-Bayen (Map pp383-5; along rue Poncelet & rue Bayen, 17e; metro Ternes; ☾8am-1pm & 4-7.30pm Tue-Sat, 8am-1pm Sun) This market street caters to the well-heeled of the 16e and 17e arrondissments.

Marché Raspail (Map pp389-91; blvd Raspail between rue de Rennes & rue du Cherche Midi, 6e; metro Rennes; ☾9am-1.30pm Tue, Fri & Sun) This traditional street market just north of the Rennes metro station features organic produce on Sunday.

Marché St-Charles (Map pp389-91; rue St-Charles & place Charles Michels, 15e; metro Charles Michels; ☾9am-1pm Fri) This market may appear somewhat far-flung off in the western 15e arrondissement, but shoppers will go any distance for its quality organic produce.

Marché St-Quentin (Map pp386-8; 85 blvd de Magenta, 10e; metro Gare de l'Est; ☾8am-1pm & 3.30-7.30pm Tue-Sat, 8am-1pm Sun) This iron-and-glass covered market, built in 1866, is a maze of corridors lined mostly with gourmet food stalls.

Place Maubert (Map pp396-9; metro Maubert Mutualité; ☾7am-2pm Tue-Sat) This market spread over a small triangle of intersecting streets reigns over St-Germain des Prés, the most upmarket part of the bohemian 5e.

Rue Cler (Map pp389-91; metro École Militaire; ☾7am or 8am-7pm or 7.30pm Tue-Sat, 8am-noon Sun) This street in the 7e arrondissement is a breath of fresh air in a sometimes stuffy *quartier* and can almost feel like a party at the weekend when the whole neighbourhood turns out en masse.

Rue Montorgueil (Map pp386-8; rue Montorgueil between rue de Turbigo & rue Réaumur, 2e; metro Les Halles or Sentier; ☾7am or 8am-7pm or 7.30pm Tue-Sat, 8am-noon Sun) This is the closest market to Paris' 700-year-old wholesale market, Les Halles, which was moved from this area to the southern suburb of Rungis in 1969 so expect a fair number of nostalgia-seekers.

Rue Mouffetard (Map pp392-5; rue Mouffetard around rue de l'Arbalète; metro Censier Daubenton or Place Monge; ☾7am or 8am-7pm or 7.30pm Tue-Sat, 8am-noon Sun) Rue Mouffetard is the city's most photogenic market street and it's the place where Parisians send tourists (real travellers go to Marché Bastille).

MARAIS & BASTILLE

In the Marais, there are several food shops and Asian delicatessens on the odd-numbered side of rue St-Antoine, 4e (Map pp396-9) plus several supermarkets. Closer to Bastille there are lots of food shops along rue de la Roquette (Map pp392-5; metro Voltaire or Bastille) towards place Léon Blum.

Supermarkets include: **Franprix** (Map pp396-9; 135 rue St-Antoine, 4e; ☉ 9am-8.30pm Mon-Sat); **Franprix Marais branch** (Map pp396-9; 87 rue de la Verrerie, 4e; ☉ 9am-8.15pm Mon-Fri, 9am-8.30pm Sat); **Monoprix** (Map pp396-9; 71 rue St-Antoine, 4e; ☉ 9am-9pm Mon-Sat); **Monoprix Bastille branch** (Map pp392-5; 97 rue du Faubourg St-Antoine, 11e; metro Ledru Rollin; ☉ 9am-10pm Mon-Sat); **Supermarché G20** (Map pp396-9; 81-83 rue de la Verrerie, 4e; ☉ 8.30am-8.30pm Mon-Sat); **Supermarché G20 Bastille branch** (Map pp396-9; 115 rue St-Antoine, 4e; ☉ 9am-8.30pm Mon-Sat).

FAUCHON Map pp392-5   *Delicatessen*
☎ 01 53 01 91 91; 10 rue St-Antoine, 4e; metro Bastille; ☉ 8am-11pm

This branch of the famous *traiteur* chain (p264) at the corner of rue des Tournelles has picnic supplies and some of the most delectable pastries in Paris.

FROMAGERIE G MILLET
Map pp396-9   *Delicatessen*
☎ 01 42 78 48 78; 77 rue St-Antoine, 4e;
☉ 7.30am-1pm & 3.30-8pm Mon-Fri, 7.30am-1pm Sat
Great for excellent cheese.

THE ISLANDS

Along rue St-Louis en l'Île on Île de St-Louis there are a number of *fromageries* and groceries (usually closed on Sunday afternoon and all day Monday). There are more food shops on rue des Deux Ponts.

LATIN QUARTER & JARDIN DES PLANTES

Place Maubert, 5e (Map pp396-9), becomes a lively food market four mornings a week (see the boxed text p153) and there are also some great provisions shops here. There's a lively food market along rue Mouffetard (see the boxed text p153). On place Monge there's a much smaller market (Map pp392-5; place Monge, 5e; metro Place Monge; ☉ 8am-2pm Wed, Fri & Sun).

Supermarkets in the area include: **Champion** (Map pp392-5; 34 rue Monge, 5e; metro Place Monge; ☉ 8.30am-9pm Mon-Sat); **Ed l'Épicier** (Map pp392-5; 37 rue Lacépède, 5e; ☉ 9am-1pm & 3-7.30pm Mon-Fri, 9am-7.30pm Sat); **Franprix** (Map pp392-5; 82 rue Mouffetard, 5e; metro Censier Daubenton or Place Monge; ☉ 9am-8pm Mon-Sat).

CRÉMERIE DES CARMES
Map pp396-9   *Fromagerie*
☎ 01 43 54 50 93; 47ter blvd St-Germain, 5e; metro Maubert Mutualité; ☉ 7.30am-1pm & 3.30-8pm Mon-Fri, 7.30am-1pm Sat

This shop in the Latin Quarter sells cheese and high-quality dairy products.

ST-GERMAIN, ODÉON & LUXEMBOURG

With the Jardin du Luxembourg nearby, this is the perfect area for a picnic lunch. There is a large cluster of food shops on rue de Seine and rue de Buci, 6e (metro Mabillon). The renovated and covered **Marché St-Germain** (Map pp396-9; rue Lobineau, 6e; metro Mabillon), just north of the eastern end of Église St-Sulpice, has a huge array of produce and prepared food. Nearby supermarkets include: **Champion** (Map pp396-9; 79 rue de Seine, 6e; metro Mabillon; ☉ 1-9pm Mon, 8.40am-9pm Tue-Sat, 9am-1pm Sun); **Monoprix** (Map pp396-9; 52 rue de Rennes, 6e; metro St-Germain des Prés; ☉ 9am-10pm Mon-Sat).

MONTPARNASSE

Opposite the Tour Montparnasse there's an outdoor **food market** (Map pp389-91; blvd Edgar Quinet; ☉ 7am-1.30pm Wed & Sat). Supermarkets that are most convenient to the area include the following: **Franprix** (Map pp389-91; 55 av du Maine, 14e; metro Gaîté; ☉ 8.30am-8pm Mon-Sat); **Franprix Delambre branch** (Map pp389-91; 11 rue Delambre; metro Vavin; ☉ 8.30am-7.50pm Mon-Sat); and **Inno** (Map pp389-91; 29-31 rue du Départ, 14e; metro Montparnasse Bienvenüe; ☉ 9am-9.50pm Mon-Fri, 9am-8.50pm Sat).

FAUBOURG ST-GERMAIN & INVALIDES

Arguably the finest grocery store in the neighbourhood is Le Bon Marché's **La Grande Épicerie de Paris** (Map pp389-91; 26 rue de Sèvres; metro Sèvres Babylone; ☉ 8.30am-9pm Mon-Sat).

ÉTOILE & CHAMPS-ÉLYSÉES

The huge **Monoprix** (Map pp383-5; 62 av des Champs-Élysées, 8e; metro Franklin D Roosevelt; ☺ 9am-midnight Mon-Sat) at the corner of rue La Boétie has a big supermarket section in the basement.

GARE DU NORD, GARE DE LEST & RÉPUBLIQUE

Rue du Faubourg St-Denis, 10e (metro Strasbourg St-Denis or Château d'Eau), which links blvd St-Denis and blvd de Magenta, is one of the cheapest places to buy food, especially fruit and veg (shop Nos 23, 27–29 and 41–43). It has a distinctively Middle Eastern air, and quite a few of the groceries offer Turkish, North African and subcontinental specialities. Many of the food shops, including the *fromagerie* at No 54, are open Tuesday to Saturday and until noon on Sunday. Further north, you'll find **Marché St-Quentin** (Map pp386-8; metro Gare de l'Est); for details see the boxed text p153.

Supermarkets convenient to this area include: **Franprix Faubourg St-Denis branch** (Map pp386-8; 25 rue du Faubourg St-Denis, 10e; metro Strasbourg St-Denis; ☺ 9am-7.50pm Mon-Sat); **Franprix Petites Écuries branch** (Map pp386-8; 7-9 rue des Petites Écuries, 10e; metro Château d'Eau; ☺ 9am-7.50pm Mon-Sat); **Franprix Magenta branch** (Map pp386-8; 57 blvd de Magenta, 10e; metro Gare de l'Est; ☺ 9am-8pm Mon-Sat) and **Franprix Bretagne branch** (Map pp396-9; 49 rue de Bretagne, 3e; metro Arts et Métiers; ☺ 9am-8.30pm Tue-Sat, 9am-1.20pm Sun).

MÉNILMONTANT & BELLEVILLE

Supermarkets in these areas include: **Franprix Jules Ferry branch** (Map pp386-8; 28 blvd Jules Ferry, 11e; metro République or Goncourt; ☺ 8am-8pm Mon-Sat) and **Franprix Jean-Pierre Timbaud branch** (Map pp386-8; 23 rue Jean-Pierre Timbaud, 11e; metro Oberkampf; ☺ 8am-8pm Mon-Sat).

GARE DE LYON, NATION & BERCY

West of Parc de Bercy, there's a **Franprix** (Map p401; 3 rue Baron le Roy, 12e; metro Cour St-Émilion; ☺ 8.30am-2pm & 2.15-8pm Mon-Sat, 9am-2pm Sun).

15E ARRONDISSEMENT

There are many supermarkets here, including **Monoprix** (Map pp389-91; 2 rue du Commerce, 15e; metro La Motte Picquet-Grenelle; ☺ 9am-10pm Mon-Sat) and **Franprix** (Map pp389-91; 34 rue de Lourmel, 15e; metro Dupleix; ☺ 8.30am-8pm Mon-Sat).

MONTMARTRE & PIGALLE

Towards place Pigalle there are lots of groceries, many of them open until late at night; try the side streets leading off blvd de Clichy (eg rue Lepic). Heading south from blvd de Clichy, rue des Martyrs, 9e (Map pp386-8), is lined with food shops almost all the way to metro Notre-Dame de-Lorette. Supermarkets in the area include: **8 à Huit** (Map p400; 24 rue Lepic, 18e; metro Abbesses; ☺ 8.30am-9pm Mon-Sat) and **Ed l'Épicier** (Map p400; 31 rue d'Orsel, 18e; metro Anvers; ☺ 9am-8pm Mon-Sat).

ST-DENIS

The large, multi-ethnic **food market** (Map St-Denis; place Jean Jaurès; ☺ 8am-2pm Tue, Fri & Sun) across the street from the tourist office and in the **Halle du Marché**, the large covered market a short stroll away to the northwest, is known in particular for its selection of spices.

There's a **Franprix** (Map St -Denis; 34 rue de la République; ☺ 9am-1pm & 3-7.15pm Tue-Sat, 8.30am-1pm Sun) in the centre of town near the post office.

LOUVRE & LES HALLES

The area between Forum des Halles (1er) and the Centre Pompidou (4e) is filled with scores of trendy restaurants but few of them are particularly good and mostly cater to tourists. Streets lined with places to eat include rue des Lombards, the narrow streets north and east of Forum des Halles and pedestrian-only rue Montorgueil, a market street and probably your best bet for something quick. In addition, there are a number of worthwhile places in the *passages couverts*, the covered shopping arcades (p144).

If you're in search of Asian food, people flock to rue Ste-Anne and other streets of Paris' Japantown, which is just west of the Jardin du Palais Royal. There are also some good-value restaurants serving other Asian cuisine in the area.

Top Five Louvre & Les Halles Restaurants

- **Café Marley** (this page)
- **Le Grand Véfour** (opposite)
- **Le Vaudeville** (opposite)
- **Macéo** (p158)
- **Willi's Wine Bar** (p159)

AU PIED DE COCHON

Map pp396-9   *French, Brasserie*
☎ 01 40 13 77 00; 6 rue Coquillière, 1er; metro Les Halles; starters €8-19.50, mains €15-28, plat du jour €15; ☻ 24hr

This venerable establishment that once satisfied the appetites of both market porters and theatre-goers with its onion soup and *pied de cochon* (pig's foot) has become more uniformly upmarket and touristy since Les Halles was moved to the suburbs, but it still opens round the clock seven days a week. If you've never eaten a trotter before, give it a go. The plat du jour includes a glass of wine.

AUX CRUS DE BOURGOGNE

Map pp386-8   *French, Bistro*
☎ 01 42 33 48 24; 3 rue de Bachaumont, 2e; metro Les Halles or Sentier; starters €6.50-17.50, mains €13-26, menu €25; ☻ lunch & dinner to 11pm Mon-Fri

This excellent bistro on a pedestrian street just off busy rue Montorgueil has a penchant for fish and seafood – especially lobster. As its name implies, Burgundy is the wine of choice. A real plus is the open terrace in the warmer months, which allows you to enjoy your crustaceans without a side order of exhaust fumes.

BAAN BORAN Map pp386-8   *Thai*
☎ 01 40 15 90 45; 43 rue Montpensier, 1er; metro Palais Royal–Musée du Louvre; meals from €30, menu €12.50 (lunch) ☻ lunch Mon-Fri, dinner to 11.30pm Mon-Sat

The fare at this eatery, just opposite the Théâtre du Palais Royal and run by two Thai women, is not as authentic as what you'll find up in Belleville. But for some quick Asian fodder while touring the Louvre, it will do.

CAFÉ DE L'ÉPOQUE

Map pp396-9   *French, Café*
☎ 01 42 33 40 70; 35-37 Galerie Véro Dodat, 2 rue du Bouloi, 1er; metro Louvre-Rivoli; starters €8-9, mains €13-22, plat du jour €14-15.80; ☻ lunch daily, dinner to midnight Mon-Sat

The lovely old 'Café of the Time' is just that – a relic of the *belle époque* when the *passages couverts* (covered arcades) were *the* places to shop. It can be entered from the covered *passage* itself or the lovely terrace facing rue du Bouloi. The daily specials are particularly good value here.

CAFÉ DU THÉÂTRE

Map pp386-8   *French, Café*
☎ 01 42 97 59 46; 67 Galerie de Montpensier, 36 rue de Montpensier, 1er; metro Pyramides; starters €9-14, mains €13-15, plat du jour €15; ☻ lunch & dinner to 10.15pm

This civilised café facing the Jardin du Palais Royal is next door to the little-known Théâtre du Palais Royal (hence the name) and opposite the peerless **Le Grand Véfour** (p157). It's a convenient spot if visiting the covered passages around Palais Royal or even the Louvre and does great teas from 3pm to 6.15pm.

CAFÉ MARLY Map pp396-9   *French, Café*
☎ 01 46 26 06 60; cour Napoléon du Louvre, 93 rue de Rivoli, 1er; metro Palais Royal–Musée du Louvre; starters €8-21, pasta €13-23, sandwiches & snacks €10-14, mains €16-30; ☻ lunch & dinner to 1am

This classic venue, brought to us courtesy of the Coste brothers, serves contemporary French fare under the colonnades of the Louvre. The views of the glass pyramid are priceless – if you don't know you're in Paris now, you never will – and depending on how *au courant* (familiar) you are with French starlets and people who appear in *Match*, you should get an eyeful.

JOE ALLEN Map pp396-9   *American*
☎ 01 42 36 70 13; 30 rue Pierre Lescot, 1er; metro Étienne Marcel; menus €12.90 (lunch), €18 & €22.50, brunch €11.90-15; ☻ noon-midnight

An institution in Paris for some three decades, Joe Allen is a little bit of New York in Paris, with a great atmosphere and a good selection of Californian wines. There's an excellent brunch from noon to 4pm at the weekend, where many can be seen slumped over a Bloody Mary and trying to make sense of the night – or was that the morning? – before. The food is simple but finely prepared. The marinated sardine fillets served on toast are a speciality, and here's where you'll find the best hamburgers in town.

LA VICTOIRE SUPRÊME DU CŒUR

Map pp396-9   *Vegetarian*

☎ 01 40 41 93 95; 41 rue des Bourdonnais, 1er; metro Châtelet; menus €12 (lunch) & €20 (dinner); ✆ lunch & dinner to 10pm Mon-Sat

This Indian-inspired vegan restaurant is a welcome addition to the hubbub of Les Halles. Try the mango lassi or spice tea.

L'AMAZONIAL Map pp396-9   *International*

☎ 01 42 33 53 13; 3 rue Ste-Opportune, 1er; metro Châtelet; starters €7.50-15, pasta €10.50, mains €10.50-21; menus €12 (lunch), €14 & €25; ✆ noon-1am

Paris' first and largest gay restaurant has food that is nothing to write home about, but it does boast good-value *menus*. Service is very s-l-o-w but the buffed-up waiters in tight T-shirts are worth the wait. There are shows at the weekend and brunch on Sunday (noon to 5pm). The covered terrace is a plus in winter.

LE GRAND COLBERT Map pp386-8   *French*

☎ 01 42 86 87 88; 2-4 rue Vivienne, 2e; metro Pyramides; starters €9.50-16.50, mains €17.50-27, menu €26; ✆ noon-1am

This former workers' cafeteria transformed into a *fin-de-siècle* showcase is more relaxed than many of its ilk and a convenient spot for lunch if visiting Galerie Vivienne and Galerie Colbert. Don't expect gastronomic miracles, but portions are huge and service is friendly and always *correct* (according to form).

LE GRAND VÉFOUR Map pp386-8   *French*

☎ 01 42 96 56 27; 17 rue de Beaujolais, 1er; metro Pyramides; starters €60-90, mains €70-94, menus €75 (lunch) & €230 (dinner); ✆ lunch Mon-Fri & dinner to 9.30pm Mon-Thu

This 18th-century jewel on the northern edge of the Jardin du Palais Royal has been a dining favourite of the Paris elite since 1784; just look at who gets their names ascribed to each table. With chef Guy Martin at the helm, expect a voyage of discovery in one of the most beautiful restaurants in the world.

LE LOUP BLANC

Map pp386-8   *International*

☎ 01 40 13 08 35; 42 rue Tiquetonne, 2e; metro Étienne Marcel; mains €11-17.50, vegetarian platters €10-12.50; ✆ dinner to midnight Sun-Thu, 12.30am Fri & 1am Sat, brunch to 5pm Sun

This predominantly but not exclusively gay restaurant offers some inventive and inexpensive dishes: meat and fish marinated with herbs

and spices (eg cardamom, star anise, marjoram) and then grilled. For accompaniments, you can choose from up to four vegetables and grains, according to your appetite and the season: red lentils, quinoa (a South American grain), creamed corn (a must) or carrots with cumin. We like the chicken with cumin and sumac, prawns with tamarind and ginger and veal cooked in beer with juniper berries.

LE MONDE À L'ENVERS

Map pp386-8   *French*

☎ 01 40 26 13 91; 35 rue Tiquetonne, 2e; metro Étienne Marcel; menus €13.50 (lunch) & €24 (dinner); ✆ lunch & dinner to 11.30pm Tue-Sun

In the past this small and intimate gay restaurant on pedestrian-only rue Tiquetonne has taken its food much more seriously than its name – the 'World Upside Down' – would suggest. Depending on your neighbour, tables are a bit too close or not close enough; claustrophobics should enter at their own peril.

LE PETIT MÂCHON

Map pp396-9   *French, Lyons*

☎ 01 42 60 08 06; 158 rue St-Honoré, 1er; metro Palais Royal-Musée du Louvre; starters €6.50-12.50, mains €14-21, menu €16.50 (lunch); ✆ lunch & dinner to 11pm Tue-Sun

This is an upbeat bistro with Lyons-inspired specialities convenient to the Louvre. It takes its name from a Burgundian variety of *galette des rois* (kings' cake), a puff pastry filled with frangipane cream that is eaten at Epiphany (Twelfth night).

LE TAMBOUR Map pp386-8   *French, Bistro*

☎ 01 42 33 06 90; 41 rue Montmartre, 2e; metro Étienne Marcel or Sentier; starters €8-14, mains €11-15, menu €10 (lunch); ✆ 6pm-7am

'This isn't a luxury hotel!' shouts the waiter as he wipes a table with the back of his apron. The service at this bistro-café with the crazy hours is brisk, the crowd mixed and often rowdy. You'll enjoy the recycled street furniture, the straightforward cuisine (served well into the night) and the cocky, moustached staff.

LE VAUDEVILLE

Map pp386-8   *French, Brasserie*

☎ 01 40 20 04 62; 29 rue Vivienne, 2e; metro Bourse; starters €7.50-15.50, mains €15-29, menus €22.90 & €32.90; ✆ lunch & dinner to 1am

This stunning brasserie just opposite the stock exchange is to Art Deco what the **Bouillon Racine** (p168) is to Art Nouveau. Wow. OK, so it's part of the Flo chain of brasseries and restaurants with food something of a second thought, but at least you can be guaranteed a certain standard. Come for the fabulous décor – engraved glass, extravagant lighting, domed ceiling and intricate ironwork – which was designed in the 1920s by the same brothers who did **La Coupole** (p183).

LE VÉRO DODAT Map pp396-9   *French*
☎ 01 45 08 92 06; 19 Galerie Véro Dodat, 2 rue du Bouloi, 1er; metro Louvre-Rivoli; starters/mains/desserts €4/9.50/4, menus €13.50 & €15.50, plat du jour €9.50; ✆ lunch & dinner to 10.30pm Tue-Sat
This friendly little place in the heart of the Véro Dodat covered *passage* has seating both downstairs and upstairs. At lunch time it's especially popular with workers from the nearby Bourse de la Commerce.

L'ÉPI D'OR Map pp396-9   *French, Bistro*
☎ 01 42 36 38 12; 25 rue Jean-Jacques Rousseau, 1er; metro Louvre-Rivoli; starters €5-15, mains €14-20, menu €18; ✆ lunch & dinner Mon-Fri, to 10pm Sat
The 'Golden Sword' has been an institution since the *belle époque*, when it would open at 10pm to serve the 'forts des halles', the brutes who stacked the 'devils', huge bags of potatoes and cabbage, all night at the old Marché des Halles. Today it's an oh-so-Parisian bistro serving well-prepared, classic dishes – such as *gigot d'agneau* (leg of lamb) cooked for seven hours – to a surprisingly well-heeled crowd.

MACÉO Map pp386-8   *International*
☎ 01 42 97 53 85; 15 rue des Petits Champs, 1er; metro Bourse or Opéra; starters €8-18, mains €12-20, menus €29.50 (lunch) & €36; ✆ lunch Mon-Fri & dinner to 11pm Mon-Sat
From the people who brought us **Willi's Wine Bar** (p159) comes this very upper crust restaurant with second Empire décor and innovative cuisine from chef Thierry Bourbonnais (just wait for the sophisticated vegetarian menu). An address of the moment for resto-spotters.

TANA Map pp386-8   *Thai*
☎ 01 42 33 53 64; 36 rue Tiquetonne, 2e; metro Étienne Marcel; dishes €10-11.50; ✆ dinner to 11.30pm
In a street where each restaurant is more original than the next, Tana takes the cake. Customers are greeted by rather sexy Thai 'waitresses' and immediately plunged into a highly exotic

---

Brunch for Breakfast

Petit déjeuner (French breakfast) is not every Anglo-Saxon's cup of tea. For many, a croissant with butter and jam, and a cup of milky coffee do not a breakfast make. Masters of the kitchen throughout the rest of the day, French chefs don't seem up to it in the morning. Brunch, however, is a whole different ball game in today's Paris, and numerous places serve late breakfast or early lunch at the weekend (especially Sunday). Here are our three favourites.

Café Beaubourg (Map pp396-9; ☎ 01 48 87 63 96; 43 rue St-Merri, 4e; metro Châtelet-Les Halles; salads €6-11, platters €14-19.50; ✆ 8am-1am Sun-Wed, 8am-2am Thu-Sat) This upbeat minimalist café across from Centre Pompidou has been drawing a well-heeled crowd for breakfast and Sunday brunch (€12.50 to €22) on the terrace since 1986; there's always free entertainment on the *parvis* (large square) opposite.

Le Troisième Bureau (Map pp386-8; ☎ 01 43 55 87 65; 74 rue de la Folie Méricourt, 11e; metro Oberkampf; starters €6.40-10.70, mains €14.50-25, menus €10.60 & €13 (lunch); ✆ lunch & dinner to midnight Mon-Fri, noon-2am Sat & Sun) the 'Third Office' is a pub-cum-bistro with an interesting clientele where you can read, listen to music and enjoy Sunday brunch (€14.50) from 11am to 4pm.

Le Viaduc Café (Map pp392-5; ☎ 01 44 74 70 70; 43 av Daumesnil, 12e; metro Gare de Lyon; starters €8-15, mains €13-24, menu €16 (lunch); ✆ 9am-4am daily) This New York-style café-bar with a terrace in one of the glassed-in arches of the Viaduc des Arts is an excellent spot to while away the early hours and enjoy brunch (€23 and €26) with live jazz from noon to 4pm on Sunday.

Les Fous de l'Île (Map pp396-9; ☎ 01 43 25 76 67; 33 rue des Deux Ponts, 4e; metro Pont Marie; meals €19-12, menu €13 (lunch); ✆ noon-7pm Mon, noon-10pm Tue-Fri, 4-10pm Sat, noon-6pm Sun) This friendly, down-to-earth tea room, exhibition space and restaurant has great brunch on Sunday (€16 to €24) from noon to 4pm.

Pitchi Poï (Map pp396-9; ☎ 01 42 77 46 15; 9 place du Marché Ste-Catherine & 7 rue Caron, 4e; metro St-Paul; dishes €14-19, menu €21; ✆ lunch & dinner to 10.30pm daily) This convivial Eastern European Jewish restaurant on one of Paris' most picturesque squares serves traditional dishes at lunch and dinner and lighter fare such as smoked salmon and chopped chicken liver at Sunday brunch (€24; noon to 4 pm).

world where the extravagant 'hostesses' are equal to the dishes on offer. The rhinestones and faux furs are dusted off on Saturday night for a show that surprises even the initiated. The subtle flavours of the mixed hors d'oeuvre for two and the *poisson vapeur dans sa feuille de banane* (steamed fish served in a banana leaf) are both fairly authentic choices.

VOYAGEURS DU MONDE

Map pp386-8 *International*
☎ 01 42 86 17 17; 51bis rue Ste-Anne, 2e; metro Pyramides or Quatre Septembre; menus €18 & €22; ☾ lunch & dinner to 10pm Mon-Fri
Voyageurs du Monde, the complete travel shop comprising an extensive travel agency (p338), shop and exhibition spaces, also boasts a restaurant that explores the cuisine of every continent in a single menu devoted to a different country each day. It's a rather ambitious task and the results – it must be said – are not always 100% successful, but in a street where Japanese restaurants jostle for space, it's a delight to find this little culinary Babel.

WILLI'S WINE BAR

Map pp386-8 *French, Bistro*
☎ 01 42 61 05 09; 13 rue des Petits Champs, 1er; metro Bourse; starters €9-14, mains €14-19, menus €25 (lunch) & €32 (dinner); ☾ lunch & dinner to 11pm Mon-Sat
This civilised yet convivial wine bar-cum-bistro is owned by British expats who introduced the wine-bar concept to Paris in the mid-1980s. The food is excellent, the wines (especially Côtes du Rhône) well chosen and Willi's legendary status lives on – and deservedly so.

CHEAP EATS
CARIBBEAN COFFEE

Map pp396-9 *Caribbean, Creole*
☎ 01 42 33 21 30; 15 rue du Roule, 1er; metro Palais Royal Musée du Louvre; dishes €4-8, platters €14,

menus €12 (lunch) & €18.50; ☾ lunch & dinner to 11pm Tue-Sat
A somewhat camp Creole canteen and rum bar with a balcony, this is the place to come for *acras de morue* (salt-cod fritters), *boudin créole* (West Indian blood sausage) and jerk chicken. It's a simple but cheery place, the welcome is warm, the food reliable and the cocktails (€6 to €8), served till 3am, lethal.

KASTOORI Map pp386-8 *Indian, Pakistani*
☎ 01 44 53 06 10; 4 place Gustave Toudouze, 9e; metro St-Georges; starters €3.70-6.90, mains €8-11; menus €8 (lunch) & €13 (dinner); ☾ lunch Tue-Sun, dinner to 11.30pm daily
This eatery just a stone's throw from place Pigalle is a delight in summer, with its large terrace looking onto a quiet, leafy square. The excellent value set *menus* include three generous courses; if you want one dish go for the excellent vegetable biryani. The lassi (yogurt-based drink) here is a cut above the usual.

KUNITORAYA Map pp386-8 *Japanese*
☎ 01 47 03 33 65; 39 rue Ste-Anne, 1er; metro Pyramides; soups €8.50-15, noodles €9-16, menu €12.50 (lunch); ☾ 11.30am-10pm
With seating on two floors, this simple place has a wide and excellent range of Japanese noodle dishes and set lunches and dinners. If headed here for lunch, aim to arrive before 1pm or prepare to join a queue that functions as a noodle vacuum cleaner.

L'ARBRE À CANNELLE

Map pp386-8 *French, Tea Room*
☎ 01 45 08 55 87; 57 passage des Panoramas, 2e; metro Grands Boulevards; dishes €6.50-9.50; ☾ noon-6.30pm Mon-Sat
The 'Cinnamon Tree' is a lovely tea room with *tartes salées* (savoury pies; €6.50 to €7) and excellent salads (€6.25 to €9.30) The original 19th-century décor is worth a visit in itself; seating is on the ground and 1st floors.

MARAIS & BASTILLE

The Marais, filled with small restaurants of every imaginable type, is one of Paris' premier neighbourhoods for eating out.

In the direction of République there's a decent selection of ethnic places. If you're looking for authentic Chinese food but can't be bothered going to Chinatown in the 13e, check out the small noodle shops and restaurants along rue Au Maire, 3e (Map pp386-8; metro Arts et Métiers). The kosher and kosher-style restaurants along rue des Rosiers (4e), the so-called Pletzel, serve specialities from North Africa, Central Europe and Israel. Many are closed on Friday evening, Saturday and Jewish holidays. Takeaway felafel and *shwarma* (kebabs) are available at several places along the street.

Bastille is another area chock-a-block with restaurants, some of which have added a star or two to their epaulets in recent years. Narrow rue de Lappe and rue de la Roquette, 11e (Map pp392-5), just east of place de la Bastille, may not be as hip as they were a dozen years ago, but they remain popular streets for nightlife and attract a young, alternative crowd.

404   Map pp386-8   *North African, Moroccan*

☎ 01 42 74 57 81; 69 rue des Gravilliers, 3e; metro Arts et Métiers; couscous & tajines €13-23, menus €17 (lunch) & €21 (brunch); ✆ lunch Mon-Fri, dinner to midnight daily, brunch to 4pm Sat & Sun

As comfortable a Maghreb (North African) caravanserai as you'll find in Paris, the 404 not only has excellent couscous and tajines but superb grills (€10 to €21) and aniseed bread as well. The weekend *brunch berbère* (Berber brunch) is available from noon to 4pm. You'll just love the One Thousand and One Nights décor and the waiters' free-flowing uniforms.

AU BASCOU   Map pp386-8   *French, Basque*

☎ 01 42 72 69 25; 38 rue Réaumur, 3e; metro Arts et Métiers; starters/mains/desserts €9/15/7.50; ✆ lunch Mon-Fri, dinner to 10.30pm Mon-Sat

This is a popular eatery serving Basque classics such as *pipérade* (peppers, onions, tomatoes and ham cooked with scrambled eggs), *ttoro* (Basque bouillabaisse) and Bayonne ham in all its guises; thankfully local flavour is only on the plate here and not festooning the walls as is the case with so many other Basque restaurants. Round off the meal with a piece of *brebis*, a ewe's milk cheese served with *confiture de cerise* (cherry jam) or a slice of *gâteau basque*, a relatively simple layer cake filled with cream and cherry jam.

BEL CANTO   Map pp396-9   *French*

☎ 01 42 78 30 18; 72 quai de l'Hôtel de Ville, 4e; metro Hôtel de Ville or Pont Marie; menu €60; ✆ dinner to midnight Tue-Sat

If London, New York and even Budapest can have one – a restaurant where the waiters sing (arias) for their supper, that is – why can't Paris? So if you fancy Bizet with your beef, Verdi with your vegetables and Puccini with your pasta, this is the place for you.

BLUE ELEPHANT

Map pp392-5   *Thai*

☎ 01 47 00 42 00; 43 rue de la Roquette, 11e; metro Bastille; starters €9.50-13.50, mains €16.50-20, menus €19 (lunch), €44 & €48; ✆ lunch Sun-Fri, dinner to midnight Tue-Sat, to 11pm Sun

The Blue Elephant is Paris' most famous up-market Thai restaurant and part of a hip international chain. Although it has become a little too successful for its own good, the indoor tropical rainforest and well-prepared spicy dishes (look for the elephant symbols on the menu) are still worth the inflated prices.

BOFINGER

Map pp392-5   *French, Brasserie*

☎ 01 42 72 87 82; 5-7 rue de la Bastille, 4e; metro Bastille; menus €21.50 (lunch) & €31.50 (dinner); ✆ lunch & dinner to 1am Mon-Fri, noon-1am Sat & Sun

Founded in 1864, Bofinger is reputedly the oldest brasserie in Paris, though its polished Art Nouveau brass, glass and mirrors throughout suggest a redecoration a few decades later. As at most Parisian brasseries, specialities include Alsatian-inspired dishes such as *choucroute* (sauerkraut with assorted meats; €15.50 to €19), and seafood dishes (€15 to €35). Ask for a seat downstairs, under the *coupole* (stained-glass dome); it's the prettiest part of the restaurant.

BRASSERIE DES GRANDES MARCHES

Map pp392-5   *French, Brasserie*

☎ 01 43 43 90 32; 6 place de la Bastille, 12e; metro Bastille; starters €12.20-17.90, mains €17.30-29.30, menus €23 (lunch) & €33

This futuristic 'modern brasserie' next to the Opéra Bastille was designed by Elisabeth and Christian Portzamparc for the Flo group. The result has been disappointing – both in décor and food served – but it has a convenient (and much coveted) location. If you do find yourself here, settle for the lunch menu or a couple of starters.

Eating – Marais & Bastille

CAFÉ DE L'INDUSTRIE

Map pp392-5   *French, Café*
☎ 01 47 00 13 53; 16 & 17 rue St-Sabin, 11e;
metro Bastille; starters €5.10-6.80; mains €7.30-14;
🕐 10am-2am

This popular café-restaurant with neocolonial décor has now taken over the old Café Le Serail across the road, doubling its capacity. It's a pleasant space and the perfect spot to meet a friend instead of at one of the crowded cafés or bars in Bastille. Food is competitively priced but not always up to scratch; to avoid disappointment stick with the simple entrees or just graze off the fabulous dessert table (€4 to €5). Brunch (€18) is served at the weekend.

CHEZ NÉNESSE

Map pp396-9   *French, Bistro*
☎ 01 42 78 46 49; 17 rue de Saintonge, 3e; metro Filles du Calvaire; starters €3.50-14.50, mains €12-15, plat du jour €9.50; 🕐 lunch & dinner to 10.30pm Mon-Fri

Chez Nénesse is an oasis of simplicity and good taste in a district that can sometimes seem to lose the plot. The atmosphere is very 'old Parisian café' and unpretentious; the dishes made with fresh, high-quality ingredients. The *salade de mesclun au foie gras de canard* (mixed green salad with duck foie gras) or *terrine de sander* (pike-perch terrine) make excellent starters, followed by the *fricassée de volaille aux morilles* (poultry fricassee with morel mushrooms) or the more traditional *tête de veau* (calf's head).

CHEZ OMAR

Map pp396-9   *North African*
☎ 01 42 72 36 26; 47 rue de Bretagne, 3e; metro Arts et Métiers; couscous €9-24, grills €12-15;
🕐 lunch Mon-Sat, dinner to 11.30pm

Once a favourite of celebrity types, Chez Omar doesn't seem to attract the very rich or famous these days but, going by the long queue that begins to form outside mid-evening (the restaurant does not take reservations), the quality of the couscous has remained topnotch. Apart from the food and the serving staff, don't expect anything else to be North African at Chez Omar: it looks almost exactly like the corner street café it was a quarter of a century ago.

GRAND APÉTIT

Map pp392-5   *Vegetarian*
☎ 01 40 27 04 95; 9 rue de la Cerisaie, 4e; metro Bastille or Sully Morland; meals from €15, menus €10-15; 🕐 lunch Mon-Fri, dinner to 9pm Mon-Wed

Set back from Bastille in a small, quiet street, the 'Big Appetite' offers light fare such as miso soup and cereals plus strength-building dishes for big eaters only. First grab a table, then order at the bar. The menu is on a big blackboard and features delicious, filling dishes served with cereals, raw and cooked vegetables and seaweed. The ingredients are 100% organic and cooked in filtered water. There's an excellent organic and macrobiotic shop attached.

ISAMI Map pp396-9   *Japanese*

☎ 01 42 46 06 97; 4 quai d'Orléans, 4e; metro Pont Marie; menus €19-34; 🕐 lunch & dinner to 10pm Tue-Sat

Japanese customers flock to this tiny, often packed restaurant for impeccably fresh sushi and sashimi (delicacies made with sea urchins and eels are especially popular) and 'sets' that always include a small starter and a soup.

JO GOLDENBERG Map pp396-9   *Jewish*

☎ 01 48 87 20 16; 7 rue des Rosiers, 4e; metro St-Paul; starters €6-8, mains €13-15, plat du jour €13;
🕐 8.30am-midnight

This kosher-style restaurant (established 1920) is Paris' most famous Jewish eatery, but we've had complaints from readers about both the quality of the food and the service. The mixed starters and apple strudel (€6 each) are OK,

L'Encrier (p167)

Eating – Marais & Bastille

but the plats du jour and main courses don't measure up to even a generic New York deli. It appears that Jo is resting on his laurels.

LA MAIN D'OR

Map pp392-5   *French, Corsican*
☎ 01 44 68 04 68; 133 rue du Faubourg St-Antoine, 11e; metro Ledru Rollin; mains €14-17, menu €11, plat du jour €7.50; ✆ lunch & dinner to 11pm Mon-Sat

The unprepossessing 'Golden Hand' serves authentic Corsican dishes – a surprisingly elusive cuisine in the city. *Sturza preti* (spinach and fine brocciu cheese) and traditional omelette with brocciu and *jambon sec* (dried ham, matured for two years) are some of the appetisers on the menu. For mains favourites include the *tian de veau aux olives* (veal ragout) and the *daube au vin de Toraccia* (meat braised in wine). A long dining room with exposed stone walls and choir music playing in the background set the tone at what is essentially a café.

LA PERLA Map pp396-9   *Mexican, Tex-Mex*
☎ 01 42 77 59 40; 26 rue François Miron, 4e; metro St-Paul or Hôtel de Ville; starters € 6.30-8.50, mains €11-15, lunch platters €6-9; ✆ lunch & dinner to midnight

A favourite with younger Parisians, the 'Pearl' is a Californian-style Mexican bar-restaurant serving guacamole (€6.30), nachos (€5.50 to €8.50) and burritos (€7.90 to €8.40). Margaritas (€8.50 to €9.30) at the bar (✆ noon to 2am) are excellent. Happy hour is 6pm to 8pm.

LA SOUMMAM

Map pp396-9   *North African, Berber*
☎ 01 43 54 12 43; 25 rue des Grands Augustins, 6e; metro Odéon or St-Michel; starters €3.70-7.30, mains €11.50-19, menus €10.50 (lunch) & €14.30-24.50 (dinner); ✆ lunch & dinner to 11.30pm Mon-Sat

The left bank of the Seine is a long way from the North African home of the Berbers. But here, in this restaurant decorated with carpets, pottery and artworks, you can taste the unusual *tammekfoult* (a couscous of steamed vegetables accompanied by milk curds) as well as a superb veal tajine with olives, artichokes, prunes and other vegetables. The *hasban* are unique: semolina croquettes flavoured with mint and served with vegetables and chickpeas. Try an Algerian wine from Medea.

L'ALIVI Map pp396-9   *French, Corsican*
☎ 01 48 87 90 20; 27 rue du Roi de Sicile, 4e; metro St-Paul; starters €8-15, mains €14-19.50, menus €15 (lunch) & €20; ✆ lunch & dinner to 11.30pm

The 'Olive Tree' (in Corsican) is a rather fashionable Corsican restaurant in the heart of the Marais. The ingredients are fresh and refined, with brocciu cheese, charcuterie and basil featuring strongly on the menu. Try *starzapreti* (brocciu and spinach quenelles) and the unrivalled *cabri rôti* (roast kid) with a Leccia wine to fully experience the pleasures of the 'île de beauté' (beautiful isle).

L'AMBASSADE D'AUVERGNE

Map pp396-9   *French, Auvergne*
☎ 01 42 72 31 22; 22 rue du Grenier St-Lazare, 3e; metro Rambuteau; starters €9-18, mains €14-19, menu €27; ✆ lunch & dinner to 10.30pm

The 'Auvergne Embassy' is the place to head for if you are a carnivore and well and truly hungry. This 100-year-old restaurant offers traditional dishes such as the unusual *terrine d'agneau et sa vinaigrette aux cinq parfums* (lamb terrine served with a five-flavour vinaigrette). A tasty lead-up to the house speciality: *la saucisse d'Auvergne à l'aligot* (Auvergne sausage served with a potato and cheese purée). A fitting conclusion to this magnificent feast is the sublime *clafoutis*, a custard and cherry tart baked upside down like a *tarte Tatin*.

L'AMBROISIE

Map pp396-9   *French*
☎ 01 42 78 51 45; 9 place des Vosges, 4e; metro St-Paul or Bastille; starters €75-90; mains €85-98; ✆ lunch & dinner to 9.30pm Tue-Sat

Both the décor (murals, ormolu, glittering silver and mirrors catching all the glitter) and chef Bernard Pacaud's attention to detail at 'Ambrosia', an *haute cuisine* establishment housed in a lovely 17th-century townhouse on place des Vosges, could turn lunch or dinner here into the meal of a lifetime. The menu changes with the season at this eatery, which has deservedly been awarded three Michelin stars, but starters might be lobster ravioli and mains *poulard de Bresse demi-deuil à la Mère Brazier* (Bresse chicken roasted with black truffles). An unforgettable experience.

LE BISTROT DU DÔME BASTILLE

Map pp392-5   *French, Seafood*
☎ 01 48 04 88 44; 2 rue de la Bastille, 4e; metro Bastille; starters €8.70-12, mains €18.70-23; ✆ lunch & dinner to 11pm

This lovely restaurant, little sister to the more established **Dôme** (p184) in Montparnasse, awash in pale yellows, specialises in superbly prepared fish and seafood dishes. The blackboard menu changes daily. Wines are a uniform (and affordable) €18 per bottle.

LE DÔME DU MARAIS

Map pp396-9 *French*

☎ 01 42 74 54 17; 53bis rue des Francs Bourgeois, 4e; metro Rambuteau; meals from €50, menus €17 & €24 (lunch); ☸ lunch & dinner to 11pm Tue-Sat

The Marais Dôme serves both classic French dishes such as *tête de veau* and, in winter, more unusual fare like *pannequets d'escargot et de pied de cochon* (pancakes stuffed with pig's trotter and snails). The location is sublime: a pre-Revolutionary building and former auction room just down from the Archives Nationales.

LE GAI MOULIN Map pp396-9 *French*

☎ 01 48 87 47 59; 4 rue St-Merri, 4e; metro Rambuteau; menu €17; ☸ dinner to midnight

One of the capital's smallest restaurants, the 'Gay Mill' serves traditional French cuisine, including a very decently priced *menu*, to a mainly (but not exclusively) gay clientele. With the tables so close, there's no chance of not making a friend or two between (or even during) courses.

LE PETIT PICARD Map pp396-9 *French*

☎ 01 42 78 54 03; 42 rue Ste-Croix de la Bretonnerie, 4e; metro Hôtel de Ville; menus €12 (lunch), €14.50 & €21.50; ☸ lunch Tue-Fri, dinner to 11pm Tue-Sun

This popular little restaurant in the centre of gay Marais serves traditional French cuisine (try the generous *menu traditionel* at €21.50). Despite its name, the only dish from Picardy that we could spot on the menu was *flamiche aux poireaux*, a Flemish-style leek pie. The place is always packed so book well in advance.

LE RÉCONFORT Map pp396-9 *French*

☎ 01 49 96 09 60; 37 rue de Poitou, 3e; metro St-Sébastien Froissart; starters €6-10, mains €14-20, menus €13 & €17 (lunch), plat du jour €10, brunch €19; ☸ lunch & dinner to 11pm Mon-Sat, brunch noon-4pm Sun

Unusual for a restaurant in the Marais area, the 'Comfort' has generous space between tables and is quiet enough to chat without yelling. The kitchen turns out some very tasty and inventive dishes. Starters include house-made foie gras and *champignons rôtis au chèvre* (roasted mushrooms with goat's cheese). For mains, consider *morue caramélisée au vinaigre*

balsamique (caramelised cod) or *filet mignon de porc aux senteurs de Garrigue* (pork with wild herbs). Unique desserts include *tian au miel et à l'orange* (mousse-like concoction of baked orange and honey) or *glace au gingembre* (ginger ice cream) made on the premises.

LE SOFA Map pp392-5 *French*

☎ 01 43 14 07 46; 21 rue St-Sabin, 11e; metro Bréguet Sabin; starters €7-11, mains €12-14, menus €9.50 (lunch) & €19 (dinner); ☸ lunch Mon-Fri, dinner to midnight Sun-Thu, to 2am Fri & Sat

Le Sofa serves inventive starters and classic French main courses in a friendly environment. On arrival sink into the white sofa, admire the exhibition and devour the menu. Varied and stylish starters include the *roulade chinoise aux légumes* (Chinese roulade with vegetables). More-traditional main courses, such as the *pintadeau rôti aux échalotes confites* (roast guinea fowl with preserved shallots) or the *tartare de boeuf coupé au couteau* (steak tartare 'cut with a knife'), are enhanced by the inventive presentation.

LE SQUARE TROUSSEAU

Map pp392-5 *French*

☎ 01 43 43 06 00; 1 rue Antoine Vollon, 12e; metro Ledru Rollin; starters €6-10, mains €19-16, menus €20 & €25 (lunch); ☸ lunch & dinner to 11.30pm Tue-Sat

This vintage bistro with etched glass, zinc bar and polished wood panelling is comfortable rather than trendy and attracts a jolly and mixed clientele. Most people come to enjoy the lovely terrace overlooking a small park. Attached is the new **Boutique du Restaurant** (☸ 9am-3pm & 6-9pm Tue-Sat), where you can pick up that bottle of Touraine you so much enjoyed over lunch.

LE STUDIO

Map pp396-9 *Tex-Mex*

☎ 01 42 74 10 38; 41 rue du Temple, 4e; metro Rambuteau; menus €15 (lunch) and €23; ☸ lunch & dinner to 11pm Mon-Sat

This popular and trendy place is Texas as only the French could imagine the Lone Star State. Tacos, enchiladas and chimichangas are pretty average; there's no denying that the surroundings make this place what it is. Overlooking a 17th-century square and the Conservatoire de la Danse, you can hear and watch flamenco, tap, jazz and salsa lessons. There are tables in the courtyard in summer; grab a cocktail, watch super-fit bods in action and feel guilty.

L'ENOTECA   Map pp396-9   *Italian*

☎ 01 42 78 91 44; 25 rue Charles V, 4e; metro Sully Morland or Pont Marie; starters €8-13, pasta €10-13, mains €17-20; ☺ lunch & dinner to 11.30pm

The 'Vinotheque', a trattoria in the historic Village St-Paul quarter, serves *haute cuisine à l'italienne*, and there's an excellent list of Italian wines by the glass (€3 to €9). Some of the more difficult-to-find wines are on hand too. It's no secret that this is one of the few Italian wine bars in Paris to take its vino seriously. Book ahead.

LES AMIS DE MESSINA

Map pp392-5   *Italian, Sicilian*

☎ 01 43 67 96 01; 204 rue du Faubourg St-Antoine, 12e; metro Faidherbe Chaligny; antipasti €7.80-13.80, pasta €11.80-17.20, mains €17-24.90; ☺ lunch Mon-Fri, dinner to 11.30pm Mon-Sat

The décor of this wonderful little neighbourhood trattoria is stylish, with clean lines, an open kitchen and the inevitable Italian football pennant. For starters, try the *boulettes farcies* (stuffed meatballs), a speciality of Palermo. The *moules à la tomate et à l'ail* (mussels with tomato and garlic) are also noteworthy. For mains, the *escalopes farcies aux aubergines* (veal escalopes stuffed with aubergine) are a huge hit, while the *entrecôte au romarin* (rib steak with rosemary) is also a winner. Friday is fish day; watch out for the specials.

LES CAVES ST-GILLES

Map pp392-5   *Spanish*

☎ 01 48 87 22 62; 4 rue St-Gilles, 3e; metro Chemin Vert; tapas €5.50-15.70, platters €8-13; ☺ lunch & dinner to 11.30pm

This Spanish wine bar a short distance northeast of place des Vosges is the most authentic place on the Right Bank for tapas, paella (at the weekend only; €18) and sangria (€27 for 1L). If you don't believe us, just ask the Spanish expats who arrive here in droves. No reservations though, so if you arrive after 9pm, settle in to watch the football on the television and be prepared to wait.

LES GALOPINS

Map pp392-5   *French, Bistro*

☎ 01 47 00 45 35; 24 rue des Taillandiers, 11e; metro Bastille or Voltaire; starters €6-10.50, mains €11.50-18, menus €11.50 & €15 (lunch); ☺ lunch Mon-Fri, dinner to 11pm Mon-Thu, to 11.30pm Fri & Sat

This cute neighbourhood bistro greets its customers with a complementary kir or glass of beer. The décor is simple, the meals straightforward and in the best tradition of French cuisine: *poêlée de pétoncles* (pan-fried queen scallops), *magret de canard* (fillet of duck breast), *cœur de rumsteck* (tenderloin rump steak) and *compotée d'agneau aux aubergines* (lamb and eggplant ragout). It's not a secret find, so it can feel like a bit of a factory on a weekend night.

LES SANS CULOTTES

Map pp392-5   *French, Bistro*

☎ 01 48 05 42 92; 27 rue de Lappe, 11e; metro Bastille; starters €9-15, mains €10-20, menu €22; ☺ lunch & dinner to 11pm Tue-Sun

You wouldn't cross Paris to eat at Sans Culottes (the place takes its name from the working-class 'men without fancy breeches' who fought in the French Revolution) but in a neighbourhood that has all from struggling art galleries to bars it's a welcome reminder of the past when Parisians would eat here before heading off to the nearby **Balajo** (p236). The interior, with frosted glass, huge zinc bar, ornate ceilings and wooden floors, positively glows in the evening. Food is uneven, though low-priced; service warm and attentive.

LES VINS DES PYRÉNÉES

Map pp396-9   *French*

☎ 01 42 72 64 94; 25 rue Beautreillis, 4e; metro Saint Paul or Bastille; starters €5.50-13, mains €11.50-14, menu €12.50 (lunch); ☺ lunch Sun-Fri, dinner to 11.30pm

The 'Wines of the Pyrenees', in a former wine warehouse a couple of doors down from the house where Jim Morrison of the Doors died in 1971 (No 17-19), is a good place to enjoy a no-nonsense French meal with a lot of wine. The place has been able to retain its old-world charm and it's not surprising that a crowd of locals have set up headquarters here. The fish, meat and game dishes are all equally good, but worth a special mention is the foie gras and the top-notch *pavé de rumsteak* (thick rump steak). The wine list offers a wide choice of celebrated and little-known estate wines.

LIRE ENTRE LES VIGNES

Map pp392-5   *French*

☎ 01 43 55 69 49; 38 rue Sedaine, 11e; metro Bastille or Bréguet Sabin; starters €7-14, mains €13-19, menus €11 & €15 (lunch); ☺ lunch Mon-Fri, dinner to 10.30pm Mon-Sat

Hidden away in a nondescript Bastille back street, 'Read between the Vines' is an oasis

Eating – Marais & Bastille

of conviviality, reminiscent of a comfortable and spacious country kitchen. The food is fresh, imaginative and tasty, and prepared before your eyes in the corner kitchen. Try the *velouté aux choux* (cabbage soup) as a starter and follow it with the comforting *hachis Parmentier* (minced-meat hash and mashed potatoes with olive oil) served on a wooden board. And don't forget to try a nice bottle of organic wine with your meal. Indeed, this place is an oasis but whoever thought up the name should be taken out and shot.

MA BOURGOGNE

Map pp396-9   *French, Bistro*
☎ 01 42 78 44 64; 19 place des Vosges, 4e; metro Saint Paul; plat du jour €15, menu €32 (dinner); ☽ noon-1am

With its terrace under the arcades of the place des Vosges and looking onto what is arguably the most beautiful square in Paris, 'My Burgundy' is a wonderful place to have lunch or just a drink.

PICCOLO TEATRO

Map pp396-9   *Vegetarian*
☎ 01 42 72 17 79; 6 rue des Écouffes, 4e; metro St-Paul; menus €8.20-14.70 (lunch), €15.10 (lunch) & €21.50 (dinner); ☽ lunch & dinner to 11.30pm

This vegetarian restaurant is an intimate place with exposed stone walls, a beamed ceiling and cosy little tables lit by candles. The tasty *assiette végétarienne* (vegetarian plate; €12.10) is always popular but try the gratin, the speciality of the house, which combines vegetables, cream and cheese.

ROBERT ET LOUISE Map pp396-9   *French*
☎ 01 42 78 55 89; 64 rue Vieille du Temple, 3e; metro St-Sébastien Froissart; starters €7-12, mains €13-18, plat du jour €12; ☽ lunch Tue-Fri, dinner to 10pm Mon-Sat

This 'country inn', complete with its red gingham curtains, offers delightful, simple and inexpensive French food, including *côte de bœuf* (side of beef, €37), which is cooked on an open fire and prepared by a husband-and-wife team. The Robert et Louise is a dark den with a glowing hearth, carefully tended by Robert, while the attentive Louise serves up the sizzling cuts of beef. If you arrive early you can choose the farmhouse table, right next to the fireplace. Everyone passes bottles around, and spirits rise as the levels drop. A true Rabelaisian evening.

SOPRANO Map pp396-9   *Italian*
☎ 01 42 72 37 21; 5 rue Caron, 4; metro St-Paul; starters €6-12, pastas €8-13, mains €11-16, menu €16 (lunch); ☽ lunch & dinner to 11pm

This Italian restaurant with the very familiar sounding name ('Hi Tony, hi Carmela') gets the award for self-promotion; its cards, flyers and menus seem to have blanketed the capital. Still, it has moderately priced southern Italian food and overlooks the glorious place du Marché Ste-Catherine.

SWANN ET VINCENT

Map pp392-5   *Italian*
☎ 01 43 43 49 40; 7 rue St-Nicolas, 12e; metro Ledru Rollin; starters €6.80-10.70, mains €10.70-14.50, menu €13.60 (lunch); ☽ lunch & dinner to 11.45pm

If you're visiting this fine restaurant, ask for a table in the front room, which will hopefully be awash in sunlight. Unpretentious French staff, who thankfully do not fake Italian accents, can help you select from the huge blackboard, but the *soupe au céleri* (celery soup) with a dash of olive oil and the *escalope au citron et légumes al dente* (veal escalope with lemon al dente vegetables) are excellent choices. Go slow on the complimentary basket of olive and sweet herb bread, though; you need to leave room for the tiramisú. And, if you must know, Swann and Vincent are the children of the owner.

THANKSGIVING

Map pp396-9   *American, Cajun*
☎ 01 42 77 68 28; 20 rue St-Paul, 4e; metro Saint Paul; starters €8-9, mains €15-22; ☽ lunch & dinner to 11pm Wed-Sat, brunch to 4pm Sun

Thanksgiving serves all-American regional dishes. OK, you didn't come all the way to Paris for jumbalaya and gumbo, but where else are you going to find Cajun in the City of Light? We especially like the fried oysters, the spicy chicken and, for afters, the pecan pie is to die for. There's a traditional brunch on Sunday (€15 to €19).

UN PIANO SUR LE TROTTOIR

Map pp396-9   *French*
☎ 01 42 77 91 91; 7 rue Francs Bourgeois, 4e; metro Chemin Vert or Saint Paul; starters €15-32, mains €22-32, menus €19 (lunch) & €39 (dinner); ☽ lunch Tue-Sun, dinner to 11pm Tue-Sat

The 'piano' isn't exactly 'on the pavement', but it's in the front window of this charming eatery just west of the places de Vosges. The food is classic French and the welcome warm.

WALY FAY Map pp392-5 *African, Creole*
☎ 01 40 24 17 79; 6 rue Godefroy Cavaignac, 11e;
metro Charonne; starters €5.50-6.50, meze &
platters €4.50-10, mains €11.50-15; ☽ dinner to
11pm Mon-Sat

This easygoing 'loungin' restaurant' attracts a
rather hip crowd for African food with a West
Indian twist served to the sounds of soul and
jazz. For starters, the *pepe* (fish soup) is deli-
ciously smooth and highly spiced. For mains,
the *tiéboudienne* (rice, fish and vegetables) and
fish *n'dole* are recommended by the staff, but
try instead the copious *mafé* (beef simmer
in peanut sauce) served with rice and *aloco*
(fried plantain bananas); the caramelised taste
of cooked banana is a perfect addition to the
spicy main course.

CHEAP EATS

COFFEE INDIA Map pp392-5 *Indian*
☎ 01 48 06 18 57; 33-35 rue de Lappe, 11e; metro
Bastille; starters €5.40-8.40, mains €12-22, menu
€9 (lunch); ☽ lunch & dinner to 2am

Despite its confusing name, this restaurant
(and cocktail bar, lounge, tea room and café)
on busy rue de Lappe serves surprisingly
authentic southern Indian fare. After 10pm
from Thursday to Saturday a DJ plays Indian
music – from traditional to electro-acoustic.
Happy hour is from 4pm to 8pm.

CRÊPES SHOW
Map pp392-5 *French, Brittany*
☎ 01 47 00 36 46; 51 rue de Lappe, 11e; metro Ledru
Rollin; menus €7 (lunch) & €11; ☽ lunch Mon-Fri,
dinner to 1am

This unpretentious little restaurant specialises
in sweet crêpes and savoury buckwheat galettes priced between €3 and €7. OK, they may
not be the most authentic in town but the
location is convenient and the welcome warm.
There are lots of vegetarian choices, including
great salads from €7.

CHEZ HANNA
Map pp396-9 *Jewish, Kosher*
☎ 01 42 74 74 99; 54 rue des Rosiers, 4e; metro
St-Paul; starters €5-12, mains €11-13.50, menus €9 &
€11.50 (lunch), €17 & €21; ☽ 11am-2am

Chez Hanna serves Israeli and Moroccan
dishes, including *assiette royale* (€12), a generous plate of seven salads and meze. When all
else fails in the Pletzel, you're sure to find nosh
at Chez Hanna.

CHEZ HEANG Map pp392-5 *Korean*
☎ 01 48 07 80 98; 5 rue de la Roquette, 11e; metro
Bastille; barbecue €8.50-17.50, menus €9 (lunch),
€11 & €23 (dinner); ☽ lunch & dinner to midnight

Also known as 'Barbecue de Seoul', this is
where you cook your food on a grill in the middle of your table. The *fondue maison*, a kind of
spicy hotpot in which you dip and cook your
food, costs €21 per person (minimum two).

CHEZ MARIANNE
Map pp396-9 *Jewish, Kosher*
☎ 01 42 72 18 86; 2 rue des Hospitalières St-Gervais,
4e; metro St-Paul; dishes €3.50-20, sandwiches
€5.50-8; ☽ noon-midnight

This is a Sephardic (and kosher) alternative to
the Ashkenazi **Jo Goldenberg** (p161). Platters with
four/five/six different meze (eg felafel, hum-
mus), purées of eggplant and chickpeas etc
cost €12/14/16. The window of the adjoining
deli sells killer takeaway felafel sandwiches for
€4 and there's an excellent bakery attached. Set
menus include vegetarian options.

CHEZ PAUL Map pp392-5 *French, Bistro*
☎ 01 47 00 34 57; 13 rue de Charonne, 11e; metro
Ledru Rollin; starters €2.80-12.80, mains €11.50-19;
☽ lunch & dinner to 12.30am

When Central Staging orders up 'French restaurant' in Hollywood, this is what it looks like.
'Paul's' is an extremely popular bistro with traditional French main courses handwritten on
a yellowing menu and surly, cavalier service –
Paris in true form! Stick with the simplest of
dishes – the steak or foie gras with lentils – and
be prepared to wait even if you've booked.

CRÊPERIE BRETONNE FLEURIE
Map pp392-5 *French, Brittany*
☎ 01 43 55 62 29; 67 rue de Charonne, 12e; metro
Ledru Rollin or Charonne; crepes €2.10-7; ☽ lunch
Mon-Fri, dinner to 11.30pm Mon-Sat

Head here if you fancy savoury buckwheat
galettes – try the ham, cheese and egg *complète* – or a sweet crepe and wash it down
with dry *cidre de Rance* (€5.70 for 50cL). The Breton
paraphernalia and B&W photos will keep you
occupied if there's a lull in the chatter.

LE TRUMILOU Map pp396-9 *French, Bistro*
☎ 01 42 77 63 98; 84 quai de l'Hôtel de Ville, 4e;
metro Hôtel de Ville; starters €4-12, mains €12-18;
menus €14.50 & €17.50; ☽ lunch & dinner to 11pm

This no-frills bistro just round the corner from
the Hôtel de Ville and facing the posh Île de

The Restaurant is Born

In 1765 a certain Monsieur A Boulanger opened a small business in rue Bailleul in the 1er, just off rue de Rivoli, selling soups, broths and, later, the crowd-pleasing sheep's trotters in a white sauce. Above the door he hung a sign to advertise these *restaurants* (restoratives, from the verb *se restaurer*, 'to feed oneself'). The world had the first restaurant as we know it today and a new name for an eating house.

Before that time not everyone cooked at home every day of the year. Hostelries and inns existed, but they only served guests set meals at set times and prices from the *table d'hôte* (host's table); cafés only offered drinks. Monsieur Boulanger's restaurant is thought to have been the first public place where diners could order a meal from a menu that offered a range of dishes.

Other restaurants opened over the following decades, including a luxury one in Paris called La Grande Taverne de Londres in 1782. The 1789 Revolution at first stemmed the tide of new restaurants but when corporations and privileges were abolished in the 1790s, their numbers multiplied. By 1804 Paris counted some 500 restaurants, providing employment for many of the chefs and cooks who had once worked in the kitchens of the aristocracy. A typical menu at that time included 12 soups, two dozen hors d'œuvre, between 12 and 30 dishes of beef, veal, mutton, fowl and game, 24 fish dishes, 12 types of *pâtisserie* (pastries) and 50 desserts.

St-Louis square is a Parisian institution in situ for over a century. If you're looking for an authentic menu from the early 20th century and prices (well, almost) to match, you won't do better than this. The *confit de canard* and the *tête de veau sauce au gribiche* are particularly good. As the popular entertainment magazine *Nova* puts it, Le Trumilou will help recall the 'Frenchitude' of yesteryear.

L'AS DE FELAFEL

Map pp396-9   *Jewish, Kosher*
☎ 01 48 87 63 60; 34 rue des Rosiers, 4e; metro St-Paul; dishes €3.50-7; ☽ 11am-midnight Sun-Thu, noon-sunset Fri
The 'Felafel Ace' has always been our favourite place for these deep-fried balls of chickpeas and herbs (€3.50 to €4). It's always packed, particularly at weekday lunch, so avoid those times if possible.

L'ENCRIER

Map pp392-5   *French, Bistro*
☎ 01 44 68 08 16; 55 rue Traversière, 12e; metro Ledru Rollin or Gare de Lyon; starters €4-10, mains €8-15.50, menus €11 (lunch) & €15-19 (dinner); ☽ lunch Mon-Fri, dinner to 11pm Mon-Sat
A popular spot, you can always expect a relaxed atmosphere at the 'Inkwell'. For starters, the classic salmon *tartare* alternates on the menu with less-common dishes such as *cervelle des canuts* (a herbed cheese from Lyons). To follow, try the *bar entier grillé* (whole grilled bass) or delicate *joues de cochon aux épices* (pig's cheeks with spices). A variety of set menus, an open kitchen, exposed beams and a large picture window make this a lovely place.

THE ISLANDS

Famed for its ice cream as much as anything else, the Île St-Louis is generally an expensive place to eat and restaurants are few and far between. It's best suited to those looking for a light snack at one of the lovely tea rooms along rue St-Louis en l'Île, 4e (Map pp396-9; metro Pont Marie) or ingredients for a picnic along the Seine.

BRASSERIE DE L'ISLE ST-LOUIS

Map pp396-9   *French, Brasserie*
☎ 01 43 54 02 59; 55 quai de Bourbon, 4e; metro Pont Marie; ☽ 5pm-1am Thu, noon-1am Fri-Tue
Founded in 1870 and still independent, this brasserie enjoys a spectacular location on the Seine just over the footbridge between Île de St-Louis and Île de la Cité. It serves favourites such as *choucroute garnie* (sauerkraut with meat), *jarret* (veal shank), *cassoulet* (€16.50 each) and *onglet de boeuf* (prime rib of beef). You can also enjoy the location by ordering a coffee/beer (€1.10/2.30 at the bar, €2.50/4.50 at a table or on the terrace).

CHEAP EATS

BERTHILLON Map pp396-9   *Ice Cream*
☎ 01 43 54 31 61; 31 rue St-Louis en l'Île, 4e; metro Pont Marie; takeaway & shop ☽ 10am-8pm Wed-Sun, café ☽ 1-8pm Wed-Fri, 2-8pm Sat & Sun

Berthillon is to ice cream what Château Lafite Rothschild is to wine and Valhrona is to chocolate. While the fruit flavours (eg cassis) produced by this celebrated *glacier* (ice-cream maker) are justifiably renowned, the chocolate, coffee, *marrons glacés* (candied chestnuts), Agenaise (Armagnac and prunes), *noisette* (hazelnut) and *nougat au miel* (honey nougat) are much richer. The takeaway counter has one/two/three/four small scoops for €2/3.50/4.50/5.50. Choose from among 70 flavours.

LATIN QUARTER & JARDIN DES PLANTES

Rue Mouffetard (Map pp392-5; metro Place Monge or Censier Daubenton) and its side streets are filled with places to eat. It's especially popular with students, in part because of the number of stands and small shops selling baguettes, *panini* (Italian toasted bread with fillings) and crepes.

Avoid rue de la Huchette (Map pp396-9) and the labyrinth of narrow streets in the 5e across the Seine from Notre Dame. The ethnic restaurants between rue St-Jacques, blvd St-Germain and blvd St-Michel attract mainly foreign tourists, who are unaware that some people refer to rue de la Huchette and nearby streets such as rue St-Séverin and rue de la Harpe as Ruelle de la Bactérie (Bacteria Alley) because of all the meat and seafood ripening in the front windows. To add insult to injury, many of the poor souls who eat here are under the impression that this little maze is the celebrated Latin Quarter.

AL DAR

Map pp396-9   *Middle Eastern, Lebanese*
☎ 01 43 25 17 15; 8-10 rue Frédéric Sauton, 5e; metro Maubert Mutualité; meze €6.30-8.30, mains €8.80-18.50, menus €12-27 (lunch); ☾ lunch & dinner to midnight

This is a popular and reasonably authentic Lebanese restaurant with a lovely terrace open in the warmer months. For those in a hurry, attached is an excellent **delicatessen** (☾ 7am-midnight daily) with meze, little pizzas, sandwiches and the like (€3.80 to €7.80).

ANAHUACALLI

Map pp396-9   *Mexican*
☎ 01 43 26 10 20; 30 rue des Bernadins, 5e; metro Maubert Mutualité; starters €7.50-9, platters €13.50-19; ☾ lunch Sun only, dinner to 11pm Mon-Sat

The ample menu at the lovely 'House by the Water' (hey, the Seine is just due north) takes you off the usual beaten track of Mexican food, starting with the delicate *napolitos compuestos* (cactus salad). The *poulet et sa sauce d'amandes et noix de cajou* (chicken in almond and cashew sauce) and the *fajitas et leurs haricots* (fajitas and beans) are light years from the typical fare. Doused in *rompope* (an eggnog-like drink), the chocolate cake looks like an Aztec pyramid and will have you raising a glass to *la cuchina mexicana*.

BOUILLON RACINE

Map pp396-9   *French, Bistro*
☎ 01 44 32 15 60; 3 rue Racine, 6e; metro Cluny La Sorbonne; starters €7-11.50, mains €12-17, menus €15 (lunch) & €25; ☾ lunch & dinner to 11pm

We've visited, inspected and eaten in lots and lots of historical restaurants in our day, but we've never – ever – seen anything quite like the Bouillon Racine, a 'soup kitchen' built in 1906 to feed city workers. It's an Art Nouveau palace and a positive delight. Oh, and the food? Not bad classic French dishes like *caille confite* (preserved quail) and *cochon de lait* (milk-fed pork) satisfy a lot more than does the service, which is rushed and rather sloppy.

CHEZ LÉNA ET MIMILLE

Map pp392-5   *French*
☎ 01 47 07 72 47; 32 rue Tournefort, 5e; metro Censier Daubenton; starters/mains/desserts €7/14/7 (lunch), menu €35 with wine (dinner); ☾ lunch Tue-Fri, dinner to 11pm Mon-Sat

This intimate but elegant restaurant has one of the most fabulous terraces in Paris, overlooking a little park with a fountain. And the food is excellent; seize the rare opportunity to

---

Top Five Latin Quarter & Jardin des Plantes Restaurants

- Bouillon Racine (this page)
- Chez Léna et Mimile (this page)
- Fogon St-Julien (opposite)
- Le Coco de Mar (p170)
- Mavrommatis (p179)

taste *pieds de cochon farcis* (stuffed pig's trotters). Classic mains with a twist include *gigot d'agneau à la crème de chorizo* (leg of lamb with spicy Spanish sausage) and *ravioles de pétoncles à la crème safranée* (queen scallop ravioli with saffron cream).

FOGON ST-JULIEN

Map pp396-9   *Spanish*

☎ 01 43 54 31 33; 10 rue St-Julien le Pauvre, 5e; metro St-Michel; menus €20 (lunch), €35 (dinner); ✆ lunch Sat & Sun, dinner to midnight Tue-Sun

Fogon St-Julien, which some say is the best Spanish restaurant in Paris (not an oxymoron, it would appear, to those of us still unconvinced by *la cuchina española*), goes well beyond 'tapas mania', serving up a half-dozen excellent paellas (vegetable, rabbit, chicken, seafood). Try the *arroz negro*, rice blackened with squid ink and hiding shrimps, cuttlefish and chunks of fish. Having said that the atmosphere is a little severe and lacks the simplicity and friendliness of a traditional bodega.

FOUNTI AGADIR

Map pp392-5   *North African, Moroccan*

☎ 01 43 37 85 10; 117 rue Monge, 5e; metro Censier Daubenton; menus €15 & €18 (lunch); ✆ lunch & dinner to 10.30pm Tue-Sun

This popular Moroccan restaurant serves some of the best couscous and tajines (€12.90 to €17) and pastillas (€7 to €8) on the Left Bank.

LA MOSQUÉE DE PARIS

Map pp392-5   *North African*

☎ 01 43 31 38 20; 39 rue Geoffroy St-Hilaire, 5e; metro Censier Daubenton or Place Monge; starters & small dishes €4-12, mains €11-25; ✆ lunch & dinner to 10.30pm

The central **Mosquée de Paris** (p97) has an authentic restaurant serving couscous (€11 to €25) and tajines (€12 to €16). There's also a North African–style **tea room** (✆ 9am-midnight) to enjoy a cup of peppermint tea (€2.50).

LA TOUR D'ARGENT Map pp396-9   *French*

☎ 01 43 54 23 31; 15 quai de la Tournelle, 5e; metro Cardinal Lemoine or Pont Marie; meals from €180,

Tarts Too Good to Forget

Parisians love *sucreries* (sweet or sugary things) and fruit, and judging from the eye-catching and saliva-inducing window displays at pastry shops throughout the city, they can't get enough of either in combination. But trying to compile a list of the best *pâtisseries* in Paris is like setting out to determine the length of a piece of string – it can just go on and on and on. We asked half a dozen of our sweet-toothed colleagues at Lonely Planet's Paris office to choose their favourites, based on their *spécialités de la maison* (house specialities). The proof, as they say, is in the pudding.

Au Levain du Marais (Map pp396-9; ☎ 01 42 78 07 31; 32 rue de Turenne, 3e; metro St-Paul; ✆ 7am-8pm Tue-Sat) Specialities include *tartes aux fruits* (fruit tarts), *macarons au citron* (lemon macaroons) and two dozen speciality breads.

Dalloyau (Map pp383-5; ☎ 01 42 99 90 00; 101 rue du Faubourg St-Honoré, 8e; metro St-Philippe du Roule; ✆ 9am-9pm) Specialities include *pain aux raisins* (raisin bread), *millefeuille* (pastry layered with cream) and *tarte au citron* (lemon tart).

Finkelsztajn (Map pp396-9; ☎ 01 42 72 78 91; 27 rue des Rosiers, 4e; metro St-Paul; ✆ 11am-7pm Mon, 10am-7pm Wed-Sun) This pâtisserie has scrumptious Jewish and Central European-style breads and pastries, including apple strudel and poppy-seed cakes.

Gérard Mulot (Map pp396-9; ☎ 01 43 26 85 77; 76 rue de Seine, 6e; metro Odéon; 6.45am-8pm Thu-Tue) Specialities include various fruit tarts (peach, lemon, apple), *tarte normande* (apple cake) and *mabillon* (caramel mousse with apricot conserves).

Jean Millet (Map pp389-91; ☎ 01 45 51 49 80; 103 rue St-Dominique, 7e; metro École Militaire; ✆ 9am-7pm Mon-Sat, 8am-1pm Sun) Specialities include *délice au chocolat praliné* (a heavenly almond and chocolate concoction) and *bavarois d'abricots* (a cold moulded mousse dessert of cream and apricot fruit purée).

Ladurée (Map pp383-5; ☎ 01 40 75 08 75; 75 av des Champs-Élysées, 8e; metro George V; ✆ 8.30am-7pm Mon-Sat, 10am-7pm Sun) Specialities include *macarons au chocolat* (chocolate macaroons) and *macarons à la pistache* (pistachio macaroons).

Stohrer (Map pp386-8; ☎ 01 42 33 38 20; 51 rue Montorgueil, 2e; metro Les Halles or Sentier; ✆ 7.30am-8.30pm) Specialities include *galette des rois* (kings' cake; puff pastry with frangipane cream) and *marrons glacées* (candied chestnuts).

menu €65 (lunch); 🕒 lunch Wed-Sun, dinner to 9pm Tue-Sun

Famous for its *caneton* (duckling) prepared in a myriad of ways, La Tour d'Argent is equally famous for its stunning views of the Seine and Notre Dame. Book well in advance (eight to 10 days before for lunch, three weeks ahead for dinner) and make sure to try the signature *quenelles de brochet* (pike-perch dumplings). The 'Silver Tower' has been around since 1582 so it must be doing something right.

LE BUISSON ARDENT

Map pp392-5   French, Bistro

☎ 01 43 54 93 02; 25 rue Jussieu, 5e; metro Jussieu; menus €15 (lunch) & €28 (dinner); 🕒 lunch & dinner to 10.30pm Mon-Fri

A modern bistro with the curious name of the 'Burning Bush', this place serves inventive starters (feta ravioli) and mains such as pork tenderloin with ceps and polenta in a subdued but upbeat atmosphere. With the university so close, expect a well-informed crowd at lunch.

LE COCO DE MER

Map pp392-5   Seychelles, Creole

☎ 01 47 07 06 64; 34 blvd St-Marcel, 5e; metro St Marcel; mains €15-22, menu €30; 🕒 lunch Tue-Sat, dinner to 10.30pm Mon-Sat

Done up like a blue clapboard beach hut, this is one of the few places in Paris you'll be able to dine with your feet in the sand and banana leaves and coconuts overhead. The real show, though, is on your plate with fish fresh from the turquoise waters of the Indian Ocean and Caribbean Sea: *carpaccio d'espadon fumé* (carpaccio of smoked swordfish) and *filet de bourgeois mariné cru aux herbes et au citron vert* (marinated fish with herbs and lime). The '*découverte*' or 'discovery' menu is a great option, allowing you to compare the flavours of *requin au tamarin* (shark with tamarind) and *vindail de dorade coryphène* (dolphin fish).

LE COSI Map pp392-5   French, Corsica

☎ 01 43 29 20 20; 9 rue Cujas, 5e; metro Luxembourg; starters €8.50-15, mains €15.50-20; 🕒 lunch & dinner to 11.15pm Mon-Sat

Based in what was a popular student bistro for some four decades, Le Cosi is a Corsican restaurant that occasionally strays to other Mediterranean lands. Lovely, upbeat surrounds, large picture windows and inventive (yet authentic) dishes.

LE TOURNEBRIDE

Map pp392-5   French, Auvergne

☎ 01 43 31 42 98; 104 rue Mouffetard, 5e; metro Censier Daubenton; meals from €15, plat du jour €11 🕒 lunch Mon-Sat

The Tournebride's restaurant section is closed in the evening (though the bar stays open till 2am), so come here at lunch time, when you can savour simple but well-prepared Auvernge cuisine in the company of journos from the nearby offices of *Le Monde*. The real treasure here though is the bleu d'Auvergne (blue-veined cheese), straight from the countryside, and alone worth the trip to rue Mouffetard. The beautifully presented *aumônière* (a pear-filled crepe served with orange-flavoured cream) adds just the right touch of sweetness to the meal.

LE VIGNERON

Map pp392-5   French, Southwest

☎ 01 47 07 29 99; 18-20 rue du Pot de Fer, 5e; metro Place Monge; starters €6-18, mains €11-24, menus €10.50 & €13.50 (lunch), €16.50 & €25 (dinner); 🕒 lunch & dinner to midnight

The 'Wine Grower', one of the better French restaurants in the Mouffetard quarter (not as prestigious a superlative as you might think), specialises in southwest cuisine. There are any number of *menus* available throughout the day and a new annexe next door handles overflow during the busiest months.

LES QUATRE ET UNE SAVEURS

Map pp392-5   Vegetarian

☎ 01 43 26 88 80; 72 rue du Cardinal Lemoine, 5e; metro Cardinal Lemoine; menus €13 (lunch), €22 & €25; 🕒 lunch Sun-Fri, dinner to 10.30 Sun-Thu & Sat

Set back from the place de la Contrescarpe, this bright restaurant is extremely popular among health-food lovers. All ingredients are fresh and guaranteed 100% organic to satisfy the clientele. Whet your appetite with mû tea (16 plants and roots including clove, peony, thistle and liquorice), then enjoy the hearty, delectable *assiette complète au seitan* (mixed plate with cooked wheat gluten) served with artistically presented *crudités* (white radishes pickled in plum vinegar, seaweed, beans, rice and millet). Vegans be warned that fish is served here.

(Continued on page 179)

1 Façade, Musée de l'Érotisme (p128) **2** Tomb, Cimetière du Montparnasse (p209) **3** Grave of Edith Piaf, Cimetière du Père Lachaise (p193)

1 Sunday afternoon, Can
St-Martin (p122) *2* Picnic
Jardin des Plantes (p96)
3 Sculpture, Jardin des
Tuileries (p82)

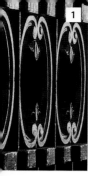

Fence detail, Jardin des Tuileries (p82) **2** Serres Tropicales (Tropical Greenhouse), Jardin des Plantes (p96) **3** Jardin du Luxembourg (p107)

1 Boat race, Jardin du Luxembourg (p107)
2 Man napping, Champs-Élysées (p117)
3 Newlyweds, Sacré Cœur (p127)

1 Volleyball match, Jardin
  du Luxembourg (p107)
2 Cyclists, av des
  Champs-Élysées (p118)
3 Banner advertising the
  Paris Olympic bid

1 Jam session, Canal St-Martin (p122) 2 Shop front Montparnasse
3 Latin Quarter (p93)

Blanc Nati

1 Façade detail, Palais du Luxembourg (p107) **2** Street scene, the Marais (p86) 3 Shakespeare & Company Bookshop (p260), Latin Quarter

1 View from Sacré Cœur
(p127), Montmartre
 2 Eiffel Tower, view from
Tour Montparnasse (p108)
3 Église du Dôme and Hôtel
des Invalides (p112), view
from Tour Montparnasse

(Continued from page 170)

LES VIGNES DU PANTHÉON

Map pp392-5   *French, Southwest*
☎ 01 43 54 80 81; 4 rue des Fossés St-Jacques, 5e; metro Luxembourg; starters €8-9, mains €15-18, menus €15 (lunch) & €26 (dinner); ☺ lunch & dinner to 10pm Mon-Fri

This charming eatery, owned and managed by a husband-and-wife team, stands out for its southwest-inspired food and choice of wines, but service can be chaotic. It's just a few paces down the hill from the Panthéon.

L'ÉTOILE DU BERGER

Map pp392-5   *French, Savoie*
☎ 01 43 26 38 87; 42 rue de la Montagne Ste-Geneviève, 5e; metro Maubert Mutualité; starters €6-12, mains €14-18, menu €22; ☺ lunch Sat & Sun, dinner to midnight

The 'Shepherd's Star', a Savoyard restaurant done up like a mountain chalet, specialises in *raclette* (Swiss cheese dish, €16 to €18), eaten with boiled potatoes and pickles, and fondue (cheese €16; beef €18). Here, try one of the big, wheel-shaped Savoy cheeses such as Beaufort, a grainy member of the French *gruyère* family that tastes slightly fruity and is head and shoulders above the rest.

MAVROMMATIS Map pp392-5   *Greek*
☎ 01 43 31 17 17; 5 rue du Marché des Patriarches, 5e; metro Censier Daubenton; mains €17-26, menus €19 (lunch) & €29; ☺ lunch & dinner to 11pm Tue-Sun

If your experience of Greek food in Paris is of takeaway outlets and restaurants in rue de la Huchette and streets like rue Saint Séverin in the Latin Quarter, visit Mavrommatis to discover the real thing. It's hard to choose between the assortment of *tarama* (fish roe dip), *aubergines fumées* (smoked aubergine) and tzatziki, on one hand, and the *salade grecque* (tomatoes, lettuce, peppers and feta), on the other. Delicious *moussaka* or the *crépines d'agneau sur lit de tomates, courgettes et pommes de terre* (lamb tripe with tomatoes, zucchini and potatoes) doesn't make it any easier. Wash it down with a retsina and you'll be swearing there's nothing like Greek food.

PERRAUDIN Map pp392-5   *French*
☎ 01 46 33 15 75; 157 rue St-Jacques, 5e; metro Luxembourg; starters €6-15, mains €14-23, menus €18 (lunch) & €26 (dinner); ☺ lunch & dinner to 10.30pm Mon-Fri

Perraudin is a traditional French restaurant that hasn't changed much since the late 19th century. For classics such as *bœuf bourguignon* (€14), *gigot d'agneau* (leg of lamb, €15) or *confit de canard* (€15), try this reasonably priced place. Starters vary; if the *flamiche* (leek pie from northern France) is on, order that.

SAVANNAH CAFÉ

Map pp392-5   *International*
☎ 01 43 29 45 77; 27 rue Déscartes, 5e; metro Cardinal Lemoine; starters €7-14, pasta €12.50-13.50, grills €12.50-14.50; ☺ 7-11pm Mon-Sat

The food at this charming little bistro just north of the Place de la Contrescarpe is as eclectic as its carnival-like decorations and choice of world music; tabouli mixes with tortellini and *fromage blanc* (cream cheese) with baklava. This place remains a godsend in an area overrun with tourist traps.

TAO Map pp392-5   *Vietnamese*
☎ 01 43 26 75 92; 248 rue St-Jacques, 5e; metro Luxembourg; soups & salads €7-8, mains €8.50-13; ☺ lunch & dinner to 10.30pm Mon-Sat

An upmarket Asian restaurant, Tao serves some of the best Vietnamese cuisine in the Latin Quarter. The fried spring rolls are wonderfully crisp, while the pan-fried shrimps, served on a bed of crunchy Chinese cabbage, are perfect. The *soupe de cheveux d'ange* (angel hair noodle soup) comes with mushrooms. Tao offers vege versions of many dishes, and different combinations of courses to suit every appetite.

CHEAP EATS
KOUTCHI

Map pp392-5   *Middle Eastern, Afghani*
☎ 01 44 07 20 56; 40 rue du Cardinal Lemoine, 5e; metro Cardinal Lemoine; starters €4-5, mains €8-13, menus €8 (lunch) & €15 (dinner); ☺ lunch Mon-Fri, dinner to 11pm Mon-Sat

Koutchi is an Afghan restaurant with décor reminiscent of a Central Asian caravanserai. Specialities: Afghan salads (€4 to €5), meat dishes (€10 to €13) and desserts (€4 to €5).

LA PETIT LÉGUME

Map pp392-5   *Vegetarian*
☎ 01 40 46 06 85; 36 rue des Boulangers, 5e; metro Cardinal Lemoine; salads €10.70-12.90, dishes €6.90-9, menus €8.55-14; ☺ lunch & dinner to 10pm Mon-Sat

The 'Little Vegetable', a tiny place on a narrow road, is a great choice for house-made vegetarian fare.

LA VOIE LACTÉE

Map pp392-5 *Turkish*

☎ 01 46 34 02 35; 34 rue du Cardinal Lemoine, 5e; metro Cardinal Lemoine; starters €5.50-6, mains €8.50-10, menus €9.50 & €12 (lunch), €14 & €17 (dinner); ✆ lunch & dinner to 11pm Mon-Sat

The 'Milky Way' is a Turkish place with modern and traditional Anatolian cuisine, including a buffet of Turkish meze and salads. For mains go for the grills, especially the various types of meatballs on offer. Come Thursday night for some specially prepared dishes.

LE FOYER DU VIETNAM

Map pp392-5 *Vietnamese*

☎ 01 45 35 32 54; 80 rue Monge, 5e; metro Place Monge; dishes €3.10-6.50, menu €8.40; ✆ lunch & dinner to 10pm Mon-Sat

The 'Vietnam Club' is a favourite meeting place among the capital's Vietnamese community. It's nothing but a long room with peeling walls and tables covered in oilcloths and plastic flowers; a small photo of Ho Chi Minh on the wall completes the picture. If you're up for a one-dish meal choose one of the hearty house specialities – 'Saigon' or 'Hanoi' soup (noodles, soya beans and pork flavoured with lemon grass, coriander and chives) – and all dishes are available in either medium or large servings.

LE JARDIN DES PÂTES

Map pp392-5 *Vegetarian*

☎ 01 43 31 50 71; 4 rue Lacépède, 5e; metro Cardinal Lemoine; starters & light dishes €3.30-4.50, salads €8, mains €7.50-12; ✆ lunch & dinner to 11pm

The 'Garden of Pastas' may not be strictly vegetarian but it is 100% *bio* (organic) and offers as many types of noodle as you can care to name – barley, buckwheat, rye, wheat, rice, chestnut and so on – all served with the freshest of ingredients. One especially delicious dish is barley pasta with salmon, crème fraîche, seaweed and leeks. There's also a **13e arrondissment branch** (Map pp380-2; ☎ 01 45 35 93 67; 33 blvd Arago, 13e; metro Les Gobelins), which keeps the same hours.

MACHU PICCHU

Map pp392-5 *South American*

☎ 01 43 26 13 13; 9 rue Royer Collard, 5e; metro Luxembourg; starters €5.50-7, mains €9-13.50, plat du jour €5.90, menu €8 (lunch); ✆ lunch Mon-Fri, dinner to 11pm Mon-Sat

Peruvian food? Doesn't that mean guinea pig fricassee? Apparently not always and this small place serves up excellent grilled meat and seafood dishes from a tiny kitchen. It has a bargain-basement lunch *menu*.

TASHI DELEK
Map pp392-5 *Tibetan*

☎ 01 43 26 55 55; 4 rue des Fossés St-Jacques, 5e; metro Luxembourg; soups €3.50-4, Tibetan bowls €5.35-6.25, menus €12 (lunch) & €18 (dinner); ✆ lunch & dinner to 11pm Mon-Sat

An intimate little place whose name approximates *tashi dele*, or 'bonjour' in Tibetan, Tashi Delek offers food that may not be gourmet but it is tasty and inexpensive. For starters, try the *tangmok* (ravioli and vegetable soup), followed by the delicious *daril seu* (meatballs with garlic, ginger and rice) or the *momok* (large vegetable or meat ravioli). Wash everything down with traditional or salted-butter tea, and don't forget the desserts, including the delicious *dressil* (yogurt with dried fruit). There are also four vegetarian choices (€6.40 to €8.40).

TEA CADDY
Map pp396-9 *Tea Room*

☎ 01 43 54 15 56; 14 rue St-Julien le Pauvre, 5e; metro St-Michel; salads €9.50-11, light meals €8.50-11.80, sandwiches €7.50-9; ✆ noon-7pm Wed-Mon

Arguably the most English of the 'English' tea rooms in Paris, this institution founded in 1928 is a fine place to break for tea (€5.50 to €7.50) and pastries (about €7) after a tour of nearby Notre Dame, Ste-Chapelle or the Conciergerie.

Le Dôme (p184) bar

ST-GERMAIN, ODÉON & LUXEMBOURG

Rue St-André des Arts (Map pp396-9; metro St-Michel or Odéon) is lined with restaurants, including a few down the covered passage de Rohan. There are lots of eateries between Église St-Sulpice and Église St-Germain des Prés as well, especially along rue des Canettes, rue Princesse and rue Guisarde. Carrefour de l'Odéon (metro Odéon) has a cluster of lively bars, cafés and restaurants. Place St-Germain des Prés itself is home to celebrated cafés such as Les Deux Magots and Café de Flore (p222) as well as the equally celebrated Brasserie Lipp.

BRASSERIE LIPP Map pp396-9   French

☎ 01 45 48 53 91; 151 blvd St-Germain, 6e; metro St-Germain des Prés; starters €7.70-17.70, mains €15.50-18; ⌚ noon-1am

The Lipp is a wood-panelled café-brasserie that was opened as the Brasserie des Bords du Rhin by one Léonard Lipp in 1880. Politicians rub shoulders with intellectuals, while waiters in black waistcoats, bow ties and long white aprons serve brasserie favourites like *choucroute garnie* (€16.60) and *tête de veau*. Many people will make a fuss about sitting downstairs rather than upstairs, which is the nonsmoking section and considered nowheresville; Lippistes call it *L'Enfer* (Hell). Look smart and like you know what you're doing; you might find yourself in the window seat – *le Paradis* (Heaven) – watching and being watched and watching being watched.

CHEZ ALBERT Map pp396-9   French

☎ 01 46 33 22 57; 43 rue Mazarine, 6e; metro Odéon; starters €6-24, mains €17-22, menus €17 (lunch) & €28 (dinner); ⌚ lunch & dinner to 10.30pm Tue-Sat

This place offers authentic Portuguese food (not easy to come by in Paris despite the large Portuguese population). Try *porc Alentejana aux palourdes* (pork cooked with clams in a casserole) or any of the numerous *bacalhau* (salt-dried cod) dishes. Excellent mains also include the generous *viande á la planche* (meat platter) for two and *arroz de mariscos*, paella abounding in seafood. There's also a good selection of Portuguese wines. The atmosphere is very pleasant and it's a good place for families – a rare commodity indeed in the very flash neighbourhood of St-Germain des Prés.

FISH LA BOISSONNERIE

Map pp396-9   French, Seafood

☎ 01 43 54 34 69; 69 rue de Seine, 6e; metro Mabillon; starters €7, mains €14, menu €21.50 (lunch); ⌚ lunch & dinner to 10.45pm Tue-Sun

A hybrid of a Mediterranean place run by a New Zealander and a Cuban-American, Fish, with its rustic communal seating and bon-

Top Five St-Germain & Montparnasse Restaurants

- Fish La Boissonnerie (this page)
- La Cagouille (p183)
- Le Dôme (p184)
- Le Golfe de Naples (p182)
- Le Mâchon d'Henri (p182)

homie, has surely taken its cue from London, where such places have been a mainstay for several years. The wine selection is excellent and the wonderful old mosaic on the front (which actually says *'la poissonnerie'* indicating it was a fishmonger) is a positive delight.

LA CAFETIÈRE

Map pp396-9   French, Corsican

☎ 01 46 33 76 90; 21-23 rue Mazarine, 6e; metro Odéon; starters €12-15, mains €17-21, menu €20 (lunch); ⌚ lunch & dinner to midnight Tue-Sat

With a shop sign in front of *la tête de Maure* (a Moor's head swaddled in a white bandana and wearing a hooped earring) there's no mistaking what you'll find inside the inaptly named 'Coffee Pot': *la cuisine corse* (Corsican cuisine). Try the *stufatu*, a fragrant stew made (in this case) with veal. There is also excellent prosciutto-like *coppa*, charcuterie such as *lonzo* and fresh *brocciu* cheese.

L'ARBUCI Map pp396-9   French, Brasserie

☎ 01 44 32 16 00; 25 rue de Buci, 6e; metro Mabillon; meals from €35, menus €15.50 & €20 (lunch); ⌚ noon-1am

Though this retro-style brasserie recently got an all-marble, all-glass makeover, the specialities remain: seafood (especially oysters) and spit-roasted beef, chicken, pork, salmon and – for dessert – pineapple. All-you-can-eat access to oysters of modest size costs €25. From midnight to daybreak Thursday to Saturday there's live jazz in the basement.

LE MÂCHON D'HENRI

Map pp396-9   *French, Lyons & Mediterranean*
☎ 01 43 29 08 70; 8 rue Guisarde, 6e; metro St-Sulpice or Mabillon; starters €6-8, mains €12-13; ⏱ lunch & dinner until 11.15pm

A very Parisian bistro in an area awash with bars, this *mâchon* (in Lyons, a restaurant serving light meals) serves Lyon-inspired dishes with, go figure, a Mediterranean twist. Numerous dishes include *poivrons grillés à l'huile d'olive* (grilled capsicum with olive oil) and *terrine de courgettes et son coulis de tomates* (courgette terrine with tomato coulis). Regional dishes such as *saucisson de Lyon* (Lyon sausage) and sumptuous *boudin noir aux pommes* (black pudding with apple) come in generous serves. Rustic décor and excellent service makes this an easy pick.

LE PETIT ZINC

Map pp396-9   *French, Brasserie*
☎ 01 42 86 61 00; 11 rue St-Benoît, 6e; metro St-Germain des Prés; starters €13-19.50, mains €19.50-43; menu €23 & €28 (lunch); ⏱ noon-2am

The 'Little Bar' is a wonderful brasserie, serving traditional French cuisine and regional specialities from the southwest in true Art Nouveau splendour. The term bistro is used loosely here; you'll feel more like you're in a starred restaurant so book ahead and dress accordingly.

CHEAP EATS

AMORINO Map pp396-9   *Ice Cream*
☎ 01 43 26 57 46; 4 rue de Buci, 6e; metro St-Germain des Prés; €3.40-5; ⏱ noon-midnight Sun-Thu, 1pm-midnight Fri & Sat

Though not as dedicated *lécheurs* (lickers) as some, we're told that **Berthillon** (p167) has serious competition and Amorino's home-made ice cream (yogurt, caramel, kiwi, strawberry etc) is, in fact, better. Expect long queues here and at the **Luxembourg branch** (Map pp389-91; ☎ 01 42 22 66 86; 4 rue Vavin, 6e; metro Vavin).

GUEN MAÏ Map pp396-9   *Vegetarian*
☎ 01 43 26 03 24; rue Cardinal & 2bis rue de l'Abbaye, 6e; metro St-Germain des Prés or Mabillon; soups €4.50, mains €7-10.50; ⏱ lunch Mon-Sat

On a corner and with two entrances, Guen Maï is essentially a health food shop, with a kitchen serving up macrobiotic, organic plats du jour and soups. It's a cosy, friendly place and, as the name suggests, the dishes are Asian-inspired. Try one of the wonderful juices.

INDONESIA Map pp392-5   *Indonesian*
☎ 01 43 25 70 22; 12 rue de Vaugirard, 6e; metro Luxembourg; menus €9-12.50 (lunch), €13-19 (dinner); ⏱ lunch Sun-Fri, dinner to 10.30pm

One of a couple of Indonesian restaurants in town, this unimaginatively named eatery has all the old favourites, from an elaborate, nine-dish *rijstafel* (rice with side dishes; €23) to *lumpia* (a type of spring roll; €4.50), *rendang* (€8.50) and *gado-gado* (€5). A half-dozen *menus* are available at dinner alone. The traditional décor, incense and the gentle rhythm of the gamelan orchestra combine to make this a very special place opposite the Jardin du Luxembourg.

LE GOLFE DE NAPLES

Map pp396-9   *Italian, Pizzeria*
☎ 01 43 26 98 11; 5 rue de Montfaucon, 6e; metro Mabillon; starters €8-13, pizza & pasta dishes €9.50-14, mains €11-18.50; ⏱ lunch & dinner to 11pm

Despite its location in the heart of tourist town, the 'Gulf of Naples' has some of the best pizza and fresh pasta in Paris – but more elaborate main courses are somewhat disappointing. Don't forget to try the *assiette napolitaine*, a plate of grilled fresh vegetables (€13.50).

POLIDOR Map pp396-9   *French*
☎ 01 43 26 95 34; 41 rue Monsieur le Prince, 6e; metro Odéon; starters €4-12, mains €7-12, menus €9 (lunch), €18 & €26; ⏱ lunch & dinner to 12.30am Mon-Sat, to 11pm Sun

A meal at Polidor, a quintessentially Parisian *crémerie-restaurant*, is like a trip to Victor Hugo's Paris – the restaurant and its décor date from 1845. Everyone knows about it and it's pretty touristy. Still, *menus* of tasty, family-style French cuisine are available. Specialities include *bœuf bourguignon* (€10), *blanquette de veau* (veal in white sauce; €11) and the most famous *tarte Tatin* (caramelised apple pie; €5) in Paris. Don't bother booking in advance; you'll just have to wait anyway.

Table setting, Le Dôme (p184)

MONTPARNASSE

Since the 1920s, the area around blvd du Montparnasse has been one of the city's premier avenues for enjoying that most Parisian of pastimes: sitting in a café and checking out the scenery on two legs. Many younger Parisians now consider the area somewhat *démodé* and touristy and avoid it. Around metro Vavin blvd du Montparnasse is home to a number of legendary places, made famous between the wars by writers (p141) and artists such as Picasso, Dalí and Cocteau. Before the Russian Revolution, these cafés attracted exiles, including Lenin and Trotsky.

Montparnasse offers all types of eateries, especially traditional creperies, as Gare Montparnasse is where Bretons arriving in Paris to look for work would disembark (and apparently venture no further). There are three creperies at 20 rue d'Odessa (Map pp389–91) alone and at least half a dozen more round the corner on rue du Montparnasse.

AQUARIUS

Map pp380-2   *Vegetarian*

☎ 01 45 41 36 88; 40 rue de Gergovie, 14e; metro Pernéty or Plaisance; starters €4-7, mains €7.80-12, menus €11 (lunch), €12.50 & €15 (dinner); ☽ lunch & dinner to 10.30pm Mon-Thu, to 11pm Fri & Sat

This vegetarian restaurant, the first to open in Paris, offers meals inspired by traditional French cuisine. From classic *chèvre chaud* (warm goat's cheese) to *ravioles de Romans* (French-style ravioli), starters are substantial. For the main course, meat has been replaced with tofu or gluten-based seitan. You can enjoy lasagna, cassoulet or *tartiflette* (a baked potato and cheese concoction). Organic wines are on offer as well. The outermost of three rooms, where smoking is permitted, opens onto a little garden that is pleasantly cool in summer. There is a smaller **Aquarius branch** (Map pp396-9; ☎ 01 48 87 48 71; 54 rue Ste-Croix de la Bretonnerie, 4e; metro Rambuteau) in the Marais that keeps the same hours.

DIX VINS

Map pp389-91   *French*

☎ 01 43 20 91 77; 57 rue Falguière, 15e; metro Pasteur; menu €18.50; ☽ lunch Tue-Sat, dinner to 11pm Mon-Sat

This tiny restaurant, on the far side of Montparnasse, is so successful that you will probably have to wait at the bar even if you've booked. Not such a bad thing, of course, in a temple devoted to Bacchus as you'll be able to sample one of the carefully chosen wines. The unique set menu may offer *merlan frit en colère sauce tartare* ('angry' fried whiting with a tartare sauce) – very agreeable despite its name – or a tempting *boudin noir* (black pudding), followed by an excellent *canette rôtie sauce au poivre* (roast duckling with pepper sauce). Excellent value, good service and stylish décor combine to form a true winner.

LA CAGOUILLE

Map pp380-2   *French, Seafood*

☎ 01 43 22 09 01; 10-12 Place Constantin Brancusi, opp 23 Rue de l'Ouest, 14e; metro Gaîté; meals from €45, menus with wine €23 & €38; ☽ lunch & dinner to 10.30pm

Chef Gérard Allemandou, one of the best seafood cooks in Paris, gets rave reviews for his fish and shellfish dishes at this café-restaurant. The €23 *menu* (lunch and dinner) is one of the better deals in the capital. Stick with it, and don't be tempted by the pricier *carte* (menu).

LA COUPOLE

Map pp389-91   *French, Brasserie*

☎ 01 43 20 14 20; 102 blvd du Montparnasse, 14e; metro Vavin; starters €7.50-12.50, mains €13.50-18.50, menus €17.50 (lunch), €22.90 & €32.90; ☽ 8am-1am Sun-Thu, to 1.30am Fri & Sat

Here there are famous mural-covered columns (painted by such artists as Brancusi and Chagall), dark wood-panelling, soft lighting and hardly any changes since the days of Sartre, Soutine, Man Ray and the dancer Josephine Baker. The reason for visiting this enormous, 450-seat brasserie, designed by the Solvet brothers and opened in 1927, is thus history not gastronomy. You can book for lunch, but have to queue for dinner; though there's always breakfast (€4.50 to €7.50).

L'ASSIETTE

Map pp380-2   *French, Southwest*

☎ 01 43 22 64 86; 181 rue du Château, 14e; metro Gaîté; meals from €50, menu €35 (lunch); ☽ lunch & dinner to 10.30pm Wed-Sun

This engaging bistro, with its ever-changing menu, is a bit off the beaten track southwest of the Cimitière du Montparnasse but has an unusual claim to fame: a woman chef. It's pricey for a bistro but the freshness and quality of the produce and the precision of the preparation and cooking would seem to justify the cost. The wine list is well considered but you won't find a bottle of wine for less than €50.

LE CAMÉLÉON Map pp389-91 *French, Bistro*
☎ 01 43 20 63 43; 6 rue de Chevreuse, 6e; metro Vavin; starters €6-18, mains €15-22, menu €22 (lunch); ⏰ lunch Mon-Fri, dinner to 11pm Mon-Sat

Head for the 'Chameleon' if you want to try out a 'nouveau bistro'; the red-tile floor, honey-coloured ceiling and friendly atmosphere make it a little island of calm. The cook does all sorts of things well, especially the *ravioles de homard* (lobster ravioli; €17) and *saucisse fumée d'Auvergne au purée maison* (smoked Auvergne sausage with mash *à la française*; €15). You might also consider *selle d'agneau à la fleur de thym* (lamb saddle with thyme).

LE DÔME Map pp389-91 *French, Seafood*
☎ 01 43 35 25 81; 108 blvd du Montparnasse, 14e; metro Vavin; starters €12.50-23, mains €30.50-56; ⏰ lunch & dinner to 12.30am

An Art Deco extravaganza dating from the 1930s, Le Dôme is a monumental place for a meal, with the emphasis on the freshest of oysters, shellfish and fish dishes such as *sole meunière* (sole sautéed in butter and garnished with lemon and parsley). It's safest to stick with the basics at this historical venue and leave fussier dishes to the upstarts.

CHEAP EATS
DIETETIC SHOP
Map pp389-91 *Vegetarian*
☎ 01 43 35 39 75; 11 rue Delambre, 14e; metro Vavin, Edgar Quinet; small dishes €5.50-8.10, salads €5.50-9.10, platters €9-10.80; ⏰ lunch Mon-Sat, dinner to 10.30pm Mon-Fri

In this tiny, no-nonsense eatery you can choose your meal from the kitchen in the middle of the room. Among the cold dishes, there's a homemade vegetable pâté, *caviar d'algues marines* (seaweed 'caviar') with pasta and an assortment of raw vegetables or lentils served with smoked tofu and raw vegetables. Hot dishes include soups, couscous and more innovative specialities such as *tarte aux graines germées* (bean sprout tart). The Dietetic Shop is essentially just that – a place selling vegetarian and organic products with a few tables added. Arrive early as reservations are not taken.

MUSTANG CAFÉ
Map pp389-91 *Mexican, Tex-Mex*
☎ 01 43 35 36 12; 84 blvd du Montparnasse, 14e; metro Montparnasse Bienvenüe; starters €6-13.50, salads €6.70-9, mains €7.50-13.30; ⏰ 8am-5am

A café that *almost* never sleeps, the Mustang has passable Tex-Mex combination platters and nachos from €7.50 to €13.30, fajitas for €12.50 and burgers from €8.90 to €10.60. Come here when the rest of Paris has gone to bed. Happy hour, when all drinks are half-price, is between 4pm and 8pm.

THUY LONG
Map pp389-91 *Vietnamese*
☎ 01 45 49 26 01; 111 blvd de Vaugirard, 6e; metro St-Placide or Montparnasse Bienvenüe; starters €7.50-11, pasta €12-15, mains €13.50-16, menus €11 & €15 (lunch), €20.50; ⏰ 11am-8pm Mon-Thu, to 9pm Fri & Sat

Thuy Long, a tiny café just north of the Gare Montparnasse, offers some of the best-value Vietnamese food in Paris. Try the generous bowl of *pho* (soup of noodles with beef) or the *bo bun* (rice noodles with beef, small spring rolls and vegetables). It's hectic here at lunch time; visit in the afternoon.

FAUBOURG ST-GERMAIN & INVALIDES
This district, effectively the 7e arrondissement, has the reputation of being rather staid and that's not too far from the truth; it seems there's a ministry on every other block. The National Assembly sits sentry by the river alongside the Musée d'Orsay, and visible from every angle is the Tour Eiffel's elaborate ironwork. The district's restaurants and other catering options reflect this world, at once serious and diligent and carefree and on holiday.

IL VIAGGIO Map pp389-91 *Italian*
☎ 01 45 55 80 75; 34 rue de Bourgogne, 7e; metro Varenne; starters €13.50-22, pasta €16-23, mains €22-26, 2-/3-course menus €24/30 (lunch); ⏰ lunch Mon-Fri, dinner to 11pm Mon-Sat

The intimate interior, irreproachable service, and stylish food and wine make the 'Journey' one of the most elegant Italian restaurants in Paris. Predictably, various sorts of pasta figure on the short, classic menu, but there are

Top Five Faubourg St-Germain, Invalides & Eiffel Tower Area Restaurants

- Il Viaggio (opposite)
- L'Atelier de Joël Robouchon (this page)
- La Cantine Russe (p186)
- La Cigale (this page)
- Thoumioux (p186)

also delicious antipasti (notably the very tasty Parma ham and mozzarella) and some subtle variations on veal – the meat that rules in Italy. With the National Assembly just round the corner, the clientele is top-heavy with politicians.

LA CIGALE Map pp389-91   *French*
☎ 01 45 48 87 87; 11bis rue Chomel, 7e; metro Sèvres-Babylone; starters €6.50-8, soufflés €8.70-15.60, mains €15.50-20.50; ☽ lunch Mon-Fri, dinner to 11pm Mon-Sat

For the past decade, Gérard Idoux, the undisputed soufflé master of Paris, has won the hearts (and bellies) of a loyal clientele. Customers can choose from 60 to 80 savoury or sweet soufflés. The *soufflés aux morilles* (morel mushrooms), *aux oursins* (sea urchins) and *au potiron* (pumpkin) are autumn favourites. In summer, don't miss the *soufflé aux abricots*

(apricot soufflé). The menu changes monthly and constantly attracts new regulars.

L'ATELIER DE JOËL ROBOUCHON
Map pp389-91   *International*
☎ 01 42 22 56 56; 5 rue de Montalembert, 7e; metro rue du Bac; starters €13-53, small dishes €7-25, mains €23-48; ☽ lunch & dinner to midnight

More Soho than St-Germain, this palace of gastronomy overseen by His Royal Highness 'King' Joël Robouchon is an understated mix of red leather seats and black lacquer bars (there are no individual tables). The cuisine is 'modern mix' (ie everything goes) and you can run the gamut by ordering any of the small dishes (*tapas à la française*, for lack of a better term) on offer. An extensive world tour, but with all of Paris along for the ride, it's well worth it.

LE 7E SUD Map pp389-91   *Mediterranean*
☎ 01 44 18 30 30; 159 rue de Grenelle, 7e; metro La Tour Maubourg; salads & starters €8-12, platters €12, mains €15-18; ☽ lunch & dinner to midnight

The cosmopolitan '7th South' specialises in bringing together the full gamut of Mediterranean flavours and the décor, with its long tables and low lighting, has a warm, eastern feel, especially in the vaulted cellar. Organise your own culinary itinerary by starting with light-as-a-feather *fritellis calamares grecs* (Greek-style calamari). For mains have a stopover in Italy

Painting, L'Atelier de Joël Robouchon (above)

with *rigatoni ricotti au jambon de Parme* (rigatoni with Parma ham), a tajine in the purest Moroccan tradition or a mixed kebab on a bed of baby beans from the market. This is a great spot to meet up with friends as the food comes in generous servings so you can easily share dishes.

THOUMIOUX

Map pp389-91 *French, Brasserie*
☎ 01 47 05 49 75; 79 rue St-Dominique, 7e; metro La Tour Maubourg; starters €8-20, mains €17-25, menus €14 (lunch) & €33; 🕐 lunch & dinner to 11.45pm

Founded in 1923, Thoumioux is an institution just south of the Quai d'Orsay and popular with politicians and tourists alike. The cassoulet (€18) is justifiably renowned for its quality and size though you might also try such favourites as *saumon aux lentilles* (€13; salmon with lentils) or *tête de veau* (€18).

CHEAP EATS
BANGA DE MAYOTTE

Map pp389-91 *Madagascan, Creole*
☎ 01 45 66 84 44; 33 rue Rousselet, 7e; metro Duroc; menus €9.15 (lunch) & €14.50 (dinner); 🕐 lunch Mon-Fri, dinner to 11pm Tue-Sat

This tiny restaurant, through a narrow hallway and courtyard, is not easy to find. But it's worth the trouble for those wishing to sample the cuisine of Mayotte (Mahore in English), a tiny island to the northwest of Madagascar. The dishes borrow heavily from Creole cuisine: delicious, fresh *sambos* (small flaky pastries stuffed with beef, herbs and spices), *cari de poulet au lait de coco* (chicken curry with coconut milk) and banana baked in its skin then sprinkled with rum. The food may be simple and the choice limited, but the owner's sunny disposition is limitless.

EIFFEL TOWER AREA & 16E ARRONDISSEMENT

The 16e arrondissement is perhaps the most chichi and snobby part of Paris, the kind of area where a waiter will ask a fluent though non-native speaker of French whether they would like *la carte en anglais* (English menu). It's not everyone's *tasse de thé* (cup of tea) but a couple of its ethnic restaurants are worth a visit.

LA CANTINE RUSSE

Map pp389-91 *Russian*
☎ 01 47 20 65 17; 26 av de New York, 16e; metro Alma Marceau; menus €12 & €20, plat du jour €9; 🕐 lunch & dinner to 10pm Tue-Sat

Founded for students at the prestigious Conservatoire Rachmaninov in 1923, the 'Russian Canteen' is still strong seven decades later. At communal tables you can savour herrings served with blinis, eggplant 'caviar', *pojarski* (chicken meatballs with dill), beef Stroganov, *chachliks* (marinated lamb kebabs) and, to complete the tableau, *vatrouchka* (cream-cheese cake). Everything is delicious and the atmosphere is utterly charming.

LA CHAUMIÈRE EN CHINE

Map pp383-5 *Chinese*
☎ 01 47 20 85 56; 26 av Pierre 1er de Serbie, 16e; metro Alma Marceau; starters €8-9, mains €9.50-17.50; 🕐 lunch & dinner to 10.30pm Mon-Sat

Parisian in the know warn against eating in ethnic restaurants outside ethnic *quartiers*, but the Chinese embassy just next door makes the 'Thatched Cottage in China' a notable exception to the rule. The largely Chinese clientele favour the *crabes mous en friture* (soft-shell crab fritters), made with a crustacean fished in the waters of Vietnam and Madagascar, the *canard farci* (stuffed duck) and pungent fermented beancurd – as should you.

ÉTOILE & CHAMPS-ÉLYSÉES

The 8e arrondissement appears to have been born under a lucky star. Its avenues radiate from place Charles de Gaulle – also known as place de l'Étoile or simply Étoile – and among them is the av des Champs-Élysées. From the Arc de Triomphe to the place de la Concorde, the 'Elysean Fields' rules unchallenged. With very few exceptions, eateries lining this touristy thoroughfare offer little value for money, but restaurants in the surrounding areas can be excellent.

FOUQUET'S Map pp383-5 *French*
☎ 01 47 23 70 60; 99 av des Champs-Élysées, 8e;
metro George V; starters €21-45, mains €28-56,
plat du jour €20; ☺ 8am-2am
You couldn't get more 'downtown Paris' than
this café-brasserie that bears a striking resemblance to a spiffy London pub with its flocked
red wallpaper and polished wood surfaces. Its
location on the very pavement of the Champs-
Élysées raises its prices considerably, though
the food is rather good – especially the fish
dishes.

GRAINDORGE Map pp383-5 *Belgian*
☎ 01 47 64 33 47; 11 rue de l'Arc de Triomphe, 17e;
metro Charles de Gaulle-Étoile; starters €11-20,
mains €22-26, menus €28 (lunch) & €32 (dinner);
☺ lunch Mon-Fri, dinner to 11pm Mon-Sat
The name of this stylish restaurant, with its
soft lighting, burgundy chairs and banquettes,
and Art Deco touches, means 'barley grain'
and alludes to the great breweries of Flanders
(check out the drinks list). The chef's signature
dish is *potjevleesch*, four different kinds of meat
cooked slowly together and served in aspic,
though you'll find plenty of other meat and
fish choices that hint at the Low Countries.

L'ARDOISE
Map pp383-5 *French, Bistro*
☎ 01 42 96 28 18; 28 rue du Mont Thabor, 1er; metro
Concorde or Tuileries; menu €30; ☺ lunch & dinner to
11pm Wed-Sun
This is a little bistro with no menu as such (*ardoise* means 'blackboard', which is all there is),
but who cares? The food – rabbit stuffed with
plums and beef fillet with morels, prepared dex-
trously by chef Pierre Jay (ex-Tour d'Argent) –
is superb and the *prix fixe* (set menu) offers
excellent value. L'Ardoise is bound to attract a
fair number of tourists due to its location, but
generally they are also on a culinary quest.

LE MAN RAY
Map pp383-5 *Fusion*
☎ 01 54 88 36 36; 34 rue Marbœuf, 8e; metro Franklin D Roosevelt; starters €7-23, mains €24-29, menus
€27 & €35; ☺ lunch & dinner to midnight
Named after our main man Man Ray, the surrealist photographer, this is the place for the
beau monde of the Right Bank to celebrity spot.
It serves lots of uninspired fusion food; come
here for the scenery not the fodder. The bar,
open till 2am daily, turns into a club on Friday
till 5am.

L'ÉTOILE VERTE
Map pp383-5 *French*
☎ 01 43 80 69 34; 13 rue Brey, 17e; metro Charles de
Gaulle-Étoile; starters €6.50-14.50, mains €10.50-22,
menu €11.50 (lunch), €18 & €25 (with wine);
☺ lunch & dinner to more than 11pm
Founded more than half a century ago, the
'Green Star' is where all the old French classics remain – the onion soup, the snails, the
rabbit. When one of us was a student in Paris
(back when the Lascaux cave paintings in
Périgord were still wet) this was the place for
both Esperanto speakers (a green star is their
symbol) and students on a splurge. That may
have changed somewhat but the lunch *menu*
is still one of the best deals in the district.

MAISON PRUNIER
Map pp383-5 *French*
☎ 01 44 17 35 85; 16 av Victor Hugo, 16e; metro
Charles de Gaulle-Étoile; starters €18-65, mains
€26-45, menu €60 (lunch); ☺ lunch & dinner to
midnight Mon-Sat
A venerable restaurant founded in 1925, the
Prunier is as famed for its Art Deco interior as
for its own brand of caviar, and fish and seafood
dishes. This is definitely a place for celebrations;
hang the expense and order the famous caviar
(€29 to €74).

P'TIT BOUCHON GOURMAND
Map pp383-5 *French*
☎ 01 40 55 03 26; 5 rue Troyon, 17e; metro Charles
de Gaulle-Étoile; starters €14-24, mains €16-28, menu
€25; ☺ lunch Mon-Fri, dinner to 11pm Mon-Sat
An institution for almost a quarter of a century in the Breton seaside town of La Baule,
'Greedy's Little Wine Bar' has arrived in *la capi-
tale* dressed up in theatrical reds and blacks.
Try the voluptuous *camembert rôti sur son lit
de salade* (roasted camembert with salad) followed by the *millefeuille de boudin noir aux
pommes* (black pudding in layered pastry with
apples). The owners offer a warm welcome.

Top Five Étoile, Champs-Élysées & Clichy Restaurants

- Á la Grande Bleue (p188)
- Charlot, Roi des Coquillages (p188)
- L'Ardoise (this page)
- Macis et Muscade (p189)
- Spoon, Food & Wine (p188)

Eating – Étoile & Champs-Élysées

SPOON, FOOD & WINE

Map pp383-5 *Fusion*

☎ 01 40 76 34 44; 14 rue de Marignan, 8e; metro Franklin D Roosevelt; starters €10-19.50, mains €24-40, menus €37 (lunch) & €43; ☾ lunch & dinner to 11pm Mon-Fri

Here diners are invited to mix and match their own main courses and sauces – grilled calamari, say, with a choice of satay, curry and Béarnaise sauces or humus and aubergine salad with samosas. It has an unheard of (for Paris) selection of New World and other European wines, with only a small proportion being French.

CHEAP EATS

LINA'S Map pp386-8

☎ 01 40 15 94 95; 4 rue Cambon, 1er; metro Concorde; salads €4.50-6.10, sandwiches €3.50-7; ☾ 9.30am-4.30pm Mon-Fri, 10am-5.30pm Sat

This branch of a popular chain of sandwich and soup bars across Paris (some 19 outlets so far) has upmarket sandwiches, salads and soups. Other outlets include **Bercy** (Map p401; ☎ 01 43 40 42 42; 104 rue de Bercy; metro Bercy) and **Opéra** (Map pp386-8; ☎ 01 47 03 30 29; 7 av de l'Opéra, 1er; metro Pyramides).

CLICHY & GARE ST-LAZARE

Unlike their neighbour to the west, these areas are not gentrified in the least. Indeed, heading east in the 8e arrondissement, by the time you reach Gare St-Lazare, the shops and architecture have changed and another journey has begun. Around place de Clichy and the eponymous avenue leading north and south from it, a maze of small streets with a pronounced working-class character stretches out, a pocket of old Paris that has survived. These are happy hunting grounds for ethnic eateries and restaurants with character.

À LA GRANDE BLEUE

Map pp380-2 *North African, Berber*

☎ 01 42 28 04 26; 4 rue Lantiez, 17e; metro Brochant or Guy Moquet; starters €4.50-7, mains €8.90-18, menu €9.50 (lunch); ☾ lunch Mon-Fri, dinner to 11pm Mon-Sat

'At the Deep Blue Sea' has rare *crepes berbères* (Berber crepes; €7 to €10.50), unusual barley couscous (€10 to €18) prepared in the style of the Berbers (Kabyles) of eastern Algeria as well as the normal semolina variety (€8.90 to €15), and the savoury-sweet *pastilla au poulet* (chicken pastilla; €16.50). Add to that the cool blue and yellow décor, art on the walls and warm welcome and you've got a winner.

BISTRO DES DAMES

Map pp383-5 *French*

☎ 01 45 22 13 42; 18 rue des Dames, 17e; metro Place de Clichy; starters €6-11, mains €11-14, plats du jour €9.90-14; ☾ lunch & dinner to 2am

The Bistro des Dames, the restaurant of **Hôtel Eldorado** (p298), will appeal to lovers of simple, authentic cuisine, such as hearty salads, tortillas and glorious charcuterie platters of *pâté de campagne*, authentic Guéméné *andouille* sausage (a smoked sausage made of pork tripe usually eaten cold) and paper-thin Serrano ham. The dining room, which looks out onto the street, is lovely, but during those humid Parisian summers it's the cool and tranquillity of the small back garden that pulls in the punters.

CHARLOT, ROI DES COQUILLAGES

Map pp383-5 *French, Seafood*

☎ 01 53 20 48 00; 12 place de Clichy, 9e; metro Place de Clichy; starters €10.60-24.50, mains €19-38, menus €25 & €30 (lunch); ☾ lunch & dinner to midnight Sun-Wed, to 1am Thu-Sat

'Charlot, the King of Shellfish' is an Art Deco palace that some Parisians think is the best place in town for no-nonsense seafood. The seafood platters and oysters are why everyone is here, but don't ignore the wonderful fish soup and mains like grilled sardines and *sole meunière*.

CHEZ JEAN

Map pp386-8 *French*

☎ 01 48 78 62 73; 8 rue St Lazare, 9e; metro Notre Dame de Lorette; starters €13-20, mains €25-35, menu €33; ☾ lunch Mon-Fri, dinner to 10.30pm Mon-Sat

This stylish gourmet restaurant manages to balance just the right amount of sophistication and genuine warmth. Dark-red banquette seats liven up the large, quiet dining room. The owner does the rounds of the tables, ensuring that customers are happy. A sample meal might include *fricassée de langoustines* (scampi) served with a julienne of vegetables, *magret de canard rôti au miel et ses navets et échalotes confites* (honey-roasted fillet of duck breast served with preserved turnips and shallots) and a modern version of profiteroles – a scoop of vanilla ice cream between two crunchy, chocolate-coated meringues.

LA GAIETÉ COSAQUE

Map pp383-5   *Russian*

☎ 01 44 70 06 07; 6 rue Truffaut, 17e; metro Place de Clichy or Rome; starters €1.30-16, mains €13-18, menus €10.50 (lunch), €17 & €21 (dinner) ☽ lunch & dinner to 11.45pm Mon-Sat

Northeast of place de Clichy, this bistro-like restaurant is the place for *zakuski* (Russian starters), typically drunk with ice-cold vodka. Among the stand-outs are *salades de choux blancs aux baies roses* (salads with cabbage and berries), the various herring dishes and aubergine 'caviar'. If you're stumped, try one of the mixed platters (€15 to €32). Hearty main dishes include lamb kebab and *koulibiaca* (pie filled with fish, rice, veg and boiled eggs).

LE BOUCLARD Map pp383-5   *French*

☎ 01 45 22 60 01; 1 rue Cavalotti, 18e; metro Place de Clichy; starters €8-15, mains €15-33, menu €17 (lunch); ☽ lunch & dinner to 11.30pm

This bistro's style of cooking is called 'la cuisine grand-mère' in honour of the owner's great-grandmother, who hailed from the southwest of France and contributed most of the recipes. Try the *terrine de lapereau en gelée de porto et ciboulette* (rabbit terrine in aspic; €9) and the *magret de canard grillé entier et tartiné de son foie gras* (roasted duck breast with foie gras; €20). There are also smaller 'tasting' portions.

MACIS ET MUSCADE

Map pp383-5   *French*

☎ 01 42 26 62 26; 110 rue Legendre, 17e; metro La Fourche; starters €8-11, mains €11-17, desserts €8, menus €13 & €16 (lunch), €24 (dinner); ☽ lunch Sun & Tue-Fri, dinner to 10.30pm Tue-Thu, to 11pm Fri & Sat

The owner of this excellent restaurant, a former *parfumeur*, tells diners that he aims to excite their 'olfactory and gustatory emotions with harmonious combinations of different ingredients and natural, unrefined products'. If that's too much of a mouthful, stick with what's on the plate: a *feuilleté de maroilles et sa salade à l'essence de ciste* (Maroilles cheese and a

rose-essence salad), perhaps, or *carré d'agneau à l'infusion de thym* (loin of lamb with thyme). The menu uses herbs and oils to evoke a particular landscape or region of France. People rave about the Sunday brunch (€20).

TY COZ Map pp386-8   *French, Brittany*

☎ 01 48 78 42 95; 35 rue St-Georges, 9e; metro St-Georges; dishes €18-21, seafood trays €38, menu €26 (dinner); ☽ lunch & dinner to 10pm Tue-Sat

Ty Coz (a corruption of *ti kozh* or 'old house') may be as Breton as a *fest-noz* (traditional Breton) festival, but don't expect crepes unless it's sweet ones for dessert. This is the place for excellent seafood, be it scallops, crabs or cured salmon, and the salads are a highlight. The nautical theme is a little kitsch; just pretend you're sitting on the dock of the bay of Cancale.

CHEAP EATS

ADDIS ABABA Map pp386-8   *Ethiopian*

☎ 01 42 80 06 78; 56 rue Notre Dame de Lorette, 9e; metro St Georges; starters €5, mains €10-15; ☽ lunch & dinner to 11.45pm

Ethiopian cuisine is always a rarity, but especially in Pigalle. At this lacklustre eatery, you might begin with *blé concassé au beurre et piment* (cracked wheat with butter and chilli) or *mousse au lentilles* (lentil mousse) and continue with Ethiopian *tartare* (cooked or raw!); or graze on the mixed platter of beef, lentils, spinach, cheese and cabbage. Each course is served in the traditional way: on a platter-sized piece of soft but slightly elastic *injera* bread, which you use to eat with your fingers.

LA MAFFIOSA DI TERMOLI

Map pp383-5   *Italian, Pizzeria*

☎ 01 55 30 01 83; 19 rue des Dames, 17e; metro Place de Clichy; pizzas €6.40-8.60, pasta dishes €6.10-7.60; ☽ lunch Mon-Sat, dinner to 11pm

These guys have some 40 pizzas that are too good to ignore, as well as decent garlic bread with or without Parma ham. They do a thriving takeaway business, too.

OPÉRA & GRANDS BOULEVARDS

The neon-lit blvd Montmartre (Map pp386-8; metro Grands Boulevards or Richelieu Drouot) and nearby sections of rue du Faubourg Montmartre (neither of which are anywhere near the neighbourhood of Montmartre) form one of the Right Bank's most animated café and dining districts. This area also has a couple of French restaurants that could almost be declared national monuments. A short distance to the north there's a large selection of kosher Jewish and North African restaurants (Map pp386–8) on rue Richer, rue Cadet and rue Geoffroy Marie, 9e, south of metro Cadet.

HARD ROCK CAFÉ

Map pp386-8 *American*

☎ 01 53 24 60 00; 14 blvd Montmartre, 9e; metro Grands Boulevards; starters €6-14, mains €11.70-21, menus €7.50-12 (lunch); ☽ noon-1am Sun-Thu, noon-2am Fri & Sat

Housed in the theatre where Maurice Chevalier once crooned, the Hard Rock looks like it does the world over. Here it attracts businesspeople for lunch and a mix of tourists and young, trendy Parisians at night. Half-price happy hour is between 5pm and 8pm weekdays.

JULIEN Map pp386-8 *French, Brasserie*

☎ 01 47 70 12 06; 16 rue du Faubourg St-Denis, 10e; metro Strasbourg St-Denis; starters €6-16, mains €13.50-28, menus with wine €22.90 & €32.90; ☽ lunch & dinner to 1am

Located in the less-than-salubrious neighbourhood of St-Denis, Julien offers food that you wouldn't cross town for. But – *mon Dieu!* – the décor and the atmosphere: it's an Art Nouveau extravaganza perpetually in motion and a real step back in time. Service is always excellent here; you'll feel welcome at any time of day.

LE BISTRO DE GALA

Map pp386-8 *French*

☎ 01 40 22 90 50; 45 rue du Faubourg Montmartre, 9e; metro Le Peletier; menus €26, €30 & €40 (tasting menu); ☽ lunch Mon-Fri, dinner to 11.30pm Mon-Sat

Movie posters crowd the walls but the *cuisine traditionelle* at this cinephile's den is

Painting, Le Chansonnier (p192)

Top Five Opéra, Grands Boulevards, Gare du Nord & Gare de l'Est Restaurants

- Julien (this page)
- La Marine (p192)
- Le Chansonnier (p192)
- Le Roi du Pot au Fer (this page)
- Terminus Nord (p193)

anything but an act. The set menus offer dishes based on fresh market produce: *croustillants de boudin, compote depommes aux épices et salade mesclun* (crispy black pudding, stewed apple with spices and mixed green salad) and *marmite de joues de cochon, petits oignons caramélisés* (pig's cheeks with caramelised baby onions). The chef, Thierry Jack-Roch, worked at **Chez Jean** (p188) before taking over this stylish and welcoming bistro.

LE ROI DU POT AU FEU

Map pp383-5 *French*

☎ 01 47 42 37 10; 34 rue Vignon, 9e; metro Havre Caumartin; starters €4-6, mains €15-17, 2-/3-course menus €21/25; ☽ noon-10.30pm Mon-Sat

The typical Parisian bistro atmosphere, '30s décor and checked tablecloths all add to the charm of the 'King of Hotpots'. What you really want to come here for is a genuine *pot au feu*, a stockpot of beef, aromatic root vegetables and herbs stewed together, with the stock served as an entree and the meat and vegetables as the main course. Other offerings – the chef's terrine, leeks *à la vinaigrette, hachis Parmentier* (chopped beef with potatoes), crème caramel, *tarte Tatin* or chocolate mousse, and the complementary cornichons at the start – are equally traditional fare but less noteworthy. You drink from an open bottle of wine and pay for what you've consumed.

LES AILES Map pp386-8 *Jewish, Kosher*

☎ 01 47 70 62 53; 34 rue Richer, 9e; metro Cadet; starters €6-17, mains €18-23; ☽ lunch & dinner to 11.30pm

Next door to the Folies-Bergère, the 'Wings' is a kosher North African (Sephardic) place that has superb couscous with meat or fish (€18 to €23) and grills. Don't even consider a starter; you'll be inundated with little plates of salad, olives etc before you can say 'Shalom'. Pre-ordered, pre-paid Sabbath meals are also available.

LES DIAMANTAIRES

Map pp386-8   *Lebanese, Armenian*
☎ 01 47 70 78 14; 60 rue La Fayette, 9e; metro Cadet;
starters €7-12, mains €12-25, menus €18 (lunch),
€30 & €38 (dinner); ⏰ lunch & dinner to 11pm
Mountains of marble, lashings of gilt, plaster
statues and a white piano make the 'Diamond
Dealers' the perfect setting for a Levantine ope-
retta. It's a favourite of Greek furriers, Armenian
jewellers and Lebanese businessmen; expect
wonderful platters of meze and authentic (and
hard to find) Armenian cuisine. In the evening,
the Kazarian brothers sing; on the weekend,
you can't even hear yourself think.

MOTHER EARTH'S Map pp386-8   *Organic*
☎ 01 47 70 06 88; 40 rue du Faubourg Montmartre,
9e; metro Le Peletier; plat du jour €10, menus €8.50
(lunch) & €14.50; ⏰ lunch & dinner to 10pm Mon-Fri
Situated at the back of a minuscule courtyard,
this place is more of a '60s-style eatery with
a homey dining room and Formica décor. At
lunch time, regulars make themselves at home
and, without a moment's hesitation, order the
assiette zen (zen platter; €13), a hearty dish
comprising all kinds of grains (bulghur wheat,
brown rice, semolina and buckwheat), vegetables and a fillet of fish. For drinks, try the
delightful home-made apple juice.

WALLY LE SAHARIEN

Map pp386-8   *North African*
☎ 01 42 85 51 90; 36 rue Rodier, 9e; metro
St-Georges or Cadet; menus €23.50 (lunch) & €40.40
(dinner); ⏰ lunch & dinner to 10.30pm Tue-Sat

'Wally the Saharan' is several cuts above most
Maghreb restaurants in Paris, offering couscous in its pure Saharan form – without stock
or vegetables, just a finely cooked grain served
with a delicious sauce, and excellent tajines.
It's fixed price here at both lunch and dinner.

CHEAP EATS

CHARTIER Map pp386-8   *French, Bistro*
☎ 01 47 70 86 29; 7 rue du Faubourg Montmartre, 9e;
metro Grands Boulevards; starters €1.60-5.70, mains
€7.50-9.50; menus €14.90-18 (with wine);
⏰ lunch & dinner to 10pm
Chartier is a real gem that is justifiably famous
for its 330-seat *belle époque* dining room, virtually unaltered since 1896. With a 25/50cL
pitchet (pitcher) of wine for €1.60/2.60, you
should spend no more than €15 per person
at this budget restaurant. It's substantial but
don't expect gourmet though the *mont blanc*
(chestnut puree with crème fraîche) remains
one of our favourites. Reservations are not accepted so expect a queue.

HAYNES Map pp386-8   *American, Southern*
☎ 01 48 78 40 63; 3 rue Clauzel, 9e; metro
St-Georges; starters €7, mains €8-16; ⏰ dinner to
midnight Tue-Sat
A legendary, funky hang-out established by an
African-American ex-GI in 1947, Haynes dishes
up genuine shrimp gumbo, fried chicken, bar-
becued ribs and cornbread. There's usually a
lively crowd for the blues, dance and performance art sessions on Friday and Saturday from
8.30pm or 9pm (€6).

GARE DU NORD, GARE DE L'EST & RÉPUBLIQUE

These areas offer all types of food but most notably Indian and Pakistani, which can be
elusive in Paris. There's a cluster of brasseries and bistros around the Gare du Nord. They're
decent options for a first (or final) meal in the City of Light.

CHEZ JENNY Map pp386-8   *French, Alsace*
☎ 01 44 54 39 00; 39 blvd du Temple, 3e; metro
République; starters €6-18.50, mains €16.50-27, menus
€17 & €24; ⏰ noon-midnight Sun-Thu, noon-1am
Fri & Sat
This cavernous, 1930s-style brasserie (now part
of the Flo chain of restaurants) serves a gargantuan *choucroute garnie* (sauerkraut cooked
in wine and served with assorted prepared
meats; €17-22), but we suspect that most
people visit to admire the stunning marquetry of Alsatian scenes on the 1st floor. A quick
and tasty lunch at Chez Jenny is *flammekuche*

(€10), an Alsatian-style tart made with cream,
onion, bacon and cheese. It's served here with
a glass of wine.

CHEZ PAPA (ESPACE SUD-OUEST)

Map pp386-8   *French, Southwest*
☎ 01 42 09 53 87; 206 rue La Fayette, 10e; metro Lois
Blanc; starters €9.15-10.20, salads €7.05-12.30,
mains €13.05-16.15; ⏰ 11.30am-1am
It must be one of the craziest scenes in Paris:
a restaurant filled to capacity most nights with
almost every diner eating the same thing. Oh,
sure, Chez Papa serves all sorts of southwest

speciality, including *cassoulet* and *garbure* (€15.80), but most are here for the famous *salade Boyarde*, an enormous bowl filled with lettuce, tomato, sautéed potatoes, two types of cheese and ham – all for the princely sum of €7.05 (or €7.80 if you want two fried eggs thrown in).

DA MIMMO

Map pp386-8   *Italian*

☎ 01 42 06 44 47; 39 blvd de Magenta, 10e; metro Jacques Bonsergeant; starters €6.50-14, pizza €11-13, pasta dishes €14-24, mains €16.50-21.50, menu €26; ☯ lunch & dinner to 11.30pm Mon-Sat

Neither the less-than-salubrious neighbourhood nor the relatively high prices are enough to keep fans away from Domenico Sommella's eatery and its authentic Neapolitan cuisine. Naples is, of course, the birthplace of pizza – try one with rocket for starters and forget about pizzas of the past. For mains, there's a profusion of fish and *palourdes* or *tellines* (clams), abundant use of white truffles and an unusual *chevreau au four* (oven-baked kid).

LA 25E IMAGE

Map pp386-8   *French*

☎ 01 40 35 80 88; 9 rue des Récollets, 10e; metro Gare de l'Est; meals from €15 (lunch) & €22 (dinner); ☯ lunch Mon-Fri, dinner to 11.30pm Mon-Sat

The original, painted-tile ceiling of this former bakery is still intact and brightly coloured ceramic tables give this 'bar-galerie-resto' a lively, upbeat feel. The '25th Image' (it's a reference to the number of frames per second on moving film) has simple, very authentic cuisine: *tarte aux légumes et au chèvre* (vegetable and goat's cheese tart), or a copious *salade savoyarde* (Reblochon cheese tartines, grilled cubes of bacon, crème fraîche and hot potatoes). The service is excellent and welcome warm.

LA MARINE Map pp386-8   *French*

☎ 01 42 39 69 81; 55bis quai de Valmy, 10e; metro République; starters €6.80-8.40, mains €15.70-18, menu €10.70 (lunch); ☯ lunch & dinner to 11.30pm Mon-Sat

This large and airy bistro overlooking the Canal St-Martin is the flavour of the season among *les branchés du quartier* (neighbourhood trendies), who sip and nibble on dishes like *mille-feuille de rouget au beurre d'agrumes* (mullet in layered pastry with citrus butter) and *brick de poisson à la crème d'ortie* (fish fritter with nettle cream). The terrace is an absolute delight in the warmer months.

LA TOCCATA Map pp386-8   *Italian*

☎ 01 40 21 04 59; 52 av de la République, 11e; metro Parmentier; starters €7.50-11, pasta €12-15, mains €13.50-16, menus €11 & €15 (lunch), €20.50; ☯ dinner to midnight Mon-Sat

It's said (by the French, of course) that Neapolitan cuisine still bears traces of the French occupation in the 18th century and makes abundant use of seafood: *il piatto del guarracino* (local bouillabaisse) and sardines in escabèche. Also to die for is the *fusili al ragú* (ham, bacon, onion, and meat cooked in wine for six hours). Occasional theme nights are organised with Neapolitan singing, *scopa* (card game) championships and readings by Italian authors.

LE CHANSONNIER Map pp386-8   *French*

☎ 01 42 09 40 58; 14 rue Eugène Varlin, 10e; metro Château Landon or Louis Blanc; starters €6-12, mains €13.50-15, menus €10.50 (lunch) & €23.50; ☯ lunch Mon-Fri, dinner to 11pm Mon-Sat

If ever there was ever a perfect example of a *restaurant du quartier*, the 'Singer', named after Lyonnais socialist singer/songwriter Pierre Dupont (1821–70), is it. With its curved zinc bar and Art Nouveau mouldings, it could be a film set. The food is authentic, excellent and very substantial; the €23.50 menu includes *terrine maison à valonté* (all you can eat of four types of terrine). The *saucisson de Lyon* (Lyon sausage) is an excellent starter while the *daube de joue de bœuf* (beef stewed in a rich broth with herbs and veg) is the main course of choice.

LE MAURICIEN FILAO

Map pp386-8   *Mauritian, Creole*

☎ 01 48 24 17 17; 9 passage du Prado, 10e; metro Strasbourg St-Denis; meals from €10; ☯ lunch & dinner to 10pm

This hole-in-the-wall canteen in passage du Prado, a derelict covered arcade accessible from 12 rue du Faubourg St-Denis and 18-20 blvd St-Denis, serves cheap but tasty Mauritian cuisine such as spicy *rougaille de bœuf* (a Creole dish made of beef fillet cooked with onions, garlic, ginger, chilli and coriander). It's won the approval of several readers. Only certain dishes from the main menu are available daily.

LE PARIS-DAKAR

Map pp386-8   *African, Senegalese*

☎ 01 42 08 16 64; 95 rue du Faubourg St-Martin, 10e; metro Gare de l'Est; starters €6, mains €10-15, menus €9 (lunch), €22.70-30.35 (dinner); ☯ lunch Tue-Thu, Sat & Sun, dinner to 1am Tue-Sun

This is a little bit of Senegal in Paris where Mamadou has reigned as the 'King of Dakar' for more than 15 years. Specialities here include *yassa* (chicken or fish marinated in lime juice and onion sauce; €12) and *mafé Cap Vert* (lamb in peanut sauce; €11.60). There's live African music in the ground-floor bar every night.

LE RÉVEIL DU XE

Map pp386-8 *French, Auvergne*
☎ 01 42 41 77 59; 35 rue du Château d'Eau, 10e; metro Chateau d'Eau; starters €8.80, mains €10.50-13; ☽ lunch Mon-Sat, dinner to 9.30pm Tue
The 'Awakening of the 10th Arrondissement', taking its name from a left-wing newspaper of the late 19th century, is an authentic and historic institution, where hearty and flavoursome family cooking is served in a friendly atmosphere. Produce from the Auvergne dominates the menu: *tripoux* (small parcels of highly seasoned sheep's or calf's tripe), *pounti* (a hash of bacon, Swiss chard and onions bound with milk and eggs) and, of course, cheese.

LE SPORTING

Map pp386-8 *International*
☎ 01 46 07 02 00; 3 rue des Récollets, 10e; metro Gare de l'Est; starters €6-7.50, mains €13-16; ☽ lunch & dinner to 10.30pm
This is one of the more sophisticated café-restaurants along the Canal St-Martin and the minimalist décor – all browns and ash greys – suggests an up-to-the-moment bar in London. Brunch on Sunday (noon to 4pm) is when Le Sporting is at its busiest.

MADRAS CAFÉ

Map pp386-8 *Indian*
☎ 01 42 05 29 56; 180 rue du Faubourg St-Denis, 10e; metro Gare du Nord; mains & thalis €6; ☽ lunch & dinner to midnight
You wouldn't cross town to eat at this simple restaurant with specialities from both northern and southern India, but if you've just arrived at or just about to leave from the Gare du Nord and need a curry fix, this café is right around the corner.

TERMINUS NORD

Map pp386-8 *French, Brasserie*
☎ 01 42 85 05 15; 23 rue de Dunkerque, 10e; metro Gare du Nord; starters €6.50-15.50, mains €13.50-28, menus €22.90 & €32.90 (both with wine); ☽ 8am-1am
The 'North Terminus' has a copper bar, waiters in white uniforms, brass fixtures and mirrored walls that look as they did when it opened in 1925. Breakfast (from €8) is from 8am to 11am,

and full meals are served continuously from 11am to 12.30am.

CHEAP EATS

CHEZ SÉBASTIEN Map pp386-8 *Turkish*
☎ 01 42 78 58 62; 22 passage Vendôme, 3e; metro République; dishes from €4; ☽ 11.30am-8pm Mon-Sat
This simple little Turkish café on two levels in a scruffy *passage* south of place de la République is just the ticket if you're looking for something cheap, filling and tasty to eat 'on the thumb' (ie on the run) as the French say. Try any of the meze or the Iskender kebab, lamb slices served with pide bread and yogurt.

CHIAAPAS Map pp386-8 *Tex-Mex, Indian*
☎ 01 53 26 09 39; 171 rue la Fayette, 10e; metro Gare du Nord; starters €3.80-5, mains €6.50-9, menus €7.50 (lunch) & €10.50 (dinner); ☽ lunch & dinner to midnight
It's not like we go out looking for the truly weird and sometimes wonderful; from time to time these places just jump out and bite us on the bottom. An easy slide from the Gare du Nord, Chiaapas holds the dubious distinction of being the only restaurant serving both Tex-Mex and Indian food. It's Indian owned, which would normally suggest you go for the latter. But with the piñata décor and salsa playing, we'll go for the former any time.

LE CAMBOGE Map pp386-8 *Cambodian*
☎ 01 44 84 37 70; 10 av Richerand, 10e; metro Goncourt; starters €2-8.50, mains €6.50-9; ☽ lunch & dinner to 11.30pm Mon-Sat
Hidden in a quiet street between the gargantuan Hôpital St-Louis and Canal St-Martin, this favourite spot among students serves enormous *rouleaux de printemps* (spring rolls), and the ever-popular *pique-nique cambodgien* ('Cambodian picnic' of rice vermicelli and sautéed beef, which you wrap up in lettuce leaves). The food tastes home-made – the vegetarian platters (€6 to €7.50) are especially good – and the staff always run off their feet. Try to arrive before 9pm so you don't have to wait for a table.

PASSAGE BRADY

Map pp386-8 *Indian, Pakistani*
46 rue du Faubourg St-Denis & 33 blvd de Strasbourg, 10e; metro Château d'Eau; ☽ lunch & dinner to 11pm
Joining rue du Faubourg St-Denis and blvd de Strasbourg in the 10e, this derelict covered

arcade could easily be in Calcutta. Its incredibly cheap Indian, Pakistani and Bangladeshi cafés offer among the best-value lunches in Paris (meat curry, rice and a tiny salad from €5, chicken or lamb biryani for €5 to €8, thalis for €12); there are dinner menus from €7.60 to €25. There are lots of places to choose from, but the pick of the crop are **Pooja** (Map pp386-8; ☎ 01 48 24 00 83; 91 passage Brady), **Roi du Kashmir** (Map pp386-8; ☎ 01 48 00 08 85; 76 passage Brady) and **Shalimar** (Map pp386-8; ☎ 01 45 23 31 61; 59 passage Brady).

MÉNILMONTANT & BELLEVILLE

In the northern part of the 11e and into the 19e and 20e arrondissements, Rue Oberkampf and its extension, rue de Ménilmontant, are popular with diners and denizens of the night, though rue Jean-Pierre Timbaud, running parallel, is stealing some of their glory these days. Rue de Belleville and the streets running off it are dotted with Chinese, Southeast Asian and a few Middle Eastern places; blvd de Belleville has some kosher couscous restaurants, most of which are closed on Saturday.

AU VILLAGE

Map pp386-8   *African, Senegalese*

☎ 01 43 57 18 95; 86 av Parmentier, 11e; metro Parmentier; mains €11-16, menu €30; ☽ dinner to midnight Sun-Thu, to 12.30am Fri & Sat

If you think this restaurant on the av Parmentier looks just like all the others, you're in for a surprise. In a small, narrow room with soft lighting, the décor transports diners to a Senegalese village. The atmosphere is warm, friendly and a bit hip. Newcomers to African cuisine can choose from a range of classic Senegalese dishes such as *aloco* (fried plantain bananas with red sauce), followed by the delicious, lightly spiced fish *yassa* or the hearty *mafé*. For dessert, check out the amazing *thiakry* (semolina and cream cheese salad).

BISTROT FLORENTIN

Map pp386-8   *Italian*

☎ 01 43 55 57 00; 40 rue Jean-Pierre Timbaud, 11e; metro Parmentier; starters €6-11.50, pasta €9-14, mains €12.50-16, menu €11 (lunch); ☽ lunch Mon-Fri, dinner to 11pm Mon-Sat

The 'Florentine Bistro' has excellent Italian fare in cosy surroundings. Grilled, finely seasoned eggplant for starters, tiramisú as light as a feather for dessert and between those two courses, a wide choice of mains and pastas. The *penne à la crème d'artichaut et aux truffes* (penne with cream, artichokes and truffles) is superb as is the *ravioli aux épinards et au fromage, sauce aux cèpes* (spinach and cheese ravioli with a cep mushroom sauce).

BISTROT GUILLAUME

Map pp392-5   *French Bistro*

☎ 01 47 00 43 50; 5 rue Guillaume Bertrand, 11e; metro St-Maur; starters €9.50-18, mains €12.50-15, menus €12 (lunch), €18.50 & €24 (dinner); ☽ lunch Mon-Fri, dinner to 11pm Mon-Sat

This smart bistro, close to the flashy rue Oberkampf, has a dozen tables with gingham tablecloths arranged around a polished wooden bar. Add a few Venetian dolls, a touch of greenery and background music from Vivaldi to Abba et voilà: 'Bill's Place'. The *ravioles de saumon crème ciboulette* (ravioli with salmon, cream and chives) will tickle your tastebuds; for mains, the menu offers a range of traditional provincial dishes such as *jarret de porc sur choucroute* (pork knuckle with sauerkraut), but also more enlightened *chou farci au saumon* (stuffed cabbage with salmon). Expect friendly, attentive service.

CHEZ RAMONA   Map pp386-8   *Spanish*

☎ 01 46 36 83 55; 17 rue Ramponeau, 20e; metro Belleville; dishes from €4; ☽ dinner to 11.30pm Tue-Sun

Tucked away in an anonymous Belleville street, this family restaurant looks just like a small neighbourhood grocery store from the outside, but enter and climb the spiral staircase and you'll be welcomed with checked tablecloths and statuettes of the Virgin Mary. Enjoy the background flamenco as you savour

---

Top Five Ménilmontant & Belleville Restaurants

- Juan et Juanita (opposite)
- L'Ave Maria (opposite)
- Le Pavillon Puebla (p196)
- Le Villaret (p196)
- Thai Classic (p197)

a real paella or any of the other dishes on the somewhat limited menu: *anchois frais avec tomates* (fresh anchovies with tomatoes) and the excellent *gambas à l'ail* (king prawns with garlic). A few words of advice: Chez Ramona operates on Spanish time, so it's better to arrive after 10pm.

JUAN ET JUANITA Map pp386-8 *French*
☎ 01 43 57 60 15; 82 rue Jean-Pierre Timbaud, 11e; metro Parmentier or Couronnes; starters €5.50, mains €13-15, menu €15; 🕐 dinner to 2am Tue-Sat

Run by two young women, this place stands out for its over-the-top, slightly camp décor and the exceedingly high standards of its kitchen. Menu features include a New Age *tajine d'agneau aux abricots secs* (lamb tajine with dried apricots), *mignon de porc au raifort* (tenderloin of pork with horseradish) and *soupe de mangues et sa glace vanille* (mango soup with vanilla ice cream).

KRUNG THEP Map pp386-8 *Thai*
☎ 01 43 66 83 74; 93 rue Julien Lacroix, 20e; metro Pyrénées; starters €7-8.50, vegetarian dishes €5.50-7, mains €8.50-18; 🕐 dinner to 11pm

The 'Bangkok' (in Thai) is a small (some might say cramped) kitsch place with all our favourites (and then some – there are 130 dishes on the menu): green curries, *tom yam gung* and fish or chicken steamed in banana leaves. The steamed shrimp ravioli and stuffed crab will hit the spot.

LA GRAND MÉRICOURT
Map pp392-5 *French*
☎ 01 43 38 94 04; 22 rue de la Folie Méricourt, 11e; metro St-Ambroise; starters €11-17, mains €14-18, menus €14, €17 & €27; 🕐 lunch & dinner to 10.30pm Mon-Sat

Young chef Gregory Merten offers his version of *'la cuisine créative'* (basically traditional French that is light on oils and fat and heavy on seasonal produce) in a very English, almost fussy (floral wallpaper, wooden floors, starched white tablecloths and napkins) place just a stone's throw from trendy rue Oberkampf.

L'AVE MARIA Map pp386-8 *Fusion*
☎ 01 47 00 61 73; 1 rue Jacquard, 11e; metro Parmentier; dishes €11-14; 🕐 lunch Mon-Fri, dinner to midnight

This place is like a Brazilian or African canteen, a chic and colourful greasy spoon combining flavours of the southern hemisphere and creating hearty, hybrid and harmonious dishes. You might be treated to *bœuf mijoté aux noyaux de palmes rouges* (beef stew with red palm seeds), served with cassava and baby white aubergine. Tropical fruit, wild, unknown grasses, and heavenly vegetation provide a lush garnish and an extra touch of exoticism. The music livens up towards midnight and dancing carries on to 2am.

LE BARATIN Map pp386-8 *French, Bistro*
☎ 01 43 49 39 70; 3 rue Jouye-Rouve, 20e; metro Pyrénées or Belleville; meals from €35, menu €15 (lunch); 🕐 lunch Tue-Fri, dinner to midnight Tue-Sat

This animated wine bar just a step away from the lively Belleville quarter offers some of the best French food in the 20e. The wine selection (by the glass or carafe) is excellent; most are under €30 a bottle.

LE C'AMELOT Map pp392-5 *French, Bistrot*
☎ 01 43 55 54 04; 50 rue Amelot, 11e; metro St-Sébastien Froissart; menus €16 & €23 (lunch), €32 (dinner); 🕐 lunch Tue-Fri, dinner to midnight Mon-Sat

The 'Street Peddler', making an awkward pun with the name of the street it's on, is the perfect little neighbourhood bistro, but it's on everyone's list so book well in advance. For starters, the *tarte feuilletée de sardines marinées et confit d'oignons* (pastry tart with marinated sardines and onion confit) is a discovery. The *agneau de Lozère rôti, de l'ail en chemise et des haricots coco mitonnés au jus* (roast lamb cooked with whole cloves of garlic and borlotti beans simmered in the juice) offers a perfect combination of flavours.

LE CLOWN BAR
Map pp392-5 *French, Bistro*
☎ 01 43 55 87 35; 114 rue Amelot, 11e; metro Filles du Calvaire; starters €10, mains €13-15, menus €13.50 (lunch) & €18 (dinner); 🕐 lunch Mon-Sat, dinner to midnight

A wonderful wine bar-cum-bistro next to the Cirque d'Hiver, the Clown Bar is like a museum with its painted ceilings, mosaics on the wall, lovely zinc bar and circus memorabilia that touches on one of our favourite themes: the evil clown. The food is simple and unpretentious traditional French; the charcuterie platter is substantial and goes well with a half-bottle of Brouilly, while the *Parmentier de boudin aux pommes* (black pudding Parmentier with apple) is deservedly one of the restaurant's most popular dishes.

LE KITCH

Map pp392-5 *French, Café*

☎ 01 40 21 94 14; 10 rue Oberkampf, 11e; metro Filles du Calvaire; starters €5.50-7.50, mains €8-14, menu €10 (lunch); ⏱ lunch Mon-Fri, dinner to midnight

Le Kitch has a lot of what its misspelled name suggests: curtains of plastic flowers, orange-coloured Christmas trees, rubber carafes and Formica tabletops with mismatched cutlery. And the food? Well, Mediterranean-inspired soups, curries, gazpacho – anything luridly coloured. Our French colleagues tell us that it's quite possible to enjoy kitsch and good taste at the same time. We still think it's a place to experience rather than digest. The bill will arrive rolled up in a hair curler.

LE PAVILLON PUEBLA

Map pp386-8 *French, Catalonia*

☎ 01 42 08 92 62; cnr av Simon Bolivar & rue Botzaris, parc des Buttes-Chaumont, 19e; metro Buttes-Chaumont; meals from €50, menus €33 & €65; ⏱ lunch & dinner to 10.30pm Tue-Sat

An exquisite restaurant in a Second Empire-style pavilion right in the parc des Buttes-Chaumont, Le Pavillon Puebla attracts people not so much for its wonderful seafood dishes but for its open terrace in the summer. The restaurant's undisputed centrepiece is its Catalonian menu; try the *coca aux escargots et à la ventrêche* (crunchy puff pastry with snails and bacon) and *pinyata des pêcheurs d'Ouille* (a delicious, subtle mixture of braised fish served in a casserole). The desserts, including *figues rôties au vin de Banyuls* (roast figs with Banyuls, a fortified wine from Roussillon), live up to expectations.

LE PÉCHÉ MIGNON

Map pp392-5 *French*

☎ 01 43 57 68 68; 5 rue Guillaume Bertrand, 11e; metro St-Maur; menus €18.50 (lunch), €22 & €26 (dinner); ⏱ lunch Tue-Sun, dinner to 11pm Tue-Sat

So, what is your weakness at the 'Weakness'? The house speciality – *pied de cochon caramélisé avec sa confiture d'oignons et sa petite salade fraîche* (caramelised pig's foot with onion marmalade and small fresh salad) may have our knees buckling but we positively swoon over the *grenadine de veau et sa tapenade de champignons à l'huile de noisette* (sliced veal with a tapenade of mushrooms and hazelnut oil). The menu changes with the seasons; pity the service is so slow.

LE POROKHANE

Map pp386-8 *African, Senegalese*

☎ 01 40 21 86 74; 3 rue Moret, 11e; metro Ménilmontant or Parmentier; starters €5-8, mains €10.50-16.50, menu €10; ⏱ dinner 7pm-2am

A large dining room in hues of ochre and terracotta, Le Porokhane is a popular meeting place for Senegalese artists in Paris and live *kora* (a traditional string instrument) music is not unusual at the weekend. Try the *tiéboudienne* (rice, tomatoes and other vegetables and fish), and *yassa* (chicken or fish marinated in lime juice and served with preserved onions) and *mafé*.

LE REPAIRE DE CARTOUCHE

Map pp392-5 *French*

☎ 01 47 00 25 86; 8 blvd des Filles du Calvaire & 99 rue Amelot, 11e; metro St-Sébastien Froissart; starters €8-12, mains €17-30, desserts €6, menu €22 (lunch); ⏱ lunch & dinner to 11pm Tue-Sat

With both a front entrance and a back entrance, the 'Cartridge Den' is an old-fashioned place that takes a very modern, innovative approach to French food under the direction of young Norman chef Rodolphe Paquin. As its name implies and the rifle on the wall underscores, it focuses on meat and game, though there are some excellent fish and shellfish dishes on the menu.

LE VILLARET Map pp386-8 *French*

☎ 01 43 57 89 76; 13 rue Ternaux, 11e; metro Parmentier; starters €7-15, mains €18-25, menus €20 & €25 (lunch), tasting menu €46 (dinner); ⏱ lunch Mon-Fri, dinner to 11.30pm Mon & Tue, to 1am Wed-Sat

An excellent neighbourhood bistro serving very rich food, Le Villaret has diners coming from across Paris to sample the house specialities. The *velouté de cèpes à la mousse de foie gras* (cep mushroom soup with foie gras mousse), the *solette au beurre citronné* (baby sole with lemon-flavoured butter) and the *gigot d'agneau de Lozère rôti et son gratin de topinambours* (roast lamb with Jerusalem artichoke gratin) are all recommended but only the chef knows what will be available as he changes the menu daily.

LES JUMEAUX Map pp392-5 *French*

☎ 01 43 14 27 00; 73 rue Amelot, 12e; metro St-Sébastien Froissart or Chemin Vert; menus €27 (lunch) & €32 (dinner); ⏱ lunch & dinner to 10.30pm Tue-Sat

The 'Twins' is owned and run by a pair of men much changed from their picture, at the entrance, as babies. There's not much to say about the décor except that crockery is different for each person and each course; it's the food that demands attention. Start with *galette de foie gras chaud aux oignons et citrons confits* (buckwheat crepe with warm foie gras and preserved onions and lemons) and move on to the extraordinary flavours offered by the *coquilles Saint-Jacques à la purée de pois cassés, sauce pamplemousse rose* (scallops with split-pea puree and pink-grapefruit sauce). The grand finish has to be the *mousse au chocolat noire au jus de café et zestes d'orange* (chocolate mousse with coffee and orange zest sauce).

CHEAP EATS

AU TROU NORMAND

Map pp386-8   *French*
☎ 01 48 05 80 23; 9 rue Jean-Pierre Timbaud, 11e; metro Oberkampf; starters €3-7.50, mains €6.50-12.50, desserts €3.50-6; ☽ lunch & dinner to 11.30pm Mon-Sat

With a change of ownership, this place is no longer the bargain-basement cafeteria of the 11e arrondissement. Still, the food, in keeping with the surrounds, is simple, and the portions generous. There are no fewer than 35 starters to choose from; main courses include various cuts of beef (tournedos, steak etc) and other meat dishes, served with house-made chips.

LA PIRAGUA

Map pp392-5   *South American, Colombian*
☎ 01 40 21 35 98; 6 rue Rochebrune, 11e; metro St-Ambroise; starters €4-6.50, mains €10-13, menus €16 & €18; ☽ dinner to 11.30pm Mon-Thu, to midnight Fri & Sat

This small, brightly coloured eatery, which pays homage to a type of canoe, has Colombian favourites such as various *ceviche* (fish marinated in lemon juice) dishes and *badeja paisa* (a concoction of chopped meat, kidney beans, rice and the kitchen sink). The list of Chilean wines is excellent, and there's good Latin American music here too.

LAO SIAM
Map pp386-8   *Thai*
☎ 01 40 40 09 68; 49 rue de Belleville, 19e; metro Belleville; starters €5.50-8.50, rice & noodles €4.50-8.40, mains €5.40-10.70; ☽ lunch & dinner to 11.30pm

This Thai-Chinese place, with neon lights and Spartan décor, looks like any other Asian restaurant in Belleville. But it's doing something right because it's always packed. Perhaps it's the more than 120 dishes on the menu – from the classic beef and duck with coconut milk and bamboo to the more unusual *méduse à la citronnelle* (jellyfish with lemon grass) – or the specially large smoking section, rare in Paris.

NEW NIOULLAVILLE

Map pp386-8   *Chinese*
☎ 01 40 21 96 18; 32 rue de l'Orillon, 11e; metro Belleville or Goncourt; starters €5.30-6, rice & noodles €6.90-9, mains €7-14, menus €7.30-12; ☽ lunch & dinner to 12.45am

This cavernous, 500-seat place resembles the Hong Kong stock exchange on a busy day. The food is a bit of a mishmash – dim sum sits next to beef satay, as do scallops with black bean alongside Singapore noodles, though whether they do so comfortably is another matter. Order carefully and you should be able to approach authenticity.

THAI CLASSIC
Map pp386-8   *Thai*
☎ 01 42 40 78 10; 41 rue de Belleville, 19e; metro Belleville; soups €6.50-8, dishes €5-8; ☽ lunch Mon-Sat & dinner to 11.30pm daily

This tiny place offers some of the most authentic Thai food in Paris and has all your favourite Thai dishes, including soups. About a half-dozen of the choices are vegetarian. Service could be a bit more friendly, though.

GARE DE LYON, NATION & BERCY

The waterfront southwest of Gare de Lyon has had a new lease of life in recent years. The development of the old wine warehouses in **Bercy Village** (p124) attract winers and diners till the wee hours. There are loads of decent restaurants on the roads fanning out from huge place de la Nation.

ATHANOR

Map pp392-5   *Romanian*
☎ 01 43 43 49 15; 4 rue Crozatier, 12e; metro Reuilly Diderot; starters €6.50-10.50, mains €15-19, menus €12 (lunch) & €23 (dinner), plat du jour €8-10; ☽ lunch Sun-Fri, dinner to 10.30pm Mon-Sat

It's not easy to get a fix of Romanian cuisine in Paris but Athanor can provide. The décor, puppets, red curtains and candle light, is theatrical in the extreme; grab a vodka (or two) and tune in to the baroque music. Try the grilled blinis with *tarama* (fish roe dip) and herrings in cream. Seasoned freshwater fish is the speciality of the house though you musn't miss the *sarmale* (stuffed cabbage), the national dish. There's also a *menu surprise* (€15) that changes according to what's fresh at the market.

CAFÉ CANNELLE

Map pp392-5 *North African, Moroccan*
☎ 01 43 70 48 25; 1bis rue de la Forge Royale, 11e; metro Ledru Rollin; starters €5.50-10.50, mains €11.50-15; ☽ dinner to midnight

The 'Cinnamon Café' is a festive Moroccan restaurant run by Algerians who do couscous and tajines with a twist (eg semolina flavoured with cinnamon, orange-blossom water and almonds served as a dessert). It's a little place so you should book in advance.

CHEZ RÉGIS Map pp392-5 *French*
☎ 01 43 43 62 84; 27ter blvd Diderot, 12e; metro Gare de Lyon; starters €7-9, mains €13-15, menus €14 & €18, plat du jour €11; ☽ lunch Sun-Fri, dinner to 10.30pm Mon-Sat

There should be more places like Chez Régis, which specialises in *cuisine de bonne femme* (home cooking). The eponymous young owner has worked hard to preserve the original décor of this attractive bistro (established in 1908), adding a few modern touches: background jazz and a good-value menu of traditional favourites. For a starter, try the delectable baby *ravioles* (ravioli) and follow with the excellent *magret de canard a sel de Guérande* (fillet of duck breast with Guérande sea salt) and a perfect *tarte Tatin*. Pluses are the organic bread, fine wines and crepe brunch (€14) on Sunday.

COMME COCHONS Map pp392-5 *French*
☎ 01 43 42 43 36; 135 rue de Charenton, 12e; metro Gare de Lyon; starters €7-9, mains €15-18, menu €13 (lunch); ☽ lunch & dinner to 11pm Mon-Sat

You may not be attracted by the name of 'Like Pigs' but the excellent traditional dishes and the sunny terrace can help to change your mind. This bistro is like a page out of the past; only the contemporary paintings on the wall by a local artist will keep you in the present. Among the specialities are *paleron aux endives meunières* (beef served with endives) and *ganache de chocolat noir aux grillotines* (a rich dark-chocolate concoction).

Top Five Nation, Bercy, 13e & 15e Arrondissements Restaurants

- **Chez Gladines** (p200)
- **Khun Akorn** (this page)
- **Kim Anh** (p201)
- **Le Troquet** (p201)
- **L'Oulette** (opposite)

KHUN AKORN

Map pp380-2 *Thai*
☎ 01 43 56 20 03; 8 av de Taillebourg, 11e; metro Nation; starters €7.60-9.20, mains €11.50-13; ☽ lunch & dinner to 11pm Tue-Sun

Khun Akorn, an airy Thai restaurant near place de la Nation, is an oasis of sophistication and good taste – in every sense. Among the traditional dishes, the *soupe de crevettes pimentées à la citronnelle* (shrimp soup seasoned with lemon grass), and the beef and chicken satays with scrumptious peanut sauce are outstanding. Among the more innovative offerings, try *fruits de mer grillés sauce barbecue maison* (grilled seafood with the chef's barbecue sauce) or the *larmes du tigre* ('tears of the tiger'; grilled fillet of beef marinated in honey and herbs). According to the menu, the tiger is crying because he wants more. In fine weather head for the upstairs terrace.

LA BANANE IVOIRIENNE

Map pp392-5 *African, Côte d'Ivoire*
☎ 01 43 70 49 90; 10 rue de la Forge Royale, 11e; metro Ledru Rollin; starters €4-6, mains €8.50-15.50; ☽ dinner to midnight Tue-Sat

The 'Ivoirian Banana' serves West African specialities in a relaxed and friendly setting. There's live African music starting at 10pm on Friday.

LANNA STORE

Map pp392-5 *Asian*
☎ 01 43 56 10 52; 5 rue de Reuilly, 12e; metro Faidherbe Chaligny; starters €9-10, Thai salads €6.80-11.80, mains €10-15; ☽ lunch Mon-Sat

Cloisonne with your curry? A Buddha with a bowl of *bami* (Thai noodle soup)? This unique concept melds shopping and eating; everything you see – from rosewood Chinese antiques to silk cushion covers – is for sale, as is the antique Asian table at which you're sitting. There's a brief but eclectic menu; the charming couple who own the joint can advise you on what to eat and what to buy.

LE MANSOURIA

Map pp392-5   *North African, Moroccan*

☎ 01 43 71 00 16; 11 rue Faidherbe, 11e; metro
Faidherbe Chaligny; starters €7-16, mains €13-24,
menu €29 & €44 (with wine); ☙ lunch Wed-Sat,
dinner to 11pm Mon-Sat

This is an especially attractive Moroccan restaurant that serves excellent milk-fed steamed lamb, if not the best *kascsou* (couscous) and *touagin* (tajine) in town. One downside is that the place has become so popular that bookings at night are for time-limited sittings.

LES AMOGNES

Map pp392-5   *French*

☎ 01 43 72 73 05; 243 rue du Faubourg St-Antoine,
11e; metro Faidherbe Chaligny; menus €29 & €33;
☙ lunch & dinner to 11pm Tue-Sat

This quiet place with its faux cottage frontage offers discreet service and an atmosphere that is *correcte* (proper), even provincial. A meal here is a quintessentially French – rather than Parisian – experience and *haute cuisine* at a reasonable price. Chef Thierry Coué is especially adept at desserts.

L'OULETTE Map p401   *French, Southwest*

☎ 01 40 02 02 12; 15 place Lachambeaudie, 12e;
metro Cour St-Émilion; starters €14-25, mains

€22-34, menus €28 (lunch) & €45; ☙ lunch & dinner
to 10.15pm Mon-Fri

The 'Little Saucepan' (in the patois of Languedoc) is a lovely restaurant with a terrace overlooking a pretty church in a rather dreary neighbourhood. Chef Marcel Baudis's *menu du marché* (market menu) might include *soupe de poisson à la crème de coquillages au safran* (fish soup with saffron cream) and *suprême de pintade farci d'un hachis de trompettes de la mort et d'échalotes* (guinea fowl stuffed with wild mushrooms and shallots). There is an excellent selection of coffees from around the world.

CHEAP EATS
LA PARTIE DE CAMPAGNE

Map p401   *French*

☎ 01 43 40 44 00; 36 cour St-Émilion, 12e; metro Cour
St-Émilion; starters from €6, pies & tartines €9-11.50,
platters €9.90-12.90; ☙ 8am-midnight

Located in one of the old *chais* (wine warehouses) of Bercy, the 'Country Outing' serves some of the best food in the area. Business people and strollers from the Jardin de Bercy sit cheek by jowl at a large communal table set up at the back of the room, and order off a menu that includes cassoulet, pies and soups. To finish, try the *tarte aux figues fourrée à la pistache* (fig tart with pistachio filling).

13E ARRONDISSEMENT & CHINATOWN

Until the opening of the high-tech Météor metro line (No 14) linking Gare St-Lazare with the Bibliothèque Nationale de France François Mitterrand, few travellers ventured as far south as this unless they were in search of authentic Chinese food. But all that has changed. And dozens of Asian restaurants – not just Chinese ones – line the main streets of Paris' Chinatown, including av de Choisy, av d'Ivry and rue Baudricourt.

Another wonderful district for an evening out is the Butte aux Cailles southwest of place d'Italie. It's chock-a-block with interesting addresses.

AU PET DE LAPIN

Map p401   *French, Southwest*

☎ 01 45 86 58 21; 2 rue Dunois, 13e; metro
Bibliothèque; starters €4.50-7.50, mains €7.50-16,
menu €12; ☙ lunch & dinner to 10pm Tue-Sat

This strangely named place (in French something useless isn't worth 'a rabbit's fart') promises quality food from southwest France and delivers – at very reasonable prices: spinach salad with bacon (€4), foie gras terrine (€10.50) and *échine de porc à la moutarde de Meaux* (loin of pork with Meaux mustard; €12). In autumn, the menu will delight lovers of game and in summer there's alfresco (outdoor) dining.

CHEZ JACKY

Map p401   *French*

☎ 01 45 83 71 55; 109 rue du Dessous des Berges,
13e; metro Bibliothèque; starters €15-26, mains
€18-27, menu €30; ☙ lunch & dinner to 10.30pm
Mon-Fri

In the shadow of the national library, Chez Jacky is a serious, traditional restaurant with thoughtful service and a nice, old-fashioned provincial atmosphere. The three brothers in charge know how to find good regional produce and present it with great panache, even if originality isn't their cardinal virtue.

L'AUDIERNES

Map p401 *French, Brasserie*
☎ 01 44 24 86 23; 22 rue Louise Weiss, 13e; metro Chevaleret; starters €3.70-12, mains €9.60-18.30, menu €11.80; ☯ lunch Mon-Sat

In an annexe of the Department of the Economy & Finance, this brasserie-bar serves well-prepared and traditional French dishes to demanding civil servants. The contemporary décor gives the place a lively feel; the menu is good (if hardly original), featuring such dishes as *bœuf à l'échalote* (beef with shallots), *pavé de rumsteck* (thick-cut rump steak), *faux-filet* (beef sirloin) and a range of main course salads with cutesy names. There's also a lovely terrace where you can sit on sunny days.

L'AVANT-GOÛT

Map pp380-2 *French, Bistro*
☎ 01 53 80 24 00; 26 rue Bobillot, 13e; metro Place d'Italie; starters €8, mains €15, menus €12 (lunch) & €26; ☯ lunch & dinner to 11pm Tue-Fri

A prototype of the Parisian 'neo-bistro' (classical yet modern), the 'Foretaste' has chef Christophe Beaufront serving some of the most inventive modern cuisine around. It can get noisy, though, and there are occasional lapses in service but the food is well worth it. For starters, try the *ravioles de thon et de morue avec velouté de crustacés* (tuna and cod ravioli with a seafood velouté sauce) followed, in season, by the *sanglier de sept heures et sa polenta croustillante* (wild boar cooked for seven hours with crunchy polenta).

LE TEMPS DES CÉRISES

Map pp380-2 *French*
☎ 01 45 89 69 48; 18-20 rue de la Butte aux Cailles, 13e; metro Corvisart or Place d'Italie; menus €12.50 & €22; ☯ lunch Mon-Fri, dinner to 11.30pm Mon-Fri, to midnight Sat

The 'Time of Cherries' (ie 'wine and roses'), an easygoing restaurant run by a workers' cooperative, keeps regulars coming back for more with its good, solid fare (rabbit with mustard, steak with fries) and low prices. It's in the heart

of the Butte aux Cailles quarter and provides the quintessential Parisian night out.

CHEAP EATS
CHEZ GLADINES

Map pp380-2 *French, Basque*
☎ 01 45 89 70 10; 30 rue des Cinq Diamants, 13e; metro Corvisart; starters €4.50-7.50, mains €8-11.50, menu €10 (lunch); ☯ lunch & dinner to midnight Mon-Fri, to 1am Sat & Sun

This lively Basque bistro in the heart of the Buttes aux Cailles quarter is always a hoot and you're bound to meet someone at one of the communal tables. Most people come for the enormous 'meal-in-a-bowl' salads (€6.50 to €9), but the traditional Basque specialities, such as *pipérade* (omelette with tomatoes and peppers), *poulet basque* (chicken cooked with tomatoes, onions, peppers and white wine), are also worth consideration.

LA FLEUVE DE CHINE

Map pp380-2 *Chinese*
☎ 01 45 82 06 88; 15 av de Choisy, 13e; metro Porte de Choisy, dishes €7.60-16.50; ☯ lunch & dinner to 11pm Fri-Wed

The 'River of China', which can also be reached through the Tour Bergame housing estate at 130 blvd Masséna, has some of the most authentic Cantonese and Hakka food to be found in Paris and, as is typical, both the surroundings and the service are forgettable. Go for the superb dishes cooked in clay pots.

SINORAMA Map pp380-2 *Chinese*
☎ 01 53 82 09 51; 118 av de Choisy & 23 rue du Docteur Magnan, 13e; metro Tolbiac or Place d'Italie; starters €4-15, mains €8.50-17, rice & noodles €4.50-8, menu €9 (lunch); ☯ lunch & dinner to 2am

This airport hangar of a Chinese restaurant with two entrances and a camp name serves good Shanghainese dishes, with a smattering of Cantonese choices. It's loud, frantic, and service is cavalier at best – an authentic Chinese restaurant.

15E ARRONDISSEMENT

Solidly working class until well after WWII, the 15e arrondissement has become more gentrified and residential over the years. Av de la Motte-Picquet, blvd Pasteur and av Félix Faure are peaceful places. But the 15e arrondissement offers much more than bourgeois homes and institutions. Parisians flock to the shops and restaurants that line rue de la Convention, rue de Vaugirard, rue St-Charles, rue du Commerce and those south of blvd de Grenelle.

EL FARES

Map pp389-91   *Middle Eastern, Lebanese*
☎ 01 47 83 54 38; 166 blvd de Grenelle, 15e; metro
Cambronne; starters €5-5.50, mixed meze €10, grills
€11-15.50; ☻ lunch & dinner to 11pm
The décor's banal but who came for the surrounds? The tabouli, *mtabal* (eggplant purée
with sesame and lemon) and *labni* (cow's milk
cheese) make delicious cold starters, while
scrumptious felafels, chicken wings and layered cheese dishes are served warm. Big eaters
will go for the *chiche taouk* (kebab of marinated chicken fillets) or the traditional *kefta*
(mincemeat kebab with onions and parsley).

FEYROUZ

Map pp389-91   *Middle Eastern, Lebanese*
☎ 01 45 78 07 02; 8 rue de Lourmel, 15e; metro
Dupleix; starters €7.65-9.50, grills €16.50-19.50, menus
€11 & €15.50 (lunch), €20.50 (dinner); ☻ 7am-2am
This bright, busy *traiteur* (delicatessen) has excellent Lebanese meze and other dishes to
take away and a small restaurant in the back
where you can enjoy them *sur place* (on the
spot). The clientele and the family running
the establishment are straight out of a Woody
Allen movie set in the Lebanon.

KIM ANH Map pp389-91   *Vietnamese*
☎ 01 45 79 40 96; 49 av Émile Zola, 15e; metro
Charles Michels; starters €10-12, mains €19-32,
menu €34; ☻ dinner to 11.15pm Tue-Sun
The antithesis of the typically Parisian canteen-
style Vietnamese restaurant, Kim Anh greets
its customers with tapestries, white tablecloths
and fresh flowers. What's more, the freshness
of the food, elaborate presentation and quality service make eating here a pleasure. The
éminçé de bœuf à la citronnelle (beef with lemon
grass) is a skilful combination of flavours and
the *éventail de brochettes au bœuf, poulet et
porc* (assortment of beef, chicken and pork
satays) offers a variety of tastes. For something
really sensational try caramelised langoustine.

LA GITANE Map pp389-91   *French*
☎ 01 47 34 62 92; 53bis av de la Motte-Picquet, 15e;
metro La Motte-Picquet Grenelle; starters €4.90-14.70,
mains €12.60-17.80; ☻ lunch & dinner to 11pm
Mon-Sat
Over the past two decades the 'Gypsy' has established itself as an ideal spot to have lunch.
While not exceptional, everything here bears
the mark of good taste and high quality. The
carpaccio de saumon frais à l'aneth (carpaccio

of fresh salmon with dill) and the *terrine de
Saint-Jacques à la sauce aigrelette* (scallop terrine with a vinegary sauce) are nice starters.
In winter, a favourite dish is *cassoulet avec ses
haricots tarbais* (cassoulet with Tarbes beans).

LAL QILA Map pp389-91   *Indian*
☎ 01 45 75 68 40; 88 av Émile Zola, 15e; metro
Charles Michels; starters €6-9, curries €10-11, menus
€12 (lunch), €21 & €25; ☻ lunch & dinner to 11.30pm
Outside it's Disneyland meets the Red Fort of
Delhi; inside the stucco colonnade and multi-
coloured mirrors make this restaurant feel
like a true Bollywood set. Kitsch it may be,
but the food is hardly B grade. Main roles are
played by such classics as fish curry or chicken
biryani as well as less known ones like chicken
shami kebab. Special award goes to shahi
korma, lamb served with cream of cashew flavoured with cardamom and cinnamon.

LE TIPAZA

Map pp389-91   *North African, Moroccan*
☎ 01 45 79 22 25; 150 av Émile Zola, 15e; metro av
Émile Zola; starters €4.60-11.50, mains €12 (lunch) &
17 (dinner); ☻ lunch & dinner to midnight
This relatively classy Moroccan place has good
couscous (€11.70 to €14.80), tajines (€13.80 to
€15) and grills (€12.80 to €17) done on a wood
stove. Service is warm and efficient.

LE TROQUET Map pp389-91   *French, bistro*
☎ 01 45 66 89 00; 21 rue François Bonvin, 15e; metro
Sèvres Lecourbe; menus €23 & €25 (lunch), €28 &
€30 (dinner); ☻ lunch & dinner to 11pm Tue-Sat
Young Basque chef Christian Etchebest takes
'ordinary' things and puts a spin on them: veal
bouillon flavoured with aniseed and served
with vegetable quenelles, caramelised pork
on puréed vegetables, and seared whiting
on a bed of fresh green beans. Breathtaking
presentation and startling tastes and a restaurant that changes its menu every day according
to what's on offer at the market will get our
vote any time. The décor is nothing special,
but top-flight service brightens things up.

L'OS À MOËLLE

Map pp380-2   *French, Bistro*
☎ 01 45 57 27 27; 3 rue Vasco de Gama, 15e; metro
Lourmel; menus €27 (lunch) & €32 (dinner);
☻ lunch Tue-Sat, dinner to 11.30pm Tue-Thu,
to midnight Fri & Sat
The 'Marrowbone' is well worth a trip to the
far-flung southwestern 15e and chef Thierry

Eating – 15e Arrondissement

Faucher (ex-Hotel Crillon) offers one of the best and most affordable *menus dégustation* (sampling menus) in town. The six-course menu (portions are modest) could include such delicacies as scallops with coriander, sea bass in cumin butter, half a quail with endives and chestnuts and the chef's award-winning chocolate quenelle with saffron cream.

SAWADEE Map pp389-91 — *Thai*
☎ 01 45 77 68 90; 53 av Émile Zola, 15e; metro Charles Michels; starters €6-13.50, mains €11-14, menu €13.50 (lunch); ☽ lunch & dinner to 10.30pm Mon-Sat

For 20 years this well-known restaurant, a short walk from the banks of the Seine, has been bidding *sawadee* (welcome) to lovers of Thai food. Don't be put off by the décor, which is rather cold and impersonal – the sophisticated cuisine more than makes up for it. You'll be able to enjoy the classic dishes of Siam, such as prawn or chicken soup flavoured with lemon grass, spicy beef salad (a real treat), or satay sticks (chicken, beef, lamb and pork) with peanut sauce. There may not be many surprises, but this delicious traditional fare, rich in flavours and scents, evokes another world.

MONTMARTRE & PIGALLE

The 18e arrondissement, where you'll find Montmartre and the northern half of place Pigalle, thrives on crowds and little else. When you've got Sacré Coeur, place du Tertre and its portrait artists and Paris literally at your feet, who needs decent restaurants? But that's not to say everything is a write-off in this well-trodden tourist area. You just have to pick and choose a bit more carefully than elsewhere in Paris. The restaurants along rue des Trois Frères (Map p400), for example, are generally a much better bet than their touristy counterparts in and around place du Tertre.

AU PETIT BUDAPEST
Map p400 — *Hungarian*
☎ 01 46 06 10 34; 96 rue des Martyrs, 18e; metro Abbesses; starters €7.50-15, mains €10.50-16, menus €13.50 (lunch) & €17.50; ☽ lunch Thu-Sun, dinner to midnight Tue-Sun
With old etchings and the requisite Gypsy music, the owner (a former artist) has recreated the atmosphere of a late-19th-century Hungarian *csárda* (traditional inn). From the *paprikash au bœuf épicé* (beef paprika) to the *gâteau au fromage blanc* (cream cheese cake), there are refined versions of popular Hungarian dishes. The *crepe à la Hortobagy* (crepe with meat and crème fraîche) is delicious.

AUX NÉGOCIANTS Map p400 — *French*
☎ 01 46 06 15 11; 27 rue Lambert, 18e; metro Château Rouge; starters €6-10, mains €12-15, ☽ lunch Mon-Fri, dinner to 10.30pm Tue-Fri
This old-style wine bar is just far enough from the madding crowds of Montmartre to attract a faithful local clientele. Patés, terrines, traditional mains like *boeuf bourguinon*, and wine paid for according to consumption – it feels like the Paris of the 1950s.

AYUTTHAYA Map p400 — *Thai*
☎ 01 42 64 19 53; 5 rue Houdon, 18e; metro Pigalle; meals from about €24, menu €15; ☽ lunch & dinner to 11.30pm Tue-Sun

They say you shouldn't eat ethnic outside of ethnic neighbourhoods but for 20 years this little eatery just up from place Pigalle has been exalting the flavours of Siam. The dishes are delicate and flavoursome if not particularly big. *Poisson en morceaux à la vapeur et au jus de coco* (steamed pieces of fish with coconut milk), cold *salade de bœuf à la menthe* (beef salad with mint) and *seiches sautées au basilic* (sautéed cuttlefish with basil) will impress lovers of Thai cuisine and convert newcomers.

CHEZ PLUMEAU Map p400 — *French*
☎ 01 46 06 26 29; 4 place du Calvaire, 18e; metro Abbesses; starters €8.50-15, mains €14-19, menus €24 & €29.50; ☽ lunch & dinner to 11.30pm daily Apr-Oct, lunch & dinner to 10.30pm Thu-Mon Nov-Mar
Once the popular Auberge du Coucou restaurant and cabaret, today's 'Feather Duster' caters mostly to tourists fresh from having their

Top Five Montmartre & Pigalle Restaurants
- **Chez Toinette** (opposite)
- **Il Duca** (opposite)
- **La Maison Rose** (opposite)
- **Le Mono** (opposite)
- **Relais Gascon** (p204)

portraits done on the place du Tertre. But for a tourist haunt it's not bad and the lovely back terrace is great on a warm spring afternoon.

CHEZ TOINETTE Map p400 _French_
☎ 01 42 54 44 36; 20 rue Germain Pilon, 18e; metro Abbesses; meals from €23; ⏰ dinner to 11pm Tue-Sat
The atmosphere of this convivial restaurant is rivalled only by its fine cuisine. In the heart of one of the capital's most touristy neighbourhoods, Chez Toinette has kept alive the tradition of old Montmartre with its simplicity and culinary expertise. Game lovers won't be disappointed; _perdreau_ (partridge), _biche_ (doe), _chevreuil_ (roebuck) and the famous _filet de canard à la sauge et au miel_ (fillet of duck with sage and honey) are the house specialities and go well with a glass of Bordeaux.

IL DUCA Map p400 _Italian_
☎ 01 46 06 71 98; 26 rue Yvonne le Tac, 18e; metro Abbesses; starters €7-12, pasta €10-13, mains €15-17, menu €14; ⏰ lunch & dinner to 11pm Mon-Fri, to midnight Sat & Sun
The 'Duke' is an intimate little Italian restaurant with good, straightforward food, including shop-made pasta. The selection of Italian wine and cheese is phenomenal and themed weeks, with various regions and types of produce, are scheduled throughout the year.

LA MASCOTTE Map p400 _French, Seafood_
☎ 01 46 06 28 15; 52 rue des Abbesses, 18e; metro Abbesses; starters €6.50-12, mains €16-22; menus €15 (lunch) & €26, plat du jour €14; ⏰ lunch & dinner to 10pm Tue-Sat
The 'Mascot' is a small and unassuming restaurant that could be easily missed among the hordes of competitors in this touristy area. It's a friendly spot much frequented by regulars who can't get enough of its seafood and regional cuisine. In winter, don't hesitate to sample the wide variety of seafood, especially the shellfish. In summer sit on the terrace and savour the delicious _fricassée de pétoncles_ (fricassee of queen scallops). Meat lovers won't be disappointed by the Corrèze pork, Aubrac beef and various regional delicacies such as Auvergne sausage and Troyes _andouillette_. The wide range of estate wines is a big plus.

LE REFUGE DES FONDUS
Map p400 _French, Savoie_
☎ 01 42 55 22 65; 17 rue des Trois Frères, 18e; metro Abbesses or Anvers; menu €15; ⏰ dinner 7pm-2am

This odd place has been a Montmartre favourite for almost 40 years. The single _menu_ provides an aperitif, hors d'oeuvre, red wine (or beer or soft drink) in a _biberon_ (baby bottle) and a good quantity of either _fondue savoyarde_ (melted cheese) or _fondue bourguignonne_ (meat fondue; minimum two people). The last sitting is at midnight.

CHEAP EATS
AU GRAIN DE FOLIE
Map p400 _Vegetarian_
☎ 01 42 58 15 57; 24 rue de la Vieuville, 18e; metro Abbesses; menus €8-15; lunch & dinner to 11.30pm Mon-Sat, noon-11am Sun
This hole-in-the-wall macrobiotic eatery has excellent vegetarian pâté and vegan quiche.

LA MAISON ROSE Map p400 _French_
☎ 01 42 57 66 75; 2 rue de l'Abreuvoir, 18e; metro Lamarck Caulaincourt; starters €7.80-13, mains €14.50-16.50, menu €14.50; ⏰ lunch & dinner to 10.30pm daily Mar-Oct, lunch Thu-Mon, dinner to 9pm Mon, Thu-Sat Nov-Feb
Looking for the quintessential Montmartre bistro? Head for the tiny 'Pink House' just north of the Place du Tertre.

LE MONO Map p400 _African, Togolese_
☎ 01 46 06 99 20; 40 rue Véron, 18e; metro Abbesses or Blanche; meals from €20; ⏰ dinner to 1am Thu-Tue
Le Mono offers Togolese and other West African specialities, including _lélé_ (flat, steamed cakes of white beans and shrimp; €5), _azidessi_ (beef or chicken with peanut sauce; €9.50), _gbekui_ (goulash with spinach, onions, beef, fish and shrimp; €10.50) and _djenkoumé_ (grilled chicken with semolina noodles; €10.50). The rum-based punches are excellent (and lethal).

LE SOLEIL GOURMAND
Map p400 _French, Mediterranean_
☎ 01 42 51 00 50; 10 rue Ravignan, 18e; metro Abbesses; dishes €9-12.50; ⏰ lunch & dinner to 11pm
The 'Greedy Sun' is a cheery little restaurant run by twin sisters that exudes the south of France through its warm décor and simple dishes such as salads, savoury tarts and oven-baked _bricks_ (stuffed fritters). Treat yourself to the _tarte aux oignons, poivrons, raisins et pignons grillés_ (tart with onion, green peppers, grapes and grilled pine nuts) and any of the home-made ice creams: gingerbread, almond milk, tiramisù or wild peach.

RELAIS GASCON

Map p400   *French, Southwest*

☎ 01 42 58 58 22; 6 rue des Abbesses, 18e; metro Abbesses; starters €5.50-7, mains €9-12, menus €8 (lunch), €12.50 & €18; ☻ lunch & dinner to midnight

A short stroll from place des Abbesses, this has a relaxed atmosphere and authentic regional cuisine at rock-bottom prices. The *salade géante* (giant salad, a house speciality) and the *confit sud-ouest* will satisfy big eaters, while the Basque *pipérade* and *tartiflette* are equally tasty and filling. After, try the traditional *gâteau basque* (a simple layer cake filled with cream and cherry jam) or a *crème brûlée*.

Top Five Eat Streets

- **Passage Brady** (p193) This covered arcade is the place to come for Indian, Pakistani and Bangladeshi food
- **Place de Clichy** (p188) The maze of small streets fanning out from this square is an excellent area to seek out ethnic eateries and restaurants
- **Rue Montorgueil** (p155) A pedestrians-only market street and one of the best places around for something quick
- **Rue Mouffetard** (p168) Not just a food market but an excellent street to find ethnic and French restaurants in the budget category
- **Rue Richer, rue Cadet & rue Geoffroy Marie** (p189) These three streets have a large range of excellent kosher and North African restaurants

---

OUTSIDE THE WALLS: BEYOND CENTRAL PARIS

LA DÉFENSE

For the most part La Défense is fast-food territory, but there are a number of independent outlets from which to choose.

BISTRO ROMAIN Map p133   *International*
☎ 01 40 81 08 08; 37 Le Parvis; lunch menu €10.95, dinner menus €15.90 & €22.70;
☻ 11.30am-10pm

Overlooking the Parvis, this chain restaurant is good for something cheap and cheerful.

BRASSERIE DU TOIT DE LA GRANDE ARCHE Map p133   *French*
☎ 01 49 07 27 27; lunch menu €15;
☻ lunch noon-3.30pm, bar with snacks 10am-7pm

Sitting atop the Grande Arche, this brasserie offers acceptable food at lunch and some of the best views in Paris from 110m up.

LE PETIT BOFINGER
Map p133   *French, Brasserie*
☎ 01 46 92 46 46, 1 place du Dôme; menus €19.50 & €24; ☻ lunch & dinner until 11pm

Formerly Le Petit Dôme (it sits under what was once the IMAX Dôme), this glassed-in dining room is a perennial favourite of La Défense *gens d'affaires* (businesspeople).

ST-DENIS

There are a number of restaurants in the modern shopping area around the Basilique de St-Denis metro station.

AU PETIT BRETON
Map p135   *French, Bretagne*
☎ 01 48 20 11 58; 18 rue de la Légion d'Honneur; menus €10 & €12, plat du jour €8; ☻ 8.30am-3.30pm Mon-Sat

'At the Little Breton' is a decent spot for a light lunch of *galettes* (a savoury version of crepes) and dry cider, or a snack of sweet crepes.

LE CAFÉ DE L'ORIENT Map p135 *Tea Room*
☎ 01 48 20 30 83; Chemin des Poulies, teas €2.30-3.50, cocktails €5-6; ☻ noon-midnight

If you fancy some North African mint tea and pastries, a toke on the hookah or a cocktail, this is a comfortable café with overstuffed cushions northeast of the basilica.

LES ARTS Map p135   *North African, French*
☎ 01 42 43 22 40; 6 rue de la Boulangerie; starters €4.90-9.50, couscous €7.9-19.20, tajines €9.50-12.50; ☻ lunch Tue-Sun, dinner to 10.30pm Mon-Sat

This central restaurant with French and Maghreb cuisine comes recommended by locals.

Drinking 207

Louvre & Les Halles 208
Marais & Bastille 208
The Islands 220
Latin Quarter & Jardin des Plantes 221
St-Germain, Odéon & Luxembourg 222
Montparnasse 223
Faubourg St-Germain & Invalides 224
Concorde & Madeleine 224
Clichy & Gare St-Lazare 224
Opéra & Grands Boulevards 225
Gare du Nord, Gare de l'Est & République 225
Ménilmontant & Belleville 226
Gare de Lyon, Nation & Bercy 227
13e Arrondissement & Chinatown 228
Montmartre & Pigalle 228

Music 229

Rock, Pop & Indie 229
Classical 230
Jazz & Blues 231
World & Latino 232
French Chansons 233

Clubbing 234

Cinema 238

Theatre 239

Comedy 240

Opera 241

Dance 242

Entertainment

Entertainment

Entertainment options are endless in this city of culture, with classical music concerts, dance performances (both corps de ballet and the most avant-garde of modern) and plays staged throughout the year. Locally cultivated drama and dance is among the most enjoyable in Europe, but the schedule of foreign performances can also be very impressive. Parisians, like most French, have always had a very special predilection for the cinema and film attendance is very high. Paris is not just for culture vultures, however. The number of drinking spots is on the increase as Parisians discover the joys of a pint and happy hour. The city's clubs, while not as throbbing as those in London, cater to every taste and passing trend and you could very well have a better chance of getting tickets to big international acts here than you would at home.

Information & Listings

It's virtually impossible to sample the richness of Paris' entertainment scene without first taking a close look at either *Pariscope* (€0.40) or *L'Officiel des Spectacles* (€0.35), both of which come out on Wednesday and are available at any newsstand. *Pariscope* includes a six-page insert at the back in English courtesy of London's *Time Out* magazine, though many people think *L'Officiel des Spectacles* is easier to use. The weekly magazine *Zurban* (www.zurban.com in French; €0.80), which also appears on Wednesday and touts itself as the complete guide for all your evenings out in Paris and the Île de France offers a fresher look at entertainment and has gained quite a loyal following over recent years. *Les Inrockuptibles* (www.lesinrocks.com in French; €2.90) is a national culture and entertainment weekly but, predictably, the lion's share of the information concerns Paris.

For up-to-date information on clubs and the music scene, pick up a copy of *LYLO* (short for *les yeux, les oreilles*, meaning 'ears and eyes'), a free booklet of 50 pages or so with excellent listings of rock concerts and other live music. It is available at many cafés, bars and clubs across town. The monthly magazine *Nova* (www.novaplanet.com in French, €3) is an excellent source for information on clubs and the music scene; its *Hot Guide* listings insert is particularly useful. Check out any of the Fnac outlets (opposite), especially the ones in the Forum des Halles shopping centre, Bastille and the Champs-Élysées, for free flyers, schedules and programmes.

Le Balajo (p236)

Other excellent sources for what's on include Radio FG on 98.2 mHz FM (www.radiofg.com in French) and Radio Nova on 101.5 mHz FM.

You can also check out www.france-techno.fr (in French) or www.flyersweb.com (in French) for up-to-date information on the club scene.

Tickets & Reservations

You can buy tickets for cultural events at many ticket outlets, including Fnac (rhymes with 'snack') and Virgin Megastore branches, for a small commission. Both accept reservations, ticketing by phone and the Internet, and most credit cards. Tickets generally cannot be returned or exchanged unless a performance is cancelled.

AGENCE MARIVAUX Map pp386-8

☎ 01 42 97 46 70; 7 rue de Marivaux, 2e; metro Richelieu Drouot; ⏰ 11.30am-7.30pm Mon-Fri, noon-4pm Sat

Agence Marivaux is just opposite the Opéra Comique.

AGENCE PERROSSIER & SOS THÉÂTRES Map pp383-5

☎ 01 42 60 58 31, 01 44 77 88 55; www.perrossier.com in French, www.sostheatres.com in French; 6 place de la Madeleine, 8e; metro Madeleine; ⏰ 10am-7pm Mon-Sat

This agency with two names faces the Église de la Madeleine.

FNAC

☎ 08 92 68 36 22; www.fnac.com in French; ⏰ 10am-7.30pm Mon-Sat

Fnac has 10 outlets in Paris with *billeteries* (ticket offices) including **Fnac Champs Élysées** (Map pp383-5; ☎ 01 53 53 64 64; 74 av des Champs Élysées, 8e; metro Franklin D Roosevelt; ⏰ 10am-midnight Mon-Sat, 11am-midnight Sun); **Fnac Forum** (Map pp396-9; ☎ 01 40 41 40 00; Forum des Halles shopping centre,

Level 3, 1-7 rue Pierre Lescot, 1er; metro Châtelet Les Halles); **Fnac Montparnasse** (Map pp389-91; ☎ 01 49 54 30 00; 136 rue de Rennes, 6e; metro St-Placide); **Fnac Musique Bastille** (Map pp392-5; ☎ 01 43 42 04 04; 4 place de la Bastille, 12e; metro Bastille; ⏰ 10am-8pm Mon-Sat); **Fnac Étoile** (Map pp383-5; ☎ 01 44 09 18 00; 26-30 av des Ternes, 17e; metro Ternes) and **Fnac St-Lazare** (Map pp383-5; ⏰ 01 55 31 20 00; 109 rue St-Lazare, 9e; metro St-Lazare; ⏰ 10am-7.30pm Mon-Wed, Fri & Sat, 10am-9.30pm Thu).

VIRGIN MEGASTORE

www.virginmega.fr in French

Virgin has a half-dozen megastores in the capital including **Barbès** (Map p400; ☎ 01 56 55 53 70; 15 blvd Barbès, 18e; metro Barbès Rochechouart; ⏰ 10am-10pm Mon-Sat); **Champs-Élysées** (Map pp383-5; ☎ 01 49 53 50 00; 52-60 av des Champs-Élysées, 8e; metro Franklin D Roosevelt; ⏰ 10am-midnight Mon-Sat, noon-midnight Sun) with a large *billeterie* in the basement and **Galerie du Carrousel du Louvre** (Map pp396-9; ☎ 01 44 50 03 10; 99 rue de Rivoli, 1er; metro Palais Royal Musée du Louvre; ⏰ 10am-8.30pm Mon & Tue, 10am-9.30pm Wed-Sun) with a ticket office in the shopping centre behind the inverted glass pyramid.

Discount Tickets

KIOSQUE THÉÂTRE Map pp383-5

(opp 15 place de la Madeleine, 8e; metro Madeleine; ⏰ 12.30-7.45pm Tue-Sat, 12.30-3.45pm Sun)

On the same day of the performance, the theatre sells tickets to plays and other events (concerts, operas, ballets etc) at half price plus commission of about €2.50. Remember though that the seats are almost always the most expensive ones in the stalls or 1st balcony. There's also a **Montparnasse Kiosque Théâtre** (Map pp389-91; parvis Montparnasse, 15e; metro Montparnasse Bienvenüe) between Gare Montparnasse and Tour Montparnasse, which keeps the same hours.

DRINKING

Traditionally drinking in Paris revolved around a café, where a *demi* looked more like an eyewash than 330mL of beer. But all that has changed and the number of drinking establishments has mushroomed in recent years, especially in the Marais and along the Grands Boulevards. Happy hour – sometimes extending to as late as 9pm – has brought the price of a pint of beer, a glass of wine or a cocktail down to pricey, rather than extortionate, levels. Many cafés in Paris also have important literary and/or historical associations (p141).

LOUVRE & LES HALLES

BANANA CAFÉ Map pp396-9

☎ 01 42 33 35 31; 13 rue de la Ferronnerie, 1er; metro Châtelet; 🕙 4pm-7am

The gay cruise bar of the '90s, the Banana (so subtle, these French, with their names) is on two levels and continues to attract a tattooed and buffed-up crowd that likes to have drag queens and go-go dancers (weekends) around them. Sunday is Hold-Up. Happy hour is 6pm to 9pm. History buffs might like to know that that in 1610 the former Huguenot king, Henri IV, was assassinated by a Catholic fanatic named François Ravaillac while passing in his carriage just in front of this spot.

CAFÉ OZ Map pp396-9

☎ 01 40 39 00 18; 18 rue St-Denis, 1er; metro Châtelet; 🕙 3pm-2am Sun-Thu, 3pm-3am Fri & Sat Apr-Oct; 5pm-2am Sun-Thu, 5pm-3am Fri & Sat Nov-Mar

This militantly Aussie pub is bubbling with the kind of enthusiasm (well, let's just call it that) you'd expect from any place with a Down Under theme. Everything is made of wood, old Foster's posters adorn the walls, and the décor and lighting evoke the ochre tones of the Australian landscape. Cocktails (€6 or at happy hour €5) and strictly Aussie beers in bottles (€5 to €6) and on tap (€5.50 a schooner) will help you to conjure up the Outback. Happy hour is 6pm to 8pm. There's also a **Pigalle branch** (Map p400; ☎ 01 40 16 11 16; 1 rue de Bruxelles, 9e; metro Blanche), which keeps the same hours.

LE FUMOIR Map pp396-9

☎ 01 42 92 00 24; 6 rue de l'Amiral Coligny, 1er; metro Louvre-Rivoli; 🕙 11am-2am

Brought to you by the owners of the **China Club** (p210), the 'Smoking Room' is a huge bar/café just opposite the Louvre with a gentleman's club theme. It's friendly, lively and quite good fun. Food (set meals €17.50 to €27.60) is available from noon to 3pm and 7.30pm to midnight but does not get top marks. If you want

to eat, stick to afternoon tea or Sunday brunch (€20). Happy hour is 6pm to 8pm.

MURPHY'S HOUSE Map pp396-9

☎ 01 42 60 20 14; 166 rue St-Honoré, 1er; metro Palais Royal Musée du Louvre; 🕙 10am-midnight Mon-Thu, 10am-2am Fri & Sat

You wouldn't travel far for this Irish-in-name-only pub full of local office workers and sport on big-screen, but with the Louvre just opposite it's a convenient place for a post-educational pint, especially during happy hour (€4.60, from 6pm to 8pm).

PAPOU LOUNGE Map pp396-9

☎ 01 44 76 00 03; 74 rue Jean Jacques Rousseau, 1er; metro Louvre-Rivoli; 🕙 10am-2am Mon-Fri, 11am-2am Sat, 5pm-midnight Sun

This bar-restaurant feels authentic, perhaps because the two brothers who own the place share a fascination for the *papous* (papuans) and Papua New Guinea. It's perfect for a drink after a movie at the Forum des Halles and the owners' tribal masks, carvings and travel pics on the wall may give you itchy feet.

MARAIS & BASTILLE

AMNÉSIA Map pp396-9

☎ 01 42 72 16 94; 42 rue Vieille du Temple, 4e; metro Hôtel de Ville; 🕙 10am-2am

Amnésia is not the place to go to forget but to meet and chat. It's a cosy, warmly lit, popular place, with comfy sofas and a more mixed clientele than most gay bars; more living room than lounge really. Beers start at €3.50, cocktails from €5.50 to €8.50.

AU PETIT FER À CHEVAL Map pp396-9

☎ 01 42 72 47 47; 30 rue Vieille du Temple, 4e; metro Hôtel de Ville or St-Paul; 🕙 9am-2am

A slightly offbeat bar-restaurant named after its horseshoe-shaped *zinc* (counter), this tiny place is often filled to overflowing with friendly regulars. And it's no wonder; it's got one of the best people-watching vantage points in the Marais. Food (*plat du jour* €12, sandwiches from €4) is available from noon to 1.15am.

BARRIO LATINO Map pp392-5

☎ 01 55 78 84 75; 46-48 rue du Faubourg St-Antoine, 11e; metro Bastille; 🕙 11.30am-2am

Squeezing the salsa craze for everything it's worth, the 'Latin Quarter', owned by the Buddha Bar people, is an enormous bar and restaurant (spread over three floors) that attracts Latinos, Latino wannabes and Latino wanna-haves. Cocktails (€9 to €10.50) are not the strongest in town, but the *mojitos* go down a treat.

BAZ'ART CAFÉ Map pp392-5
☎ 01 42 78 62 23; 36 blvd Henri IV, 4e; metro Bastille; ⏰ 8am-midnight

This café, whose name sounds suspiciously like 'bizarre' in English, is just southwest of Bastille but could be a million miles away. It's a stylish place with friendly service and good-value food (starters €6.80 to €15.95, mains €11.40 to €19.40, lunch menu €17). Sunday brunch (€18 to €22) is served from noon to 5pm.

BLISS KFÉ Map pp396-9
☎ 01 55 34 98 81; 30 rue du Roi de Sicile, 4e; metro St-Paul; ⏰ 5.30pm-2am

This lesbian café-cum-lounge bar in what was once a boulangerie-patisserie (note the glass mural advertising 'croissants and hot breads at all hours' outside) at the corner of rue des Écouffes, is a stylish newcomer to the Marais, with a New York vibe and a somewhat mixed crowd. Guys are welcome, and there's a club downstairs on Friday and Saturday nights.

BOCA CHICA Map pp392-5
☎ 01 43 57 93 13; 58 rue de Charonne, 11e; metro Ledru Rollin; ⏰ 10am-2am Sun-Thu, 10am-5am Fri & Sat

This enormous place with three large bars on two floors attracts a very trendy crowd (just check out the models and the tans) and serves decent tapas (€5.50 to €12). Happy hour is from 4pm to 8pm (to 10pm on Monday) when a glass (€3.10) and litre (€14.60) of sangria and cocktails are half-price.

BOTTLE SHOP Map pp392-5
☎ 01 43 14 28 04; 5 rue Trousseau, 11e; metro Ledru Rollin; ⏰ 11.30am-2am

You won't be a stranger for long in this place; it's packed full of regulars, who will soon make you feel welcome. The friendly conversation (mostly English) is just as big a drawcard as the contemporary art and cocktails (€6 to €8). It's almost a perfect mix of an American pub and a French café.

CAFÉ DES PHARES Map pp392-5
☎ 01 42 72 04 70; 7 place Bastille, 4e; metro Bastille; ⏰ 7am-3am Sun-Thu, 7am-4am Fri & Sat

The 'Beacons Café' is best known as the city's original *philocafé* (philosophers' café), established by the late philosopher and Sorbonne professor Marc Sautet (1947–98). If you feel like debating such topics as 'What is a fact?' and 'Can people communicate?', head for the Phares at 11am on Sunday. It sounds posy in the extreme and it is but – hey! – this is Paris. If you need sustenance of a more mundane sort, salads are €8.50 to €9, *croque-monsieur* (grilled ham & cheese sandwich, €6 to €8), omelettes €5.50 to €7 and a set lunch is €8.50.

CAFÉ LÉOPARD Map pp392-5
☎ 01 40 09 95 99; 149 blvd Voltaire, 11e; metro Charonne; ⏰ 9am-2am Mon-Sat

Café Léopard was once a standard bistro, but it has been done up with all sorts of recycled bric-a-brac to give it a bright, funky look and feel. Here they know how to put on a show without planning it: theatre, music (house and techno) and video viewings are improvised in a relaxed, fun atmosphere. The clients are a real mixture, like the décor, but veer towards the arty. There's a good-quality *menu* (€12.50) available at lunch and dinner to 11pm.

Entertainment – Drinking

Gay & Lesbian Venues

The Marais (4e), especially those areas around the intersection of rue Ste-Croix de la Bretonnerie and rue des Archives, and eastwards to rue Vieille du Temple, has been Paris' main centre of gay and – to a lesser extent – lesbian nightlife for over two decades. There are also a few bars and clubs within walking distance of blvd de Sébastopol. Other venues are scattered throughout the city.

A gay night out for guys just has to start at the **Open Café** (p220) or the quieter **Quetzal** (p219); if you're up for cruising this early in the game, **Le Cox** (p219) is just next door to the Open Café. The hottest gay club at the moment is the **Red Light** (p238) but for a more relaxed evening of carousing and cruising try **Le Scorp** (p237). For clubs where all your needs are taken care of *in situ*, *La crème de la crème* (best of the best) is **Le Depôt** (p237), but it must be said that **La Station** (p236) is more personable.

Girls might have a drink at **Bliss Kfé** (above) or **Les Scandaleuses** (p220) before heading on to **Le Pulp** (p237).

CHINA CLUB Map pp392-5

☎ 01 43 43 82 02; 50 rue de Charenton, 12e; metro Ledru Rollin or Bastille; ⏰ 7pm-2am Sun-Thu, 7pm-3am Fri & Sat

This stylish establishment, behind the Opéra Bastille, is done up like a tropical gentlemen's club. It has a huge bar with high ceilings on the ground floor, a *fumoir* (smoking room) complete with glowing fire for cigar aficionados on the 1st floor and a jazz club called **Le Sing Song** (done up to look like Shanghai circa 1930) is in the cellar. Happy hour (all drinks €6) is 7pm to 9pm. Starters cost €7.20 to €10.50, mains €12.20 to €29 and dim sum €6.50 to €8. The good-value *menus* cost €18 and €28.

HAVANITA CAFÉ Map pp392-5

☎ 01 43 55 96 42; 11 rue de Lappe, 11e; metro Bastille; ⏰ noon-2am Mon-Fri, 4pm-2am Sat

Havanita Café is a bar-restaurant decorated with posters and murals inspired – like the food and drink – by all things Cuban. The main courses (€13.20 to €16.50) are excellent and huge; if only peckish, just go for a starter (€6.90 to €15). Happy hour, when cocktails are €5.50 instead of €8.30, is from opening to 8pm.

IGUANA CAFÉ Map pp392-5

☎ 01 40 21 39 99; 15 rue de la Roquette, 11e; metro Bastille; ⏰ 9am-4pm Sun-Thu, 9am-5am Fri & Sat

The Iguana is a two-level café-pub with a lovely backlit bar and a clientele of 20 to 30 year olds. Cocktails, which are excellent, cost €9 to €10, beer on tap costs €4 to €7 and brunch (€15 and €18) is served from 11am to 5pm on Saturday and Sunday.

INTERFACE BAR Map pp392-5

☎ 01 47 00 67 15; 34 rue Keller, 11e; metro Ledru Rollin; ⏰ 4pm-2am Sun-Thu, 5pm-4am Fri & Sat

No, not 'in yer face'… This is a very laid-back neighbourhood gay bar that attracts locals and habitués of the nearby **Gay & Lesbian Centre** (p343).

JOKKO BAR Map pp396-9

☎ 01 42 74 35 96; 5 rue Elzévir, 3e; metro St-Paul or Chemin Vert; ⏰ 5pm-12.30am Wed-Sun

Part of a little African colony recently established on this quiet Marais backstreet and part of the CSAO group (p255), Jokko is a delightful spot with colourful décor, great world music and rum-based cocktails from €8. There are concerts most nights at 7.30pm and rotating exhibitions.

LA CHAISE AU PLAFOND Map pp396-9

☎ 01 42 76 03 22; 10 Rue du Trésor, 4e; metro Hôtel de Ville or St-Paul; ⏰ 9.30am-2am

The 'Chair on the Ceiling' is a peaceful and warm place, with wooden tables outside on a pedestrian-only side street. It's a real oasis in the frenzy of the Marais.

LA RENAISSANCE Map pp392-5

☎ 01 43 79 83 09; 87 rue de la Roquette, 11e; metro Voltaire; ⏰ 8.30am-8pm Mon, 8.30am-midnight Tue-Sat, 9.30am-8pm Sun

If you're looking for the quintessential Parisian *café du quartier* (neighbourhood café) not too far from Bastille, head for this simple, unaffected place. Regulars drop in for a late breakfast, a drink or a meal at one of the pavement tables. Intrepid souls can enjoy the house speciality: steak tartare (raw minced steak).

LA TARTINE Map pp396-9

☎ 01 42 72 76 85; 24 Rue de Rivoli, 4e; metro St-Paul; ⏰ 8am-2am

A wine bar where little has changed since the days of gas lighting (the fixtures are still in place), this place offers 15 selected reds, whites and rosés for €8 to €10 *le pot* (46mL). There's not much to eat except sandwiches and, of course, lots of *tartines*.

L'APPAREMMENT CAFÉ Map pp396-9

☎ 01 48 87 12 22; 18 rue des Coutures St-Gervais, 3e; metro St-Sébastien Froissart; ⏰ noon-2am Mon-Fri, 4pm-2am Sat, 12.30pm-midnight Sun

Tucked not so 'Apparently' behind the Musée Picasso and at a merciful distance from the 'shopping highways' that rue des Francs Bourgeois and nearby streets have become, this oasis of peace looks like a private living room. Not a single lapse of taste mars the studied untidiness: wood panelling, the odd leather sofa, parlour games here and there, dog-eared books (but not *too* dog-eared) and cool (not *too* cool) service. Sunday brunch (€19) is served to 4pm.

L'ARMAGNAC Map pp392-5

☎ 01 43 71 49 43; 104 rue de Charonne & 24 rue Jules Vallès, 11e; metro Charonne; ⏰ 7.30am-2am Mon-Fri, 10.30am-2am Sat & Sun

A bustling lunch spot with *plat du jour* (dish of the day) €10 and *tartines* (slices of bread with toppings or garnishes) €6.50 to €7 by day, the

(Continued on page 219)

Entertainment – Drinking

1 Café, Champs-Élysées (p117) 2 Parisian reading Le Monde, Rue Mouffetard 3 Café, place des Vosges (p87)

1 *L'Encrier (p167)*
2 *Le Chansonnier (p192)*
3 *Café, place de la Bastille (p90)*

1 Le Dôme (p184) *2* Cheese for sale, Rue Mouffetard (p153) *3* L'Atelier de Joël Robouchon (p185)

1 *Église St-Eustache (p85)*
2 *Café Oz (p208)* 3 *Le Bala*
(p236)

214

1 *Le Batofar (p236)* **2** *Moulin Rouge (p242)* **3** *Point Virgule (p240)*

1 *Antoine et Lili (p266)*
2 *Tobacconist, Rue Mouffetard* 3 *Shakespeare Company bookshop (p260)*

1

3

2

*1 Kenzo (p277) **2** Louis Vuitton (p262) **3** Hermès (p264)*

1 Monet's garden, Giverny
(p326) *2* Portail Royal
figures (p323), Cathèdrale
Notre Dame, Chartres
3 Château de Fontaine-
bleau, Fontainebleau (p31

(Continued from page 210)

'Armagnac' has just the right levels of smoke, noise and local flavour by night to give it the authenticity that more self-conscious bars closer to Bastille struggle to replicate. It was once a bistro – check out the old furniture and mouldings on the ceiling – and the music is a comfortable mix of classic French and funk.

LE CAFÉ DU PASSAGE Map pp392-5

☎ 01 49 29 97 64; 12 rue de Charonne, 11e; metro Ledru Rollin; ☺ 6pm-2am

Wine buffs will appreciate this chic, somewhat exclusive bar, where customers can relax in armchairs while sampling Loire vintages from the wide range on offer (18 available by the glass for between €5 and €12). Conversation is easy in this quiet place and light meals and snacks such as pasta, risotto and salads (€12 to €15) are available.

LE CENTRAL Map pp396-9

☎ 01 48 87 99 33; 33 Rue Vieille du Temple, 4e; metro Hôtel de Ville; ☺ 4pm-2am Mon-Fri, 2pm-2am Sat & Sun

Founded in 1980, the Central, part of the hotel of that name (p286) is the oldest gay bar still open in Paris and it's pretty comatose these days. Still, therein lies its charm. Happy hour – what they call *apéro détente* (aperitive relaxation), is from 6pm to 8pm.

LE COFFEE SHOP Map pp396-9

☎ 01 42 74 24 21; 3 rue Ste-Croix de la Bretonnerie, 4e; metro Hôtel de Ville; ☺ 10am-2am

This small, almost exclusively gay café is a convenient pit stop if you're of the persuasion and about to drop from shopping. The gay bookshop **Les Mots à la Bouche** (p256) is just opposite.

LE COX Map pp396-9

☎ 01 42 72 08 00; 15 rue des Archives, 4e; metro Hôtel de Ville; ☺ noon-2am

This small gay bar attracts an interesting (and maybe interested) cruisy crowd throughout the evening. OK, we don't like the in-your-face name either but what's a boy to do? Happy hour is 6pm to 9pm.

LE LÈCHE-VIN Map pp392-5

☎ 01 43 55 98 91; 13 rue Daval, 11e; metro Bastille; ☺ 6.30pm-1.30am Mon-Sat, 5pm-midnight Sun

A divine surprise in a crass and vulgar neighbourhood, the 'Wine Licker' is an irreverent shambles of religious bric-a-brac, with an electric pietà, Pope John XXIII plates, a Last Supper bathmat and icons of the Virgin Mary everywhere. Be aware, however, that eternal damnation is just a visit to the toilet away (see the boxed text on p236).

LE PICK CLOPS Map pp396-9

☎ 01 40 29 02 18; 16 rue Vieille du Temple, 4e; metro Hôtel de Ville or St-Paul; ☺ 7.30am-2am Mon-Sat, 9am-3am Sun

This retro café-bar, all shades of yellow and lit by neon, has Formica tables, ancient bar stools and plenty of mirrors. It's a great place for that last drink – either alone or with company. The clientele, which includes both regulars and passing trade, is hip but friendly.

LE QUETZAL Map pp396-9

☎ 01 48 87 99 07; 10 rue de la Verrerie, 4e; metro Hôtel de Ville; ☺ 5pm-5am

This place, just opposite rue des Mauvais Garçons (literally 'Bad Boys' Street'), which has been its name since 1540 when brigands congregated here, is a dimly lit, modern bar popular with 30-something gay men and one of very few attitude-free places in the Marais. It's not nearly as popular as it was a few short years ago – oh, you fickle Parisians – but a decent spot for a quiet drink and chat. Happy hour is 5pm to 9pm when pints are €3.30.

LES ÉTAGES Map pp396-9

☎ 01 42 78 72 00; 35 rue Vieille du Temple, 4e; metro Hôtel de Ville; ☺ 3.30pm-2am

The 'Storeys' is upstairs on the two upper floors with distressed surrounds: graffiti on the walls, big *faux* (fake) leather armchairs and ceilings about to implode. The drinks aren't cheap (around €7.50 for cocktails) but happy hour is, generously, from 3.30pm to 9pm when most are only €4. Check out the ancient Bakelite telephone.

LES PHILOSOPHES Map pp396-9

☎ 01 48 87 49 64; 28 rue Vieille du Temple, 4e; metro St-Paul; ☺ 9am-2am

A Marais stalwart, the 'Philosophers' does a booming trade as a bistro at meal times (*menus* €15.50 and €26, Sunday brunch €18) and as a café before, after and in between. Though it is decidedly not a *philocafé* like the **Café des Phares** (p209), it has aspirations (see the boxed text p236).

LES SCANDALEUSES Map pp396-9

☎ 01 48 87 39 26; 8 rue des Écouffes, 4e; metro Hôtel de Ville; ⏰ 6pm-2am

Just up from the more homely and relaxed **Bliss Kfé** (p209) the 'Scandalous' is a glossy and lively women-only (accompanied men are welcome, however) bar in the Marais. It is popular with artists and designers, and has guest DJs at the weekend. Beer (from €3.60) and cocktails (from €7.20); happy hour is 6pm to 8pm.

MIXER BAR Map pp396-9

☎ 01 48 87 55 44; 23 rue Ste-Croix de la Bretonnerie, 4e; metro Hôtel de Ville; ⏰ 5pm-2am

A place that uses a blender as its logo has a name that says it all: high-voltage techno, electro and house music of all flavours, gay (with a sprinkling of hetero), parties and chill-out sessions. Beers cost €3.30 to €4.40. Happy hour is 6pm to 8pm.

OPEN CAFÉ Map pp396-9

☎ 01 42 72 26 18; 17 rue des Archives, 4e; metro Hôtel de Ville; ⏰ 11am-2am

The Open – think huge, overflowing terrace in the warmer months – is where most boyz of most ages head after work and before moving on to bigger and better things. It's packed, but more social than cruisy. Happy hour is 6pm to 9pm.

PAUSE CAFÉ Map pp392-5

☎ 01 48 06 80 33; 41 rue de Charonne, 11e; metro Ledru Rollin; ⏰ 7.30am-2am Mon-Sat, 9am-8.30pm Sun

At meal times, this bar operates mostly as a restaurant, but you can still take advantage of the large terrace for a drink during the day or a weekend brunch. Just that wee bit away from Bastille, Pause is frequented mainly by local inhabitants and workers.

PURE MALT BAR Map pp396-9

☎ 01 42 76 03 77; 4 rue Caron, 4e; metro St-Paul; ⏰ 5pm-2am

Just south of the lovely place du Marché Ste-Catherine and a short distance from the place des Vosges, the Pure Malt concentrates mainly on single malt whisky (though beer is available at €6 a pint). More than 150 types of whisky are on hand to try at €7 to €17 a glass.

QUIET MAN Map pp396-9

☎ 01 48 04 02 77; 5 rue des Haudriettes, 3e; metro Rambuteau; ⏰ 5pm-2am Sun-Thu, 4pm-2am Fri & Sat

This is about the most authentic Irish pub Paris has to offer, with a real live Irish owner and musicians playing Irish music. The only thing fake about it is its name, which comes from John Ford's 1952 film starring John 'Call Me Paddy' Wayne. There are traditional sets in the basement every night from 8pm to 1am. Happy hour is from 5pm to 8pm.

SANZ SANS Map pp392-5

☎ 01 44 75 78 78; 49 rue du Faubourg St-Antoine, 11e; metro Bastille; ⏰ 9am-2am Sun-Thu, 9am-5am Fri & Sat

This is one of the liveliest and most colourful (in every sense) drinking spots on the Bastille beat; expect to meet every and anyone here. By day the red velvet décor seems a tad cheesy and overdone. There's a menu with international specials (starters cost €6.50 to €9, mains €9.50 to €15, *plat du jour* €9) and music changes with the DJ every night: acid jazz, hip-hop, soul, funk and house.

STOLLY'S Map pp396-9

☎ 01 42 76 06 76; 16 rue de la Cloche Percée, 4e; metro Hôtel de Ville; ⏰ 4.30pm-2am

This expatty, Anglophone bar on a tiny street just above rue de Rivoli is always crowded, particularly during the 4.30pm to 8pm happy hour, when a 1.6L pitcher of cheap *blonde* (that's the house lager – not the Monroe look-alike propping up the bar) costs €11 and cocktails (usually €5.50 to €7.50) cost €4.60. When big football matches are on and you're looking forward to a quiet drink, go elsewhere.

WAX Map pp392-5

☎ 01 40 21 16 16; 15 rue Daval, 11e; metro Bastille; ⏰ 6pm-2am

Wax is a 'retro-futuristic' (think *A Clockwork Orange*) bar and club with yellow and red plastic furniture and walls, portholes on the walls and DJs playing most electronic. Happy hour is from 6pm to 9pm. Next door to **Le Léche Vin** (p219).

THE ISLANDS

LA CHARLOTTE EN ÎLE Map pp396-9

☎ 01 43 54 25 83; rue St-Louis en l'Île 24, Île de St-Louis, 4e; metro Pont Marie; ⏰ noon-8pm Thu-Sun

This tiny place is one of the loveliest *salons de thé* (tearooms) in all of Paris and definitely worth crossing the bridge for. The fairy-tale theme adds flavour (as if any is needed) to the chocolate and pastries (€2.60 to €5), and the three dozen or so teas on offer are superbly chosen. There's a unique 'piano tea' from 4pm to 8pm on Friday.

TAVERNE HENRI IV Map pp396-9
☎ 01 43 54 27 90; 13 place du Pont Neuf, Île de la Cité, 1er; metro Pont Neuf; ☯ 9am-4pm & 6-9pm Mon-Fri, 9am-4pm Sat
One of the very few places to drink on the Île de la Cité, the 'Henry IV Tavern' is a serious wine bar and decent place for a nibble, with a choice of *tartines* (€5 to €8), as well as *charcuterie* (cold cooked meats), cheese and quiche (€4.50 to €10). This place attracts lots of legal types from the nearby Palais de Justice and has become something of an institution. Great for people-watching.

LATIN QUARTER & JARDIN DES PLANTES

CAFÉ AUSSIE Map pp392-5
☎ 01 43 54 30 48; 184 rue St-Jacques, 5e; metro Luxembourg; ☯ 4pm-2am Mon-Sat
Although its ties with Café Oz (p208) on the Right Bank have been irrevocably cut, this French-owned café-pub retains its Australian theme – sort of. It has some decent beers and cider on tap, including Beamish and Strongbow (€6.50 a pint, €5 at happy hour), plus Australian wines from €3 a glass. Happy hour is from 4pm to 8pm.

CAFÉ DELMAS Map pp392-5
☎ 01 43 26 51 26; 2 place de la Contrescarpe, 5e; metro Cardinal Lemoine; ☯ 8am-2am Sun-Thu, 8am-4am Fri & Sat
The Delmas occupies one of the most enviable positions in Paris: overlooking the idyllic place de la Contrescarpe at the top of rue Mouffetard. Although located in a solidly student neighbourhood, the café is surprisingly cosmopolitan, and you'll hear (and meet) all types here.

FINNEGAN'S WAKE Map pp392-5
☎ 01 46 34 23 65; 9 rue des Boulangers, 5e; metro Jussieu; ☯ 11am-2am Mon-Fri, 6pm-2am Sat
Irish pub meets Latin Quarter; this is probably the first time you'll walk into a drinking establishment where the vast majority of those bending their elbows have read the James Joyce classic, *Finnegan's Wake*. Good fun – if a bit heavy. Happy hour is 6pm to 9pm.

LA LUCIOLE Map pp392-5
☎ 01 45 31 08 24; 51 rue Censier Daubenton, 5e; metro Censier; ☯ 11.30am-7pm Tue-Sun
What has to be one of the most tastefully decorated (and expensive) tearooms in Paris (€6 for tea and a piece of cake, *menus* €15 and €25), the 'F'Firefly' is nevertheless worth a visit for the rainbow-hued crockery on the table and the artwork on the walls. Brunch (€25) is served from 11.30am to 3pm Sunday.

LE CROCODILE Map pp392-5
☎ 01 43 54 32 37; 6 rue Royer Collard, 5e; metro Luxembourg; ☯ 10.30pm-6am Mon-Sat
This bar has been dispensing cocktails (more than 200 on the list) since 1966 – apparently the 1970s were '*épiques*' (epics) here – and continues on. It's one of the few places in Paris where you may experience a 'lock-in' (the bar staff locks the door on drinkers at closing, allowing the drinking to go on).

LE PIANO VACHE Map pp392-5
☎ 01 46 33 75 03; 8 rue Laplace, 5e; metro Maubert Mutualité; ☯ noon-2am Mon-Fri, 9pm-2am Sat & Sun
Just down the hill from the Panthéon, the 'Mean Piano' is a throwback to the 1970s, with some 1980s Goth just to keep on top of things. Very studenty and 'underground' as the films would have us understand the term. Great music (guest DJs) and a good crowd of *very* mixed ages. Happy hour is from opening to 9pm Monday to Friday.

LE RALLYE Map pp396-9
☎ 01 43 54 29 65; 11 Quai de la Tournelle, 5e; metro Maubert Mutualité; ☯ 7.30am-2am Mon-Fri, 9.30am-2am Sat & Sun
A 1950s-style Provençal café where the speciality is, as you'd expect, *pastis* (aniseed liquer). The Tintin-themed décor is not so easily explained. Most of the daytime customers come from the *quartier*, some in search of the cheap lunch *menu*, others to pick up their *boules* for a game of *pétanque* on the banks of the nearby river Quai. The evening crowd is young, lively and from all over the city.

LE SALON EGYPTIEN Map pp392-5
☎ 01 43 25 58 99; 77 rue du Cardinal Lemoine, 5e; metro Cardinal Lemoine; ☯ 11.30am-2am
People come here mainly to smoke hookahs (€4.60), which have become all the rage at Middle Eastern cafés in recent years, and you'll smell the intoxicating aromas of apricot,

honey, apple and strawberry as soon as you walk through the door. Settle into a large pouf and sip tea or the unusual *karkadet* (a hibiscus-derived beverage), or nibble on Middle Eastern pastries. For more intimacy, there are five small rooms adjoining the main lounge.

LE VIEUX CHÊNE Map pp392-5

☎ 01 43 37 71 51; 69 rue Mouffetard, 5e; metro Place Monge; ☺ 4pm-2am Sun-Thu, 4pm-5am Fri & Sat

The 'Old Oak', a rue Mouffetard institution popular with students, has a long history. A revolutionary circle met here in 1848, when most of Europe was in turmoil, and it was a popular *bal musette* (dancing club) in the late 19th and early 20th centuries. Some believe it's the oldest bar in the city. There's jazz on weekends, and happy hour is from opening to 9pm.

LE VIOLON DINGUE Map pp392-5

☎ 01 43 25 79 93; 46 rue de la Montagne Ste-Geneviève, 5e; metro Maubert Mutualité; ☺ 8pm-4.30am Tue-Sat

The 'Crazy Violin' (it's a pun on the expression *le violon d'Ingres*, meaning 'hobby' in French, as the celebrated painter Jean Auguste Dominique Ingres (see p28) used to fiddle in his spare time) is a loud, lively American-style bar that attracts lots of young English-speakers. During happy hour (8pm to 10pm) a pint of beer (usually €5.50 to €6) is €3 to €4 and most mixed drinks (usually €6 to €9) are half-price. Add about €1 to prices after 1.30am at the weekend. American and British sporting events on the large-screen TV lure in the punters and there's lots of flirting here – especially in the cellar bar, the Dingue Lounge.

L'ENVOL QUÉBÉCOIS Map pp392-5

☎ 01 45 35 53 93; 30 rue Lacépède, 5e; metro Jussieu; ☺ 4pm-2am

Should you be a *québécois(e)* (native of Quebec) in Paris in search of a chinwag in *joual* (French slang spoken in Quebec) or one who misses home, you couldn't do better than the 'Quebec Flight', which functions as both a pub and a kind of cultural centre.

MAISON DE LA VANILLE Map pp392-5

☎ 01 43 25 50 95; 8 rue du Cardinal Lemoine, 5e; metro Cardinal Lemoine; ☺ 11.30am-7pm Wed-Sat, 2.30-7pm Sun

This sweet-scented Creole café specialises in vanilla in all its guises and it all comes from the island of Réunion. Try the *thé à la mauricienne*

(Mauritian-style tea with milk and cardamom) and the sumptuous *gâteau à la patate douce* (sweet potato cake). On a gloomy winter's day, the décor – coconut palms, fans and primary colours – is certain to lift your spirits.

ST-GERMAIN, ODÉON & LUXEMBOURG

CAFÉ DE FLORE Map pp396-9

☎ 01 45 48 55 26; 172 blvd St-Germain, 6e; metro St-Germain des Prés; ☺ 7.30-1.30am

This Art Deco café, where the red, upholstered benches, mirrors and marble walls haven't changed since the days when Sartre, de Beauvoir, Camus and Picasso bent their elbows and wagged their chins here, is slightly less touristy than the **Deux Magots** (opposite). Expect a mixed bag of lunching ladies, business-people and foreigners in search of the past. The terrace is a popular place to sip beer (€7.50 for 400mL), the house Pouilly Fumé (€7.50 a glass or €29 a bottle) or coffee (€4).

CAFÉ DE LA MAIRIE Map pp396-9

☎ 01 43 26 67 82; 8 place St-Sulpice, 6e; metro St-Sulpice; ☺ 7am-2am Mon-Sat

The 'Town Hall Café' is a bustling and laid-back place on two floors frequented by students, writers and, since the late 1980s, film producers attracted by its tattered Left Bank ambience. A beer costs €2.10 at the counter and €3.60 if you manage to sit down. The terrace is a fine place to while away half an afternoon in fine weather.

COOLÍN Map pp396-9

☎ 01 44 07 00 92; 15 rue Clément, 6e; metro Mabillon; ☺ 10.30am-2am Mon-Sat, 1pm-2am Sun

This rather upscale Irish pub (actually more like a French café) in a renovated covered market is a friendly refuge from what can be a some-what unwelcoming *quartier*. There's live music from 5.30pm to 8.30pm on Sunday (and from 9pm on Tuesday from September to June). Happy hour is from 5pm to 8pm. The place really fills up when there's a football match on the giant screen.

LA PALETTE Map pp396-9

☎ 01 43 26 68 15; 43 rue de Seine, 6e; metro Mabillon; ☺ 8am-2am Mon-Sat

This *fin-de-siècle* café and erstwhile stomping ground of Cézanne and Braque attracts art dealers and collectors from nearby galleries, as well as fashion people. At around €8 a cocktail and €4 for a *pression* (draught beer), this is an expensive place for any serious drinking. There have been reports that the service (and the welcome) can be, well, uneven.

LE 10 Map pp396-9
☎ 01 43 26 66 83; 10 rue de l'Odéon, 6e; metro Odéon; ⏱ 5.30pm-2am

The '10', an institution with both local and foreign university students and au pairs, is a cellar pub with smoke-darkened posters on the walls and an eclectic selection on the jukebox with everything from jazz and the Doors to Yves Montand. Sangria, the house speciality, is always at the ready. It's the ideal spot for plotting the next revolution or conquering a lonely heart. Happy hour is from 6pm to 9pm.

LE COMPTOIR DES CANNETTES
Map pp396-9
☎ 01 43 26 79 15; 11 rue des Canettes, 6e; metro Mabillon; ⏱ noon-2am Tue-Sat, closed Aug

The 'Bottle Counter', is better known as Chez Georges. Upstairs is a friendly wine bar straight out of Orwell's *Down and Out in Paris and London*. In the cellar (open from 10pm) is a fusty, studenty pub with photos of musicians who played here in the 1960s and 1970s. Bottled beer starts at about €3.50 (€4 after 10pm).

LES DEUX MAGOTS Map pp396-9
☎ 01 45 48 55 25; 170 blvd St-Germain, 6e; metro St-Germain des Prés; ⏱ 7am-1am

This erstwhile literary haunt, with a name derived not from a couple of white worms, but from the two *magots* (grotesque figurines) of Chinese dignitaries at the entrance, dates from 1914. It is best known as the favoured hangout of Sartre, Hemingway, Picasso and Breton. It may be a touristy thing to do but everyone has to sit on the terrace of the Deux Magots at least once and have a coffee (€4), beer (€5.50) or the famous shop-made hot chocolate served in porcelain jugs (€6).

L'URGENCE BAR Map pp396-9
☎ 01 43 26 45 69; 45 rue Monsieur le Prince, 6e; metro Luxembourg; ⏱ 9pm-2am Mon-Sat

The 'Emergency Room Bar', just south of the École de Médecine, takes the ER theme and runs with it; hospital phobics should stay away. It is all in good fun, but the service can be a bit slow. Try to have some, er, patience. Cocktails are around €9.

MOOSEHEAD BAR Map pp396-9
☎ 01 46 33 77 00; 16 rue des Quatre Vents, 6e; metro Odéon; ⏱ 4pm-2am Mon-Fri, 11am-2am Sat & Sun

This friendly pub that is forever Canada was established in 1999 and has become a mecca for homesick Canucks. Pints are from €5.50, cocktails €7; happy hour is from 4pm to 9pm.

MONTPARNASSE
CUBANA CAFÉ Map pp389-91
☎ 01 40 46 80 81; 47 rue Vavin, 6e; metro Vavin; ⏱ 11am-3am Sun-Wed, 11am-5am Thu-Sat

The 'Cuban Café' is the perfect place for a couple of 'starter' drinks before carrying on to the nearby La Coupole (p183), with Cuban cocktails (€7.30) reduced to €5.30 at happy hour (5pm to 7.30pm). Tapas are €1.60 to €7.40 and Sunday Cuban brunch (available noon to 5pm) costs €18.50. For those who indulge in cigars, there's a *salon fumoir* (smoking lounge) equipped with comfy old leather armchairs and oil paintings of daily life in Cuba decorating the walls.

LA CLOSERIE DES LILAS Map pp392-5
☎ 01 40 51 34 50; 171 blvd du Montparnasse, 6e; metro Port Royal; ⏱ noon-2am

As anyone who has read Hemingway will know, what is now the American Bar at the 'Lilac Enclosure' is where Papa did a lot of writing, drinking and eating of oysters (€11.40 to €20.40 a half-dozen). Brass plaques tell you exactly where he and other luminaries such as Picasso, Apollinaire, Man Ray, Sartre and Beckett whiled away the hours. In fact the place touts itself as 'the oldest literary café in Paris'; have a look at some of the testimonials of the rich and famous reprinted on the placemats. The décor is warm and romantic and the terrace is superb in the warmer months. Starters cost €6.50 to €15.50, mains €15.50 to €25 and there's a *menu* for €43 in the adjoining brasserie-restaurant.

LE ROSEBUD Map pp389-91
☎ 01 43 35 38 54; 11 bis rue Delambre, 14e; metro Edgar Quinet or Vavin; ⏱ 7pm-2am

Like the sleigh of that name in Citizen Kane, the Rosebud harkens back to the past. In this case it's the Montparnos (painters and writers who frequented Montparnasse during the neighbourhood's golden years of the early 20th century). The setting is quiet and elegant with polished wood and aged leather upholstery, and the staff are highly cultivated mixologists. Try a champagne cocktail or whisky sour.

Entertainment – Drinking

LE SELECT Map pp389-91

☎ 01 42 22 65 27; 99 blvd du Montparnasse, 6e; metro Vavin; 🕐 7.30-2.30am

Along with **La Coupole** (p183) and **Le Dôme** (p184) this café is a great Montparnasse institution. It has changed very little since it opened in 1923. It's a favourite student hangout early in the evening; regulars tend to take over as the night wears on. *Tartines* made with Poilâne bread (a famous bakery, see p261) are a speciality here (€5 to €15), but you can also have full meals (starters €9.50 to €17, mains €15.50 to €18.50, plat du jour €14.50). Food is served from noon to 1am.

FAUBOURG ST-GERMAIN & INVALIDES

CAFÉ DU MUSÉE RODIN Map pp389-91

☎ 01 44 18 61 10; 77 rue de Varenne, 7e; metro Varenne; 🕐 9.30am-6.45pm Tue-Sun Apr-Sep, 9.30am-4.45pm Tue-Sun Oct-Mar

A serene beauty pervades the garden of the **Musée Rodin** (p111) with the great master's sculptures popping up from among the roses and lime trees that line the pathways. If the weather is fine, you can have a drink and a snack at one of the tables hidden behind the trees (entry to garden €1).

CAFÉ THOUMIEUX Map pp389-91

☎ 01 45 51 50 40; 4 rue de la Comète, 7e; metro La Tour Maubourg; 🕐 noon-2am Mon-Fri, 5pm-2am Sat

This café and tapas bar attached to the **Thoumieux brasserie** (p186) is just a hop, skip and a jump from Invalides and the bustle of shops on rue St-Dominique. As a result its single, long room is always full of well-heeled young people who seem to enjoy the Iberian ambience. Tapas (€7 to €13) go perfectly with San Miguel beer (€4) or a flavoured vodka, with no fewer than 40 different types (including chocolate and watermelon) on offer.

CONCORDE & MADELEINE

BUDDHA BAR Map pp383-5

☎ 01 53 05 90 00; 8 rue Boissy d'Anglas, 8e; metro Concorde; 🕐 noon-2am Mon-Fri, 6pm-midnight Sat & Sun

The Buddha Bar is an ultra-hip bar-restaurant just up from the start of the av des Champs-Élysées, an area once considered *très démodé* (very out of fashion), but now enjoying a new lease of life since its renovation in the mid-1990s. A large Buddha still lords over all

here but the clientele is increasingly suits and people who have the bar's CDs. With all the security, it's a chore to actually enter and get to a table or the bar. Go at least once for a look – even if you don't have one of the CDs. Cocktails go for €12 to €14. If you plan to eat starters are €11 to €29, mains €18 to €35, while lunch and dinner *menus* are €32 and €60.

CRICKETER PUB Map pp383-5

☎ 01 40 07 01 45; 41 rue des Mathurins, 8e; metro St-Augustin or Madeleine; 🕐 11am-2am Mon-Fri, 4pm-2am Sat & Sun

This almost genuine English pub (that was supposedly transported to Paris lock, stock and barrel from Ipswich) is a last refuge for homesick Brits, with Newcastle Brown and Strongbow on tap (€4 to €5 a *demi*). Have chips with salt and vinegar, pick up the *Sun* and throw a few darts – you've crossed the Channel without even realising it. Quiz night is Tuesday at 9pm.

HEMINGWAY BAR Map pp383-5

☎ 01 43 16 30 30; Hôtel Ritz Paris, 15 place Vendôme, 1er; metro Madeleine; 🕐 6.30pm-2am Tue-Sat

This bar, in one of the world's most celebrated and expensive hotels, is a paean to Papa and it's where he imbibed once he made a name for himself. The legend lives on that during the liberation of Paris, Hemingway was personally put in charge of the bar – complete with jeep and machinegun. Fabulous décor, excellent drinks and cocktails (from €20), and expert bar staff.

CLICHY & GARE ST-LAZARE

AU 24 Map pp383-5

☎ 01 42 94 29 65; 24 rue Biot, 17e; metro Place de Clichy; 🕐 11am-3pm & 7pm-2am Tue-Fri, 7pm-2am Sat & Sun

Four small coffee tables and a few bench seats along the wall – that's all there is to the 'At the 24'. But the hostess warmly invites customers to take a seat, have a chat, and order something to drink (a punch, maybe, €5) or nibble (plat du jour with entrée or dessert €9). There's *vin de pays* ('country wine') from a particular named village or region), beer, punch and *charcuterie*, cheese and soup (which changes daily) on offer.

LE WEPLER Map pp383-5

☎ 01 45 22 53 24; 14 place de Clichy, 18e; metro Place de Clichy; 🕐 noon-1am

Though this large café-brasserie founded in 1892 is known for its oysters and other seafood, the Wepler's greatest appeal is sitting with a drink on the large covered terrace, enjoying the hubbub and scenery of place de Clichy.

LUSH BAR Map pp383-5

☎ 01 43 87 49 46; 16 rue des Dames, 17e; metro Place de Clichy; ☺ 10am-2am Mon-Fri, noon-2am Sat & Sun
This stylish new bar next to the equally stylish **Hôtel Eldorado** (p298) is already famous for its cocktails, particularly white Russians. Get here at happy hour (4pm to 7pm Monday to Friday, 8pm to 10pm Saturday) when cocktails (usually €6.50 to €8) are only €5.

OPÉRA & GRANDS BOULEVARDS

BUSHWACKER'S Map pp383-5

☎ 01 44 94 95 64; 10 rue de Caumartin, 9e; metro Havre-Caumartin or Opéra; ☺ noon-2am
Despite the casual name, this is a very upscale Australian-themed bar in the financial district. Stuffed wallabies, didgeridoos and flat screen TVs predominate, and the circular bar – with a wide range of Australian and English beers – is good for encouraging interaction with other customers.

CAFÉ NOIR Map pp386-8

☎ 01 40 39 07 36; 65 rue Montmartre, 2e; metro Sentier; ☺ 8am-2am Mon-Fri, 3pm-2am Sat
Right on the edge of the Sentier garment district, the 'Black Café' may be a bit off the beaten track but it's a great draw for both Anglophone and French imbibers, attracted by the friendly and very hip ambience, well into the night. Wouldn't it be great if all locals were like this one!

HARRY'S NEW YORK BAR Map pp383-5

☎ 01 42 61 71 14; 5 rue Daunou, 2e; metro Opéra; ☺ 10.30am-4am
One of the most popular American-style bars in the prewar years, when there were several dozen in Paris, Harry's once welcomed such habitués as writers F Scott Fitzgerald and Ernest Hemingway. They no doubt sampled the bar's unique cocktail creation: the Bloody Mary (€9.60). The Cuban mahogany interior dates from the mid-19th century and was brought over from a Manhattan bar in 1911. Beer costs €5.40 and cocktails (270 to choose from) in the basement piano bar cost €10.10. If sustenance (€8 to €11) is required, try a club sandwich. Apparently it's the best one in Paris.

LA CHAMPMESLÉ Map pp386-8

☎ 01 42 96 85 20; 4 rue Chabanais, 2e; metro Pyramides; ☺ 2pm-2am Mon-Thu, 2pm-dawn Fri & Sat
This is the oldest lesbian bar in the city, established in 1979 when gay life was all but underground in Paris. This intimate and friendly bar plays mellow music, has art on the walls and schedules regular theme nights, including a cabaret of French *chansons* (songs) at 10pm on Thursday and sometimes Saturday. Beer or fruit juice from €6.

O'SULLIVAN'S Map pp386-8

☎ 01 40 26 73 41; 1 blvd Montmartre, 2e; metro Grands Boulevards; ☺ noon-2am Sun-Tue, noon-5am Wed-Fri, 1pm-5am Sat
The bars and cafés on or just off the seemingly interminable Grands Boulevards are some of the best venues for a night on the town if you don't feel like crossing the Seine. And while this place may look like just another supermarket-chain Irish pub, its prominent location makes it one of the most popular (and packed) bars around. If you're searching for a bit of tranquillity, avoid the bar and the lager louts on the ground floor and head upstairs. O'Sullivan's has good live music at the weekend.

GARE DU NORD, GARE DE L'EST & RÉPUBLIQUE

CENTRE CULTUREL POUYA Map pp386-8

☎ 01 42 08 38 47; 48 bis quai de Jemmapes, 10e; metro République; ☺ 10am-2am
Persian musical instruments, carpets, benches and low tables adorn this little tearoom on the banks of the Canal St-Martin. You can sip Kurdish cardamom tea (€2.50) or nibble on some pastries (€2), but that's about it for Iranian specialties. Tequila and whisky, however, are also available.

CHEZ PRUNE Map pp386-8

☎ 01 42 41 30 47; 71 quai de Valmy, 10e; metro République; ☺ 8am-2am Mon-Sat, 10am-2am Sun
This Soho-boho café is the venue that put the Canal St-Martin on the map. Most people come here for the vibe and *mojitos,* though there are decent dishes (€9 to €11.50) available at lunch, and snacks throughout the evening.

CHEZ WOLF MOTOWN BAR

Map pp386-8

☎ 01 46 07 09 79; 81-83 blvd de Strasbourg, 10e; metro Gare de l'Est; 🕙 24hr except 6am-7pm Sat

This little find is the place to come in the lonely wee hours when you've got a thirst and a few bob but, alas, no friends. You can drink at any time of day but food (soups and salads €5.50 to €9.50, mains €8.50 to €13.50) is *only* available from 11am to 5pm. Both the staff and the patrons are exceptionally friendly here. The place almost feels like a club.

L'APOSTROPHE Map pp386-8

☎ 01 42 08 26 07; 23 rue de la Grange aux Belles, 10e; metro Colonel Fabien; 🕙 7.30am-2am Mon-Fri, 4.30pm-2am Sat & Sun

It's hard not to like this local institution, a *bar musicale* (bar with music) with unbeatable prices and large picture windows that let you soak up the first rays of the sun should you still be out on a crawl at that time. Just a stone's throw from the Canal St-Martin, it still feels a million miles away from that trendy scene.

LE RELAIS DU NORD Map pp386-8

☎ 01 48 78 03 51; 22 rue de Dunkerque, 10e; metro Gare du Nord; 🕙 6am-9pm

This gem of an Art Nouveau café is a short distance to the west of the Gare du Nord and an excellent, down-to-earth choice if you're in the mood to celebrate your departure or arrival with a drink or a light meal.

LE VERRE VOLÉ Map pp386-8

☎ 01 48 03 17 34; 67 rue de Lancry, 10e; metro Jacques Bonsergent; 🕙 10.30am-11pm Tue-Sat, 11am-8pm Sun

The tiny 'Stolen Glass' – a wine shop with a couple of tables – is just about the most perfect wine bar in Paris, with excellent wines from southeastern France (€18 to €54 a bottle) and expert advice. Unpretentious and hearty *plats du jour* average €11.

MÉNILMONTANT & BELLEVILLE

AU PETIT GARAGE Map pp386-8

☎ 01 48 07 08 12; 63 rue Jean-Pierre Timbaud, 11e; metro Parmentier; 🕙 10am-2am

You don't know the meaning of 'grunge' and 'distressed' until you walk into 'At the Little Garage', a former butchers that may just have some dried blood still decorating the walls. As its name would imply, this is part of the Parisian garage scene, which means punks who shower and comb their hair.

BOTECO Map pp386-8

☎ 01 43 57 15 47; 131 rue Oberkampf, 11e; metro Parmentier; 🕙 9am-2am

This jewel of a Brazilian bar is the watering hole of choice along rue Oberkampf. Super *cäpirinhas*, cocktails made from Brazilian *cachaça* (a sugarcane-based alcohol), lime juice, sugarcane syrup and ice, are a reasonable €5.50, and the music will get you up every time. If peckish, there are Brazilian platters (€7.50 to €13).

CAFÉ CHARBON Map pp386-8

☎ 01 43 57 55 13; 109 rue Oberkampf, 11e; metro Parmentier; 🕙 9am-2am Sun-Thu, 9am-4am Fri & Sat

With its antique-cum-postmodern ambience, the 'Coal Café' was the first of the hip cafés and bars to catch on in Ménilmontant and it still pulls in the punters with house punch (€6) and decent food (starters €6 to €7, mains €9.50 to €12). Brunch (€12) is served from noon to 5pm on Saturday and Sunday.

CANNIBALE CAFÉ Map pp386-8

☎ 01 49 29 95 59; 93 rue Jean-Pierre Timbaud, 11e; metro Couronnes; 🕙 8.30am-2am

'Cannibal Café' couldn't be more welcoming, with its grand rococo-style bar topped with worn zinc, wood panelling, Formica tables and red leatherette bench seats. It's a laid-back, almost frayed alternative to the groovy pubs and bars of rue Oberkampf, and the perfect place to linger over a coffee (€2) or grab a quick beer (€2 a *demi* or €6.50 a pint). If you get hungry, keep your eye off your neighbour's thigh and order from the extensive menu (€6 to €14). Breakfast is €7 and brunch (served between noon and 4pm at the weekend) is €16.50.

L'ARAM Map pp392-5

☎ 01 48 05 57 79; 7 rue de la Folie Méricourt, 11e; metro St-Ambroise; 🕙 noon-2am Mon-Sat, 4pm-midnight Sun

Just a few streets away from the *branché* (trendy) bars of Oberkampf, this *café-bar théâtre* is definitely not one of those places where drinking is the main event. Plenty of other things happen here too – exhibitions, theatre performances, community TV broadcasts and clairvoyant readings, which are all the rage in Paris at the moment. There is usually an 'events night' on Thursday at around 9pm.

Even without all the entertainment, l'Aram is worth discovering for its friendly service and somewhat kitsch décor.

L'AUTRE CAFÉ Map pp386-8
☎ 01 40 21 03 07; 62 rue Jean-Pierre Timbaud, 11e; metro Parmentier; 🕐 8am-1.30am Mon-Fri, 11.30am-1.30am Sat & Sun,

The 'Other Café' helped move some of the after-dark action north from rue Oberkampf to rue Jean-Pierre Timbaud. It attracts a young mixed crowd of locals, artists and party-goers with its long bar, huge open space, relaxed environment and reasonable prices (*plats du jour* €9 to €12). A springboard for young artists, the Autre Café organises exhibition openings and film screenings. There are also philosophical afternoon teas for children. A small lounge upstairs is available and it's a great place to do a little work; you can plug in your laptop anywhere around the room.

LE MÉCANO BAR Map pp386-8
☎ 01 40 21 35 28; 99 rue Oberkampf, 11e; metro Parmentier; 🕐 9pm-2am

Housed in a former mechanics' workshop established in 1832, this hip café-bar is a good place to meet before heading elsewhere along rue Oberkampf. There are DJs from 8pm Thursday to Saturday and occasional themed nights. Starters are €4 to €13, mains €10 to €15.

LE PRAVDA Map pp386-8
☎ 01 48 06 19 76; 49 rue Jean-Pierre Timbaud, 11e; metro Parmentier; 🕐 5pm-2am Mon-Sat, noon-4pm Sun

Retro Russian bars like le Pravda were alright in their time and place but are now just a wee bit, well, passé? Still, it's an excuse to down vodka shots (€3.30 to €4.30) flavoured with honey, chilli and herbs and tuck into a Ruso-Med brunch (€15) on Sunday.

LES ABATS-JOUR À COUDRE
Map pp386-8
☎ 06 16 24 08 54; 115 rue Oberkampf, 11e; metro Ménilmontant; 🕐 5pm-2am

South of place de la République, rue Oberkampf and its eastern extension, rue Ménilmontant, have some of the most interesting and unusual cafés and bars. A good example is this lively, down-to-earth pub with sewing machine tables to match its bizarre name – 'Lampshades to Sew'. Happy hour is 4pm to 9pm and there's live music at the weekend.

POP IN Map pp392-5
☎ 01 48 05 56 11; 105 rue Amelot, 11e; metro St-Sébastien Froissart; 🕐 6.30pm-1.30am Tue-Sun

This rather cool space in limbo land has excellent cocktails (€5.50) and a downstairs club with DJ that attracts a fun crowd.

GARE DE LYON, NATION & BERCY

BAR À VINS NICOLAS
Map p401
☎ 01 43 40 12 11; 24 cour St-Émilion, 12e; metro Cour St-Émilion; 🕐 noon-11.30pm

Run by the giant Nicolas wine retailer, this little wine bar has lower-shelf wines for €2 to €3.50 a glass; the vintage stuff costs €4 to €8. Salads, cheese platters and other edibles are €7 to €12. In fine weather, do anything to bag a seat on the back terrace.

BISTROT À VIN JACQUES MÉLAC
Map pp392-5
☎ 01 43 70 59 27; 42 rue Léon Frot, 11e; metro Charonne; 🕐 9am-midnight Tue-Sat

The eponymous owner of this wine bar and former vintner, Jacques Mélac takes his wine very seriously, offering a wide choice by the glass (€2.90 to €4) or bottle (€14 to €36). Light meals (omelettes, salads, *plats du jour*) are available at lunch and dinner.

CHAI 33 Map p401
☎ 01 53 44 01 01; 33 cour St-Émilion, 12e; metro Cour St-Émilion; hnoon-2am

The converted wine warehouses in Bercy Village house a variety of restaurants and bars, including this enormous new wine-oriented concept space with a restaurant, lounge, tasting room and shop. Wine (both French and foreign) is divided into six categories and colour-coded: red is 'fruity and intense', green is 'light and spirited' etc. We never thought we'd see this happen in Paris but, all in all, it seems to work well. There are cocktails (€8) and decent food here too.

FROG AT BERCY VILLAGE
Map p401
☎ 01 43 40 70 71; 25 cour St-Émilion, 12e; metro Cour St-Émilion; 🕐 noon-2am

Just about the largest English-style pub in Paris, the Frog at Bercy Village (as the name suggests there are other branches – three more in Paris and two more elsewhere in France) has a range of British beers, and brews five of its own lagers on site. Pints are €6 or €4.50 at happy hour (6pm to 8pm Monday to Friday). There's a lunch *menu* for €12; if ordering à la carte count on spending about €25.

LA FLÈCHE D'OR CAFÉ
Map pp380-2
☎ 01 43 72 04 23; 102 bis rue de Bagnolet, 20e; metro Alexandre Dumas; ☼ 6pm-2am Tue-Fri, 11am-2am Sat, noon-2am Sun

Just over 1km northeast of place de la Nation, the 'Golden Arrow' is a smoky music bar in a former railway station on the outer edge of central Paris. It attracts a young arty and alternative crowd; this could very well be Berlin. The big café serves food (lunch and dinner *menus* €11 and €17) till 1.30am and does a decent brunch (€13) noon to 4pm on Sunday. There's music (usually live) daily at 9pm. With a solid reputation for promoting young talent, the Flèche d'Or has become a hip place for Parisians to start a night on the town.

LES FUNAMBULES
Map pp392-5
☎ 01 43 70 83 70; 12 rue Faidherbe, 11e; metro Faidherbe Chaligny; ☼ 7.30am-2am Mon-Sat, 10am-8.30pm Sun

Like so many small cafés in east Paris, the 'Tightrope Walkers' has been transformed into a fashionable bar. While the original architecture provides character, nowadays the terrace is crammed with beautiful people on warm summer evenings. The rest of the year customers take shelter inside under the stunning coffered ceiling and enjoy a cocktail at the bar or a snack in the back room.

13E ARRONDISSEMENT & CHINATOWN

LE MERLE MOQUEUR Map pp380-2
☎ 01 45 65 12 43; 11 rue de la Butte aux Cailles, 13e; metro Corvisart; ☼ 5pm-2am

The pimple of a hill called the Butte aux Cailles southwest of place d'Italie is great for a night out. Boasting the largest selection of rum punches we've ever seen (€5), the 'Mocking Bird' is the perfect place for an aperitif before crossing the street for a meal at **Le Temps des Cérises** (p200) or up the road at the **L'Avant-Goût** (p200). Happy hour is from 5pm to 8pm.

MONTMARTRE & PIGALLE

CORCORAN'S CLICHY Map p400
☎ 01 42 23 00 30; 110 blvd de Clichy, 18e; metro Blanche; ☼ 11.30am-5am

OK, so it's just another Irish pub. But with the entrance to the Cimetière de Montmartre just paces away, Corcoran's is a great place to stop off on your way to or from paying obeisance to Zola or Stendhal. And it feels right somehow, just at the start of a quiet cul-de-sac.

EDWARD & SON Map p400
☎ 01 44 92 90 91; 10 blvd de Clichy, 18e; metro Pigalle; ☼ 4pm-2am Mon-Thu, noon-2am Fri & Sat

About as Éireannach as good food and the colour orange, this place in the style of an old Irish pub has a decent happy hour: 4pm to 8pm for beers and 7pm to 9pm for cocktails.

JUNGLE MONTMARTRE Map p400
☎ 01 46 06 75 69; 32 rue Gabrielle, 18e; metro Abbesses; ☼ 11am-2am

A corner of West Africa on an outcrop of the Butte Montmartre. We'd walk a million miles for the ginger punch (€3), which soon gets you chatting and boogieing. The atmosphere is hyper-festive thanks to nonstop DJ mixes and a *kora* (West African stringed instrument) player nearly every night. West African dishes such as chicken *yassa* (onion and lemon-based sauce) and beef *mafé* (peanut-based stew; €11.50) are available to 1am.

LA FOURMI Map p400
☎ 01 42 64 70 35; 74 rue des Martyrs, 18e; metro Pigalle; ☼ 8am-2am Mon-Thu, 10am-4am Fri-Sun

A trendy Pigalle hang-out, the 'Ant' marches all day and night, and is a convenient place to meet before heading off to the clubs. People flock here for the ultra-hip décor – zinc, patina, mirrors and, above all, a superb 'hedgehog' centre light – as well as the atmosphere, music and unbridled conversation. Fleeting and fashionable perhaps, but lively and friendly too. If you're hungry the *plat du jour* costs €8.50.

LE CHÀO BÀ Map p400
☎ 01 46 06 72 90; 22 blvd de Clichy, 18e; metro Pigalle; ☼ 8.30am-2am Sun-Thu, 9am-4am Fri & Sat

This café-restaurant, transformed from the old-style Café Pigalle, is straight out of the film *Indochine*. It serves great cocktails (from €8.50) in goldfish-bowl-sized glasses, and somewhat bland Franco-Vietnamese food (starters €6 to

€10, rice and noodle dishes €9.50 to €10, mains €11.50 to €19.50). And don't hesitate to ask what *chào bà* means.

LE DÉPANNEUR Map p400
☎ 01 40 16 40 20; 27 rue Fontaine, 9e; metro Blanche; 🕐 24hrs

The 'Repairman', an American diner with post-modern frills, is open round the clock and has plenty of tequila and fancy cocktails (from €6). Beer costs €4.50 to €5.50. Lunch and dinner *menus* cost €11 and €15 and the *plat du jour* is €9. There are DJs after 11pm from Thursday to Saturday.

LE SANCERRE Map p400
☎ 01 42 58 08 20; 35 rue des Abbesses, 18e; metro Abbesses; 🕐 7am-2am Sun-Thu, 7am-4am Fri & Sat

Le Sancerre is a popular, rather brash bistro-cum-bar that's often crowded to capacity in the evening, especially on Saturday. It may look somewhat scruffy, but the place is hip and the service always tops. Beer starts at €3.20 and cocktails are €8 to €10. Food includes breakfast (€7.50 to €10) and two *plats du jour* (€10 to €12) served from 11.30am to 11.30pm.

OLYMPIC CAFÉ Map pp386-8
☎ 01 42 52 29 93; 20 rue Léon, 18e; metro Château Rouge; 🕐 7pm-2am Mon-Sat

This community bar in the Goutte d'Or neigh-bourhood is full of surprises. From plays and film screenings to concerts of Afro punk, Bal-kan folk, hip-hop, klezmer and so on in the basement, this is a breeding ground for crea-tive, young people bursting with original ideas. Events are €5 to €7 and drinks are in the €3 range. The monthly program available at the bar also includes events at the **Lavoir Moderne Parisien** (Map pp386-8; ☎ 01 42 52 09 14; 35 rue Léon, 18e), another springboard for young talent just down the road.

MUSIC
ROCK, POP & INDIE

There's rock, pop and indie music at bars, cafés and clubs around Paris, and a number of venues regularly host acts by interna-tional performers. It's often easier to see big-name Anglophone acts in Paris than in their home countries. The most popular stadiums and other big venues for interna-tional acts are the **Palais Omnisports de Paris-Bercy**

(Map p401; ☎ 08 25 03 00 31, 01 46 91 57 57; www.bercy.fr in French; 8 blvd de Bercy, 12e; metro Bercy) in Bercy; the **Stade de France** (☎ 08 92 70 09 00, 01 55 93 00 00; www.stadedefrance.fr; rue Francis de Pressensé, ZAC du Cornillon Nord, 93216 St-Denis La Plaine; metro St-Denis-Porte de Paris) in St-Denis; and **Le Zénith** (Map pp380-2; ☎ 01 42 08 60 00; www.le-zenith.com in French; 211 av Jean Jaurès, 19e; metro Porte de Pantin) at the Cité de la Musique in Parc de la Villette, 19e.

CAFÉ DE LA DANSE Map pp392-5
☎ 01 47 00 57 59; www.cafedeladanse.com in French; 5 passage Louis-Philippe, 11e; metro Bastille; admission €10-20; 🕐 box office noon-6pm Mon-Fri

Located just a few metres down a small pas-sage from 23 rue de Lappe, the 'Dance Café' is a large auditorium with 300 to 500 seats. Almost every day between 7.30pm and 9pm, it plays host to rock and world music concerts, dance performances, musical theatre and poetry readings.

LA CIGALE Map p400
☎ 01 49 25 89 99; 120 blvd de Rochechouart, 18e; metro Anvers or Pigalle; admission €22-45; 🕐 box office noon-7pm Mon-Fri

The 'Cicada' is an enormous old music hall seating up to 2000 people and hosting inter-national rock, jazz and folk groups, and dance and variety performances. There's seating in the balcony and dancing up front when the crowd begins to groove.

LE BATACLAN Map pp392-5
☎ 01 43 14 35 35; www.bataclan.fr in French; 50 blvd Voltaire, 11e; metro Oberkampf or St-Ambroise; admission €15-50; 🕐 box office 11am-7pm Mon-Sat

Built in 1864 and Maurice Chevalier's debut venue in 1910, this small concert hall draws some French and international acts. It also masquerades as a theatre and dance hall. Le Bataclan usually opens from 8pm for concerts. Attached is the wonderful **Bataclan Café** (☎ 01 49 23 96 33; 🕐 7am-2am).

L'ÉLYSÉE-MONTMARTRE Map p400
☎ 01 44 92 45 36, 01 55 07 16 00; www.elyseemont martre.com; 72 blvd de Rochechouart, 18e; metro Anvers; admission €10-34

A huge old music hall with a great sound sys-tem, L'Élysée-Montmartre is one of the bet-ter venues in Paris for one-off rock and indie concerts. It opens at 7.30pm for concerts. It becomes a popular club on Friday and Saturday from midnight to 6am; the bimonthly Saturday Le Bal attracts an eclectic crowd with its live bands.

L'OLYMPIA Map pp383-5
☎ 08 92 68 33 68; 28 blvd des Capucines, 9e; metro Opéra; admission €20-50; ☉ box office noon-7pm Mon-Fri

The Olympia has hosted all the big names – both French and international – over the years and remains a great venue for manageable-size concerts.

CLASSICAL

Paris plays host to dozens of orchestral, organ and chamber-music concerts each week.

CHÂTELET-THÉÂTRE MUSICAL DE PARIS Map pp396-9
☎ 01 40 28 28 40; www.chatelet-theatre.com in French; 2 rue Édouard Colonne, 1er; metro Châtelet; concert tickets €9-60, opera €11-106, ballet €9-62; ☉ box office 11am-7pm, no performances Jul-Aug

The central Théâtre du Châtelet hosts concerts (including ones by the Orchestre de Paris) as well as operas, ballets and theatre performances. Classical music is also performed at 11am on Sunday (€20) and at 12.45pm on Monday, Wednesday and Friday (€9). Tickets go on sale 14 days before the performance date at the box office. Subject to availability, anyone under 26 or over 65 can get reduced-price tickets from 15 minutes before curtain time.

SALLE PLEYEL Map pp383-5
☎ 01 45 61 53 00; 252 rue du Faubourg St-Honoré, 8e; metro Ternes

This highly regarded hall dating from the 1920s hosts many of Paris' finest classical music concerts and recitals. It was closed in July 2002 for a three-year renovation.

THÉÂTRE DES CHAMPS-ÉLYSÉES Map pp383-5
☎ 01 49 52 50 50; www.theatrechampselysees.fr in French; 15 av Montaigne, 8e; metro Alma Marceau; tickets €5-120; ☉ box office 1-7pm Mon-Sat

This prestigious Right Bank orchestral and recital hall holds concerts throughout the year. It also serves as a theatre called the **Comédie des Champs-Élysées** (☎ 01 53 23 99 19; www.comedie deschampselysees.com).

THÉÂTRE MOGADOR Map pp383-5
☎ 01 53 32 32 00; 25 rue Mogador, 9e; metro St-Lazare

The Orchestre de Paris is playing at Théâtre Mogador while renovation of the Salle Pleyel is completed.

Église St-Eustache (p85)

Music with Spirit

Many of Paris' churches contain organs celebrated for their size and/or sound quality, so the churches are popular venues for classical music concerts and organ recitals. The concerts don't keep to any fixed schedule, but are advertised on posters around town. Admission fees can vary, but they usually range from €10 for children and students to €19 for adults.

Notre Dame Cathedral (Map pp396-9; ☎ 01 42 34 56 10; tickets €10-40) There's usually a free organ concert some time between 4.30pm and 5.15pm on Sunday, especially in winter.

Ste-Chapelle (Map pp396-9; ☎ 01 53 73 78 51; Île de la Cité, 1er) Also holds classical concerts from April to October. The cheapest seats cost around €17 (€12 for students under 26).

Église Royale du Val-de-Grâce (Map pp392-5; ☎ 01 42 01 47 67; 277bis rue St-Jacques, 5e; metro Port Royal; adult/child €18.30/12.20) Concerts are held in this exquisite church from November to June.

Other noted concert venues with similar admission fees:

American Church (Map pp389-91; ☎ 01 42 50 96 18; 65 quai d'Orsay, 7e; metro Pont de l'Alma)

Église de la Madeleine (Map pp383-5; ☎ 01 44 51 69 00; rue Royale, 8e; metro Madeleine)

Église St-Étienne du Mont (Map pp292-5; ☎ 01 43 54 11 79; 1 rue St-Etienne du Mont, 5e; metro Cardinal Lemoine)

Église St-Eustache (Map pp396-9; ☎ 01 42 36 31 05; 2 impasse St-Eustache, 1er; metro Les Halles)

Église St-Germain des Prés (Map pp396-9; ☎ 01 43 25 41 71; 3 place St-Germain des Prés, 6e; metro St-Germain des Prés)

Église St-Julien le Pauvre (Map pp396-9; ☎ 01 42 26 00 00; 1 rue St-Julien le Pauvre, 5e; metro St-Michel)

Église St-Paul-St-Louis (Map pp396-9; ☎ 01 42 72 30 32; 7 passage St-Paul, 4e; metro St-Paul)

Oratoire du Louvre (Map pp396-9; ☎ 01 43 26 36 18; 145 rue St-Honoré, 1er; metro Louvre-Rivoli)

JAZZ & BLUES

After WWII, Paris was Europe's most important jazz centre and, though the style commands just a niche following today, the city's better clubs and cellars attract top international stars. The **Banlieues Bleues** (Suburban Blues; ☎ 01 49 22 10 10; www .banlieuesbleues.org), a jazz festival held in St-Denis and other Paris suburbs in March and early April, attracts big-name talent.

CAFÉ UNIVERSEL Map pp392-5

☎ 01 43 25 74 20; 267 rue St-Jacques, 5e; metro Port Royal; admission free; 🕓 9.30pm-2am Mon-Sat

The 'Universal Café' attracts a mix of students and jazz lovers with its live music, with everything from bebop and Latin sounds to vocal jazz sessions.

LE BAISER SALÉ Map pp396-9

☎ 01 42 33 37 71; 58 rue des Lombards, 1er; metro Châtelet; admission free-€22; 🕓 7pm-late

The 'Salty Kiss' is one of several jazz clubs on the same street. The *salle de jazz* (jazz room) on the 1st floor has concerts of pop rock and chansons at 7pm and Afro-jazz and jazz fusion

at 10pm. The cover charge depends on the act; it's free during the *soirée bœuf* (jam session) on Monday night. The bar on the ground floor opens from 6pm to 6am.

LE CAVEAU DE LA HUCHETTE

Map pp396-9

☎ 01 43 26 65 05; 5 rue de la Huchette, 5e; metro St-Michel; adult €10.50 Sun-Thu, €13 Fri & Sat, student €9; 🕓 9pm-2.30am Sun-Thu, 9pm-3.30am Fri, 9pm-4am Sat

Housed in a medieval *caveau* (cellar) that was used as a courtroom and torture chamber during the Revolution, this club is where virtually all the jazz greats have played since the end of WWII. It's touristy, but the atmosphere can be more electric than at the more serious jazz clubs. Sessions start at 9.30pm.

LE DUC DES LOMBARDS Map pp396-9

☎ 01 42 33 22 88; www.jazzvalley.com/duc; 42 rue des Lombards, 1er; metro Châtelet; admission €12-20; 🕓 9pm-4am

A cool venue decorated with posters of jazz greats (including the eponymous Duke), this place attracts a far more relaxed (and less reverent) crowd than the other jazz clubs in the same street. The ground-floor bar vibrates from 9pm, when sets start, to 4am nightly.

LE PETIT JOURNAL ST-MICHEL
Map pp392-5

☎ 01 43 26 28 59; www.petitjournalsaintmichel.com in French; 71 blvd St-Michel, 5e; metro Luxembourg; admission €15.25-40; ⏱ 8pm-2am Mon-Sat

The 'Little Newspaper' is a sophisticated jazz venue, with everything from Dixieland and vocals to big band and swing. Sets start at 9.15pm and last till 1am; Monday night jam sessions are free.

L' OPUS Map pp386-8

☎ 01 40 34 70 00; 167 quai de Valmy, 10e; metro Louis Blanc; admission free-€15; ⏱ 8pm-2am Sun & Tue-Thu, 8pm-4am Fri & Sat,

Housed in a former officers' mess by the Canal St-Martin, the Opus has moved on from hip-hop to the cool sounds of jazz, soul, blues, gospel and *zouk* (a blend of African and Latin American dance rhythms). It's a club-cum-concert venue and there are *menus* for €33 and €40 (obligatory Thursday to Saturday).

NEW MORNING Map pp386-8

☎ 01 45 23 51 41; www.newmorning.com in French; 7-9 rue des Petites Écuries, 10e; metro Château d'Eau; admission €14.50-21; ⏱ 8pm-2am, box office 4.30-7.30pm Mon-Fri

New Morning is a well-regarded auditorium that hosts jazz concerts as well as blues, rock, funk, salsa, Afro-Cuban and Brazilian music three to seven nights a week at 9pm, with the second set ending at about 1am. Tickets are available at the box office, but can usually be purchased at the door.

SUNSET & SUNSIDE Map pp396-9

☎ 01 40 26 46 60 (Sunset), 01 40 26 21 25 (Sunside); 60 rue des Lombards, 1er; metro Châtelet; admission €10-22; ⏱ 9.30pm-4am Mon-Sat

This trendy club with two separate cellars – Sunset with electric jazz and concerts beginning at 10pm, Sunside with acoustics and concerts at 9pm – attracts musicians and actors (both film and theatre).

WORLD & LATINO

Sono mondiale (world music) is a very big deal in Paris and you'll hear everything from Algerian *raï* and other North African

music to Senegalese *mbalax* and West Indian *zouk* at clubs. But nothing has caught on in the past decade like Latino music, especially Cuban salsa.

BISTROT LATIN Map pp396-9

☎ 01 42 77 21 11; 20 rue du Temple, 4e; metro Hôtel de Ville; admission €6-9; ⏱ 7pm-1am Mon, Wed & Thu, 7pm-2am Fri-Sun

This friendly bistro-club upstairs from the cinema Le Latina (p239) has tango Wednesday to Saturday and salsa on Sunday. Admission includes dance classes from 7pm to 8.30pm.

CITÉ DE LA MUSIQUE Map pp380-2

☎ 01 44 84 44 84; www.cite-musique.fr; 221 av Jean Jaurès, 19e; metro Porte de Pantin; tickets €6-34; ⏱ box office noon-6pm Tue-Sat, 10am-6pm Sun, to 8pm on the day of performance

The 'City of Music' at the Parc de la Villette hosts every imaginable type of music and dance, from Western classical to North African and Japanese, in its oval-shaped, 1200-seat main auditorium. Concerts are in the little **Amphithéâtre du Musée de la Musique** on Saturday (4.30pm) and Sunday (3pm). Get tickets from the box office opposite the main auditorium next to the Fontaine aux Lions (Lion Fountain).

CONSERVATOIRE NATIONAL SUPÉRIEUR DE MUSIQUE ET DE DANSE Map pp380-2

National Higher Conservatory of Music & Dance; ☎ 01 40 40 45 45; www.cnsmdp.fr; 209 av Jean Jaurès, 19e; metro Porte de Pantin; ⏱ box office noon-6pm Tue-Sat, 10am-6pm Sun, to 8pm on the day of performance

On the other side of the fountain from the Cité de la Musique (but sharing the same box office) students put on free orchestra concerts and recitals several times a week, in the afternoon or evening.

LA CASA 128 Map pp386-8

☎ 01 48 01 05 71; www.casa128.com in French; 128 rue La Fayette, 10e; metro Gare du Nord; admission €10; ⏱ 8pm-6am Thu-Sat

This club prides itself on its *chaud et chalereux* (hot and warm) Latino, tropical and Caribbean atmosphere and sounds.

LA JAVA Map pp386-8

☎ 01 42 02 20 52; 105 rue du Faubourg du Temple, 10e; metro Goncourt; admission €8-16; ⏱ 11pm-5am Thu-Sat, 2-7pm Sun

Built in 1922 this is the dance hall where Édith Piaf (see the boxed text p234) got her first break, and it now reverberates to the sound of live salsa and other Latino music. There's a *thé dansant* (tea dance) on Sunday.

LATINA CAFÉ Map pp383-5

☎ 01 42 89 98 89; 114 av des Champs-Élysées, 8e; metro George V; admission free-€15.25; ☼ 9am-5am Mon-Thu, 9am-6am Fri, 10am-6am Sat, 10am-5am Sun

More of a temple dedicated to salsa than a café, the Latina has a *bodeguita* (little bar) and tapas bar (tapas €3.50 to €8) on the ground floor (*demi* of beer €4.60, cocktails from €8), a restaurant and the Bar Hacienda on the 1st floor, and a club with a stage and live bands in the basement. Radio Latina broadcasts from here live from 9pm to 11.30pm on Thursday.

LES ÉTOILES Map pp386-8

☎ 01 47 70 60 56; 61 rue du Château d'Eau, 10e; metro Château d'Eau; admission €9-19; ☼ 9pm-4am Thu-Sat

Paris' first music hall, opened in 1856 and still going strong, features live Latin bands and an *ambiente popular* (easygoing atmosphere) three nights a week. Entry is €9; for €10 more you get dinner and a dance class at 11pm.

MONTECRISTO CAFÉ Map pp383-5

☎ 01 45 62 30 86; 68 av des Champs-Élysées, 8e; metro Franklin D Roosevelt; admission €10-15; ☼ 24hr

This bar-restaurant brings mainstream Latin music to the Right Bank and the tourists can't get enough of it. A DJ plays salsa from 10pm; go on Monday or Tuesday night when there's classic salsa from the 1970s and 1980s.

OPUS LATINO Map pp389-91

☎ 01 40 61 08 66; 33 rue Blomet, 15e; metro Volontaires; admission €5-10; ☼ 10pm-2am Tue-Sun

The former premises of Bal Nègre, this restaurant-bar has a fabulous oak dance floor. Admission is for nondiners; those eating here (*menus* €25 and €30) get in free. One-hour salsa classes (€9) start at 8pm for beginners and 9pm for intermediates Tuesday to Saturday.

SATELLITE CAFÉ Map pp392-5

☎ 01 47 00 48 87; www.satellit-café.com; 44 rue de la Folie Méricourt, 11e; metro Oberkampf; admission €10; ☼ 8pm-3am Tue-Thu, 10pm-6am Fri & Sat

The 'Satellite Café' is a great venue for world music and is not as painfully trendy as some

others in Paris. Come here to hear everything from blues and flamenco to tango and Peruvian folk music. Beer costs €7; cocktails from €9 to €12. The admission fee includes two drinks.

FRENCH CHANSONS

When French music comes to mind, most people hear accordions and *chansonniers* (cabaret singers) such as Édith Piaf, Jacques Brel, Georges Brassens and Léo Ferré. But though you may stumble upon buskers performing *chansons françaises* (French songs) or playing *musette* (accordion music) in the market, it can sometimes be difficult to catch traditional French music in a more formal setting. Following are a handful of venues where you're sure to hear it – both the traditional and the modern forms.

AU LAPIN AGILE Map p400

☎ 01 46 06 85 87; www.au-lapin-agile.com; 22 rue des Saules, 18e; metro Lamarck Caulaincourt; adult €24, students except Sat €17 ☼ 9pm-2am Tue-Sun

This rustic cabaret venue in Montmartre was favoured by artists and intellectuals in the early 20th century and chansons are still performed here. Poetry is read six nights a week starting at 9.30pm. Admission includes one drink. The name derives from *Le Lapin à Gill*, a mural of a rabbit jumping out of a cooking pot. The mural is by caricaturist André Gill and can still be seen on the western exterior wall.

CHEZ ADEL Map pp386-8

☎ 01 42 08 24 61; 10 rue de la Grange aux Belles, 10e; metro Jacques Bonsergent; admission free; ☼ noon-2am

Chez Adel is a truly Parisian concept: Syrian hosts with guest *chansonniers* (as well as Gypsy, folk and world music) performing most nights to a mixed and very enthusiastic crowd. There's a *formule* (set meal) for €6 and a *menu* for €8. The part-Parisian part-Eastern décor of this simple bistro looks better as the owners' punch goes down.

CHEZ LOUISETTE Map pp380-2

☎ 01 40 12 10 14; Marché aux Puces de St-Ouen; metro Porte de Clignancourt; ☼ noon-6pm Sat-Mon

This little bistro is one of the highlights of a visit to Paris' largest **flea market** (p268). Market-goers crowd around little tables to eat lunch (mains €12 to €20) and hear old-time *chanteuses* and *chanteurs* (they change regularly)

Édith Piaf: Urchin Sparrow

Like her US contemporary Judy Garland, Édith Piaf was not just a singer but a tragic and stoic figure who the nation took to its heart and has never let go.

She was born Édith Giovanna Gassion to a street acrobat and a singer in the working-class district of Belleville in 1915. Piaf's early childhood was spent with her maternal grandmother, an alcoholic who neglected her, and later with her father's parents in Normandy, who ran a local brothel. At age nine she toured with her father, but left home at 15 to sing alone in the streets of Paris. Her first employer, Louis Leplée, called her *la môme piaf* (urchin sparrow) and introduced her to the cabarets of the capital.

In 1935 Leplée was murdered and Piaf faced the streets again. But along came Raymond Asso, an ex-French Legionnaire who became her Pygmalion, forcing her to break with her pimp and hustler friends, putting her in her signature black dress and inspiring her first big hit, *Mon légionnaire* (My Legionnaire) in 1937. When he succeeded in getting her a contract at what is now La Java (p232), one of the most famous Parisian music halls of the time, her career skyrocketed.

This frail woman, who sang about street life, drugs, unrequited love, violence, death and whores, seemed to embody all the miseries of the world yet sang in a husky, powerful voice with no self-pity. Her tumultuous love life earned her the reputation as *une dévoreuse d'hommes* (a man-eater), but she launched the careers of several of her lovers, including Yves Montand and Charles Aznavour. Another of her many lovers was world middleweight boxing champion Marcel Cerdan; he was killed in a plane crash while flying over to join her on tour in the US in 1949. True to form, Piaf insisted that the show go on after learning of his death and fainted on stage in the middle of *L'Hymne à l'amour* (Hymn to Love), a song inspired by Cerdan.

After suffering injuries in a car accident in 1951, Piaf began drinking heavily and became addicted to morphine. Her health declined quickly but she continued to sing around the world, including New York's Carnegie Hall in 1956, and recorded some of her biggest hits such as *Je ne regrette rien* (No, I regret nothing), *Milord* (My Lord) etc. In 1962, frail and once again penniless, Piaf married a 20-year-old hairdresser called Théophanis Lamboukas (aka Théo Sarapo), recorded the duet *À quoi ça sert l'amour?* (What Use Is Love?) with him and left Paris for the South of France, where she died the following year. Some two million people attended her funeral in Paris, and the grave of the beloved and much missed Urchin Sparrow at Père Lachaise Cemetery is still visited and decorated by thousands of her loyal fans each year. Interest in her life and work continues unabated, as was seen in early 2004 when the City of Paris sponsored a highly successful and interactive exhibition *Piaf, la Môme de Paris* (Piaf, the Urchin Sparrow of Paris).

belt out numbers by Piaf and other classic French singers, accompanied by accordion music; you might even get to see an inspired diner jump up to dance *la guingette* (jig) in the aisles.

L'ATTIRAIL Map pp386–8

☎ 01 42 72 44 42; 9 rue au Maire, 3e; metro Arts et Métiers; admission free; ⏱ 10.30am-1.30am

With its cheap *pots* (460mL bottle) of wine and free concerts of *chansons françaises* and world music (Gypsy rap, Irish sets, southern Italian folk and pop) almost daily at 8.30pm, this North African enclave in the heart of Paris' original Chinatown attracts a large crowd of students. At an amazing Formica bar, which snakes its way down one side of a long room covered with posters, manic but friendly customers are served by an easy-going staff.

LE LIMONAIRE Map pp386–8

☎ 01 45 23 33 33; 18 cité Bergère, 9e; metro Grands Boulevards; admission free; ⏱ 6pm-midnight Tue-Sun

This little wine bar is one of the best places to listen to traditional French *chansons* but come here only if you're serious about the genre; the crowd is almost reverential. Singers (who change regularly) perform at 1pm Tuesday to Saturday and at 7pm on Sunday. Be generous when the hat comes your way.

CLUBBING

The clubs and other dancing venues favoured by the Parisian party people change frequently and many are officially private. Single men may not be admitted – even if their clothes are subculturally appropriate – simply because they're men on their own. Women, on the other hand, get in for free on some nights. It's always easier to get into the club of your choice during the week, when things may be hopping even more than they are at the weekend.

Remember that Parisians tend to go out in groups and don't mingle as much as Anglo-Saxons do. The truly trendy crowd considers showing up before 1am a serious breach of good taste. Admission fees almost always include one alcoholic drink.

Paris is great for music (techno remains very popular) and there are some mighty fine DJs based here. Latino and Cuban salsa music is also huge. Theme nights at clubs are common, so it's best to consult the publications and websites (p206) before making plans.

AU TANGO Map pp386-8

☎ 01 42 72 17 78; www.boite-a-frissons.fr; 13 rue au Maire, 3e; metro Arts et Métiers; admission €5-6.50; 🕙 10.30pm-6am Fri & Sat, 5-11pm Sun

Formerly an Afro-Caribbean *club frotti/frotta* (roughly 'rub club'), the 'Tango' now bills itself as a *boîte à frissons* (quivering club), with a mixed gay and lesbian crowd bent on doing the same. The atmosphere and style is retro; there isn't much high-tech in this place.

CLUB ZED Map pp396-9

☎ 01 43 54 93 78; 2 rue des Anglais, 5e; metro Maubert Mutualité; admission €8-16; 🕙 10.30pm-3am Thu, 11pm-5.30am Fri & Sat

This is a slightly sleazy club (in a fun way) in a vaulted cellar. The DJs favour rock 'n' roll, jazz, swing and salsa; it's got kind of a '50s feel and sound to it all. *Garçons non accompagnés* (unaccompanied boys) may not be allowed in.

DUPLEX Map pp383-5

☎ 01 45 00 45 00; www.leduplex.fr in French; 2bis av Foch, 16e; metro Charles de Gaulle-Étoile; admission €15-19; 🕙 11pm-6am Tue-Sun

This stylish club, just west of place Charles de Gaulle, makes for happy hunting grounds for the well-heeled residents (and their offspring) of the chi-chi 16e arrondissement. This is the place to meet your millionaire.

FOLIES PIGALLE Map p400

☎ 01 48 78 55 25; 11 place Pigalle, 9e; metro Pigalle; admission free-€20; 🕙 midnight-dawn Tue-Sat, 7pm-midnight Sun

Folies Pigalle is a heaving place with a mixed gay and straight crowd that is great for cruising from the balcony above the dance floor. There are theme nights and concerts (usually at 2am) throughout the week. Sunday is the *ethnik et gay* tea dance, called 'Black, Blanc, Beur' (slang for North African; €6), with R & B, dance, techno, house and oriental.

FULL METAL Map pp396-9

☎ 01 42 72 30 05; 40 rue des Blancs Manteaux, 4e; metro Rambuteau; 🕙 5pm-4am Sun-Thu, 5pm-6am Fri & Sat

Full Metal is another very serious men-only cruising bar and is heavy stuff most nights till the wee hours. There's a demanding fetishist dress code most nights, leather, rubber, sports attire, uniforms – including Wednesday's CIA – Cuir (leather) in Action. Happy hour is 5pm to 8pm.

GIBUS Map pp386-8

☎ 01 47 00 78 88; www.gibus.fr in French; 18 rue du Faubourg du Temple, 11e; metro République; admission free-€18; 🕙 11pm-dawn Tue-Sat

Gibus, an enormously popular cave-like venue, halfway between Canal St-Martin and place de la République, has hard techno on Tuesday with Thermo Tek, acid and trance on Wednesday with Virtual Moon, and techno on Thursday with Parisjuana Night.

LA CHAPELLE DES LOMBARDS
Map pp392-5

☎ 01 43 57 24 24; 19 rue de Lappe, 11e; metro Bastille; admission €15-19; 🕙 11pm-dawn Tue-Sun

This perennially popular Bastille dance club has salsa, R & B, reggae, funk and *zouk* – in a word, a bit of everything. Concerts take place at 8.30pm on Thursday and Friday.

LA COUPOLE Map pp389-91

☎ 01 43 27 56 00; 102 blvd du Montparnasse, 14e; metro Vavin; admission €12-16; 🕙 9.30pm-3am Thu, 11.30pm-5.30am Fri, 10am-5pm Sat

Sadly the basement of this celebrated brasserie (p183), from the time of the 'Roaring Twenties' ,no longer hosts its Tuesday salsa night that single-handedly passed on Latin fever to *le tout Paris,* but other favourite theme nights live on: *L'Attitud' Caraïbes* with *zouk,* reggae/funk on Thursday, hip-hop and R & B on Friday, and Cheers with house and garage on Saturday.

LA FAVELA CHIC Map pp386-8

☎ 01 40 21 38 14; www.favelachic.com in French; 18 rue du Faubourg du Temple, 10e; metro République; admission free; 🕙 7.30pm-2am Tue-Fri, 9.30pm-4am Sat

Next to **Gibus** (above), the ambience is more *favela* (shantytown) than chic in this restaurant-cum-dancehall whose motto is 'Disorder

Skip to the Loo

In Paris a trip to the toilet at a bar or restaurant can often go beyond the merely utilitarian. A short stretch of rue Vieille du Temple (4e) in the Marais is particularly well endowed. Check out the unusual conveniences at La Chaise au Plafond (p210) – you'll enjoy the Norman cow theme – while the toilets at Au Petit Fer a Cheval (p208) are straight out of a Flash Gordon film. But our favourites in these parts are the stainless-steel ladies and gents at Les Philosophes (p219), with philosophy texts on display and deep-and-meaningful thought-provokers lit up on the back wall: *'Que dois faire?'* (What should I do?); *'Que m'est-il permis d'espérer?'* (What am I allowed to hope for?); *'Je doute j'ai conscience'* (I doubt I have a conscience).

Closer to Bastille (11e) the decorations in the restrooms at Le Lèche-Vin (p219) are a little bit of heaven – or is that hell? – itself after the pious imagery at the bar. At L'Autre Café (p227), men and women meet at a back-to-back washbasin, and are excused for momentarily thinking they've been reincarnated as the opposite sex.

For Indian kitsch straight out of Bollywood, Lal Qila (p201) in the 15e arrondissement is worth the trip, while the sophisticated Asian-inspired toilets at Khun Akorn (p198) in the 11e arrondissement will transport you to the other side of the world. For vast and beautiful spaces evocative of a time when the upper classes spared no expense to fit out their bogs, visit the loos at the China Club (p210) in the 12e arrondissement, where everything is made of marble, wood and glass. On the other hand, using the stone urinal at Buddha Bar (p224) in the 8e arrondissement, which flushes in the wink of an (electric) eye, can feel almost irreverent.

and Progress' (an iconoclastic jab at Brazil's national motto 'Ordem e Progresso'). This is 'Paree de Janeiro', where Brazilians and French alike get down to the frenetic mix of samba, *baile* (dance) funk and Brazilian pop. La Favela Chic has by far the best *câpirinhas* (cocktails made from a sugarcane-based alcohol, lime juice, sugarcane syrup and shaved ice).

LA GUINGUETTE PIRATE Map p401
☎ 01 53 61 08 49; opp 11 quai François Mauriac, 13e; metro Quai de la Gare or Bibliothèque; admission €6-12; ☾ 7pm-2am Tue-Sat, 5pm-midnight Sun
The 'Pirate Dance Café' is another floating *boîte* (club), this time in a three-masted Chinese junk referred to as *'la dame de Canton'* (the lady from Canton). It usually hosts concerts at 8pm – from pop and indie to electro and hip-hop – and the crowd is young and energetic.

LA LOCOMOTIVE Map p400
☎ 01 53 41 88 88; www.laloco.com in French; 90 blvd de Clichy, 18e; metro Blanche; admission €6-20; ☾ 11pm-6am Tue-Sun
La Loco is an enormous, ever-popular disco on three levels featuring three dance floors and three styles of music. It has long been one of the favourite dancing venues for teenage out-of-towners hot to bop. Most popular is house evening BPM (Beats per Minute) on Friday.

LA STATION Map pp396-9
☎ 01 42 78 88 49, 01 42 21 03 53; 80 quai de l'Hôtel de Ville, 4e; metro Hôtel de Ville; ☾ 2pm-6am Mon-Thu, 2pm-7am Fri-Sun

What was L'Arène for many years remains true to form. This is for gay blokes who are seriously OFB (out for business). It's got dark rooms and cubicles on two levels and heats up (boils over, rather) from around midnight. Take the usual precautions. There's a strip show on Thursday (11pm) and a DJ from 10pm on Sunday. Happy hour is from 9pm to 11pm and 2am to 3am.

LE BALAJO Map pp392-5
☎ 01 47 00 07 87; 9 rue de Lappe, 11e; metro Bastille; admission €8-17; ☾ 9pm-4.30am Tue-Thu, 11pm-5.30am Fri & Sat, 3-7.30pm Sun
A mainstay of Parisian nightlife since 1936, this ancient ballroom is a bit lower shelf these days but still hosts a number of popular theme nights. Tuesday to Thursday is salsa and Latino music (Wednesday throws in a little rock too), on Friday and Saturday DJs play rock, disco, R & B and house. From 3pm to 7.30pm on Sunday, DJs play old-fashioned *musette* (accordion music) – waltz, tango, cha-cha – for aficionados of retro tea-dancing.

LE BATOFAR Map p401
☎ 01 56 29 10 33; www.batofar.net in French; opp 11 quai François Mauriac, 13e; metro Quai de la Gare or Bibliothèque; admission free-€12; ☾ 9pm-midnight Mon & Tue, 9pm or 10pm-4am, 5am or 6am Wed-Sun
What looks like a mild-mannered tugboat moored near the imposing Bibliothèque Nationale de France, is a rollicking dancing spot that attracts some top international techno and funk DJ talent. Jazz concerts usually take place on Monday and Tuesday evening.

LE CITHÉA Map pp386-8

☎ 01 40 21 70 95; 114 rue Oberkampf, 11e; metro Parmentier or Ménilmontant; admission free-€4; ⏳ 5pm-5.30am Tue-Thu, 10pm-6.30am Fri & Sat

This popular and ever-hopping concert venue has bands playing soul, Latin and funk, but especially world music and jazz, usually from 10.30pm with DJs from 1am. Wine and beer cost €4 to €7, cocktails are €8 to €10.

LE DÉPÔT Map pp396-9

☎ 01 44 54 96 96; 10 rue aux Ours, 3e; metro Rambuteau or Étienne Marcel; admission €6-12; ⏳ 2pm-8am

With a spanking new cop shop just next door you'd think this strictly men-only bar on the 'Street of the Bears' would be a titch more subdued. Fat chance. The 'Depot' is a bigger and slightly more upscale version of **La Station** (opposite) with the same sorts of nooks, crannies and goings-on. Theme nights with DJs scheduled throughout the week, including Wednesday's naff Boum disco and a Sunday tea dance.

LE MOLOKO Map p400

☎ 01 48 74 50 26; 26 rue Fontaine, 9e; metro Blanche; admission free-€9; ⏳ 8pm-7am

A very popular *bar de nuit* with an eclectic mix of the classic (red velvet) and the provocative, and a split personality. From 8.30pm it's café-theatre with improvisations and musical comedy and from 11pm dancing on the ground floor, nattering above and cruising everywhere. Hotfunk, with funk, soul, disco and R & B, is Wednesday night.

LE NOUVEAU CASINO Map pp386-8

☎ 01 43 57 57 40; www.nouveaucasino.net in French; 109 rue Oberkampf, 11e; metro Parmentier; admission free-€18; ⏳ 9pm or 11pm-2am or 6am

The 'New Casino', the bar-club-concert venue annexe of the **Café Charbon** (p226), has made quite a splash since opening in 2000, with its electronic live music concerts and DJs. It has a huge dance floor and some pretty impressive acoustic and video systems.

LE PULP Map pp386-8

☎ 01 40 26 01 93; 25 blvd Poissonnière, 2e; metro Grands Boulevards; admission €9-10; ⏳ midnight-6am Thu-Sun

Le Pulp, on the ground floor of **Le Scorp** (right), is Paris' pre-eminent girls-only (mixed on Thursday) club. Lots of cruising going on here and there are musical soirées at the weekend.

LE QUEEN Map pp383-5

☎ 01 53 89 08 90; www.queen.fr; 102 av des Champs-Élysées, 8e; metro George V; admission €9-18 ⏳ midnight-6am

The king (as it were) of gay discos in Paris, Le Queen now reigns more supreme with special theme parties open to all, such as the slightly cheesy Disco Queen on Monday night and Break (drum and bass) on Wednesday night.

LE RÉSERVOIR Map pp392-5

☎ 01 43 56 39 60; 16 rue de la Forge Royale, 11e; metro Ledru Rollin; admission free-€12; ⏳ 8pm-2am Mon-Thu, 8pm-4am Fri & Sat, noon-2am Sun

This east Paris warehouse turned restaurant-club is a place to party, not to share a romantic dinner for two. It's an impressive, cave-like space lit with candles. There's an imposing stage in the centre of the room where concerts take place most nights at 11pm. The music is eclectic – pop, tango, Latino, jazz etc – and the clientele glamour-puss.

LE SCORP Map pp386-8

☎ 01 40 26 28 30; 25 blvd Poissonnière, 2e; metro Grands Boulevards; admission free-€15; ⏳ 11.45pm-6.30am Wed & Thu, midnight-7.30am Fri & Sat

The Scorp – short for 'scorpion' – may have metamorphosed in a place called Le Vogue by the time you read this but what's in a name? This is one of the more relaxed gay dance clubs in Paris. There's a different musical theme most nights such as Oh La La, with a *chansons françaises* vibe, on Thursday.

LE WAGG Map pp396-9

☎ 01 55 42 22 00; 62 rue Mazarine, 6e; metro Odéon; admission €10-12; ⏳ 11pm-5am Wed-Sun

Clerkenwell meets St-Germain in the former Whisky a Go-Go, now a UK-style Conran club associated with the popular Fabric in London. Dress light; the temperature rises as the night wears on. Friday is house and electro, with the likes of Draghixa and Putafranges.

LES BAINS Map pp386-8

☎ 01 48 87 01 80; www.lesbains-club.com in French; 7 rue du Bourg l'Abbé, 3e; metro Étienne Marcel; admission €16-20; ⏳ 11pm-5am Mon-Sat

Housed in a refitted old Turkish *hammam*, the 'Baths' is still renowned for its surly, selective bouncers on the outside even though celebrities and star-struck revellers are now scarce inside; just look at the paucity of Porsches, Rollers and BMWs waiting at the kerb. Wednesday is Be Fly, with mainly house and garage. There's a decent restaurant on the 2nd floor featuring Italian and Thai cuisine.

RED LIGHT Map pp389-91
☎ 01 42 79 94 94; 34 rue du Départ, 14e; metro Montparnasse Bienvenüe; admission €20; ⏲ 11pm-6am Thu-Sun
This underground (literally) venue at the foot of the Tour Montparnasse has become the destination of choice for the young gay crowd, especially on Saturday house nights.

REX CLUB Map pp386-8
☎ 01 42 36 10 96; 5 blvd Poissonnière, 2e; metro Bonne Nouvelle; admission €8-13; ⏲ 11.30pm-6am Wed-Sat
This club is indisputably the hottest place in town for house (Thursday and Saturday) and techno (Friday), and attracts Paris' top DJ talent. The best nights are Wednesday's Massive (drum and bass) and Friday's Automatik (the techno event of the week in the capital).

SLOW CLUB Map pp396-9
☎ 01 42 33 84 30; 130 rue de Rivoli, 1er; metro Châtelet or Louvre-Rivoli; admission €8.50-15; ⏲ 10pm-3am Tue & Thu, 10pm-4am Fri-Sun

Top Five Clubs
- La Favela Chic (p235)
- Le Nouveau Casino (p237)
- Red Light (left)
- Rex Club (left)
- Slow Club (left)

This is an unpretentious dance and jazz club (concerts from 10pm), housed in a deep cellar once used to ripen bananas imported from the Caribbean. It attracts a very mixed-age crowd and is more an institution than just a club. The music varies from night to night, but includes jazz, boogie, bebop, swing and reggae.

STUDIO 287 Map pp380-2
☎ 01 48 34 00 00; 33 av de la Porte d'Aubervilliers, 18e; metro Porte de la Chapelle; admission €10-16; ⏲ 11pm-5am Tue-Thu, 11pm-noon Fri & Sat
By far the city's biggest dance club, with a capacity for 2000 gyrating and sweating bods. This club in the northern reaches of Paris may be a bit too commercial for some, but Thursday's Studio 54 disco packs them in and Kit-Kat afters at the weekend often last till noon.

Entertainment – Cinema

CINEMA

Pariscope and *L'Officiel des Spectacles* (p206) list Paris' cinematic offerings alphabetically by their French title followed by the English (or German, Italian, Spanish etc) one. Going to the cinema in Paris does not come cheap: expect to pay up to €9 for a first-run film. Students and those under 18 or over 60 usually get discounts of about 25% except on Friday nights, all day Saturday and until the evening on Sunday. On Wednesday (and sometimes Monday) most cinemas give discounts of 20% to 30% to everyone. The first film of the day (usually before noon) at some cinemas is half-price.

If a movie is labelled 'v.o.' or 'VO' (for *version originale*) it means it will be sub-titled rather than dubbed (labelled 'v.f.', for *version française*). Thus English-language films marked 'v.o.' will still be in English.

Beyond the cinemas showing Hollywood blockbusters, the following are noteworthy.

CINÉMA DES CINÉASTES Map pp383-5
☎ 01 53 42 40 20, 08 36 68 97 17; 7 av de Clichy, 17e; metro Place de Clichy; adult €6.50-7.20, student & child €5.50-5.70, morning screenings €4.80
Founded by the three Claudes (Miller, Berri and Lelouch) and *Betty Blue* director Jean-Jacques Beneix, the 'Film-makers' Cinema' is a three-screen theatre dedicated to quality cinema, be it French or foreign, but always avant-garde. Thematic seasons, documentaries and meet-the-director sessions round out the repertoire.

CINÉMATHÈQUE FRANÇAISE
☎ 01 56 26 01 01; www.cinemathequefrancaise.com in French; adult/student & child €4.70/3
This national institution almost always leaves its foreign offerings – often rarely screened classics – in their original versions. There are two *salles*, the main one at **Palais de Chaillot** (Map pp383-5; 7 av Albert de Mun, 16e; metro Trocadéro or Iéna), which you enter from the Jardins du Trocadéro. Screenings are from Wednesday to Sunday. Check the website for exact times. The more conveniently located

but less dramatic **Grands Boulevards branch** (Map pp386-8; 42 blvd de Bonne Nouvelle, 10e; metro Bonne Nouvelle) has screenings daily.

FORUM DES IMAGES Map pp396-9

☎ 01 44 76 62 00; www.forumdesimages.net in French; 1 Grande Galerie, Porte St-Eustache, Forum des Halles, 1er; metro Les Halles; adult/senior, student & under 26 €5.50/4.50; ☷ 1-10pm Tue, 1-9pm Wed-Sun

This archive cinema beneath the sprawling Forum des Halles is a superb place to see rarely screened and little known films, especially ones that deal with Paris as a theme or have the City of Light as the setting. There are usually between four and five screenings a day.

LE CHAMPO Map pp396-9

☎ 01 43 54 51 60; www.lechampo.com in French; 51 rue des Écoles, 5e; metro St-Michel or Cluny la Sorbonne; adult/student & child €7/5.50, 2pm matinee €4.50

The Champo, one of the most popular of the many Latin Quarter cinemas, features classics and retrospectives looking at the films of actors and directors such as Alfred Hitchcock, Jacques Tati, Alain Resnais, Frank Capra and Woody Allen. There are two *salles* (halls), one of which has wheelchair access.

LE LATINA Map pp396-9

☎ 01 42 78 47 86; www.lelatina.com in French; 20 rue du Temple, 4e; metro Hôtel de Ville; adult/student, under 20 & everyone Mon & Tue €6.50/5.50

This cinema, which dates back more than 90 years, is the premier spot in Paris for catching films in Spanish and Portuguese. It has two *salles*, one with 180 seats and one with 60 seats, and there are themed festivals and retrospectives scheduled. Some three films are usually screened each day.

MK2 BIBLIOTHÈQUE Map p401

☎ 08 92 69 84 84; www.mk2.com in French; 128-162 av de France, 13e; metro Quai de la Gare; adult/student/child €9/6.50/4.50, everyone before noon €4.50

This branch of the ever-growing chain (10 outlets at last count) is the most ambitious yet, with 14 screens, café, brasserie, restaurant and late-night bar. MK2 cinemas show both blockbusters and studio films so there's always something for everyone.

THEATRE

Entertainment – Theatre

Almost all of Paris' theatre productions, including those originally written in other languages, are performed in French. There are a few English-speaking troupes around, though; look for ads on metro poster boards and in English-language periodicals such as *FUSAC* (p206), *Paris Voice* and *The Irish Eyes*, which are free at English-language bookshops, pubs and so on, as well as the website www.parisfranceguide.com. Apart from the celebrated **Théâtre des Bouffes du Nord** (p240), theatres that occasionally stage productions in English include **Théâtre de Nesle** (Map pp396-9; ☎ 01 46 34 61 04; 8 rue de Nesle, 6e; metro Odéon or Mabillon); **Théâtre des Déchargeurs** (Map pp396-9; ☎ 01 42 36 00 02; 3 rue des Déchargeurs, 1er; metro Châtelet); and **Théâtre de Ménilmontant** (Map pp380-2; ☎ 01 46 36 03 43; 15 rue du Retrait, 20e; metro Gambetta).

For booking agencies for theatre tickets see p207.

COMÉDIE FRANÇAISE Map pp396-9

☎ 08 25 10 16 80; www.comedie-francaise.fr; place Colette, 1er; metro Palais Royal-Musée du Louvre; tickets €5-32; ☷ box office 11am-6pm Tue-Sat, 1-6pm Sun & Mon

Founded in 1680 during the reign of Louis XIV, the 'French Comedy' theatre bases its repertoire around the works of the classic French playwrights such as Molière, Racine, Corneille, Beaumarchais, Marivaux and Musset, though in recent years contemporary and even non-French works have been staged.

There are three venues: the main Salle Richelieu on place Colette just west of the Palais Royal; the **Comédie Française Studio Théâtre** (Map pp396-9; ☎ 01 44 58 98 58; Galerie du Carrousel du Louvre, 99 rue de Rivoli, 1er; metro Palais Royal-Musée du Louvre; hbox office 1-5pm Wed-Mon); the **Théâtre du Vieux Colombier** (Map pp389-91; ☎ 01 44 39 87 00; 21 rue du Vieux Colombier, 6e; metro St-Sulpice; ☷ box office 11am-6pm Tue-Sat, 1-6pm Sun & Mon).

Tickets for regular seats cost €10 to €32; tickets for the 95 places near the ceiling (€5) go on sale one hour before curtain time (usually 8.30pm), which is when those under 27 can purchase any of the better seats remaining for €7.50 to €10. The discount tickets are available from the window round the corner from the main entrance and facing place André Malraux.

ODÉON-THÉÂTRE DE L'EUROPE

Map pp396-9

☎ 01 44 41 36 36; www.theatre-odeon.fr in French; place de l'Odéon, 6e; metro Odéon

This huge, ornate theatre built in the early 1780s often puts on foreign plays in their original languages (subtitled in French), and hosts theatre troupes from abroad. At the time of writing the Odéon was undergoing complete renovation (until 2005) during which time plays were being staged at the **Ateliers Berthier** (Map pp380-2; ☎ 01 44 85 40 40; 8 blvd Berthier, 17e; metro Porte de Clichy; tickets €13-26; ☺ box office 11am-6.30pm Mon-Sat). People over 60 get a discount on the pricier tickets, while students and those under 30 can get good reserved seats for as little as €7.50.

THÉÂTRE DE LA BASTILLE

Map pp392-5

☎ 01 43 57 42 14; www.theatre-bastille.com in French; 76 rue de la Roquette, 11e; metro Bastille or Voltaire; adult/concession €19/12.50; ☺ box office 10am-6pm Mon-Fri, 2-6pm Sat

One of the best fringe theatre venues in Paris, with two spaces and a variety of experimental works: spoken word, movement and music.

THÉÂTRE DE LA VILLE-SALLE DES ABBESSES Map p400

☎ 01 42 74 22 77; www.theatredelaville-paris.com in French; 31 rue des Abbesses, 18e; metro Abbesses; adult €15-29, student €11; ☺ box office 5-8pm Tue-Sat, 1hr before matinee

This red-and-cream neoclassical building in Montmartre mainly stages the contemporary dramatic productions of the **Théâtre de la Ville** (p242), but also some music and dance.

THÉÂTRE DES BOUFFES DU NORD

Map pp386-8

☎ 01 46 07 34 50; www.bouffesdunord.com in French; 37bis blvd de la Chapelle, 10e; metro La Chapelle; adult €14-24.50, concession €8-17; ☺ box office 11am-6pm Mon-Sat

Perhaps best known as the Paris base of Peter Brooks' and Stéphane Lissner's experimental troupes, this theatre in the northern reaches of the 10e and just north of the Gare du Nord also hosts works by other directors (eg Stéphane Braunschweig, Krzysztof Warlikowski), as well as classical and jazz concerts.

COMEDY

Though it may come as a surprise to some, Parisians do like to laugh, and the capital is not short of comedy clubs where comedians such as Bourvil, Fernandel, Bernard Blier, Louis de Funès, Francis Blanche, Jean Poiret and Michel Serrault have enjoyed enormous popularity over the years. Among contemporary stars are the *pied noirs* (Algerian-born French) comics Elie Kakou and Guy Bedos (the latter is left-wing which, among this generally conservative group, is comical in itself) and the French-Arab comedian Smaïn.

CAFÉ DE LA GARE Map pp396-9

☎ 01 42 78 52 51; www.cafe-de-la-gare.fr.st in French; 41 rue du Temple, 4e; metro Hôtel de Ville or Rambuteau; Sun-Thu adult €15-20, under 26 €10

The 'Station Café' in the erstwhile mews of a Marais *hôtel particulier* (private mansion) is one of the best and most innovative café-theatres in Paris, with acts ranging from comic theatre and stand-up to reinterpreted classics.

HÔTEL DU NORD Map pp386-8

☎ 01 53 19 98 88; www.anythingmatters.com; 102 quai de Jemmapes, 10e; metro République; tickets €20-22

The 'Hotel of the North', which figured in Marcel Carné's eponymous 1938 film starring Arletty, hosts Laughing Matters a couple of times a week at 8.30pm, the best place in town for English-language belly laughs, with a regular stream of stand-ups from across the Channel and the pond.

POINT VIRGULE Map pp396-9

☎ 01 42 78 67 03; 7 rue Ste-Croix de la Bretonnerie, 4e; metro Hôtel de Ville; Sun-Fri adult €15, student €12

The tiny 'Semicolon', which celebrated its silver anniversary in 2003, is a popular comedy spot in the Marais offering café-theatre at its best – stand-up comics, performance artists, musical acts. The quality is variable, but it's great fun nevertheless and the place has a reputation for discovering new talent. There are three shows daily at 8pm, 9.15pm and 10.30pm.

OPERA

The **Opéra National de Paris** (ONP; ☎ 08 92 89 90 90; www.opera-de-paris.fr in French) splits its performance schedule between the Palais Garnier, its original home built in 1875, and the modern Opéra Bastille, which opened in 1989. Both opera houses also stage ballets and classical-music concerts performed by the ONP's affiliated orchestra (p230) and ballet companies (p242). The season runs from September to July.

OPÉRA BASTILLE Map pp392-5
2-6 place de la Bastille, 12e; metro Bastille;
opera €6-114, ballet €13-70, chamber music €6-16

Most Parisians aren't keen on this 2700-seat venue, the main opera house in the capital, and shedding its exterior tiles onto the pavement in retrospect seems to have been the least of its teething problems. It's now performing superbly, however, and tickets are available from its **box office** (Map pp392-5; 130 rue de Lyon, 11e; ☎ 11am-6.30pm Mon-Sat) from 14 days before the date of the performance. According to local opera buffs, the only way to ensure a seat is to book by post (120 rue de Lyon, 75576 Paris CEDEX 12) some two months in advance. To have a shot at the cheapest (ie worst) seats in the house (€6, €10 and €20), you have to stop by the box office the day tickets go on sale – exactly 14 days before the performance (on Monday if the performance is on a Sunday). If there are unsold tickets, people under 26 or over 65 and students can get excellent seats for €20, only 15 minutes before the curtain goes up.

OPÉRA COMIQUE Map pp386-8
☎ 08 25 00 00 58; www.opera-comique.com in French; 5 rue Favart, 2e; metro Richelieu Drouot; tickets €7-100

The 'Comic Opera' is a century-old hall that premiered of many important French operas. It continues to host classic and less-known operas. Get tickets from **Fnac** (p207) or **Virgin** (p207) and directly from the **box office** (☉ 9am-9pm Mon-Sat, 11am-7pm Sun & 1hr before performances) on the southwest side of the theatre. Subject to availability, students and those under 26 can buy unsold tickets for less than €10.

PALAIS GARNIER Map pp383-5
place de l'Opéra, 9e; metro Opéra

The city's original opera house is smaller and more glamorous than its Bastille counterpart, and boasts perfect acoustics. Due to its odd shape, a some seats have limited or no visibility. Ticket prices and conditions (including last-minute discounts) at the **box office** (place de l'Opéra, 9e; ☉ 11am-6.30pm Mon-Sat) are almost the same as those at the **Opéra Bastille** (left).

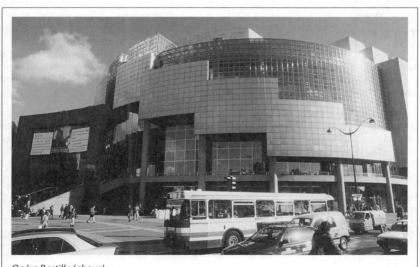

Opéra Bastille (above)

They Certainly Can Cancan

Paris' risqué cabaret revues – those dazzling, pseudo-bohemian productions where the women wear two beads and a feather (or was that two feathers and a bead?) – are about as representative of the Paris of the 21st century as crocodile-wrestling is of Australia or broncobusting of the USA. But they continue to draw in the crowds as they did in the days of Toulouse-Lautrec and Aristide Bruant and can be a lot of fun.

Crazy Horse (Map pp383-5; ☎ 01 47 23 32 32; www.lecrazyhorseparis.com; 12 av George V, 8e; metro Alma Marceau) This popular cabaret, whose dressing (or, rather, undressing) rooms were featured in Woody Allen's film What's New Pussycat? (1965), has been promoting what it calls l'art du nu (nudity) for over half a century. Shows, lasting 1¾ hours, are at 8.30pm and 11pm from Sunday to Friday and at 7.30pm, 9.45pm and 11.50pm on Saturday. Admission including two drinks costs €49/69/90 at the bar/mezzanine/orchestra and €110 in the orchestra with a half-bottle of champagne. Admission for students is €29 with one drink.

Folies-Bergère (Map pp386-8; ☎ 01 44 79 98 98; www.foliesbergere.com in French; 32 rue Richer, 9e; metro Cadet) The cabaret where the African-American exotic dancer Josephine Baker made her debut and where none other than Charlie Chaplin, WC Fields and Stan Laurel appeared on stage together one night in 1911 is celebrated for its high-kicking, pink feather-clad cancan dancers but has been staging more mainstream musicals lately such as Fame and Snow White. Times vary but shows are usually at 8.30 or 9pm Tuesday to Sunday and admission is €32 to €62.

Le Lido de Paris (Map pp383-5; ☎ 01 40 76 56 10; www.lido.fr; 116bis av des Champs-Élysées, 8e; metro George V) Founded at the close of WWII, the Lido gets top marks for its ambitious sets and the lavish costumes of its 70 artistes. Nightly shows cost €80 at 9.30pm and €60 (€80 on Friday and Saturday) at 11.30pm and €69 to watch from the bar with two drinks. With dinner, entry to the 9.30pm show costs €140, €170 and €200, depending on the menu chosen and includes a half-bottle of champagne per person.

Moulin Rouge (Map p400; ☎ 01 53 09 82 82; www.moulinrouge.fr; 82 blvd de Clichy, 18e; metro Blanche). Ooh la la... This legendary cabaret founded in 1889, whose dancers appeared in Toulouse-Lautrec's celebrated posters, sits under its trademark red windmill (actually a 1925 replica of the 19th-century original). The champagne dinner show (at 7pm) costs €130, €145 or €160. The show at 9pm with half a bottle of champers costs €92; at 11pm it drops to €82.

Paradis Latin (Map pp392-5; ☎ 01 43 25 28 28; www.paradis-latin.com; 28 rue du Cardinal Lemoine, 5e; metro Cardinal Lemoine) This cabaret, which also dates back to 1889, is known for its extravagant, nonstop performances of songs, dances and nightclub numbers. The staff, including the waiters, often participate. The show begins at 9.30pm Wednesday to Monday and costs €75, including half a bottle of champagne or two drinks. A ticket including dinner at 8pm costs €109, €139 or €200 depending on the menu you choose.

DANCE

The **Ballet de l'Opéra National de Paris** (www.opera-de-paris.fr in French) performs at both the **Palais Garnier** (p241) and the **Opéra Bastille** (p241). Other important venues for both classical and modern dance are the **Châtelet-Théâtre Musical de Paris** (p230) and **Théâtre des Champs-Élysées** (p230) as well as the **Théâtre de la Bastille** (p240).

LE REGARD DU CYGNE Map pp380-2
☎ 01 43 58 55 93; 210 rue de Belleville, 20e; metro Place des Fêtes; adult/concession €13/10; ⊙ box office 1-3pm Mon-Fri

Le Regard du Cygne (Look of the Swan) is a great performance space in Belleville where many of Paris' young and daring talents in movement, music and theatre congregate to perform.

If you're in the mood for some innovative modern dance, performance or participation, this is the place. There are discounts for students and seniors half an hour before curtain time.

THÉÂTRE DE LA VILLE Map pp396-9
☎ 01 42 74 22 77; www.theatredelaville-paris.com in French; 2 place du Châtelet, 4e; metro Châtelet; tickets €15-25; ⊙ box office 11am-7pm Mon, 11am-8pm Tue-Sat

While the Théâtre de la Ville also hosts theatre and music, it's most celebrated for its avant-garde dance productions by such noted choreographers as Merce Cunningham, Angelin Preljocaj and Pina Bausch. Depending on availability, students and people under 27 can buy up to two tickets for €11 or €12.50 each on the day of the performance. There are no performances in July and August.

Sports, Health & Fitness

Watching Sport   244
Football   244
Rugby   245
Tennis   245
Cycling   245
Horse Racing & Showjumping   245

Outdoor Activities   246
Cycling   246
Skating   247
Boules & Bowling   248
Tennis   248

Health & Fitness   248
Gyms & Fitness Clubs   248
Swimming   249
Turkish Baths   249
Yoga   250

Sports, Health & Fitness

Parisians love to watch sport, but if you're feeling more active while in the French capital, getting involved in sport can be as simple as slipping into some swimming gear, putting yourself behind handlebars or wrapping your hand around a racquet.

WATCHING SPORT

For details of upcoming sporting events, consult the sports daily *L'Équipe* (www.lequipe .fr in French; €0.80) or *Figaroscope* (www.figaroscope.fr in French), an entertainment and activities supplement published with *Le Figaro* daily newspaper each Wednesday.

Most big international sporting events are held at the magnificent **Stade de France** (☎ 08 92 70 09 00; www.stadefrance.com; rue Francis de Pressensé, ZAC du Cornillon Nord, 93216 St-Denis La Plaine) at St-Denis (p136).

FOOTBALL

France's home matches (friendlies and qualifiers for major championships) are held at the Stade de France (p244, tickets €12 to €70), which was built especially for the 1998 World Cup.

The city's only top-division football team, **Paris-St-Germain** (☎ 01 47 43 71 71; www.psg .fr in French), wears red and blue and plays its home games at the 45,500-seat **Parc des Princes** (Map pp380-2; ☎ 08 25 07 50 78; 24

Information

The best single source of information on sports in Paris – both spectator and participatory – but in French only is the 500-page *Parisports: Le Guide du Sport à Paris* (www.sport.paris.fr in French) available free from the **Mairie de Paris** (Map pp396-9; ☎ 08 20 007 575; www.paris.fr; Hôtel de Ville, 29 rue de Rivoli, 4e; metro Hôtel de Ville).

Ice-skating, l'Hôtel de Ville (p87)

rue du Commandant Guilbaud, 16e; metro Porte de St-Cloud; tickets €12-80; ☾ box office 9am-9pm Mon-Sat) built in 1972. Tickets are also available at the more centrally located **Boutique PSG** (☎ 01 56 69 22 22; www.psg.fr in French; 27 av Champs Elysées, 8e; metro Franklin D Roosevelt; ☾ 10am-7.45pm Mon-Thu, 10am-9.45pm Fri & Sat, noon-7.45pm Sun).

RUGBY

Rugby has a strong following in the southwest of France with the favourite teams being Toulouse, Montauban and St-Godens. Paris-based **Stade Français CASG** (☎ 01 40 71 71 00; www.stade.fr) catapulted the capital to rugby fame and fortune with its defeat of the favourites, Toulouse, in the national championship in 2003. Stade Français CASG play their home games at the **Stade Jean Bouin** (Map pp380-2; ☎ 01 46 51 00 75; 26 av du Général Sarrail, 16; metro Exelmans), with room for 10,000 spectators, just north of the Parc des Princes. Tickets are available at the **stadium box office** (☎ 01 46 51 00 75; tickets €5-35; ☎ 11am-2pm & 3-7pm Tue-Fri, 2-7pm Mon & Sat) and at Fnac outlets (p207) throughout Paris. The finals of the Championnat de France de Rugby take place in late May and early June.

France's home games in the *Tournoi des VI Nations* (Six Nations Tournament) are held in March and April and involve France, England, Scotland, Wales, Ireland and Italy. France won the Six Nations title with a 44–5 victory over Ireland in April 2002 and again in March 2004 by beating England 24-21.

TENNIS

In late May and early June the tennis world focuses on the clay surface of 16,500-seat **Stade Roland Garros** (Map pp380-2; ☎ 01 47 43 48 00, 01 47 43 52 52; www.rolandgarros .com in French; av Gordon Bennett, 16e; metro Porte d'Auteuil) in the Bois de Boulogne for Les Internationaux de France de Tennis (French Open), the second of the four Grand Slam tournaments. Tickets are quite expensive and very hard to come by; bookings must usually be made by the previous March.

The top indoor tournament is the Open de Tennis de la Ville de Paris (Paris Tennis Open), which usually takes place in late October or early November at the **Palais Omnisports de Paris-Bercy** (Map p401; ☎ 01 40 02 60 60; www.bercy.fr in French; 8 blvd de Bercy, 12e; metro Bercy). Tickets are available from the **stadium box office** (☎ 08 92 39 04 90, from abroad 33-1 46 91 57 57; ☾ 11am-6pm Mon-Sat) or from Fnac (p207) and Virgin Megastore outlets (p207) in central Paris.

CYCLING

The Tour de France (www.letour.fr) is the world's most prestigious bicycle race. For three weeks in July, 189 of the world's top cyclists (in 21 teams of nine) take on a 3000km-plus route.

The route changes each year, but three things remain constant – the inclusion of the Alps, the Pyrenees and, since 1974, the race's finish on the av des Champs-Élysées. The final day varies from year to year but is usually the 3rd or 4th Sunday in July, with the race finishing sometime in the afternoon. If you want to see this exciting event, find a spot at the barricades before noon.

The race itself is divided into 22 stages: the prologue, a short time trial used essentially to put a rider (the prologue's winner) in the leader's jersey for the first stage; two more time trials; five or six stages in the mountains; and some long flat stages.

There's usually one rest day. Each stage is timed and the race's overall winner is the rider with the lowest aggregate time. The smallest winning margin was in 1989, when American Greg LeMond beat enigmatic Parisian Laurent Fignon by eight seconds after 23 days and 3285km of racing.

Track cycling, a sport at which France excels, is usually held in the velodrome of the **Palais Omnisports de Paris-Bercy** (Map p401; ☎ 01 40 02 60 60; www.bercy.fr in French; 8 blvd de Bercy, 12e; metro Bercy).

HORSE RACING & SHOWJUMPING

One of the cheapest ways to spend a relaxing afternoon in the company of Parisians of all ages, backgrounds and walks of life is to go to the races. The most accessible of the Paris areas' seven racecourses is **Hippodrome d'Auteuil** (Map pp380-2; ☎ 01 40 71 47 47; www.france-galop.com; Champ de Courses d'Auteuil, Bois de Boulogne, 16e; metro Porte d'Auteuil) in the south-eastern corner of the Bois de Boulogne, which hosts steeplechases from February to late June or early July and early September to early December.

Races are held about six times a month (check the Hippodrome d'Auteuil website for exact days), with half a dozen or so heats scheduled between 2pm and 5.30pm. There's no charge to stand on the *pelouse* (lawn) in the middle of the track, but a seat in the *tribune* (stands) costs about €3 for adults and €1.50 for students and seniors on weekdays. On Sunday it is €4 and €2. Those under age 18 get in free. Race schedules are published in almost all of the national newspapers. If you can read French, pick up a copy of *Paris Turf* (€1.15), the horse-racing daily.

Showjumping is all the rage and the Jumping International de Paris, held in early March at the **Palais Omnisports de Paris-Bercy** (Map p401; ☎ 01 40 02 60 60; www.bercy .fr in French; 8 blvd de Bercy, 12e; metro Bercy), attracts thousands of fans.

OUTDOOR ACTIVITIES

The entertainment weeklies *Pariscope* and *L'Officiel des Spectacles* (p206) have up-to-date information in French on every imaginable sort of activity. For more information on Paris' sporting activities and facilities, consult the free *Parisports: Le Guide du Sport à Paris* (p244) or ring **Mairie de Paris** (☎ 08 20 00 75 75).

CYCLING

Including tracks in the Bois de Boulogne (16e) and Bois de Vincennes (12e), Paris now has some 220km of bicycle lanes running throughout the city, as well as a dedicated lane running parallel to some two-thirds of the blvd Périphérique. At the same time, on Sundays and holidays throughout most of the year, large sections of road are reserved for pedestrians, cyclists and skaters under a scheme called 'Paris Respire' (Paris Breathes).

The **Mairie de Paris** (Map pp396-9; ☎ 08 20 00 75 75; www.paris.fr; Hôtel de Ville, 29 rue de Rivoli, 4e; metro Hôtel de Ville) produces a free booklet called *Paris à Vélo* (Paris by Bicycle) with itineraries, rules and regulations listed as well as a map called *À Paris Sortez Vos Vélos* (In Paris Get Out Your Bikes). More detailed is *Paris de Poche: Cycliste et Piéton* (Pocket Paris: Cyclist and Pedestrian; €3.50), which is available in most bookshops.

Bicycles on Public Transport

Bicycles are not allowed on the metro except on line No 1 on Sunday and public holidays. You can, however, take your bicycle to the suburbs on some RER lines on weekdays before 6.30am, between 9am and 4.30pm, after 7pm, and all day at the weekend and on public holidays. More lenient rules apply to SNCF commuter services. Contact SNCF (p337) for details.

For information on guided bicycle tours in Paris, see p77.

Bicycle Hire

BIKE 'N' ROLLER Map pp389-91
☎ 01 45 50 38 27; 38 rue Fabert, 7e; metro Invalides; 3hr/1 day €9/12; 🕑 10am-8pm Mon-Sat, 10am-6.30pm Sun

This place just north of the Hôtel des Invalides hires out bicycles as well as inline skates (p247).

FAT TIRE BIKE TOURS Map pp389-91
☎ 01 56 58 10 54; www.fattirebiketours.com; 24 rue Edgar Faure, 15e; metro La Motte-Piquet Grenelle; 1hr/day/weekend/week/month €2/15/25/50/65; 🕑 9am-7pm

Formerly known as Mike's Bike Tours, Fat Tire rents out three-speeds and also does bike tours (p77).

GEPETTO & VÉLOS Map pp392-5
☎ 01 43 54 19 95; www.gepetto-et-velos.com; 59 rue du Cardinal Lemoine, 5e; metro Cardinal Lemoine; half-/full-day €7.50-15, weekend/week €23/50; 🕑 9am-1pm & 2-7.30pm Tue-Sat, 9am-1pm & 2-7pm Sun

There is another **5e arrondissement branch** (Map pp392-5; 🕑 01 43 37 16 17; 46 rue Daubenton, 5e; metro Censier Daubenton; 🕑 9am-1pm & 2-7.30pm Mon-Sat) to the south that opens on Monday.

MAISON ROUE LIBRE Map pp396-9

☎ 08 10 44 15 34; www.rouelibre.fr; Forum des Halles, 1 passage Mondétour, 1er; metro Les Halles; 1hr/half-day/10hr-day/24hr-day/weekend €3/8/12/14/20; ⏱ 9am-7pm mid-Jan–mid-Dec

Sponsored by RATP, the city's public transport system, this is the best place to rent a bicycle in Paris. There are hourly, daily, weekly, monthly and yearly rates. Seniors, students and those aged under 26 get a 10% discount. Insurance, helmet and baby seat are included. The deposit is €150 along with some form of identification. From 9am to 7pm on Saturday and Sunday from April to October, Roue Libre bikes can also be rented from 'cyclobuses' (bikes stored on big buses) in various locations around the city including one at **Bercy** (Map p401; Parking SAEMES, 210 quai de Bercy, 12e; metro Cour St-Émilion) and at **La Villette** (Map pp386-8; 23 quai de la Loire, 19e; metro Laumière).

PARIS À VÉLO, C'EST SYMPA!

Map pp392-5

☎ 01 48 87 60 01; www.parisvelosympa.com in French; 37 blvd Bourdon, 4e; metro Bastille; ⏱ 9.30am-1pm & 2-6.30pm Mon-Fri, 9am-7pm Sat & Sun Apr-Oct; 9.30am-1pm & 2-6pm Mon-Fri, 9am-6pm Sat & Sun Nov-Mar

This association with the cringey name (Paris by Bike is Nice!) also rents tandems, which are the price of two bikes. There's a deposit of €200 (€610 for a tandem), which can be made with a credit card. If you need repairs done, **Vélo Bastille** (☎ 01 48 87 60 80, fax 01 48 87 61 01), at the same address, can do work on all bike models seven days a week.

SKATING

Be it on tarmac or ice, skating has taken Paris by storm in recent years.

Inline Skating

Inline skaters might want to join in one of the two so-called Skating Rambles (Randonnées en Roller) organised weekly throughout the year, that attract up to 10,000 participants. The **Pari Roller Ramble** (☎ 01 43 36 89 81; www.pari-roller.com in French) leaves place Raoul Dautry, 14e (Map pp389-91; metro Montparnasse Bienvenuë), the plaza between gare Montparnasse and Tour Montparnasse, at 10pm Friday, returning at 1am. The **Rollers & Coquillages Ramble** (☎ 01 44 54 07 44; www.rollers-coquillages.org) de-

parts from blvd Bourdon, 4e (Map pp392-5; metro Bastille), every Sunday at 2.30pm, returning between 5.30pm and 6pm.

BIKE 'N' ROLLER Map pp389-91

☎ 01 45 50 38 27; 38 rue Fabert, 7e; metro Invalides; half-day/full-day €9/12; ⏱ 10am-8pm Mon-Sat, 10am-6.30pm Sun

This place has bicycles, *rollers* (inline skates), *quads* (roller skates) and *trottinettes* (scooters) for rent. Elbow/knee guards cost €1/1.50.

NOMADES Map pp392-5

☎ 01 44 5 54 07 44; www.nomadeshop.com in French; 37 blvd Bourdon, 4e; metro Bastille; half-day/full-day weekdays €5/8, half-day/full-day weekends €6/9, weekend €16, Mon-Fri €23, full week €30; ⏱ 11am-1pm & 2-7pm Mon-Fri, 10am-7pm Sat, 10am-6pm Sun

This enormous shop next to **Paris à Vélo, C'est Sympa!** (this page) is the Harrods for roller heads and, as well as renting skates, it sells equipment and accessories and gives courses at five different levels. Elbow and knee guards/helmets cost €1/2. You must leave a deposit of €150 or an identity card or passport.

Ice-Skating

From early December to early March, the city of Paris and the adjoining *département* of Hauts-de-Seine maintain several outdoor ice-skating rinks, including **Patinoire de l'Hôtel de Ville** (Map pp396-9; ☎ 08 20 00 75 75; metro Hôtel de Ville; ⏱ noon-10pm Mon-Thu, noon-midnight Fri, 9am-midnight Sat, 9am-10pm Sun), **Patinoire de Montparnasse** (Map pp389-91; ☎ 08 20 00 75 75; place Raoul Dautry, 14e; metro Montparnasse Bienvenuë; ⏱ noon-8pm Mon-Fri, 9am-8pm Sat & Sun) and **Patinoire du Parvis de la Défense** (Map La Défense; ☎ 01 47 74 84 24; metro La Défense Grande Arche; ⏱ noon-2pm & 4.30-7.30pm Mon, Thu & Fri, 9.30am-7.30pm Wed, Sat & Sun). **Patinoire Sonja Henie** (☎ 01 40 02 60 60; www.bercy.fr in French; 8 blvd de Bercy, 12e; metro Bercy; adult/student & under 26 €4/3, Fri & Sat night €6/4; ☎ 3-6pm Wed, 9.30am-12.30am Fri, 3-6pm & 9.30pm-12.30am Sat, 10am-2pm & 3-6pm Sun Sep-May) is an ice-skating rink inside the Palais Omnisports de Paris-Bercy (use the garden-facing north entrance) and is open year-round except in summer. Access to the rinks is free, but *patins* (skates) cost €5 to rent.

BOULES & BOWLING

France's most popular traditional games are *boules* and the similar, but less formal *pétanque*, which aren't unlike lawn bowls but are played on a gravel or sandy pitch known as a *boulodrome*, scratched out wherever a bit of flat, shady ground can be found. The object is to get your *boules* (biased metal balls) as close as possible to the *cochonnet* (little piggy), or jack, the small wooden target ball thrown at the start. *Boules* are especially popular in southern France, but you may come across a group (usually men) playing in the Jardin du Luxembourg, which has several *boulodromes*.

Bowling is surprisingly popular in Paris and there are more than 24 tenpin alleys in the city. The three listed are among the best and/or most central. Prices for games depend on the time and day of the week.

AMF BOWLING DE MONTPARNASSE
Map pp389-91

☎ 01 43 21 61 32; 25 rue du Commandant René Mouchotte, 14e; metro Montparnasse Bienvenüe; games €2.25-6.50, set price from €16, shoes €2; ☯ 10-2am Sun-Thu, 10-4am Fri, 10-5am Sat

This centre just opposite the Gare Montparnasse has 16 alleys. A *forfait* (set price) allows multiple games, depending on the time and the day of the week.

AMF BOWLING DE PARIS Map pp380-2

☎ 01 53 64 93 00; Jardin d'Acclimitation, route du Mahatma Gandhi, 16e; metro Porte de Neuilly; games €2.45-6.55, shoe rental €1.85; ☯ 10-3am Sun-Thu, 10-5am Fri & Sat

Super-modern centre with 24 alleys on the northern edge of the Bois de Boulogne.

BOWLING MOUFFETARD Map pp392-5

☎ 01 43 31 09 35; 13 rue Gracieuse & 73 rue Mouffetard, 5e; metro Place Monge; games €2.30-5.50, set price €8.40-12.90, shoes €1.70; ☯ 3pm-2am Mon-Fri, 10-2am Sat & Sun

This intimate and friendly bowlodrome with eight alleys has two entrances.

TENNIS
MAIRIE DE PARIS

☎ 08 20 00 75 75; www.sport.paris.fr; 1hr covered court/open court €11.40/5.75, under 26 €6.10/3.20, everyone before 11am on weekdays €6.10/3.20

This organisation has some 170 covered and open tennis courts in 44 different locations that can be hired (hours vary considerably) provided you have a **Carte Paris Sports** (Mairie de Paris, Direction de la Jeunesse et des Sports, BP 4121, 75163 Paris CEDEX 04) which is available free by post. Courts can be reserved in advance by **Minitel** (p350) but *not* by the Internet at present. The following are three very central tennis centres with courts available for hire. **Luxembourg** (Map pp392-5; ☎ 01 43 25 79 18; Jardin du Luxembourg, 6e; metro Luxembourg) has six courts for hire, **Candie** (Map pp392-5; ☎ 01 43 55 84 95; rue Candie, 11e; metro Ledru Rollin) has two courts and **Neuve Saint Pierre** (Map pp396-9; ☎ 01 42 78 21 04; 5-7 rue Neuve St Pierre, 4e; metro St Paul) has one court.

HEALTH & FITNESS
GYMS & FITNESS CLUBS

Like everywhere else in the world these days, gyms and fitness clubs are a penny a barrel in Paris and several allow short-term memberships.

CLUB MED GYM

☎ 08 20 20 20 20; www.clubmedgym.com

This extremely well-equipped chain with a dozen gym outlets (many of them were part of the now defunct Gymnase Club group) allows single entry for €40. A 10-entry *carnet* costs €320. Convenient locations include **Palais Royal** (Map pp396-9; ☎ 01 40 20 03 03; 147 bis rue St-Honoré, 1er; metro Palais Royal-Musée du Louvre; ☯ 7.30am-10pm Mon-Fri, 9am-7pm Sat, 9am-5pm Sun), **République** (Map pp386-8; ☎ 01 47 00 69 98; 10 place de la République, 11e; metro République; ☯ 7.30am-10pm Mon-Fri, 8am-7pm Sat, 9am-5pm Sun) and **Montparnasse** (Map pp389-91; ☎ 01 45 44 24 35; 149 rue de Rennes, 6e; metro St-Placide; ☯ 8am-10pm Mon-Fri, 8am-8pm Sat, 9am-2pm Sun).

CLUB QUARTIER LATIN Map pp396-9

☎ 01 55 42 77 88; www.clubquartierlatin.com in French; 19 rue de Pontoise, 5e; metro Maubert Mutualité; pool single entry €3.40, 10-entry carnet €28.20; gym single entry €16, 10-entry carnet €140; ☯ 9am-midnight Mon-Fri, 9.30am-7pm Sat & Sun

This no-frills gym above **Piscine Pontoise-Quartier Latin** (opposite) also has squash courts. Check with the gym for class details and times.

Sports, Health & Fitness – Health & Fitness

ESPACE VIT' HALLES Map pp396-9

☎ 01 42 77 21 71; www.vithalles.com; 48 rue Rambuteau, 3e; metro Rambuteau; single visit €25, 10-entry carnet €179; ⏲ 8am-10.30pm Mon-Fri, 10am-7pm Sat, 10am-6pm Sun

This squeaky clean health club just north of Forum des Halles gets fabulous reviews from both local residents and blow-ins especially for its exercise classes.

SWIMMING

Paris has some 35 swimming pools open to the public; check with the **Mairie de Paris** (☎ 08 20 00 75 75; www.paris.fr) for the pool nearest to you. Most are short-length pools and finding a free lane for laps can be nigh on impossible. Opening times vary widely, but avoid Wednesday afternoon and Saturday when kids off from school take the plunge. Unless noted otherwise the entry cost for municipal pools in Paris is adults €2.40 and under-21s €1.35. A *carnet* of 10 tickets is €19.80 and €11.40.

PISCINE DE LA BUTTE AUX CAILLES
Map pp380-2

☎ 01 45 89 60 05; 5 place Paul Verlaine, 13e; metro Place d'Italie; ⏲ 7-8am, 11.30am-1pm & 4.30-6.30pm Tue, 7am-6.30pm Wed, 7-8am & 11.30am-6pm Thu & Fri, 7-8am & 10am-6pm Sat, 8am-5.30pm Sun

This positively stunning pool, built in 1924 and now a listed building, takes advantage of the lovely warm water issuing from a nearby artesian well.

PISCINE PONTOISE-QUARTIER LATIN
Map pp396-9

☎ 01 55 42 77 88; 18 rue de Pontoise, 5e; metro Maubert Mutualité; single entry adult/concession €3.40/, 10-entry carnet €28.20; ⏲ 7-8.30am, 12.15-1.30pm & 4.30-8.45pm, 9-11.45pm Mon & Tue, 7-8.30am, 12.15-8.45pm, 9-11.45pm Wed, 7-8.30am, 12.15-1.30pm & 4.30-7.15pm, 9-11.45pm Thu,

Top Five Sport Venues

- AMF Bowling de Paris (p248)
- Espace Vit' Halles (p249)
- Hammam de la Mosquée de Paris (p249)
- Patinoire de l'Hôtel de Ville (p247)
- Piscine de la Butte aux Cailles (p249)

7-8.45am, noon-1.30pm & 4.30-8pm, 9-11.45pm Fri, 10am-7pm Sat, 8am-7pm Sun

This beautiful Art Deco-style pool in the heart of the Latin Quarter measures 33m by 15m.

PISCINE ROGER LE GALL Map pp380-2

☎ 01 44 73 81 12; 34 boulevard Carnot, 12e; metro Porte de Vincennes; ⏲ noon-2pm & 5-8pm Mon, noon-2pm & 5-9pm Tue, Thu & Fri, 8am-9pm Wed, 10am-7pm Sat, 8am-7pm Sun

Readers tell us that this is one of the best public pools in Paris, but the blvd Périphérique is a little too close for our comfort.

PISCINE SUZANNE BERLIOUX
Map pp396-9

☎ 01 42 36 98 44; Level 3, Forum des Halles, 10 place de la Rotonde, 1er; metro Les Halles; adult/child 4-15 €3.80/3, 10-entry carnet €35/28.95; ⏲ 11.30am-10pm Mon, Tue, Thu & Fri, 10am-10pm Wed, 9am-7pm Sat & Sun

This 50m by 20m pool surrounded by a tropical garden is in the bowels of Paris' largest shopping centre; always busy, but fun.

Water Parks

AQUABOULEVARD Map pp380-2

☎ 01 40 60 10 00; www.aquaboulevard.com in French; 4 rue Louis Armand, 15e; metro Balard; adult/child 3-12 €20/10; ⏲ 9am-11pm Mon-Thu, 9am-midnight Fri, 8am-midnight Sat, 8am-11pm Sun

A huge recreational centre in southwest Paris with a wide range of activities for adults and kids, including a swimming pool, a 'beach' and aquatic park, tennis, squash, golf practice, gym, restaurants and so on.

TURKISH BATHS

One of the best places to relax after a day slogging through the streets and museums of Paris is in a *hammam* (Turkish bath).

HAMMAM DE LA MOSQUÉE DE PARIS
Map pp392-5

☎ 01 43 31 18 14, 01 43 31 38 20; 39 rue Geoffroy St-Hilaire; metro Censier Daubenton or Place Monge admission €15; ☎ men 2-9pm Tue, 10am-9pm Sun; women 10am-9pm Mon, Wed, Thu & Sat, 2-9pm Fri

The massages here cost €1 per minute in 10-minute blocks. There are several 'combination' tickets available, including the *formule orientale* (Oriental set menu), which includes admission to the *hammam*, a 10-minute massage and a couscous meal with drink for €58.

HAMMAM DES GRANDS BOULEVARDS Map pp386-8

☎ 01 48 01 03 05; 28 blvd de Bonne Nouvelle, 10e; metro Bonne Nouvelle; admission €21-23; ☽ men 1-10pm Tue, 1-8pm Fri; women 1-5pm Sat; mixed with bathing suit required 2-10pm Mon, 1-5pm Wed, 5-9pm Sat, 1-9pm Sun, mixed with naturist association card required 5-10pm Wed, 1-10pm Thu

This bath has two eucalyptus *hammam*s (where the *hammams* are steamed with eucalyptus), sauna, cold pool etc.

HAMMAM PACHA Map St-Denis

☎ 01 48 29 19 66; 147 rue Gabriel Péri, St-Denis; metro Basilique de St-Denis; admission €27; ☽ noon-midnight Mon-Wed & Fri, 10am-midnight Thu, 10am-8pm Sat & Sun

This *hammam* reserved for women only is one of the better ones around, though it is in far-flung St-Denis.

YOGA

One of the most active yoga centres in Paris, the **Fédération Inter-Enseignements de Hatha Yoga** (Hatha Yoga Teachings Federation; Map pp383-5; ☎ 01 42 60 31 10; www .fidhy.asso.fr in French; 322 rue St-Honoré, 1er; metro Tuileries), organises courses at various Paris venues. Check its website for exact locations, times and costs.

Louvre & Les Halles	253
Marais & Bastille	254
Île St-Louis	258
Latin Quarter & Jardin des Plantes	258
St-Germain, Odéon & Luxembourg	260
Faubourg St-Germain & Invalides	261
Étoile & Champs-Élysées	262
Concorde & Madeleine	263
Opéra & Grands Boulevards	265
Gare du Nord, Gare de l'Est & République	266
Gare de Lyon, Nation & Bercy	267
Montmartre & Pigalle	267
Outside the Walls: Beyond Central Paris	267

Shopping

Shopping

Paris is a wonderful place to shop, whether you're someone who can afford an off-the-peg Cartier diamond bracelet or you're an impoverished *lèche-vitrine* (literally 'window-licker') who just enjoys what you see behind glass. From the ultra-chic couture houses of av Montaigne and the cubby-hole boutiques of the Marais to the vast underground shopping centre at Les Halles and the flea-market bargains at St-Ouen, Paris is a city that knows how to make it, how to display it and how to charge for it.

Paris has everything for sale but stick to the tried and the true: fashion, jewellery, fine food and wine, professional kitchenware, beauty products, and quality gifts and souvenirs.

Credit cards (most commonly Visa) are accepted at retail outlets everywhere but travellers cheques are not.

Opening Hours

Opening times in Paris are notoriously anarchic, with each store setting its own hours. Most shops will be open at least from 10am to 6pm five days a week (including Saturday) but they may open earlier, close later, close for lunch (usually 1pm to 2pm or 2.30pm) or for a full or half-day on Monday or Tuesday. In general, only shops in tourist areas (eg the Champs-Élysées and the Marais) open on Sunday, though most are open during the sales in January and June. Many larger shops and department stores also have a *nocturne* – one late shopping night (usually to 10pm on Thursday) a week.

Van Cleef & Arpels (p264)

Consumer Taxes

If you're not a resident of the EU, you can get a TVA (vat; sales tax) refund of up to 17%, provided you have spent more than €182 in any one store (see Tax & Refunds, p349).

Bargaining

Many stores (eg large department stores and some 'duty-free' shops), will give discounts of 10% to foreign-passport holders if asked. Otherwise bargaining is reserved for flea markets.

LOUVRE & LES HALLES

The area around the Louvre and Les Halles is a good area to shop for things like gifts and kitchenware. There's no shortage of fashion boutiques as well.

A SIMON Map pp386-8   *Household Goods*
☎ 01 42 33 71 65; http://simon-a.com; 48 & 52 rue Montmartre, 2e; metro Étienne Marcel;
🕑 1.30-6.30pm Mon, 9am-6.30pm Tue-Sat
A more modern kitchenware shop than nearby **E Dehillerin** (p254), A Simon has more pots, pans, mixing bowls and utensils than you thought imaginable in two shops.

ANNA JOLIET
Map pp386-8   *Gifts & Souvenirs*
☎ 01 42 96 55 13; passage du Perron, 9 rue de Beaujolais, 1er; metro Pyramides; 🕑 10am-7pm Mon-Sat
This wonderful (and tiny) shop at the northern end of the Jardin du Palais Royal specialises in

music boxes, both new and old. Just open the door and see if you aren't tempted in.

CARROUSEL DU LOUVRE
Map pp396-9   *Shopping Centre*
☎ 01 43 16 47 10; www.carrouseldulouvre.com;
99 rue de Rivoli, 1er; metro Palais Royal-Musée du Louvre; 🕑 8.30am-11pm
Built around IM Pei's **inverted glass pyramid** (p80) beneath the place du Carrousel, this shopping centre contains some three dozen upmarket shops, restaurants and even the **Comédie Française Studio Théâtre** (p239).

DIDIER LUDOT
Map pp386-8   *Clothing & Accessories*
☎ 01 42 96 06 56; 19-20 & 23-24 Galerie de Montpensier, 1er; metro Palais Royal-Musée du Louvre; 🕑 11am-7pm Mon-Sat
Formed from old galleries that have been joined together, this fabulous shop in the

Top Five Shops for Gifts

- **2 Mille & 1 Nuits** (below)
- **Anna Joliet** (p253)
- **CSAO Boutique**(p255)
- **E Dehillerin** (below)
- **Musée & Compagnie** (p267)

equally fabulous **Galerie de Montpensier** (p145) just up from the Palais Royal is crammed with pre-loved couture creations from yesteryear, including original Chanel suits from the 1950s and Hermès bags and accessories – all sold for half the original price.

E DEHILLERIN
Map pp396-9   *Household Goods*
☎ 01 42 36 53 13; 18-20 rue Coquillière, 1er; metro Les Halles; 🕙 8am-12.30pm & 2-6pm Mon, 8am-6pm Tue-Sat

This shop spread over two floors and dating back to 1820 carries the most incredible selection of professional-quality *matériel de cuisine* (kitchenware). You're sure to find something even the most well-equipped kitchen is lacking. These items might include a *coupe volaille* (poultry scissors), *turbotiére* (turbot poacher), or even a *poëlon escargots* (snail pan), with six or 12 holes.

LA MAISON DE L'ASTRONOMIE
Map pp396-9   *Hobby Items*
☎ 01 42 77 99 55; 33-35 rue de Rivoli, 4e; metro Hôtel de Ville; 🕙 10am-6.40pm Tue-Sat

If you've ever had the inclination to gaze at the stars, visit this large shop just west of

the Hôtel de Ville. The 1st floor is positively crammed with telescopes, some of which can run into the tens of thousands of euros. It also stocks astronomical books, periodicals and sky maps.

LA SAMARITAINE
Map pp396-9   *Department Store*
☎ 01 40 41 20 20; www.lasamaritaine.com; 19 rue de la Monnaie, 1er; metro Pont Neuf; 🕙 9.30am-7pm Mon-Wed & Fri, 9.30am-10pm Thu, 9.30am-8pm Sat

The 'Samaritan' is in two buildings between Pont Neuf and 142 rue de Rivoli, 1er. The main store's biggest draw is the outstanding view from the rooftop restaurant and café; the building devoted to men's fashion has a large sports department in the basement.

LOUVRE DES ANTIQUAIRES
Map pp396-9   *Antiques*
2 place du Palais Royal; www.louvre-antiquaires.com; metro Palais Royal-Musée du Louvre; 🕙 11am-7pm Tue-Sun Sep-Jun, 11am-7pm Tue-Sat Jul & Aug

This extremely elegant 'mall' houses some 250 antique shops spread over three floors and is filled with *objets d'art*, furniture, clocks and classical antiquities – affordable for anyone with a king's ransom. The basement is an Aladdin's cave of jewellery shops.

ROXY LIFE SHOP
Map pp386-8   *Clothing & Accessories*
☎ 01 42 36 50 38; 42 rue Étienne Marcel, 2e; metro Étienne Marcel; 🕙 10.30am-7.30pm Mon-Sat

This funky little boutique just down from place des Victoires sells hip street and party clothes.

MARAIS & BASTILLE

The Marais has a growing number of fashionable clothing shops and is a good place to look for streetwear. For more everyday clothing, there are lots of shops along rue de Rivoli, which gets less expensive as you move east into the 4e. The southern end of rue de Turenne, 4e (Map pp396–9), is packed with design and clothes boutiques. Another interesting area is along rue des Francs Bourgeois (3e and 4e) leading out of place des Vosges.

2 MILLE & 1 NUITS
Map pp396-9   *Gifts & Souvenirs*
☎ 01 48 87 07 07; 13 rue des Francs Bourgeois, 4e; metro Chemin Vert or St-Paul; 🕙 11am-7.30pm

The large '2001 Nights' shop at the end of a courtyard just off rue des Francs Bourgeois has colourful gifts and decorative items with a Middle Eastern theme. Some of the stuff for sale – a silver cup with a handle made from

antelope horn, for example – is just this side of kitsch, but it's all good fun.

À L'OLIVIER
Map pp396-9   *Food & Drink*
☎ 01 48 04 86 59; 23 rue de Rivoli, 4e; metro St-Paul; 🕙 9.30am-1pm & 2-7pm Mon-Sat

'At the Olive Tree' has been *the* place for oil, from olive and walnut to soy and sesame, since 1822. Good vinegars, jams and honeys, too.

ABOU D'ABI BAZAR

Map pp396-9 *Clothing & Accessories*

☎ 01 42 77 96 98; 10 rue des Francs Bourgeois, 3e;
metro St-Paul; ☺ 2-7pm Sun & Mon, 10.30am-7.15pm
Tue-Sat

This fashionable boutique with the odd name
is a treasure-trove of smart and affordable
ready-to-wear pieces from young designers
such as Paul & Joe, Isabel Marant and Vanessa
Bruno.

BAINS PLUS

Map pp396-9 *Household Goods*

☎ 01 48 87 83 07; 51 rue des Francs Bourgeois, 3e;
metro Hôtel de Ville or Rambuteau; ☺ 11am-7.30pm
Tue-Sat, 2-7pm Sun

A bathroom supplier for the 21st century true
to its name, 'Baths Plus' stocks luxurious robes
and gowns, soaps and oils, shaving brushes
and mirrors.

BAZAR DE L'HÔTEL DE VILLE

Map pp396-9 *Department Store*

☎ 01 42 74 90 00; www.bhv.fr in French; 14 rue du
Temple, 4e; metro Hôtel de Ville; ☺ 9.30am-7.30pm
Mon, Tue, Thu & Fri, 9.30am-9pm Wed, 9.30am-8pm Sat

BHV is a straightforward department store –
apart from its huge but hopelessly chaotic
hardware/DIY department in the basement,
with every type of hammer, power tool, nail,
plug or hinge you could ask for. Service is
decidedly in the DIY vein too.

BOUTIQUE PARIS-MUSÉES

Map pp396-9 *Gifts & Souvenirs*

☎ 01 42 74 13 92; 29 bis rue des Francs Bourgeois, 4e;
metro Chemin Vert or St-Paul; ☺ 2-7pm Mon,
11am-1pm, 2-7pm Tue-Sun

This lovely boutique stocks museum reproductions, especially of art and sculpture on exhibit
at museums run by the City of Paris, such as
the Musée Carnavalet and the Musée d'Art
Moderne de la Ville de Paris.

CSAO BOUTIQUE

Map pp396-9 *Gifts & Souvenirs*

☎ 01 44 54 55 88; 1-3 rue Elzévir, 3e; metro St-Paul
or Chemin Vert; ☺ 11am-7pm Tue-Fri, 11am-7.30pm
Sat, 2-7pm Sun

This wonderful gallery and shop, owned and
operated by the charitable Compagnie du
Sénégal et de l'Afrique de l'Ouest (CSAO;
Senegal and West Africa Company), distributes
the work of African artists and craftspeople.

Many of the colourful fabrics and weavings
are exquisite and the handmade recycled
items – handbags and caps from soft-drink
cans, lamp shades from tomato paste tins –
are both amusing and heartbreaking. CSAO is
worth at least a visit.

FNAC MUSIQUE Map pp392-5 *Music*

☎ 01 43 42 04 04; 4 place de la Bastille, 12e;
metro Bastille; ☺ 10am-8pm Mon-Sat

Fnac's flagship music store at Bastille has a
huge variety of local and international music.

GALERIE & ATELIER PUNCINELLO

Map pp396-9 *Art & Antiques*

☎ 01 42 72 00 60; 16 rue du Parc Royal, 4e;
metro St-Paul; ☺ 2-7pm Tue-Sat

This delightful gallery and workshop stocks
masks, shields, spears and other collectibles
and antiques from Oceania and Southeast
Asia. The items coming from Irian Jaya in Indonesia are particularly fine though expensive;
a carved shield will set you back €2700 and a
woven body mask €1860. The workshop can
make a unique stand or plinth for your prized
piece in wood, bronze or plexiglass.

Clothing Sizes
Measurements approximate only, try before you buy

Women's Clothing						
Aus/UK	8	10	12	14	16	18
Europe	36	38	40	42	44	46
Japan	5	7	9	11	13	15
USA	6	8	10	12	14	16
Women's Shoes						
Aus/USA	5	6	7	8	9	10
Europe	35	36	37	38	39	40
France only	35	36	38	39	40	42
Japan	22	23	24	25	26	27
UK	3½	4½	5½	6½	7½	8½
Men's Clothing						
Aus	92	96	100	104	108	112
Europe	46	48	50	52	54	56
Japan	S		M	M		L
UK/USA	35	36	37	38	39	40
Men's Shirts (Collar Sizes)						
Aus/Japan	38	39	40	41	42	43
Europe	38	39	40	41	42	43
UK/USA	15	15½	16	16½	17	17½
Men's Shoes						
Aus/UK	7	8	9	10	11	12
Europe	41	42	43	44½	46	47
Japan	26	27	27½	28	29	30
USA	7½	8½	9½	10½	11½	12½

ISSEY MIYAKE
Clothing & Accessories

You can purchase the avant-garde designs of Issey Miyake at his eponymous store, **Issey Miyake** (Map pp396-9; ☎ 01 48 87 01 86; 5 place des Vosges, 4e; 🕙 11am-7pm Mon-Sat). His designs are also available at **Pleats Please** (Map pp396-9; ☎ 01 40 29 99 66; 3 rue des Rosiers, 4e; 🕙 11am-7pm Mon-Sat) and the nearby **Apoc** (Map pp396-9; ☎ 01 44 54 07 05; 47 rue des Francs Bourgeois, 4e; 🕙 11am-7pm Tue-Sat), his lab-style boutique designed by Erwan and Ronan Bouroullec.

LA BOUTIQUE DES INVENTIONS
Map pp396-9   *Gifts & Souvenirs*

☎ 01 42 71 44 19; Village St-Paul, 13 rue St-Paul, 4e; metro St-Paul; 🕙 1am-7pm Wed-Sun

This unique shop in the heart of Village St-Paul, a delightful little shopping square with antique shops, galleries and boutiques, is a forum for inventors and their inventions. Be the first on the block to own a shaker that sprinkles its own salt, a pepper grinder that twists itself or a miraculous filter that turns water into wine. Lots of wacky designs too.

LA CHARRUE ET LES ÉTOILES
Map pp396-9   *Gifts & Souvenirs*

☎ 01 48 87 39 07; 19 rue des Francs Bourgeois, 4e; metro St-Paul or Chemin Vert; 🕙 11am-7pm

Presumably named after Sean O'Casey's 1926 play (though the Irish connection is lost on us) the 'Plough and Stars' may look like just another gift shop, but it stocks an unusual collection of figurines modelled after celebrated works of art. It's worth a browse for an unusual gift or souvenir.

LA MAISON DU CERF-VOLANT
Map pp392-5   *Toys*

☎ 01 44 68 00 75; 7 rue de Prague, 12e; metro Ledru Rollin; 🕙 11am-2pm & 3-7pm Tue-Sat

The 'Kite House' has just that – kites in every conceivable size, shape and colour and kits to make them. You'll also find quite a nice collection of boomerangs.

LE PALAIS DES THÉS
Map pp396-9   *Food & Drink*

☎ 01 48 87 80 60; 64 rue Vieille du Temple, 3e; metro Hôtel de Ville or St-Paul; 🕙 10am-8pm

The 'Palace of Teas' is not as well established as **Mariage Frères** (right) but the selection is as large and the surroundings more 21st century. There are three other outlets in Paris including

a **6e branch** (Map pp389-91; ☎ 01 42 22 03 98; 61 rue du Cherche Midi, 6e; metro Rennes).

LES MOTS À LA BOUCHE
Map pp396-9   *Books*

☎ 01 42 78 88 30; www.motsbouche.com in French; 6 rue Ste-Croix de la Bretonnerie, 4e; metro Hôtel de Ville; 🕙 11am-11pm Mon-Sat, 2-8pm Sun

'On the Tip of the Tongue' is Paris' premier gay bookshop. Most of the left-hand side of the ground floor is devoted to English-language books, including some guides and novels. If you're feeling naughty, go downstairs.

LES RUCHERS DU ROY
Map pp396-9   *Food & Drink*

☎ 01 42 72 02 96; 37 rue du Roi de Sicile, 4e; metro St-Paul; 🕙 11am-1pm & 3-8pm Tue-Sun

The 'Apiaries of the King' sells honey and apiarian products fit for a king – especially its pure royal jelly, a substance secreted by worker bees and fed to future queens. It sells dozens of types of honey including those made from *miels monofloraux* (one type of flower), *miels polyfloraux* (a number of blossoms) and various *miels des régions* (regional honeys).

LIBRAIRIE DE L'HÔTEL DE SULLY
Map pp396-9   *Books*

☎ 01 44 61 21 75; 62 rue St-Antoine, 4e; metro St-Paul; 🕙 10am-6pm Tue-Sun

This early-17th-century aristocratic mansion housing the body responsible for many of France's historical monuments, the **Centre des Monuments Nationaux** (p88), has one of the best bookshops in town for titles related to Paris. From historical texts and biographies to picture books and atlases, it's all here.

L'OURS DU MARAIS
Map pp396-9   *Toys*

☎ 01 42 77 60 43; 18 rue Pavée, 4e; metro St-Paul; 🕙 11.30am-7.30pm Tue-Sat, 2-7.30pm Sun

'Marais Bear' doesn't focus on Smoky or Yogi but on teddy – there are more versions of the popular stuffed animal in this crowded shop than you could fill a den with.

MARIAGE FRÈRES
Map pp396-9   *Food & Drink*

☎ 01 42 72 28 11; www.mariagefreres.com in French; 30 rue du Bourg Tibourg, 4e; metro Hôtel de Ville; 🕙 shop 10.30am-7.30pm, tearooms noon-7pm

Founded in 1854, this is Paris' first and arguably its finest tea shop, with 500 varieties from more than 30 countries. Mariage Frères has

Best Areas to Shop

Unlike many other cities, Paris does not have a shopping 'centre' as such and browsing can be a fascinating way to discover hidden parts of the city. Many *quartiers* – and even streets – still specialise in a single product or art. Areas such as the Latin Quarter (p258) and St-Paul are good for stationery and books, and the Marais (p254) has hip boutiques and quirky speciality stores. Other great shopping areas are Opéra and Grands Boulvevards (p265), St-Germain (p260) and Sentier. The area known as the Triangle d'Or (Golden Triangle) near the av des Champs-Élysées is where the *haute couture* fashion houses are.

While Paris' myriad boutiques – still the heart and soul of shopping here – are often worth a visit in themselves, some of its *grands magasins* (department stores) like Le Bon Marché are Art Nouveau extravaganzas and La Samaritaine and Galeries Lafayette also have fabulous views out over the rooftops of the city. All offer quality and very stylish items in one convenient location that will go down a treat at home. Remember that the department stores hold their biannual *soldes* (sales) in January and June.

Paris' *marchés aux puces* (flea markets) are well and truly picked over but they can be great fun if you're in the mood to browse for unexpected diamonds in the rough through all the *brocante* (second-hand goods) and bric-a-brac on display, see the boxed text p152.

Shopping Streets

Passage de l'Industrie 10e (Map pp386-8; metro Château d'Eau) Shops specialise in equipment and tools for *coiffeurs* (hairdressers).

Place Vendôme 1er (Map pp383-5; metro Tuileries) Jewellery, luxury goods.

Rue de Paradis 10e (Map pp386-8; metro Château d'Eau) Famed for its crystal, glass and tableware shops.

Rue de Rivoli & Les Halles 1er & 2e (Map pp396-9; metro Chtelet or Louvre Rivoli) International brands, clothes, shoes, books, music, toys, perfume.

Rue des Abbesses 18e (Map p400; metro Abbesses) Vintage clothing, streetwear, fabrics, music.

Rue Drouot 9e (Map pp386-8; metro Richelieu Drouot) Shops sell almost nothing but collectible postage stamps.

Rue du Faubourg St-Honoré 8e (Map pp383-5; metro St-Philippe du Roule or Madeleine) Haute couture, jewellery, luxury goods, art galleries.

Rue du Pont Louis-Philippe 4e (Map pp936-9; metro Pont Marie) Has all manner of high-quality paper goods and stationery for sale.

Rue Keller 11e (Map pp392-5; metro Ledru Rollin) Comic books and action hero videos, DVDs and bric-a-brac.

Rue Martel 10e (Map pp386-8; metro Château d'Eau) If you're in the market for a sewing machine come here, it's chock-a-block with the things.

Rue Réaumur 3e (Map pp386-8; metro Arts et Métiers) Lots of jewellery shops.

Rue Victor Massé 9e (Map pp386-8; metro Pigalle) Musical instruments.

two other outlets – a **6e branch** (Map pp396-9; ☎ 01 40 51 82 50; 13 rue des Grands Augustins; metro Odéon) and an **8e branch** (Map pp383-5; ☎ 01 46 22 18 54; 260 rue du Faubourg St-Honoré; metro Tuileries) as well as concessions in four major department stores: **La Samaritaine** (p254), **Le Bon Marché** (p261), **Galeries Lafayette** (p265) and **Le Printemps** (p265).

MÉLODIES GRAPHIQUES

Map pp396-9   *Gifts & Souvenirs*
☎ 01 42 74 57 68; 10 rue du Pont Louis-Philippe, 4e; metro Pont Marie; ☽ 2-7pm Mon, 11am-7pm Tue-Sat
'Graphic Melodies' carries all sorts of items made from exquisite Florentine *papier à cuve*

(paper hand-decorated with marbled designs). There are several other fine stationery shops along the same street.

PRODUITS DES MONASTÈRES

Map pp396-9   *Food & Drink*
☎ 01 48 04 39 05; 10 rue des Barres, 4e; metro Hôtel de Ville or Pont Marie; ☽ 10am-noon & 2.30-6.30pm Tue-Sat, 12.30-1pm Sun
This shop on an ancient cobbled street just down from Église St-Gervais sells jams, biscuits, cakes, muesli, honeys, herbal teas and other comestibles made at Benedictine and Trappist monasteries in Jerusalem. The staff is particularly friendly and helpful.

RED WHEELBARROW BOOKSTORE

Map pp396-9 *Books*

☎ 01 48 04 75 08; 22 rue St-Paul, 4e; metro St-Paul; ⏱ 10am-7pm Mon-Sat, 2-6pm Sun

This somewhat earnest English-language bookshop has arguably the best selection of literature and 'serious reading' in Paris and a helpful, well-read staff. Around the corner, the **Red Wheelbarrow Children's Bookstore** (Map pp396-9; ☎ 01 42 77 42 17; 13 rue Charles V, 4e; metro St-Paul; ⏱ noon-6pm Wed-Sun) stocks books for kids as well as university texts for students. All in all, the Wheelbarrows are very welcome additions to the English-language book trade in Paris.

ROUL'TABILLE Map pp396-9 *Toys*

☎ 01 42 74 38 18; 23 rue de Rivoli, 4e, metro St-Paul; ⏱ 10am-7pm Tue-Sun

They may be toys but they're for big boys – and girls! Billiard tables, pinball machines (which are called *flippers* in French), video games and smaller items such as chessboards, decks of cards and the ever-popular French board game, *Le Cochon qui rit* (Laughing Pig).

SIC AMOR Map pp396-9 *Jewellery*

☎ 01 42 76 02 37; 20 rue du Pont Louis-Philippe, 4e; metro Pont Marie; ⏱ 10.30am-2pm & 3-7pm Tue-Sat, 3-7pm Sun & Mon

This shop sells contemporary jewellery by local designers from a shop opposite the headquarters of the all-but-moribund Partie Communiste Française.

SLIP

Map pp396-9 *Clothing & Accessories*

☎ 01 42 77 53 23; 6 rue du Grenier St-Lazare, 3e; metro Rambuteau; ⏱ 2-7.30pm Mon, noon-7.30pm Tue-Sat

This is for the guy who has everything and likes to let everyone know just that. It's a shop totally devoted to men's underwear – from G-strings and thongs to Y-fronts and boxers.

TUMBLEWEED

Map pp396-9 *Toys*

☎ 01 42 78 06 10; 19 rue de Turenne, 4e; metro St-Paul or Chemin Vert; ⏱ 11am-7pm Mon-Sat, 2-7pm Sun

This little shop, which specialises in *l'arsinart d'art ludique* (crafts of the playing art), stocks wonderful wooden toys, some of which look too nice to play with. The jack-in-the-box collection is especially fine.

ÎLE ST-LOUIS

GALERIE ALAIN CARION

Map pp396-9 *Gifts & Souvenirs*

☎ 01 43 26 01 16; 92 rue St-Louis en l'Île, 4e; metro Pont Marie; ⏱ 10.30am-1pm & 2-7.30pm Tue-Sat

This small boutique has a stunningly beautiful collection of museum-quality minerals, crystals, fossils and meteorites from 40 different countries, some of them in the form of earrings, brooches and pendants.

LA PETITE SCIERIE

Map pp396-9 *Food & Drink*

☎ 01 55 42 14 88; 60 rue St-Louis en l'Île, 4e; metro Pont Marie; ⏱ 11am-8pm

This little hole-in-the-wall called the 'Little Sawmill' on posh rue St-Louis en l'Île sells every permutation of edibles produced by and made from ducks, with the emphasis – *naturellement* – on foie gras (€30 for 180g). The products come direct from the farm with no middle party involved so you can be assured of the highest quality. If duck is not your thing, there is also a nice line of asparagus products.

LIBRAIRIE ULYSSE

Map pp396-9 *Books*

☎ 01 43 25 17 35; 26 rue St-Louis en l'Île, 4e; metro Pont Marie; ⏱ 2-8pm Tue-Sat

The 'Ulysses Bookshop' is a delightful store full of travel guides, maps, 20,000 back issues of *National Geographic* and sage advice from owner Catherine Domain.

LATIN QUARTER & JARDIN DES PLANTES

The Latin Quarter is a particularly good hunting ground for bookshops and sporting goods.

ABBEY BOOKSHOP Map pp396-9 *Books*

☎ 01 46 33 16 24; www.abbeybookshop.com; 29 rue de la Parcheminerie, 5e; metro Cluny-La Sorbonne; ⏱ 10am-7pm Mon-Sat

The Abbey is a mellow Canadian-owned bookshop, not far from place St-Michel known for its free tea and coffee, and good selection of new and used works of fiction and nonfiction. Ask about the weekend hikes around Paris.

AU VIEUX CAMPEUR

Map pp396-9   *Outdoor Gear*

☎ 01 53 10 48 48; www.auvieuxcampeur.fr in French; 48 rue des Écoles, 5e; metro Maubert Mutualité or Cluny La Sorbonne; ☷ 11am-7.30pm Mon-Wed & Fri, 11am-9pm Thu, 10am-7.30pm Sat

This popular sporting gear chain in the Latin Quarter, just east of rue St-Jacques between blvd St-Germain and rue des Écoles, has more than 20 outlets. Each specialises in equipment for a specific kind of outdoor activity: hiking, mountaineering, cycling, skiing, snowboarding, scuba diving, canyoning etc. Camping equipment is sold at several shops, including those at 18 rue du Sommerard, 3 rue de Latran and 6 rue Thénard; check the website for the appropriate outlet.

EOL' MODELISME

Map pp396-9   *Hobby Items*

☎ 01 43 54 01 43; www.eol-model.fr in French; 62 blvd St-Germain, 5e; metro Maubert Mutualité; ☷ 10am-7pm Tue-Sat

This shop sells expensive toys for big boys and girls, including every sort of model imaginable – from radio-controlled aircraft to large wooden yachts. The main shop, right by the metro entrance, has an amazing collection of tiny cars. There are two nearby branches, **No 55** (Map pp396-9; blvd St-Germain, 5e) and **No 70** (Map pp396-9; blvd St-Germain, 5e) that keep the same hours.

JADIS ET GOURMANDE

Map pp392-5   *Food & Drink*

☎ 01 43 26 17 75; 88 blvd de Port Royal, 5e; metro Port Royal; ☷ 1-7pm Mon, 9.30am-7pm Tue & Wed, 9.30am-7.30pm Thu-Sat

This shop at the southern end of the Jardin du Luxembourg sells chocolate, chocolate and more chocolate in every conceivable shape and size. There are three other outlets in town, including an **8e branch** (Map pp383-5; ☎ 01 42 25 06 04; 49 bis av Franklin D Roosevelt, 8e).

LA MAISON DE LA VANILLE

Map pp392-5   *Food & Drink*

☎ 01 43 25 50 95; 8 rue du Cardinal Lemoine, 5e; metro Cardinal Lemoine; ☷ 11.30am-7pm Wed-Sat, 2.30-7pm Sun

This sweet-scented Creole shop, which has a café, specialises in vanilla in all its guises and it all comes from the island of Réunion. Try the *thé à la mauricienne* (Mauritian-style tea with milk and cardamom) and the sumptuous *gâteau à la patate douce* (sweet potato cake). On a gloomy winter's day, the décor – coconut palms, fans, primary colours – and heady scents are bound to lift your spirits.

LIBRAIRIE GOURMANDE

Map pp396-9   *Books*

☎ 01 43 54 37 27; www.librairie-gourmande.fr in French; 4 rue Dante, 5e; metro Maubert Mutualité; ☷ 10am-7pm Mon-Sat

---

St-Sulpice Chic

The largest group of chic clothing boutiques in the fashionable 6e – many of them run by younger and more daring designers – is northwest of place St-Sulpice.

There are also some ultra-chic clothing, footwear and leather-goods shops along rue du Cherche Midi. A bit to the southwest, just south of Le Bon Marché department store (p261), rue St-Placide has lots of attractive shops (Map pp389-91) selling clothes and shoes, mainly – but not exclusively – for women. Reasonably priced clothing and shoe shops are legion along the southern half of rue de Rennes.

Shops are open from 10am or 10.30am to 7pm or 7.30pm Monday to Saturday.

Celine (Map pp389-91; ☎ 01 45 48 58 55; 58 rue de Rennes, 6e)

Christian Lacroix (Map pp396-9; ☎ 01 46 33 48 95; 2-4 place St-Sulpice, 6e)

Fausto Santini (Map pp389-91; ☎ 01 45 44 39 40; 4ter rue du Cherche Midi, 6e)

Il Bisonte (Map pp389-91; ☎ 01 42 22 08 41; 17 rue du Cherche Midi, 6e)

JB Martin (Map pp389-91; ☎ 01 45 44 29 40; 13 rue du Cherche Midi, 6e)

Kenzo (Map pp389-91; ☎ 01 45 44 27 88; 60-62 rue de Rennes, 6e)

Sonia Rykiel men (Map pp389-91; ☎ 01 45 44 83 19; 194 blvd St-Germain, 6e); **women** (Map pp389-91; ☎ 01 49 54 60 60; 175 blvd St-Germain, 6e) For more information see p275.

Yves Saint Laurent Rive Gauche Homme (Map pp396-9; ☎ 01 43 26 84 40;12 place St-Sulpice, 6e;

Femme (Map pp396-9; ☎ 01 43 29 43; 6 place St-Sulpice, 6e)

Not only do the French love to talk about food, they love to write about it as well, and this tasteful bookshop is the place to discover the secrets of French food, wine and the culinary arts.

SHAKESPEARE & COMPANY

Map pp396-9   *Books*

☎ 01 43 26 96 50; 37 rue de la Bûcherie, 5e; metro St-Michel; ☯ noon-midnight

Paris' most famous English-language bookshop has a varied collection of new and used books, including used paperback novels, but the place has been resting on its laurels and is now an expensive tourist trap. Poetry readings are held at 8pm on most Mondays, and there's a library on the 1st floor. This isn't the original Shakespeare & Company owned by Sylvia Beach, who published James Joyce's *Ulysses*; that was closed by the Nazis.

ST-GERMAIN, ODÉON & LUXEMBOURG

This area, especially Odéon, is a great spot to shop for gifts and souvenirs.

ALBUM Map pp396-9   *Hobby Items*

☎ 01 43 25 85 19; 8 rue Dante, 5e; metro Maubert Mutualité; ☯ 10am-8pm Mon-Sat

Album specialises in *bandes dessinées* (comic books), which have an enormous following in France, with everything from Tintin and Babar to erotic comics and the latest Japanese manga. There's a **blvd St-Germain branch** (Map pp396-9; ☎ 01 53 10 00 60; 67 blvd St-Germain, 5e) just around the corner.

CACAO ET CHOCOLAT

Map pp396-9   *Food & Drink*

☎ 01 46 33 77 63; 29 rue du Buci, 6e; metro Mabillon; ☯ 10.30am-7.30pm Mon-Sat, 11am-1.30pm & 2.30-7pm Sun

You haven't tasted chocolate (a veritable religion in France) till you've tasted it here. 'Cocoa and Chocolate' is a contemporary and

Top Five Bookshops

- **Abbey Bookshop** (p258)
- **Librairie Ulysse** (p258)
- **Red Wheelbarrow Bookstore** (p258)
- **Tea and Tattered Pages** (p262)
- **Village Voice** (this page)

exotic take on chocolate, showcasing the cocoa bean in all its guises, both solid and liquid. The citrus flavours, spices and even chilli are guaranteed to tempt you back. There are two other outlets including a **Marais branch** (Map pp396-9; ☎ 01 42 71 50 06; 36 rue Vieille du Temple, 4e; metro St-Paul; ☯ 11am-7.30pm).

CROCODISC Map pp392-5   *Music*

☎ 01 43 54 47 95; 40-42 rue des Écoles, 5e; metro Maubert Mutualité; ☯ 11am-7pm Tue-Sat

This place has a good selection of new and used African, Oriental, Caribbean and soul as well as pop and rock. For jazz and blues try **Crocojazz** (Map pp392-5; ☎ 01 46 34 78 38; 64 rue de la Montagne Ste-Geneviève, 5e) just around the corner.

L'ÎLE DU DÉMON

Map pp396-9   *Art, Jewellery*

☎ 01 43 26 92 53; 13 rue Bonaparte, 6e; metro St-Germain des Prés; ☯ 10am-1pm & 1-7pm Mon-Sat

'Devil's Island' sells tribal masks and collectibles from Africa though there are some from Southeast Asia as well. There is also some interesting jewellery.

ODIMEX PARIS

Map pp396-9   *Household Goods*

☎ 01 46 33 98 96; 17 Rue de l'Odéon, 6e; metro Odéon; ☯ 10.30am-6.30pm Mon-Sat

This shop sells teapots in all their guises: little ones, big ones, sophisticated ones, comic ones and very expensive ones. Some of the Japanese teapots are particularly beautiful.

VILLAGE VOICE Map pp396-9   *Books*

☎ 01 46 33 36 47; www.villagevoicebookshop.com; 6 rue Princesse, 6e; metro Mabillon; ☯ 2-8pm Mon, 10am-8pm Tue-Sat, 2-6pm Sun

With an excellent selection of contemporary North American fiction and European literature, lots of readings and other events and helpful staff, the Village Voice is many people's favourite English-language bookshop in Paris.

VOYAGEURS & CURIEUX

Map pp396-9   *Antiques*

☎ 01 43 26 14 58; 2 rue Visconti, 6e; metro St-Germain des Prés; ☯ 2-7pm Wed-Sat

This wonderful shop devoted to the 'travellers and curious' looks and feels like an 18th-century cabinet of curiosities collected from around the world: chalices made from coconut shells, unusual feathers and beads, and odd masks.

FAUBOURG ST-GERMAIN & INVALIDES

This is the area where you'll find the lion's share of Paris' top-end antique shops and art galleries.

CARRÉ RIVE GAUCHE

Map pp389-91 *Art & Antiques*
☎ 01 42 60 70 10; www.carrerivegauche.com; quai Voltaire, rue de l'Université, rue des St-Pères not & rue du Bac; metro Rue du Bac or Solférino; 🕙 10am-6pm Mon-Sat

Not a shop but a group of 120 fine-art and antique galleries, the 'Left Bank Square' is just east of the Musée d'Orsay and is bordered by quai Voltaire and the Seine to the north, rue de l'Université to the south, rue des St-Pères to the east and rue du Bac to the west. It represents one of the finest groupings of shops and merchants not just in Paris but in the world and should not be missed.

FROMAGERIE BARTHELEMY

Map pp389-91 *Food & Drink*
☎ 01 42 22 82 24; 51 rue de Grenelle, 7e; metro Rue du Bac; 🕙 8am-1pm & 4-7.15pm Tue-Fri, 8am-1.30pm & 3.30-7.15pm Sat

This cheese maker has fans not just in Paris but also in Fontainebleau where there is another store (p317). The idyllic scene painted on glass on the exterior wall is museum quality.

LE BON MARCHÉ

Map pp389-91 *Department Store*
☎ 01 44 39 80 00; www.bonmarche.fr; 24 rue de Sèvres, 7e; metro Sèvres Babylone; 🕙 9.30am-7pm Mon-Wed & Fri, 10am-9pm Thu, 9.30am-8pm Sat

Built by Gustave Eiffel as Paris' first department store in 1852, the 'Good Market' (which also means 'bargain') is less frenetic than its rivals across the river, but no less chic. Men's and women's fashions are both sold. Its glorious grocery store, **La Grande Épicerie de Paris** (p154), is in store No 2.

MADELEINE GÉLY

Map pp389-91 *Clothing & Accessories*
☎ 01 42 22 63 35; 218 blvd St-Germain, 7e; metro St-Germain des Prés; 🕙 10am-7pm Tue-Sat

Founded in 1834, Madeleine Gély is the place to come if you're in the market for a bespoke cane or umbrella.

POILÂNE

Map pp389-91 *Food & Drink*
☎ 01 45 48 42 59; www.poilane.fr; 8 rue du Cherche Midi, 6e; metro Sèvres Babylone; 🕙 7.15am-8.15pm Mon-Sat

Truly a legend in its own lunch time, Poilâne is the most famous *boulangerie* (bakery) in Paris and bakes perfect wholegrain bread (€3.80 a loaf) using traditional sourdough leavening and sea salt. Every loaf is an original. There's also a **15e branch** (Map pp389-91; ☎ 01 45 79 11 49; 49 blvd de Grenelle; metro Dupleix).

Display, Fromagerie Barthelemy (above)

SENNELIER

Map pp389-91 *Hobby Items*

☎ 01 42 60 72 15; 3 quai Voltaire, 7e; metro St-Germain des Prés; ☼ 9.30am-12.30pm & 2-6pm Tue-Sat

If your visit to the Musée d'Orsay left you inspired, drop in at Sennelier to find the source of all those vibrant colours. This artists' colour merchant has been in business for well over a century and still makes paints using rare pigments, and supplies other artists' materials.

TEA AND TATTERED PAGES

Map pp389-91 *Books*

☎ 01 40 65 94 35; 24 rue Mayet, 6e; metro Duroc; ☼ 11am-7pm Mon-Sat, noon-6pm Sun

This is the best and most comprehensive shop selling used English-language books in Paris. There are some 15,000 volumes squeezed on to two floors – guys, do us a favour and take off your backpacks *before* you enter – and a lovely tea room in the back where you can sip, munch and browse (teas from €3, sweet and savoury snacks from €3.80).

ÉTOILE & CHAMPS-ÉLYSÉES

The av des Champs-Élysées is not quite the shopping street it was, but just off it you'll find a number of interesting boutiques and arguably the best map shop in Paris.

BRÛLERIE DES TERNES

Map pp383-5 *Food & Drink*

☎ 01 46 22 52 79; 10 rue Poncelet, 17e; metro Charles de Gaulle-Étoile; ☼ 9am-2pm & 3.30-7.30pm Tue-Fri, 9am-7.30pm Sat, 9am-1pm Sun

---

Triangle d'Or

Some of the fanciest clothes in Paris are sold by the *haute couture* houses of the 'Golden Triangle' (metro Franklin D Roosevelt or Alma Marceau), an ultra-chic neighbourhood in the 8e whose corners are at the Arc de Triomphe, av des Champs-Élysées, av Marceau, place de l'Alma and av Franklin D Roosevelt. The Asian customers gathered outside such shops as Louis Vuitton are trying to buy in bulk for resale back home and may ask for your assistance. This is not allowed and you should avoid them. Among some of the big names represented are those listed below. Unless noted otherwise, the boutiques are open from 10am or 10.30am to 7pm or 7.30pm Monday to Saturday.

Barbara Bui (Map pp383-5; ☎ 01 42 25 05 25; 50 av Montaigne, 8e) For more information see p274.

Celine (Map pp383-5; ☎ 01 56 89 07 91; 36 av Montaigne, 8e)

Chanel (Map pp383-5; ☎ 01 47 23 74 12; 40-42 av Montaigne, 8e) For more information see p271.

Christian Dior (Map pp383-5; ☎ 01 40 73 54 44; 30-32 av Montaigne, 8e) For more information see p271.

Christian Lacroix (Map pp383-5; ☎ 01 47 20 68 95; 26 av Montaigne, 8e) For more information see p274.

Courrèges (Map pp383-5; ☎ 01 53 67 30 00; 40 av Montaigne, 8e) For more information see p273.

Emilio Pucci (Map pp383-5; ☎ 01 47 20 04 45; 36 Montaigne, 8e)

Gianfranco Ferre (Map pp383-5; ☎ 01 49 52 02 74; 44 av George V, 8e)

Givenchy (Map pp383-5; ☎ 01 44 31 51 25, 01 44 31 51 09; 3 & 8 av George V, 8e) For more information see p272.

Gucci (Map pp383-5; ☎ 01 56 69 80 80; 60 av Montaigne, 8e)

Inès de la Fressange (Map pp383-5; ☎ 01 47 23 98 94; 14 av Montaigne, 8e)

Jean-Paul Gaultier (Map pp383-5; ☎ 01 44 43 00 44; 44 av George V, 8e) For more information see p274.

Lolita Lempicka (Map pp383-5; ☎ 01 40 70 96 96; 78 av Marceau, 8e) For more information see p274.

Louis Vuitton (Map pp383-5; ☎ 01 53 57 24 00; 101 av des Champs-Élysées, 8e), **Montaigne branch** (Map pp383-5; ☎ 01 45 62 47 00; 22 av Montaigne, 8e) For more information see p273.

Nina Ricci (Map pp383-5; ☎ 01 40 88 64 51; 39 av Montaigne, 8e),

Plein Sud (Map pp383-5; ☎ 01 47 20 42 43; 2 av Montaigne, 8e)

Prada (Map pp383-5; ☎ 01 53 23 99 40; 10 av Montaigne, 8e)

Ungaro (Map pp383-5; ☎ 01 53 57 00 00; 2 av Montaigne, 8e)

Valentino (Map pp383-5; ☎ 01 47 23 64 61; 17-19 av Montaigne, 8e)

The 'Ternes Roaster' is probably the best coffee roaster, grinder and shop in Paris. There's also a **16e branch** (Map pp389-91; ☎ 01 45 25 15 08; 28 rue de l'Annonciation, 16e; metro Boulainvilliers).

ESPACE IGN

Map pp383-5 *Books*
☎ 01 43 98 80 00; www.ign.fr in French; 107 rue La Boétie, 8e; metro Franklin D Roosevelt; ⏰ 9.30am-7pm Mon-Fri, 11am-12.30pm & 2-6.30pm Sat
This is the place to find a full selection of Institut Géographique National (IGN) maps, as well as atlases, globes, walking maps, city plans, compasses, satellite images, historic maps and guidebooks.

FROMAGERIE ALLÉOSSE

Map pp383-5 *Food & Drink*
☎ 01 46 22 50 45; 13 rue Poncelet, 17e; metro Termes; ⏰ 9am-1pm & 4-7pm Tue-Sat, 9am-1pm Sun
This is without a doubt the best cheese shop in Paris and worth a trip across town. Cheeses are grouped and displayed as they should be – in five main categories: *fromage de chèvre* (goat's milk cheese); *fromage à pâte persillée* (veined or blue cheese); *fromage à pâte molle* (soft cheese); *fromage à pâte demi-dure* (semi-hard cheese); and *fromage à pâte dure* (hard cheese).

GUERLAIN

Map pp383-5 *Cosmetics & Perfume*
☎ 01 45 62 52 57; 68 av des Champs-Élysées, 8e; metro Franklin D Roosevelt; ⏰ 10.30am-8pm Mon-Sat, 3-7pm Sun
Guerlain is Paris' most famous *perfumerie*, and its shop, dating from 1912, is one of the most beautiful in the city. With its shimmering mirror and marble décor, it's a reminder of the former glory of the Champs-Élysées.

SÉPHORA

Map pp383-5 *Cosmetics & Perfume*
☎ 01 53 93 22 50; www.sephora.com; 70 av des Champs-Élysées, 8e; metro Franklin D Roosevelt; ⏰ 10am-1am Mon-Sat, noon-1am Sun
Séphora's flagship store features over 12,000 fragrances and cosmetics, most of which you can sample with no pressure to buy. This place is a madhouse, even into the wee hours.

VIRGIN MEGASTORE

Map pp383-5 *Music*
☎ 01 49 53 50 00; 52-60 av des Champs-Élysées, 8e; metro Franklin D Roosevelt; ⏰ 10am-midnight Mon-Sat, noon-midnight Sun
This French-owned version of the huge British music and bookshop chain has the largest music collection in Paris, as well as English-language books and a decent café-restaurant.

CONCORDE & MADELEINE

Though they don't have quite the cachet of the boutiques of the Triangle d'Or (p262), there is another group of couture houses and exclusive clothing and accessories stores just north of place de la Concorde along rue du Faubourg St-Honoré, 8e (metro Madeleine or Concorde), and its eastern extension, rue St-Honoré (metro Tuileries). The boutiques following are open from 10am or 10.30am to 7pm or 7.30pm Monday to Saturday.

BOUTIQUE MAILLE

Map pp383-5 *Food & Drink*
☎ 01 40 15 06 00; 6 place de la Madeleine, 8e; metro Madeleine; ⏰ 10am-7pm Mon-Sat
Who said Parisian stores are no longer specialised? This outlet on the southeastern corner of lovely place de Madeleine specialises in mustards. There are shelf items or the store can make up for you some two dozen different varieties – from mustard with Dijon cassis (to be served with game or fowl) and mustard with honey and nuts (to serve with *charcuterie* and vinaigrette) to mustard with Cognac (to serve with red meats). There is a range of exclusive vinegars too.

CAVIAR KASPIA

Map pp383-5 *Food & Drink*
☎ 01 42 65 66 21; www.kaspia.fr; 17 place de la Madeleine, 8e; metro Madeleine; ⏰ boutique 9am-1am Mon-Sat, tasting room noon-1am Mon-Sat
This place sells the finest beluga, sevruga and oscietra caviar from the Iranian and Russian sections of the Caspian Sea for from €136 to €272 per 100g, depending on the quality. Locally farmed caviar d'Aquitaine is a mere €87 per 100g.

CÉCILE ET JEANNE Map pp383-5 *Jewellery*
☎ 01 42 61 68 68; 215 rue St-Honoré, 1er; metro Tuileries; ⏰ 11am-7pm Mon-Sat

All that Glitters

Around place Vendôme, 1er (metro Tuileries) you'll find quite a few high-end jewellery shops. Such baubles don't come cheap so security is high. Expect to have to wait and be scrutinised before being buzzed in. There are more such shops nearby along rue de Castiglione (1er), which runs south of the square, and rue de la Paix (2e), which runs north.

Cartier (Map pp383-5; ☎ 01 44 55 32 50; www.cartier.com; 7 place Vendôme, 1er; 🕑 10.30am-6.30pm Mon-Sat) Jeweller and watchmaker to the stars.

Patek Philippe (Map pp383-5; ☎ 01 42 44 17 77; www.patek.com; 10 place Vendôme, 1er; 🕑 10.30am-6.30pm Mon-Fri, 11am-12.30pm & 2-6.30pm Sat) Specialises in watches and other timepieces.

Van Cleef & Arpels (Map pp383-5; ☎ 01 53 45 45 45; www.vancleef.com; 22 place Vendôme, 1er; 🕑 10.30am-6.30pm Mon-Sat)

These two are young jewellery designers making a splash in Paris with their colourful and arty jewellery and must-have handbags.

FAUCHON Map pp383-5 *Food & Drink*
☎ 01 47 42 60 11; 26-30 place de la Madeleine, 8e; metro Madeleine; 🕑 8.30am-7pm Mon-Sat
Paris' most famous caterer has six departments in two buildings selling the most incredibly mouth-watering delicacies from *pâté de foie gras* to *confitures* (jams). Fruit – the most perfect you've ever seen – includes exotic items from Southeast Asia (mangosteens, rambutans etc). There are a dozen smaller outlets throughout the city, including a **Bastille branch** (p154).

HÉDIARD Map pp383-5 *Food & Drink*
☎ 01 43 12 88 88; www.hediard.fr; 21 place de la Madeleine, 8e; metro Madeleine; 🕑 8.30am-8.30pm Mon-Sat
This famous luxury food shop established in 1854 consists of two adjacent sections selling prepared dishes, teas, coffees, jams, wines, pastries, fruits, vegetables and so on as well as a popular **tea room** (🕑 8.30am-7pm Mon-Sat).

HERMÈS Map pp383-5 *Clothing & Accessories*
☎ 01 40 17 47 83; 24 rue du Faubourg St-Honoré, 8e
This is the place to shop for luxury scarves.

IL POUR L'HOMME
Map pp383-5 *Gifts & Souvenirs*
☎ 01 42 60 43 56; 209 rue St-Honoré, 1er; metro Tuileries; 🕑 10.30am-7pm Mon-Sat
Housed in what was once a paint shop with 19th-century display counters and chests of drawers, 'It for the Man' has everything a guy could want and not really need – from hip flasks and cigar cutters to shaving brushes and designer tweezers.

LA MAISON DE LA TRUFFE
Map pp383-5 *Food & Drink*
☎ 01 42 65 53 22; www.maison-de-la-truffe.com in French; 19 place de la Madeleine, 8e; metro Madeleine; 🕑 shop 9am-9pm Mon-Sat, eating area 11am-9pm Mon-Sat
The 'House of Truffles' is the place for tasting these fine fungi – French black from late October to March, Italian white (over €450 per 100g) from mid-October to December. There's a small sit-down area where you can sample dishes made with the prized fungus, dishes from €28 to €36 and a *menu* (set menu) €55.

LA MAISON DU MIEL
Map pp383-5 *Food & Drink*
☎ 01 47 42 26 70; 24 rue Vignon, 9e; metro Madeleine; 🕑 9.15am-7pm Mon-Sat
This shop, which has been trading since 1898 (but 'only' since 1905 from this address) stocks over 40 kinds of honey priced from €3.85 (sunflower) to €8.20 (Corsican wildflower) for 500g. A kg of honey will cost from €6 to €14.50, depending on the type.

MADELIOS
Map pp383-5 *Clothing & Accessories*
☎ 01 53 45 00 00; 23 blvd de la Madeleine, 8e; metro Madeleine; 🕑 10am-7pm Mon-Sat
This is a one-stop shop for men and has a fine selection of classic and modern suits, shoes and casual wear, a hairdressing and beauty salon, café and exhibition space.

NICOLAS Map pp383-5 *Food & Drink*
☎ 01 42 68 00 16; 31 place de la Madeleine, 8e; metro Madeleine; 🕑 9am-8pm Mon-Sat
This is just one of dozens of branches of the nationwide wine chain founded in 1822. It has a vast and wide-ranging selection – from

Shopping – Concorde & Madeleine

lower-shelf (but good-quality and recommended) house labels from €3 to Bordeaux *grands crus* upwards of €60. The staff is very well informed and always ready to give advice.

WH SMITH

Map pp383-5   *Books*

☎ 01 44 77 88 99; www.whsmith.fr; 248 rue de Rivoli, 1er; metro Concorde; ☺ 9am-7.30pm Mon-Sat, 1-7.30pm Sun

This branch of the British-owned chain has 70,000 titles and a good selection of magazines and Paris-related titles, but the staff can be surly and unhelpful and can (or will) not speak English.

YVES SAINT LAURENT

Map pp383-5   *Clothing & Accessories*

☎ 01 42 65 74 59; Femmes 38 rue du Faubourg St-Honoré, 8e; Hommes ☎ 01 53 05 80 80; 32 rue du Faubourg St-Honoré, 8e

As on the Left Bank, Yves Saint Laurent has separate boutiques almost side by side for both men and women.

OPÉRA & GRANDS BOULEVARDS

The area around Opéra and the Grands Boulevards is where you'll find Paris' most popular *grands magasins* (department stores).

BRENTANO'S

Map pp383-5   *Books*

☎ 01 42 61 52 50; www.brentanos.fr; 37 av de l'Opéra, 2e; metro Opéra; ☺ 10am-7.30pm Mon-Sat

Situated midway between the Louvre and Palais Garnier, this US-based chain is a good shop for tracking down books from the US, including fiction, business and children's titles, and magazines.

DROUOT   Map pp386-8   *Antiques*

☎ 01 48 00 20 20; www.gazette-drouot.com; 7-9 rue Drouot, 9e; metro Richelieu Drouot; ☺ sales 2 or 2.30-6pm

Paris' most established auction house has been selling fine lots for more than a century. Bidding is in rapid-fire French (also now available on the Internet) and a 10% to 15% commission is charged on top of the purchase price.

Viewings (always a vicarious pleasure) are from 11am to 6pm the day before and 10.30am to 11.30am the morning of the auction. Details can be found in the weekly *Gazette de l'Hôtel Drouot*, available at the auction house and selected newsstands on Friday, and on the house's website.

GALERIES LAFAYETTE

Map pp383-5   *Department Store*

☎ 01 42 82 34 56; www.galerieslafayette.com; 40 blvd Haussmann, 9e; metro Auber or Chaussée d'Antin; ☺ 9.30am-7.30pm Mon-Wed, Fri & Sat, 9.30am-9pm Thu

A vast *grand magasin* (department store) in two adjacent buildings linked by a pedestrian bridge over rue de Mogador, Galeries Lafayette features over 75,000 brand-name items and has a wide range of fashion and accessories. There's a fine view from the rooftop restaurant. A fashion show (☎ 01 42 82 30 25 to book a seat) takes place at 11am every Tuesday year-round with another show at 2.30pm on Friday April to October. The recently *dévoilé* (let's say 'unveiled') lingerie department measures 2600 sq metre, the largest underwear shop in the world. The new 10,000 sq metre **Lafayette Maison** (Map pp383-5; 35 blvd Haussmann, 9e; metro Auber or Chaussée d'Antin) in the building once occupied by Marks & Spencer has each floor dedicated to a particular room in the house.

LE PRINTEMPS

Map pp383-5   *Department Store*

☎ 01 42 82 50 00; www.printemps.com; 64 blvd Haussmann, 9e; metro Havre Caumartin; ☺ 9.35am-7pm Mon-Wed, Fri & Sat, 9.35am-10pm Thu

The 'Spring' (as in the season) is actually three separate stores – *de la Mode* (women's fashion), *de l'Homme* (for men) and *de la Beauté et Maison* (for beauty and household goods) – offering a staggering display of perfume, cosmetics and accessories, as well as established and up-and-coming designer wear. There's a fashion show under the 7th floor cupola at 10am on Tuesday. Reservations are not required.

LEGRAND FILLES & FILS

Map pp386-8   *Food & Drink*

☎ 01 42 60 07 12; 7-11 Galerie Vivienne, 1 rue de la Banque, 2e; metro Pyramides; ☺ 11am-7pm Mon-Sat

This shop sells not just fine wines but all the accoutrements: corkscrews, tasting glasses, decanters etc. Just opposite is a new wine bar and tasting room.

LES CAVES AUGÉ

Map pp383-5 *Food & Drink*
☎ 01 45 22 16 97; 116 blvd Haussmann, 8e; metro
St-Augustin; 🕑 1-7.30pm Mon, 9am-7.30pm Tue-Sat

The 'Augé Cellars' should be the wine shop for you if you're following the advice of Marcel Proust. It's now under the stewardship of knowledgeable sommelier Marc Sibard.

GARE DU NORD, GARE DE L'EST & RÉPUBLIQUE

These areas cater more to working-class Parisians. Workaday department stores and shops proliferate; boutiques and fancy jewellers are thin on the ground.

ANTOINE ET LILI

Map pp386-8 *Gifts & Souvenirs*
☎ 01 40 37 41 55; www.antoineetlili.com; 95 quai
de Valmy, 10e; metro République or Gare de l'Est;
🕑 11am-2.30pm & 3.30-7pm Mon, 11am-2.30pm &
3.30-8pm Tue-Fri, 10am-8pm Sat, 11.30am-7.30pm Sun
Do *not* enter this huge shop spread through three townhouses with a hangover. The décor (shocking pink, chartreuse, blinding yellow) will have you begging for mercy. It sells *art tribu*, although it's hard to see what makes luridly coloured pillows and household goods 'tribal'. Still it's fun and highly original.

DARTY Map pp386-8 *Electronics*
☎ 01 42 79 79 31; www.darty.com in French; 1 av de
la République, 11e; metro République;
🕑 10am-7.30pm Mon-Sat

The best place to seek out adaptors and other electrical goods is any branch of the electronics chain Darty including this outlet. There's also a **Ternes branch** (Map pp383-5; ☎ 01 42 79 79 30; 8°av des Ternes, 17e; 🕑 10am-7.30pm Mon-Sat) north of Étoile.

JAMIN PUECH

Map pp386-8 *Clothing & Accessories*
☎ 01 40 22 08 32; www.jamin-puech.com; 61 rue
d'Hauteville, 10e; metro Poissonière;
🕑 10am-2pm & 3-7pm Mon-Sat
Handbag as a work of a art? Assert your individuality, honey, with a completely original *sac* (bag) by Isabelle Puech and Benoît Jamin. They're available in an innovative range of fabrics and designs.

Tati (opposite)

GARE DE LYON, NATION & BERCY

The upmarket boutiques of Bercy have transformed the 12e arrondissements and are always packed with shoppers.

BERCY VILLAGE

Map p401 *Shopping Centre*

☎ 01 40 02 90 80; www.bercyvillage.com; Cour St-Émilion; metro Cour St-Émilion, 12e; ⌚ 11am-9pm

This redevelopment of a row of 19th-century *chais* (wine warehouses) in southeast Paris contains dozens of shops, bars and restaurants, including **Musée & Compagnie** (p267) and the **Chai 33** (p227) wine bar.

MARCHÉ AUX PUCES D'ALIGRE

Map pp392-5 *Flea Market*

place d'Aligre, 12e; metro Ledru Rollin; ⌚ 7am-1.30pm Tue-Sun

Smaller but more central than Paris' other flea markets, the one at place d'Aligre is one of the best places to rummage through boxes of clothes and accessories worn decades ago by those fashionable (and not-so-fashionable) Parisians.

MUSÉE & COMPAGNIE

Map p401 *Gifts & Souvenirs*

☎ 01 40 02 98 72; 40-42 Cour St-Émilion, 12e; metro Cour St-Émilion; ⌚ 11am-9pm.

This shop sells top-end copies of all those knick-knacks and dust-collectors you admired in the museum but couldn't have: *Mona Lisa*, *Venus de Milo*, Celtic jewellery and so on. All fakes, of course – but good ones.

MONTMARTRE & PIGALLE

These are good areas for cut-price (and cut-label) fashion. The Goutte d'Or is a less-than-salubrious district in the 18e that features a collection of shops and stalls where young designers sell their creations and assorted frippery. The most fertile hunting grounds are on rue des Gardes, which runs south from rue Myrha to rue de la Goutte d'Or.

LA CITADELLE

Map p400 *Clothing & Accessories*

☎ 01 42 52 21 56; 1 rue des Trois Frères, 18e; metro Abbesses; ⌚ 11am-8pm Mon-Sat, 2-7pm Sun

This designer discount shop hidden away on rue des Trois Frères in Montmartre has some real finds from new French and Italian designers. Look out for labels like Noir Ebène, Les Chemins Blancs and Petit Bateau T-shirts.

TATI

Map pp386-8 *Department Store*

☎ 01 55 29 50 00; 4 blvd Rochechouart, 18e; metro Barbès Rochechouart; ⌚ 10am-7pm Mon-Fri, 9.15am-7pm Sat

With its war cry of *les plus bas prix* (the lowest prices) – and quality to match – Tati has been Paris' great working-class department store for 50 years. Don't be surprised to see trendy Parisians searching for street cred and fighting for bargains hidden in the crammed bins and piled onto tables. There's a smaller **3e branch** (Map pp386-8; ☎ 01 48 87 72 81; 174 rue du Temple, 3e; metro République) as well.

OUTSIDE THE WALLS: BEYOND CENTRAL PARIS

Venture beyond central Paris for shopping malls and flea markets.

LA VALLÉE VILLAGE *Shopping Centre*

☎ 01 60 42 35 00; www.valueretail.com; 3 cours de la Garonne, 77700 Serris; ⌚ 10am-8pm Mon-Sat May-Sep, 10am-7pm Mon-Sat Oct-Apr, 11am-7pm Sun

This shopping centre within the **Disneyland Resort** (p329), 30km east of Paris, contains some 60 big-name outlets – from Christian Lacroix to Kenzo and Versace – offering discounts on last season's clothing, accessories and tableware. To get there from central Paris, take RER line A4 (€5.80, 30 to 35 minutes) and get off at Val d'Europe station. Alternatively **Cityrama** (p78) runs a coach (adult/child 3-11 yrs €15/10) from 4 place des Pyramides, 1er (metro Tuileries) at 10.15am on Tuesday, Thursday and Sunday, returning at 4pm. Be sure to book in advance.

MARCHÉ AUX PUCES DE LA PORTE DE VANVES

Map pp380-2 *Flea Market*

av Georges Lafenestre & av Marc Sangnier, 14e; metro Porte de Vanves; ⌚ 7am-6 or 7pm Sat & Sun

The Porte de Vanves flea market is the smallest and, some say, friendliest of the lot. Av Georges Lafenestre has lots of 'curios' that don't quite qualify as antiques. Av Marc Sangnier is lined with stalls of new clothes, shoes, handbags and household items for sale.

MARCHÉ AUX PUCES DE MONTREUIL

Map pp380-2   *Flea Market*

av du Professeur André Lemière, 20e; metro Porte de Montreuil; ⏱ 7.30 or 8am-6 or 7pm Sat-Mon

Established in the 19th century, the Montreuil flea market is known for its quality second-hand clothes and designer seconds. The 500 stalls also sell engravings, jewellery, linen, crockery, old furniture and appliances.

MARCHÉ AUX PUCES DE ST-OUEN

Map pp380-2   *Flea Market*

www.les-puces.com; rue des Rosiers, av Michelet, rue Voltaire, rue Paul Bert & rue Jean-Henri Fabre, 18e; metro Porte de Clignancourt; ⏱ 9 or 10am-7pm Sat-Mon

This vast flea market founded in the late 19th century and said to be Europe's largest, has 2500-odd stalls grouped into 10 *marchés* (market areas), each with its own speciality (eg Marché Serpette and Marché Biron for antiques, Marché Malik for second-hand clothing). For more information about the market and its stalls check out www.libertys.com or www.vernaison.com.

Fashion

Bespoke & Off the Peg	270
In the Beginning	271
Classic Couturiers	271
Accessories Actually	273
Designers du Jour	273
World Fashion in Paris	275
One of Your Own	276

Fashion

FASHION IS NOT SOMETHING THAT EXISTS IN DRESSES ONLY. FASHION IS IN THE SKY, IN THE STREET; FASHION HAS TO DO WITH IDEAS, THE WAY WE LIVE, WHAT IS HAPPENING.

Coco Chanel

Chanel was right – fashion is everywhere, and nowhere is that more apparent than in Paris. Style is a way of life and second nature to most Parisians, whose flair and elegance is imitated around the world. While window-shopping here nowadays, you may be forgiven for thinking that Paris has been consumed by international retail giants like Zara, Gap and H&M. But don't despair; surprisingly original and inspired outfits can be found tucked away in the backstreet boutiques of every arrondissement and even in such high-street shops as Monoprix. Though hardly slaves to fashion, Parisians are and probably always will be loyal to French labels.

BESPOKE & OFF THE PEG

Haute couture (literally 'high sewing') refers to the exquisite made-to-measure apparel that a *maison de couture* (fashion house) produces. In the past, clientele included royalty, aristocracy and stars of the silver screen; today this elite group of about 2000 women worldwide

Kenzo store (p277)

includes all the above, as well as rock stars and football wives. A single creation can cost up to €60,000 and take 400 hours to assemble.

Prêt-à-porter means 'ready-to-wear'. Most established couturiers also have a ready-to-wear line; other designers concentrate solely on the more affordable *prêt-à-porter*.

Haute couture catwalk shows are scheduled in mid-January for the spring/summer collections and early July for the autumn/winter ones. *Prêt-à-porter* collections come several months later.

The catwalk shows are part of a tightly packed schedule, with four cities hosting them back to back: New York followed by London, Milan and then Paris. The high-profile Paris shows are still recognised as being the most influential, a cut (as it were) above the rest.

And just how influential are the *haute couture* and *prêt-à-porter* shows? By the time this guide reaches your hands, you'll be able to judge for yourselves. Do women on the boulevards look like Marc Jacob's Cleopatra, Jean-Paul Gaultier's saloon bar cowgirls or like Ginger Rogers as reinvented by Viktor & Rolf? Do their partners resemble Elvis clones or teddy boys as envisaged by John Galliano? Or have they gone all high-tech, inspired by clothes paraded at the same time on a catwalk in Cannes: mood-changing jackets and jewels that tingle when someone is trying to get in touch?

IN THE BEGINNING

The man who in effect created Paris *haute couture* was not French as you'd expect, but from the other side of what the French called La Manche ('Sleeve'), also known as the English Channel. Charles Frederick Worth (1825–95; www.charlesfrederickworth.org) arrived in Paris at the age of 20. Within a year he was working at the fashionable house of Gagelin et Opigez on the rue de Richelieu (2e). Worth, who became known as 'the Napoleon of costumers', revolutionised fashion by banishing the crinoline (stiffened petticoat), lifting hemlines up to the oh-so-shocking ankle length and presenting his creations on live models. His clientele read like a who's who of European nobility and included Eugénie, consort of Emperor Napoleon III. Paul Poire, a one-time Worth employee, would further revolutionise the industry by getting rid of corsets and creating unstructured body-hugging clothes. The House of Worth stayed in the family for four generations until the 1950s.

CLASSIC COUTURIERS

Following is a far-from-complete list of couturiers who have had the greatest impact on Paris fashion over the decades. The best single website for individual couturiers is that of the Fédération Française de la Couture du Prêt à Porter des Couturiers et des Créateurs de Mode (French Federation of Couture, Designer Ready-to-Wear Clothing and Fashion Creators; www.modeaparis.com) though we've listed the individual houses' sites as well. Many of the couturiers are located in the Triangle d'Or (see the boxed text, p262 near the av des Champs-Elysées.

Christian Dior

Christian Dior (1905–57; www.dior.com) caused a sensation in 1947 when he unveiled his small-waisted, full-skirted 'new-look'. After a period of wartime austerity, Dior's creations helped re-establish Paris as the world fashion capital. In the 1950s, Dior went on to virtually dictate fashion styles and when he died, his creations accounted for half of France's fashion exports. Yves Saint Laurent (p272), who had been hired as an assistant in 1953, was appointed chief designer after Dior's death. Flamboyant British designer John Galliano (1960–; www.johngalliano.com), who also has his own line, is the latest to take up the coveted position.

Coco Chanel

Think classic French style, think Chanel. At the same time visionary and perfectionist, Gabrielle 'Coco' Chanel (1883–1971; www.chanel.com) revolutionised 20th-century fashion by shunning corsetry and dressing women in comfortable, often mannish clothes. Starting her career as a milliner in 1912, Chanel launched her fashion house in the early 1920s. By 1925 she had presented her signature cardigan jacket and the following year saw the arrival of her celebrated 'little black dress'. Chanel was the first fashion designer to create a boutique that offered clients the opportunity to try on a total look in a relaxed environment. Fashion passes but Chanel's creations have stood the test of time. Karl Lagerfeld, Chanel's successor, reinvents and reinterprets the Chanel look each season.

Hubert de Givenchy

A classic couturier from the golden age of Paris fashion, Hubert de Givenchy (1927–; www .givenchy.com) opened his own *maison de couture* in 1952. A pioneer, Givenchy was the first to present a luxury collection of women's ready-to-wear. Audrey Hepburn and, to a lesser extent, Jacqueline Kennedy, became the label's unofficial style ambassadors in the '50s and '60s. In recent years the house of Givenchy has appointed a succession of British designers as creative directors, including Ozwald Boateng (1967–; www.ozwaldboateng .com) to Givenchy menswear in 2003.

Jean-Louis Scherrer

Jean-Louis Scherrer (1936–; www.modeaparis.com) founded his *maison de couture* house in 1962, after having worked alongside Yves Saint Laurent at Dior, and at Louis Féraud. His original creations include classic blazers and cocktail dresses with floral, animal prints or polka dots. Scherrer's label had a change of image in 2002, when Ritu Beri became the first Indian to be appointed as chief designer of a prestigious French label.

Louis Féraud

Louis Féraud (1920–99; www.modeaparis.com) established his reputation as couturier to the stars and starlets of the 1950s – from Ingrid Bergman to Brigitte Bardot. His slogan *'Louis Féraud adore les femmes'* (Louis Féraud loves women) worked wonders and in the following decade he went on to open boutiques around the world.

Pierre Cardin

Pierre Cardin (1922–; www.chanel.com) presented his first *haute couture* collection in 1953 followed by his initial *prêt-à-porter* line some six years later. Cardin rose to stardom in the 1960s when, alongside André Courrèges (p273) and Paco Rabanne, he championed a futurist geometric look. The first designer to license his name, Cardin has spent a lifetime building an empire that stretches from *haute couture* to olive oil and from Tokyo to Texas via Beijing and Belarus.

Yves Saint Laurent

Many believe that the golden age of *haute couture* came to an end in 2002 when Yves Saint Laurent (1936–; www.ysl.com) announced he was closing his custom-made dressmaking business. The darling of the fashion world for almost half a century, he started out at age 17 working for the then 'King of Paris fashion', Christian Dior, and opened his own fashion house in 1962, followed by his first *prêt-à-porter* boutique, Rive Gauche, in 1966. The 'Swinging '60s' were a time of frenzied activity for the creative young designer, with Saint Laurent shocking traditional Parisians with designs that would go on to become classics: trouser suits with tuxedo tops, safari jackets and see-through blouses. His passion for the arts shone through with his stylish geometric dresses and other creations inspired by the Ballets Russes and the work of Abstract painter Piet Mondrian, while his 1960s Beat collection was the first *haute couture* assemblage influenced by clothes being worn in the streets.

Celebrated as the man who re-imagined women's fashion, Yves Saint Laurent will go down in fashion history as perhaps the most brilliantly inspired of the great couturiers.

ACCESSORIES ACTUALLY

Many visitors coming to Paris make a trip to Louis Vuitton for handbags or luggage, or to Hermès for scarves a top priority. Both labels go back to the mid-18th century.

Hermès

This fashion house (www.hermes.com) was founded in 1837 by saddle-maker Thierry Hermès, and the company is currently in the hands of the seventh generation of Hermès; its logo – a horse-drawn carriage – reflects the company's original business. The famous scarves were first launched in 1930 and are considered by many to be *the* fashion accessory. Jean-Paul Gaultier (p274) presented his first collection for Hermès in 2004.

Louis Vuitton

Louis Vuitton (1821–92; www.vuitton.com) opened his first luggage and trunk shop in 1854 after working as the Empress Eugenie's personal packer. The ever-popular canvas bag with the 'LV' monogram was created as far back as 1896. In 1987, Louis Vuitton merged with the Champagne *maison* Moët Hennessy to form the powerful LVMH group. American-born Marc Jacobs (1963–; www.marcjacobs.com) is now the creative director.

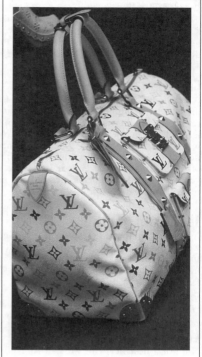

Louis Vuitton bag

DESIGNERS DU JOUR

Chic Parisians of the 21st century are spoiled for choice. Depending on their mood, they can choose Jean-Paul Gaultier or Christian Lacroix for a more carefree style of fashion, or opt for agnès b or Sonia Rykiel for a slightly more sober style. Incarnating the new independent spirit are such designers as Isabel Marant (1967–; www.modeaparis.com) and Vanessa Bruno (1967–), two more rising stars of the Paris fashion scene.

agnès b

Style and photography guru agnès b (1941–; www.agnesb.fr) excels in extremely wearable, durable and comfortable (yet sometimes quirky) clothes. Perhaps the most affordable of the established Parisian designers, agnès b opened her first boutique almost 30 years ago in rue du Jour (1er) in Les Halles (p253) where it and a handful of others remain to this day. Women of all ages from Les Halles to Hong Kong now sport the agnès b look.

André Courréges

Space age designer André Courréges (1923–; www.courreges.com) trained with the House of Balenciaga (p275) and opened his own house in 1961. He hit the headlines in the 1960s with his pure white and silver, precision-cut, mini-skirted, cat-suited, moon-girl look. His stark, squeaky-clean space style hasn't changed much since then, but tastes have and now he's back in fashion.

Barbara Bui

When Franco-Vietnamese Barbara Bui (www.barbarabui.fr in French) opened her boutique Kabuki in rue Etienne Marcel (1er) just over 10 years ago, it had pieces by herself and other designers. It was an instant success and Bui went on to open her own shop (p253) next door followed by others in New York and Milan.

Christian Lacroix

A native of Arles in the south of France, Christian Lacroix (1951–; www.christian-lacroix .fr) is the man who put sunshine into *haute couture*. Creating with a colourful palette that recalls the Mediterranean, Lacroix is often theatrical; taffeta and lace flirt with denim and knits in contemporary combinations. Lacroix joined Jean Patou in 1981, produced his first *prêt-à-porter* collection in 1986 and opened his own *maison de couture* in 1987. In 1994 he created his Bazar collection, zapping between folklore and different eras, a celebration of the melting pot that Paris had become. He went on to launch his Jeans collection two years later, the first collection combining past, present and future with denim as the common denominator.

Jean-Paul Gaultier

Jean-Paul Gaultier (1952–; www.jeanpaul-gaultier.com), the shy kid from the Paris suburbs, worked for Pierre Cardin in the 1970s (after Gaultier's mother had sent some of his designs to Cardin) and later for Jean Patou. In 1975 Gaultier launched his own label and, influenced by the punk movement in London, quickly became known as the *enfant terrible* of the fashion world, with his granny's corsets, men dressed in skirts and bracelets cut from tin cans. In 1990, Gaultier put Madonna in her signature conical bra. Totally obsessed with fashion, Gaultier continues to surprise, seduce and innovate.

Lolita Lempicka

No, not a designer with Russian roots, but a fashion house (www.fragrancex.com) that pays homage to the eponymous character in Nabokov's novel and to the Polish-American Art Deco painter Tamara de Lempicka (1898–1980). Founded by Josiane Pividal (1954–) and her husband Joseph (who have since legally changed their names to Lolita and Joseph-Marie Lempicka) in 1983. Their first boutique, which opened in the Marais a year later, was an immediate success. Lolita Lempicka designs are often inspired by the fashion of the 1940s, beautifully tailored and feminine suits that combine modern with retro.

Queer Eye for the Metrosexual

Parisian metrosexuals – straight guys who have embraced facials and shopping with women – are taking a leaf out of their gay brothers' lifestyle and grooming manual, and superstores and specialist shops now cater to their every whim and need.

Citadium (Map pp383-5; ☎ 01 55 31 74 00; 50 rue Caumartin, 9e; metro Havre Caumartin; ⏰ 9.35am-7pm Mon-Wed, Fri & Sat, 9.35am-10pm Thu) A streetwear superstore, also part of the Printemps group, is located next door to the department store.

Madelios (Map pp383-5; ☎ 01 53 45 00 00; 23 blvd de la Madeleine, 1er; metro Madeleine; ⏰ 10am-7pm Mon-Sat) A kilometre to the southwest of Citadium, this store has 100 specialist labels spread across 5000 sq metres, with everything from Dior to Dunhill.

Nickel (Map pp396-9; ☎ 01 42 77 41 10; 48 rue des Francs Bourgeois, 3e; metro St-Paul; ⏰ 11am-7.30pm Mon, Tue, Fri & Sat, 11am-9pm Wed & Thu) Another must-visit for the metrosexual is this boutique and *institut de beauté* (beauty institute), which has the best morning-after refresher gels in town.

Printemps de l'Homme (p265) Recently renovated and has six floors of everything from suits to sportswear, with creations from some of the funkiest and coolest designers around (Paul Smith, Comme des Garçons, Helmut Lang).

Sonia Rykiel

In May 1968, while students were busy demonstrating on the streets of the Latin Quarter, Sonia Rykiel (1930–; www.soniarykiel.com) was opening her first boutique around the corner. Her philosophy has always been that women should adapt fashion for themselves rather than blindly follow trends. Rykiel is famous for re-inventing the sweater (she is known as 'the Queen of Knitwear'), exposing seams inside out and eliminating lining and hems. Her boutiques (p259) are amongst the best for sales.

WORLD FASHION IN PARIS

From the Italian surrealist Elsa Schiaparelli (1890–1973) to the Spaniard Balenciaga (1895–1972), Paris *haute couture* has always attracted creators from other countries, and today 'Paris Mondial' (p147) is very much *à la mode* (in style) and a spawning ground for much creativity and new talent. In recent years, British designers, including Alexander McQueen, John Galliano, Julien MacDonald and Stella McCartney, have been particularly visible while Japanese designers such as Issey Miyake, Yohji Yamamoto, Junko Shimada, Hanae Mori and Rei Kawakubo of Comme des Garçons have added a touch of minimalism with unstructured fashions, sharp lines and innovative fabrics.

Azzedine Alaïa

Tunisian-born Azzedine Alaïa (1951–) studied sculpture at the École des Beaux-Arts de Tunis before moving to Paris in 1975. He worked with Dior and Guy Laroche before setting up his own label in 1981. One of the most influential designers of the last 20 years, Alaïa, now in partnership with Prada, is best known for his skin-tight sculptural silhouettes.

Erotokritos

Erotokritos, born of Greek parents in Cyprus, worked with Thierry Mugler before launching his own label in 1994. He quickly gained a reputation for chic and colourful casual clothing and opened his own boutique in 1996.

Fayçal Amor

Born in Tangiers to a Moroccan father and a Russian mother, Fayçal Amor (1949–) was destined to be an economist, but instead changed direction and got involved in the fashion world, developing new dyeing techniques and working closely with Moroccan fabric makers. He moved to Paris in 1980 and started his label Plein Sud in 1986. His multicultural influences shine through in his creations.

Hedi Slimane

With an Italian mother, Tunisian father and Brazilian grandmother, Hedi Slimane (1971–) personifies *la mode globale)*. With several years spent at Yves Saint Laurent and Dior, Slimane is out to completely redefine men's fashion.

Hussein Chalayan

Hussein Chalayan (1970–) excels in faux-Hawaiian print frocks depicting scenes from the recent (and menacing) history of Cyprus, where the Turkish-speaking Chalayan was born. Chalayan's creations could be called fashion for thinkers.

Martin Margiela

The most Parisian of Belgian designers, Martin Margiela (1957–) set up his own *maison* in 1988 and has a boutique that is an immaculate (and windowless) white space. His clothes bear a blank label and can be recognised by their white stitching and other visible sewing techniques.

Espace Créateurs

In the heart of Paris this **space** (Map pp396-9; Level -1, Forum des Halles, 1-7 rue Pierre Lescot, 1er; metro Châtelet-Les Halles; ☼ 10am-7.30pm Mon-Sat) opened in 1997 and is dedicated to up-and-coming creators and designers. It's a living clothes lab and has helped launch the careers of now established designers such as Isabel Marant, Xuly Bët and Erotokritos. Espace Créateurs has eight boutiques housing some 60 designers. If it's unusual hats you're after, check out Marie Brickler's La Ma in this complex. Other boutiques of interest include the following.

Boutique 102 (☎ 01 42 21 12 62) Has designs by Moloko.

Boutique 102 For creative accessories and bags, visit Abyss.

Boutique 105A (☎ 01 39 09 56) Features designs by Xuly Bët, Frédérique Fimat, Pedro Williams Borquez and Gianna et Moi.

Boutique 105A Chapeaux Marguerite.

Boutique des 10 (☎ 01 40 41 00 64) Has the J des Chapeaux line.

Red Space (☎ 01 45 08 44 93) Ziké more creative accessories and bags.

Ocimar Versolato

Born in São Paolo, Brazil, Ocimar Versolato (1961–) has a collection based on the theme of multicultural mixing and is into dressing Japanese as Africans and Africans as Russians. His philosophy is that as an international form of expression, fashion can and must integrate all cultures.

Viktor & Rolf

A recent 10-year retrospective at the Musée des Arts Décoratifs was dedicated to the cerebral Dutch design duo of Viktor & Rolf (1969–), well known for their dynamic and distorted forms.

Xuly Bët

Kouyaté Lamine Badian (1962–), the Mali-born designer behind the label, is Africa's ambassador to the Paris fashion world. He studied architecture, and it shows in the structured styling of his clothes. Badian designs crossover, funky fashion, blending cultures and styles, and perfectly capturing the spirit of today's urban young. His creations are figure-hugging often in knits and Lycra, which are sometimes hand-dyed in Senegal. One of his special touches is the stitching of seams on the outside of his garments.

ONE OF YOUR OWN

Most French couturiers have their own boutiques in the capital – the Right Bank is traditionally the epicentre of Parisian fashion – but it's also possible to see impressive ready-to-wear designer collections at the major department stores (p257). In recent years Paris' most famous fashion strips, department stores and boutiques have undergone massive face-lifts by such interior designers as Philippe Starck and Andrée Putmann, and have revealed 'new looks' every bit as important as that of Dior in 1947.

If you're keen to acquire designer or label garments and your budget is not equal to the GNP of a medium-sized African nation, consider scheduling your trip to Paris during the biannual *soldes* (sales). Winter sales normally start the first week of January and the summer ones in the second week of June. They usually last between five and six weeks, and some 30% of Paris' annual retail turnover is done during these periods.

At other times, check out the designer outlets, which sell overbuys and unsold stock from the previous year's collections or one-off samples and clothes worn by models for fashion shoots or shows. *Dépôt-ventes* (resale stores) sell used (often barely used) clothes and accessories from a quarter to half off the original price. Most stores offer both established designer – many women want to be up-to-date on a permanent basis and sell off their designer clothes as soon as the season changes – and lesser known labels, so there's something for every budget.

Along with the designer shops and boutiques of the so-called Golden Triangle (see the boxed text on p262), the rue du Faubourg St-Honoré and rue St-Honoré (p263), place des Victoires and Les Halles (p253) and parts of St-Germain (p260), as well as the streetwear shops and outlets of Marais (p254), the following boutiques, concept stores, designer outlets and *dépôt-ventes* come highly recommended.

ALTERNATIVES Map pp396-9

☎ 01 42 78 31 50; 18 rue du Roi de Sicile, 4e; metro St-Paul; 🕓 11am-1pm & 2.30-7pm Tue-Sat

This men's and women's resale shop has great bargains in superb condition and is an excellent place to pick up Japanese designer wear at a third of the original price. You'll also find Miu Miu, Prada, Martin Margiela and Isabel Marrant here.

COLETTE Map pp383-5

☎ 01 55 35 33 90; www.colette.fr; 213 rue St-Honoré, 1er; metro Tuileries; 🕓 10.30am-7.30pm Mon-Sat

This highly successful concept store is Japanese inspired and an ode to style over all else. Its selection and display of clothes, accessories and odds and ends is exquisite. Featured designers include Alexander McQueen, Marko Matysik and Lulu Guinness but it doesn't stop there. Check out the limited edition Nike sneakers, Prada handbags, designer hairpins and cutting-edge clocks. The Water Bar in the basement features still and sparkling mineral waters from around the world.

KENZO Map pp396-9

☎ 01 73 04 20 00; www.kenzo.com; 1 rue Pont Neuf, 1er; metro Pont Neuf; 🕓 10.30am-8pm Mon-Sat

The new Kenzo Paris flagship store is in one of the former Samaritaine department store buildings. It's a tantalising temple to fashion and beauty over four floors and, while Kenzo himself may have retired from designing in 1999, Sardinian Antonio Marras has brought a new *joie de vivre* to the label.

KILIWATCH Map pp386-8

☎ 01 42 21 17 37; 64 rue Tiquetonne, 2e; metro Étienne Marcel; 🕓 2-7pm Mon, 11am-7pm Tue-Sat

This enormous barn of a stop is filled with rack after rack of colourful, original street and club wear, plus a startling range of second-hand clothes and accessories, which are all in reasonable condition.

KOKON TO ZAI Map pp386-8

☎ 01 42 36 92 42; 48 rue Tiquetonne, 2e; metro Étienne Marcel; 🕓 11.30am-7.30pm Mon-Sat

This tiny shop with a clubby atmosphere was set up by Paris-based Macedonian designers. It stocks cutting-edge styles from designers like Viktor & Rolf, as well as one-offs.

LE MOUTON À CINQ PATTES

Map pp396-9

☎ 01 43 29 73 56; 19 rue Grégoire de Tours, 6e; metro Odéon; 🕓 10.30am-7.30pm Mon-Fri, 10.30am-8pm Sat

The 'Sheep with Five Legs' specialises in heavily discounted designer clothing from last year's range. All items are new but most are *dégriffé* (their labels have been torn out). If you can spot a Jean-Paul Gaultier or Vivienne Westwood without a label, you'll walk away with a discount of up to 70%.

L'ÉCLAIREUR Map pp396-9

☎ 01 48 87 10 22; 9 89; www.leclaireur.com; 3ter rue des Rosiers, 4e; metro St-Paul; 🕓 11am-7pm Mon-Sat

Armand Hadida was one of the first to mix fashion and design for sale in his rue des Rosiers boutique, where you'll find John Galliano and Dries Van Noten rubbing shoulders with objects by Garouste & Bonetti and Ron Arad. The 'Enlightener' is part art space, part lounge and part deconstructionist fashion statement. There is also another branch in the **Marais** (Map pp396-9; ☎ 01 44 54 22 11; 12 rue Malher, 4e; metro St-Paul)

L'HABILLEUR Map pp396-9

☎ 01 48 87 77 12; 44 rue de Poitou, 3e; metro St-Sébastien Froissart; 🕓 11am-8pm Mon-Sat

The 'Dresser' has discount designer duds, including some avant-garde designers, for up to 70% off original prices. This boutique generally stocks last season's collections – Plein Sud, Vivienne Westwood and Prada for women, Helmut Lang for men – but they never look dated.

Fashion – One of Your Own

MARIA LUISA Map pp383-5

☎ 01 47 03 96 15; 1 rue Cambon, 1er; metro Concorde; ⊗ 10.30am-7pm Mon-Sat

A trustworthy selection of classic and avant-garde designers (including Alexander McQueen, Stella McCartney and Helmut Lang), this shop also has some very tasty swimwear. Around the corner you'll find an **accessories branch** (Map pp383-5; ☎ 01 47 03 48 08; 40 rue Mont Thabor, 1er) and a **menswear branch** (Map pp282-5; ☎ 01 42 60 89 83; 19bis rue Mont Thabor, 1er).

MARITHÉ ET FRANÇOIS GIRBAUD
Map pp386-8

☎ 01 53 40 74 20; www.girbaud.com; 38 rue Etienne Marcel, 2e; metro Étienne Marcel; ⊗ noon-7pm Mon, 10am-7pm Tue-Sat

This globetrotting designer couple from the 1960s claim to have introduced the world to bell bottoms, as well as to the technique of stonewashing. They consider themselves 'jeanologists' having devoted themselves to 'jeanetic engineering' for over 30 years. As influential in Tokyo as they are in Paris, Marithé et François Girbaud is an anti-fashion attitude. There is another branch in the **6e arrondissement** (Map pp389-91; ☎ 01 53 40 74 20; 7 rue du Cherche Midi, 6e; metro Sèvres Babylone).

ONWARD Map pp396-9

☎ 01 55 42 77 56; 147 blvd St-Germain, 6e; metro St-Germain des Prés; ⊗ 11am-7pm Mon-Sat

Formerly called Kashiyama, Onward is a clean, modern-looking boutique that stocks fashion-forward clothes from some 20 up-and-coming designers such as People of the Labyrinth and Hussein Chalayan.

RÉCIPROQUE Map pp383-5

☎ 01 47 04 30 28, 01 47 04 82 24; 88 & 95 rue de la Pompe, 16e; metro Rue de la Pompe; ⊗ 11am-7pm Tue-Fri, 10.30am-7pm Sat

The biggest *dépôt-vente* in Paris with half a dozen shops on the same street, 'Converse' has rack after rack of Chanel suits as well as bits and pieces from Christian Lacroix, Hermès, Prada, Thierry Mugler, Issey Miyake, John Galliano, Gucci and Dolce & Gabbana. It's an excellent place to pick up bags and shoes.

Louvre & Les Halles	284
Marais & Bastille	285
The Islands	289
Latin Quarter & Jardin des Plantes	290
St-Germain, Odéon & Luxembourg	294
Montparnasse	296
Faubourg St-Germain & Invalides	297
Étoile & Champs-Élysées	297
Clichy & Gare St-Lazare	298
Opéra & Les Grands Boulevards	298
Gare du Nord, Gare de l'Est & République	299
Ménilmontant & Belleville	301
Gare de Lyon, Nation & Bercy	302
13e Arrondissement & Chinatown	302
15e Arrondissement	302
Montmartre & Pigalle	302
Outside the Walls: Beyond Central Paris	304

Sleeping

Sleeping

Paris has a very wide choice of accommodation options that caters for all budgets throughout much of the city. There are four basic types: deluxe and top-end hotels, some of which count among the finest in the world; mid-range hotels, many of which have personalities all of their own and by and large offer very good value when compared with similarly priced places to stay in other European capitals; adequate but generally uninspiring budget hotels; and hostels, which run the gamut from cramped hellholes to party places with bars worth a visit in their own right. In this chapter, accommodation options are listed according to the sections of the city as outlined in the Quarters & Arrondissements chapter. The last two types of accommodation (budget hotels and hostels) can be found under the heading Cheap Sleeps.

Since 1994 the city of Paris has levied a *taxe de séjour* (tourist tax) of between €0.20 (camp sites, unclassified hotels) to €1.20 (four-star hotels) per person per night on all forms of accommodation.

Accommodation Services

The **Paris tourist office**, notably the **Gare du Nord** centre (p351) can find you a place to stay for the night of the day you stop by. The price for booking a hostel is €1.20; a one-star hotel costing €40 to €70 for a double room is €3; and a two-star for €60 to €100 costs €4. For a three-star hotel costing €100 to €150 for a double, you'll pay €6; for a four-star costing €150 to €450 it's €7.60; and for a four-star luxe hotel costing €260 to €730 it's €8.

Some travel agencies (p338) can also book reasonably priced accommodation. The student travel agency **OTU Voyages** (Map pp396-9; ☎ 01 40 29 12 22, 08 25 00 40 24; www .otu.fr in French; 119 rue St-Martin, 4e; metro Rambuteau; ☯ 9.30am-6.30pm Mon-Fri, 10am-5pm Sat), directly across the *parvis* (square) from the Centre Pompidou, can *always* find you accommodation, even in summer. You pay for the accommodation plus a finder's fee of €12, and the staff gives you a voucher to take to the hotel. Prices for singles cost around €35, doubles start at about €40. Be prepared for long queues in the high season.

An agency that arranges B&B stays in Paris and gets good reviews from readers is **Alcôve & Agapes** (☎ 01 44 85 06 05; fax 01 44 85 06 14; info@paris-bedandbreakfast.com), meaning 'alcoves & feasts'. Expect to pay €45 to €100 for a double. **Frendy** (www.frendy.com) is an accommodation booking service (mostly apartments and B&Bs) for gays and lesbians.

Accommodation Styles & Price Ranges

HOTELS

Hotels in Paris are inspected by authorities and classified into six categories – from no star to four-star 'L' (for *luxe*), the French equivalent of five stars. All hotels must display their rates (including Value Added Tax; VAT) both outside the hotel and in the guestrooms.

Paris may not be able to boast the number of cheap hotels it did a decade ago, but the choice is still more than ample, especially in the Marais, around the Bastille and near the major train stations off the Grands Boulevards. Places with one star or the designations 'HT' (Hôtel de Tourisme) or 'NN' (Nouvelle Norme), which signifies that a hotel is awaiting its rating but assures you of a certain standard of comfort, are much of a muchness. Remember: the overall consideration at these places is cost, never quality. We've said it before and we'll say it again: you get what you pay for. Be advised also that many budget hotels in Paris do not accept credit cards.

When calculating accommodation costs, assume you'll spend about €30 for a washbasin-equipped double in a budget hotel (count on closer to €50 if you want your own shower). Bear in mind that you may be charged from around €2 to as much as €5 to use communal showers in budget hotels. If you can't go without your daily ablutions, it is often a false economy staying at such places.

Mid-range hotels in Paris offer some of the best value for money of any European capital. Hotels at this level always have bathroom facilities. All rooms have showers or baths unless noted otherwise. These hotels charge between €65 and €150 for a double and generally offer excellent value, especially at the higher end.

Top-range places run the gamut from tasteful and discreet boutique hotels to palaces with 100+ rooms and will cost two people up to about €250 a night. Anything above that falls into the deluxe category. See the boxed text (p291).

Breakfast (usually a simple continental affair of bread, croissants, butter, jam and coffee or tea) is served at most hotels with two or more stars and costs from about €6.

Some hotels in Paris have different rates according to the season and are noted as such throughout the chapter. The high season is from June to August, while the low season is from November to March.

HOSTELS

Paris is awash in hostels, but such budget accommodation isn't as cheap as it used to be here. Beds under €20 are increasingly rare – especially in summer – so two people who don't mind sleeping in the same bed may find basic rooms in budget hotels a less-expensive proposition. Groups of three or four will save even more if they share two or three beds in a budget hotel.

Showers are always free at hostels in Paris and rates include breakfast. Internet access (about €1 for 15 minutes) is available at almost all the hostels listed here. If you don't have your own sheet bag, sheets can be rented at most hostels for a one-off charge of €2.50. Towels cost €1.

Some hostels only allow guests to stay a maximum of three nights, particularly in summer. Places that have upper age limits (for example, 30) tend not to enforce them except at the busiest of times. Only the official *auberges de jeunesse* (youth hostels) require guests to present Hostelling International (HI) cards or their equivalent. Curfew – if enforced – is generally at 1am or 2am.

Sleeping

Exterior of Hotel Ritz Paris (p291).

HOMESTAYS & B&BS

Under an arrangement known as *hôtes payants* (literally 'paying guests') or *hébergement chez l'habitant* (lodging with the occupants of private homes), students, young people and tourists can stay with French families. In general you rent a room and, for an additional fee, have access to the family's kitchen in the evening.

One well-established agency that organises homestays is **Accueil Familial des Jeunes Étrangers** (Map pp389-91; ☎ 01 42 22 50 34; accueil@afje-paris.org; 23 rue du Cherche Midi, 6e; metro Sèvres Babylone). It can find you a room with a family for €465 to €540 per month, including breakfast, or €534 to €610 with evening access to the kitchen. For stays of less than a month, expect to pay from €23 (or €25 with access to the kitchen) per day. There's a subscription fee of about €25 per month for longer stays.

In addition, many language schools (p340) can arrange homestays for their students.

SERVICED APARTMENTS

Serviced flats – like staying in a hotel without all the extras – are an excellent option for those staying longer than a week, particularly if you're part of a small group. There are quite a few locations around Paris.

APART'HOTELS
CITADINES   *Serviced Apartment*
☎ 08 25 33 33 32, 01 41 05 79 05 from abroad;
www.citadines.com

This (now international) chain has studios and apartments at 17 properties in Paris, including those listed below. Prices vary depending on the season and the property but, in general, a small studio for two people with cooking facilities for just under a week costs €105 to €249 per night and a one-bedroom flat sleeping four costs €179 to €375. For stays longer than six days there's a discount of 10% to 15%, and for 30 days and over about 20% to 25%.

Bastille Nation (Map pp392-5; ☎ 01 40 04 43 50; bastillenation@citadines.com; 14-18 rue de Chaligny, 12e; metro Reuilly Diderot), **Les Halles** (Map pp396-9; ☎ 01 40 39 26 50; resa@citadines.com; 4 rue des Innocents, 1er; metro Châtelet-Les Halles), **Maine Montparnasse** (Map pp389-91; ☎ 01 53 91 27 00; maine@citadines.com; 67 av du Maine, 14e; metro Gaîté), **Montmartre** (Map p400; ☎ 01 44 70 45 50; montmartre@citadines.com; 16 av Rachel, 18e; metro Blanche), **Opéra Drouot** (Map pp386-8; ☎ 01 40 15 14 00; resa@citadines.com; 18 rue Favart, 2e; metro Richelieu Drouot), **St-Germain des Prés** (Map pp396-9; ☎ 01 44 07 70 00; stgermain@citadines.com; 53 ter quai des Grands Augustins, 6e; metro St-Michel) and **Tour Eiffel** (Map pp389-91; ☎ 01 53 95 60 00; eiffel@citadines.com; 132 blvd de Grenelle, 15e; metro La Motte Picquet Grenelle).

FRANCE LOCATION   *Serviced Apartment*
☎ 01 44 89 66 70; www.france-location.fr

This chain of serviced apartments has properties around France, including in Paris. Daily

---

All in the Family

The **Paris tourist office** (p351) has a number of brochures on homestays, including one on *pensions de famille*, which are similar to B&Bs. *Pensions de famille* recommended by this tourist office include the following four places.

Pension Au Palais Gourmand (Map pp389-91; ☎ 01 45 48 24 15; www.au-palais-gourmand.fr; 3rd fl, 120 blvd Raspail, 6e; metro Vavin or Notre Dame des Champs; half-board s €39-55, d €62-79) The promisingly named 'At the Gourmet Palace' is on a busy street between the Jardin du Luxembourg and Montparnasse and convenient to everything.

Pension Les Marroniers (Map pp389-91; ☎ 01 43 26 37 71; fax 01 43 26 07 72; 78 rue d'Assas, 6e; metro Vavin or Notre Dame des Champs; half-board s/d €45/82) 'The Chestnut Trees' is in a pretty building facing the Jardin du Luxembourg and has monthly rates at 20% less. Vegetarian meals are also available.

Pension Ladagnous (Map pp389-91; ☎ 01 43 26 79 32; fax 01 43 54 60 61; 2nd fl, 78 rue d'Assas, 6e; metro Vavin or Notre Dame des Champs; s/d incl breakfast €42/58) This pension is in the same building as the Pension Les Marroniers.

Résidence Cardinal (Map pp383-5; ☎ 01 48 74 16 16; fax 01 48 74 22 25; 2nd fl, 4 rue Cardinal Mercier, 9e; metro Liège or Place de Clichy; s/d incl breakfast €35/55) This place is on a quiet street with an old fountain at the end of it.

Sleeping

282

prices quoted are for up to six nights' stay, and there is a discount of 15% or 20% after 28 days.

Résidence Le St-Germain (Map pp396-9; ☎ 01 46 34 22 33; fax 01 46 34 60 83; 16 rue Boutebrie, 5e; metro St-Michel; 2-person studio €78-91 day, €497-574 week, 4-person apt €124-158 day, €784-994 week) This property offers a choice of 11 fully equipped studios and apartments for between two and six people.

Résidence Passage Dubail (Map pp386-8; ☎ 01 44 89 66 70; fax 01 40 37 55 97; 5-7 Passage Dubail, 10e; metro Gare de l'Est; 2-person studio €76-87 day, €441-504 week, 4-person apt €115-332 day, €728-840 week) This property has studios and apartments that can accommodate up to four people.

MAEVA CITY TOLBIAC

Map p401   *Serviced Apartment*
☎ 01 53 61 62 00; tolbiac@city-maeva.com; 15 rue de Tolbiac, 13e; metro Bibliothèque; r with kitchenette for 1 & 2 people €75, for 3 & 4 people €90, €472.50/567 per week)

Effectively a hotel (p302), this property, which is close to the Bibliothèque Nationale de France (National Library), also rents fully equipped rooms for longer periods.

RÉSIDENCE DES ARTS

Map pp396-9   *Serviced Apartment*
☎ 01 55 42 71 11; fax 01 55 42 71 00; www.hotel -and-paris.com; 14 rue Gît le Cœur, 6e; metro St-Michel; studio €130-180, ste €230-280, apt €275-340, 2-bed apt €352-430)

This lovely *résidence* in a 15th-century private mansion just west of place St-Michel feels more like a luxury hotel than a flat. Legend has it the street name came about when Henri IV, having dallied with his mistress Gabrielle d'Estrée in a nearby hotel, mused as he departed '*Ici gît mon cœur*' (here lies my heart).

RÉSIDENCE PIERRE & VACANCES

Map p400   *Serviced Apartment*
☎ 01 42 57 14 55; montmartre@pierre-vacances.fr; 10 place Charles Dullin, 18e; metro Abbesses; 2/3/4 person apt €110/121/140, 1/2 bed apt €170/215)

An attractive *résidence* in the heart of Montmartre. There's a 10% discount on stays of eight nights or more and 20% on stays of 28 days or more. Another Pierre & Vacances *résidence* is **Paris Côté Seine** (Map pp389-91; ☎ 01 55 00 67 06; fax 01 45 54 27 48; 14 rue du Théâtre, 15e; metro Charles Michels; 2-person studio €130-135, 4-person apt €180-187), with 40-sq-metre studios and one-, two- and three-bedroom apartments; rates are much lower by the month.

Reservations

During periods of heavy domestic or foreign tourism (Christmas and New Year, February-March school holidays, Easter, July and August), a hotel reservation can mean the difference between a bed in a room and a bench in a park. For really popular (location, price) places, book several months ahead.

Many hotels, especially budget ones, accept reservations only if they are accompanied by *des arrhes* (a deposit). Some places, especially those with two or more stars, don't ask for a deposit if you give them your credit card number or send them confirmation of your plans by letter, fax or email in French or clear, simple English.

Most independent hotels will hold a room only until a set hour, rarely later than 6pm or 7pm without prior arrangement. If you're arriving later than expected and you haven't prepaid or given the hotel your credit-card details, let the staff know or they might rent your room to someone else.

Long-Term Rentals

If you are interested in renting a furnished flat, consult one of the many agencies listed under the heading 'Location Appartements Meublés' on sheets distributed by the **Paris tourist office** (p351) and on its website. Organisations that help find accommodation for students who will be in Paris for at least a semester are listed under 'Logements pour Étudiants'.

The hardest time to find an apartment – especially a cheap one – in Paris is in September and October, when everyone is back from their summer holidays and students are searching for digs for the academic year. Moderately priced places are easiest to find towards the end of university semesters – ie between Christmas and early February and July to September.

Sleeping

About €450 a month will get you a tiny garret room with a washbasin but no telephone, no proper place to cook and no private toilet. There may not even be a communal shower. These rooms, often occupied by students, are usually converted *chambres de bonne* (maid's quarters) on the 6th or 7th floors of old apartment buildings without lifts, but in decent neighbourhoods.

Small (15 to 30 sq metres) unfurnished/furnished studios with attached toilet start from about €16.50 per sq metre per month. Thus a one-bedroom apartment will cost about €800 and a studio around €500. The per-metre cost theoretically decreases the larger the place, the further away it is from the city centre and if it doesn't have a lift.

If you've exhausted your word-of-mouth sources (expats, students, compatriots living temporarily in Paris), it's a good idea to check out the bulletin boards at the American Church (p354). People who advertise there are more likely to rent to foreigners, will probably speak some English and might be willing to sign a relatively short-term contract. *FUSAC* (p348), a free periodical issued every two weeks, is another good source.

If you know some French (or someone who does), you'll be able to consult several periodicals available from newsagents: *De Particulier à Particulier* (€2.75) and *Se Loger* (€2.30), both issued on Thursday; *L'Hebdo Immobilier* (€1.90) on Wednesday; and *Les Annonces Immobiliers* (€2.40). You'll have to do your calling in French, though. If you have access to a telephone, you could place a wanted ad in *De Particulier à Particulier* and have people call you.

RENTAL AGENCIES

Allô Logement Temporaire (Map pp396-9; ☎ 01 42 72 00 06; alt@claranet.fr; 1st fl, 64 rue du Temple, 3e; metro Rambuteau; ☽noon-8pm Mon-Fri) is a nonprofit organisation that links flat-owners and foreigners looking for furnished apartments for periods of one week to one year. Small furnished studios of between 18 and 30 sq metres cost €460 to €765 per month, depending on the location. October, when university classes resume, is the hardest month to find a place, but over summer and into September it's usually possible to rent something within a matter of days. Before any deals are signed, the company will arrange for you to talk to the owner by phone, assisted by an interpreter if necessary. There is a €50 annual membership fee and, in addition to the rent and one month's deposit (paid directly to the owner), a charge of €35 for each month you rent.

LOUVRE & LES HALLES

The area encompassing the Musée du Louvre and the Forum des Halles, effectively the 1er and a small slice of the 2e, is more disposed to welcoming top-end travellers, but there are some decent mid-range places to choose from as well.

GRAND HÔTEL DE CHAMPAIGNE

Map pp396-9   *Hotel*
☎ 01 42 36 60 00; www.hotelchampaigneparis.com; 17 rue Jean Lantier, 1er; metro Châtelet; s €125-172, d €135-193, tw €214-276

This very comfortable, three-star hotel is housed in the former Hôtel des Tailleurs, a stonecutters' mansion built in 1562 on a quiet street between rue de Rivoli and the Seine. Some of the 43 guestrooms (eg the Louis XIII-style room) are *almost* over the top but, well, this is Paris. Enjoy.

HÔTEL BRIGHTON Map pp383-5   *Hotel*
☎ 01 47 03 61 61; www.esprit-de-france.com; 218 rue de Rivoli, 1er; metro Tuileries; s €115-155, d €115-226, tr €164-252, ste from €226

This three-star establishment, now part of the seven-property Esprit de France group of hotels, has 65 lovely rooms but is a wee bit tatty for this part of town. The rooms overlooking the Jardin des Tuileries are the most popular; those on the 4th and 5th floors afford views over the trees to the Seine. Service is good here and the welcome warm.

HÔTEL LE RELAIS DU LOUVRE
Map pp396-9   *Hotel*

☎ 01 40 41 96 42; www.relaisdulouvre.com; 19 rue des Prêtres St-Germain l'Auxerrois, 1er; metro Chatelet; s with shower/bath €99/128, d & tw with bath €145-180, tr €180, ste €205-244

If you are someone who likes style but in a traditional sense, choose this lovely 21-room hotel just west of the Louvre and south of the Église St-Germain l'Auxerrois. It was given a face-lift for the millennium.

HÔTEL ST-HONORÉ
Map pp396-9   *Hotel*

☎ 01 42 36 20 38; paris@hotelsthonore.com; 85 rue St-Honoré, 1er; metro Châtelet; s/d/tw/q €59/74/83/92

This upgraded, 29-room hotel is between the Palais Royal and the Seine and at the eastern end of a very upmarket shopping street. It offers some fairly cramped rooms, and a few more spacious ones for three and four people.

HÔTEL VICTOIRES OPÉRA
Map pp386-8   *Hotel*

☎ 01 42 36 41 08; www.hotelvictoiresopera.com; 56 rue de Montorgueil, 2e; metro Sentier; s & d €214-275, ste from €330

The two dozen rooms of this ultra-minimalist, four-star hotel right on a lively, pedestrians-only market street are attractive, understated and soundproofed.

CHEAP SLEEPS

This part of the 1er and 2e is very central, but don't expect to find tranquillity or many bargains here.

Both airports are linked to nearby metro Châtelet-Les Halles by the RER (Réseau Express Régional).

CENTRE INTERNATIONAL DE SÉJOUR BVJ PARIS-LOUVRE
Map pp396-9   *Hostel*

☎ 01 53 00 90 90; bvj@wanadoo.fr; 20 rue Jean-Jacques Rousseau, 1er; metro Louvre-Rivoli; per person dm €25, d €28, incl breakfast

This modern, 200-bed hostel run by the Bureau des Voyages de la Jeunesse (Youth Travel Bureau) has bunks in a single-sex room for two to eight people. Guests should be aged under 35. Rooms are accessible from 2.30pm on the day you arrive and all day after that. There are no kitchen facilities and showers are in the hallway. There is usually space in the morning, even in summer, so stop by as early as you can.

The **Centre International de Séjour BVJ Paris-Quartier Latin** (Map pp392-5; ☎ 01 43 29 34 80; bvj@wanadoo.fr; 44 rue des Bernardins, 5e; metro Maubert Mutualité; 1/2/6-bed r per person €35/28/26) is a 138-bed Left Bank branch hostel with the same rules, though at this place all rooms have showers and telephones.

HÔTEL DE LILLE PÉLICAN
Map pp396-9   *Hotel*

☎ 01 42 33 33 42; 8 rue du Pélican, 1er; metro Palais Royal-Musée du Louvre; s/d/tr with washbasin €35/43/65, d with shower €50

This old-fashioned but clean 13-room hotel down a quiet side street has recently been given a face-lift. Some of its rooms have just washbasin and bidet, with communal showers in the hallway (€4.50), but most now have their own shower. The friendly and helpful manager speaks good English.

HÔTEL TIQUETONNE
Map pp386-8   *Hotel*

☎ 01 42 36 94 58; fax 01 42 36 02 94; 6 rue Tiquetonne, 2e; metro Étienne Marcel; s with washbasin/shower €24/36, d with shower €44

If you're looking for good-value digs smack in the middle of party town, this vintage 47-room cheapie on a cobbled street may not be inspirational but it's clean and comfortable. Some rooms are quite large.

MARAIS & BASTILLE

There are quite a few top-end hotels in the heart of the Marais as well as in the vicinity of the elegant place des Vosges, and the choice of lower-priced one- and two-star hotels is excellent. Two-star comfort is less expensive closer to the Bastille in the neighbouring 11e, however.

GRAND HÔTEL MALHER

Map pp396-9 *Hotel*

☎ 01 42 72 60 92; www.grandhotelmalher.com;
5 rue Malher, 4e; metro St-Paul; low season s €86-95,
d €103-112, ste €155-175, high season s €103-115,
d €118-132, ste €155-175

This friendly, family-run establishment has 31
nicely appointed rooms and a pretty courtyard
at the back. Some of the public areas have
been recently renovated, including the lobby.

HÔTEL AXIAL BEAUBOURG

Map pp396-9 *Hotel*

☎ 01 42 72 72 22; www.axialbeaubourg.com; 11 rue
du Temple, 4e; metro Hôtel de Ville; s €110-125, d/tw
€155/165

With 39 newly refurbished 'new look' rooms in
the heart of the Marais, the Axial Beaubourg
has a name that says it all: modern mixed with
historic. It's very upbeat and convenient to
almost everything.

HÔTEL BAUDELAIRE BASTILLE

Map pp392-5 *Hotel*

☎ 01 47 00 40 98; www.tonichotel.com; 12 rue de
Charonne, 11e; metro Bastille or Ledru Rollin; s with
shower €62-65, d with shower & toilet €65-72,
tr €72-82, q €90-100

Formerly the Pax and now part of the small
chain called Tonic Hotels with three properties
elsewhere in France, the one-star Baudelaire
Bastille offers 46 large, spotless rooms but
does not have a lift.

*Room in Hôtel Caron de Beaumarchais
(above)*

HÔTEL CARON DE BEAUMARCHAIS

Map pp396-9 *Boutique Hotel*

☎ 01 42 72 34 12; www.carondebeaumarchais.com;
12 rue Vieille du Temple, 4e; metro St-Paul; d €120-152

You have to see this award-winning themed
hotel to believe it. Decorated like an 18th-
century private house contemporary with
Beaumarchais – who wrote *Le Mariage de
Figaro* (The Marriage of Figaro) at No 47 on this
street – the hotel has a prized 18th-century
pianoforte and candelabras in its front room,
and 44 stylish (though small) guestrooms.

HÔTEL CASTEX Map pp392-5 *Hotel*

☎ 01 42 72 31 52; www.castexhotel.com; 5 rue
Castex, 4e; metro Bastille; s €95-115, d €120-140,
ste €190-220; ⌨

Equidistant from the Bastille and the Marais,
the Castex got a major face-lift in 2003 and has
retained some of its 17th-century elements, including a vaulted stone cellar used as a breakfast room, terracotta tiles on the floor and Toile
de Jouy wallpaper. Unusual for a small hotel in
Paris, the Castex is fully air-conditioned.

HÔTEL CENTRAL BASTILLE

Map pp392-5 *Hotel*

☎ 01 47 00 31 51; fax 01 47 00 77 29; 16 rue de la
Roquette, 11e; metro Bastille; s/d/tw/tr €50/70/70/90,
incl breakfast

This 22-room hotel is nothing special among
the line-up of budget hotels in the Bastille,
but the welcome is warm and there's a 10%
discount after three days.

HÔTEL CENTRAL MARAIS

Map pp396-9 *Hotel*

☎ 01 48 87 56 08; www.hotelcentralmarais.com;
2 rue Ste-Croix de la Bretonnerie, 4e; metro Hôtel de
Ville; r €87, ste €110

This small, seven-room hotel in the centre of
gay land Paris caters essentially for gay men,
though lesbians are also welcome. Bear in
mind that there is only one bathroom for
every two rooms and the suite for up to four
people demands a minimum stay of three
nights. After 3pm reception is round the corner in the bar **Le Central** (p219).

HÔTEL DAVAL Map pp392-5 *Hotel*

☎ 01 47 00 51 23; hoteldaval@wanadoo.fr; 21 rue
Daval, 11e; metro Bastille; s €65-69, d €69-97

This 21-room property is a clean and central
option if you're looking for budget accommodation just off place de la Bastille.

HÔTEL DE LA BRETONNERIE

Map pp396-9 *Hotel*

☎ 01 48 87 77 63; www.bretonnerie.com; 22 rue St-Croixe de la Bretonnerie, 4e; metro Hôtel de Ville; s & d €110-145, tr & q €170, ste €180-205

This is a very charming three-star in the heart of the Marais nightlife area dating from the 17th century. The décor of each of the 22 rooms and seven suites is unique, and some rooms have four-poster and canopy beds.

HÔTEL DE LA PLACE DES VOSGES

Map pp392-5 *Hotel*

☎ 01 42 72 60 46; fax 01 42 72 02 64; hotel.place .des.vosges@gofornet.fr; 12 rue de Birague, 4e; metro Bastille; s €101, d with shower €101-120, tw with bath €106-120, ste €140, incl breakfast

This superbly situated two-star hotel south of place des Vosges has rather average rooms, though the public areas are quite impressive. There's a tiny lift from the 1st to 4th floors.

HÔTEL DE NICE Map pp396-9 *Hotel*

☎ 01 42 78 55 29; fax 01 42 78 36 07; 42 bis rue de Rivoli, 4e; metro Hôtel de Ville; s/d/tr €65/100/120

This is an especially warm, family-run place with 23 comfortable rooms. Some rooms have balconies high above busy rue de Rivoli. Reception is on the 1st floor.

HÔTEL DU 7E ART Map pp396-9 *Hotel*

☎ 01 44 54 85 00; hotel7art@wanadoo.fr; 20 rue St-Paul, 4e; metro St-Paul; s with washbasin €59, s & d with shower or bath & toilet €75-130, tw €85-130

This themed 23-room hotel on the south side of rue St-Antoine is a fun place for film buffs (*le septième art*, or 'the seventh art', is what the French call cinema), with a B&W-movie theme throughout, right down to the tiled floors and bathrooms. Oddly, almost all the posters and memorabilia relate to old Hollywood films, with not a reference to a French film in sight.

HÔTEL DU BOURG TIBOURG

Map pp396-9 *Hotel*

☎ 01 42 78 47 39; www.hoteldubourgtibourg.com; 19 du Bourg Tibourg, 4e; metro Hôtel de Ville or St-Paul; s €150, d €200-250, ste €350

This 30-room property, the former Hôtel Rivoli Notre Dame, has been totally revamped by designer Jacques Garcia, he of Hôtel Costes fame and one of the most fashionable interior designers in Paris at the moment. The result: romantic 'French' combined with a hint of Oriental neogothic.

HÔTEL JEANNE D'ARC

Map pp396-9 *Hotel*

☎ 01 48 87 62 11; www.hoteljeannedarc.com; 3 rue de Jarente, 4e; metro St-Paul; small/large s €57/70, d €80, tw/tr/q €95/112/140

This charming 36-room hotel near lovely place du Marché Ste-Catherine is a great little base for your peregrinations among the museums, bars and restaurants of the Marais, Village St-Paul and the Bastille. But everyone knows about it, so book early. Do not confuse this two-star place with the two-star Grand Hôtel Jeanne d'Arc in the unlovely 13e.

HÔTEL LE COMPOSTELLE

Map pp396-9 *Hotel*

☎ 01 42 78 59 99; fax 01 40 29 05 18; 31 rue du Roi de Sicile, 4e; metro Hôtel de Ville; s/d with shower & toilet €60/89, d with bath €96

This is a tasteful 25-room place at the more tranquil end of the Marais not far from the place des Vosges and surrounded by excellent restaurants, but the welcome could be a titch warmer.

HÔTEL LYON MULHOUSE

Map pp392-5 *Hotel*

☎ 01 47 00 91 50; www.1-hotel-paris.com; 8 blvd Beaumarchais, 11e; metro Bastille; s €60-85, d €68-75, tw €80-85, tr €90-95, q €100-115

This former post house, from where carriages would set out for Lyon and Mulhouse, has been a hotel since the 1920s and has 40 quiet and quite comfortable rooms. Place de la Bastille and the Marché Bastille (p152) on blvd Richard Lenoir are just around the corner.

HOTEL NEW CANDIDE

Map pp392-5 *Hotel*

☎ 01 43 79 02 33; www.new-hotel.com; 3 rue Pétion, 11e; metro Voltaire; s €71-90, d €79-107

This 48-room hotel within easy striking distance of the Bastille and the Marais offers relatively good value and is very convenient to the Marché Bastille (p152) on blvd Richard Lenoir.

HÔTEL PRATIC Map pp396-9 *Hotel*

☎ 01 48 87 80 47; www.hotelpratic.com; 9 rue d'Ormesson, 4e; metro St-Paul; s/d with washbasin & toilet €59/77, s/d with shower €87/98, s/d with bath & toilet €102/117, tr with bath & toilet €135

This 23-room hotel, which is opposite the delightful place du Marché Ste-Catherine has been thoroughly renovated and the décor – exposed beams, gilt frames and striped wallpaper – is almost too much. Rather pricey for what you get, frankly.

HÔTEL ROYAL BASTILLE

Map pp392-5   *Hotel*

☎ 01 48 05 62 47; hroyalbastille@hotmail.com; 14 rue de la Roquette, 11e; metro Bastille; s/d/tr/ q from €78/87/104/123

More upmarket than most of the other lower-priced hotels along lively rue de la Roquette in the Bastille, the pleasant 29-room Royal Bastille is good value.

HÔTEL ST-LOUIS MARAIS

Map pp396-9   *Hotel*

☎ 01 48 87 87 04; www.saintlouismarais.com; 1 rue Charles V, 4e; metro Sully Morland; small/ large s €59/91, d/tw/tr €107/125/140

This especially charming hotel within a 17th-century convent is more Bastille than Marais but still within easy walking distance of the latter. Wooden beams, terracotta tiles and heavy drapes tend to darken the 16 rooms but certainly add to the atmosphere.

HÔTEL ST-MERRY

Map pp396-9   *Hotel*

☎ 01 42 78 14 15; www.hotelmarais.com; 78 rue de la Verrerie, 4e; metro Châtelet; d & tw €160-230, tr €205-275, ste €335-407

The interior of this 11-room hostelry, with beamed ceilings, church pews and confessionals, and wrought-iron candelabra, is a Gothic historian's wet dream; you have to see the architectural elements of room No 9 and the furnishings of No 20 to believe them. It's all a bit of *faux* fun.

HÔTEL SAINTONGE MARAIS

Map pp396-9   *Hotel*

☎ 01 42 77 91 13; www.hotelmarais.com; 16 rue Saintonge, 3e; metro Filles du Calvaire; s €90-105, d €110-115, ste €170

This charming 23-room hotel, with exposed beams, vaulted cellar and period furniture, is really more Oberkampf/République than the Marais. But with the Musée Picasso practically next door, let's not quibble. You'll get much more bang for your buck here than in the more central parts of the Marais, include at the Saintonge's sister property, the **Hôtel St-Merry** (p288).

HÔTEL SÉVIGNÉ Map pp396-9   *Hotel*

☎ 01 42 72 76 17; www.le-sevigne.com; 2 rue Malher, 4e; metro St-Paul; s €62, d €72-84, tw €78-84, tr €99

This 30-room hotel in the heart of the Marais and named after the celebrated Marquise de Sévigné (1626–96), whose letters give us such a wonderful insight into 17th-century Paris, is excellent value for its location.

CHEAP SLEEPS

The Marais is one of the liveliest parts of the Right Bank and its hostels are among the city's finest. Despite massive gentrification, there are also some less expensive hotels left. East of the Bastille, the relatively untouristed 11e is generally made up of unpretentious, working-class areas and is a good way to see 'real' Paris up close.

GRAND HÔTEL DU LOIRET

Map pp396-9   *Hotel*

☎ 01 48 87 77 00; hoteloiret@aol.com; 8 rue des Mauvais Garçons, 4e; metro Hôtel de Ville or St-Paul; s & d with washbasin €45, s/d with shower & toilet €55/60, s/d/tr with bath & toilet €70/80/90

This 29-room budget hotel in the heart of gay Maris is very popular with young male travellers, not just because it is within easy walking distance of just about everything after dark but because it sits – or does it lie? – on 'Street of the Bad Boys'. Only 16 of the rooms have shower or bath and toilet; the rest share facilities off the corridors.

HÔTEL BAUDIN Map pp392-5   *Hotel*

☎ 01 47 00 18 91; hotelbaudin@wanadoo.fr; 113 av Ledru Rollin, 11e; metro Ledru Rollin; s/d with washbasin €29/36, s/d with shower & toilet €40/49, s/d with bath & toilet €46/54, tr €54-72

This once-grand, old-fashioned hostelry has 17 brightly coloured rooms. Hall showers are free and the welcome is warm.

HÔTEL DE LA HERSE D'OR

Map pp392-5   *Hotel*

☎ 01 48 87 84 09; hotel.herse.dor@wanadoo.fr; 20 rue St-Antoine, 4e; metro Bastille; s/d with washbasin €38/45, d with shower/bath & toilet €58/60

This friendly, 35-room place on busy rue St-Antoine has partially renovated, serviceable rooms off a long stone corridor. Hall showers cost €2. And, BTW, *herse* in French is not 'hearse' but 'portcullis'. So let's just call it the 'Golden Gate Hotel'.

HÔTEL LES SANS CULOTTES

Map pp392-5 *Hotel*

☎ 01 48 05 42 92; fax 01 48 05 08 56; 27 rue de Lappe, 11e; metro Bastille; s/d €53.50/63

The rooms in this nine-room hotel above a nice little bistro of the same name (p164) are on the small size but are clean, tidy and very central. Be warned that there is no lift here.

HÔTEL RIVOLI Map pp396-9 *Hotel*

☎ 01 42 72 08 41; 44 rue de Rivoli or 2 rue des Mauvais Garçons, 4e; metro Hôtel de Ville; s/d with washbasin €27/35, s/d with shower €35/39, d with bath & toilet €49

Long an LP favourite (no pretending who we are – or are not – with these guys), the Rivoli is forever cheery but not as dirt cheap as it once was, with 20 basic, somewhat noisy rooms. Showers are free, and the front door is locked from 2am to 7am.

MAISON INTERNATIONALE DES JE-UNES POUR LA CULTURE ET LA PAIX

Map pp392-5 *Hostel*

☎ 01 43 71 99 21; mij.cp@wanadoo.fr; 4 rue Titon, 11e; metro Faidherbe Chaligny; dm €20

This hostel with 166 beds is 1.3km east of place de la Bastille. It offers accommodation in Spartan, comfortable but rather institutional dormitory rooms for up to eight people, and there's a curfew between 2am and 6am. The upper age limit of 30 is not strictly enforced. Telephone reservations are accepted, but your chance of finding a bed is greatest if you call or stop by between 8am and 10am. The maximum stay is theoretically three days but you can usually stay for a week if there is room.

MAISON INTERNATIONALE DE LA JEUNESSE ET DES ÉTUDIANTS

Map pp396-9 *Hostel*

☎ 01 42 74 23 45; www.mije.com

The MIJE runs three hostels in attractively renovated 17th- and 18th-century *hôtels particuliers* in the heart of the Marais, and it's difficult to think of a better budget deal in Paris. Costs are the same for all three. A bed in a shower-equipped, single-sex dorm sleeping four to eight people is €27 and per person in a single/double/triple €42/32/28. Rooms are closed from noon to 3pm, and curfew is from 1am to 7am. The maximum stay is seven nights. Individuals can make reservations at any of the three MIJE hostels listed below by emailing (info@mije.com) or calling the central switchboard; reception will hold you a bed till noon. During summer and other busy periods, there may not be space after mid-morning. There's an annual membership fee of €2.50.

MIJE Le Fourcy (6 rue de Fourcy, 4e; metro St-Paul) This 207-bed branch is the largest of the three. There's a cheap eatery here called Le Restaurant, which offers a three-course *menu* (fixed-price meal with two or more courses) including a drink for €10.50, and a two-course *formule* (similar to a *menu* but allows choice of whichever two of three courses you want) plus drink for €8.50.

MIJE Le Fauconnier (11 rue du Fauconnier, 4e; metro St-Paul or Pont Marie) This 125-bed hostel is two blocks south of MIJE Le Fourcy.

MIJE Maubuisson (12 rue des Barres, 4e; metro Hôtel de Ville or Pont Marie) This 103-bed place – and the pick of the three in our opinion – is half a block south of the *mairie* (town hall) of the 4e.

THE ISLANDS

The smaller of the two islands in the Seine, the Île St-Louis, is by far the more romantic and has a string of excellent top-end hotels. It's an easy walk from central Paris.

ÎLE DE LA CITÉ
Cheap Sleeps

Believe it or not, the only hotel on the Île de la Cité is a budget one.

HÔTEL HENRI IV Map pp396-9 *Hotel*

☎ 01 43 54 44 53; 25 place Dauphine, 1er; metro Pont Neuf or Cité; s €24-31, d €31-36, tr with washbasin €42, d with shower €44, d with shower/bath & toilet €55/68, incl breakfast

This decrepit place, with 20 tattered, worn rooms, is popular for its location, location and location on the tip of the Île de la Cité. It's impossible to find a hotel more romantic at such a price; just don't stay in bed too long. Hall showers cost €2.50. Book well in advance.

ÎLE ST-LOUIS

HÔTEL DE LUTÈCE

Map pp396-9 *Hotel*

☎ 01 43 26 23 52; www.hotel-ile-saintlouis.com; 65 rue St-Louis en l'Île, 4e; metro Pont Marie; s/d/tr €133/158/172

An exquisite 23-room hotel and more country than city, the Lutèce is under the same friendly and helpful management as the **Hôtel des Deux Îles** (below). The comfortable rooms are tastefully decorated and the location is one of the most desirable in the city.

HÔTEL DES DEUX ÎLES

Map pp396-9 *Hotel*

☎ 01 43 26 13 35; www.hotel-ile-saintlouis.com; 59 rue St-Louis en l'Île, 4e; metro Pont Marie; s & d €140, tw €158

This atmospheric 17-room hotel has rustic furnishings and an open fire in the lobby but some of the guestrooms are disappointingly small.

HÔTEL ST-LOUIS Map pp396-9 *Hotel*

☎ 01 46 34 04 80; www.hotel-saint-louis.com; 75 rue St-Louis en l'Île, 4e; metro Pont Marie; d/tw €130/145, ste €210

The third hotel lining posh rue St-Louis en l'Île has 19 appealing but unspectacular rooms, though the public areas are lovely. The breakfast room in the basement dates from the early 17th century.

LATIN QUARTER & JARDIN DES PLANTES

There are dozens of attractive two- and three-star hotels in the Latin Quarter, including a cluster near the Sorbonne and another group along the lively rue des Écoles. Mid-range hotels in the Latin Quarter are very popular with visiting academics, so rooms are hardest to find when conferences and seminars are scheduled (usually from March to July and October). In general this area offers better value among top-end hotels than the neighbouring 6e does. The Luxembourg and Port Royal RER stations are linked to both airports by RER and Orlyval.

COMFORT INN MOUFFETARD

Map pp392-5 *Chain Hotel*

☎ 01 43 36 17 00; www.mouffetard.paris.comfort-inn.fr; 56 rue Mouffetard, 5e; metro Place Monge; s/d €89/119

This inn may not be what you had in mind when you decided on Paris but it's not entirely without charm on this lovely pedestrians-only street. And it's a hop, skip and a jump from delightful place de la Contrescarpe and one of the best food markets in Paris.

FAMILIA HÔTEL Map pp392-5 *Hotel*

☎ 01 43 54 55 27; fax 01 43 29 61 77; www.hotel-paris-familia.com; 11 rue des Écoles, 5e; metro Cardinal Lemoine; s/d with shower & toilet €73.50/90, d/tw/tr/q with bath & toilet €100/102/143.50/180, incl breakfast

This very welcoming and well-situated hotel has attractive sepia murals of Parisian landmarks in its 30 rooms. Eight rooms have little balconies, from which you can glimpse Notre Dame. The flower-bedecked windows make the front of the hotel one of the most attractive in the quarter.

GRAND HÔTEL ST-MICHEL

Map pp392-5 *Hotel*

☎ 01 46 33 33 02; www.grand-hotel-st-michel.com; 19 rue Cujas, 5e; metro Luxembourg; s/d €120/170, ste €220

This very well-situated 46-room hotel is far away from the din of blvd St-Michel, making it feel almost remote. Some of the rooms have a balcony and the attached *salon de thé* (tea room) is quite pleasant.

HÔTEL CLUNY SORBONNE

Map pp392-5 *Hotel*

☎ 01 43 54 66 66; www.hotel-cluny.fr; 8 rue Victor Cousin, 5e; metro Luxembourg; s €69-74, d/tr/q €78/122/130,

This hotel, surrounded by buildings of La Sorbonne where Rimbaud and Verlaine dallied in 1872, has 23 pleasant, well-kept rooms; room No 63 has fabulous views of the college and the Panthéon. The lift may be the size of a telephone box but it will accommodate most travellers and their hatboxes. Service could be better here.

Top of the Class: Paris' Finest Deluxe Hotels

Some of Paris' most opulent hotels are so famous that they have lent their names to the English lexicon.

Hôtel Bel Ami St-Germain des Prés (Map pp396-9; ☎ 01 42 61 53 53; www.hotel-bel-ami.com; 7-11 rue St-Benoit, 6e; metro St-Germain des Prés; s & d €260-380, ste €490) This 115-room minimalist palace housed in a converted 18th-century print works is so streamlined that you'd be forgiven for thinking you'd landed in London. The renovated public areas (all soft greens) are a delight, but standard rooms are on the smallish size.

Hôtel Costes (Map pp383-5; ☎ 01 42 44 50 00; fax 01 42 44 50 01; www.hotelcostes.com; 239 rue St-Honoré, 1er; metro Concorde; s & d €350-800, ste from €1200) Jean-Louis Costes' eponymous 83-room hotel offers a 'luxurious and immoderate home away from home' to the visiting style-Mafia. Outfitted in over-the-top (and very camp) Second Empire castoffs, it remains a darling of the rich and famous.

Hôtel de Crillon (Map pp383-5; ☎ 01 44 71 15 00; www.crillon.com; 10 place de la Concorde, 8e; metro Concorde; s €480-575, d €575-855, ste from €945, larger ste from €1400) This colonnaded, 200-year-old palace, whose sparkling public areas (including Les Ambassadeurs restaurant, with two Michelin stars) are sumptuously decorated with chandeliers, original sculptures, gilt mouldings, tapestries and inlaid furniture, is the epitome of French luxury. The 157 rooms are spacious and most have floor-to-ceiling marble bathrooms.

L'Hôtel (Map pp396-9; ☎ 01 44 41 99 00; www.l-hotel.com; 13 rue des Beaux Arts, 6e; metro St-Germain des Prés; low season s & d €248-529, high season s & d €272-625, ste from €529/625) With 20 rooms and tucked away in a quiet quay-side street, the place with the most minimal of names is the stuff of romantic Paris legends. Rock- and film-star patrons alike fight to sleep in room No 16 where Oscar Wilde died a century ago or in the mirrored Art Deco room (No 36) of legendary dancer Mistinguett. This was also a home away from home for the Argentine writer Jorge Luis Borges (1899–1986), who stayed here many times in the late 1970s and early '80s. Über-designer Jacques Garcia did the most recent renovations.

Hôtel Luxembourg Parc (Map pp392-5; ☎ 01 53 10 36 50; www.hotelluxparc.com; 42 rue de Vaugirard, 6e; metro Luxembourg; s & d €200-300, ste €475) This is a stunner of a 23-room hotel overlooking the Jardin du Luxembourg. It's very convenient to the Sénat and the Palais du Luxembourg, and the American novelist William Faulkner holed up here in 1925 (p144).

Mélia Colbert Boutique Hotel (Map pp396-9; ☎ 01 56 81 19 00; melia.colbert@solmelia.com; 7 rue l'Hôtel Colbert, 5e; metro Maubert Mutualité; s & d €260-390, tr & q €442-549, ste €494-602) This 37-room hotel that unabashedly calls itself a 'boutique hotel' has a glorious front courtyard and a namesake address. Well-heeled friends swear by this discreet property.

Hôtel Meurice (Map pp383-5; ☎ 01 44 58 10 10; www.meuricehotel.com; 228 rue de Rivoli, 1er; metro Tuileries; s €490-650, d €650-800, ste from €800) Counting 60 rooms and facing the Jardin des Tuileries, the Meurice's gold leaf and Art Nouveau glass positively gleam after a major renovation. It's a member of the Dorchester group of hotels.

Hôtel Relais Christine (Map pp396-9; ☎ 01 40 51 60 80; www.relais-christine.com; 3 rue Christine, 6e; metro Mabillon or St-Michel; s & d €325-425, ste from €475) Part of the prestigious Chateaux et Hôtels de France chain, the Relais Christine is a beautiful 51-room property with an unforgettable courtyard entrance off a quiet street, back garden, and a spa and fitness centre built in and around an original 13th-century cellar.

Hôtel Ritz Paris (Map pp383-5; ☎ 01 43 16 35 29; www.ritzparis.com; 15 place Vendôme, 1er; metro Opéra; s & d Nov-Apr & Jul-Aug €580-680, s & d May-Jun & Sep-Oct €630-730, junior ste €800-1030, 1-bed ste €1050-1500) One of the world's most celebrated hotels, the Ritz – is there any other? – has 162 sparkling rooms and suites. Its L'Espadon restaurant has two Michelin stars and the **Hemingway Bar** (p224) is where the American author imbibed once he'd made a name for himself – and could afford it.

La Villa St-Germain des Prés (Map pp396-9; ☎ 01 43 26 60 00; www.villa-saintgermain.com; 29 rue Jacob, 6e; metro St-Germain des Prés; s & d from €240-335, ste from €440) This 32-room hotel helped set what has become a standard of the Parisian accommodation scene: small, minimalist, discreet. Fabrics, lighting, soft furnishing – all are of the utmost quality and taste.

Hotel Ritz Paris (p291)

away in a courtyard off a medieval street with its own garden; if the weather isn't suitable to have breakfast there, you'll enjoy the old-fashioned breakfast just as much. James Joyce lived in one of the courtyard flats in 1921 (p141). The owners will make you feel at home.

HÔTEL DU PANTHÉON

Map pp392-5   *Hotel*

☎ 01 43 54 32 95; www.hoteldupantheon.com; 19 place du Panthéon, 5e; metro Luxembourg; s €99-213, d €99-223, tr €184-244, f €198-426

In the shadow of the capital's largest secular mausoleum and just uphill from the Jardin du Luxembourg, the 'Pantheon Hotel' is an attractive 36-room property that feels almost more 'deluxe' than 'top-end'. Rates vary widely according to the season but in any case, booking via the Internet will save you at least 15%.

HÔTEL ESMERALDA

Map pp396-9   *Hotel*

☎ 01 43 54 19 20; fax 01 40 51 00 68; 4 rue St-Julien le Pauvre, 5e; metro St-Michel; s with washbasin/shower/bath €35/65/80, d with shower & toilet €80, d with bath & toilet €85-95, tr/q from €110/180

This renovated 19-room inn tucked away in a quiet street with full views of Notre Dame has been everyone's secret 'find' for years, so book well in advance. This is about as central Latin Quarter as you're ever going to get.

HÔTEL GAY-LUSSAC

Map pp392-5   *Hotel*

☎ 01 43 54 23 96; fax 01 40 51 79 49; 29 rue Gay Lussac, 5e; metro Luxembourg; s/d €33/49, s/d with shower €55/64, s/d with shower & toilet €59/68.50, tr/q with shower & toilet €90/95, incl breakfast

The Gay-Lussac is a 35-room hotel with a lot of character in the southern part of the Latin Quarter. Though the single rooms are small, the others are large and have high ceilings.

HÔTEL HENRI IV   Map pp396-9   *Hotel*

☎ 01 46 33 20 20; www.hotel-henri4.com; 9-11 rue St-Jacques, 5e; metro St-Michel Notre Dame or Cluny La Sorbonne; s/d/tr €128/146/165

This three-star place awash in antiques, old prints and fresh flowers is a Latin Quarter oasis mere steps from Notre Dame and the Seine. It's part of the same group as the **Hôtel de Lutèce** (p290) and the **Hôtel des Deux Îles** (p290) on the Île de St-Louis, but do *not* confuse this hotel with the bare-bones budget hotel of the same name on the Île de la Cité (p289).

HÔTEL DE L'ESPÉRANCE

Map pp392-5   *Hotel*

☎ 01 47 07 10 99; hotel.esperance@wanadoo.fr; 15 rue Pascal, 5e; metro Censier Daubenton; s with shower/bath & toilet €68/76, d with shower/bath & toilet €73/84, tw/tr €84/99

The 'Hotel of Hope', just a couple of minutes' walk south of lively rue Mouffetard, is a quiet and immaculately kept 38-room place with *faux* antique furnishings and a warm welcome. Larger rooms have two double beds.

HÔTEL DES GRANDES ÉCOLES

Map pp392-5   *Hotel*

☎ 01 43 26 79 23; www.hotel-grandes-ecoles.com; 75 rue du Cardinal Lemoine, 5e; metro Cardinal Lemoine or Place Monge; s & d €105-130, tr €125-150

This wonderful 51-room hotel just north of place de la Contrescarpe has one of the loveliest situations in the Latin Quarter, tucked

HÔTEL LA DEMEURE

Map pp380-2 & Map pp392-5   *Hotel*

☎ 01 43 37 81 25; www.hotel-paris-lademeure.com;
51 blvd St-Marcel, 13e; metro Les Gobelins;
s/d €119/141, ste €198

This self-proclaimed *'hotel de caractère'* owned
and operated by a charming father-son team
is just a bit away from the action at the bottom of the 5e. But the refined elegance of
its 43 rooms, the almost 'clubby' public areas
and the wrap-around balconies of the corner rooms make it worth going the extra
distance.

HÔTEL MINERVE Map pp392-5   *Hotel*

☎ 01 43 26 26 04; www.hotel-paris-minerve.com;
13 rue des Écoles, 5e; metro Cardinal Lemoine;
s with shower & toilet €79-101, d with shower €93,
d with bath €109-125, tr €145

This 54-room hotel in two buildings is owned
by the same family who run the Familia Hôtel
(p290). It has a reception area kitted out in
Oriental carpets and antique books, which
the affable owner/manager Erich Gaucheron
collects, and some of the rooms have been
enlarged. We like the frescoes of French monuments and reproduction 18th-century wallpaper. Some 10 rooms have small balconies,
eight with views of Notre Dame and two have
tiny courtyards that are swooningly romantic.

HÔTEL RÉSIDENCE HENRI IV

Map pp392-5   *Hotel*

☎ 01 44 41 31 81; www.residencehenri4.com; 50 rue
des Bernadins, 5e; metro Maubert Mutualité; s & d
€93-155, 1-2 person apt €130-200, 3-person apt
€149-230, 4-person apt €169-260

This exquisite late 19th-century hotel, which
is at the end of a quiet cul-de-sac near the
Sorbonne and opposite leafy Square Paul
Langevin, has nine rooms and five apartments
with kitchenette (microwave, fridge, stove,
crockery). Rates vary widely according to the
season and there's a 15% discount if you book
on the Internet.

HÔTEL RÉSIDENCE MONGE

Map pp392-5   *Hotel*

☎ 01 43 26 87 90; www.hotelmonge.com; 55 rue
Monge, 5e; metro Place Monge; s €65-84, d & tw
€80-130, tr €110-150

This spotless and well-managed hotel has 36
newly renovated rooms right in the thick of
things.

HÔTEL ST-CHRISTOPHE

Map pp392-5   *Hotel*

☎ 01 43 31 81 54; www.charm-hotel-paris.com;
17 rue Lacépède, 5e; metro Place Monge; s €104-113,
d €115-125

This classy small hotel with 31 well-equipped
rooms is located on a quiet street between
rue Monge in the Latin Quarter and the Jardin
des Plantes. It's part of the Logis de France
umbrella association, always a sign of quality.

HÔTEL ST-JACQUES

Map pp392-5   *Hotel*

☎ 01 44 07 45 45; www.hotel-saintjacques.com in
French; 35 rue des Écoles, 5e; metro Maubert Mutualité; s €50-75, d €85-112, tr €105-135

This adorable 35-room hotel has balconies
overlooking the Panthéon. Audrey Hepburn
and Cary Grant, who filmed some scenes of
Charade a half-century ago, would com-
mend the mod cons that now complement
the original 19th-century details (ornamented
ceilings, iron staircase and so on), but sadly
the service seems to have slipped a notch
or two since our last visit. The singles are
relatively spacious, but not all rooms have
toilets.

SELECT HÔTEL

Map pp392-5   *Boutique Hotel*

☎ 01 46 34 14 80; www.selecthotel.fr; 1 place de la
Sorbonne, 5e; metro Cluny La Sorbonne; d €139-165,
tw €149-165, tr €169-179, ste €202

What was formerly a popular student hotel,
the Select has been transformed into an Art
Deco mini-palace, with an atrium with water
feature, an 18th-century vaulted breakfast
room and 68 stylish guestrooms.

TIMHÔTEL QUARTIER LATIN

Map pp392-5   *Chain Hotel*

☎ 01 43 31 25 64; www.timhotel.com; 71 rue Monge,
5e; metro Place Monge; s & d €125-150

Unusual for the Timhotel chain, which has
two-star properties by and large, the 33-room
Timhotel Quartier Latin has three stars, presumably because of the quality of its décor – a
kind of *Paris moderne* – and the generous size
of its rooms.

CHEAP SLEEPS

The northern section of the 5e close to the
Seine has been popular with students and
young people since the Middle Ages.

GRAND HÔTEL DU PROGRÈS

Map pp392-5   *Hotel*

☎ 01 43 54 53 18; fax 01 56 24 87 80; 50 rue Gay Lussac, 5e; metro Luxembourg; s/d/tr €35/42/55, s/d with shower & toilet €46/54, incl breakfast

This budget, 26-room hotel has been a student favourite for generations. It has washbasin-equipped singles and large, old-fashioned doubles with a view and morning sun.

YOUNG & HAPPY HOSTEL

Map pp392-5   *Hostel*

☎ 01 47 07 47 07; www.youngandhappy.fr; 80 rue Mouffetard, 5e; metro Place Monge; dm €20-22, d per person €23-25

This is a friendly though slightly tatty place in the centre of the most happening area of the Latin Quarter. It's popular with a slightly older crowd nowadays. The rooms are shut tight from 11am to 4pm but the reception stays open; the 2am curfew is strictly enforced. Beds are in smallish rooms for two to four people with washbasins.

Rates differ according to the season. In summer, the best way to get a bed is to stop by at about 9am.

ST-GERMAIN, ODÉON & LUXEMBOURG

St-Germain des Prés is a delightful area to stay and offers some excellent mid-range hotels. The three-star hotels in this area are around St-Germain des Prés.

ARTUSHOTEL

Map pp396-9   *Boutique Hotel*

☎ 01 43 29 07 20; www.artushotel.com; 34 rue de Buci, 6e; metro St-Germain des Prés; s & d with shower €190, tw with shower/bath €220/235, ste €300-320

This must-see, must-stay-at boutique hotel is so very cool it should be in London. Graffiti-covered staircase, guestroom doors painted by individual artists and instruction plaques for the staff that say things like 'Go Ahead Make My Bed' – and all a stone's throw from place St-Germain des Prés.

DELHY'S HÔTEL Map pp396-9   *Hotel*

☎ 01 43 26 58 25; delhys@wanadoo.fr; 22 rue de l'Hirondelle, 6e; metro St-Michel; s with washbasin €40-58, s with shower €66-73, d with washbasin €58-64, d with shower €72-79, tw with washbasin €62-68, tw with shower €76-83, tr €96-113

This 21-room hotel, through the arch from 6 place St-Michel, has neat but simple rooms

Door, Artushotel (above)

that are surprisingly quiet given the fracas that is usually taking place a whisper away. Hall showers cost €4.

GRAND HÔTEL DE L'UNIVERS

Map pp396-9   *Hotel*
☎ 01 43 29 37 00; www.hotel-paris-univers.com; 6 rue Grégoire de Tours, 6e; metro Odéon; s €130-170, d & tw €150-185, ste €200-215

The public areas of this hotel in an original 15th-century townhouse are a baroque dream (or nightmare, depending on your taste), though the 34 guestrooms are up-to-date. It's part of the same stable as the **Hôtel St-Germain des Prés** (p296), a short distance northwest.

HÔTEL D'ANGLETERRE

Map pp396-9   *Hotel*
☎ 01 42 60 34 72; www.hotel-dangleterre.com; 44 rue Jacob, 6e; metro St-Germain des Prés; s €130-220, d €140-230, ste €270-300

The 'England Hotel' is a beautiful 27-room property in a quiet street close to busy blvd St-Germain and Musée d'Orsay. The loyal guests breakfast in the courtyard patio of this former British Embassy, where the Treaty of Paris ending the American Revolution was signed and where Hemingway once lodged (p142). Duplex suite No 51 at the top has beamed ceilings and is the finest in the house.

HÔTEL DE DANEMARK

Map pp389-91   *Boutique Hotel*
☎ 01 43 26 93 78; www.hoteldanemark.com; 21 rue Vavin, 6e; metro Vavin; s €112-145, d €125-145

This positively scrumptious boutique hotel southwest of the Jardin du Luxembourg has 15 very tastefully furnished rooms – there's original artwork in each, some gaze onto Henri Sauvage's Carreaux Metro, an Art Nouveau tiled apartment building designed in 1912, and the higher priced rooms have Jacuzzis. Montparnasse and all its bars and brasseries are a short walk away.

HÔTEL DE NESLE Map pp396-9   *Hotel*

☎ 01 43 54 62 41; fax 01 43 54 31 88; 7 rue de Nesle, 6e; metro Odéon or Mabillon; s with shower €50-60, d with shower/bath €75/100

The Nesle is a relaxed, colourfully decorated hotel with 20 rooms and different themes – from Molière and Africa to 1001 Nights – in a quiet street west of place St-Michel. There's

also a lovely garden at the back. Reservations are only accepted by telephone and usually only up to a few days in advance.

HÔTEL DE ST-GERMAIN

Map pp389-91   *Hotel*
☎ 01 45 48 91 64; www.hotel-de-saint-germain.fr; 50 rue du Four, 6e; metro Sèvres Babylone; s €95-105, d €105-120, ste €210-240

Staying in this immaculate, 30-room hotel really does feel like staying at a friend's place – a 'home away from home' as the marketing blurb says. The breakfast room with all the newspapers and the teapots on display is particularly *coquette* (cute).

HÔTEL DES DEUX CONTINENTS

Map pp396-9   *Hotel*
☎ 01 43 26 72 46; www.2continents-hotel.com; 25 rue Jacob, 6e; metro St-Germain des Prés; s €135, d €145-155, tw €155, tr €190

The 'Two Continents Hotel' (surely the name is to lure Americans over) is a very pleasant 41-room establishment with spacious rooms in a quiet street. The mural in the breakfast room is an early morning eye-opener.

HÔTEL DES MARRONNIERS

Map pp396-9   *Hotel*
☎ 01 43 25 30 60; www.hotel-marronniers.com; 21 rue Jacob, 6e; metro St-Germain des Prés; s €110, d €150-165, tw €155-170, tr €185-205, q €245

At the end of a small courtyard, the 'Chestnut Trees Hotel' has 37 less-than-huge rooms with veranda and a magical garden at the back. It's a real oasis in the heart of St-Germain.

HÔTEL DU GLOBE

Map pp396-9   *Boutique Hotel*
☎ 01 43 26 35 50; fax 01 46 33 62 69; 15 rue des Quatre Vents, 6e; metro Odéon; r with toilet €55, r with shower & toilet €70-90, r with bath & toilet €105

The 'Globe Hotel' is an eclectic, if somewhat dusty, caravanserai with 15 rooms, each with its own theme. We especially like room No 12, which has a canopy bed.

HÔTEL LE CLOS MÉDICIS

Map pp396-9   *Hotel*
☎ 01 43 29 10 80; www.closmedicis.com; 56 rue Monsieur le Prince, 6e; metro Luxembourg; s €140, d €170-185, tw €210, tr €250, ste €250-450

Someone has taken an 18th-century building and spun it into the 21st century, with 38 tasteful grey-and-burgundy guestrooms. History stays in the lobby, with its antiques and open fire. The inner courtyard is a delight in fine weather.

HÔTEL MICHELET ODÉON

Map pp396-9 *Hotel*

☎ 01 53 10 05 60; www.hotelmicheletodeon.com; 6 place de l'Odéon, 6e; metro Odéon; s €70, d €82.50-92.50, tw €93-100, tr €116, q €127

Opposite the Odéon-Théâtre de l'Europe (p240) and just a minute's walk from the Jardin du Luxembourg, this 42-room, two-star hotel has tasteful, generously proportioned rooms.

HÔTEL ST-ANDRÉ DES ARTS

Map pp396-9 *Hotel*

☎ 01 43 26 96 16; hsaintand@wanadoo.fr; 6 rue St-André des Arts, 6e; metro Odéon; s/d/tw/tr/q €64/82/87/102/112, incl breakfast

This is a 31-room hotel on a lively, restaurant-lined thoroughfare. All of the rooms have shower or bath and toilet.

HÔTEL ST-GERMAIN DES PRÉS

Map pp396-9 *Hotel*

☎ 01 40 46 83 63; www.hotel-paris-saint-germain .com; 36 rue Bonaparte, 6e; metro St-Germain des Prés; s €130-160, d with shower €150-180, d with bath €160-195, ste €255

Situated just up from the cafés and hubbub of place St-Germain des Prés and south of the Seine, this fabulously appointed 30-room hotel would be a top choice in its own right (we love the room with the four-poster bed), but many come here in order to say they've laid their head (if nothing else) where Henry Miller did (p143).

CHEAP SLEEPS

The well-heeled 6e has very little in the way of budget offerings.

HÔTEL DES ACADÉMIES

Map pp389-91 *Hotel*

☎ 01 43 26 66 44; fax 01 43 26 03 72; 15 rue de la Grande Chaumière, 6e; metro Vavin; s with washbasin/shower €39/53, d with shower €53-65

This 21-room hotel located between Jardin du Luxembourg and the former artists' quarter of Montparnasse has been run by the same friendly family since 1920. It retains an authentic 1950s feel and offers clean, cheap and basic lodgings. Hall showers are a pricey €5.

MONTPARNASSE

Just east of Gare Montparnasse (the train station that is also home to metro Montparnasse Bienvenüe), there are a number of two- and three-star places on rue Vandamme and rue de la Gaîté – though the latter is rife with sex shops and peep shows. Gare Montparnasse is served by Air France buses from both airports. Place Denfert Rochereau is also linked to both airports by Orlybus, Orlyval and RER.

HÔTEL AVIATIC Map pp389-91 *Hotel*

☎ 01 53 63 25 50; www.aviatic.fr; 105 rue de Vaugirard, 6e; metro Montparnasse Bienvenüe; s €130-170, d €155-199, tr €165-210

This 43-room hotel with charming, almost Laura Ashley-style décor has been in the business since 1856, so it must be doing something right. The conservatory is a breath of fresh air in the heart of Paris.

HÔTEL DE PARIS

Map pp389-91 *Hotel*

☎ 01 43 22 10 13; fax 01 40 47 07 58; 51 av du Maine, 14e; metro Montparnasse Bienvenüe; s €68-80, d €75-90, tr €83-90

This simple hotel with the equally simple name has 54 rooms with little balconies overlooking the Gare Montparnasse.

HÔTEL DELAMBRE Map pp389-91 *Hotel*

☎ 01 43 20 66 31; www.hoteldelambre.com; 35 rue Delambre, 14e; metro Montparnasse Bienvenüe; s €65-85, d €80-95, tr & q €140

This attractive 30-room hotel just east of the Gare Montparnasse takes wrought iron as a theme and uses it both in functional pieces and decorative items throughout.

HÔTEL MIRAMAR Map pp389-91 *Hotel*

☎ 01 45 48 62 94; www.hotelmiramar75.com in French; 6 Place Bienvenüe, 15e; metro Montparnasse Bienvenüe; s/d/tr/q €76/85/124/139

This soundproofed hotel with 37 smallish rooms on the corner of blvd Vaugirard is recommended only because of its location: opposite the Tour Montparnasse and the Gare Montparnasse.

HÔTEL ODESSA MONTPARNASSE

Map pp389-91   *Hotel*

☎ 01 43 20 64 78; www.paris-hotel-odessa.com;
28 rue d'Odessa, 14e; metro Montparnasse Bienvenüe;
s €66-69, d €78-83, tw €90, tr €100, q €105

This hotel on the street of creperies (p183)
and just around the corner from the brasseries
and bistros of Montparnasse has 42 bright,
good-sized rooms and offers good value for
money.

VILLA MODIGLIANI

Map pp389-91   *Hotel*

☎ 01 56 54 20 00; www.vacancesbleues.com; 13 rue
Delambre, 14e; metro Montparnasse Bienvenüe;
s €110-116, d €127-133

The 100 rooms of this ultra-posh 'villa hotel'
spread though a series of 19th-century buildings set away from rue Delambre. There are
substantial discounts for stays of six nights
or more.

CHEAP SLEEPS

The budget places in the 14e don't usually
see many foreign tourists.

CELTIC HÔTEL Map pp389-91   *Hotel*

☎ 01 43 20 93 53; hotelceltic@wanadoo.fr; 15 rue
d'Odessa, 14e; metro Edgar Quinet; s with washbasin/
shower €43/54, d with shower & toilet €57-63, tr with
shower & toilet €72

This 29-room hotel is an old-fashioned place
that has undergone only partial modernisa-

tion. It has pretty bare singles and doubles,
but the Gare Montparnasse is only 200m
away.

HÔTEL DE BLOIS Map pp380-2   *Hotel*

☎ 01 45 40 99 48; fax 01 45 40 45 62; 5 rue des
Plantes, 14e; metro Mouton Duvernet; s/d with washbasin €40/42, s/d with shower €43/45, s/d with shower
& toilet €46/49, tr with bath €61

This very friendly, 25-room establishment just
off the av du Maine offers smallish singles and
doubles, and fully equipped triples.

HÔTEL DE L'ESPÉRANCE

Map pp389-91   *Hotel*

☎ 01 43 21 63 84; info@esperancehotelparis.com;
45 rue de la Gaîté, 14e; metro Gaîté; s with shower &
toilet €55-60, d with shower & toilet €65-70

This 14-room place along a street lined with
sex shops has had a somewhat cheesy refit
but remains good value for what and where
it is.

PETIT PALACE HÔTEL

Map pp380-2   *Hotel*

☎ 01 43 22 05 25; petitpalace@hotelsparisonline
.com; 131 av du Maine, 14e; metro Gaîté; s €54-61,
d €61-69, tr €69

This friendly and rather ambitiously named
two-star hotel has been run by the same
family for half a century. It has 44 smallish
but spotless rooms, and all have showers and
toilets.

FAUBOURG ST-GERMAIN & INVALIDES

The 7e is a lovely arrondissement in which to stay, but apart from the northeast section –
the area east of Invalides and opposite the Louvre – it's fairly quiet here.

HÔTEL LENOX ST-GERMAIN

Map pp389-91   *Hotel*

☎ 01 42 96 10 95; hotel@lenoxsaintgermain.com;
9 rue de l'Université, 7e; metro Rue du Bac; s €115-120,
d €140-150, tw €142-160, ste €255-270

This hotel has 34 simple, comfortable rooms
and a late-opening 1930s-style bar, attracting a
chic clientele. The Art Deco décor is a treat and
the leather armchairs more than comfortable.

HÔTEL THOUMIEUX

Map pp389-91   *Hotel*

☎ 01 47 05 49 75; www.thoumieux.com in French; 79
rue St-Dominique, 7e; metro La Tour Maubourg;
s/d €107/115

This three-star hotel, which is above the popular brasserie **Thoumioux** (p186), has 10 well-
appointed rooms, and is a stone's throw from
the Musée d'Orsay and Invalides.

ÉTOILE & CHAMPS-ÉLYSÉES

Like the 1er, the 8e is for the most part
home to deluxe hotels (see the boxed text,
p291), though there are a few top-end
favourites in the vicinity of place Charles
de Gaulle.

HÔTEL ÉLYSÉE CERAMIC

Map pp383-5 *Hotel*

☎ 01 42 27 20 30; www.elysees-ceramic.com; 34 av de Wagram, 8e; metro Charles de Gaulle-Étoile; s/d/tr/q €180/200/223/246

The 'Elysian Ceramic' should be avoided by bulls who like china shops and people in glasshouses with a penchant for throwing stones. It's a 57-room, three-star hostelry on well-to-do av de Wagram made of sculpted and painted Art Nouveau ceramic (well, at least the façade is). It's been here since 1904.

CLICHY & GARE ST-LAZARE

These areas offer some excellent medium-range reasonably priced top-end hotels. The better deals are away from Gare St-Lazare but there are several places along rue d'Amsterdam beside the station worth checking out.

HÔTEL BRITANNIA Map pp383-5 *Hotel*

☎ 01 42 85 36 36; fax 01 42 85 16 93; 24 rue d'Amsterdam, 9e; metro St-Lazare; s & d with shower/bath €78/85, tr with shower or bath €94

This 46-room place with narrow hallways but pleasant, clean rooms is just opposite Gare St-Lazare and a quick walk to the *grands magasins* (department stores) on blvd Haussmann. The triples are on the small side, though.

HÔTEL CONCORDE ST-LAZARE

Map pp383-5 *Hotel*

☎ 01 40 08 44 44; www.concordestlazare-paris.com; 108 rue St-Lazare, 8e; metro St-Lazare; s & d €300-430, ste from €575

Built in 1889 as the Grand Hôtel Terminus, this fabulous 266-room railway hotel has now been totally restored, declared a historical monument and must be seen to be believed. Make sure you bring a compass; the corridors are enormous.

HÔTEL DU CALVADOS

Map pp383-5 *Hotel*

☎ 01 48 74 39 31; hotelcalvados@wanadoo.fr; 20 rue d'Amsterdam, 9e; metro St-Lazare; s €70-85, d €106.50-115

A thorough refurbishment several years ago has transformed this 25-room hotel just up from Gare St-Lazare into a very affordable three-star property.

HÔTEL FAVART Map pp386-8 *Hotel*

☎ 01 42 97 59 83; fax 01 40 15 95 58; www.hotel-paris-favart.com; favart.hotel@wanadoo.fr; 5 rue Marivaux, 2e; metro Richelieu Drouot; s/d/tr €85/108/130

With 37 rooms facing the Opéra Comique, the Favart is a stylish Art Nouveau hotel that feels like it never let go of the *belle époque* (literally 'beautiful age'). If you're interested in shopping at the big department store on blvd Haussmann, this is an excellent choice.

CHEAP SLEEPS

Clichy offers a couple of very unusual places to stay in the budget category.

HÔTEL ELDORADO Map pp383-5 *Hotel*

☎ 01 45 22 35 21; eldoradohotel@wanadoo.fr; 18 rue des Dames, 17e; metro Place de Clichy; s/d/tr with shower €45/60/80

This boho place is one of Paris' grooviest finds: a welcoming, well-run place with 40 colourfully decorated rooms in a main building on a quiet street and in an annexe with a private garden at the back. Is this really Paris? The excellent **Bistro des Dames** (p188) next door, which belongs to the hotel, is a bonus.

STYLE HOTEL Map pp383-5 *Hotel*

☎ 01 45 22 37 59; fax 01 45 22 81 03; 8 rue Ganneron, 18e; metro La Fourche; s with shower €43, d without/with shower €34/48, tr €55, q €65

This 36-room hotel just north of place de Clichy and west of Cimetière de Montmartre is a titch rough around the edges but loaded with character and the welcome is charming. There's a lovely little courtyard, but no lift.

OPÉRA & LES GRANDS BOULEVARDS

The avenues around blvd Montmartre are a popular nightlife area and a lively area in which to stay.

HÔTEL CHOPIN Map pp386-8 *Hotel*

☎ 01 47 70 58 10; fax 01 42 47 00 70; 46 passage Jouffroy, entrance at 10 blvd Montmartre, 9e; metro Grands Boulevards; s €57, s with shower & toilet €64-72, d with shower & toilet €73-84, tr with shower & toilet €97

The Chopin, dating back to 1846, is down one of Paris' most delightful 19th-century *passages couverts* (covered shopping arcades; p144). It may be a little faded, but it's still enormously evocative of the *belle époque* and the welcome is always warm. After the arcade closes at 10pm, ring the *sonnette de nuit* (night doorbell).

HÔTEL DES ARTS Map pp386-8   *Hotel*
☎ 01 42 46 73 30; hdag@free.fr; 7 Cité Bergère, 9e; metro Grands Boulevards; s with shower/bath €68/74, d with shower/bath €74/82, tr €92/98

The new management have transformed what was once a funky place to stay with loads of character (and resident parrot) into just another two-star hotel. But some things never change. The 'Arts Hotel' still has 25 rooms and it remains in a quiet little alley off rue du Faubourg Montmartre. There are seven other hotels on this street, including **Hotel Victoria** (below).

HÔTEL LANGLOIS Map pp383-5   *Hotel*
☎ 01 48 74 78 24; www.hotel-langlois.com; 63 rue St-Lazare, 9e; metro Trinité; s €79-89, d €89-99, tw/ste €99/132

Built in 1870, the hotel formerly known as the Hôtel des Croisés has retained its charming *belle époque* look and feel despite a massive makeover in 1997. Its 27 rooms and suites are unusually large for a small-ish hotel in Paris, and it's very convenient to the department stores on the blvd Haussmann.

HÔTEL PELETIER HAUSSMANN OPÉRA Map pp386-8   *Hotel*
☎ 01 42 46 79 53; www.peletieropera.com; 15 rue Le Peletier, 9e; metro Richelieu Drouot; s €70-75, d €78-86, tr €86-100

This is a pleasant, 26-room hotel just off blvd Haussmann and close to the big department stores. There are attractive packages available at the weekend, depending on the season.

HOTEL VICTORIA Map pp386-8   *Hotel*
☎ 01 47 70 20 01; fax 01 48 01 08 43; 2bis-4 Cité Bergère, 9e; metro Grands Boulevards; s €68-87, d €74-93, tr €93-12

This 107-room old-style hotel in a quiet alley-way just off the Grands Boulevards is a good choice if you're looking for mid-range accommodation on the Right Bank.

HÔTEL VIVIENNE Map pp386-8   *Hotel*
☎ 01 42 33 13 26; paris@hotel-vivienne.com; 40 rue Vivienne, 2e; metro Grands Boulevards; s with shower €50, d with shower/shower & toilet/bath & toilet €65/77/80, tw/tr €86/100

The public areas of this cheery place have undergone refurbishment recently, and it's a wise choice if you want to be close to the Palais Royal or the Vivienne and Colbert passages (p145).

PAVILION OPÉRA BOURSE
Map pp386-8   *Boutique Hotel*
☎ 01 53 34 12 12; www.leshotelsdeparis.com; 15 rue Geoffroy Marie, 9e; metro Grands Boulevards; s €190, d €210-250, tr €300

Just north of the Grands Boulevards and around the corner from the Folies-Bergère, this 'charming pavilion' is one of the nicest of the 25 properties owned or managed by Les Hôtels de Paris. Each of its 31 rooms is kitted out in Art Deco style with a twist – a jungle theme. It's not oppressive – bit of faux zebra and leopard skin here, brass antelope 'horns', palm fronds over there. Somehow it all works.

VILLA OPÉRA DROUOT
Map pp386-8   *Boutique Hotel*
☎ 01 48 00 08 08; www.leshotelsdeparis.com; 2 rue Geoffroy Marie, 9e; metro Grands Boulevards; s €217, d €267-298, ste €337

This 'prestige villa', just down from its sister 'hotel', Pavilion Opéra Bourse (above), evokes the Paris of the *belle époque*. The 30 rooms (including four duplex suites) have musical themes and are swathed in silk and velvet.

GARE DU NORD, GARE DE L'EST & RÉPUBLIQUE

There are a few two- and three-star places around the train stations in the 10e that are convenient if you're catching an early train to London or want to crash immediately upon arrival.

GRAND HÔTEL DE PARIS
Map pp386-8   *Hotel*
☎ 01 46 07 40 56; grand.hotel.de.paris@gofornet.com; 72 blvd de Strasbourg, 10e; metro Gare de l'Est; s/d/tr/q €74/79/96/112

Grand Hôtel de Paris is well-run establishment just south of the Gare de l'Est on blvd de Strasbourg. It has 49 soundproofed rooms and a tiny lift, and is a pleasant place to stay if you're in the area.

HÔTEL AULIVIA OPÉRA

Map pp386-8   *Hotel*
☎ 01 45 23 88 88; www.astotel.com; 4 rue des Petites Écuries, 10e; metro Château d'Eau; s €90, d €100-120, tr €150.

This 32-room, three-star Best Western Hotel is just opposite the jazz club **New Morning** (p232) and a host of restaurants, including the Subcontinental eateries of **Passage Brady** (p193).

HÔTEL FRANÇAIS Map pp386-8   *Hotel*

☎ 01 40 35 94 14; www.hotelfrancais.com; 13 rue du 8 Mai 1945, 10e; metro Gare de l'Est; s €77-81, d €84-91, tr €109-116; P

This two-star hotel facing the Gare de l'Est has 71 attractive, almost luxurious rooms (some with balconies). Parking – always difficult around the train stations – in the hotel garage costs a steep €8.

HÔTEL GARDEN OPÉRA

Map pp386-8   *Hotel*
☎ 01 47 70 40 75; www.gardenopera.com; 65 rue du Château d'Eau, 10e; metro Château d'Eau; s €70-85, d €80-90, tr €95-110

This 32-room hotel is one of the nicest and cleanest in the area, and just up from the Grands Boulevards (but nowhere near either Opéra). Some of the rooms have parquet floors. Generous discounts are available after stays of six nights.

NORD HÔTEL Map pp386-8   *Hotel*

☎ 01 45 26 43 40; www.nordhotel.com; 37 rue de St-Quentin, 10e; metro Gare du Nord; s €60-79, d €89, tr €109

Just opposite the Gare du Nord, the 'North Hotel' has 46 clean and quiet rooms with shower or bath.

NORD-EST HÔTEL Map pp386-8   *Hotel*

☎ 01 47 70 07 18; hotel.nord.est@wanadoo.fr; 12 rue des Petits Hôtels, 10e; metro Poissonnière; s/d/tr/q €62/72/92/115

This unusual 30-room hotel charmingly located on the 'Street of Little Hotels' is set away from the street and fronted by a small terrace. It is convenient to both the Gare du Nord and the Gare de l'Est.

CHEAP SLEEPS

The areas east and northeast of the Gare du Nord and Gare de l'Est have always had a more than ample selection of hotels and now you'll also find a hostel within striking distance. Place de la République is convenient for the nightlife areas of Ménilmontant.

Gare du Nord is linked to Charles de Gaulle airport by RER and RATP (Régie Autonome des Transports Parisians) bus No 350, and to Orly airport by Orlyval. Bus No 350 to/from Charles de Gaulle airport also stops right in front of the Gare de l'Est.

AUBERGE DE JEUNESSE JULES FERRY

Map pp386-8   *Hostel*
☎ 01 43 57 55 60; www.fuaj.fr; 8 blvd Jules Ferry, 11e; metro République or Goncourt; dm €19.50, d per person €20

This official hostel, three blocks east of place de la République, is somewhat institutional and the rooms could be cleaner, but the atmosphere is fairly relaxed. Beds are in two- to six-person rooms, which are locked between 10.30am and 2pm for housekeeping, and there is no curfew. You'll have pay an extra €3 per night if you don't have an HI card or equivalent. The only other official hostel in central Paris is the **Auberge de Jeunesse Le D'Artagnan** (Map pp380-2; ☎ 01 40 32 34 56; www.fuaj.fr; 80 rue Vitruve, 20e; metro Porte de Bagnolet; dm €20.60), which is far from the centre of the action but just one metro stop from the Gare Routière Internationale de Paris-Galliéni (International Bus Terminal). It has rooms with two to eight beds, big lockers, laundry facilities, a bar, cinema, and the same rules and regulations as the Jules Ferry hostel. It is the largest hostel in France, with 439 beds on seven floors.

HÔTEL AQUARELLE

Map pp386-8   *Hotel*
☎ 01 48 05 79 76; fax 01 48 05 58 28; 38 blvd du Temple, 11e; metro République or Filles du Calvaire; d/tw/tr/ste €60/67/75/92

This lovely, 32-room place due south of the place de la République would be that much more attractive if it wasn't on such a busy street. Still, the location couldn't be better if you're planning to graze and/or cruise rue Oberkampf.

HÔTEL DE NEVERS

Map pp386-8   *Hotel*
☎ 01 47 00 56 18; www.hoteldenevers.com; 53 rue de Malte, 11e; metro République; s & d with washbasin €32, s & d with shower €42, s & d with shower & toilet

€45, tw with shower & toilet €48, tr with shower & toilet €60-74

This excellent-value 34-room budget hotel is around the corner from place de la République, and within easy walking distance of the pubs, bars and restaurants of Ménilmontant. Hyper-allergenics may think twice about staying here; there are three cats on hand to greet you. It's a family-run place and gay-friendly.

HÔTEL LA VIEILLE FRANCE

Map pp386-8 *Hotel*

☎ 01 45 26 42 37; la.vieille.france@wanadoo.fr; 151 rue La Fayette, 10e; metro Gare du Nord; d with washbasin €42, d with shower/bath & toilet €58/64, tr €78-90

'The Old France' is a 34-room place with relatively spacious and pleasant rooms. At least one reader has written to complain about the noise, however. Hall showers are free.

HÔTEL LIBERTY Map pp386-8 *Hotel*

☎ 01 42 08 60 58; libertyhotel@wanadoo.fr; 16 rue de Nancy, 10e; metro Château d'Eau; s/d with washbasin €29/35, s/d with shower €37/43, s/d with shower & toilet €40/50

The Liberty is a 1st-floor hotel with clean, partially renovated but very plain rooms. Hall showers cost €1.50.

HÔTEL LONDRES ET ANVERS

Map pp386-8 *Hotel*

☎ 01 42 85 28 26; fax 01 42 80 04 73; 133 blvd Magenta, 10e; metro Gare du Nord; s €45-64, d €62-83, tr €86-94

This 65-room hotel just north of the Gare du Nord is no great shakes, but it's a reliable budget place to stay if it's late or you've missed your train back to London (or Anvers for that matter).

PEACE & LOVE HOSTEL

Map pp386-8 *Hostel*

☎ 01 46 07 65 11; www.paris-hostels.com; 245 rue La Fayette, 10e; metro Jaurès or Louis Blanc; dm €17-210, d per person €21-26

This modern-day hippy hang-out is a groovy though chaotically run hostel with beds in smallish, shower-equipped rooms for two to four people. There's a great kitchen and eating area, but most of the action seems to revolve around the ground floor bar (open till 2am) that boasts more than 10 types of beer, including the cheapest *blondes* (that's lagers) in Paris.

SIBOUR HÔTEL Map pp386-8 *Hotel*

☎ 01 46 07 20 74; sibour.hotel@wanadoo.fr; 4 rue Sibour, 10e; metro Gare de l'Est; s & d with washbasin €35, s & d with toilet €40, s/d/tr/q with shower & toilet €50/58/63/80

This friendly place has 45 well-kept rooms, including some old-fashioned ones. Hall showers cost €3.

MÉNILMONTANT & BELLEVILLE

The Ménilmontant nightlife area is an excellent area in which to spend the night, but the selection of accommodation in all price categories is surprisingly limited.

HÔTEL BEAUMARCHAIS

Map pp392-5 *Boutique Hotel*

☎ 01 53 36 86 86; www.hotelbeaumarchais.com; 3 rue Oberkampf, 11e; metro Filles du Calvaire; s €69-85, d €99, ste €140

This brighter-than-bright 31-room boutique hotel with its emphasis on sunbursts and bold colours, particularly orange and yellow, is just this side of kitsch. But it makes for a different Paris experience and fits in with its surroundings very well indeed. Some rooms look onto a small leafy courtyard.

HÔTEL DU VIEUX SAULE

Map pp396-9 *Hotel*

☎ 01 42 72 01 14; www.hotelvieuxsaule.com; 6 rue Picardie, 3e; metro Filles du Calvaire; low season s €76-91, d €106-136, VIP r €121-151, high season s €91-106, d €121-151, VIP r €136-166

The flower-bedecked 'Old Willow Tree' is a 31-room hostelry in the northern Marais and something of a 'find' because of its slightly unusual location. There's a tranquil little garden, and the original 16th-century vaulted cellar (now breakfast room) has antique copper utensils on display. The five rooms on the VIP (4th) floor have been renovated.

Top Five Boutique Hotels

- Artushotel (p294)
- Hôtel Bel Ami St-Germain des Prés (p291)
- Hôtel Caron de Beaumarchais (p286)
- Hôtel de Danemark (p295)
- Villa Royale Pigalle (p303)

GARE DE LYON, NATION & BERCY

The development of Bercy Village, with its selection of restaurants and bars, has done much to resuscitate the 12e.

CHEAP SLEEPS

The neighbourhood around Gare de Lyon has a few budget hotels and a popular independent hostel.

HOSTEL BLUE PLANET

Map pp392-5   *Hostel*

☎ 01 43 42 06 18; www.hostelblueplanet.com; 5 rue Hector Malot, 12e; metro Gare de Lyon; dm €18.30-21

This 43-room hostel is very close to Gare de Lyon – convenient if you're heading south or west at the crack of dawn. Dorm beds are in rooms for three or four people; it closes between 11am and 3pm but there's no curfew.

13E ARRONDISSEMENT & CHINATOWN

The 13e is where you'll find the Bibliothèque Nationale de France, as well as the *péniches* (barges) on the Seine fitted out with music clubs and restaurants, such as Le Batofar and La Guinguette Pirate (p236).

MAEVA CITY TOLBIAC

Map p401   *Chain Hotel*

☎ 01 53 61 62 00; tolbiac@city-maeva.com; 15 rue de Tolbiac, 13e; metro Bibliothèque; s & d €75, tr & q €90

This conversion, with 87 rooms and studios, stands out not for its amenities but for its location – it's a stone's throw from the Bibliothèque Nationale de France and the Seine. Rooms are available for longer periods (p283).

CHEAP SLEEPS

The southern 13e is a happy hunting ground for budget hotels.

HÔTEL DES BEAUX-ARTS

Map pp380-2   *Hotel*

☎ 01 44 24 22 60; www.hotel-beaux-arts.fr in French; 2 rue Toussaint Féron, 13e; metro Tolbiac; s & d with washbasin & toilet €34-37, with shower & toilet s €46, d €54-58, tr €59

This 25-room hotel just north of the metro Tolbiac has a lovely little garden and is run by a friendly, dynamic young couple. It's a great budget choice if you don't mind going the distance.

15E ARRONDISSEMENT

The 15e, some people's least favourite arrondissement in Paris, offers some decent accommodation options, especially when it comes to chain hotels.

LE RELAIS DE PARIS CAMBRONNE

Map pp389-91   *Chain Hotel*

☎ 01 44 49 63; www.lesrelaisdeparis.fr; 166 blvd de Grenelle, 15e; metro Cambronne; s & d €95, tr €118

It may be part of a chain, with some 15 other properties in central Paris, but this 54-room hotel offers predictable comfort and services, and is within easy walking distance of Unesco to the east and the Eiffel Tower to the west.

CHEAP SLEEPS
ALOHA HOSTEL

Map pp389-91   *Hostel*

☎ 01 42 73 03 03; www.aloha.fr; 1 rue Borromée, 15e; metro Volontaires; Nov-Apr/May-Oct dm €19/22, Nov-Apr/May-Oct d per person €22.50/25

The Aloha is a laid-back and safe hostel north of rue de Vaugirard. The rooms, which have two to six beds and sometimes a shower, are locked from 11am to 5pm (though reception remains open) and curfew is 2am. Kitchen facilities are available.

MONTMARTRE & PIGALLE

Montmartre, encompassing the 18e and the northern part of the 9e, is one of the most charming neighbourhoods in Paris. There is a bunch of top-end hotels in the area, and the attractive two-star places on rue Aristide Bruant are generally less full in July and August than in the spring and autumn.

COMFORT HÔTEL PLACE DU TERTRE

Map p400 *Chain Hotel*

☎ 01 42 55 05 06; www.comfort-placedutertre.com; 16 rue Tholozé, 18e; metro Abbesses or Blanche; s €95, d & tw €100

It's anyone's guess how the Comfort Inn/Hotel people get away with naming this 46-room property after Montmartre's most popular square when, in fact, it's 400m to the northeast (and that's as the crow flies). But for location and quality, the price is right.

HÔTEL DES 3 POUSSINS

Map pp386-8 *Hotel*

☎ 01 53 32 81 81; www.les3poussins.com; 15 rue Clauzel, 9e; metro St-Georges; s €130-175, d & tw €145-175, tr & q €210, 1-person studio €140-190, 2-person studio €155-190, 3-4 person studio €225

The 'Hotel of the Three Chicks' (as in, ahem, little chickens) is a lovely property due south of place Pigalle. It has 40 rooms, half of which are small studios with their own cooking facilities.

HÔTEL DES ARTS Map p400 *Hotel*

☎ 01 46 06 30 52; www.arts-hotel-paris.com; 5 rue Tholozé, 18e; metro Abbesses or Blanche; s €64, d & tw €78, tr €94

Part of the Logis de France group, the 'Arts Hotel' is a friendly and attractive 50-room place convenient for both place Pigalle and Montmartre. Towering over it is the old-style windmills Moulin de la Galette.

HÔTEL IBIS SACRÉ CŒUR

Map p400 *Chain Hotel*

☎ 01 46 06 99 17; www.ibishotel.com; 100 blvd Rochechouart, 18e; metro Anvers; s & d €69-75

If you're the type of person who likes to know exactly what they're getting, you could do worse than this 68-room chain hotel smack dab in the middle of Montmartre. Prices depend on the day of the week and the season.

HÔTEL REGYNS MONTMARTRE

Map p400 *Hotel*

☎ 01 42 54 45 21; www.regynsmontmartre.com; 18 place des Abbesses, 18e; metro Abbesses; s €65-85, d & tw €75-110, tr €99-120

This 22-room hotel should be one of your first choices if you want to stay in old Montmartre. It's just opposite the Abbesses metro station, which happens to have one of the best preserved Art Nouveau entrance canopies designed by Hector Guimard. Some of the rooms have views.

HÔTEL UTRILLO Map p400 *Hotel*

☎ 01 42 58 13 44; fax 01 42 23 93 88; adel.utrillo@wanadoo.fr; 7 rue Aristide Bruant, 18e; metro Abbesses or Blanche; s €61, d with shower/bath €73/79, tr €91

This friendly 30-room hotel is very nicely decorated and can even boast a small sauna.

TIMHÔTEL MONTMARTRE

Map p400 *Chain Hotel*

☎ 01 42 55 74 79; www.timhotel.com; 11 rue Ravignan (place Émile Goudeau), 18e; metro Abbesses; s & d €130-145, tr €150-170, q €215

This 60-room hotel is a good choice if you place more value on location than room size. Rooms are neat and modern; some on the 4th and 5th floors have stunning views of the city.

TIMHÔTEL ST-GEORGES

Map p400 *Hotel*

☎ 01 48 74 01 12; www.timhotel.com; 21 blvd de Clichy, 9e; metro Pigalle; s & d €95, tr €135

This recently renovated chain hotel has 74 rooms, most of which look out onto a courtyard garden or up to the Butte de Montmartre (Montmartre Hill) and Sacré Cœur.

VILLA ROYALE PIGALLE

Map p400 *Boutique Hotel*

☎ 01 55 31 78 78; www.leshotelsdeparis.com; 2 rue Duperré, 9e; metro Pigalle; s & d €210-310, ste €350

Part of the swish Les Hôtels de Paris chain, each of the 34 rooms in this 'luxury villa' just might be a Pigalle madam's boudoir – what, with every shade of red on the spectrum represented, the sash curtains and the gilded taps. Could be just the place and the district to stay in for that dirty (real or imagined) weekend. Oooo la la, indeed.

CHEAP SLEEPS

The flat area around the base of the Butte de Montmartre has some surprisingly good deals. The lively, ethnically mixed area east of Sacré Cœur can be a bit rough; some people say it's prudent to avoid Château Rouge metro station at night. Both the 9e and the 18e have fine and recommended hostels.

HÔTEL BONSÉJOUR Map p400 *Hotel*

☎ 01 42 54 22 53; fax 01 42 54 25 92; 11 rue Burq, 18e; metro Abbesses; s with washbasin €22-25, d with washbasin €30-32, d with shower €38-40, tr €53

The 'Good Stay' is at the end of a quiet street in Montmartre. Some rooms (eg Nos 14, 23, 33, 43 and 53) have little balconies and at least one room (No 55) offers a fleeting glimpse of Sacré Cœur. It's a simple place to stay – no lift, linoleum floors etc – but comfortable and very friendly. Hall showers cost €2.

HÔTEL DES CAPUCINES
MONTMARTRE Map p400 *Hotel*

☎ 01 42 52 89 80; fax 01 42 52 29 57; 5 rue Aristide Bruant, 18e; metro Abbesses or Blanche; s €45-50, d €54-60, tr €60-70

This is a decent, family-run hotel with 30 rooms on a small street awash with places to stay.

HÔTEL DU MOULIN
Map p400 *Hotel*

☎ 01 42 64 33 33; www.hotelmoulin.com; 3 rue Aristide Bruant, 18e; metro Abbesses or Blanche; s €54-66, d €59-76, tw €73-79

This quiet little hotel has 27 good-sized rooms with toilet and bath or shower. The Korean family who own the place are very kind. Check out their crazy website.

LE VILLAGE HOSTEL Map p400 *Hostel*

☎ 01 42 64 22 02; www.villagehostel.fr; 20 rue d'Orsel, 18e; metro Anvers; per person Nov–mid-Mar/mid-Mar-Oct dm €20/21.50, d €23/25 & tr €21.50/23

'The Village' is a fine 25-room hostel with beamed ceilings and views of Sacré Cœur. Dorm beds are in rooms for four to six people, and all rooms have showers and toilet. Kitchen facilities are available, and there is a lovely outside terrace. Rooms are closed between 11am and 4pm; curfew is 2am.

WOODSTOCK HOSTEL
Map pp386-8 *Hostel*

☎ 01 48 78 87 76; www.woodstock.fr; 48 rue Rodier, 9e; metro Anvers; per person Oct-Mar/Apr-Sep dm €15/20, d €17/23

Woodstock Hostel is down the hill from raucous place Pigalle in a quiet, residential quarter. Dorm beds are in rooms sleeping four to six people, and there's also a kitchen. Rooms are shut between 11am and 3pm; the curfew is 2am. High season rates also apply over Christmas and the New Year .

OUTSIDE THE WALLS: BEYOND CENTRAL PARIS

Both Aéroport Charles de Gaulle and Aéroport d'Orly have a wide selection of places to stay, including mid-range Ibis hotels. In fact, the former has three Ibis properties.

HÔTEL IBIS PARIS CDG AÉROPORT
GARES *Chain Hotel*

☎ 01 49 19 19 19; www.ibishotel.com; s & d €75-89, tr from €109, f up to 5 people €132

Next to Aéroport Roissy Charles de Gaulle 1 train station, this hotel has two stars and 556 rooms. It is linked to the Aéroport Roissy Charles de Gaulle terminals by shuttle bus.

HÔTEL IBIS PARIS ORLY
AÉROPORT *Chain Hotel*

☎ 01 56 70 50 50; www.ibishotel.com; 3-person r €59-82, q from €95

This large, modern 300-room chain hotel at Aéroport d'Orly is linked to both terminals by the ADP shuttle bus. It offers all the standard amenities.

Chateaux 307
Cathedrals 307
Art Towns 308
Theme Parks 308

Versailles 308

Fontainebleau 313

Vaux-le-Vicomte 317

Chantilly 318

Senlis 321

Chartres 322

Giverny 326

Auvers-sur-Oise 327

Disneyland Resort Paris 329

Parc Astérix 330

Excursions

Excursions

Paris is encircled by the Île de France ('Island of France') a 12,000-sq-km area shaped by five rivers: the Epte (northwest), the Aisne (northeast), the Eure (southwest), the Yonne (southeast) and the Marne (east). The region was the seed from which the kingdom of France grew, beginning about AD 1100.

Today, the excellent rail and road links between the French capital and the exceptional sights of the Île de France and neighbouring *départements* (administrative divisions) make the region especially popular with day-trippers from Paris. At the same time, the many woodland areas around the city, including the forests of Fontainebleau and Chantilly, offer unlimited outdoor activities.

In Paris visit the **Espace du Tourisme d'Île de France** (Tourism Office for Île de France; Map pp396-9; ☎ 08 26 16 66 66, or from abroad ☎ 33-1 44 50 19 98; www.pidf.com; Galerie du Carrousel du Louvre; 99 rue de Rivoli, 1er; metro Palais Royal-Musée du Louvre; ☯ 10am-7pm) in the lower level of the Carrousel du Louvre shopping centre next to IM Pei's inverted glass pyramid. Staff can provide you with a wealth of information about the region.

If you're visiting the region under your own steam, pick up a copy of IGN's 1:250,000 scale map *Île de France* (€4.90) or the more compact 1:100,000 scale *Paris et Ses Environs* (€3.70) both available from the Espace IGN outlet (p263) just off the av des Champs-Élysées.

All of the accommodation options listed in this section have showering facilities unless otherwise stated.

CHATEAUX

Not all of France's most celebrated chateaux are in the Loire Valley. In fact **Versailles** (p308), seat of the royal court for more than a century and one of the most extravagant palaces in the country, is a mere 21km southwest of Paris. **Chantilly** (p318) north of Paris is especially well-known for its artwork and wonderful gardens while **Fontainebleau** (p313) to the south of Paris is one of the largest and most important Renaissance chateaux in France. **Vaux-le-Vicomte** (p317), just 20km north of Fontainebleau, is a much smaller version of Versailles (in fact, the same architects and landscape artist worked on both) and, for many, much more accessible as a result.

CATHEDRALS

If you haven't had your fill of grand churches in Paris, travel the extra distance southwest to **Chartres** (p322), where the cathedral is one of the greatest achievements of Western architecture and contains some of the finest examples of medieval stained glass in Europe. The cathedral at **Senlis** (p321) to the north of Paris, parts of which influenced the construction of the cathedral at Chartres, is just a hop, skip and a jump from Chantilly and its wonderful chateau.

Vaux-le-Vicomte (left)

Organised Tours

If you're pressed for time or don't want to do it yourself, several companies organise excursions to destinations outside Paris. Children four to 11 generally pay half-price.

Cityrama (Map pp386-8; ☎ 01 44 55 61 00; www.cityrama.fr; 4 place des Pyramides, 1er; metro Tuileries)
This well-established outfit has half-day trips to Versailles (€36 to €61), Chartres (€51), Vaux-le-Vicomte (€57), and Fontainebleau and Barbizon (€57), as well as many combination trips such as Versailles apartments and Chartres (€91) and Versailles apartments and Fontainebleau (€95).

Paris Vision (Map pp383-5; ☎ 01 47 42 27 40; www.parisvision.com; 1 rue Auber, 9e; metro place de l'Opéra)
This company has eight-hour trips to Versailles and nine-hour ones to Giverny and Versailles, and Auvers-sur-Oise and Giverny. All cost €135.

Touringscope (Map pp386-8; ☎ 01 53 34 11 91; www.touringscope.com; 11 bis blvd Haussman, 9e; metro Richelieu Drouot) Touringscope has full day trips (usually eight hours) to Versailles (€92, including lunch), Versailles and Giverny (€100) and Versailles and Chartres (€100).

ART TOWNS

Giverny (p326), where Claude Monet lived and painted from 1883 to 1926, is in the northwest just over the border from the Île de France in Normandy, but still easily accessible from the capital. Less visited but only 35km north of Paris is **Auvers-sur-Oise** (p327), where van Gogh arrived in May 1890, painted prolifically for just over two months, and then died in the upstairs bedroom of a cheap inn from a self-inflicted bullet wound.

THEME PARKS

It may not be everyone's *tasse de thé* (cup of tea) but the kids have decided it's theirs – **Disneyland Resort Paris** (p329) is now the most popular fee-charging destination in Europe. If globalisation and cultural imperialism have you concerned, however, a home-grown alternative to the American theme park is **Parc Astérix** (p330). What's more, it's closer to Paris.

VERSAILLES

The prosperous, leafy and very bourgeois suburb of Versailles (population 85,300) is the site of the grandest and most famous palace in France. It served as the kingdom's political capital and the seat of the royal court for more than a century from 1682 to 1789, the year Revolutionary mobs massacred the palace guard and dragged Louis XVI and Marie-Antoinette back to Paris, where they eventually had their heads lopped off.

The enormous **Château de Versailles** was built in the mid-17th century during the reign of Louis XIV (1643–1715) – the Roi Soleil (Sun King) – to house the entire court of 6000 people, and to project at home and abroad the absolute power of the French monarchy. Its scale and décor also reflect Louis XIV's taste for profligate luxury and his appetite for self-glorification. To accomplish this he hired four very talented men: the architect Louis Le Vau; Jules Hardouin-Mansart, who took over from Le Vau in the mid-1670s; the painter and interior designer Charles Le Brun; and the landscape artist André Le Nôtre, whose workers flattened hills, drained marshes and relocated forests to lay out seemingly endless gardens, ponds and fountains.

Le Brun and his hundreds of artisans decorated every moulding, cornice, ceiling and door of the interior with luxurious and ostentatious appointments: frescoes, marble, gilt and woodcarvings, with themes and symbols drawn from Greek and Roman

Did You Know?

The chateau at Versailles counts 700 rooms, 2153 windows, 352 chimneys and 28 acres of roof set on 900 hectares of garden, park and wood. The walls and rooms are adorned with 6300 paintings, 2000 sculptures and statues, 15,000 engravings and 5000 decorative art objects and furnishings.

mythology. The **Grand Appartement du Roi** (King's Suite), for example, includes rooms dedicated to Hercules, Venus, Diana, Mars and Mercury. The opulence reaches its peak in the **Galerie des Glaces** (Hall of Mirrors), a 75m-long ballroom with 17 huge mirrors on one side and, on the other, an equal number of windows looking out on the gardens.

The chateau has undergone relatively few alterations since its construction, though almost all the interior furnishings disappeared during the Revolution, and many of the rooms were rebuilt by Louis-Philippe (ruled 1830–48), who opened part of the chateau to the public. A €370 million renovation and maintenance program begun in late 2003 will affect 25 different areas of the chateau and take 17 years.

The chateau complex consists of four main sections: the palace building, a 580m-long structure with innumerable wings, grand halls and sumptuous bedchambers (only parts of which are open to the public); the vast gardens, canals and pools to the west of the palace; the two smaller palaces – the Grand Trianon and, a few hundred metres to the east, the Petit Trianon and the Hameau de la Reine (Queen's Hamlet).

The **Grands Appartements** (State Apartments), the main section of the palace building, includes the Galerie des Glaces, the **Appartement de la Reine** (Queen's Suite), the **Musée de l'Histoire de France** (Museum of French History) and other halls and apartments. **Les Grandes Heures du Parlement** (Landmarks in the History of French Parliament), a rather esoteric exhibit on the history of France's Assemblée Nationale, is in the souther wing of the chateau.

The section of the vast gardens nearest the palace, laid out between 1661 and 1700 in the formal French style, is famed for its geometrically aligned terraces, flowerbeds, tree-lined paths, ponds and fountains. The many statues of marble, bronze and lead were by the most talented sculptors of the period. The more pastoral English-style **Jardins du Petit Trianon** have meandering, sheltered paths.

The **Grand Canal**, 1.6km long and 62m wide, is oriented to reflect the setting sun. It's traversed by the 1km-long **Petit Canal**, creating a cross-shaped body of water with a perimeter of over 5.5km. Louis XIV used to hold boating parties here. In summer you can paddle around the Grand Canal in four-person rowing boats; the dock is at the canal's eastern end. The **Orangerie**, built under the Parterre du Midi (a flowerbed) on the southwestern side of the palace by Le Vau in 1663, houses exotic plants in winter.

The gardens' largest fountains are the 17th-century **Bassin de Neptune** (Neptune's Fountain), 300m north of the palace and the **Bassin d'Apollon** (Apollo's Fountain), built in 1668 at the eastern end of the Grand Canal. The straight side of the Bassin de Neptune abuts a small, round pond graced by a winged dragon. Emerging from the water in the centre of the Bassin d'Apollon is Apollo's chariot, pulled by rearing horses. There are **Grande Perspective** and **Grandes Eaux Musicales** fountain displays during the warmer months.

In the middle of the park, about 1.5km northwest of the main building, are two smaller palaces, each surrounded by neat flowerbeds. The pink-colonnaded **Grand Trianon** was built in 1687 for Louis XIV and his family as a place of escape from the rigid etiquette of the court. Napoleon I had it renovated in the Empire style.

Transport

Distance from Paris 21km

Direction Southwest

Travel time 35 minutes by RER/train

Car Route A13 from Porte de St-Cloud. Exit 'Versailles Château'.

Bus No 171 (€1.30 or one metro/bus ticket) from Pont de Sèvres (15e) to place d'Armes every eight to 15 minutes daily, with the last bus leaving Versailles just before 1am. It's faster to go by RER and you'll have to get to/from Pont de Sèvres metro station on line No 9.

RER The RER line C5 (€2.35) from Paris' Left Bank RER stations to Versailles-Rive Gauche station is only 700m southeast of the chateau and close to the tourist office. There are up to 70 trains a day (half that number on Sunday), and the last train back to Paris leaves shortly before midnight. RER line C8 (€2.35) links Paris' Left Bank with Versailles-Chantiers station, a 1.3km walk from the chateau.

Train From Paris' Gare St-Lazare (€3.20) SNCF operates about 70 trains a day to Versailles-Rive Droite, which is 1.2km from the chateau. The last train to Paris leaves just after midnight. Versailles-Chantiers is also served by some 30 SNCF trains a day (20 on Sunday) from Gare Montparnasse; all trains on this line continue to Chartres (€9.90; 45 to 60 minutes).

VERSAILLES

0 ———————————— 500 m
0 ———————————— 0.3 miles

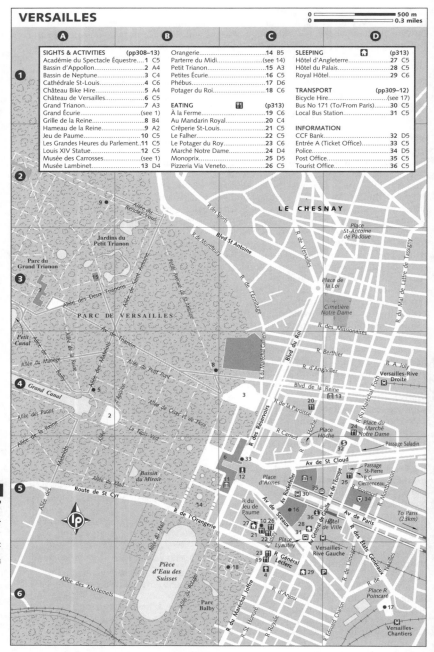

SIGHTS & ACTIVITIES	(pp308–13)
Académie du Spectacle Équestre....**1**	C5
Bassin d'Appollon....................**2**	A4
Bassin de Neptune..................**3**	C4
Cathédrale St-Louis..................**4**	C6
Château Bike Hire....................**5**	A4
Château de Versailles................**6**	C5
Grand Trianon..........................**7**	A3
Grand Écurie............................(see 1)
Grille de la Reine......................**8**	B4
Hameau de la Reine..................**9**	A2
Jeu de Paume..........................**10**	C5
Les Grandes Heures du Parlement..**11**	C5
Louis XIV Statue........................**12**	C5
Musée des Carrosses..................(see 1)
Musée Lambinet........................**13**	D4

| Orangerie..............................**14** | B5 |
| Parterre du Midi......................(see 14) |
Petit Trianon..........................**15**	A3
Petites Écurie..........................**16**	C5
Phébus..................................**17**	D6
Potager du Roi........................**18**	C6

EATING	🍴	(p313)
À la Ferme..............................**19**	C6
Au Mandarin Royal..................**20**	C4
Crêperie St-Louis......................**21**	C5
Le Falher................................**22**	C5
Le Potager du Roy....................**23**	C5
Marché Notre Dame..................**24**	D4
Monoprix................................**25**	D5
Pizzeria Via Veneto..................**26**	C5

SLEEPING	🛏	(p313)
Hôtel d'Angleterre....................**27**	C5
Hôtel du Palais........................**28**	C5
Royal Hôtel............................**29**	C6

TRANSPORT	(pp309–12)
Bicycle Hire............................(see 17)
Bus No 171 (To/From Paris)........**30**	C5
Local Bus Station......................**31**	C5

INFORMATION	
CCF Bank..............................**32**	D5
Entrée A (Ticket Office)..............**33**	D5
Police....................................**34**	D5
Post Office..............................**35**	C5
Tourist Office..........................**36**	C5

The much smaller, ochre-coloured **Petit Trianon**, built in the 1760s, was redecorated in 1867 by Empress Eugénie (the consort of Napoleon III) who added Louis XVI-style furnishings similar to the uninspiring pieces that now fill its 1st-floor rooms.

A bit further north is the **Hameau de la Reine** (Queen's Hamlet), a mock village of thatched cottages constructed from 1775 to 1784 for the amusement of Marie-Antoinette, who liked to play milkmaid here. Because so many people consider it a must-see destination, Versailles attracts more than three million visitors a year. The best way to avoid the queues is to arrive first thing in the morning; if you're interested in just the Grands Appartements, another good time to get here is about 3.30pm or 4pm. The queues are longest on Tuesday, when many of Paris' museums are closed, and on Sunday.

If you have a Carte Musées et Monuments (p341), you don't have to wait in the queue – go straight to Entrée B2 (Entrance B2). The entrance for disabled visitors is Entrée H, northwest of entrance A and you can ring ☎ 01 30 83 76 20 for information.

Like its chateau, the attractive town of **Versailles**, crisscrossed by wide boulevards, is a creation of Louis XIV. Most of today's buildings, however, date from the 18th and 19th centuries. Av de St-Cloud, av de Paris and av de Sceaux, the three wide thoroughfares that fan out eastwards from place d'Armes in front of the chateau, are separated by two stables dating from the late 17th century. The recently restored **Grande Écurie** (Big Stables) contains the **Musée des Carrosses** (Coach Museum) as well as the **Académie du Spectacle Équestre** (Academy of Equestrian Arts), where riding and dressage displays are held. The **Petite Écurie** (Little Stables) is occupied by Versailles' celebrated school of architecture.

Some 100m south of the Petite Écurie is the **Jeu de Paume** (Royal Tennis Court), which was built in 1686 and played a pivotal role in the Revolution less than a century later (see the boxed text below). South of this is **Le Potager du Roi** (King's Kitchen Garden), which was built on nine hectares of land in the late 17th century to meet the enormous catering requirements of the court. It retains its original patch divisions as well as some very old apple and pear orchards, and produces 70 tonnes of vegetables and fruit a year.

In the same *quartier* (neighbourhood), one of the prettiest in Versailles, is the neoclassical (and slightly baroque) **Cathédrale St-Louis**, a harmonious if austere work by Hardouin-Mansart built between 1743 (when Louis XV himself laid the first stone) and 1754, and made a cathedral in 1802. It is known for its 3636-pipe Cliquot organ and is decorated with a number of interesting paintings and stained-glass panels. To the northeast of the chateau just around the corner from the Versailles-Rive Drite train station and housed in a lovely 18th-century residence, the **Musée Lambinet** (Lambinet Museum) displays 18th-century furnishings (ceramics, sculpture, paintings and furniture) and objects connected with the history of Versailles, including the all-important Revolutionary period.

Sights & Information

Académie du Spectacle Équestre (Academy of Equestrian Arts; ☎ 01 39 02 07 14; Grande Écurie, 1 av Rockefeller, Versailles; morning dressage adult/student & child 5-16 €7/3; ☯ 9am-1pm Tue-Fri, 11am-3pm Sat & Sun)

Appartement de Louis XIV & **Appartements du Dauphin et de la Dauphine** (King's Chamber; Château de Versailles; 1hr audioguide adult €4.50, child under 10 free; ☯ 9am-5.30pm Apr-Oct, 9am-4.30pm Nov-Mar) This audioguide is available at Entrée C and buying tickets here is also a good way to avoid the queues at Entrée A.

Cathédrale St-Louis (☎ 01 39 50 40 65; 4 place St-Louis, Versailles; ☯ 8.30am-noon & 2-7.45pm)

CCF bank (17-19 rue du Maréchal Foch, Versailles; ☯ 9am-5pm Mon-Fri)

Tennis Court Oath

In May 1789, in an effort to deal with the huge national debt and to moderate dissent by reforming the tax system, Louis XVI convened at Versailles the *États-Généraux* (States General), a body made up of over 1000 deputies representing the three 'estates': the nobility, the clergy and the so-called Third Estate, representing the middle classes.

When the Third Estate's representatives, who formed the majority of the delegates, were denied entry to the usual meeting place of the *États-Généraux*, they met separately in a room of the *Jeu de Paume* (Royal Tennis Court), where, on 17 June, they constituted themselves as the National Assembly. Three days later they took the famous *Serment du Jeu de Paume* (Tennis Court Oath), swearing not to dissolve the assembly until Louis XVI had accepted a new constitution. This act of defiance sparked demonstrations of support and, less than a month later, a mob in Paris stormed the prison at Bastille.

Excursions – Versailles

Château de Versailles (p308)

Château bike hire (☎ 01 39 66 97 66; Château de Versailles; half-/1hr €2.50/5, half-/full day €10.50/12; ⏰ 10am-close Mon-Fri, 1pm-close Sat & Sun Jun–mid-Sep; 10am-close Sat & Sun Feb-May & mid-Sep–Nov) Rent these bicycles from kiosks at Petite Venise at the eastern end of the Grand Canal and next to Grille de la Reine. The bike hire closes when the gardens close, which varies according to season.

Château de Versailles (☎ 01 30 83 78 00, 01 30 83 77 77; www.chateauversailles.fr; Château de Versailles; Passport 10-17 Apr-Oct adult/child €20/6, Nov-Mar €14.50/4; ⏰ 9am-6.30pm Tue-Sun Apr-Oct, 9am-5.30pm Tue-Sun Nov-Mar) The Passport allows entry via Entrée B2 to the Grands Appartements, Appartement de Louis XIV, the Trianons, the gardens, Musée des Carrosses and fountain displays.

Château English-language guided tours (☎ 01 30 83 77 88; Château de Versailles; 1-/1½-/2hr tours adult €4/6/8, child 10-17 €2.70/4.20/5.50; ⏰ 9am-3.45pm Tue-Sun Nov-Mar, 9am-4pm Tue-Sun Apr-Oct) Tickets for the tours only are sold at Entrée D; they begin across the courtyard at Entrée F and must be booked ahead. All tours require you to purchase a ticket to the Grands Appartements. If you buy it at Entrée C or Entrée D you can later avoid the Grands Appartements queue at Entrée A by going straight to Entrée B.

Château gardens (Château de Versailles; adult/child under 18 €3/free, Apr-Oct admission free for all after 6pm, Nov-Mar admission free; ⏰ 9am-sunset Apr-Oct, 8am–5.30-6.30pm Nov-Mar)

Grand Canal rowing boats (☎ 01 39 66 97 66; Château de Versailles; per half-/1hr €8/11; ⏰ Mar-Nov)

Grande Perspective & Grandes Eaux Musicales fountain displays (Château de Versailles; adult/student & child over 11 €6/4.50, admission free for all after 4.50pm; ⏰ 11am-noon & 3.30-5pm Sat early-May–late-Sep, 11am-noon & 3.30-5pm Sun early-Apr–early-Oct) On the same days the Bassin de Neptune flows for 10 minutes from 5.20pm.

Grand Trianon & Petit Trianon (Château de Versailles; adult before/after 3.30pm €5/3, child under 18 free; ⏰ noon-6.30pm Apr-Oct, noon-5.30pm Nov-Mar)

Grands Appartements (State Apartments; Château de Versailles; adult before/after 3.30pm €7.50/5.30, child under 18 free, 1hr audioguide €4.50; ⏰ 9am-6.30pm Tue-Sun Apr-Oct, 9am-5.30pm Tue-Sun Nov-Mar) This is the main section of the palace that can be visited without a guided tour. Tickets are on sale at Entrée A, to the right of the equestrian statue of Louis XIV as you approach the palace.

Jeu de Paume (Royal Tennis Court; ☎ 01 30 83 77 88; 1 rue du Jeu de Paume, Versailles; admission free; ⏰ 2-5pm Sat & Sun May-Sep)

Le Potager du Roi (King's Kitchen Garden; ☎ 01 39 24 62 62; 10 rue du Maréchal Joffre, Versailles; adult weekday/weekend €4.50/6.50, student & child 6-18 €3; ⏰ 10am-6pm Apr-Oct)

Les Grandes Heures du Parlement (Landmarks in the History of the French Parliament; ☎ 01 39 25 70 70; www.assemblee-nationale.fr; Château de Versailles; adult/18-25/under 18 €3/2.20/free; ⏰ 9am-6.30pm Tue-Sun Apr-Oct, 9am-5.30pm Tue-Sun Nov-Mar) Admission cost includes a taped commentary.

Musée des Carrosses (Coach Museum; ☎ 01 30 83 77 88; Grande Écurie, 1 av Rockefeller, Versailles; adult/child child under 18 €2/free; ⏰ noon-6.30pm Tue-Sun Mar-Sep)

Musée Lambinet (Lambinet Museum; ☎ 01 39 50 30 32; 54 blvd de la Reine, Versailles; adult/concession €5/2.50, 1st Sun of the month free; ⏰ 2-6pm Tue, Thu, Sat & Sun, 1-6pm Wed, 2-5pm Fri)

Office de Tourisme de Versailles (Tourist Office; ☎ 01 39 24 88 88; www.versailles-tourisme.com; 2 bis av de Paris, Versailles; ⏰ 9am-7pm Apr-Oct; 9am-6pm Tue-Sat, 9am-5pm Sun & Mon Nov-Mar) The tourist office has themed guided tours (adult/child €8/4) of the city and chateau throughout the week year-round.

Phébus bike hire (☎ 01 39 20 16 60; www.phebus.tm.fr in French; place Raymond Poincaré, Versailles; 30 min/1hr/day/week/month €5/10/12/16/25; ⏰ 7.15am-7.45pm Mon-Fri, 11am-5pm Sat & Sun) This place in front of the Versailles-Chantiers train station rents bicycles; a deposit of €300 is required.

Post office (av de Paris, Versailles; ⏰ 8am-7pm Mon-Fri, 8am-noon Sat) On the opposite side of av de Paris from the tourist office.

Versailles Tour (☎ 01 39 20 16 20; www.phebus.tm.fr in French; place Raymond Poincaré, Versailles; ride/day pass €1.30/4; ⏰ 10am-4pm Tue-Sun late-Apr–Jun, Sep & Oct, to 5pm Jul & Aug) This is a jump-on, jump-off tour bus run by Phébus that makes a circuit from the Versailles-Rive Droite train station to place St-Louis, taking in the chateau and most other sights along the way up to seven times a day.

Eating

À la Ferme (☎ 01 39 53 10 81; 3 rue du Maréchal Joffre, Versailles; starters €6-10, mains €10.50-15, 2-/3-course menus €15.50/19; ⏰ lunch & dinner to 11pm Wed-Sun) 'At the Farm' specialises in grilled meats and the cuisine of southwest France. It's next door to Potager du Roy and is much cheaper and more relaxed.

Au Mandarin Royal (☎ 01 39 50 48 03; 5 rue de Ste-Geneviève, Versailles; lunch menu €10, dinner menus €13.60 & €18; ⏰ lunch Tue-Sun & dinner to 11pm Mon-Sat) This is a decent restaurant not far from the Musée Lambinet has Vietnamese dishes as well.

Crêperie St-Louis (☎ 01 39 53 40 12; 33 rue du Vieux Versailles, Versailles; menus €9-14; ⏰ lunch & dinner to 11pm) This is a cosy place with Breton specialities including sweet and savoury crêpes and galettes (€3 to €7.50).

Le Falher (☎ 01 39 50 57 43; 22 rue Satory, Versailles; starters €14-20, mains €23-25, lunch menu €22, dinner menus €29 & €46; ⏰ lunch Mon-Fri & dinner to 10.30pm Tue-Sat) This quiet and elegant place not far from the palace has French gastronomic *menus* (set menus).

Le Potager du Roy (☎ 01 39 50 35 34; 1 rue du Maréchal Joffre, Versailles; lunch menu including wine €23, dinner menus €32 & €47; ⏰ lunch & dinner to 10.30pm Tue-Sat) This is a refined place with traditional *cuisine bourgeoise* (French home cooking).

Pizzeria Via Veneto (☎ 01 39 51 03 89; 20 rue Satory, Versailles; ⏰ lunch & dinner to 11pm) Has pizzas and pasta dishes (€7 to €11).

CHEAP EATS

Marché Notre Dame (place du Marché Notre Dame, Versailles; ⏰ 7.30am-1.30pm Tue, Fri & Sun) If headed for this outdoor food market from the tourist office, enter via passage Saladin (33 av de St-Cloud). There are also food halls (⏰ 7am-1pm & 3.30-7.30pm Tue-Sat, 7am-2pm Sun) surrounding the market place.

Monoprix (9 rue Georges Clemenceau, Versailles; ⏰ 8.30am-8.55pm Mon-Sat) This department store north of av de Paris has a large supermarket section.

Sleeping

Hôtel d'Angleterre (☎ 01 39 51 43 50, hotelangleterre@voila.fr; 2 bis rue de Fontenay, Versailles; s & d with washbasin & toilet €35, s & d with shower & toilet €65-71, tr & q €86). Less than 300m from the chateau entrance and around the corner from the Jeu de Paume, this charming 18-room hotel has decent-sized and very modern rooms.

Hôtel du Palais (☎ 01 39 50 39 29, hotelpalais@ifrance .com; 6 place Lyautay, Versailles; d with washbasin €38, d with shower €50-55) This well-kept 24-room place is an inexpensive, but very central place across the street from the Versailles-Rive Gauche train station and in front of the local bus station.

Royal Hôtel (☎ 01 39 50 67 31; www.royalhotel.fr.st; 23 rue Royale, Versailles; s & d with shower & toilet €49-58, d with bath & toilet €61, tr with bath & toilet €70) This place has 35 bare but adequate rooms in the delightful Quartier St-Louis neighbourhood.

FONTAINEBLEAU

The town of Fontainebleau (population 15,800) is renowned for its elegant Renaissance chateau – one of France's largest royal residences – with splendid furnishings that make it particularly worth visiting. It's much less crowded and pressured than Versailles. The town itself has a number of fine restaurants and night spots – you're bound to have a fine time here – and it is surrounded by the beautiful **Forêt de Fontainebleau**, a favourite hunting ground of many French kings.

Château de Fontainebleau (p314)

Distance from Paris 67km

Direction Southeast

Travel time 35 to 60 minutes by SNCF train

Car Route A6 from Porte d'Orléans, direction Lyon. Exit 'Fontainebleau'.

Train Up to 30 daily SNCF commuter trains link Paris' Gare de Lyon with Fontainebleau-Avon station (€7.30)

Bus The train station is linked with central Fontainebleau (€1.30), 2km to the southwest, every 10 minutes from about 6am until about 9.30pm (11.30pm on Sunday) The last train back to Paris leaves Fontainebleau a bit after 9.45pm weekdays, just after 10pm on Saturday and sometime after 10.30pm on Sunday.

SNCF A package (adult/child 10-17/child 4-9 €20/16/8) includes return transport from Paris, bus transfers and admission to the chateau.

The enormous, 1900-room **Château de Fontainebleau** (the list of former tenants or visitors is like a who's who of French royalty) is one of the most beautifully decorated and furnished chateaux in France. Walls and ceilings are richly adorned with wood panelling, gilded carvings, frescoes, tapestries and paintings. The parquet floors are of the finest woods, the fireplaces decorated with exceptional carvings, and many of the pieces of furniture are originals dating back to the Renaissance.

The first chateau on this site was built sometime in the early 12th century and enlarged by Louis IX a century later. Only a single medieval tower survived the energetic Renaissance-style reconstruction undertaken by François I (ruled 1515–47), whose superb artisans, many of them brought over from Italy, blended Italian and French styles to create what is known as the First School of Fontainebleau. The *Mona Lisa* once hung here amid other fine works of art of the royal collection.

During the latter half of the 16th century, the chateau was further enlarged by Henri II (ruled 1547–59), Catherine de Médicis and Henri IV (ruled 1589–1610), whose Flemish and French artists created the Second School of Fontainebleau. Even Louis XIV got in on the act: it was he who hired Le Nôtre to redesign the gardens.

Fontainebleau, which was not damaged during the Revolution (though its furniture was stolen or destroyed), was beloved by Napoleon, who also had a fair bit of restoration work carried out. Napoleon III was another frequent visitor.

During WWII, the chateau was turned into a German headquarters. After it was liberated by US General George Patton in 1944, part of the complex served as Allied and then NATO headquarters from 1945 to 1965.

The **Grands Appartements** (State Apartments) include a number of outstanding rooms. The spectacular **Chapelle de la Trinité** (Trinity Chapel), with ornamentation dated from the first half of the 17th century, is where Louis XV married Marie Leczinska in 1725 and where the future Napoleon III was christened in 1810. **Galerie François 1er** (François 1 Gallery), a jewel of Renaissance architecture, was decorated from 1533 to 1540 by Il Rosso, a Florentine follower of Michelangelo. In the wood panelling, François I's monogram appears repeatedly along with his emblem, a dragon-like salamander.

The **Salle de Bal** (Ballroom), a 30m-long room dating from the mid-16th century that was also used for receptions and banquets, is renowned for its mythological frescoes, marquetry floor and Italian-inspired coffered ceiling. The large windows afford views of the Cour Ovale and the gardens. The gilded bed in the 17th- and 18th-century **Chambre de l'Impératrice** (Empress' Bedroom) was never used by Marie-Antoinette, for whom it was built in 1787. The gilding in the **Salle du Trône** (Throne Room), the royal bedroom before the Napoleonic period, is in three shades: gold, green and yellow.

The **Petits Appartements** (Small Apartments) were the private apartments of the emperor and empress and the **Musée Napoléon 1er** (Napoleon I Museum) contains personal effects – uniforms, hats, coats – ornamental swords and knick-knacks that belonged to Napoleon and his relatives. Neither has fixed opening hours, and they must be visited with a guide for a separate fee. Ask at the main ticket counter.

As successive monarchs added their own wings to the chateau, five irregularly shaped courtyards were created. The oldest and most interesting is the **Cour Ovale** (Oval Courtyard), no longer oval but U-shaped due to Henri IV's construction work. It incorporates the

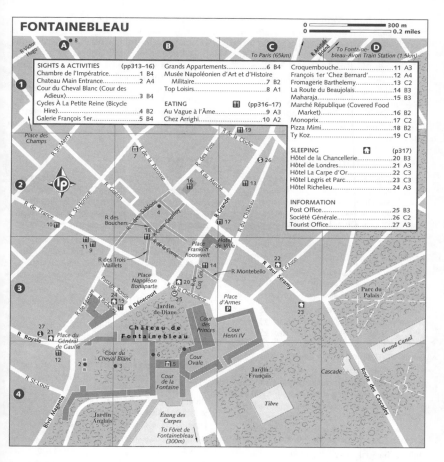

FONTAINEBLEAU

0 ——————— 300 m
0 ——————— 0.2 miles

SIGHTS & ACTIVITIES	(pp313–16)
Chambre de l'Impératrice	1 B4
Chateau Main Entrance	2 A4
Cour du Cheval Blanc (Cour des Adieux)	3 B4
Cycles À La Petite Reine (Bicycle Hire)	4 B2
Galerie François 1er	5 B4
Grands Appartements	6 B4
Musée Napoléonien d'Art et d'Histoire Militaire	7 B2
Top Loisirs	8 A1

EATING	🍴	(pp316–17)
Au Vague à l'Âme		9 A3
Chez Arrighi		10 A2
Croquembouche		11 A3
François 1er 'Chez Bernard'		12 A4
Fromagerie Barthelemy		13 C2
La Route du Beaujolais		14 B3
Maharaja		15 B3
Marché République (Covered Food Market)		16 B2
Monoprix		17 C2
Pizza Mimi		18 B2
Ty Koz		19 C1

SLEEPING	🏠	(p317)
Hôtel de la Chancellerie		20 B3
Hôtel de Londres		21 A3
Hôtel La Carpe d'Or		22 C3
Hôtel Legris et Parc		23 C3
Hôtel Richelieu		24 A3

INFORMATION		
Post Office		25 B3
Société Générale		26 C2
Tourist Office		27 A3

keep, the sole remnant of the medieval chateau. The largest courtyard is the **Cour du Cheval Blanc** (Courtyard of the White Horse), from where you enter the chateau. Napoleon, about to be exiled to Elba in 1814, bid farewell to his guards from the magnificent 17th-century **double-horseshoe staircase** here. For that reason the courtyard is also called the Cour des Adieux (Farewell Courtyard).

On the northern side of the chateau is the **Jardin de Diane**, a formal garden created by Catherine de Médicis. Le Nôtre's formal, 17th-century **Jardin Français** (French Garden) or Grand Parterre, is east of the **Cour de la Fontaine** (Fountain Courtyard) and the **Étang des Carpes** (Carp Pond). The **Grand Canal** was excavated in 1609 and predates the canals at Versailles by over half a century. The informal **Jardin Anglais** (English Garden), laid out in 1812, is west of the pond. The **Forêt de Fontainebleau**, crisscrossed by paths, begins 500m south of the chateau.

The **Musée Napoléonien d'Art et d'Histoire Militaire** (Napoleonic Museum of Art & Military History), not to be confused with the similarly named museum in the chateau itself, is housed in a 19th-century mansion and has seven rooms filled with military uniforms and weapons. Particularly lovely **gardens** surround the mansion.

The **Forêt de Fontainebleau**, the 20,000-hectare wood surrounding the town, is one of the loveliest forests in the region. The national hiking trails **GR1** and **GR11** are excellent for jogging, walking, cycling, horse riding, and climbing. The area is covered by IGN's 1:25,000 scale

Excursions – Fontainebleau

Forêt de Fontainebleau map (No 2417OT; €9). The tourist office sells the *Guide des Sentiers de Promenades dans le Massif Forestier de Fontainebleau* (€7.60), whose maps and text (in French) cover almost 20 walks in the forest, as well as the comprehensive *La Forêt de Fontainebleau* (€12.50), published by the Office National des Forêts, with almost 32 walks.

Rock-climbing enthusiasts have long come to the forest's sandstone ridges, rich in cliffs and overhangs, to hone their skills before setting off for the Alps. If you want to give it a go, contact **Top Loisirs** about equipment hire and instruction. Two gorges worth visiting are the **Gorges d'Apremont**, about 7km northwest of Fontainebleau near **Barbizon** (home of the 19th-century Barbizon school of landscape painting), and the **Gorges de Franchard**, a few kilometres south of Gorges d'Apremont. The tourist office sells the comprehensive *Fontainebleau Climbs* (€25), newly translated into English.

Sights & Information

Château de Fontainebleau (☎ 01 60 71 50 70; Château de Fontainebleau; www.musee-chateau-fontainebleau.fr in French; adult/18-25/child under 18 €5.50/4/free, 1st Sun of the month for all €4; ⏰ 9.30am-6pm Wed-Mon Jun-Sep, 9.30am-5pm Wed-Mon Oct-May) Conducted tours of the Grands Appartements in English usually depart at 2.30pm July to September from the staircase near the ticket windows, but check with staff.

Château gardens & courtyards (Château de Fontainebleau; admission free; ⏰ 9am-7pm May-Sep, 9am-6pm Mar, Apr & Oct, 9am-5pm Nov-Feb).

Cycles À La Petite Reine (☎ 01 60 74 57 57; 32 rue des Sablons, Fontainebleau; €5 per hr, half-/full-day Mon-Fri €10/13, half-/full-day Sat & Sun €13/16, week €54; ⏰ 9am-7.30pm Mon-Sat, 9am-6pm Sun) This place rents out mountain bikes and requires a deposit (credit card accepted) of €305.

Musée Napoléonien d'Art et d'Histoire Militaire (Napoleon Museum of Art & Military History; ☎ 01 60 74 64 89; 88 rue St-Honoré, Fontainebleau; adult/student & child 12-18 €2.50/1.70, child under 12 free; ⏰ 2-5.30pm Tue-Sat; gardens ⏰ 10am-7pm Mon-Sat mid-Mar–mid-Nov, 10am-5pm Tue-Sat mid-Nov–mid-Mar)

Office de Tourisme de Pays de Fontainebleau (Tourist Office; ☎ 01 60 74 99 99; www.fontainebleau-tourisme .com; 4 rue Royale, Fontainebleau; ⏰ 10am-6pm Mon-Sat, 10am-12.30pm & 3-5pm Sun Apr-Oct, 10am-1pm Sun Nov-Mar). The tourist office in a converted petrol station a couple of hundred metres west of the chateau hires out bicycles (half-/full-day €15/19) as well as self-paced audioguide tours (€4.60) of both the palace and the Forêt de Fontainebleau in English, each lasting 30 minutes.

Petits Appartements & Musée Napoléon 1er (Small Apartments & Napoleon 1 Museum; Château de Fontainebleau; adult/18-25/under 18 €3/2.30/free)

Post office (2 rue de la Chancellerie, Fontainebleau; ⏰ 8.15am-7pm Mon-Fri, 8.15am-noon Sat)

Société Générale (102 rue Grande, Fontainebleau; ⏰ 8.35am-12.30pm & 1.30-5.25pm Mon-Fri, 8.35am-12.30pm & 1.30-4.25pm Sat).

Top Loisirs (☎ 01 60 74 08 50; www.toploisirs.fr; 16 rue Sylvain Collinet, Fontainebleau)

Eating

Au Vague à l'Âme (☎ 01 60 72 10 32; 39 rue de France, Fontainebleau; crêpes & galettes €2.50-7.50, menus €25 & €35; ⏰ lunch Tue-Sun, dinner to 1am Tue-Sat) This café-restaurant is the place to come for Breton specialities including fresh oysters and an oyster terrine to die for.

Chez Arrighi (☎ 01 64 22 29 43; 53 rue de France, Fontainebleau; starters €9-20, mains €13.50-23.50, menus €18.80, €23.50 & €31.80; ⏰ lunch & dinner to 11pm Tue-Sun) An elegant place – arguably the best restaurant in Fontainebleau – with traditional cuisine.

Croquembouche (☎ 01 64 22 01 57; 43 rue de France, Fontainebleau; lunch menu €20, dinner menu €32; ⏰ lunch Fri-Tue, dinner to 10.30pm Thu-Sat, Mon & Tue) This excellent traditional French restaurant is just down the road from Chez Arrighi.

François 1er 'Chez Bernard' (☎ 01 64 22 24 68; 3 rue Royale, Fontainebleau; starters €6.90-18.90, mains €14.50-18.60, lunch/dinner menu €15/€28; ⏰ lunch & dinner to 11pm) This double-barrelled eatery has excellent specialities from Normandy, with an emphasis on seafood. Expect to pay about €35 per person if ordering à la carte.

La Route du Beaujolais (☎ 01 64 22 27 98; 3 rue Monte-bello, Fontainebleau; starters €7-14, mains €12-20, lunch menu €12, dinner menus €17 & €24; ⏰ lunch & dinner to 11pm) The 'Beaujolais Way' is no great shakes, but it's central and serves reliable and copious Lyonnaise dishes.

Maharaja (☎ 01 64 22 14 64; 15 rue Dénecourt, Fontainebleau; starters €3.50-7.50, mains €5.50-17.50, lunch menus €9 & €14, dinner menu €15; ⏰ lunch & dinner to midnight Mon-Sat) The Maharaja has curries (€7.50 to €9) and tandoori dishes (€5.50 to €17.50) as well as standard starters such as pakoras and samosas.

Pizza Mimi (☎ 01 64 22 70 77; 17 rue des Trois Maillets, Fontainebleau; pizzas & pasta €6-11.90, mains €10.90-11.90; ⏰ lunch & dinner to 11pm) Just around the corner from Fontainebleau's nightlife strip, Mimi has the usual pizzas and pasta, and more elaborate Italian main courses.

Ty Koz (☎ 01 64 22 00 55; 18 rue de la Cloche, Fontainebleau; crêpes & galettes €2.60-8.20; ⏰ lunch & dinner to 10pm) This little Breton place a small alleyway north of the centre has excellent crêpes and galettes.

Excursions – Fontainebleau

CHEAP EATS

Fromagerie Barthelemy (☎ 01 64 22 21 64; 92 rue Grande, Fontainebleau; 🕐 8.30am-12.30pm & 3.30-7.30pm Tue-Thu, 8am-1.30pm & 3.30-7.30pm Fri & Sat, 8.30am-12.30pm Sun) This branch of the famous cheesemongers in Paris (p261) is one of the finest cheese shops in the Île de France.

Marché Republique (rue des Pins, Fontainebleau; 🕐 8am-1pm Tue, Fri & Sun) Fontainebleau's covered food market is just north of the central pedestrian area.

Monoprix (58 rue Grande, Fontainebleau; 🕐 8.45am-7.45pm Mon-Sat, 9am-1pm Sun) This department store has a supermarket section on the 1st floor.

Sleeping

Fontainebleau has a wide range of accommodation suitable for all budgets but some of its top-end hotels are very fine indeed.

Hôtel de la Chancellerie (☎ 01 64 22 21 70; hotel.chancellerie@gofornet.com; 1 rue de la Chancellerie, Fontainebleau; s/d/tr €35/40/58) This hotel opposite the post office has 25 old-fashioned, but comfortable and spotless rooms. Rates are about €10 more from April to October.

Hôtel de Londres (☎ 01 64 22 20 21; www .hoteldelondres.com; 1 place du Général de Gaulle, Fontainebleau; s & d €90-105, ste €125-150) This classy 12-room hotel opposite the chateau's main entrance is a very comfortable place to stay. Some rooms (including Nos 2 & 10) have balconies with stunning views of the chateau.

Hôtel La Carpe d'Or (☎ 01 64 22 28 64; fax 01 64 22 39 95; 7 rue d'Avon, Fontainebleau; s/d/tr/q €39/53/63/63) This partially renovated hotel east of the place d'Armes has 16 basic but comfortable rooms.

Hôtel Legris et Parc (☎ 01 64 22 24 24; legris .et.parc@wanadoo.fr; 36 rue Paul Seramy & 6 rue d'Avon, Fontainebleau; s €46-50, d €61-95, tr €102-145) This lovely 32-room hotel in a 17th-century residence where Racine apparently once laid his head abuts the palace park and stands beside a synagogue built in 1861 and razed by the Nazis in 1941. The hotel has a lovely swimming pool and an excellent restaurant called L'Éden.

Hôtel Richelieu (☎ 01 64 22 26 46; fax 01 64 23 40 17, 4 rue Richelieu, Fontainebleau; s €41-57, d €46-62) This 18-room hotel just north of the chateau is part of the Logis de France group – always a sign of quality – and has an excellent wine bar and bistro called Le Bacchus.

VAUX-LE-VICOMTE

The privately owned **Château de Vaux-le-Vicomte** and its magnificent gardens 20km north of Fontainebleau were designed and built by Le Brun, Le Vau and Le Nôtre between 1656 and 1661 as a precursor to their more ambitious work at Versailles.

Unfortunately, Vaux-le-Vicomte's beauty turned out to be the undoing of its owner, Nicolas Fouquet, Louis XIV's minister of finance.

It seems that Louis, seething with jealousy that he had been upstaged at the chateau's official opening, had Fouquet thrown into prison, where he died in 1680.

Today visitors can view the interior of the chateau, including the fabulous **dome**, the **André Le Nôtre Exhibition** in the chateau's basement, the delightful formal **gardens** with elaborate *jeux d'eau* (fountain displays) in season and the **Musée des Équipages** (Carriage Museum) in the castle stables. A visit by night when the chateau is lit by 2000 candles is a never-to-be-forgotten experience.

Transport

Distance from Paris 61km

Direction Southeast

Travel time 60 minutes by car or by RER and by taxi

Car Route N6 from Paris and then A5a (direction Melun & exit 'Voisenon'); from Fontainebleau N6 and N36

RER Line D2 from Paris (€7) to Melun, 6km to southwest, then taxi (€15 & €20)

Sights & Information

Château de Vaux-le-Vicomte (☎ 01 64 14 41 90; www.vaux-le-vicomte.com; adult/senior, student & child 6-16 €12/9.50, candlelight visit €15/13, exhibit, garden & museum only €7; 🕐 10am-1pm & 2-6pm Mon-Fri, 10am-6pm Sat & Sun late-Mar–mid-Nov; candlelight visits

8pm-midnight Fri July & Aug, Sat May–mid-Oct) Audioguides available for €2.

Gardens (🕐 10am-6pm late-Mar–mid-Nov)

Fountain displays (🕐 3-6pm, 2nd & last Sat, late-Mar-Oct)

Musée des Équipages (Carriage Museum; 🕐 10am-1pm & 2-6pm Mon-Fri, 10am-6pm Sat & Sun late-Mar–mid-Nov)

CHANTILLY

The elegant town of Chantilly (population 10,900) is best known for its imposing, but largely reconstructed chateau surrounded by parkland, gardens, lakes and a vast forest. The chateau is just over 2km east of the train station. The most direct route is to walk along av de la Plaine des Aigles through a section of the Forêt de Chantilly, but you'll get a better sense of the town by taking av du Maréchal Joffre and rue de Paris to rue du Connétable, Chantilly's principal thoroughfare.

The **Château de Chantilly**, which was left in a shambles after the Revolution, is of interest mainly because of its gardens and a number of superb paintings. It consists of two attached buildings, which are entered through the same vestibule. The **Petit Château** was built around 1560 for Anne de Montmorency (1493–1567), who served six French kings as *connétable* (high constable), diplomat and soldier and died whilst fighting Protestants during the Counter-Reformation. The attached Renaissance-style **Grand Château**, completely demolished during the Revolution, was rebuilt by the duke of Aumale, son of King Louis-Philippe, from 1875 to 1885.

The Grand Château, to the right as you enter the vestibule, now contains the **Musée Condé**. Its unremarkable 19th-century rooms feature furnishings, paintings and sculptures haphazardly arranged according to the whims of the duke. He donated the chateau to the Institut de France at the

Transport

Distance from Paris 48km

Direction North

Travel time 30/45 minutes by train/RER

Car Route A1 from Paris, exit No 7 'Survilliers-Chantilly'; route N16 from Porte de La Chapelle

RER Line D1 from Gare de Lyon, Châtelet-Les Halles or Gare du Nord Paris (€7.45) to Chantilly-Gouvieux station

Train Paris' Gare du Nord is linked to Chantilly by SNCF commuter trains that, with RER trains, total almost 40 a day (about 20 on Sunday). The last train back to Paris departs daily just before midnight.

end of the 19th century on the condition that the exhibits were not reorganised and would be open to the public. The most remarkable works are hidden away in a small room called the **Sanctuaire**, including paintings by Raphael, Filippino Lippi and Jean Fouquet.

The Petit Château contains the **Appartements des Princes** (Princes' Suites), which are straight ahead from the entrance. The highlight here is the **Cabinet des Livres**, a repository of 700 manuscripts and over 30,000 volumes, including a Gutenberg Bible and a facsimile of the *Très Riches Heures du Duc de Berry*, an illuminated manuscript dating from the 15th century that illustrates the calendar year for both the peasantry and

Château de Chantilly (above)

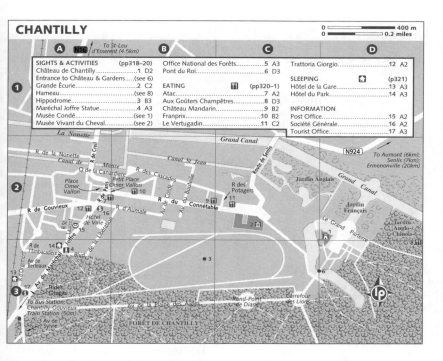

CHANTILLY

0 —————— 400 m
0 —————— 0.2 miles

SIGHTS & ACTIVITIES	(pp318–20)	Office National des Forêts	5 A3	Trattoria Giorgio	12 A2
Château de Chantilly	1 D2	Pont du Roi	6 D3		
Entrance to Château & Gardens	(see 6)			SLEEPING	(p321)
Grande Écurie	2 C2	EATING	(pp320–1)	Hôtel de la Gare	13 A3
Hippodrome	3 B3	Atac	7 A2	Hôtel du Park	14 A3
Hameau	(see 8)	Aux Goûters Champêtres	8 D3		
Maréchal Joffre Statue	4 A3	Château Mandarin	9 B2	INFORMATION	
Musée Condé	(see 1)	Franprix	10 B2	Post Office	15 A2
Musée Vivant du Cheval	(see 2)	Le Vertugadin	11 C2	Société Générale	16 A2
				Tourist Office	17 A3

the nobility. The **chapel**, to the left as you walk into the vestibule, has woodwork and stained-glass windows dating from the mid-16th century and was assembled by the duke in 1882.

The chateau's excellent, but long-neglected **gardens** were once among the most spectacular in France. The formal **Jardin Français** (French Garden), whose flowerbeds, lakes and Grand Canal were laid out by Le Nôtre in the mid-17th century, is northeast of the main building. To the west, the 'wilder' **Jardin Anglais** (English Garden) was begun in 1817. East of the Jardin Français is the rustic **Jardin Anglo-Chinois** (Anglo-Chinese Garden), created in the 1770s. Its foliage and silted-up waterways surround the **Hameau**, a mock village dating from 1774 whose mill and half-timbered buildings inspired the Hameau de la Reine at Versailles. Crème Chantilly – cream beaten with icing and vanilla sugar and dolloped on everything sweet that doesn't move in France – was born here (see the boxed text p320).

The chateau's **Grande Écurie** (stables), built between 1719 and 1740 to house 240 horses and over 400 hounds, are next to Chantilly's famous **Hippodrome** (racecourse), inaugurated in 1834. Today the stables house the **Musée Vivant du Cheval** (Living Horse Museum), whose 30 pampered and spoiled equines live in luxurious wooden stalls built by Louis-Henri de Bourbon (seventh Prince de Condé). Displays, in 31 rooms, include everything from riding equipment to horse toys and portraits, drawings and sculptures of famous nags. Make sure you stick around for the 30-minute **Présentation Équestre Pédagogique** (Introduction to Dressage), included in the admission price.

South of the chateau is the 6300-hectare **Forêt de Chantilly** (Chantilly Forest), once a royal hunting estate and now crisscrossed by a variety of walking and riding trails. In some areas, straight paths laid out centuries ago meet at multi-angled *carrefours* (crossroads). Long-distance trails that pass through the Forêt de Chantilly include the **GR11**, which links the chateau with the town of Senlis (p321) and its wonderful cathedral; the **GR1**, which goes from Luzarches (famed for its cathedral, parts of which date from the 12th century) to Er-menonville; and the **GR12**, which goes northeastward from four lakes known as the Étangs de Commelles to the Forêt d'Halatte.

Château de Whipped Cream

Like every other self-respecting French chateau three centuries ago, the palace at Chantilly had its own *hameau* (hamlet), complete with *laitier* (dairy) where the lady of the household and her guests could play at being milkmaids, as Marie-Antoinette did at Versailles. But the cows at Chantilly's dairy took their job rather more seriously than their fellow bovine actors at other faux dairies, and news of the *crème chantilly* (sweetened whipped cream) served at the hamlet's teas became the talk (and envy) of aristocratic 18th-century Europe. The future Habsburg Emperor Joseph II clandestinely visited this *'temple de marbre'* (marble temple), as he called it, to try out the white stuff in 1777, and when the Baroness of Oberkirch tasted the goods she cried: 'Never have I eaten such good cream, so appetising, so well prepared.'

The area is covered by IGN's 1:25,000 scale map *Forêts de Chantilly, d'Halatte and d'Ermenonville* (No 2412OT; €9). The 1:100,000 scale map *Carte de Découverte des Milieux Naturels et du Patrimoine Bâti* (€6.50), available at the tourist office, indicates sites of interest (eg churches, chateaux, museums and ruins). The **Office National des Forêts** (ONF, National Forests Office) publishes a good walking guide for families called *Promenons-Nous dans les Forêts de Picardie: Chantilly Halatte & Ermenonville* (€7.50). Mountain bikers might want to pick up a copy of the detailed *Les Cahiers de la Randonnée VTT: Forêts de Chantilly et d' Ermenonville* (€13) available from the tourist office.

Sights & Information

Château de Chantilly (☎ 03 44 62 62 62; www.chateau dechantilly.com; Château de Chantilly; adult/child 12-17/child 4-11 €7/6/2.80; ☉ chateau 10am-6pm Jul-Aug, 10am-6pm Wed-Mon Mar-Jun, Sep & Oct, 10.30am-12.45pm & 2-5pm Wed-Mon Nov-Feb; park 10am-6pm Mar-Oct, 10am-12.45pm & 2-6pm Nov-Feb) Admission allows entry to the chateau, Musée Condé and park. You can also only visit the park (adult/child 4-11 €3/2). Combination tickets include the park and canal boat ride (adult/child 4-11 €8/5); the chateau, museum, park and canal boat ride adult/child 12-17/child 4-11 €13/11/7); the chateau, museum, park, canal boat and mini-train ride through park (adult/child 12-17/child 4-11 €15/13/9).

Musée Vivant du Cheval (Living Horse Museum; ☎ 03 44 57 13 13; www.musee-vivant-du-cheval .fr; Chantilly; adult/child 12-17/child 4-11 €8/6.50/5.50; ☉ 10.30am-6.30pm Mon-Fri, to 7pm Sat & Sun May & Jun; 10.30am-6.30pm Mon & Wed-Fri, from 2pm Tue, to 7pm Sat & Sun Jul & Aug; 10.30am-6.30pm Wed-Mon, to 7pm Sat & Sun Apr, Sep & Oct; 10.30am-6.30pm Sat & Sun, from 2pm Mon & Wed-Fri Nov-Mar.

Office National des Forêts (ONF, National Forests Office; ☎ 03 44 57 03 88, www.onf.fr in French; 1 av de Sylvie, Chantilly; ☉ 8.30am-noon & 2-5pm Mon-Fri) This office is just southeast of the tourist office. Ask the staff about organised forest walks.

Office de Tourisme de Chantilly (Tourist Office; ☎ 03 44 67 37 37; www.chantilly-tourisme.com; 60 av du Maréchal Joffre, Chantilly; ☉ 9.30am-12.30pm & 1.30-5.30pm Mon-Sat, 10.30am-1.30pm Sun May-Sep, 9.30am-12.30pm & 1.30-5.30pm Mon-Sat Oct-Apr) The tourist office is just round the corner from the train station. Ask the staff for a copy of *Circuit Touristique en Ville*, a pamphlet with a 23-stop walk around town starting from the tourist office.

Post office (26 av du Maréchal Joffre, Chantilly; ☉ 9am-12.15pm & 1.45-6pm Mon-Fri, 9am-12.30pm Sat).

Présentation Équestre Pédagogique (Introduction to Dressage; ☉ 11.30am, 3.30pm & 5.30pm Apr-Oct, 3.30pm Mon-Fri, 11.30am, 3.30pm & 5.15pm Sat & Sun Nov-Mar)

Société Générale (1 av du Maréchal Joffre, Chantilly; ☉ 8.30am-12.15pm & 1.45-5.30pm Mon-Thu, 8.30am-12.15pm & 1.45-6.30pm Fri, 9.30am-3.25pm Sat)

Eating

Aux Goûters Champêtres (☎ 03 44 57 46 21; Château de Chantilly; menus €16, €26 & €34; ☉ 11am-7pm Apr-Oct) This fine restaurant in the windmill of the park's Hameau has local specialities on the menu and is a wonderful place for lunch, particularly during the summer.

Château Mandarin (☎ 03 44 57 00 29; 62 rue du Connétable, Chantilly; starters €3-5.50, mains €6.50-15, lunch menu €12; ☉ lunch & dinner to 10.30pm Tue-Sun) This is a decent Chinese restaurant a short distance west of the Grande Écurie. It has Thai and Vietnamese dishes too.

Le Vertugadin (☎ 03 44 57 03 19; 44 rue du Connétable, Chantilly; starters €8-15, mains €15-25, lunch menu €15, dinner menu €23; ☉ lunch & dinner to 11pm Mon-Sat) This is a very friendly and highly recommended restaurant with excellent *menus* and a walled-in garden that is a delight in summer.

Trattoria Giorgio (☎ 03 44 57 00 48; av du Maréchal Joffre, Chantilly; starters €6.90-11.50, pasta €7.90-11, mains €11.50-18.10, lunch menu €9.90; ☉ lunch & dinner to 11.30pm) This very central Italian restaurant is just the ticket for a pizza or more ambitious meal en route to the train station.

CHEAP EATS

Atac (5 petit place Omer Vallon, Chantilly; ☺ 8.30am-7.30pm Mon-Sat) This large supermarket is midway between the train station and the chateau.

Franprix (132 rue du Connétable, Chantilly; ☺ 8.30am-12.30pm & 2.30-7.30pm Tue-Thu, 8.30am-7.30pm Fri & Sat, 8.30am-1pm Sun)

Sleeping

Hôtel de la Gare (☎ 03 44 62 56 90, 06 81 60 16 39; fax 03 44 62 56 99; place de la Gare, Chantilly; s & d €49)

This rambling hotel with a dozen rooms opposite the train station is a surprisingly pleasant place with recently renovated shower-equipped doubles. The only drawback is the Star d'un Star karaoke club that wails from 8pm to 1am daily on the 1st floor.

Hôtel du Parc (☎ 03 44 58 20 00; www.bestwestern.fr; 36 av du Maréchal Joffre, Chantilly; s €78-88, d €86-96, tr €98-108, ste €112) This 57-room, architecturally bankrupt place is no great shakes, but it's part of the Best Western chain so you can expect a reasonable standard of service. Cheaper rooms face the street.

SENLIS

Senlis (population 16,250), just 10km northeast of Chantilly, is an attractive medieval town of winding cobblestone streets, Gallo-Roman ramparts and towers. It was a royal seat from the time of Clovis to Henri IV and contains four fine **museums** and an important 12th-century cathedral.

The Gothic **Cathédrale de Notre Dame**, which is entered through the south portal, was built between 1150 and 1191. The cathedral is unusually bright, but the stained glass, though original, is generally unexceptional. The magnificent carved stone **Grand Portal** (1170), on the western side facing place du Parvis Notre Dame, has statues and a central relief relating to the life of the Virgin Mary. It is believed to have been the inspiration for the portal at the cathedral in Chartres.

Sights & Information

Banque de Picardie (2 rue Bellon; ☺ 8.45am-12.30pm & 2-5.30pm Mon-Fri, 8.45am-12.30pm & 2-4.30pm Sat) At the corner of rue St-Hailaire southeast of the cathedral.

Cathédrale de Notre Dame (place Notre Dame; ☺ 8am-6pm)

Office de Tourisme de Senlis (☎ 03 44 53 06 40; off .tourisme-senlis@ wanadoo.fr; place du Parvis Notre Dame; ☺ 10am-12.30pm & 2-6.15pm Mon-Sat, 10.30am-1pm & 2.30-6.15pm Sun Mar-Oct; 10am-12.30pm & 2-5pm Mon-Sat, 11.15am-1pm & 2.30-5pm Sun Nov-Feb) The tourist office is just opposite (and west of) the cathedral.

Senlis museums (adult/senior & student 17-25 €4/2; ☺ 10am-noon & 2-6pm Mon, Thu & Fri, 2-6pm Wed, 11am-1pm & 2-6pm Sat & Sun) One ticket allows entry to the **Musée d'Art et d'Archéologie** (Museum of Art & Archaeology; ☎ 03 44 32 00 83; place Notre Dame); the **Musée de la Vénerie** and **Musée des Spahis** (☎ 03 44 32 00 81), with exhibits relating to hunting and to the North African cavalry garrisoned in Senlis; and the **Musée de l'Hôtel de Vermandois** (☎ 03 44 32 00 82; place du Parvis Notre Dame), which looks at the history of Senlis.

Eating & Sleeping

Hostellerie de la Porte Bellon (☎ 03 44 53 03 05; www.portebellon.com; 51 rue Bellon; s with shower €52-65, d with shower €55-68, s with bath €65-70, d with bath €68-73). This wonderful 18-room hotel is housed in an

18th-century manor a couple of hundred metres east of the cathedral. The garden surrounding the property is a delight and the restaurant (starters €8.90-19, mains €17-24, lunch menu €21, dinner menus €23, €27 & €36; ☺ lunch daily & dinner to 9.30pm Mon-Sat) is worth a visit in itself.

Le Scaramouche (☎ 03 44 53 01 26; 4 place Notre Dame; starters €10-22, mains €14-35, menus €24, €35 & €58; ☺ lunch & dinner to 10.30pm Thu-Mon) This upmarket restaurant is the best and most central place for a meal while visiting the cathedral or museums.

Market (rue St-Hilaire; ☺ 8am-1pm Tue & Fri) Surrounding the open-air market southwest of the cathedral are a number of relatively cheap places to eat including pizzerias, crêperies and cafés.

Excursions – Senlis

CHARTRES

The magnificent 13th-century cathedral of Chartres, crowned by two very different spires – one Gothic, the other Romanesque – rises from rich farmland and dominates the medieval town (population 40,250) around its base. The cathedral's varied collection of relics – particularly the Sainte Voile, the 'holy veil' said to have been worn by the Virgin Mary when she gave birth to Jesus – attracted many pilgrims during the Middle Ages, who contributed to the building and extending of the cathedral. With its astonishing blue stained glass and other treasures, the cathedral at Chartres is a must-see for any visitor to Paris.

The 130m-long **Cathédrale Notre Dame**, one of the crowning architectural achievements

Transport

Distance from Paris 88km

Direction Southwest

Travel time 55 to 70 minutes by train

Car Route A6 from Paris' Porte d'Orléans (direction Bordeaux-Nantes) then route A10 & A11 (direction Nantes); exit 'Chartres'

Train More than 30 SNCF trains a day (20 on Sunday) link Paris' Gare Montparnasse (€11.80) with Chartres, all of which pass through Versailles-Chantiers (€9.90, 45 to 60 minutes). The last train back to Paris leaves Chartres a bit after 9pm weekdays, just before 9pm on Saturday and sometime after 10pm on Sunday.

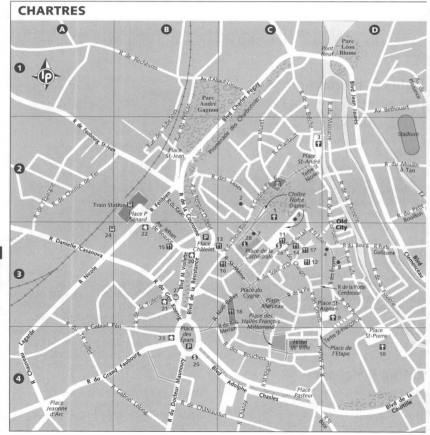

of Western civilisation, was built in the Gothic style during the first quarter of the 13th century. It was built to replace a Romanesque cathedral that had been devastated, along with much of the town, by fire on the night of 10 June 1194. Because of effective fund-raising among the aristocracy and donated labour from the common folk, construction took only 30 years, resulting in a high degree of architectural unity. It is France's best-preserved medieval cathedral, having been spared post-medieval modifications, the ravages of war and the iconoclastic Reign of Terror (see the boxed text p324).

All three of the cathedral's entrances to the west, north and south have superbly ornamented triple **portals**, but the west entrance, **Portail Royal**, is the only one that predates the fire. Carved between 1145 and 1155, its superb statuary, whose features are elongated in the Romanesque style, represent the glory of Christ in the centre, and the Nativity and Ascension to the right and left, respectively. The structure's other main Romanesque feature is the 103m-high **Clocher Vieux** (Old Bell Tower; also called the Tour Sud, or 'South Tower'), which was begun in the 1140s. It is the tallest Romanesque steeple still standing.

A visit to the 112m-high **Clocher Neuf** (New Bell Tower), also known as the Tour Nord (North Tower), is well worth the ticket price and the climb up the long, spiral stairway. Access is just behind the cathedral bookshop. A 70m-high platform on the flamboyant Gothic spire, built from 1507 to 1513 by Jehan de Beauce after an earlier wooden spire burned down, affords superb views of the three-tiered flying buttresses and the 19th-century copper roof, turned green by verdigris.

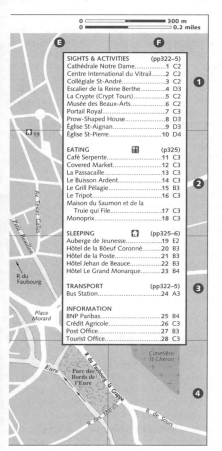

SIGHTS & ACTIVITIES	(pp322–5)
Cathédrale Notre Dame	1 C2
Centre International du Vitrail	2 C2
Collégiale St-André	3 C2
Escalier de la Reine Berthe	4 D3
La Crypte (Crypt Tours)	5 C2
Musée des Beaux-Arts	6 C2
Portail Royal	7 C3
Prow-Shaped House	8 D3
Église St-Aignan	9 D3
Église St-Pierre	10 D4

EATING 🍴	(p325)
Café Serpente	11 C3
Covered Market	12 C3
La Passacaille	13 C3
Le Buisson Ardent	14 C3
Le Grill Pélagie	15 B3
Le Tripot	16 C3
Maison du Saumon et de la Truie qui File	17 C3
Monoprix	18 C3

SLEEPING 🛏	(pp325–6)
Auberge de Jeunesse	19 E2
Hôtel de la Bœuf Coronné	20 B3
Hôtel de la Poste	21 B3
Hôtel Jehan de Beauce	22 B3
Hôtel Le Grand Monarque	23 B4

TRANSPORT	(pp322–5)
Bus Station	24 A3

INFORMATION	
BNP Paribas	25 B4
Crédit Agricole	26 C3
Post Office	27 B3
Tourist Office	28 C3

The cathedral's 172 extraordinary **stained-glass windows**, almost all of which are 13th-century originals, comprise one of the most important collections of medieval stained glass in Europe. The three most important windows dating from before the 13th century are in the wall above the west entrance, below the rose window. Survivors of the fire of 1194 (they were made around 1150), the windows are renowned for the depth and intensity of their blue tones, which have become known as 'Chartres blue'.

If you want to see more stained glass up close and in more modern guises, trek down the hill from the cathedral's north portal to the **Centre International du Vitrail** (International Stained-Glass Centre) located in a half-timbered former granary.

The cathedral's 110m-long **crypt**, a tombless Romanesque structure built in 1024 around a 9th-century predecessor is the largest in France. Guided tours in French (with a written English translation) lasting 30 minutes are available year-round.

The most venerated object in the cathedral is the **Sainte Voile** (Holy Veil) relic, which originally formed part of the imperial treasury of Constantinople but was offered to Charlemagne by the Empress Irene when the Holy Roman Emperor proposed marriage to her in AD 802. It has been in Chartres since 876 when Charles the Bald presented it to the town. The cathedral was built because the veil survived the 1194 fire. It is contained in a cathedral-shaped reliquary and is currently displayed in a small side chapel off the eastern aisle.

Excursions – Chartres

Chartres' **Musée des Beaux-Arts** (Fine Arts Museum), accessed most easily via the gate next to the cathedral's north portal, is in the former Palais Épiscopal (Bishop's Palace), built in the 17th and 18th centuries. The museum's collections include 16th-century enamels of the Apostles made by Léonard Limosin for François I, paintings from the 16th to 19th centuries and polychrome wooden sculptures from the Middle Ages.

Chartres' carefully preserved **old town** is northeast and east of the cathedral along the narrow western channel of the River Eure, spanned by a number of footbridges. From rue Cardinal Pie, the stairways called **Tertre St-Nicolas** and **rue Chantault**, the latter lined with medieval houses, lead down to the empty shell of the 12th-century **Collégiale St-André**, a Romanesque collegiate church that closed in 1791 and was damaged in the early 19th century and again during WWII.

Saved by Red Tape

The magnificent cathedral at Chartres and its priceless stained glass managed to survive the ravages of the Revolution and the Reign of Terror for the same reason that everyday life in France can often seem so complicated: the French bureaucratic approach to almost everything.

As antireligious fervour was reaching fever pitch in 1791, the Revolutionaries decided that the cathedral deserved something more radical than mere desecration: demolition. The question was how to accomplish that. To find an answer, they appointed a committee, whose admirably thorough members deliberated for four or five years. By that time the Revolution's fury had been spent, and – to history's great fortune – the plan was shelved.

Along the river's eastern bank, **rue de la Tannerie** and its extension **rue de la Foulerie**, are lined with flower gardens, millraces and the restored remnants of riverside trades: wash houses, tanneries and the like. **Rue aux Juifs** (Street of the Jews) on the western bank has been extensively renovated. Half a block down the hill there's a riverside promenade. Up the hill **rue des Écuyers** has many structures dating from around the 16th century, including a half-timbered, **prow-shaped house** at No 26 with its upper section supported by beams. At No 35 is the **Escalier de la Reine Berthe** (Queen Bertha's Staircase) a tower-like covered stairwell clinging to a half-timbered house that dates back to the early 16th century.

There are also some old half-timbered houses on **rue du Bourg** and **rue de la Poissonnerie**; on the latter, look for the magnificent **Maison du Saumon** (Salmon House), also known as the Maison de la Truie qui File (House of the Spinning Sow) at No 10–14. It has carved consoles of the Archangel Gabriel and Mary, Archangel Michael slaying the dragon and, of course, the eponymous salmon and is now a restaurant.

From **place St-Pierre**, you get a good view of the flying buttresses holding up the 12th- and 13th-century **Église St-Pierre**. Once part of a Benedictine monastery founded in the 7th century, it was outside the city walls and thus vulnerable to attack; the fortress-like, pre-Romanesque **bell tower** attached to it was used as a refuge by monks and dates from around 1000. The fine, brightly coloured **clerestory windows** in the nave, choir and apse date from the early 14th century.

To the northwest **Église St-Aignan**, built in the early 16th century, is interesting for its wooden barrel-vault roof (1625), arcaded nave and painted interior of faded blue and gold floral motifs (circa 1870). The stained glass and the Renaissance Chapelle de St-Michel date from the 16th century.

The **Train Touristique de Chartres** makes a 35-minute circuit around the city in season.

Sights & Information

BNP Paribas (7-9 place des Épars; ⌚ 8.30am-noon & 1.30-5.35pm Tue, 8.50am-noon & 1.45-5.35pm Wed-Fri, 8.30am-noon & 1.30-4.45pm Sat)

Cathédrale Notre Dame de Chartres (☎ 02 37 21 22 07; www.cathedrale-chartres.com in French; place de la Cathédrale; ⌚ 8.30am-7.30pm) Excellent English-language audioguide tours (25/45/70 min €2.90/3.80/5.65) with three different themes can be hired from the cathedral shop. French-language guided tours

(adult/senior/student & child under 18 €6/4/3; ⌚ 3pm daily, 10.30am Tue-Sat Apr-Oct, 2.30pm Nov-Mar) also depart from here.

Centre International du Vitrail (International Stained Glass Centre; ☎ 02 37 21 65 72; www.centre-vitrail.org; 5 rue du Cardinal Pie, Chartres; adult/senior, student & child €4/3; ⌚ 9.30am-12.30pm & 1.30-6pm Mon-Fri, 10am-12.30pm & 2.30-6pm Sat & Sun)

Clocher Neuf (New Bell Tower; Cathédrale Notre Dame de Chartres; adult/18-25/under 18 €4.60/3.10/free, admission free on the 1st Sun of some months; 🕑 9.30am-noon & 2-5.30pm Mon-Sat & 2-5.30pm Sun May-Aug; 9.30am-noon & 2-4.30 Mon-Sat, 2-4.30pm Sun Sep-Apr)

Crédit Agricole (1 Cloître Notre-Dame, Chartres; 🕑 8.45am-12.30pm & 1.50-5.30pm Tue-Fri, 8.45am-12.30pm & 1.50-4pm Sat)

Crypt (Cathédrale Notre Dame de Chartres; adult/senior, student & child 7-18 €2.60/2; 🕑 11am Mon-Sat, 2.15pm, 3.30pm, 4.30pm & 5.15pm daily late-Jun–late-Sep; 11am Mon-Sat, 2.15pm, 3.30pm & 4.30pm daily Apr–late-Jun, late-Sep-Oct; 11am Mon-Sat & 4.15pm daily Nov-Mar) Guided tours of the crypt in French (with a written English translation) lasting 30 minutes start at La Crypte. At other times they begin at the shop below the North Tower in the cathedral.

Église St-Aignan (place St-Aignan, Chartres; 🕑 9am-noon & 2-6pm)

Église St-Pierre (place St-Pierre, Chartres; 🕑 9am-noon & 2-6pm)

English-language tours (Cathédrale Notre Dame de Chartres; adult/senior/student €6/4/3; 🕑 noon & 2.45pm Mon-Sat Apr–early-Nov) are conducted by Chartres expert Malcolm Miller (☎ 02 37 28 15 58; fax 02 37 28 33 03).

La Crypte (☎ 02 37 21 56 33; 18 Cloître Notre Dame) The cathedral-run shop selling religious items and souvenirs, from April to October.

Musée des Beaux-Arts (Fine Arts Museum; ☎ 02 37 36 41 39; 29 Cloître Notre Dame, Chartres; adult/student & senior €2.45/1.20; 🕑 10am-noon & 2-6pm Mon & Wed-Sat, 2-6pm Sun May-Oct; 10am-noon & 2-5pm Mon & Wed-Sat, 2-5pm Sun Nov-Apr)

Office de Tourisme de Chartres (Tourist Office; ☎ 02 37 18 26 26; info@otchartres.fr; place de la Cathédrale, Chartres; 🕑 9am-7pm Mon-Sat, 9.30am-5.30pm Sun Apr-Sep; 10am-6pm Mon-Sat, 10am-1pm & 2.30-4.30pm Sun Oct-Mar) The tourist office, across the square from the cathedral's main entrance, rents self-paced English-language audioguide tours (€5.50/8.50 for one or two persons) of the medieval city lasting 1½ hours.

Post office (place des Épars; 🕑 8.30am-7pm Mon-Fri, 8.30am-noon Sat) The main post office is housed in an impressive neo-Gothic building with fin-de-siècle mosaics on the front.

Train Touristique de Chartres (Chartres Tourist Train; ☎ 02 37 25 88 50; adult/child 3-10 €5.50/3.20; 🕑 10.30am-6pm late-Mar–early-Nov)

Eating

Café Serpente (☎ 02 37 21 68 81; 2 Cloître Notre Dame, Chartres; salads & omelettes €5.20-11.50, dishes €13.50-15; 🕑 10am-1pm) This atmospheric brasserie and salon de thé (tearoom) is conveniently located opposite the cathedral.

La Passacaille (☎ 02 37 21 52 10; 30 rue Ste-Même, Chartres; starters €3.70-8.10, mains €9.90-12.40; 🕑 lunch & dinner to 10.30pm) This welcoming Italian place has particularly good pizzas (€7.10 to €10.10) and fresh pasta (€8.10 to €9.50).

Le Buisson Ardent (☎ 02 37 34 04 66; 10 rue au Lait, Chartres; starters €9.50-16, mains €13-22, lunch menu €18, dinner menu 22; 🕑 lunch Thu-Tue & dinner to 10.30pm Mon, Tue, Thu-Sat) The 'Burning Bush' is a charming, old-style place with good-value menus.

Le Grill Pélagie (☎ 02 37 36 07 49; 1 av Jehan de Beauce, Chartres; starters €3.70-7.90, mains €9.90-14.80, menus €11.50-18.50; 🕑 lunch & dinner to 11pm Mon-Sat) This is a popular place specialising in grills and Tex-Mex dishes such as guacamole and quesadillas (€6.50) and fajitas (€13.80 to €15.60).

Le Tripot (☎ 02 37 36 60 11; 11 place Jean Moulin, Chartres; starters €11-19, mains €13.50-24, lunch menu €15, dinner menus €22.50, €28.50 & €37.50; 🕑 lunch Tue-Sun, dinner to 9.30pm Tue-Sat) This wonderful little place just down from the cathedral is one of the best bistros in Chartres.

Maison du Saumon et de la Truie qui File (☎ 02 37 36 28 00; 10-14 rue de la Poissonnerie, Chartres; starters €9.50-14.50, mains €15-19.50, menu €19.70; 🕑 lunch Tue-Sun, dinner to 11.30pm Tue-Sat) Housed in the medieval house of the same name, this place tries to have something for everyone – Alsatian choucroute, Hungarian goulash, Moroccan tajine, pirozhki, fish – and ends up nothing but confused. Come here for the venue.

CHEAP EATS

Covered market (place Billard, Chartres; 🕑 7am-1pm Sat) This market just off rue des Changes south of the cathedral dates from the early 20th century. There are a lot of food shops surrounding it.

Monoprix (21 rue Noël Ballay & 10 rue du Bois Merrain, Chartres; 🕑 9am-7.30pm Mon-Sat) This department store with two entrances has a supermarket on the ground floor.

Sleeping

Auberge de Jeunesse (☎ 02 37 34 27 64; fax 02 37 35 78 85; 23 av Neigre, Chartres; dm €11) Reception at this hostel, which is about 1.5km east of the train station via blvd Charles Péguy and blvd Jean Jaurès, opens from 2pm to 10pm and curfew is 10.30pm in winter and 11.30pm in summer. To get there from the train station, take bus No 5 (direction Mare aux Moines) to the Rouliers stop.

Le Grand Monarque (☎ 02 37 18 15 15; www.bw-grand -monarque.com; 22 place des Épars, Chartres; s €85-107, d €105-120, tr €145-155) This three-star hotel is supposedly Chartres' finest, but some of the public areas and the 54 guestrooms now have a frayed look to them.

Hôtel de la Poste (☎ 02 37 21 04 27; www.hotel poste-chartres.com; 3 rue du Général Koenig, Chartres; s with shower/bath €57/62, d €71.50/77.50; €94/117) This 57-room two-star property just off the place des Épars offers excellent value.

Hôtel du Bœuf Couronné (☎ 02 37 18 06 06; fax 02 37 21 72 13; 15 place Châtelet, Chartres; s with washbasin & toilet/with shower/with bath €27/40/43, d €30/50/57) This cosy, Logis de France affiliated guesthouse in the centre of everything offers excellent value and has a memorable restaurant (menus €22 & €26; ☯ lunch & dinner to 11pm) with generous menus.

Hôtel Jehan de Beauce (☎ 02 37 21 01 41; www .contact-hotel-chartres.com; 19 av Jehan de Beauce, Chartres; s/d with washbasin & toilet €29/36, s with shower €43-48, d with shower €50-55, s with bath €48-52, d with bath €55-59, tr €55-61) If you're looking for budget accommodation this 46-room hotel has clean, but very Spartan singles, doubles and triples. It's very convenient to the train station.

GIVERNY

This small village (population 525) north-west of Paris and en route to Rouen contains **Maison de Claude Monet**, the home and flower-filled garden of one of the leading Impressionist painters and his family from 1883 to 1926. Here Monet painted some of his most famous series of works, including *Décorations des Nymphéas* (Water Lilies). Unfortunately, the hectare of land that Monet owned here has become two distinct areas, cut by the Chemin du Roy, a small railway line that has been converted into what is now the busy D5 road.

The northern area of the property is **Clos Normand**, where Monet's famous pastel pink and green house and the **Atelier des Nymphéas** (Water Lilies studio) stand. These days the

Transport

Distance from Paris 76km

Direction Northwest

Travel time 70 minutes by train to Vernon and bus

Car Route A13 from Paris' Port de St-Cloud (direction Rouen); exit No 14 to route N15 (direction Vernon & Giverny)

Train From Paris' Gare St-Lazare there are two early-morning trains to Vernon (€10.90) from where Transport Val de Seine buses (☎ 02 32 71 06 39; €1.90) depart for Giverny, 7km to the northwest. There's roughly one train an hour back to Paris between 5pm and 9pm.

studio is the entrance hall, adorned with precise reproductions of his works and ringing with cash-register bells from busy souvenir stands. Outside are the symmetrically laid-out gardens. Visiting the house and gardens is a treat in any season. From early to late spring, daffodils, tulips, rhododendrons, wisteria and irises appear, followed by poppies and lilies. By June, nasturtiums, roses and sweet peas are in blossom. Around September, there are dahlias, sunflowers and hollyhocks.

From the Clos Normand's far corner, a tunnel leads under the D5 to the **Jardin d'Eau** (Water Garden). Having bought this piece of land in 1895 after his reputation had been established (and his bank account had swelled), Monet dug a pool, planted water lilies and constructed the famous **Japanese bridge**, which has since been rebuilt. Draped with purple wisteria, the bridge blends into the asymmetrical foreground and background, creating the intimate atmosphere for which the 'Painter of Light' was famous.

The **Musée d'Art Américain** (American Art Museum) contains a fine collection of the works of many of the American Impressionist painters who flocked to France in the late 19th and early 20th centuries. It's housed in a modern building about 100m northwest of the Maison de Claude Monet.

Sights & Information

Maison de Claude Monet (☎ 02 32 51 28 21; www .fondation-monet.com; 84 rue Claude Monet; adult/ student/child 7-12 €5.50/4/3, house €1.50, garden €4; ☯ 9.30am-6pm Tue-Sun Apr-Oct)

Musée d'Art Américain (☎ 02 32 51 94 65; www.maag .org; 99 rue Claude Monet; adult/senior & student/ child 12-18 €5.50/4/3, audioguide €1; ☯ 10am-6pm Tue-Sun Mar, Apr, mid-Jul–Oct; 9.30am-6.30pm Tue-Sun May–mid-Jul, 10am-6pm Thu-Sun Nov)

Office de Tourisme de Vernon (☎ 02 32 51 39 60; tourisme.vernon@wanadoo.fr; 36 rue Carnot; ☯ 9.30am-noon & 2.30-6.30pm Tue-Sat, 10am-noon Sun Apr-Sep, 10am-noon & 2-5pm Tue-Sat Oct-Mar) The clos-est tourist office is in Vernon, 7km to the northwest.

If travelling by train you can stop here before carrying on by bus to Giverny. Otherwise check the excellent Valley of the Impressionists website (www.giverny-art.com).

Eating & Sleeping

Auberge du Vieux Moulin (☎ 02 32 51 46 15; 21 rue de la Falaise; menus €12-24; ⊙ lunch Tue-Sun, dinner to 10.30pm Sat) The lovely little 'Old Mill Inn' a couple of hundred metres east of the Maison de Claude Monet is an excellent place for lunch and has a lovely terrace.

Hôtel La Musardière (☎ 02 32 21 03 18; fax 02 32 21 60 00; 123 rue Claude Monet; s & d €55-70) This lovely 10-room hotel evocatively called the 'Idler' and set amidst a lovely garden is less than 100m northeast of the Maison de Claude Monet.

AUVERS-SUR-OISE

On 20 May 1890 the painter Vincent van Gogh left a mental asylum in Provence and moved to this small village (population 6800) north of Paris on the Oise River both to reacquaint himself with the light he was so familiar with in his native Holland and to be closer to his friend and benefactor Dr Paul Ferdinand Gachet (1828–1909). He set to work immediately, producing at least one painting or sketch every day until his death on 29 July.

Today Auvers-sur-Oise is predominantly a shrine to the great Impressionist painter, and many sights, including five museums, are related to his short stay and large body of work created here. Foremost is the so-called **Maison de Van Gogh** (van Gogh's House), actually the Auberge Ravoux, where the artist stayed during his 70 days here. Apart from the restaurant (p328) on the ground floor, for the most part it's empty though there's an excellent video on van Gogh's life and work, and the bedroom in which he fatally wounded himself is strangely moving.

Northwest of the Maison de van Gogh is the **Maison-Atelier de Daubigny**, the house and studio of the artist Charles-François Daubigny (1818–78) who began the practice of painting *en plein air* (outside) and whose work is considered a precursor to Impressionism. The studio was decorated from top to bottom by the artist with some help from the painters Camille Corot (1796–1875) and Honoré Daumier (1808–79). It is positively stunning.

The sprawling 17th-century **Château d'Auvers**, to the west of the Maison-Atelier de Daubigny, has an audiovisual presentation on van Gogh and other Impressionists who found their way here at some stage, including Paul Cézanne (1839–1906) and Camille Pissarro (1830–1903). Along the way don't miss the opportunity of visiting the **Musée de l'Absinthe**, the unique Absinthe Museum that traces the history of the liqueur that may (or may not have) been the cause of van Gogh's downfall (see the boxed text p329).

A trip to Auvers-sur-Oise should include a visit to the **Église Notre Dame**, subject of van Gogh's *L'Église d'Auvers* (1890) and the **cemetery** where he is buried beside his brother Théo. Note that most places worth seeing in Auvers-sur-Oise are closed in winter.

Transport

Distance from Paris 35km

Direction North

Travel time 70 minutes by train & bus

Car Route A15 from Paris' Porte de Clichy; exit 7 to route N184 (direction Beauvais), exit 'Méry-sur-Oise'

RER Line A3 from Gare de Lyon or Châtelet-Les Halles (€4.50) to Cergy Préfecture station then bus No 95-07 (destination Butry)

Train From Gare du Nord or Gare St-Lazare to Pontoise, change to train heading for Creil and alight at Auvers-sur-Oise. There is a SNCF package (adult/child 6-9 €14.60/8.70) that includes return transport from Paris, bus transfers and admission to the Château d' Auvers. The last train to Paris leaves just after 9pm weekdays and sometime after 10.30pm at the weekend.

Sights & Information

Cemetery (Chemin des Vallées)

Château d'Auvers (☎ 01 34 48 48 45; www .chateau-auvers.fr; rue de Léry; adult/student & child 6-18 €10/6, families €21-25; ⊙ 10.30am-6pm Tue-Fri, 10.30am-6.30pm Sat & Sun Apr-Sep; 10.30am-4.30pm Tue-Fri, 10.30am-5.30pm Sat & Sun Oct-Dec & mid-Jan-Mar)

Église Notre Dame (rue Daubigny)

Maison-Atelier de Daubigny (☎ 01 34 48 03 03; 61 rue Daubigny; admission €5, child under 5 free; ⊙ 2-6.30pm Thu-Sun early-Apr–early-Nov)

AUVERS-SUR-OISE

| 0 | 500 m |
| 0 | 0.3 miles |

SIGHTS & ACTIVITIES (pp327–9)
Cemetery..............................1 C2
Château d'Auvers...................2 A2
Église Notre Dame..................3 C2
Maison de Van Gogh................4 B3
Maison-Atelier de Daubigny.......5 B2
Musée de l'Absinthe................6 B2

EATING 🍴 (pp328–9)
Café de la Paix......................7 B3

SLEEPING 🛏 (pp328–9)
Auberge Ravoux...................(see 4)
Hostellerie du Nord.................8 C3

INFORMATION
Post Office............................9 B3
Société Générale....................10 B3
Tourist Office........................11 B3

Maison de Van Gogh (Auberge Ravoux; ☎ 01 30 36 60 60; 52 rue du Général de Gaulle; adult/family/child under 18 €5/10/free; ☯ 10am-6pm Tue-Sun mid-Mar–mid-Nov) Enter from rue de la Sansonne.

Musée de l'Absinthe (☎ 01 30 36 83 26; 44 rue Callé; adult/student/child under 15 €4.50/3.80/free; ☯ 2-6pm Wed, from 11am Thu-Sun mid-Jun–mid-Sep; 11am-6pm Sat & Sun Oct-May)

Office de Tourisme d'Auvers-sur-Oise (Tourist Office; ☎ 01 30 36 10 06; www-auvers-sur-oise in French; rue de la Sansonne; ☯ 9.30am-12.30pm & 2-6pm Apr-Oct; 9.30am-12.30pm & 2-5pm Nov-Mar) In the delightful Manoir des Colombières, runs an excellent 15-minute tour in English and French that helps put the town's contribution to the Impressionist school of art in perspective.

Post office (place de la Mairie; ☯ 9am-noon & 2.30-5.30 Mon-Fri, 9am-noon Sat)

Sociéte Générale (17 rue du Général du Gaulle; ☯ 9am-noon & 2-5.30pm Mon-Fri, 9am-noon & 2-5pm Sat)

Eating & Sleeping

Auberge Ravoux (☎ 01 30 36 60 63; 52 rue du Général de Gaulle; menus €24 & €30; ☯ lunch Tue-Sun & dinner to 9pm Tue-Sat) What could be a more appropriate way to celebrate the life of Vincent van Gogh than by having lunch or dinner in the house in which he died? The Auberge Ravoux has been a *café d'artistes* (or so they claim) since 1876, so it predates van Gogh's fateful sojourn by more than a dozen years.

Café de la Paix (☎ 01 30 36 73 23; 11 rue du Général de Gaulle; starters €9-10, mains €15-16, menu €12; ☯ 7am-8.30pm Wed-Mon) If the Ravoux is full, head across the road to this cheap and very cheerful café.

Hostellerie du Nord (☎ 01 30 36 70 74; www.hostellerie dunord.fr; 6 rue du Général de Gaulle; s & d €92-122, ste €183) This lovely inn is housed in a 17th-century building that was one of the first post offices in France. Each of the eight beautifully appointed rooms and suites is named after an artist with a connection to Auvers-sur-Oise.

DISNEYLAND RESORT PARIS

It took almost €4.6 billion and five years of work to turn the beet fields east of the capital into Europe's first Disney theme park, which opened in 1992 amid much fanfare and controversy. Although Disney stockholders were less than thrilled with the park's performance for the first few years, what was originally known as Euro-Disney is now very much in the black, and the many visitors – mostly families with young children – can't seem to get enough.

Disneyland Resort Paris consists of three main areas: the **Disney Village**, with its five hotels, shops, restaurants and clubs; **Disneyland Park** with its five theme parks; and **Walt Disney Studios**, which brings film, animation and television production to life. The first two are separated by the RER and TGV train stations; Walt Disney Studios is next to Disneyland Park. Moving walkways whisk visitors to the sights from the far-flung car park.

Disneyland Park is divided into five *pays* (lands). **Main Street, USA**, just inside the main entrance and behind the Disneyland Hotel, is a spotless avenue reminiscent of Norman Rockwell's idealised small-town America

Transport

Distance from Paris 32km

Travel time 35 to 40 minutes by RER

Direction East

Car Route A4 from Porte de Bercy, direction Metz-Nancy and exit No 14

RER Line A4 to Marne-la-Vallée/Chessy, Disneyland's RER station from central Paris (€6). Trains run every 15 minutes or so, with the last train back to Paris at about 12.20am.

circa 1900, complete with Disney characters let loose among the crowds. The adjoining **Frontierland** is a re-creation of the 'rugged, untamed American West'.

Adventureland evoking the Arabian Nights and the wilds of Africa (among other exotic lands portrayed in Disney films), is home to that old favourite, Pirates of the Caribbean, as well as Indiana Jones and the Temple of Peril: a roller coaster that spirals through 360 degrees – in reverse! **Fantasyland** brings fairy-tale characters such as Sleeping Beauty, Pinocchio, Peter Pan and Snow White to life; you'll also find 'It's a Small World' here. **Discoveryland** features a dozen high-tech attractions and rides (including Space Mountain and Orbitron) and futuristic films at Videopolis that pay homage to Leonardo da Vinci, George Lucas and – for a bit of local colour – Jules Verne.

Walt Disney Studios, which opened in March 2002, has a sound stage, production backlot and animation studios that help illustrate up close how films, television programs and cartoons are produced.

Absinthe: Spirit of the Age

It was what marijuana was to the 1960s, and cocaine was to the 1980s. But until absinthe became the drink of choice among artists, artistes and the under-classes (and thus gained in notoriety), it had been a bourgeois favourite, sipped quietly and innocuously in cafés around the land. It was only when the creative world discovered the wormwood-based liqueur and its supposed hallucinogenic qualities that it took off, and everyone from Verlaine, Rimbaud, Wilde, Manet, Degas, Toulouse-Lautrec and, of course, van Gogh wrote about it, painted or drank it. Whether or not it was the *fée verte* (green fairy), as absinthe was known during the *belle époque*, that pushed van Gogh over the edge is not known. Some say he was so poor he couldn't even afford this relatively cheap libation and instead sometimes ate paint containing lead, which may have driven him mad instead. More than anything else the availability and low cost of the spirit led to widespread alcoholism and in 1915, having just entered into war against Germany and its allies, France found it prudent to ban the drink altogether.

Sights & Information

Disneyland Resort Paris (☎ 01 60 30 60 30, UK 0 87 05 03 03 05, USA 407-WDISNEY or 407-934 7639; www .needmagic.com; **Disneyland Park** (Apr-Oct adult/child 3-11 €40/30, Nov-Mar €39/29; ☯ 9am-8pm daily except from 10am Mon-Fri early-May–mid-Jun & Sep-Mar, to 11pm early-Jul–Aug; **Walt Disney Studios Park** (Apr-Oct adult/child 3-11 €40/30, Nov-Mar €39/29; ☯ 9am-6pm late-Jun–early-Sep, 10am-6pm Mon-Fri, 9am-6pm Sat & Sun early-Sep–late-Jun) One-day admission fees include unlimited access to all rides and activities in *either* Disneyland Park or Walt Disney Studios Park. Those who opt for the latter, however, can also enter Disneyland Park three hours before it closes. Multiple-day passes are also available: a **Passe-Partout** (adult/child €49/39) allows entry to both parks for one day while a **Hopper Ticket** (adult/child €109/84 high season, €105/78 low season) allows you to enter and leave both parks as you like over three days, which need not be consecutive but must be used within three years.

Eating & Sleeping

There are 50 restaurants at Disneyland Paris, including venues like the **Silver Spur Steakhouse** in Frontierland and **Annette's Diner** in Disney Village. Depending on the restaurant most have adult *menus* for between €20 and €28 and a children's one for €10. Disneyland Park restaurant hours change according to the season; those in Disney Village are open from 11am or 11.30am to about midnight daily. You are not allowed to picnic inside Disneyland Resort Paris.

Each of the resort's six **hotels** (central booking ☎ 01 60 30 60 30; fax 01 64 74 59 20) has its own all-American theme, reflected in the design, décor, restaurants and entertainment. All of the rooms have two double beds (or, in the case of the Hôtel Cheyenne, one double bed and a set of bunk beds) and can sleep up to four people. Free shuttle buses link the hotels with the parks.

Rates are highest during July and August and around Christmas; on Friday and Saturday nights and during holiday periods from April to October; and on Saturday nights from mid-February to March. The cheapest rates are available on most weeknights (ie Sunday to Thursday or, sometimes, Friday) from January to mid-February, from mid-May to June, for most of September, and from November to mid-December. Most guests stay on some sort of package.

Disneyland Hôtel (d per person €258-599) This 496-room property at the entrance to the two parks bills itself as a 'lavish Victorian fantasy' and is the pinnacle of Disneyland Resort Paris accommodation.

Hôtel Cheyenne (d per person €105-184) The 14 timber-framed buildings of this 1000 room hotel – each with its own hokey name – are arranged to resemble a Wild West frontier town.

Hôtel Santa Fe (d per person €69-139) This 1000-room hotel, which offers the most affordable accommodation in the resort itself, has an American Southwest style.

PARC ASTÉRIX

A local alternative to Disneyland Paris (p329), Parc Astérix is northeast of Paris just beyond Roissy Charles de Gaulle airport. Like Disneyland, it's divided into a number of 'regions' – the Village of the Gauls, the Roman Empire, Ancient Greece, the Middle Ages, Old Paris and so on – and there are lots of rides, including a particularly hair-raising roller coaster called *Tonnère de Zeus* (Zeus' Thunder) and the *Oxygénarium flume*. The Three Musketeers also figure prominently.

Information

Parc Astérix (☎ 08 91 67 67 11; www.parcasterix .com; adult half-/full-day €32/60, child 3-11 half-/full-day €23/42; ☯ 10am-6pm April; 10am-6pm Tue-Thu, 9.30am-7pm Sat & Sun May–mid-Jul, 9.30am-7pm mid-Jul-Aug, 10am-6pm Wed, Sat & Sun Sep–early-Oct) Tickets including admission and all transport to/from the park (adults/children 3-11 €36.85/25.60) are available at most RER and SNCF stations in central Paris.

Transport

Distance from Paris 36km

Travel time 50 to 60 minutes by RER & bus

Direction Northeast

Car Route A1, Parc Astérix exit between exit Nos 7 and 8

RER Line B3 from Châtelet or Gare du Nord to Aéroport Charles de Gaulle 1 train station then Courriers Île-de-France bus (adult/child 3-11 €5.65/4.20 return); every half-hour 9.30am to 6.30pm, return from the park every half hour from 4.30pm to 7pm or 8pm.

Transport 332

Air	332
Bicycle	334
Boat	334
Bus	334
Car & Motorcycle	335
Metro & RER Networks	336
Taxi	337
Train	337
Tram & Funicular	338
Travel Agents	338

Practicalities 338

Accommodation	338
Business	339
Children	339
Climate	340
Courses	340
Customs	341
Disabled Travellers	341
Discount Cards	341
Electricity	342
Embassies	342
Emergency	342
Gay & Lesbian Travellers	343
Holidays	343
Internet Access	344
Laundry	344
Legal Matters	345
Maps	346
Medical Services	346
Metric System	346
Money	346
Newspapers & Magazines	347
Pharmacies	348
Photography	348
Post	348
Radio	348
Safety	349
Tax & Refunds	349
Telephone	349
Television	350
Time	351
Tipping	351
Toilets	351
Tourist Information	351
Visas	352
Websites	353
Women Travellers	353
Work	353

Directory

Directory

TRANSPORT
AIRLINES

Aer Lingus (EI; ☎ 01 70 20 00 72; www.aerlingus.com)

Air Canada (AC; ☎ 08 25 88 08 81; www.aircanada.com)

Air France (AF; ☎ 08 20 82 08 20, arrivals & departures 08 92 68 10 48; www.airfrance.com)

Air Littoral (FU; ☎ 08 25 83 48 34; www.air-littoral.fr)

Air New Zealand (NZ; ☎ 01 40 53 82 83; www.airnz.com)

British Airways (BA; ☎ 08 25 82 54 00; www.british-air ways.com)

British Midland (BD; ☎ 01 41 91 87 04; www.flybmi.com)

Continental Airlines (CO; ☎ 01 42 99 09 09; www.con tinental.com)

Delta Air Lines (DL; ☎ 08 00 35 40 80; www.delta.com)

Easyjet (U2; ☎ 08 25 08 25 08; www.easyjet.com)

KLM (KL; ☎ 08 90 71 07 10; www.klm.com)

Lufthansa Airlines (LH; ☎ 08 20 02 00 30; www.luft hansa.com)

Northwest Airlines (NW; ☎ 08 90 71 07 10; www.nwa.com)

Qantas Airways (QF; ☎ 08 20 82 05 00; www.qantas.com)

Ryanair (FR; ☎ 08 92 68 20 73; www.ryanair.com)

Scandinavian Airlines (SAS; ☎ 08 20 32 53 35; www .scandinavian.net)

Singapore Airlines (SQ; ☎ 01 53 65 79 01; www .singaporeair.com)

Thai Airways International (TG; ☎ 01 44 20 70 80; www.thaiair.com)

United Airlines (UA; ☎ 08 10 72 72 72; www.ual.com)

US Airways (US; ☎ 08 10 63 22 22; www.usairways.com)

Virgin Atlantic (VS; ☎ 08 00 52 85 28; www.virgin -atlantic.com)

AIRPORTS

Paris has two main international airports: Aéroport d'Orly and Aéroport Roissy Charles de Gaulle. A third airport at Beauvais handles flights by some charter companies and Ryanair.

Aéroport d'Orly

The older and smaller of Paris' two major airports, **Orly** (ORY; ☎ 01 49 75 15 15, flight info 08 92 68 15 15; www.adp.fr) is 18km south of the city. Air France and some other international carriers (eg Iberia and TAP Air Portugal) use Orly-Ouest (the west terminal). A driverless overhead rail, linking Orly-Ouest with Orly-Sud, is part of the Orlyval system and functions as a free shuttle between the terminals.

The following are the public-transport options to/from Orly airport. Apart from RATP bus No 183, all services call at both terminals. Tickets for the bus services are sold on board. With certain exceptions, children between the ages of two and 11 pay half-price.

Air France Bus No 1 (☎ 08 92 35 08 20; www.cars-air france.com in French; one way/return €7.50/12.75; 30-45 min; every 15 min, 6am-11.30pm from Orly, 5.45am-11pm from Paris) This *navette* (shuttle bus) runs to/from the eastern side of **Gare Montparnasse** (Map pp389-91; rue du Commandant René Mouchotte, 15e; metro Montparnasse Bienvenüe) as well as **Aérogare des Invalides** (Map pp389-91; metro Invalides) in the 7e. On your way into the city, you can ask to get off at metro Porte d'Orléans or metro Duroc.

Jetbus (☎ 01 69 01 00 09; €5.15; 55 min; every 15-20 min, 6.43am-10.49pm from Orly, 6.15am-10.15pm from Paris) With the exception of RATP bus No 183, Jetbus is the cheapest way to get to/from Orly. It runs to/from metro Villejuif Louis Aragon, which is a bit south of the 13e on the city's southern fringe. From there a regular metro/bus ticket will get you into the centre of Paris.

Orlybus (☎ 08 92 68 77 14; €5.70; 30 min; every 15-20 min 6am-11.30pm from Orly, 5.35am-11pm from Paris) This RATP bus runs to/from metro Denfert Rochereau (Map pp380-2) in the 14e, and makes several stops in the eastern 14e in each direction.

Orlyval (☎ 08 92 68 77 14; €8.80 to/from Paris, €10.65 to/from La Défense; 33 min to Paris, 50 min to La Défense; every 4-12 min, 6am-11pm each direction) This RATP service links Orly with the city centre via a shuttle train and the RER (see p336). A driverless shuttle train runs between the airport and Antony RER station (eight minutes) on RER line B, from where it's an easy journey into the city; to get to Antony from the city (26 minutes), take line B4 towards St-Rémy-lès-Chevreuse. Orlyval tickets are valid for travel on the RER and for metro travel within the city.

RATP Bus No 183 (☎ 08 92 68 77 14; €1.30 or one metro/bus ticket; one hour; every 35 min, 5.35am-8.35pm each direction) This is a slow public bus that links Orly-Sud (only) with metro Porte de Choisy (Map pp380-2), at the southern edge of the 13e.

RER C (☎ 08 90 36 10 10; €5.35; 50 min; every 12-20 min, 5.45am-11pm each direction) An Aéroports de Paris (ADP) shuttle bus links the airport with RER line C at Pont de Rungis-Aéroport d'Orly RER station. From the city, take a C2 train towards Pont de Rungis or Massy-Palaiseau. Tickets are valid for onward travel on the metro.

Along with public transport the following private options are available:

Allô Shuttle (☎ 01 34 29 00 80; www.alloshuttle.com) All provide door-to-door service for about €25 per single person (from about €15 to €18 per person for two or more). Book in advance and allow for numerous pick-ups and drop-offs. Some readers have written to say that some shuttle-van services are less than reliable.

Taxi To/From central Paris and Orly will cost about €40 and take 20 to 30 minutes

Paris Airports Service (☎ 01 46 80 14 67; www.parisair portservice.com),

World Shuttle (☎ 01 46 80 14 67; www.world-shuttles.com)

Shuttle Van PariShuttle (☎ 08 00 69 96 99; www.pari shuttle.com)

Aéroport Roissy Charles de Gaulle

Northeast of Paris in the suburb of Roissy, **Roissy Charles de Gaulle** (CDG; ☎ 01 48 62 22 80, 08 92 68 15 15; www.adp.fr), 30km consists of three terminals, appropriately named Aérogare 1, 2 and 3. Aérogares 1 and 2 are used by international and domestic carriers. Aérogare 3 is used mainly by charter companies.

Roissy Charles de Gaulle has two train stations: Aéroport Charles de Gaulle 1 (CDG1) and the sleek Aéroport Charles de Gaulle 2 (CDG2). Both are served by commuter trains on RER line B3. A free shuttle bus links all of the terminals with the train stations.

There are various public-transport options for travel between Aéroport Roissy Charles de Gaulle and Paris. Tickets for the bus services are sold on board. With certain exceptions, children between two and 11 pay half-price.

Air France bus No 2 (☎ 08 92 35 08 20; www.cars-air france.com in French; one way/return €10/17; 35-50 min; every 15 min, 5.45am-11pm each direction) Links the airport with two locations on the Right Bank: near the Arc de Triomphe just outside **2 av Carnot, 17e** (Map pp383-5; metro Charles de Gaulle-Étoile) and the **Palais des Congrès de Paris** (Map pp383-5; blvd Gouvion St-Cyr, 17e; metro Porte Maillot).

Air France bus No 4 (☎ 08 92 35 08 20; www.cars-air france.com in French; one way/return 11.50/19.55; 45-55

min; every 30 min, 7am-9pm from the airport, 7am-9.30pm from Paris) Links the airport with **Gare de Lyon** (Map pp392-5; 20bis blvd Diderot, 12e; metro Gare de Lyon) and **Gare Montparnasse** (Map pp389-91; rue du Commandant René Mouchotte, 15e; metro Montparnasse Bienvenüe).

RATP Bus Nos 350 (☎ 08 92 68 77 14; €3.90 or three metro/bus tickets; 1¼hr, every 30 min, 5.45am-7pm each direction) Links Aérogares 1 and 2 with **Gare de l'Est** (Map pp386-8; rue du 8 Mai 1945, 10e; metro Gare de l'Est) and **Gare du Nord** (Map pp386-8; 184 rue du Faubourg St-Denis, 10e; metro Gare du Nord).

RATP Bus No 351 (☎ 08 92 68 77 14; €3.90 or three metro/bus tickets; 55 min; every 30 min, 6am-9.30pm from the airport, 6am-8.20pm from Paris) Links the eastern side of **place de la Nation** (Map pp380-2; av du Trône, 11e; metro Nation) with Roissy Charles de Gaulle.

RER B (☎ 08 90 36 10 10; €7.75; 30 min; every 4-15 min, 4.56am-11.40pm in each direction) RER line B3 links CDG1 and CDG2 with the city. To get to the airport take any RER line B train whose four-letter destination code begins with E (eg EIRE) and a shuttle bus (every five to eight minutes) will take you to the correct terminal. Regular metro ticket windows can't always sell RER tickets to the airport so you may have to buy one at the RER station where you board.

Roissybus (☎ 08 92 68 77 14; €8.20; 60 min; every 15-20 min, 5.45am-11pm in each direction) This public bus links both terminals with **rue Scribe** (Map pp383-5; metro Opéra) behind the Palais Garnier in the 9e.

In addition to the public-transport options you can use the following:

Shuttle Van The four companies in the Orly section (see p332) will take you from Roissy Charles de Gaulle to your hotel for €25 for a single person, or €15 to €18 for two or more people. Book in advance.

Taxi To/from the city centre cost from €40 to €55, depending on the traffic and time of day.

Between Orly & Roissy Charles de Gaulle

Air France bus No 3 (☎ 08 92 35 08 20; www.cars -airfrance.com in French; €15.50; every 30 min 6am-10.30pm; journey time 50-60 min) This bus runs between Orly and Roissy Charles de Gaulle and is free for Air France passengers making flight connections.

Taxi The fare from one airport to the other should cost around €56. Count on one hour's travel time.

Aéroport Paris-Beauvais

Eighty kilometres north of Paris, the **Aéroport Paris-Beauvais** (BVA; ☎ 03 44 11 46 86; www.aeroport

beauvais.com) is used by charter companies and Ryanair for its discount European flights, including those between Paris and Dublin, Shannon and Glasgow.

Express Bus (☎ 08 92 68 20 64; 1-1¼hr; 8.40am to 10.10pm from Beauvais, 5.45am-7.15pm from Paris) Leaves **Parking Pershing** (Map pp383-5; 1 blvd Pershing, 17e; metro Porte Maillot), just west of the Palais des Congrès de Paris, three hours before each Ryanair departure (you can board up to 15 minutes before) and leaves the airport 20 to 30 minutes after each arrival, dropping passengers off just south of the Palais des Congrès on Place de la Porte Maillot. Tickets can be purchased from **Ryanair** (☎ 03 44 11 41 41) at the airport or from a kiosk in the parking lot.

Taxi Between central Paris and Beauvais costs €110 during the day, and €150 at night and all day Sunday.

Websites

As well as airline websites (see p332), there are a number of efficient online resources for buying good-value plane tickets. Some of the best include the following:

Anyway (www.anyway.fr in French)

Bargain Holidays (www.bargainholidays.com)

Cheap Flights (www.cheapflights.co.uk)

easyvols (www.easyvols.com in French)

ebookers (www.ebookers.com)

e-mondial (www.e-mondial.com in French)

Go Voyages (www.govoyages.com in French)

Last Minute (www.lastminute.com)

Opodo (www.opodo.com)

Travelocity (www.travelocity.com)

Voyages SNCF (www.voyages-sncf.com in French)

BICYCLE

For detailed information on where and how to cycle in Paris, see p246.

BOAT

Batobus (☎ 01 44 11 33 99; www.batobus.com; adult/child 2-6 1-day pass €11/6, 2-day pass €13/7; every 25 min 10am-7pm, 10am-9pm Jun-Sep), a fleet of five glassed-in trimarans, docks at small piers below the following eight locations. As you can jump on and off at will, Batobus can be used as a form of transport.

Champs-Élysées (Map pp383-5; Port des Champs-Élysées, 8e; metro Champs-Élysées Clemenceau)

Musée du Louvre (Map pp396-9; quai du Louvre, 1er; metro Palais Royal-Musée du Louvre)

Hôtel de Ville (Map pp396-9; metro Hôtel de Ville; quai de l'Hôtel de Ville, 4e)

Jardin des Plantes (Map pp392-5; quai St-Bernard, 5e; metro Jussieu)

Notre Dame (Map pp396-9; quai Montebello, 5e; metro St-Michel)

St-Germain des Prés (Map pp396-9; quai Malaquais, 6e; metro St-Germain des Prés)

Musée d'Orsay (Map pp389-91; quai de Solférino, 7e; metro Musée d'Orsay)

Eiffel Tower (Map pp389-91; Port de la Bourdonnais, 7e; metro Champ de Mars-Tour Eiffel)

For pleasure cruises on the Seine, Canal St-Martin and Canal de l'Ourcq, see p77.

BUS
Local

Paris' bus system, which is operated by the Régie Autonome des Transports Parisiens (RATP; see p336), runs from 5.45am to 8.30pm Monday to Saturday; after that another 20 lines continue until 12.30am. Services are drastically reduced on Sunday and public holidays when buses run from 7am to 8.30pm. Key *service en sorée* (evening service) routes – distinct from the Noctambus overnight services described later in this section – are: No 26 between the Gare St-Lazare and Cours de Vincennes via Gare du Nord and Gare de l'Est; No 38 linking Châtelet and Porte d'Orléans via blvd St-Michel; No 92 from Gare Montparnasse to place Charles de Gaulle and back via Alma Marceau; and No 95 between Porte de Montmartre and Porte de Vanves via Opéra and St-Germain. Bus fares in the evening and on Sunday and public holidays are the same as those for regular daytime services, and all passes are honoured.

NIGHT BUSES

After the metro lines have finished their last runs at about 1am, the Noctambus network of night buses links place du Châtelet (1er) and av Victoria, just west of the Hôtel de Ville (Map pp396-9) in the 4e, with most parts of the city and the suburbs. Look for the symbol of a little black owl silhouetted against a yellow quarter moon. All 18 Noctambus lines (designated A to V, with N, O, Q and U missing) depart hourly weekdays and half-hourly at weekends (from 1am to 5.30am).

Noctambus services are free if you have a Carte Orange, Mobilis or Paris Visite pass for the zones in which you are travelling. Otherwise, a single ride costs €2.60 and allows one immediate transfer onto another Noctambus.

TICKETS & FARES
Short bus rides (ie one or two bus zones) cost one metro/bus ticket (see p336); longer rides require two tickets. Transfers to other buses or the metro are not allowed on the same ticket. Travel to the suburbs costs up to three tickets, depending on the zone. Special tickets valid only on the bus can be purchased from the driver.

Whatever kind of single-journey ticket you have, you must cancel (oblitérer) it in the composteur (cancelling machine) next to the driver. If you have a Carte Orange, Mobilis or Paris Visite pass (see p337), just flash it at the driver when you board. Do not cancel the magnetic coupon that accompanies your pass.

Long Distance
Eurolines (Map pp396-9; ☎ 01 43 54 11 99, 08 92 89 90 91; www.eurolines.fr; 55 rue St-Jacques, 5e; metro Cluny-La Sorbonne; ☒ 9.30am-6.30pm Mon-Fri, 10am-1pm & 2-6pm Sat), an association of more than 30 national and private bus companies that links Paris with points all over Western and Central Europe, Scandinavia and Morocco, can book you seats and sell you tickets. The **Gare Routière Internationale de Paris-Galliéni** (Map pp380-2; ☎ 08 92 89 90 91; 28 av du Général de Gaulle; metro Gallieni), the city's international bus terminal, is in the inner suburb of Bagnolet.

CAR & MOTORCYCLE
The easiest way to turn a stay in Paris into an uninterrupted series of hassles is to arrive by car. If driving the car doesn't destroy your holiday sense of spontaneity, parking the damn thing will. But while driving in Paris is nerve-wracking, it is not impossible – except for the faint-hearted or indecisive. The fastest way to get across the city is usually via the blvd Périphérique (Map pp380–2), the ring road that encircles the city.

Hire
You can get a small car (eg a Renault Twingo) for one day, without insurance and 250km mileage, from around €71 with Budget. Most of the larger companies listed below have offices at the airports and several are also represented at **Aérogare des Invalides** (Map pp389–91; metro Invalides) in the 7e.

Avis (☎ 08 02 05 05 05; www.avis.fr)

Budget (☎ 08 25 00 35 64; www.budget.fr in French)

Europcar (☎ 08 25 35 83 58; www.europcar.fr in French)

Hertz (☎ 08 25 86 18 61; www.hertz.fr)

Smaller agencies often offer much more attractive deals. For example, Rent A Car Système has an economical-class car from €30 per day and €0.30 per km, €45/69 a day with 100/300km, €90 for a weekend with 500km and €199 for seven days with 800km. The companies listed here offer reasonable rates; a wider selection is in the Yellow Pages under 'Location d'Automobiles: Tourisme et Utilitaires'. It's a good idea to reserve at least three days ahead, especially for holiday weekends and during the summer.

ADA (☎ 08 25 16 91 69; www.ada-location.com in French) ADA has a dozen branches in Paris including: **8e arrondissement** (Map pp383-5; ☎ 01 42 93 65 13; 72 rue de Rome, 8e; metro Rome); **11e arrondissement** (Map pp386-8; ☎ 01 48 06 58 13; 34 av de la République, 11e; metro Parmentier)

easyCar (www.easycar.com) Britain's budget car-rental agency hires mini Mercedes from €13 a day plus extras, and Smart cars (from €8) from these branches: **Montparnasse** (Map pp389-91; Parking Gaîté, 33 rue du Commandant René Mouchotte, 15e; metro Gaîté); **place Vendôme** (Map pp383-5; ☎ /fax 01 40 15 60 17; 1er; metro Tuileries or Opéra). Both are in underground car parks and are fully automated systems; you must book in advance and fill in all the forms on line on location.

Rent A Car Système (☎ 08 91 70 02 00; www.rentacar.fr) Rent A Car has 16 outlets in Paris, including: **Gare du Nord** (Map pp386-8; ☎ 01 42 80 31 31; 2 rue de Compiègne, 10e; metro Gare du Nord); **Bercy** (Map pp401; ☎ 01 43 45 98 99; 79 rue de Bercy, 12e; metro Bercy); **16e arrondissement** (Map pp380-2; ☎ 01 42 88 40 04; 84 av de Versailles, 16e; metro Mirabeau).

If you've got the urge to look like you've just stepped into (or out of) a B&W French film from the 1950s, a motor scooter will fit the bill perfectly.

Free Scoot (Map pp392-5; ☎ 01 44 93 04 03; www.free-scoot.com; 144 blvd Voltaire, 11e; metro Voltaire; 9am-1pm & 2-7pm Mon-Fri) Rents out 50cc scooters for per day (9am-6pm)/24-hour day/weekend/week €30/35/75/145, and 125cc scooters for €45/55/110/245. Prices include third-party insurance as well as two helmets, locks, raingear and gloves. To rent a 50cc scooter you must be at least 21 and leave a credit-card deposit of €1300. For a 125cc one, the minimum age is 23 and the deposit is €1600 deposit. There's also a branch in the **5e arrondissement** (Map pp396-9; ☎ 01 44 07 06 72; 63 quai de la Tournelle, 5e; metro Maubert Mutualité).

Parking

In many parts of Paris you have to pay €1.50 to €2 an hour to park your car on the street. Municipal parking garages usually charge €2.60 an hour and between €20 and €23 for 24 hours.

Parking fines are €11 to €33, depending on the offence and its gravity, and parking attendants dispense them with great abandon. You pay them by purchasing a *timbre amende* (fine stamp) for the amount written on the ticket from any *tabac* (tobacconist), affixing the stamp to the preaddressed coupon and dropping it in a letter box.

METRO & RER NETWORKS

Paris' underground network, which is run by the RATP (Régie Autonome des Transports Parisians), consists of two separate but linked systems: the Métropolitain, known as the *métro*, with 14 lines and 372 stations; and the Réseau Express Régional (RER), a network of suburban lines (designated A to E and then numbered) that pass through the city centre. When giving the names of stations in this book, the term 'metro' is used to cover both the Métropolitain and the RER system within Paris proper.

Information

Metro maps of various sizes and degrees of detail are available for free at metro ticket windows. RATP *Paris 1* provides plans of metro, RER, bus and tram routes in central Paris; *Paris 2* superimposes the same over street maps; and *Île-de-France 3* covers the area around Paris. *Touristes: Grand Plan Touristique* combines all three and adds tourist information.

For information on the metro, RER and bus systems, contact **RATP** (☎ 08 92 68 77 14 in French, ☎ 08 92 68 41 14 in English ☯ 6am-9pm daily; www.ratp.fr in French). For itineraries, traffic and so on, log onto www.citefutee .com (in French).

Metro

Each metro train is known by the name of its terminus. On maps and plans each line has a different colour and number (from one to 14); the latter are now used by Parisians when differentiating the lines.

Blue-on-white *direction* signs in metro and RER stations indicate the way to the correct platform for your line. On lines that split into several branches (like line Nos 3, 7 and 13), the terminus served by each train is indicated on the cars with back-lit panels.

Older black-on-orange signs marked *correspondance* (transfer) and newer ones listing the lines in their individual colours show how to reach connecting trains. In general, the more lines that stop at a station, the longer the transfer will take – and some (eg those at Châtelet and Montparnasse Bienvenüe) are *very* long indeed.

White-on-blue *sortie* signs indicate the station exits from which you have to choose. You can get your bearings by checking the *plan du quartier* (neighbourhood map) posted at each exit.

The last metro train on each line begins its run sometime between 12.35am and 1.04am. The metro starts up again around 5.30am.

RER

The RER is faster than the metro but the stops are much further apart. Some attractions, particularly those on the Left Bank (eg the Musée d'Orsay, Eiffel Tower and Panthéon), can be reached far more conveniently by the RER than by metro.

RER lines are known by an alphanumeric combination – the letter (A to E) refers to the line, the number to the spur it will follow somewhere out in the suburbs. As a rule of thumb, even-numbered RER lines head for Paris' southern or eastern suburbs while odd-numbered ones go north or west. All trains whose four-letter codes (indicated both on the train and on the lightboard) begin with the same letter share the same terminus. Stations served are usually indicated on electronic destination boards above the platform.

TICKETS & FARES

The same RATP tickets are valid on the metro, the RER (for travel within the city limits), buses, trams and the Montmartre funicular. They cost €1.30 if bought individually and €10 (€5 for children four to 11) for a *carnet* (book) of 10. Tickets are sold at all metro stations, though not always at every entrance. Ticket windows and vending machines accept most credit cards.

One metro/bus ticket lets you travel between any two metro stations for a period of two hours, no matter how many transfers are required. You can also use it on the RER for travel within zone 1. However, a single ticket cannot be used to transfer from the metro to a bus, from a bus to the metro or between buses.

Always keep your ticket until you exit from your station; you may be stopped by a *contrôleur* (ticket inspector) and will have to pay a fine (€20 to €40 on the spot), if you don't have a valid ticket.

TRAVEL PASSES

The cheapest and easiest way to use public transport in Paris is to get a **Carte Orange**, a combined metro, RER and bus pass whose accompanying magnetic coupon comes in weekly and monthly versions. You can get tickets for travel in two to eight urban and suburban zones but, unless you'll be using the suburban commuter lines extensively, the basic ticket valid for zones 1 and 2 should be sufficient.

A weekly Carte Orange (*coupon hebdomdaire*) costs €14.50 for zones 1 and 2, and is valid from Monday to Sunday. It can be purchased from the previous Thursday until Wednesday; from Thursday weekly tickets are available for the following week only. Even if you'll only be in Paris for three or four days, it may work out cheaper than buying carnets and it will certainly cost less than buying a daily Mobilis or Paris Visite pass (see p337). The Carte Orange monthly ticket (*coupon mensuel*; €48.60 for zones 1 and 2) begins on the first day of each calendar month; you can buy one from the 20th of the preceding month. Both are on sale in metro and RER stations from 6.30am to 10pm and at certain bus terminals. You can also buy your Carte Orange coupon from vending machines and, if you have a French postal address, on the RATP website (www.ratp.fr).

When buying a Carte Orange for the first time, take a passport-size photograph (four photos are available from photo booths in train and many metro stations for €4) of yourself to any metro or RER ticket window. Request a Carte Orange (which is free) and the kind of coupon (weekly or monthly) you'd like. To prevent tickets from being used by more than one person, you must write your surname (*nom*) and first name (*prénom*) on the Carte Orange, and the number of your Carte Orange on the weekly or monthly coupon you've bought.

TOURIST PASSES

The Mobilis and Paris Visite passes are valid on the metro, RER, SNCF's suburban lines (see below), buses, night buses, trams and the Montmartre funicular railway. No photo is needed but write your card number on the ticket.

The **Mobilis** card coupon allows unlimited travel for one day in two to eight zones (€5.20 to €18.30). It is available at all metro and RER stations as well as SNCF stations in the Paris region. You would have to make at least six metro trips in a day (based on the carnet price) in zones 1 and 2 to break even on this pass.

Paris Visite passes, which allow the holder discounted entry to certain museums and activities as well as discounts on transport fares, are valid for either three, five or eight zones. The version covering one to three zones costs €8.35/13.70/18.25/26.65 for one/two/three/five days. Children four to 11 pay €4.55/6.85/9.15/13.70. The passes can be purchased at larger metro and RER stations, SNCF offices in Paris, and the airports.

TAXI

The *prise en charge* (flag-fall) is €2. Within the city limits, it costs €0.62 per km for travel between 7am and 7pm Monday to Saturday (*Tarif A*; white light on meter), and €1.06 per km from 7pm to 7am, all day Sunday and public holidays (*Tarif B*; orange light on meter). Travel in the suburbs (*Tarif C*) is €1.24 per km.

There's a €2.60 surcharge for taking a fourth passenger, but most drivers refuse to accept more than three people for insurance reasons. Each piece of baggage over 5kg costs €0.90 extra, an animal costs €0.60 and pick-ups from SNCF mainline stations cost another €0.70.

Radio-dispatched taxi companies, on call 24 hours, include:

Alpha Taxis (☎ 01 45 85 85 85)

Artaxi (☎ 01 42 41 50 50)

Taxis Bleus (☎ 01 49 36 10 10)

Taxis G7 (☎ 01 47 39 47 39)

Taxis Radio 7000 (☎ 01 42 70 00 42)

Taxis-Radio Étoile (☎ 01 42 70 41 41)

TRAIN
Suburban

The RER and the commuter lines of the **SNCF** (Sociéte' Nationale des Chemins de Fer; ☎ 08 91 36 20 20, 08 91 67 68 69 for timetables;

www.sncf.fr) serve suburban destinations outside the city limits (ie zones 2 to 8). Purchase your ticket *before* you board the train or you won't be able to get out of the station when you arrive. You are not allowed to pay the additional fare when you get there.

If you are issued with a full-sized SNCF ticket for travel to the suburbs, validate it in one of the time-stamp pillars *before* you board the train. You may also be given a *contremarque magnétique* (magnetic ticket) to get through any metro/RER-type turnstiles on the way to/from the platform. If you are travelling on a multizone Carte Orange, Paris Visite or Mobilis pass, do *not* punch the magnetic coupon in one of SNCF's time-stamp machines. Most, but not all RER/SNCF tickets purchased in the suburbs for travel to the city allow you to continue your journey by metro. For some destinations, tickets can be purchased at any metro ticket window; for others you'll have to go to an RER station on the line you need in order to buy a ticket.

Mainline & International

Paris has six major train stations, each of which has its own metro station: Gare d'Austerlitz (13e), Gare de l'Est (10e), Gare de Lyon (12e), Gare du Nord (10e), Gare Montparnasse (15e) and Gare St-Lazare (8e). Each station handles passenger traffic to different parts of France and the rest of Europe. Information for **SNCF mainline services** (☎ 08 92 35 35 35; www.sncf .com) is available by phone or Internet.

All the stations have left-luggage offices or lockers. They cost €3.40/5/7.50 for 48 hours for a medium/large/extra large bag. After that it costs €4.50 a day. Be warned that most left-luggage offices and lockers are closed to the public from about 11.15pm to between 6.15am and 6.45am.

TRAM & FUNICULAR

Paris has two tram lines: T1 links the northern suburb of St-Denis with Noisy le Sec on RER line E2 via metro Bobigny Pablo Picasso on metro line No 5; T2 runs south along the Seine from La Défense to the Issy Val de Seine RER station on line C. However it is unlikely that most visitors will make use of either. The national and Île de France governments have undertaken an ambitious scheme to extend these lines around Paris over the next decade so that eventually they will completely encircle Paris about 5km outside the Périphérique.

One form of transport that most travellers will use is the Montmartre funicular, which whisks visitors up the southern slope of Butte de Montmartre from square Willette (metro Anvers) to Sacré Cœur.

TRAVEL AGENTS

You'll find travel agencies everywhere in Paris but the following are among the largest and offer the best service (if not always deals):

Forum Voyages (www.forum-voyages.fr in French; ☉ 9.30am-7pm Mon-Sat) Has nine outlets in Paris, including branches at: **Opéra** (Map pp386-8; ☎ 01 42 61 20 20; 11 av de l'Opéra, 1er; metro Pyramides); **Latin Quarter** (Map pp392-5; ☎ 01 53 10 50 50; 28 rue Monge, 5e; metro Cardinal Lemoine)

Latin Nouvelles Frontières (☎ 08 25 00 08 25; www .nouvelles-frontieres.fr in French; ☉ 9am-7pm Mon-Sat) Has 22 outlets around the city, including: **Opéra** (Map pp386-8; ☎ 01 42 61 02 62; 13 av de l'Opéra, 1er; metro Pyramides); **Odéon** (Map pp396-9; ☎ 01 43 25 71 35; 116 blvd St-Germain, 6e; metro Odéon)

OTU Voyages (☎ 08 20 81 78 17; www.otu.fr in French) There's a branch opposite the Centre Pompidou (see p280), plus one at **Luxembourg** (Map pp392-5; ☎ 08 25 00 40 27; 39 av Georges Bernanos, 5e; metro Port Royal; ☉ 9am-6.30pm Mon-Fri, 10am-noon & 1.15-5pm Sat)

Quarter (Map pp392-5; ☎ 01 53 10 50 50; 28 rue Monge, 5e; metro Cardinal Lemoine)

Voyageurs du Monde (Map pp386-8; ☎ 01 42 86 16 00; www.vdm.com in French; 55 rue Ste-Anne, 2e; metro Pyramides or Quatre-Septembre; ☉ 9.30am-7pm Mon-Sat) 'World Travellers' is an enormous agency with more than 10 departments dealing with different destinations. There's also a good **travel bookshop** (☎ 01 42 86 17 38; ☉ 9.30am-7pm Mon-Sat) downstairs. The agency has its own restaurant (see p159) next door serving daily specialities from around the world and a **shop & exhibition centre** (☎ 01 42 86 16 25; ☉ 9.30am-7pm Mon-Sat; 50 rue Ste-Anne) opposite.

PRACTICALITIES
ACCOMMODATION

The accommodation options in this guide are listed alphabetically by area for mid- and top-range hotels, followed by a separate 'cheap sleeps' section. When budgeting for your trip remember that hotel rates often rise in the spring and summer, while there are often bargains to be had during the late autumn and winter months.

For details on accommodation costs in Paris and useful agencies and websites for finding and booking hotels see p280.

BUSINESS

Before you leave home, it's a good idea to contact one of the main commercial offices or your embassy's trade office in Paris. These include the following:

American Chamber of Commerce (☎ 01 56 43 45 67; www.amchamfrance.org; 156 blvd Haussmann, 75008 Paris)

Australian Trade Commission (☎ 01 40 59 33 85; paris@austrade.gov.au; 4 rue Jean Rey, 75015 Paris)

Canadian Government Department of Commercial & Economic Affairs (☎ 01 44 43 29 00; www.amb-canada .fr; 35 av Montaigne, 75008 Paris)

Chambre de Commerce et d'Industrie de Paris (CCIP; ☎ 01 53 40 46 00; www.ccip.fr; 2 place de la Bourse, 75002 Paris)

France-Canada Chamber of Commerce (☎ 01 43 59 32 38; www.ccfc-france-canada.com in French; 9-11 av Franklin D Roosevelt, 75008 Paris)

Franco-British Chamber of Commerce & Industry (☎ 01 53 30 81 30; www.francobritishchamber.com; 31 rue Boissy d'Anglas, 75008 Paris)

Irish Embassy Trade Office (☎ 01 53 43 12 00; irembparis@wanadoo.fr; 4 rue Rude, 75016 Paris)

New Zealand Embassy Trade Office (☎ 01 45 01 43 10; nzembassy.paris@wanadoo.fr; 7ter rue Léonard de Vinci, 75116 Paris)

UK Embassy Trade Office (☎ 01 44 51 34 56; www .amb-grandebretagne.fr; 35 rue du Faubourg St-Honoré, 75008 Paris)

US Embassy Trade Office (☎ 01 43 12 22 22; www.amb -usa.fr; 2 av Gabriel, 75008 Paris)

If you are looking to set up a business in France and need a temporary office or secretarial assistance, contact the following:

NewWorks (Map pp383-5; ☎ 01 72 74 24 44; www .newworks.net in French; 12 rue Auber, 9e; metro Auber or Havre-Caumartin; 🕒 8.30am-8.30pm Mon-Fri) This *service bureau* chain can supply most of your office and secretarial needs and can serve as your temporary office. There are three other outlets, including **NewWorks Champs-Élysées** (Map pp383-5; ☎ 01 72 74 24 54; 10 rue du Colisée, 8e; metro Franklin D Roosevelt).

Copy-Top (www.copytop.com in French) This chain is useful for photocopying, printing etc and has more than 24 Paris branches, including **Copy-Top Voltaire** (Map pp392-5; ☎ 01 48 05 80 84; 87 blvd Voltaire, 11e; metro Voltaire; 🕒 8.30am-6pm Mon-Fri).

Business Hours

Most museums are closed on either Monday or Tuesday each week. A few places stay open until as late as 10pm one night a week, including the Louvre (Monday and Wednesday) and the Musée d'Orsay (Thursday).

Small businesses are open daily, except Sunday and often Monday. Hours are usually 9am or 10am to 6.30pm or 7pm, usually with a midday break from 1pm to 2pm or 2.30pm.

Banks usually open from 8am or 9am to between 11.30am and 1pm, and then 1.30pm or 2pm to 4.30pm or 5pm, Monday to Friday or Tuesday to Saturday. Exchange services may end 30 minutes before closing time.

Most post offices open 8am to 7pm weekdays and 8am or 9am till noon Saturdays.

Supermarkets open Monday to Saturday, though a few open on Sunday morning. Small food shops are mostly closed on Sunday and often Monday too, so Saturday afternoon may be your last chance to stock up until Tuesday.

Restaurants keep the most convoluted hours of any business in Paris (see p150).

CHILDREN

Paris abounds in places that will delight children, and there is always a special child's entry rate to paying attractions (though eligibility ages vary). Visits can be designed around a stop (or picnic) at the places listed here; more details are in the Quarters & Arrondissements chapter (see also the boxed text Top Five for Children on p107). For details about theme parks in the area, see p330 and p329.

Bastille (Map pp392-5; 4e) Playground at Port de Plaisance de Paris-Arsenal.

Bois de Boulogne (Map pp380-2) Jardin d'Acclimatation; Exploradôme.

Bois de Vincennes (Map pp380-2 & Map p401) Parc Zoologique de Paris; Parc Floral de Paris.

Champs-Élysées (Map pp383-5; 8e) Palais de la Découverte.

Eiffel Tower (Map pp389-91; 7e) Parc du Champ de Mars.

Forum des Halles (Map pp396-9; 1er) Jardin des Enfants aux Halles.

Jardin des Plantes (Map pp392-5; 5e) Ménagerie; Musée National d'Histoire Naturelle.

La Villette (Map pp380-2; 19e) Parc de la Villette; Cité des Sciences et de l'Industrie; Géode; Cinaxe.

Luxembourg (Map pp392-5; 6e) Jardin du Luxembourg.

Montmartre (Map p400; 18e) Playground at Square Willette.

Lonely Planet's *Travel with Children* by Cathy Lanigan includes all sorts of useful advice for those travelling with their little ones. If you read French, the newspaper *Libération* (see p16) produces a supplement every other month called *Paris Mômes* (Paris Kids) with listings and other information aimed at kids to age 12. An excellent website is www.babygoes2.com.

Baby-sitting

L'Officiel des Spectacles, the weekly entertainment magazine that appears on newsstands every Wednesday, lists *gardes d'enfants* (baby-sitters) available in Paris.

Après la Classe (Map p386–8; ☎ 01 42 33 75 45; 63 blvd Sébastopol, 1er; metro Châtelet les Halles) From €6 per hour (€10 subscription fee).

Baby Sitting Services (☎ 01 46 21 33 16) From €6.30 per hour (€10.90 subscription).

Étudiants de l'Institut Catholique (Map p389–91; ☎ 01 44 39 60 24; 21 rue d'Assas, 6e; metro Rennes) From €6 per hour plus €1.60 for each session.

CLIMATE

The Paris basin lies midway between coastal Brittany and mountainous Alsace and is affected by both climates. The Île de France region records the nation's lowest annual precipitation (about 575mm), but rainfall is erratic; you're just as likely to be caught in a heavy spring shower or an autumn downpour as in a sudden summer cloudburst. Paris' average yearly temperature is 15°C (6°C in January, 24°C in July), but the mercury sometimes drops below zero in winter and can climb to the mid-30s in the middle of summer.

You can find out the weather forecast in French for the Paris area by calling ☎ 08 92 68 02 75. The national forecast can be heard on ☎ 08 99 70 11 11 (€1.34 then €0.34 per minute) or read for free on the Internet at www.meteoconsult.fr.

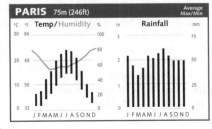

COURSES
Cooking

What better place to discover the secrets of la cuisine Française than in Paris? Courses are available at different levels and lengths of time and the cost of tuition varies widely. One of the most popular – and affordable – is **Cours de Cuisine Françoise Meunier** (Map pp386–8; ☎ 01 40 26 14 00; www.fmeunier.com; 7 rue Paul Lelong, 2e; metro Bourse), which offers three-hour courses (adult/child 12 to 14 €90/60) at 2.30pm on Tuesday and at 10.30am from Wednesday to Saturday. 'Carnets' of five/20 courses cost €400/1500.

Other major cooking schools in Paris include the following.

École de Gastronomie Française Ritz Escoffier (Map pp383–5; ☎ 01 43 16 30 50; www.ritzparis.com; 38 rue Cambon, 1er; metro Concorde)

École Le Cordon Bleu (Map pp389–91; ☎ 01 53 68 22 50; www.cordonbleu.edu; 8 rue Léon Delhomme, 15e; metro Vaugirard or Convention)

École Lenôtre (Map pp383–5; ☎ 01 45 02 21 19; www.lenotre.fr; Pavillon Élysée, 10 av des Champs-Élysées, 8e; metro Champs-Élysées Clemenceau)

Language

All manner of French-language courses, lasting from two weeks to a full academic year, are available in Paris, and many places begin new courses every month or so.

Alliance Française (Map pp389–91; ☎ 01 42 84 90 00; www.alliancefr.org; 101 blvd Raspail, 6e; metro St-Placide; office ☀ 8.30am-6pm Mon-Fri) Month-long French courses at all levels begin on the first working day of each month; registration (€50) takes place five days before. If there's space, it's possible to enrol for just two weeks. *Intensif* courses (€596) meet for four hours a day (ie 64 hours a month); *extensif* courses (€298) involve two hours of class a day (32 hours a month).

Cours de Langue et Civilisation Françaises de la Sorbonne (Map pp392–5; ☎ 01 40 46 22 11; www.fle.fr/sorbonne; 47 rue des Écoles, 5e; metro Cluny-La Sorbonne or Maubert Mutualité; ☀ 11am-4pm Mon-Fri) The Sorbonne's prestigious French Language and Civilisation Course caters for students at all levels. Costs vary: a four-week summer course starts at €480, while 20 hours a week of lectures and tutorials costs €1200 per semester. The instructors take a very academic (though solid) approach to language teaching.

Eurocentres (Map pp396–9; ☎ 01 40 46 72 00; www.eurocentres.com; 13 passage Dauphine, 6e; metro Odéon; ☀ 8.30am-6pm Mon-Fri) Paris branch of the Zürich-based chain. Two-/four-week intensive courses with 10 to 13 participants cost from €720/1392. New courses begin every two, three or four weeks.

Institut Parisien de Langue et de Civilisation Françaises (Map pp389-91; ☎ 01 40 56 09 53; www.institutparisien .com; 87 blvd de Grenelle, 15e; metro Dupleix; 🕑 8.30am-5pm Mon-Fri) Four-week courses with a maximum of 12 students per class cost €129/194/258/323 for 10/15/20/25 hours a week plus an enrolment fee (€40).

Langue Onze (Map pp386-8; ☎ 01 43 38 22 87; www .langueonzeparis.com; 15 rue Gambey, 11e; metro Parmentier; 🕑 11am-5pm Mon-Fri) This small, independent language school gets good reviews from readers. Two-/four-week intensive courses are €315/535 and evening classes (four hours a week) start at €160 a month. Classes have a maximum of nine students.

CUSTOMS

Duty-free shopping within the EU was abolished in 1999; you cannot, for example, buy tax-free goods in, say, France and take them to the UK. However, you can still enter an EU country with duty-free items from countries *outside* the EU (eg Australia, the USA).

The usual allowances apply to duty-free goods purchased at airports or on ferries originating outside the EU: 200 cigarettes, 50 cigars, 100 small cigars or 250g of loose tobacco; 2L of still wine and 1L of spirits of 22% or less, or 2L of fortified wine of 22% or less; 50g of perfume; 250cc of eau de toilette; and other duty-free goods to the value of €175.

Do not confuse these with *duty-paid* items (including alcohol and tobacco) bought at normal shops and supermarkets in another EU country and brought into France, where certain goods might be more expensive. Here allowances are more than generous: 800 cigarettes, 200 cigars, 400 small cigars or 1kg of loose tobacco; and 10L of spirits (more than 22% alcohol by volume), 20L of fortified wine or aperitif, 90L of wine or 110L of beer.

DISABLED TRAVELLERS

Paris is not particularly well equipped for *les handicapés* (disabled people): kerb ramps are few, older public facilities and bottom-end hotels usually lack lifts, and the metro, most of it built decades ago, is inaccessible for those in a wheelchair *(fauteuil roulant)*. But disabled people who would like to visit Paris can overcome these problems. Most hotels with two or more stars are equipped with lifts, and Michelin's *Guide Rouge* indicates hotels with lifts and facilities for disabled people.

Information & Organisations

The tourist office's website (www.paris-tourist office.com) lists organisations as well as some sights, accommodation and restaurants with the 'Tourisme & Handicap' sign, indicating special facilities for the disabled. The SNCF has made many of its train carriages more accessible to people with physical disabilities. A traveller in a wheelchair can travel in both the TGV and in the 1st-class carriage with a 2nd-class ticket on mainline trains provided they make a reservation by phone or at a train station at least a few hours before departure. Details are available in the SNCF booklet *Le Mémento du Voyageur à Mobilité Réduite.* Contact **SNCF Accessibilité Service** (☎ 08 00 15 47 53) for advice on planning your journey.

For information on accessibility to all forms of public transport in the Paris region, get a copy of the *Guide Practique à l'Usage des Personnes à Mobilité Réduite* from the **Syndicat des Transports d'Île de France** (☎ 01 47 53 28 00; www.stif-idf.fr).

The following organisations can provide information to disabled travellers:

Association des Paralysées de France (APF; ☎ 01 40 78 69 00, 08 00 50 05 97; www.apf.asso.fr in French; 17 blvd Auguste Blanqui, 13e) Brochures on wheelchair access and accommodation in Paris.

Groupement pour l'Insertion des Personnes Handicapées Physiques (GIHP; ☎ 01 43 95 66 36; www.gihpnational .org in French; 10 rue Georges de Porto Riche, 14e) Provides vehicles outfitted for people in wheelchairs for use within the city.

DISCOUNT CARDS

Museums, the SNCF, ferry companies and other institutions discounts to those aged under 26 (ie holders of the International Youth Travel Card, or IYTC), students with an International Student Identity Card (ISIC; age limits may apply) and *le troisième age* (those aged over 60 or 65). Look for the words *tarif réduit* (reduced rate) or *demi-tarif* (half-price tariff) and then ask if you qualify. Under-18s get an even wider range of discounts, including free admission to the *musées nationaux* (national museums run by the government) and everyone gets in free to permanent collections of city-run museums for nothing. About a dozen museums are free on the first Sunday of every month.

The **Carte Musées-Monuments** (Museums Monuments Card; ☎ 01 44 61 96 60; 1-/3-/5-day €18/36/54) is valid for entry to 37 venues in Paris – including the Louvre, Centre Pompidou and Musée d'Orsay – and another 22 in the Île de France, including parts of the chateaux at Versailles, Fontaine and Chantilly (see p318). The pass is available from the participating venues as well as the tourist office branches, Fnac outlets (see p207), RATP information desks and major metro stations.

ELECTRICITY

France runs on 220V at 50Hz AC. Plugs are the standard European type with two round pins. French outlets often have an earth (ground) pin; you may have to buy a French adapter to use even a two-pin European plug. The best place to seek out adapters and other electrical goods is the BHV department store near Hôtel de Ville (see p255) or any branch of the electronics chain Darty (see p266).

EMBASSIES

It's important to realise what your own embassy – the embassy of the country of which you are a citizen – can and can't do to help you if you get into trouble. Generally speaking, it won't be much help if the trouble you're in is remotely your own fault. Remember that you are bound by French law while travelling in France. Your embassy will not be sympathetic if you commit a crime locally, even if such actions are legal in your own country.

In genuine emergencies you might get some assistance, but only if other channels have been exhausted. For example, if you need to get home urgently, a free ticket home is exceedingly unlikely – the embassy would expect you to have insurance. If you have all your money and documents stolen, it might assist with getting a new passport, but a loan for onward travel is out of the question.

The following is a list of selected embassies and consulates in Paris. For a more complete list, consult the *Pages Jaunes* (Yellow Pages) under 'Ambassades et Consulats' or the website www.paris.org/addresses/embassies.

Australia (Map pp389-91; ☎ 01 40 59 33 00; 4 rue Jean Rey, 15e; metro Bir Hakeim)

Belgium (Map pp383-5; ☎ 01 43 80 61 00; 9 rue de Tilsitt, 17e; metro Charles de Gaulle-Étoile)

Canada (Map pp383-5; ☎ 01 44 43 29 00; 35 av Montaigne, 8e; metro Franklin D Roosevelt)

Germany (Map pp383-5; ☎ 01 42 99 78 00; 13-15 av Franklin D Roosevelt, 8e; metro Franklin D Roosevelt)

Ireland (Map pp383-5; ☎ 01 45 00 20 87; 4 rue Rude, 16e; metro Argentine)

Italy (Map pp389-91; ☎ 01 45 44 38 90; 51 rue de Varenne, 7e; metro Rue du Bac)

Netherlands (Map pp389-91; ☎ 01 43 06 61 88; 7 rue Eblé, 7e; metro St-François Xavier)

New Zealand (Map pp383-5; ☎ 01 45 00 24 11; 7ter rue Léonard de Vinci, 16e; metro Victor Hugo)

South Africa (Map pp389-91; ☎ 01 45 55 92 37; 59 quai d'Orsay, 7e; metro Invalides)

Spain (Map pp383-5; ☎ 01 44 43 18 18; 22 av Marceau, 8e; metro Alma-Marceau)

Switzerland (Map pp389-91; ☎ 01 49 55 67 00; 142 rue de Grenelle, 7e; metro Varenne)

UK (Map pp383-5; ☎ 01 44 51 31 00; 35 rue du Faubourg St-Honoré, 8e; metro Concorde) There's also a **consulate** (☎ 01 42 51 31 01; 18bis rue d'Anjou, 8e; metro Concorde).

USA (Map pp383-5; ☎ 01 43 12 21 72; 2 av Gabriel, 8e; metro Concorde) There's also a **consulate** (☎ 01 43 12 22 22; 2 rue St-Florentin, 1er; metro Concorde).

EMERGENCY

The following numbers are to be dialled in an emergency. See p346 for hospitals with 24-hour accident and emergency departments.

Ambulance (SAMU; ☎ 15, 01 45 67 50 50)

Fire brigade (☎ 18)

Police (☎ 17)

EU-wide emergency hotline (☎ 112)

Rape crisis hotline (☎ 08 00 05 95 95)

Urgences Médicales de Paris (Paris Medical Emergencies; ☎ 01 53 94 94 94, 24hr house calls 01 48 28 40 40)

SOS Médecins (☎ 01 47 07 77 77, 24hr house calls 08 00 33 24 24)

SOS Helpline (☎ 01 47 23 80 80 in English)

Lost Property

All objects found anywhere in Paris – except those picked up on trains or in train stations – are brought to the city's **Bureau des Objets Trouvés** (Lost Property Office; Map pp380-2; ☎ 01 55 76 20 20; fax 01 40 02 40 45; 36 rue des Morillons, 15e; metro Convention; ☺ 8.30am-5pm Mon & Wed, 8.30am-8pm Tue & Thu, 8.30am-5.30pm Fri Sep-Jun, 8.30am-7pm Mon-Fri Jul & Aug), which is run by the Préfecture de Police. Since telephone enquiries are impossible, the only way to find out if a lost item has been located is to go there and fill in the forms.

Items lost on the metro are held by station agents (☎ 01 44 68 20 20) for three days, before being sent to the Bureau des Objets Trouvés. Anything found on trains or stations is taken to the lost-property office (usually attached to the left-luggage office) of the relevant station. Phone enquiries (in French) are possible:

Gare d'Austerlitz (☎ 01 53 60 71 98)

Gare de l'Est (☎ 01 40 18 88 73)

Gare de Lyon (☎ 01 53 33 67 22)

Gare du Nord (☎ 01 55 31 58 40)

Gare Montparnasse (☎ 01 40 48 14 24)

Gare St-Lazare (☎ 01 53 42 05 57)

GAY & LESBIAN TRAVELLERS

Paris is home to thriving gay and lesbian communities, and same-sex couples are a common sight on its streets. In 1999 the government enacted its PACS (Pacte Civile de Solidarité) legislation, designed to give homosexual couples the same legal protection (eg regarding inheritance) as married heterosexuals, and in May 2001, Paris elected Bertrand Delanoë, a European capital's first openly gay mayor.

Information & Organisations

Most of France's major gay organisations are based in Paris. If you require a more complete list pick up a copy of *Genres*, an annual listing gay, lesbian, bisexual and transsexual organisations, at the Gay and Lesbian Centre.

Act Up-Paris (☎ 01 48 06 13 89; www.actupparis.org in French) Advice by phone is available from 2pm to 6pm on Wednesday and meetings are held every Tuesday at 7pm at the **École des Beaux-Arts** (Map pp396-9; 16 rue Bonaparte, 6e; metro St-Germain des Prés).

Association des Médecins Gais (AMG; ☎ 01 48 05 81 71; www.medecins-gays.org in French) The Association of Gay Doctors, based at the Centre Gai et Lesbien (see below), deals with gay-related health issues. Telephone advice is possible from 6pm to 8pm on Wednesday and 2pm to 4pm on Saturday.

Centre Gai et Lesbien Paris Île de France (CGL; Map pp392-5; ☎ 01 43 57 21 47; www.cglparis.org; 3 rue Keller, 11e; metro Ledru Rollin; 🕓 4-8pm Mon-Sat) The Gay and Lesbian Centre is your best single source of information in Paris.

Écoute Gaie (☎ 08 10 81 10 57; 🕓 6-10pm Mon-Fri) Established in 1982, this is the oldest hotline for gays and lesbians in Paris.

SOS Homophobie (☎ 01 43 47 09 69, 08 10 10 81 35; www.sos-homophobie.org in French; 🕓 8-10pm Sun-Fri, 2-4pm Sat) This hotline accepts anonymous calls concerning discriminatory acts against gays and lesbians.

Among some of the better websites are:

Adventice (www.adventice.com) The oldest free gay site but its cultural bent is going rather commercial.

Gay France (www.gayfrance.fr) Lots and lots of male-to-male chat.

La France Gaie & Lesbienne (www.france.qrd.org) 'Queer resources directory' for gay and lesbian travellers.

Dyke Planet (www.dykeplanet.com in French) The best French-language website for gay women.

Publications

Têtu (€5; www.tetu.com in French) is a general-interest national magazine available monthly at newsstands everywhere. Among the more serious gay publications around is *Action*, a free monthly by Act Up-Paris'. Be on the lookout for the bimonthlies *e.m@le* and *Illico*, which have interviews and articles (in French) and listings of gay clubs, bars, associations and personal classifieds. It is available free at most gay venues. The monthly magazine **Lesbia** (€4; lesbiapub@worldonline.fr) gives a rundown of what's happening around the country.

The following guidebooks list pubs, restaurants, clubs, beaches, saunas, sex shops and cruising areas; they are available from Les Mots à la Bouche bookshop (see p256).

Dyke Guide: Le Guide Lesbien (€11) The essential French-language guide for girls on the go in France and Paris.

Frommer's Gay & Lesbian Europe (€18) Contains some 130 pages on France, half of which concern Paris.

Le Petit Futé Paris Gay & Lesbien (€12) A French-language guide that goes well beyond pursuits hedonistic, with political, cultural, religious and health listings along with bars and restaurants. Highly recommended.

Spartacus International Gay Guide (€29) A male-only guide to the world with more than 80 pages devoted to France and 25 pages on Paris.

HOLIDAYS
Public Holidays

The following holidays are observed in Paris:

New Year's Day (Jour de l'An) 1 January

Easter Sunday (Pâques) Late March/April

Easter Monday (Lundi de Pâques) Late March/April

May Day (Fête du Travail) 1 May

Victory in Europe Day (Victoire 1945) 8 May

Ascension Thursday (L'Ascension) May (40th day after Easter)

Pentecost/Whit Sunday (Pentecôte) Mid-May to mid-June (7th Sunday after Easter)

Whit Monday (Lundi de Pentecôte) Mid-May to mid-June (7th Monday after Easter)

Bastille Day/National Day (Le Quatorze Juillet/Fête Nationale) 14 July

Assumption Day (L'Assomption) 15 August

All Saints' Day (La Toussaint) 1 November

Armistice Day/Remembrance Day (Le Onze Novembre) 11 November

Christmas (Noël) 25 December

School Holidays

Christmas & New Year 20 December to 4 January

February/March Runs from about 11 February to 11 March, with pupils in each of three zones off for overlapping 15-day periods.

Easter Begins a week before Easter and lasts a month, which also means pupils have overlapping 15-day holidays.

Summer Nationwide summer holidays lasts from the end of June until very early September.

INTERNET ACCESS

Some metro and RER stations (eg Miromesnil, St-Michel) offer free Internet access but there's always a huge queue. At the same time, some 50 post offices in Paris have Internet centres called **Cyberposte** (www.laposte.net), where a rechargeable card costs €7 for one hour's connection time and €4 for each additional hour. The centres generally open 8am or 9am to 7pm weekdays and till noon Saturday.

Paris is awash with Internet cafés. Among the best and/or most central:

Access Academy (Map pp396-9; ☎ 01 43 25 23 80; 60-61 rue St-André des Arts, 6e; metro Odéon; per hr approx €3.50, per day/week/month €6.80/14.90/35.70; ⊙ 8-2am) France's largest Internet café has some 400 screens, in the heart of St-Germain. Hourly rates depend on what time you log on.

Akyrion Net Center (Map pp396-9; ☎ 01 40 27 92 07; 19 rue Charlemagne, 4e; metro St-Paul; adult per 15/30/60 min €2.50/4.10/7.30, student €2/3.30/5.90; ⊙ 11am-midnight Mon-Sat, 2pm-midnight Sun) This Marais centre is popular with students at the nearby university.

Cyber C@fe (Map pp392-5; ☎ /fax 01 43 26 01 79; 42 rue Descartes, 5e; metro Cardinal Lemoine or Place Monge; per 10/30/60 min €1.25/2.50/5; ⊙ 11-1am Mon, Tue, Thu & Fri, 10-1am Wed, Sat & Sun)

Cyber Squ@re (Map pp386-8; ☎ 01 48 87 82 36; 1 place de la République; metro République;

per 5/15/30/60 min €0.75/2.30/3.80/6, per 10/20hr €45.70/76.20; ⊙ 10am-8pm Mon-Sat) This small but convivial place is entered from passage Vendôme.

Cyberbe@ubourg Internet C@fé (Map pp396-9; ☎ /fax 01 42 71 49 80; 38 rue Quincampoix, 4e; metro Châtelet-Les Halles; per 15/30/45/60 min €1.50/3/4.60/6, per 10/20/40 hr €29/44/75; ⊙ 9am-11pm)

Cybercafe Latin (Map pp389-91; ☎ 01 42 22 01 18; 35bis rue de Fleurus, 6e; metro St-Placide; per 20/30/60 min €1.50/2.20/4, per 5/10/20 hr €16/29/53; ⊙ 9.30am-8.30pm Mon-Fri, noon-7.30pm Sat)

Espace du Tourisme d'Île de France (Map pp396-9; ☎ 01 44 50 19 98; Galerie du Carrousel du Louvre, 99 rue de Rivoli, 1er; metro Palais Royal-Musée du Louvre; per min €0.15; ⊙ 10am-7pm) The bureau responsible for tourism in the Île de France has five terminals available to the public.

Luxembourg Micro (Map pp392-5; ☎ 01 46 33 27 98; www.luxembourg-micro.com; 81 blvd St-Michel, 5e; metro Luxembourg; €1/2/3 for 20/40/60 min; ⊙ 9am-11pm Mon-Sat, 10am-11pm Sun)

Metro Jungle Web Center (Map pp386-8; ☎ 01 53 01 90 62; fax 01 53 01 90 61; 30 rue de Picardie, 3e; metro République or Temple; per 15/30/60 min €1/2/4, per 6/10/20hr €17/27/46; ⊙ 10.30am-8pm) Near République.

Toonet Cyber Space (Map pp392-5; ☎ 06 32 38 46 97; 74 rue de Charonne, 11e; metro Charonne or Ledru Rollin; per 1/5/15/30hr €5/16/34/48; ⊙ 10.30am-9pm Mon-Sat)

Web 46 (Map pp396-9; ☎ 01 40 27 02 89; fax 01 40 27 03 89; 46 rue du Roi de Sicile, 4e; metro St-Paul; per 15/30/60 min €2.50/4/7, per 5hr €29; ⊙ 9.30am-midnight) A very pleasant café in the heart of the Marais.

XS Arena Luxembourg (Map pp392-5; ☎ 01 43 44 55 55; 17 rue Soufflot, 5e; metro Luxembourg; per 1/2/3/4/5hr €3/6/8/10/12; ⊙ 24hr) This minichain of Internet cafés is bright, buzzy and open round the clock, with a branch at **Les Halles** (Map pp396-9; ☎ 01 40 13 02 60; 43 rue Sébastopol, 1er; metro Les Halles).

LAUNDRY

There's a *laverie libre-service* (self-service laundrette) around every corner in Paris; your hotel or hostel can point you to one in the neighbourhood. Machines usually cost €2.80 to €3.70 for a small load (5kg to 7kg) and €5 to €5.50 for a larger (10kg to 13kg) one. Drying costs €1 for 10 to 12 minutes. Some laundrettes have self-service *nettoyage à sec* (dry-cleaning) machines.

Change machines are occasionally out of order or refuse to accept bills, so come prepared with change for the *séchoirs* (dryers) as well as the *lessive* (laundry powder) and *javel* (bleach) dispensers. Usually you deposit coins into a *monnayeur central* (central control box) – not the machine itself – and push a button that corresponds to the number of the washer or dryer you wish to operate.

The control boxes are sometimes programmed to deactivate the machines 30 minutes to an hour before closing time (laundrettes are usually open daily between about 7am and 10pm).

Among centrally located self-service laundrettes are the following:

C'Clean Laverie (Map pp386-8; 18 rue Jean-Pierre Timbaud, 11e; metro Oberkampf)

Julice Laverie (Map pp396-9; 56 rue de Seine, 6e; metro Mabillon; 22 rue des Grands Augustins, 6e; metro St-Michel)

Laverie Éclat (Map pp389-91; 69 rue Blomet, 15e; metro Vaugirad)

Laverie Libre Service is at the following locations: **Louvre & Les Halles** (Map pp396-9; 7 rue Jean-Jacques Rousseau, 1er; metro Louvre-Rivoli); **Marais & Bastille** (Map pp396-9; 35 rue Ste-Croix de la Bretonnerie, 4e; metro Hôtel de Ville); **Marais & Bastille** (Map pp396-9; 25 rue des Rosiers, 4e; metro St-Paul); **Latin Quarter** (Map pp392-5; 216 rue St-Jacques, 5e; metro Luxembourg); **Jardin des Plantes** (Map pp392-5; 63 rue Monge, 5e; metro Place Monge); **Montmartre** (Map p400; 92 rue des Martyrs, 18e; metro Abbesses); **Gare de Lyon, Nation & Bercy** (Map p401; 94 rue du Dessous des Berges, 12e; metro Bibliothèque)

Laverie Libre Service Primus has branches at: **Les Halles** (Map pp396-9; 40 rue du Roi de Sicile, 4e; metro St-Paul); **Ménilmontant & Belleville** (Map pp386-8; 83 rue Jean-Pierre Timbaud, 11e; metro Couronnes)

Laverie Miele Libre Service (Map pp392-5; 2 rue de Lappe, 11e; metro Bastille)

Laverie SBS has branches at: **Gare du Nord, Gare de l'Est & République** (Map pp386-8; 6 rue des Petites Écuries, 10e; metro Château d'Eau); **15e Arrondissement** (Map pp389-91; 20 rue de l'Abbé Groult, 15e; metro Félix Faure)

Le Bateau Lavoir (Map pp392-5; 1 rue Thouin, 5e; metro Cardinal Lemoine)

Pigalle (Map p400; 4 rue Burq, 18e; metro Blanche); **République** (Map pp386-8; 14 rue de la Corderie, 3e; metro République or Temple); **Bibliothèque** (Map p401; 94 rue du Dessous des Berges, 12e; metro Bibliothèque)

Salon Lavoir Sidea (Map p400; 28 rue des Trois Frères, 18e; metro Abbesses)

LEGAL MATTERS
Drink Driving
As elsewhere in the EU, the laws are very tough when it comes to drinking and driving, and for many years the slogan has been: '*Boire ou conduire, il faut choisir*' (roughly 'To drive or to booze, you have to choose'). The acceptable blood-alcohol limit is 0.05%, and drivers exceeding this amount face fines of up to €4500 (or a maximum of two years in jail). Licences can also be immediately suspended.

Police
Thanks to the Napoleonic Code on which the French legal system is based, the police can search anyone they want to at any time – whether or not there is probable cause.

France has two separate police forces. The Police Nationale, under the command of departmental prefects (and, in Paris, the Préfet de Police), includes the Police de l'Air et des Frontières (PAF; the border police). The Gendarmerie Nationale, a paramilitary force under the control of the Ministry of Defence, handles airports, borders and so on. During times of crisis (eg a wave of terrorist attacks), the army may be called in to patrol public places.

The dreaded Compagnies Républicaines de Sécurité (CRS) – riot-police heavies – are part of the Police Nationale. You often see hundreds of them, each bigger and butcher than the next and armed with the latest riot gear, at strikes or demonstrations. Police with shoulder patches reading 'Police Municipale' are under the control of the local mayor.

If asked a question, cops are likely to be correct and helpful but little more (though you may get a little salute). If the police stop you for any reason, be polite and remain calm. They have wide powers of search and seizure and, if they take a dislike to you, may choose to use them. The police can, without any particular reason, decide to examine your passport, visa, *carte de séjour* (residence permit) and so on.

French police are very strict about security. Do not leave baggage unattended; they're serious when they warn that suspicious objects will be summarily blown up. Your bags will be inspected and you will have to pass through security gates not only at airports but also at many public buildings (including museums and galleries) throughout the city. If asked to open your bag or backpack for inspection, please do so willingly – it's for your own safety ultimately.

MAPS

Many Parisians swear by *Paris par Arrondissement* (€13.50), which has a double-page hand-drawn street plan of each arrondissement. Some find it confusing, though it does list the nearest metro station with each street name in the index. More user-friendly is L'Indispensable's *Paris Practique par Arrondissement* (€5.50), a pocket-sized atlas with a larger format. The larger *Le Petit Parisien* (€7) has three maps for each arrondissement showing streets, metro lines and bus routes. Lonely Planet's *Paris City Map* is handy, laminated and has four plans that cover the more popular parts of town, a street index and a metro map.

The best place to find a full selection of maps is the **Espace IGN** (see p263).

MEDICAL SERVICES
Dental Care

For emergency dental care contact either of the following:

Hôpital de la Salpêtrière (Map pp392-5; ☎ 01 42 16 00 00; rue Bruant, 13e; metro Chevaleret) The only dental hospital with extended hours. After hours use the emergency entrance (Map pp392-5; 83 blvd de l'Hôpital, 13e; metro Gare d'Austerlitz; ⏰ 5.30pm-8.30am).

SOS Dentaire (Map pp380-2; ☎ 01 43 36 36 00; 87 blvd de Port Royal, 14e; metro Port Royal) A private dental office that also offers services when most dentists are off-duty (8.30pm to 11pm weekdays, 9.30am to 11pm weekends).

Hospitals

For medical emergencies see p342, otherwise hospitals in Paris include:

American Hospital in Paris (Map pp380-2; ☎ 01 46 41 25 25; www.american-hospital.org; 63 blvd Victor Hugo, 92200 Neuilly-sur-Seine; metro Pont de Levallois Bécon) Offers emergency 24-hour medical and dental care.

Hertford British Hospital (Map pp380-2; ☎ 01 46 39 22 22; http://hbh.free.fr; 3 rue Barbès, 92300 Levallois-Perret; metro Anatole France) A less-expensive English-speaking option than the American Hospital.

Hôtel Dieu (Map pp396-9; ☎ 01 42 34 81 31; place du Parvis Notre Dame, 4e; metro Cité) After 8pm use the emergency entrance on rue de la Cité.

METRIC SYSTEM

France uses the metric system, which was invented after the Revolution by the French Academy of Sciences at the request of the National Assembly, and adopted by the French government in 1795. The metric system replaced a confusing welter of traditional units of measurement that lacked all logical basis and made conversion complicated and commerce chaotic. For a conversion chart, see the inside back cover.

MONEY
ATMs

You'll find ATMs, which are known as a *DAB* (*distributeur automatique de billets*) or *point d'argent* in French, linked to the Cirrus, Maestro Visa or MasterCard networks virtually everywhere in Paris. Those without a local bank account should know that there is nearly always a transaction surcharge for cash withdrawals. You should contact your bank to find out how much this is before using ATMs too freely.

Many ATMs won't accept PIN codes with more than four digits – ask your bank how to handle this. If you normally remember your PIN code as a string of letters, translate it back into numbers, as keyboards in France may not have letters indicated.

Changing Money

In general, cash is not a very good way to carry money. Not only can it be stolen, but in France it doesn't usually offer the best exchange rates. Some banks, post offices and bureaux de change pay up to 2.5% more for travellers cheques, more than making up for the 1% commission usually charged when buying the cheques in the first place.

Post offices can offer the best exchange rates, and accept banknotes in various currencies as well as travellers cheques issued by Amex or Visa. The commission for travellers cheques is 1.5% (minimum about €4).

Commercial banks usually charge a stiff €3 to €4.50 per foreign-currency transaction (eg BNP Paribas charges 3.3% or a minimum of about €4). The rates offered vary, so it pays to compare. Banks charge roughly €3.40 to €5.30 to cash travellers cheques (eg BNP Paribas charges 1.5%, with a minimum charge of €4).

In Paris, bureaux de change are faster and easier, open longer hours and give better rates than most banks. It's best to familiarise yourself with the rates offered by the post office and compare them with those on offer at *bureaux de change*, which are not generally allowed to charge commissions. On small transactions, even exchange places with less-than-optimal rates may leave you with more euros in your pocket.

Among some of the better *bureaux de change* are the following (generally open between 10am and 6pm, some later):

Best Change (Map pp396-9; ☎ 01 42 21 46 05; 21 rue du Roule, 1er; metro Louvre Rivoli)

Bureau de Change (Map pp383-5; ☎ 01 42 25 38 14; 25 av des Champs-Élysées, 8e; metro Franklin D Roosevelt)

European Exchange Office (Map p400; ☎ 01 42 52 67 19; 6 rue Yvonne Le Tac, 18e; metro Abbesses)

Le Change du Louvre (Map pp396-9; ☎ 01 42 97 27 28; 151 rue St-Honoré, 1er; metro Palais Royal-Musée du Louvre) On the northern side of Le Louvre des Antiquaires (see p254).

Société Touristique de Services (STS; Map pp396-9; ☎ 01 43 54 76 55; 2 place St-Michel, 6e; metro St-Michel)

Thomas Cook (Map pp383-5; ☎ 01 47 20 25 14; 125 av des Champs-Élysées, 8e; metro Charles de Gaulle-Étoile)

Travelex (Map p400; ☎ 01 42 57 05 10; 82-86 blvd de Clichy, 18e; metro Blanche)

Credit Cards

In Paris, Visa (known locally as Carte Bleue) is the widely accepted credit card, followed by MasterCard (Eurocard). Amex cards can be useful at more upmarket establishments and allow you to get cash at some ATMs. In general, all three cards can be used for train travel, restaurant meals and cash advances.

When you get a cash advance on your Visa or MasterCard account, your issuer charges a transaction fee, which can be very high; check with your card issuer before leaving home. Also, many banks charge a commission of 4% (minimum around €6) for an advance.

Call the following numbers if your card is lost or stolen. It may be impossible to get a lost Visa or MasterCard reissued until you get home so two different credit cards are generally safer than one.

Amex (☎ 01 47 77 72 00, 01 47 77 70 00)

Diners Club (☎ 08 10 31 41 59)

MasterCard/Eurocard (☎ 08 00 90 23 90, 01 45 67 53 53)

Visa/Carte Bleue (☎ 08 92 70 57 05, 08 92 69 08 80)

Currency

The euro (abbreviated € and pronounced *eu-roh* in French) is the national currency of France and 11 of the 25 other member-states

of the EU (Austria, Belgium, Finland, Germany, Greece, Ireland, Italy, Luxembourg, Netherlands, Portugal and Spain). One euro is divided into 100 cents (*centimes* in French). There are seven euro notes in different colours and sizes; they come in denominations of €500, €200, €100, €50, €20, €10 and €5. The designs on the recto (generic windows or portals) and verso (imaginary bridges, map of the EU) are exactly the same in all 12 countries and symbolise openness and cooperation.

The eight coins in circulation are in denominations of €2 and €1, then one, two, five, 10, 20 and 50 cents. The 'heads' side of the coin, on which the denomination is shown, is identical throughout the 'euro zone'; the 'tails' side is peculiar to each member-state, though euro coins can be used anywhere that accepts euros, of course. In France the €2 (brassy centre with silver ring) and €1 (silver centre with brassy ring) coins portray the tree of liberty; the €0.50, €0.20 and €0.10 (all brass) ones have *la Semeuse* (or 'the Sower', a recurring theme in the history of the French franc); and the €0.05, €0.02 and €0.01 coins (all copper) portray Marianne, the symbol of the French Republic.

The euro is a stable and increasingly strong currency. In spring 2004 €1 was worth US$1.22, UK£0.66, A$1.60, C$1.64 and NZ$1.80. The latest rates are available on websites such as www.oanda.com and www.xe.com.

Travellers Cheques

The most flexible travellers cheques are issued by American Express (in US dollars or euros) and Visa, as they can be changed at many post offices.

Amex offices don't charge commission on their own travellers cheques (though they charge about 4% on other brands). If your Amex travellers cheques are lost or stolen in Paris, call ☎ 08 00 90 86 00 (24-hour, toll-free). Reimbursements can be made at the main **Amex** (Map pp383-5; ☎ 01 47 14 50 00; 11 rue Scribe, 9e; metro Auber or Opéra; 🕑 9.30am-7.30pm Mon-Fri Jun-Sep, 9.30am-6.30pm Oct-May, 9am-5.30pm Sat).

The toll-free customer service bureau for **Thomas Cook** (☎ 08 00 90 83 30) is open round the clock.

NEWSPAPERS & MAGAZINES

Among English-language newspapers widely available in Paris are the *International Herald Tribune* (€1.85), which is edited in Paris and has very good coverage of French and international news; the *Guardian* and the more compact *European Guardian*; the *Financial Times*; the *Times*; and the colourful (if lightweight) *USA Today*. English-language news weeklies that are widely available include *Newsweek*, *Time* and the *Economist*. For information about the French-language press, see p16.

The Paris-based *Fusac* (short for *France USA Contacts*), a freebie issued every fortnight, consists of hundreds of ads placed by both companies and individuals. It is distributed free at Paris' English-language bookshops, Anglophone embassies and the **American Church** (Map pp389-91; ☎ 01 40 62 05 00; www.acparis.org; 65 quai d'Orsay, 7e; metro Pont de l'Alma or Invalides; reception ☼ 9am-noon & 1-10.30pm Mon-Sat, 9am-noon & 1-7pm Sun), which functions as a community centre for English speakers and is an excellent source of information on au pair work, short-term accommodation etc. To place an ad, contact **Fusac** (☎ 01 56 53 54 54; www.fusac.fr; 26 rue Bénard, 14e; metro Alésia or Pernety; ☼ 10am-7pm Mon-Fri).

PHARMACIES

Pharmacies with extended hours include:

Pharmacie Bader (Map pp396-9; ☎ 01 43 26 92 66; 12 blvd St-Michel, 5e; metro St-Michel; ☼ 9am-9pm)

Pharmacie des Champs (Map pp383-5; ☎ 01 45 62 02 41; Galerie des Champs, 84 av des Champs-Élysées, 8e; metro George V; ☼ 24hr)

Pharmacie Européenne de la Place Clichy (Map pp383-5; ☎ 01 48 74 65 18; 6 place de Clichy, 17e; metro place de Clichy; ☼ 24hr)

Pharmacie des Halles (Map pp396-9; ☎ 01 42 72 03 23; 10 blvd de Sébastopol, 4e; metro Châtelet; ☼ 9am-midnight Mon-Sat, 9am-10pm Sun)

PHOTOGRAPHY

Kodak and Fuji colour-print film is widely available in supermarkets, photo shops and Fnac stores (see p207). Photography is rarely forbidden, except in museums and art galleries.

POST

Most post offices *(bureaux de poste)* in Paris are open 8am to 7pm weekdays and 8am or 9am till noon on Saturday. *Tabacs* (tobacconists) usually sell postage stamps.

The main **post office** (Map pp386-8; ☎ 01 40 28 76 00; 52 rue du Louvre, 1er; metro Sentier or Les Halles; ☼ 24hr), five blocks north of the eastern end of the Louvre, is open round the clock, but only for basic services such as sending letters and picking up poste restante mail (window Nos 5 to 7; €0.46 per letter). Other services, including currency exchange, are available only during regular opening hours. Be prepared for long queues after 7pm. Poste restante mail not specifically addressed to a particular branch post office will be delivered here. There is a one-hour closure from 6.20am to 7.20am Monday to Saturday and from 6am to 7am on Sunday.

Postal Codes

Each arrondissement has its own five-digit postcode, formed by prefixing the arrondissement number with '750' or '7500' (eg 75001 for the 1er arrondissement, 75019 for the 19e etc). The only exception is the 16e, which has two postcodes: 75016 and 75116. All mail to addresses in France *must* include the postcode. Cedex (*Courrier d'Entreprise à Distribution Exceptionelle*) simply means that mail sent to that address is collected at the post office rather than delivered to the door.

Postal Rates

Domestic letters weighing up to 20/50g cost €0.50/0.75. Postcards and letters up to 20/40/60g sent within the EU cost €0.50/1/1.20; €0.75/1.60/1.95 to the rest of Europe and Africa; and €0.90/1.80/2.40 to North America, Asia and Australasia.

RADIO

You can pick up a mixture of the BBC World Service and BBC for Europe in Paris on 648 kHz AM. The Voice of America (VOA) is on 1197 kHz. You can pick up an hour of Radio France Internationale (RFI) news in English at 3pm daily on 738 kHz AM.

Pocket-sized short-wave radios and the Internet make it easy to keep abreast of world news in English wherever you are. The BBC World Service can be heard on 6195 kHz, 9410 kHz and 12095 kHz (a good daytime frequency), depending on the time of day. BBC Radio 4 broadcasts on 198 kHz LW, and carries BBC World Service programming in the wee hours of the morning. The VOA broadcasts in English at various times of the day on 7170 kHz, 9535 kHz, 9760 kHz, 9770 kHz, 11805 kHz, 15205 kHz and 15255 kHz.

The following are some of the more popular French-language radio stations:

France Info (105.5 MHz FM) Operates 24-hour all news radio.

Paris Jazz (98.1 MHz FM) Jazz and blues.

Radio FG (98.2 MHz FM) Club news, gigs.

Radio France Internationale (738 kHz AM) France's official international station.

Radio Nova (101.5 MHz FM) Latino, clubs.

SAFETY

In general, Paris is a safe city and random street assaults are rare; in fact, criminal acts fell by 7% between 2002 and 2003, with thefts involving violence dropping by almost 10%. The so-called Ville Lumière (City of Light) is generally well lit, and there's no reason not to use the metro before it stops running at some time between 12.30am and just past 1am. As you'll notice, women *do* travel alone on the metro late at night in most areas, though not all who do so report feeling 100% comfortable.

Metro stations that are best avoided late at night include: Châtelet-Les Halles and its seemingly endless corridors; Château Rouge in Montmartre; Gare du Nord; Strasbourg St-Denis; Réaumur Sébastopol; and Montparnasse Bienvenüe. *Bornes d'alarme* (alarm boxes) are located in the centre of each metro/RER platform and in some station corridors.

Nonviolent crime such as pickpocketing and thefts from handbags and packs is a problem wherever there are crowds, especially packs of tourists. Places to be particularly careful include Montmartre (especially around Sacré Cœur); Pigalle; the areas around Forum des Halles and the Centre Pompidou; the Latin Quarter (especially the rectangle bounded by rue St-Jacques, blvd St-Germain, blvd St-Michel and quai St-Michel); below the Eiffel Tower; and on the metro during rush hour. Take the usual precautions: don't carry more money than you need, and keep your credit cards, passport and other documents in a concealed pouch, a hotel safe or a safe-deposit box.

TAX & REFUNDS

France's VAT is known as *TVA (taxe sur la valeur ajoutée)* and is 19.6% on most goods except medicine and books, for which it's 5.5%. Prices that include TVA are often marked *TTC (toutes taxes comprises*; literally 'all taxes included').

If you're not an EU resident, you can get a TVA refund provided that you're over 15; you'll be spending less than six months in France; you purchase goods (not more than 10 of the same item) worth at least €182 (tax included)

at a single shop; the goods fit into your luggage; you are taking the goods out of France three months after purchase; and the shop offers *vente en détaxe* (duty-free sales).

Present a passport at the time of purchase and ask for a *bordereau de vente à l'exportation* (export sales invoice). Most shops will refund less than the full 17% to which you are entitled, in order to cover the time and expense involved in the refund procedure.

As you leave France or another EU country, have all three pages of the *bordereau* validated by the country's customs officials at the airport or at the border. Customs officials will take two sheets and the stamped self-addressed envelope provided by the shop; the third copy is your receipt. Once the shop where you made your purchase receives its stamped copy, it will send you a *virement* (fund transfer) in the form you have requested. Be prepared for a wait of up to three months.

If you're flying out of Orly or Roissy Charles de Gaulle, certain shops can arrange for you to receive your refund as you're leaving the country. You must make such arrangements at the time of purchase.

For more information contact the **customs information centre** (☎ 08 25 30 82 63; www .douane.minefi.gouv.fr in French).

TELEPHONE

To call a number in Paris from outside France, dial your country's international access code, then ☎ 33 (France's country code), and then the local number, omitting the initial zero.

To call abroad from Paris, dial France's international access code (☎ 00), the country code, the area code (without the initial zero, if there is one) and the local number. International Direct Dial (IDD) calls to almost anywhere in the world can be placed from public telephones.

There are no area codes in France – you always dial the 10-digit number. Paris numbers always start with ☎ 01.

For France Télécom's domestic *service des renseignements* (directory enquiries or assistance), dial ☎ 12 (€0.80 for two enquiries). Don't be surprised if the operator doesn't speak English.

For international directory enquiries as well as reverse-charge (collect) calls, dial ☎ 3212. But be careful when using this service from a private line as it costs a whopping €3. Instead consult the phone book on the Internet (www .pagejaunes.fr, which will also link you to the white pages).

Domestic Call Rates

Local calls are relatively cheap – costing from €0.018 a minute (from €0.034 at peak time from 8am to 7pm weekdays) from a private telephone depending on the length of the call and the distance covered.

Calling mobile phones (which always start with '06' in France) will cost you €0.10 to €0.14 off-peak and €0.21 to €0.29 during peak times (usually 8am to 9.30pm weekdays, 8am to noon on Saturday).

Note that while numbers beginning with ☎ 08 00 (numéro vert) are toll-free in France, other numbers beginning with '8' are not. A numéro azur (08 01, 08 10) is charged at local rates while a numéro indigo can cost €0.12 (08 02, 08 20) or €0.15 (08 03, 08 25) per minute. The ubiquitous 08 92 numbers are always billed at an expensive €1.35 for connection then €0.34 per minute whenever you call.

International Call Rates

Daytime calls to neighbouring European countries as well as continental USA and Canada cost from €0.12 to €0.22 a minute. Reductions of about 20% generally apply from 7pm to 8am Monday to Thursday, from 7pm on Friday to 8am on Monday, and all day on public holidays. For mobile phones the discounted hours are shorter: from 9.30pm to 8am Monday to Friday and from noon on Saturday to 8am on Monday.

Full-price calls to the rest of Europe (including Russia), Australasia and most of Asia are about €0.49 per minute during peak times and €0.34 at off-peak times. The corresponding rates for most of Africa are €0.99 and €0.80.

Public Phones & Phonecards

All public phones can receive both domestic and international calls. If you want someone to call you back, just give them France's country code and the 10-digit number, usually written after the words 'Ici le…' or 'No d'appel' on the tariff sheet or on a little sign inside the phone box. Remind them to drop the '0' of the initial '01' of the number. When there's an incoming call, the words 'décrochez – appel arrive' will appear in the LCD window.

Public telephones in Paris require a télécarte (phonecard; €7.50/15 for 50/120 calling units), which can be purchased at post offices, tabacs, supermarkets, SNCF ticket windows, metro stations and anywhere you see a blue sticker reading 'télécarte en vente ici'.

You can buy prepaid phonecards in France that are up to 60% cheaper for calling abroad than the standard télécarte, however. Allô-mundo, Best Europe, EuroLatina and Kestel are among the most common. They're usually available in €7.50 and €15 denominations from tabacs, newsagents, phone shops and other sales points, especially in ethnic areas such as rue du Faubourg St-Denis (10e), Chinatown (13e) and Belleville (19e and 20e). In general they're valid for two months but the ones offering the most minutes for the least euros can expire in just a week.

Minitel

Minitel is a screen-based information service peculiar to France that was set up in the 1980s. It's useful but can be expensive to use, and the growing popularity of the Internet is giving Minitel a run for its money.

Mobile Phones

France uses GSM 900/1800, which is compatible with the rest of Europe and Australia but not with the North American GSM 1900 (though many North Americans now have GSM 1900/900 phones that do work in France) or the totally different system in Japan. If you have a GSM phone, check with your service provider about using it in France, and beware of calls being routed internationally (very expensive for a 'local' call).

Orange/France Telecom (☎ 08 00 88 14 44; www.orange.fr in French) has a €100 package that includes a mobile phone, a local phone number and 10 minutes of prepaid connection time. For more time, you can buy a prepaid Mobicarte recharge card (€10 to €100) from tabacs and other places you'd buy a télécarte; Mobicartes from €30 offering extra talk time (€5 bonus for €30, €10 bonus for €40 etc) If you don't mind changing your telephone number to a French one during your visit, you can also change your mobile telephone's SIM card (provided it's not blocked) for €30 (plus 10 minutes' talk time) and recharge with Mobicartes as you go along.

TELEVISION

Mid-range and top-end hotels frequently offer English-language cable and satellite TV, including CNN, BBC Prime, Sky and other networks. Canal+ sometimes screens nondubbed English-language films.

A variety of TV listings are sold at newsstands, including *Télérama* (€1.60), which includes a supplement of the best films of the month. Foreign films that are shown in their original language with subtitles are marked 'VO' or 'v.o.' *(version originale)*.

TIME

France uses the 24-hour clock in most instances, with the hours usually separated from the minutes by a lower-case 'h'. Thus, 15h30 is 3.30pm, 00h30 is 12.30am and so on.

France is on Central European Time, which is one hour ahead of (ie later than) GMT. During daylight-saving time, which runs from the last Sunday in March to the last Sunday in October, France is two hours ahead of GMT.

Without taking daylight-saving time into account, when it's noon in Paris it's 11am in London, 6am in New York, 3am in San Francisco, 9pm in Sydney and 11pm in Auckland.

TIPPING

French law requires that restaurant, café and hotel bills include a service charge (usually 12% to 15%); for more information, see p151. In taxis, the usual procedure is to round up to the nearest €0.50 or €1 regardless of the fare.

TOILETS

Public toilets in Paris are signposted *toilettes* or *WC*. The tan-coloured, self-cleaning cylindrical toilets you see on Paris' pavements are open 24 hours and cost €0.40.

If you are not a paying customer, café-owners do not appreciate you using their facilities. If you are desperate, try a fast-food place, major department store or even a big hotel. There are public toilets (€0.40) in front of Notre Dame cathedral, near the Arc de Triomphe, east down the steps at Sacré Cœur and in a few metro stations. Check out the wonderful Art Nouveau public toilets, built in 1905, below place de la Madeleine, 8e (Map pp383–5).

In older cafés and bars, you may find a *toilette à la turque* (Turkish-style toilet), which is what the French call a squat toilet.

TOURIST INFORMATION

The main branch of the **Office de Tourisme et de Congrès de Paris** (Paris Convention & Visitors Bureau; Map pp383–5; ☎ 08 92 68 30 00; www.paris-touristoffice.com; 25-27 rue des Pyramides, 1er;

metro Pyramides; 🕒 9am-8pm Apr-Oct, 9am-8pm Mon-Sat & 11am-7pm Sun Nov-Mar, closed 1 May) is about 500m northwest of the Louvre.

The bureau also maintains five centres (telephone numbers and website are the same as the main office) elsewhere in Paris. For details of the area around Paris, contact **Espace du Tourisme d'Île de France**, see p307.

Eiffel Tower (Map pp389-91; Pilier Nord, Parc du Champ de Mars, 7e; metro Champ de Mars-Tour Eiffel; 🕒 11am-6.45pm 2 May-Sep) At the base of the North Pillar.

Gare de Lyon (Map pp392-5; Hall d'Arrivée, 20 blvd Diderot, 12; metro Gare de Lyon; 🕒 8am-6pm Mon-Sat, closed holidays) In the arrivals hall for mainline trains.

Gare du Nord (Map pp386-8; 18 rue de Dunkerque, 10; metro Fare du Nord; 🕒 12.30-8pm, closed Christmas Day & 1 May) Under the glass roof of the Île de France departure and arrival area at the eastern end of the station.

Montmartre (Map p400; 21 place du Tertre, 18e; metro Abbesses; 🕒 10am-7pm, closed Christmas Day & 1 May)

Opéra/Grands Magasins (Map pp383-5; 11 rue Scribe, 9e; metro Auber or Opéra; 🕒 9am-6.30pm Mon-Sat, closed Christmas Day, 1 Jan & 1 May) In the same building as Amex (see p347).

These information offices are beyond central Paris, at La Défense and St-Denis:

Espace Info-Défense (☎ 01 47 74 84 24; www.ladefense .fr in French; 15 place de la Défense; 🕒 9.30am-5.30pm Mon-Fri Oct-Mar, 10am-6pm Apr-Sep) La Défense's tourist office has reams of free information, details on cultural activities and sells guides to the area's monumental art (€2.30), architecture (€5.40) and history (€6.10).

Le Kiosk (☎ 01 48 13 06 07; 6 place de la Légion d'Honneur; 🕒 11am-6pm Mon-Fri, 10am-1pm Sat) This office has information about festivals and other cultural events, such as the **Banlieues Blues** (☎ 01 49 22 10 10) jazz and blues festival in March and April and the **Festival de St-Denis** (www.festival-saint-denis.fr) from late May to late June.

Office de Tourisme de St-Denis Plaine (☎ 01 55 87 08 70; www.saint-denis-tourisme.com in French; 1 rue de la République; 🕒 9.30am-1pm & 2-6pm Mon-Sat, 10am-2pm Sun Nov-Mar; 10am-1pm & 2-4pm Sun Apr-Oct) The tourist office is 100m west of the basilica. Ask staff about free concerts in the basilica on certain Sundays at the end of August and into September.

Sources d'Europe (☎ 01 41 25 12 12; Le Socle de la Grande Arche; 🕒 10am-6pm Mon-Fri) This multimedia information centre in the base of the Grande Arche has everything you could possibly need or want to know about Europe and the European Union and there is a book and gift shop as well. You can gain access from La Défense Grande Arche metro station.

VISAS

There are no entry requirements for nationals of EU countries. Citizens of Australia, the USA, Canada and New Zealand do not need visas to visit France for up to three months. Except for people from a handful of other European countries (including Switzerland), everyone needs a 'Schengen Visa', named after the Schengen Agreement that abolished passport controls between Austria, Belgium, Denmark, Finland, France, Germany, Greece, Italy, Luxembourg, the Netherlands, Portugal, Spain and Sweden and was later ratified by the non-EU governments of Norway and Iceland. A visa for any of these countries should be valid throughout the Schengen area, but it pays to double check with the embassy or consulate of each country you intend to visit.

Visa fees depend on the current exchange rate but transit and the various types of short-stay (up to 90 days) visas all cost €35, while a long-stay visa allowing stays of more than 90 days costs €99. You will need your passport (valid for a period of three months beyond the date of your departure from France); a return ticket; proof of sufficient funds to support yourself; proof of prearranged accommodation (possibly); two passport-sized photos; and the visa fee in cash payable in local currency.

If all the forms are in order, your visa will usually be issued on the spot. You can also apply for a French visa after arriving in Europe – the fee is the same, but you may not have to produce a return ticket. If you enter France overland, your visa may not be checked at the border, but major problems can arise if the authorities discover that you don't have one later on (for example, at the airport as you leave the country).

Carte de Séjour

If you are issued a long-stay visa valid for six months or longer, you should apply for a *carte de séjour* (residence permit) within eight days of your arrival in France. Students must apply in person for a carte de séjour at the **Centre des Étudiants** (Map pp389-91; ☎ 01 53 71 51 68 for information; 13 rue Miollis, 15e; metro Cambronne or Ségur; 🕑 8.30am-4.30pm Mon-Thu, 8.45am-4pm Fri). Arrive early – the queues can be serpentine.

EU passport-holders seeking a *carte de séjour* should apply to the Service Étranger office in Salle Nord Est, which is on the ground floor next to *escalier F* (stairway F) in the Préfecture de Police (see p352).

Foreigners with non-EU passports must go to specific offices, depending on the arrondissement in which they're living or staying. The offices are usually open from 9am to 4.30pm Monday to Thursday and from 9am to 4pm Friday but it pays to check in advance.

1er, 2e, 4e-9e & 13e-16e Arrondissements (Map pp380-2; ☎ 01 53 74 14 06; Hôtel de Police, 114-116 av du Maine, 14e; metro Gaîté)

3e, 10e & 19e Arrondissements (Map pp386-8; ☎ 01 42 76 13 00; Hôtel de Police, 90 blvd de Sébastopol, 3e; metro Réaumur-Sébastopol)

11e, 12e & 20e Arrondissements (Map pp392-5; ☎ 01 43 43 24 12; Hôtel de Police, 163 rue de Charenton, 12e; metro Reuilly Diderot)

17e & 18e Arrondissements (Map pp383-5; ☎ 01 44 90 37 17; Hôtel de Police, 19-21 rue Truffaut, 17e; metro Place de Clichy or La Fourche)

Long-Stay & Student

If you would like to work, study or stay in France for longer than three months, apply to the French embassy or consulate nearest where you live for the appropriate *long séjour* (long-stay) visa. For details of au pair visas, which must be arranged *before* you leave home (unless you're an EU resident), see p354.

Unless you live in the EU, it's extremely difficult to get a visa that will allow you to work in France. For any sort of long-stay visa, begin the paperwork in your home country several months before you plan to leave. Applications cannot usually be made in a third country nor can tourist visas be turned into student visas after you arrive in France. People with student visas can apply for permission to work part-time; enquire at your place of study.

Visa Extensions

Tourist visas *cannot* be extended except in emergencies (such as medical problems). If you have an urgent problem, you should call the Service Étranger (Foreigner Service) at the **Préfecture de Police** (Map pp396-9; ☎ 01 53 71 51 68; 1 place Louis Lépine, 4e; metro Cité; 🕑 8.35am-4.45pm Mon-Thu, 8.35am-4.15pm Fri) for guidance.

If you don't need a visa to visit France, you'll almost certainly qualify for another automatic three-month stay, eg if you take the train to, say, Geneva or Brussels and then re-enter France. The fewer recent French entry stamps you have in your passport the easier this is likely to be.

If you needed a visa the first time around, one way to extend your stay is to go to a French consulate in a neighbouring country and apply for another one there.

WEBSITES

Lonely Planet's website (www.lonelyplanet .com) is a good start for many of Paris' more useful links. Other good English-language websites about Paris and France include:

France Diplomatie (www.france.diplomatie.fr) Includes lists of embassies and consulates with visa information.

French Government Tourism Office (www.francetourism .com) Official tourism site with all manner of information on and about travel in France and lots on Paris.

Mairie de Paris (www.paris.fr) Statistics and city information direct from the Hôtel de Ville.

Meteo France (www.meteoconsult.fr) Current weather conditions and five-day forecasts.

Metropole Paris (www.metropoleparis.com) Excellent online magazine in English.

Paris Pages (www.paris.org) Good links to museums and cultural events.

Paris Tourist Office (www.paris-touristoffice.com) Super site with more links than you'll ever need.

WOMEN TRAVELLERS

French women obtained suffrage in 1945 from de Gaulle's short-lived postwar government, but until 1964 a woman still needed her husband's permission to open a bank account or get a passport. Younger French women especially are quite outspoken and emancipated but self-confidence has yet to translate into equality in the workplace, where women are passed over for senior and management positions in favour of their male colleagues.

Information & Organisations

France's women's liberation movement flourished along as in other countries in the late 1960s and early 1970s, but by the mid-'80s had become moribund. For reasons that have more to do with French society than anything else, few women's groups function as the kind of supportive social institutions that exist in the USA, the UK and Australia.

The women-only **Association Maison des Femmes de Paris** (Map pp392–5; ☎ 01 43 43 41 13; http://maisondesfemmes.free.fr in French; 163 rue Charenton, 12e; metro Reuilly Diderot; ☺ office 9am-7pm Mon-Wed, 9am-5pm Thu

& Fri) is a meeting place for women of all ages and nationalities, with events, workshops and exhibitions scheduled throughout the week.

France's national **rape-crisis hotline** (☎ 08 00 05 95 95; ☺ 10am-6pm Mon-Fri) can be reached toll-free from any telephone, without using a phonecard.

An excellent all-round website for travelling women is www.journeywoman.com.

Safety Precautions

Female travellers need not fear walking around Paris; people are rarely assaulted on the street. However, the French seem to have given relatively little thought to *harcèlement sexuel* (sexual harassment), and many men still think that to stare suavely at a passing woman is to pay her a compliment.

Using the metro until late at night is generally all right, but there are certain stations you might want to avoid (see p349).

In an emergency, you can always call the **police** (☎ 17). Medical, psychological and legal services are available to people referred by the police at the **Service Médico-Judiciaire** (☎ 01 42 34 86 78; ☺ 24hr) of the Hôtel Dieu (see p346).

WORK

Although there are strict laws preventing non-EU nationals from being employed in France, it's increasingly possible to work 'in the black' (ie without the legally required documents). Au pair work is popular and can be done legally even by non-EU nationals.

For practical information on employment in Paris, consider picking up *Living & Working in Paris: Your First-Hand Introduction to This Capital City* by Alan Hart. Other useful titles include *Live and Work in France* by Victoria Pybus, *Living and Working in France: A Survival Handbook* by David Hampshire and *Living, Studying, and Working in France: Everything You Need To Know To Fulfil Your Dreams of Living Abroad* by Saskia Reilly and Lorin David Kalisky.

To work legally in France you need a *carte de séjour* (see p352). Getting one is almost automatic for EU nationals and almost impossible for anyone else except full-time students.

Non-EU nationals cannot work legally unless they obtain an *autorisation de travail* (work permit) before arriving in France. This is no easy matter, as a prospective employer has to convince the authorities that there is no French person – or other EU national, for that matter – who can do the job being offered to you.

Au Pair

Under the au pair system, single people aged 18 to about 27, who are studying in France, can live with a French family and receive lodging, full board and some pocket money in exchange for taking care of the kids, babysitting, doing light housework and perhaps teaching English to the children. Most families prefer young women, but some positions are also available for men. Many families want au pairs who are native English-speakers; knowing at least some French may be a prerequisite. For practical information, pick up the outdated but useful *Au Pair and Nanny's Guide to Working Abroad* by Susan Griffith and Sharon Legg.

By law, au pairs must have one full day off a week. Some families may provide metro passes. The family must also pay for French social security, which covers about 70% of medical expenses (get supplementary insurance if you are not an EU citizen).

Residents of the EU can easily arrange for an au pair job and a *carte de séjour* after arriving in France. Non-EU nationals who decide to look for au pair work after entering the country cannot do so legally and won't be covered by the protections provided for under French law.

Check the bulletin boards at the American Church (see p348) as well as *FUSAC* (see p348) for job ads. In the latter, you'll find au pair work listed under 'Childcare Positions'.

Information & Organisations

The fortnightly *FUSAC* (see p348) is an excellent source for job-seekers; check out the classified ads under 'Employment & Careers'.

The following agencies might be of some assistance.

Agence Nationale pour l'Emploi (ANPE; www.anpe.fr in French) France's national employment service has lists of job openings and branches throughout the city.
The following assists those residing in the 1er, 2e and 12e arrondissements: **ANPE Hôtel de Ville** (Map pp396-9; ☎ 01 42 71 24 68; 20bis rue Ste-Croix de la Bretonnerie, 4e; metro Hôtel de Ville)

Centres d'Information et de Documentation Jeunesse (www.cidj.com in French) CIDJ offices have information on housing, professional training and educational options, and notice boards with work possibilities. Its **Paris headquarters** (☎ 01 44 49 12 00; 101 quai Branly, 15e; metro Champ de Mars-Tour Eiffel; ✆ 10am-6pm Mon-Fri, 9.30am-1pm Sat) is a short distance southwest of the Eiffel Tower.

Social   356
Be Polite!   356
Meeting People   356
Going Out   356

Practical   356
Question Words   356
Numbers & Amounts   357
Days   357
Banking   357
Post   357
Phones & Mobiles   357
Internet   357
Transport   358

Food   358

Emergencies   358

Health   358
Symptoms   358

Glossary   358

Language

Language

It's true – anyone can speak another language. Don't worry if you haven't studied languages before or that you studied a language at school for years and can't remember any of it. It doesn't even matter if you failed English grammar. After all, that's never affected your ability to speak English! And this is the key to picking up a language in another country. You just need to start speaking.

Learn a few key phrases before you go. Write them on pieces of paper and stick them on the fridge, by the bed or even on the computer – anywhere that you'll see them often.

You'll find that locals appreciate travellers trying their language, no matter how muddled you may think you sound. So don't just stand there, say something! If you want to learn more French than we've included here, pick up a copy of Lonely Planet's comprehensive but user-friendly *French Phrasebook*.

SOCIAL
Be Polite!

Politeness pays dividends in Parisian daily life and the easiest way to make a good impression on Parisian merchants is always to say *Bonjour Monsieur/Madame/Mademoiselle* when you enter a shop, and *Merci Monsieur/ Madame/Mademoiselle, au revoir* when you leave. *Monsieur* means 'sir' and can be used with any adult male. *Madame* is used where 'Mrs' or 'Ma'am' would apply in English. Officially, *Mademoiselle* (Miss) relates to unmarried women, but it's much more common to use *Madame* – unless of course you know the person's marital status! Similarly, if you want help or need to interrupt someone, approach them with *Excusez-moi, Monsieur/Madame/Mademoiselle*.

Meeting People

Hello.
Bonjour/Salut. (polite/informal)
Goodbye.
Au revoir/Salut. (polite/informal)
Please.
S'il vous plaît.
Thank you (very much).
Merci (beaucoup).
Yes/No.
Oui/Non.
Do you speak English?
Parlez-vous anglais?
Do you understand (me)?
Est-ce que vous (me) comprenez?
Yes, I understand.
Oui, je comprends.

No, I don't understand.
Non, je ne comprends pas.

Could you please ...?
Pourriez-vous ..., s'il vous plaît?
  repeat that — répéter
  speak more slowly — parler plus lentement
  write it down — l'écrire

Going Out

What's on ...?
Qu'est-ce qu'on joue ...?
  locally — dans le coin
  this weekend — ce week-end
  today — aujourd'hui
  tonight — ce soir

Where are the ...?
Où sont les ...?
  clubs — clubs/boîtes
  gay venues — boîtes gaies
  places to eat — restaurants
  pubs — pubs

Is there a local entertainment guide?
Y a-t-il un programme des spectacles?

PRACTICAL
Question Words

Who?	Qui?
Which?	Quel/Quelle? (m/f)
When?	Quand?
Where?	Où?
How?	Comment?

Numbers & Amounts

0	zéro
1	un
2	deux
3	trois
4	quatre
5	cinq
6	six
7	sept
8	huit
9	neuf
10	dix
11	onze
12	douze
13	treize
14	quatorze
15	quinze
16	seize
17	dix-sept
18	dix-huit
19	dix-neuf
20	vingt
21	vingt et un
22	vingt deux
30	trente
40	quarante
50	cinquante
60	soixante
70	soixante-dix
80	quatre-vingts
90	quatre-vingt-dix
100	cent
1000	mille
2000	deux mille

Days

Monday	lundi
Tuesday	mardi
Wednesday	mercredi
Thursday	jeudi
Friday	vendredi
Saturday	samedi
Sunday	dimanche

Banking

I'd like to ...
Je voudrais ...

cash a cheque	encaisser un chèque
change money	changer de l'argent
change some travellers cheques	changer des chèques de voyage

Where's the nearest ...?
Où est ... le plus prochain?

ATM	le guichet automatique

foreign exchange office — le bureau de change

Post

Where is the post office?
Où est le bureau de poste?

I want to send a ...
Je voudrais envoyer ...

fax	un fax
letter	une lettre
parcel	un colis
postcard	une carte postale

I want to buy ...
Je voudrais acheter ...

an aerogram	un aérogramme
an envelope	une enveloppe
a stamp	un timbre

Phones & Mobiles

I want to buy a phone card.
Je voudrais acheter une carte téléphonique.
I want to make a call (to Australia/to Rome).
Je veux téléphoner (en Australie/à Rome).
I want to make a reverse-charge/collect call.
Je veux téléphoner avec préavis en PCV.
   ('PCV' is pronounced 'pay say vay')

Where can I find a/an ...?
Où est-ce quee je peux trouver ...?
I'd like a/an ...
Je voudrais ...

adaptor plug	une prise multiple
charger for my phone	un chargeur pour mon portable
mobile/cell phone for hire	louer un portable
prepaid mobile/ cell phone	un portable pré-payé
SIM card for your network	une carte SIM pour le réseau

Internet

Where's the local Internet café?
Où est le cybercafé du coin?

I'd like to ...
Je voudrais ...

check my email	consulter mon courrier électronique
get online	me connecter à l'internet

Transport

What time does the ... leave?
À quelle heure part ...?

bus	le bus
ferry	le bateau
plane	l'avion
train	le train

What time's the ... bus?
Le ... bus passe à quelle heure?

first	premier
last	dernier
next	prochain

Are you free? (taxi)
Vous êtes libre?
Please put the meter on.
Mettez le compteur, s'il vous plaît?
How much is it to ...?
C'est combien pour aller à ...?
Please take me to (this address).
Conduisez-moi à (cette adresse), s'il vous plaît.

FOOD

breakfast	le petit déjeuner
lunch	le déjeuner
dinner	le dîner
snack	un casse-croûte
eat	manger
drink	boire

Can you recommend a ...
Est-ce que vous pouvez me conseiller un ...

bar/pub	bar/pub
café	café
restaurant	un restaurant

Is service/cover charge included in the bill?
Le service est compris?

For more detailed information on food and dining out, see 'Food & Drink' on p43.

EMERGENCIES

It's an emergency!
C'est urgent!
Could you please help me/us?
Este-ce que vous pourriez m'aider/nous aider, s'il vous plaît?
Call the police/a doctor/an ambulance!
Appelez la police/un médecin/une ambulance!
Where's the police station?
Où est le commissariat (de police)?

HEALTH

Where's the nearest ...?
Où est ... le/la plus prochain/e? (m/f)

chemist (night)	la pharmacie (de nuit)
dentist	le dentiste
doctor	le médecin
hospital	l'hôpital (m)

I need a doctor (who speaks English).
J'ai besoin d'un médecin (qui parle anglais).

Symptoms

I have (a) ...
J'ai ...

diarrhoea	la diarrhée
fever	de la fièvre
headache	mal à la tête
pain	une douleur

Glossary

(m) indicates masculine gender, (f) feminine gender, (pl) plural and (adj) adjective

arrondissement (m) – one of 20 administrative divisions in Paris; abbreviated on signs as 1er (1st arrondissement), 2e or 2ème (2nd) and so on
auberge de jeunesse (f) – (youth) hostel

belle époque (f) – literally 'beautiful age'; era of elegance and gaiety characterising fashionable Parisian life in the period preceding WWI
billeterie (f) – ticket office or counter
bon vivant – a person who enjoys good food and drink
boulangerie (f) – bakery
boules (f pl) – a game played with heavy metal balls on a sandy pitch; also called *pétanque*

brasserie (f) – brewery; a restaurant usually serving food all day
brioche – small roll or cake, sometimes made with nuts, currants or candied fruits
bureau de change (m) – currency exchange bureau
bureau des objets trouvés (m) – lost and found bureau, lost property office

cacher or **casher (adj)** – kosher
carnet (m) – a book of five or 10 bus, tram, metro or other tickets sold at a reduced rate
carrefour (m) – crossroad, intersection
carte (f) – card; menu; map
carte de séjour – residence permit
chanson française (f) – literally 'French song'; traditional musical genre where lyrics are paramount
chansonnier (m) – cabaret singer

charcuterie (f) – a variety of pork products that are cured, smoked or processed, including sausages, hams, pâtés and rillettes; shop selling these products

cimetière (m) – cemetery

cour (f) – courtyard

crêpe (f) – a large, paper-thin pancake served with various fillings, both savoury and sweet

demi (m) – half; 330mL glass of beer

département (m) – administrative division of France

digestif (m) – digestive; a drink served after a meal

eau (f) – water

église (f) – church

épicerie (f) – small grocer's store

escalier (m) – stairway

espace (f) – space; outlet or branch

forêt (la) – forest

formule or **formule rapide (f)** – similar to a *menu* but allows choice of whichever two of three courses you want (eg starter and main course or main course and dessert)

fromagerie (f) – cheese shop

fumoir (f) – smoking room or chamber

galerie (f) – gallery; covered shopping arcade (also called *passage*)

galette (f) – a pancake or flat pastry, with a variety of (usually savoury) fillings; see also *crêpe*

gare or **gare SNCF (f)** – railway station

gare routière (f) – bus station

Grands Boulevards (m pl) – literally 'Great Boulevards'; the eight contiguous broad thoroughfares that stretch from place de la Madeleine eastwards to the place de la République, which were a centre of café and theatre life in the 18th and 19th centuries

grand projet (m) – huge, public edifice erected by a government or politician generally in a bid to immortalise themselves

gratin (m) – dish cooked in the oven and browned with breadcrumbs or cheese

halles (f pl) – (covered) food market

hameau (m) – hamlet

hammam (m) – steam room, Turkish bath

haute cuisine (f) – literally 'high cuisine'; classic French style of cooking typified by elaborately prepared multi-course meals

hôtel de ville (m) – city or town hall

hôtel particuliers (m pl) – private mansions

intra-muros – literally 'within the walls' (Latin); refers to central Paris

jardin (m) – garden

kir (m) – white wine sweetened with a blackcurrant (or other) liqueur

laverie (f) – laundrette

lycée (m) – secondary school

mairie (f) – city or town hall

marché – market

marché aux puces (m) – flea market

menu (m) – fixed-price meal with two or more courses; see *formule*

musée (m) – museum

nocturne (f) – late night opening at a shop, museum etc

palais de justice (m) – law courts

parvis (m) – square in front of a church or public building

passage (m) – covered shopping arcade (also called *galerie*)

pastis (m) – an aniseed-flavoured apéritif than turns cloudy when you add water

pâté (m) – potted meat; a thickish paste, often of pork, cooked in a ceramic dish and served cold (sometimes called terrine)

pâtisserie (f) – cakes and pastries; shop selling these products

pelouse (f) – lawn

pétanque (f) – see *boules*

pied-noir (m) – literally 'black foot'; French colonial born in Algeria

place (f) – place; square or plaza

plan du quartier (m) – map of nearby streets (hung on the wall near metro exits)

plat du jour (m) – daily special in a restaurant

poissonnerie (f) – fishmonger, fish shop

pont (m) – bridge

port (m) – harbour, port

port de plaisance (m) – boat harbour or marina

porte (f) – door; gate in a city wall

préfecture (f) – prefecture (ie capital of a *département*)

quai (m) – quay; railway platform

quartier (m) – quarter, district, neighbourhood

raï (m) – a type of Algerian popular music

résidence (f) – residence; hotel for long-term stays

rillettes (f pl) – shredded potted meat or fish

rive (f) – bank of a river

rond point (m) – roundabout

rue (f) – street or road

salon de thé (m) – tearoom

soldes (m pl) – sale, the sales

sono mondiale (f) world music

spectacle (m) – performance, play or theatrical show

square (m) – public garden

tabac (m) – tobacconist (also selling bus tickets, phone-cards etc)

tartine (f) – a slice of bread with any topping or garnish

télécarte (f) – phonecard

tour (f) – tower

traiteur (m) – caterer or delicatessen

vélo (m) – bicycle

vin de table (m) – table wine

voie (f) – way; train platform

Behind the Scenes

THE LONELY PLANET STORY

The story begins with a classic travel adventure: Tony and Maureen Wheeler's 1972 journey across Europe and Asia to Australia. There was no useful information about the overland trail then, so Tony and Maureen published the first Lonely Planet guidebook to meet a growing need.

From a kitchen table, Lonely Planet has grown to become the largest independent travel publisher in the world, with offices in Melbourne (Australia), Oakland (USA), London (UK) and Paris (France).

Today Lonely Planet guidebooks cover the globe. There is an ever-growing list of books and information in a variety of media. Some things haven't changed. The main aim is still to make it possible for adventurous travellers to get out there – to explore and better understand the world.

At Lonely Planet we believe travellers can make a positive contribution to the countries they visit – if they respect their host communities and spend their money wisely.

THIS BOOK

This is the 5th edition of *Paris*. The 1st edition was researched and written by Daniel Robinson and Tony Wheeler. The 2nd, 3rd and 4th editions were updated by Steve Fallon, who returned to Paris to revise, expand and update this edition. The guide was commissioned in Lonely Planet's London office, and produced by:

Commissioning Editor Sam Trafford
Coordinating Editor Charlotte Keown, Maryanne Netto, Gina Tsarouhas
Coordinating Cartographers Joelene Kowalski, Simon Tillema
Coordinating Layout Designer Pablo Gastar
Editors Michelle Coxall, Barbara Delissen, Victoria Harrison, Samantha McCrow, Kate McLeod, Kristin Odijk, Sally Steward
Cartographers Lachlan Ross
Layout Designers Adam Bextream, Yvonne Bischofberger, Steven Cann, Sally Darmody, Laura Jane, Michael Ruff, Jacqui Saunders, John Shippick, Tamsin Wilson
Cover Designer Nic Lehman
Series Designer Nic Lehman
Series Design Concept Nic Lehman, Andrew Weatherill
Managing Cartographer Mark Griffiths
Mapping Development Paul Piaia
Project Manager Glenn van der Knijff, Sally Darmody
Language Editor Quentin Frayne
Regional Publishing Manager Amanda Canning
Series Publishing Manager Gabrielle Green

Thanks to Ingmar Collinson, Michala Green, Charlotte Harrison, Nancy Ianni, Craig Kilburn, Adriana Mammarella, Kate McDonald, Darren O'Connell, Emma Sangster

Cover photographs Paris, Alexandre III Bridge, Jerry Driendl/Getty Images (top); Art Nouveau metro Chateau d'Eau sign, Martin Moos/Lonely Planet Images (bottom).

Internal photographs by Jonathan Smith/Lonely Planet Images except for the following: p99 (#3) Glenn van der Knijff/Lonely Planet Images; p60, p99 (#2), p102 (#2, 3), p103 (#1, 2, 3), p173 (#1), p176 (#3), p206, p214 (#3), p215 (#2), p244 Martin Moos/Lonely Planet Images; p102 (#1) Bethune Carmichael/Lonely Planet Images; p171 (#1), p215 (#1), p241, p266 Rob Flynn/Lonely Planet Images; p172 (#3) p318 Stephen Saks/Lonely Planet Images; p172 (#2) Juliet Coombe/Lonely Planet Images; p171 (#3), p176 (#2), p218 (#3) Neil Setchfield/Lonely Planet Images; p173 (#2) Brenda Turnnidge/Lonely Planet Images; p177 (#1) Mark Honan/Lonely Planet Images; p177 (#2) Greg Elms/Lonely Planet Images; p215 (#2) Manfred Gottschalk/Lonely Planet Images; p218 (#2), p307 Christopher Wood/Lonely Planet Images; p218 (#3) John Hay/Lonely; p312 Diana Mayfield/Lonely Planet Images; p313 Greg Gawslowski/Planet Images. All images are the copyright of the photographers unless otherwise indicated. Many of the images in this guide are available for licensing from Lonely Planet Images: www.lonelyplanetimages.com.

SEND US YOUR FEEDBACK

We love to hear from travellers – your comments keep us on our toes and help make our books better. Our well-travelled team reads every word on what you loved or loathed about this book. Although we cannot reply individually to postal submissions, we always guarantee that your feedback goes straight to the appropriate authors, in time for the next edition. Each person who sends us information is thanked in the next edition – and the most useful submissions are rewarded with a free book.

To send us your updates – and find out about LP events, newsletters and travel news – visit our award-winning website: www.lonelyplanet.com.

Note: We may edit, reproduce and incorporate your comments in Lonely Planet products such as guidebooks, websites and digital products, so let us know if you don't want your comments reproduced or your name acknowledged. For a copy of our privacy policy visit www.lonelyplanet.com/privacy.

ACKNOWLEDGMENTS

Many thanks to the RATP for the use of its transit map © RATP – CML Agence Cartographique.

THANKS

STEVE FALLON

A number of people helped in the updating of *Paris* but first and foremost stands resident Brenda Turnnidge, whose knowledge of all things Parisian – especially fashion, transport and *les bonnes addresses* – never ceases to amaze and excite. Thanks, too, to Zahia Hafs, Olivier Cirendini, Caroline Guilleminot and Chew Terrière for assistance, ideas, hospitality and/or a few laughs during what was a very grey, very bleak winter. As always, I'd like to dedicate my efforts to my partner, Michael Rothschild, whose knowledge of *menu* French grows in direct proportion to...well, never mind.

OUR READERS

Many thanks to the travellers who used the last edition and wrote to us with helpful hints, useful advice and interesting anecdotes. Your names follow:

Susan Alexander, Richard Bacon, Niti Bagchi, Lance Balcom, Lenore Baken, Nigel Beauchamp, Ann Berne, Karry Brenann, Maria Bursey, Muriel Cahen, Kenny Campbell, Sam Carter, Nikitas Chondroyannos, Elspeth Christie, Greta Cleghorn, David Cruden, Laura & Ami Diner, Susan Dumas, Colin Dunn, Benjamin Dyson, Craig Falls, Lea Feng, Mat Fitzwilliam, Alexander Forsen, Michael Foth, Margaret Frey, Jacqueline Gilmartin, John Grant, David Grumett, Anne Haas, Melanie Hall, Isabelle Hanssens, Jim Hendrickson, Evan Hirsch, Gail Hopley, Christine Hwang, Irvin Ilarde, Tony Jonkx, Marilyn Jupp, Jude Anton Jusayan, Patricia Kaddar, R Karlmarx, Dawn Keremitsis, Anke Kramm, Andreas Krueger, Marc Liberati, Nana Lim, Tita Luisa, Peter MacLean, Janina & James McBean, Robert S. Miller, Shantanu Mukherjee, Brian Murphy, Nichole Negrete, Mark Nunez, Gunnar Øregaard, Fiona Parrott, Tamas Patko, Stephane Reynolds, Anne & Peter Rolston, Linda Scira, Brenda Scofield, Neha Singhal, Jacalyn Soo, William Space, James Stern, Jill Strosser, David W. Stultz, Helen Sykes, Bill Thames, Caroline Topp, Edward Tsui, Tim van Meurs, Brigitte Voykowitsch, Matthew Wilner-Reid, Keefe Wong, Lyn and Clara Yates, Andrew Young

Notes

Notes

Notes

Notes

Notes

Index

See also separate indexes for Eating (p375), Shopping (p377) and Sleeping (p377).

13e arrondissement 125
  drinking 228
  food 199-200
15e arrondissement 126
  accommodation 302
  food 200-2
16e arrondissement 113-17
  food 186

A

Abélard, Pierre 26
absinthe 328, 329
Académie du Spectacle
  Équestre 311
Académie Française 98
accommodation 280-304,
  338-9, *see also indi-*
  vidual neighbourhoods,
  Sleeping index p377
activities, *see individual*
  activities, sports
Aéroport d'Orly 332-3
Aéroport Paris-Beauvais
  333-4
Aéroport Roissy Charles de
  Gaulle 333
Agence Marivaux 207
Agence Perrossier 207
agnès b 273
air travel 332-4
airlines 332
airports 332-4
Alaïa, Azzedine 275
ambulance services 342
American Church 231
AMF Bowling de
  Montparnasse 248
AMF Bowling de
  Paris 248
Amnésia 208
Amor, Fayçal 275
apartments 283
Aquaboulevard 249
Aquarium Tropical 131
Arc de Triomphe 117
Arc de Triomphe du
  Carrousel 82, **34**, **106**
architecture 34-42
  Art Nouveau 39
  baroque 37-8
  Carolingian 35

contemporary 40-2
controversial build-
  ings 38
Gallo-Roman 35
Gothic 36-7
Merovingian 35
modern 39-40
Neoclassicism 38-9
Renaissance 37
Romanesque 35-6
Archives Nationales 89
Arènes de Lutèce 95
Argonaut 130
arrondissements 19, 74-136
arts 22-32
  art towns 308
  metro art 84
Assemblée Nationale 111
Atelier Brancusi 85
Atelier des Nymphéas 326
Ateliers d'Artistes de
  Belleville-Les Portes
  Ouvertes 10
ATMs 346
Au 224
Au Lapin Agile 233
au pair system 354
Au Petit Fer à Cheval 208
Au Petit Garage 226
Au Tango 235
Auvers-sur-Oise 308, 327-9,
  328
Av des Champs-Élysées
  118, **135**

B

B&Bs 282
babysitting services 340
Balabus 78
ballet 32
Ballon Eutelsat 76
Balzac, Honoré 115
Banana Café 208
Banlieues Bleues 10
Bar à Vins Nicolas 227
Barbizon 316
Barbizon School 28
bargaining 253
Barrio Latino 208-9
Basilique de St-Denis 36,
  135-6

Basilique du Sacré Cœur
  127, **104**
Bassin Agam 134
Bastille 86-90
  accommodation 285-9
  drinking 208-20
  food 159-67
  shopping 254-68
Bastille Day (14 July) 11
Bateaux Mouches 78
Bateaux Parisiens 77
bathrooms 351
Batobus 334
Baudelaire, Charles 23
Baz'Art Café 209
belle epoque 68
Belleville 123-4
  accommodation 301
  drinking 226-7
  food 194-7
Bercy 124-5
  drinking 227-8
  food 197-9
  shopping 267
Bibliothèque Mazarine 98
Bibliothèque Nationale de
  France 125
Bibliothèque Publique
  d'Information 85
bicycle travel, *see* cycling
Bike 'n' Roller 246, 247
Bistrot à Vin Jacques Mélac
  227
Bistrot Latin 232
Black Death 62
Bliss Kfé 209
blues 231-2
boat travel 334, *see also*
  cruises
Boca Chica 209
Bois de Boulogne 131-2
Bois de Vincennes 130
Bonaparte, Napoleon 66-7
books 13, 25, *see also*
  literature
  architecture 39
  history 71
bookstores 260
Boteco 226
Bottle Shop 209
Bouchard, Henri 115

boules 248
Bourdelle, Antoine 109
Bourse de Commerce 85
bowling 248
Bowling Mouffetard 248
Brancusi, Constantin 30, 85
bread 47
Buddha Bar 224
Bui, Barbara 274
bus travel 334-5
Bushwacker's 225
business 339
business hours 150, 252, 339

C

cabaret revues 242
Cabinet des Livres 318
Cabinet des Monnaies,
  Médailles et Antiques 83
Café Aussie 221
Café Charbon 226
Café de Flore 222
Café de la Danse 229
Café de la Gare 240
Café de la Mairie 222
Café Delmas 221
Café des Phares 209
Café du Musée Rodin 224
Café Léopard 209
Café Noir 225
Café Oz 208, **214**
Café Thoumieux 224
Café Universel 231
canal cruises 77
Canal St-Martin 122, **176**
Canauxrama 77
cancan 242
Cannibale Café 226
Capet, Hugh 61
car hire 335-6
car parking 336
car travel 335-6
Cardin, Pierre 272
carte de séjour 352
Carte Orange 337
Catacombes 110
Cathédrale de Notre Dame
  (Senlis) 321
Cathédrale de Notre Dame
  de Paris 91-2, 231,
  2, **105**

Cathédrale Notre Dame de Chartres 322, 324, 325
Cathédrale St-Louis 311
cathedrals, see churches
Centre Culturel Pouya 225
Centre de la Mer 94
Centre des Monuments Nationaux 88
Centre des Nouvelles Industries et Technologies 133
Centre d'Informations Musicales 130
Centre Pompidou 6, 83, **100**
Chai 33 227
Chalayan, Hussein 275
Champs-Élysées 117-18, 297-8, **2**, **211**
food 186-8
shopping 262
Chanel, Coco 271
chansons française 30, 233-4
Chantilly 307, 318-21, **319**
Chapelle de la Sorbonne 94
Chapelle de la Trinité 314
Chapelle de St-Symphorien 97
Chapelle Expiatoire 120
Chapelle Royale 131
charcuterie 49
Chartres 307, 322-6, **322-3**
Château d'Auvers 327
Château de Bagatelle 131
Château de Chantilly 318, 320, **318**
Château de Fontainebleau 314-16, 316, **218**, **313**
Château de Vaux-le-Vicomte 317
Château de Versailles 308-11, 312, **312**
Château de Vincennes 131
Châtelet-Théâtre Musical de Paris 230
cheese 47
chemists 348
Chez Adel 233
Chez Louisette 233-4
Chez Prune 225
Chez Wolf Motown Bar 226
children, travel with 107, 339-40

000 map pages
000 photographs

babysitting organisations 340
Bois de Boulogne 131-2
Bois de Vincennes 130
Cité des Sciences et de l'Industrie 129-30
food 58
Jardin du Luxembourg 107
Palais de la Découverte 118
Parc de la Villette 128-9
China Club 210
Chinatown 125
drinking 228
food 199-200
Chinese New Year 9
Chirac, Jacques 8, 19, 72
Christmas Eve Mass 11
churches, see also église
Basilique de St-Denis 135-6
Basilique du Sacré Cœur 127
Cathédrale de Notre Dame de Paris 91-2, **2**, **105**
Cathédrale Notre Dame de Chartres 322
Cathédrale St-Louis 311
Chapelle de la Sorbonne 94
Cimetière de Montmartre 128
Cimetière du Montparnasse 109-10, **171**
Cimetière du Père Lachaise 6, 123-4, **171**
Cinaxe 129
cinema 10, 31, 238-9
Cinéma des Cinéastes 238
Cinémathèque Française 238-9
Cité de la Musique 130, 232
Cité des Enfants 129
Cité des Sciences et de l'Industrie 129-30
Cityrama 78, 308
classical music 230
Clichy 119-20
accommodation 298
drinking 224-5
food 188-9
climate 340
Clos Normand 326
clothing sizes 255
Club Med Gym 248

Club Quartier Latin 248
Club Zed 235
clubbing 234-8
Colette 24
Colonne de Juillet 90
Colonne Vendôme 83
Comédie Française 83, 239-40
comedy 240-1
Conciergerie 92
Concorde 118-19
drinking 224
Conservatoire National Supérieur de Musique et de Danse 232
consulates 342
cooking courses 340
Coolín 222
Corcoran's Clichy 228
costs 6, 16, 18
accommodation 280-1
food 150
taxes 253, 349
Courréges, André 273
courses 340-1
couturiers 271-2
Crazy Horse 242
credit cards 347
Crème Chantilly 319, 320
Cricketer Pub 224
cruises 77-8, **99**
Crypte Archéologique 92
Cubana Café 223
culture 11-18
books 13
customs 14-15
customs regulations 341
CyberLouvre 81
Cyberposte 344
Cycles À La Petite Reine 316
cycling 245, 246-7, 312, 316, see also Tour de France
tours 77

D
Dalí, Salvador 127
dance 32, 242
Daubigny, Charles-François 327
de Beauvoir, Simone 24, 27
de Gaulle, Charles 70
Delacroix, Eugène 98
Delanoë, Bertrand 19, 72
dental care 346
Descartes, René 26
Dior, Christian 271

disabled travellers 341
discount cards 341-2
Disneyland Resort Paris 308, 329-30
drink driving 345
drinking 51-4, 207-29
duplex 235
Duras, Marguerite 24

E
École Militaire 114
economy 18
education 15
Edward & Son 228
Église de la Madeleine 119, 231
Église du Dôme 113, **110**
Église Notre Dame (Auvers-sur-Oise) 327
Église Notre Dame de la Pentecôte 135
Église Notre Dame de l'Espérance 90
Église Royale du Val-de-Grâce 231
Église St-Aignan 324, 325
Église St-Étienne du Mont 94-5, 231
Église St-Eustache 85, 231, **214**, **230**
Église St-Germain des Prés 97, 231
Église St-Germain L'Auxerrois 82, **101**
Église St-Julien le Pauvre 231
Église St-Louis des Invalides 113
Église St-Louis en l'Île 93
Église St-Paul-St-Louis 231
Église St-Pierre 324, 325
Église St-Pierre de Montmartre 127
Église St-Sulpice 107
Eiffel Tower 114, **2**, **105**, **113**, **178**
electricity 342
embassies 342
emergency phone numbers 342-3, 346, see also inside front cover
environmental issues 19-20
Erotokritos 275
Espace Salvador Dalí 127
Espace Vit' Halles 249
Esplanade des Invalides 112

Étoile 117-18
  accommodation 297-8
  food 186-188
  shopping 262-3
Eurolines 335
exchange rates, *see inside front cover*
Explora 129
Exploradôme 132

F

fashion 270-8, *see also* shopping
  clothing sizes 255
  designer garment sales 276
  designers 271-6
  Espace Créateurs 276
  St-Sulpice 259
  Triangle d'Or 262
Fat Tire Bike Tours 77, 246
Faubourg St-Germain 110-13
  accommodation 297
  drinking 224
  food 184-6
  shopping 261-2
Féraud, Louis 272
Festival d'Automne 11
Festival du Film de Paris 10
festivals & events 9-11, *see also* music festivals
Fête de la Musique 10
Fête des Vendanges à Montmartre 11
films, *see* cinema
Finnegan's Wake 221
fire services 342
fitness clubs 248-9
Flame of Liberty Memorial 116
Flaubert, Gustave 23
Fnac 207
Foire de Paris 10
Foire du Trône 10, 131
Foire Internationale d'Art Contemporain 11
Folies-Bergère 242
Folies Pigalle 235
Fondation Dubuffet 109
Fontainebleau 307, 313-16, **315**
Fontaine des Innocents 85
Fontaine des Médicis 107
Fontaine des Quatre Évêques 107
food 44-58, 150-204, *see also* Eating index p375

booking 150
business hours 150
chain restaurants 151
costs 150
culture 45-7
custom 14, 15-16, 46-7
eateries, types of 55-8
ethnic cuisine 51
etiquette 46
fast-food 151
festivals 54-5
history 44-5, 63, 167
markets 152-3
paying 151
regional specialities 49-51
self-catering 57, 153-5
staples 47-9
tipping 151
university canteens 152
vegetarians & vegans 58
football 16, 244-5
Forêt de Chantilly 319-20
Forêt de Fontainebleau 313, 315-16
Forum des Halles 85
Forum des Images 239
French chansons 30, 233-4
French Open 10, 16, 245
French Revolution 65-6
Frog at Bercy Village 227-8
Full Metal 235
funicular 338

G

Galerie de Montpensier 83
Galerie de Valois 83
Galerie François 314
Galerie Vivienne 145, **22**, **100**
Galeries Nationales du Grand Palais 118
Gare de l'Est 121-2
  accommodation 299-301
  drinking 225-6
  food 191-4
  shopping 266
Gare de Lyon 124-5
  accommodation 302
  drinking 227-8
  food 197-9
  shopping 267
Gare du Nord 121-2
  accommodation 299, 299-301
  drinking 225-6

food 191-4
  shopping 266
Gare Montparnasse 108
Gare St-Lazare 119-20
  accommodation 298
  drinking 224-5
Gaultier, Jean-Paul 274
Gay Pride March 10
gay travellers 10, 209, 343
Géode 129
geography 19
Gepetto & Vélos 77, 246
Gibus 235
Givenchy, Hubert 272
Giverny 308, 326-7
Gorges d'Apremont 316
Gorges de Franchard 316
government 18-19
Grand Bassin 107
Grand Canal 309
Grand Château 318
Grand Palais 118
Grand Portal 321
Grand Trianon 309, 312
Grande Arche de la Défense 134, **42**, **106**
Grande Écurie 319
Grande Perspective 309, 312
Grande Pyramide 80
Grandes Eaux Musicales 309, 312
Grands Boulevards 120-1
  accommodation 298
  drinking 225
  food 189-91
  shopping 265-6
Guimard, Hector 39
Guimard synagogue 89
gyms 248-9

H

Hameau (Chantilly) 319
Hameau de la Reine 311
hammam 249-50
Hammam de la Mosquée de Paris 249
Hammam des Grands Boulevards 250
Hammam Pacha 250
Harry's New York Bar 225
Haussmann, Georges-Eugène 34
haute couture 270-1
Havanita Café 210
health & fitness 244-50
Hébert, Ernest 109

Hemingway Bar 224
Hermès 273
Hippodrome 319
Hippodrome d'Auteuil 132, 245-6
Hippodrome de Longchamp 132
history 60-72
  belle époque 68
  Carolingians 61
  Dreyfus Affair, the 68-9
  Fifth Republic 70-1
  First Empire 66-7
  First Republic 65-6
  Fourth Republic 70
  French Revolution 65-6
  Gauls 60-1
  Louis XIV 64-5
  Merovingians 61
  Middle Ages 61-2
  present, the 72
  Romans 60-1
  Reformation 63-4
  Renaissance 62-3
  republican calendar 66
  Second Empire 67-8
  Second Republic 67
  Tennis Court Oath 311
  Third Republic 68-9
  WWI 69
  WWII 69-70
holidays 343-4
homestays 282
horse racing 245-6
hospitals 346
hostels 281
Hôtel de Cluny 94
Hôtel de la Monnaie 98
Hôtel de Sully 88
Hôtel de Ville 87
Hôtel des Invalides 113, **178**
Hôtel du Nord 240
hotels 280-1, 291, 301
Hugo, Victor 23
Hunchback of Notre Dame 23
Hundred Years' War 62

I

ice-skating 247
Iguana Café 210
Île de la Cité 91-3
  accommodation 289-90
  drinking 220-1
Île St-Louis 93
  accommodation 290
  drinking 220-1

Index

Île St-Louis *continued*
food 167-8
shopping 258
immigrants 11-13
indie music 229-30
inline skating 247
Institut de France 98
Institut du Monde Arabe 96
Interface Bar 210
Internationaux de France
de Tennis 10, 16, 245
Internet access 344
Internet resources
air fares 334
airlines 332
travel information 353
Invalides 110-13, 184-6
drinking 224
shopping 261-2
Islands, The 91-3, 289-90
drinking 220-1
food 167-8
itineraries 6, 75-6

J

Jardin Alpin 96
Jardin d'Acclimatation 132
Jardin de l'Atlantique 82, 108
Jardin d'Eau 326
Jardin d'Hiver 96
Jardin des Plantes 96, **172**
Jardin des Tuileries 82,
172, **173**
Jardin du Luxembourg 82,
107, **173**, **174**, **175**
Jardin du Palais Royal 83
Jardins de l'Arche 134
Jardins du Trocadéro 115
jazz 231-2
Jazz à la Villette 11
Jeanneret, Charles-Édouard
39-40
Jeu de Paume 83, 311
Jim Morrison's grave 123
Joan of Arc 62
Jokko Bar 210
Jumping International de
Paris 10
Jungle Montmartre 228

K

kestrels 20
Kiosque Théâtre 207

000 map pages
000 photographs

L

La Casa 128 232
La Chaise au Plafond 210
La Champmeslé 225
La Chapelle des Lombards
235
La Charlotte en Île 220-1
La Cigale 229
La Closerie des Lilas 223
La Coupole 235
La Défense 133-5, **133**
food 204
La Favela Chic 235-6
La Flèche d'Or café 228
La Fourmi 228
La Goutte d'Or en Fête 10
La Grande Parade de Paris 9
La Guinguette Pirate 236
La Java 232-3
La Locomotive 236
La Luciole 221
La Palette 222-3
La Renaissance 210
La Samaritaine rooftop
terrace 86
La Station 209, 236
La Tartine 210
La Villette 128-30
Lacroix, Christian 274
language 17-18, 356-9
courses 340-1
L'Apostrophe 226
L'Apparement Café 210
L'Aram 226-7
L'Armagnac 210-19
Latin Quarter 93-7, **176**
accommodation 290-4
drinking 221-2
food 168-80
shopping 258-60
Latina Café 233
latino music 232-3
L'Attirail 234
laundrettes 344-5
L'Autre Café 227
Le 10 223
Le Baiser Salé 231
Le Balajo 236, **206**, **214**
Le Bataclan 229
Le Batofar 236, **215**
Le Bourget 136
Le Café du Passage 219
Le Caveau de la Huchette
231
Le Central 219
Le Champo 239
Le Chào Bà 228-9

Le Cithéa 237
Le Close du Montmartre 127
Le Coffee Shop 219
Le Comptoir des Cannettes
223
Le Corbusier 39-40
Le Cox 209, 219
Le Crocodile 221
Le Dépanneur 229
Le Depôt 209
Le Dépôt 237
Le Duc des Lombards 231-2
Le Fumoir 208
Le Latina 239
Le Lèche-Vin 219
Le Lido de Paris 242
Le Limonaire 234
Le Mécano Bar 227
Le Merle Moqueur 228
Le Moloko 237
Le Nouveau Casino 237
Le Petit Journal St-Michel
232
Le Piano Vache 221
Le Pick Clops 219
Le Pravda 227
Le Pulp 209, 237
Le Queen 237
Le Quetzal 219
Le Rallye 221
Le Regard du Cygne 242
Le Relais du Nord 226
Le Réservoir 237
Le rosebud 223
Le Salon Egyptien 221-2
Le Sancerre 229
Le Scorp 209, 237
Le Select 224
Le Verre Volé 226
Le Vieux Chêne 222
Le Violon Dingue 222
Le Wagg 237
Le Wepler 224-5
left luggage 338
legal matters 345
L'Élysée-Montmartre
229-30
L'Envol Québécois 222
Les Abats-Jour à Coudre
227
Les Bains 237-8
Les Deux Magots 223
Les Étages 219
Les Étoiles 233
Les Funambules 228
Les Grandes Heures du
Parlement 309, 312

Les Halles 79-86
accommodation
284-285
drinking 208
food 155-9
shopping 253
Les Philosophes 219
Les Scandaleuses 209, 220
lesbian travellers 10,
209, 343
literature 22-5 *see also*
books
literary awards 24
Lolita Lempicka 274
L'Olympia 230
L'Open Tour 78
L'Opus 232
lost property 342-3
Louis Vuitton 273, **217**, **273**
Louis XIV 64-5
Louis XVI 65-6
Louis XVI Commemorative
Mass 9
Louvre, the 80-1, **2**, **79**, **100**
L'Urgence Bar 223
Lush Bar 225
Lustiger, Jean-Marie 13
Luxembourg 97-107
accommodation 294-6
drinking 222-3

M

Madeleine 118-19
drinking 224
magazines 347-8
Mairie de Paris 246, 248
Maison-Atelier de Daub-
igny 327
Maison de Balzac 115
Maison de Claude Monet
326, **218**
Maison de la Vanille 222
Maison de l'Air 123
Maison de Van Gogh 327,
328
Maison de Victor Hugo 88
Maison du Saumon 324
Maison Européenne de la
Photographie 90
Maison Roue Libre 77, 247
Manufacture des Gobelins
125-6
maps 346
Marais 6, 86-90, **177**
accommodation 285-9
drinking 208-20
food 159-67

shopping 254-68
walking tour 138-40
Marathon International de Paris 10
Marché aux Fleurs 92
Marché aux Oiseaux 92
Margiela, Martin 275
Marie-Antoinette 65-6
Marina de Bercy 78
markets 152
medical services 346
Mémorial des Martyrs de la Déportation 92-3
Mémorial du Martyr Juif Inconnu 89
Ménagerie du Jardin des Plantes 96
Ménilmontant 123-4
  accommodation 301
  drinking 226-7
  food 194-7
metric conversions, see inside front cover
metric system 346
metro 336
  art 84
  maps 336
  safety 349
Microzoo 96
Ministère des Affaires Étrangères 111
Mission du Patrimoine Photographique 88
Mixer Bar 220
MK2 Bibliothèque 239
mobile phones 350
Monet, Claude 28, 326
money 346-7, see also inside front cover
  ATMs 346
  credit cards 347
  currency 347
  exchange 346-7
Montecristo Café 233
Montmartre 126-8, **2**, **178**
  accommodation 302-4
  drinking 228-9
  food 202-4
  shopping 267
Montparnasse 108-10, 223-4
  accommodation 296-7
  food 183-4
Montparnasse Kiosque Théâtre 207
Moosehead Bar 223
Moreau, Gustave 29

Mosquée de Paris 97
motorcycle travel 335-6
Moulin Rouge 242
Murphy's House 208
Musée-Atelier Henri Bouchard 115
Musée-Atelier Zadkine 107
Musée Bouilhet-Christofle 136
Musée Bourdelle 109
Musée Carnavalet 88
Musée Cernuschi 120
Musée Cognacq-Jay 88
Musée Condé 318
Musée Dapper 115
Musée d'Art Américain 326
Musée d'Art et d'Archéologie 321
Musée d'Art et d'Histoire 136
Musée d'Art et d'Histoire du Judaïsme 89
Musée d'Art Moderne de la Ville de Paris 116
Musée d'Art Naïf Max Fourny 127
Musée de Cluny 94
Musée de la Chasse et de la Nature 89
Musée de la Contrefaçon 132
Musée de la Curiosité et de la Magie 90
Musée de la Défense 134
Musée de la Marine 114
Musée de la Mode et du Textile 81
Musée de la Monnaie de Paris 98, **102**
Musée de la Musique 130
Musée de la Poste 109
Musée de la Poupée 89
Musée de la Préfecture de Police 95
Musée de la Publicité 81
Musée de la Vénerie 321
Musée de la Vie Romantique 128
Musée de l'Absinthe 327, 328
Musée de l'Air et de l'Espace 136
Musée de l'Armée 113
Musée de l'Assistance Publique-Hôpitaux de Paris 95-6
Musée de l'Érotisme 128, **171**

Musée de l'Évantail 122
Musée de l'Histoire de France 89
Musée de l'Histoire de la Médecine 97-8
Musée de l'Homme 114
Musée de l'Hôtel de Vermandois 136
Musée de l'Opéra 121
Musée de l'Orangerie 82-3
Musée de Montmartre 127
Musée de Notre Dame de Paris 92
Musée de Radio France 115
Musée d'Ennery 132
Musée des Arts Décoratifs 81
Musée des Arts et Métiers 90
Musée des Beaux-Arts (Chartres) 324
Musée des Beaux-Arts de la Ville de Paris 118
Musée des Égouts de Paris 116-17
Musée des Équipages 317
Musée des Spahis 321
Musée d'Orsay 111, **102**
Musée du Cristal Baccarat 115-16
Musée du Fumeur 123
Musée du Louvre 80-1, **2**, **79**, **100**
Musée du Luxembourg 107
Musée du Montparnasse 109
Musée du Parfum Fragonard 121
Musée du Stylo et de l'Écriture 115
Musée du Vin 115
Musée Édith Piaf 123
Musée Ernest Hébert 109
Musée Galliera de la Mode de la Ville de Paris 116
Musée Grévin 121
Musée Guimet des Arts Asiatiques 116
Musée Internationale de la Franc-Maçonnerie 121
Musée Jacquemart-André 119-20
Musée Jean Moulin 108
Musée Jean-Jacques Henner 120
Musée Lambinet 311, 312
Musée Maillol-Fondation Diana Vierny 111

Musée Marmottan-Monet 132
Musée Napoléonien d'Art et d'Histoire Militaire 316
Musée Napoléon 1er 314, 316
Musée National d'Art Moderne 84-5
Musée National des Arts et Traditions Populaires 132
Musée National d'Histoire Naturelle 96, **103**
Musée National du Moyen Age 6, 35, 94
Musée National Eugène Delacroix 98, **103**
Musée National Gustave Moreau 128
Musée Nissim de Camondo 120
Musée Pasteur 109
Musée Picasso 88
Musée Rodin 111, **102**
Musée Vivant du Cheval 319, 320
museums & galleries, see also musée
  Arc de Triomphe 117
  Cabinet des Monnaies, Médailles et Antiques 83
  Conciergerie 92
  Espace Salvador Dalí 127
  Fondation Dubuffet 109
  Galeries Nationales du Grand Palais 118
  Galerie François 314
  Jeu de Paume 83
  Maison de Balzac 115
  Maison de Victor Hugo 88
  Mémorial des Martyrs de la Déportation 92-3
  Mémorial du Martyr Juif Inconnu 89
  Palais de Tokyo 116
  Panthéon 94
  Ste-Chapelle 92
  Tours de Notre Dame 92
music 30-1, 229-34
  blues 231-2
  classical 230
  French chansons 30, 233-4
  indie 229-30
  jazz 231-2

music *continued*
  latino 232-3
  opera 241
  pop 229-30
  rock 229-30
  world 232-3
music festivals 10

N

Napoleon's Tomb 113
Nation 124-5
  drinking 227-8
  food 197-9
New Morning 232
New Year's Eve 11
newspapers 16, 347-8
Nomades 247

O

Observatoire
  Météorologique 108
Odéon 97-107
  accommodation 294-6
  drinking 222-3
  food 181-2
Odéon & Luxembourg
  shopping 260
Odéon-Théâtre de l'Europe
  240
Olympic Café 229
Open Café 209, 220
Opéra 120-1
  accommodation 298
  drinking 225
  food 189-91
  shopping 265-6
opera 241
Opéra Bastille 90, 241, **241**
Opéra Comique 241
Opéra National de Paris 241
Opus Latino 233
Orangerie 82-3
Oratoire du Louvre 231
organ recitals 231
organised tours 76-9
O'Sullivan's 225

P

painting 28-9
Palais de Chaillot 114
Palais de la
  Découverte 118
Palais de l'Élysée 118
Palais de Tokyo 116

Palais du Luxembourg
  107, **177**
Palais Garnier 121, 241
Palais Omnisports de Paris-
  Bercy 245
Palais Royal 83
Panthéon 94
Papou Lounge 208
Paradis Latin 242
Parc André Citroën 82
Parc Astérix 308, 330
Parc de Bagatelle 131
Parc de Belleville 82, 123
Parc de Bercy 82, 124-5
Parc de la Villette 6, 82,
  128-9
Parc de Monceau 82
Parc des Buttes-Chaumont
  82, 130
Parc du Champ de Mars 114
Parc Zoologique de Paris 131
Paris à Vélo, c'est Sympa!
  77, 247
Paris Canal Croisières 77
Paris Cycles 132
Paris Hélicoptère 76-7
Paris Jazz Festival 10
Paris Plage 11
Paris Vision 308
Paris Walking Tours 79
Pascal, Blaise 26
Patinoire de l'Hôtel de
  Ville 247
Patinoire de Montparnasse
  247
Patinoire du Parvis de la
  Défense 247
Patinoire Sonja Henie 247
Pause Café 220
Pavillon des Arts 85
Pei, IM 80
pensions de famille 282
Petit Canal 309
Petit Château 318
Petit Palais 118
Petit Train de la Défense
  133
Petit Trianon 311, 312
pharmacies 348
Phébus bike hire 312
philosophy 25-7
photography 348
Piaf, Édith 234
Picasso, Pablo 29, 88
Pigalle 126-8
  accommodation 302-4
  drinking 228-9

food 202-4
  shopping 267
Piscine de la Butte aux
  Cailles 249
Piscine Pontoise-Quartier
  Latin 249
Piscine Roger Le Gall 249
Piscine Suzanne Berlioux
  249
place de la Bastille 90, **212**
place de la Concorde 118
place de la Contrescarpe 98
place de la Madeleine 119
place de l'Hôtel de Ville 87
place des Vosges 87-8, 98,
  104, **211**
place du Marché Ste-
  Catherine 98
place du Parvis Notre
  Dame 91
place du Tertre 127
place Georges Pompidou 85
place Vendôme 83, **64**
Planétarium 129
Pletzl 89
Point Virgule 240, **215**
police services 342, 345
politics 18-19
Pont Neuf 93, **99**
Pop In 227
pop music 229-30
population 6, 11-12
Portail Royal 323, **218**
Porte St-Denis 122
Porte St-Martin 122
postal services 348
postcodes 348
Promenade Plantée 82, 124
Proust, Marcel 24
public holidays 343-4
Pure Malt Bar 220
pyramide inversée 81

Q

Quai d'Orsay 111
Quartier du Parc 134
Quetzal 209
Quiet Man 220

R

Rabelais, François 22
racism 13
radio 17, 348-9
Red Light 209, 238
Reign of Terror 66
religion 12, 13
rental agencies 284

rental properties 283-4
République 121-2
  accommodation
    299-301
  drinking 225-6
  food 191-4
  shopping 266
RER 336-7
reservations
  accommodation 283
  cultural events 207
  tables 150
  tennis courts 248
Rex Club 238
Rimbaud, Arthur 24
river cruises 77-8, **99**
rock music 229-30
Rodin, Auguste 29, 111
Rousseau, Jean-Jacques
  23, 26
rue de Furstemberg 98
rue Mouffetard 142, 153, **8**,
  213, **216**
rugby 16, 245
Rykiel, Sonia 275

S

Sacré Cœur 127, **104**
St-Denis 135-6, **135**
  food 204
St-Germain 97-107
  accommodation 294-6
  drinking 222-3
  food 181-2
  shopping 260
Saint-Laurent, Yves 272
Ste-Chapelle 92, 231, **60**
Sainte Voile 323
Salle des Gens d'Armes 92
Salle Pleyel 230
Salon International de
  L'Agriculture 9
Sanz Sans 220
Sarkozy, Nicolas 8
Sartre, Jean-Paul 24, 26-7
Satellite Café 233
Scherrer, Jean-Louis 272
school holidays 344
sculpture 29-30
self-catering 153-5
Senlis 307, 321
Serres Tropicales 96, **173**
serviced apartments 282
Seven Years' War 65
shopping 252-68, *see also*
  fashion, Shopping index
  p377

bargaining 253
clothing sizes 255
St-Sulpice 259
Triangle d'Or 262
showjumping 245-6
Six Nations Tournament 245
skating 247
Slimane, Hedi 275
Slow Club 238
Sorbonne 94
sporting events
    French Open 10, 16, 245
    Jumping International de Paris 10
    Marathon International de Paris 10
    Tour de France 11, 16, 245
sports 16, 244-50
soccer, see football
SOS Théâtres 207
Stade de France 136
Stade Roland Garros 132, 245
Stolly's 220
street numbers 78
Studio 287 238
Sunset & Sunside 232
swimming 249

T
Taverne Henri IV 221
taxes 253, 349
taxis 337
telephone services 349-50
tennis 10, 16, 245, 248
Tenniseum-Musée de Roland Garros 132
tennis courts 248
theatre 32, 239-240
Théâtre de la Bastille 240
Théâtre de la Ville 242
Théâtre de la Ville-Salle des Abbesses 240
Théâtre de Ménilmont-ant 239
Théâtre de Nesle 239
Théâtre des Bouffes du Nord 240
Théâtre des Champs-Élysées 230
Théâtre des Déchargeurs 239
Théâtre Mogador 230
thefts 349
theme parks 308

Disneyland Resort Paris 329-30
Parc Astérix 330
tickets
    bus 335
    cinema 238
    cultural events 207
    metro 336-7
    plane 334
    RER 336-7
time 6, 351
tipping 151, 351, see also inside front cover
toilets 351
Tomb of the Unknown Deportee 93
Top Loisirs 316
Total Fina Elf Coupole 133
Tour de France 11, 16, 245
Tour Jean Sans Peur 85-6, 104
Tour Montparnasse 108-9
Tour St-Jacques 86
Touringscope 308
tourist information 351
tourist passes 337
tours
    air 76-7
    bicycle 77
    boat 77-8
    bus 78, 312
    Cathédrale Notre Dame de Chartres 324, 325
    Château de Chantilly 320
    Château de Fontaine-bleau 316
    Château de Vaux-le-Vicomte 317
    Château de Versailles 312
    Cimetière du Père Lachaise 123-4
    Musée d'Orsay 111
    Musée du Louvre 81
    Opéra Bastille 90
    outside Paris 308
    walking 78-9, 138-48
Tours de Notre Dame 92
train travel 337-8
    safety 349
trams 338
travel agents 338
travel passes 337
travellers cheques 347
Turkish baths 249-250
TV 17, 350-1

U
Union Centrale des Arts Décoratifs 81

V
Van Gogh, Vincent 28-9, 327
Vaux-le-Vicomte 307, 317, 307
Vedettes du Pont Neuf 78
vegetarian travellers 58
Verlaine, Paul 24
Versailles 308-13, 311, 310
Versailles Tour 312
Versolato, Ocimar 276
Viaduc des Arts 124
Viktor & Rolf 276
Village St-Paul 98
Villon, François 22
Virgin Megastore 207
visas 352-3
visual arts 28-30
Voie Triomphale 82
Voltaire 23

W
walking tours 137-48
    Left Bank 141-4
    Marais 138-40
    multicultural areas 146-8
    Right Bank 144-6
Walt Disney Studios 329
Wars of Religion 63
water parks 249
Wax 220
women travellers 353
    safety 349, 353
work 353-4
world music 31, 232-3
Worth, Charles Frederick 271

X
Xuly Bët 276

Y
yoga 250
Yourcenar, Marguerite 24

Z
Zadkine, Ossip 107
Zola, Émile 23

EATING
404 160
À la Grande Bleue 188

À l'Olivier 254
Addis Ababa 189
Al Dar 168
Amorino 182
Anahuacalli 168
Aquarius 183
Athanor 197-8
Au Bascou 160
Au Grain de Folie 203
Au Levain du Marais 169
Au Petit Breton 204
Au Petit Budapest 202
Au Pet de Lapin 199
Au Pied de Cochon 156
Au Trou Normand 197
Au Village 194
Aux Crus de Bourgogne 156
Aux Négociants 202
Ayutthaya 202
Baan Boran 156
Banga de Mayotte 186
Bel Canto 160
Berthillon 167-8
Bistro des Dames 188
Bistro Romain 151, 204
Bistrot Florentin 194
Bistrot Guillaume 194
Blue Elephant 160
Bofinger 160
Bouillon Racine 168
Boutique Maille 263
Brasserie de l'Isle St-Louis 167
Brasserie des Grandes Marches 160
Brasserie du Toit de la Grande Arche 204
Brasserie Lipp 181
Brûlerie des Ternes 262
Buffalo Grill 152
Cacao et Chocolat 260
Café Beaubourg 158
Café Cannelle 198
Café de l'Époque 156
Café de l'Industrie 161
Café du Thèatre 156
Café Marly 156
Caviar Kaspia 263
Centre Régional des Œuvres Universitaires et Scolaires 152-3
Charlot, Roi des Coquil-lages 188
Chartier 191
Chez Albert 181
Chez Gladines 200
Chez Hanna 166

Chez Heang 166
Chez Jacky 199
Chez Jean 188
Chez Jenny 191
Chez Léna et Mimille 168-9
Chez Marianne 166
Chez Nénesse 161
Chez Omar 161
Chez Papa (Espace Sud-
    ouest) 191-2
Chez Paul 166
Chez Plumeau 202-3
Chez Ramona 194-5
Chez Régis 198
Chez Sébastien 193
Chez Toinette 203
Chiaapas 193
Coffee India 166
Comme Cochons 198
Crémerie des Carmes 154
Crêperie Bretonne Fleurie
    166
Crêpes Show 166
Da Mimmo 192
Dalloyau 169
Dietetic Shop 184
Dix Vins 183
El Fares 201
Fauchon 154, 264
Feyrouz 201
Finkelsztajn 169
Fish la Boissonnerie 181
Fogon St-Julien 169
Founti Agadir 169
Fouquet's 187
Fromagerie Alléosse 263
Fromagerie Barthelemy
    261, **48**, **261**
Fromagerie G Millet 154
Gérard Mulot 169
Graindorge 187
Grand Apétit 161
Guen Maï 182
Hard Rock Café 190
Haynes 191
Hédiard 264
Hippopotamus 152
Hôtel de Crillon 119
Il Duca 203
Il Viaggio 184-5
Indonesia 182
Isami 161
Jean Millet 169
Jo Goldenberg 161-2

Joe Allen 156
Juan et Juanita 195
Julien 190
Kastoori 159
Khun Akorn 198
Kim Anh 201
Koutchi 179
Krung Thep 195
Kunitoraya 159
La 25e Image 192
La Banane Ivoirienne 198
La Cafetière 181
La Cagouille 183
La Cantine Russe 186
La Chaumière en Chine 186
La Cigale 185
La Coupole 183
La Fleuve de Chine 200
La Gaieté Cosaque 189
La Gitane 201
La Grand Méricourt 195
La Maffiosa di Termoli 189
La Main d'Or 162
La Maison de la Truffe 264
La Maison du Miel 264
La Maison Rose 203, **150**
La Marine 192
La Mascotte 203
La Mosquée de Paris 169
La Partie de Campagne 199
La Perla 162
La Petit Légume 179
La Piragua 197
La Soummam 162
La Toccata 192
La Tour d'Argent 169-70
La Victoire Suprême du
    cœur 157
La Voie Lactée 180
Ladurée 169
Lal Qila 201
L'Alivi 162
L'Amazonial 157
L'Ambassade d'Auvergne
    162
L'Ambroisie 162
Lanna Store 198
Lao Siam 197
L'Arbre à Cannelle 159
L'Arbuci 181
L'Ardoise 187
L'As de Felafel 167
L'Assiette 183-184
L'Atelier de Joël Robouchon
    185, **185**, **213**
L'Audiernes 200
L'Avant-Goût 200

L'Ave Maria 195
Le 7e Sud 185-6
Le Baratin 195
Le Bistrot du Dôme Bastille
    162-3
Le Bistro de Gala 190
Le Bouclard 189
Le Buisson Ardent 170
Le Café de l'Orient 204
Le Camboge 193
Le Caméléon 184
Le C'amelot 195
Le Chansonnier 192, **190**,
    212
Le Clown Bar 195
Le Coco de Mer 170
Le Cosi 170
Le Dôme 184, **180**, **213**
Le Dôme du Marais 163
Le Foyer du Vietnam 180
Le Gai Moulin 163
Le Golfe de Naples 182
Le Grand Colbert 157
Le Grand Véfour 83, 157
Le Jardin des Pâtes 180
Le Kitch 196
Le Loup Blanc 157
Le Mâchon d'Henri 182
Le Man Ray 187
Le Mansouria 199
Le Mauricien Filao 192
Le Monde à L'Envers 157
Le Mono 203
Le Paris-Dakar 192-3
Le Pavillon Puebla 196
Le Péché Mignon 196
Le Petit Mâchon 157
Le Petit Picard 163
Le Petit Zinc 182
Le Porokhane 196
Le Réconfort 163
Le Refuge des Fondus 203
Le Repaire de Cartouche
    196
Le Réveil du Xe 193
Le Roi du Pot au Feu 190
Le Sofa 163
Le Soleil Gourmand 203
Le Sporting 193
Le Square Trousseau 163
Le Studio 163
Le Tambour 157
Le Temps des Cérises 200
Le Tipaza 201
Le Tournebride 170
Le Troisième Bureau 158
Le Troquet 201

Le Trumilou 166-7
Le Vaudeville 157-8
Le Véro Dodat 158
Le Viaduc Café 158
Le Vigneron 170
Le Villaret 196
Legrand Filles & Fils 265
L'Encrier 167, **161**, **212**
L'Enoteca 164
Léon de Bruxelles 152
L'Épi d'Or 158
Les Ailes 190
Les Amis de Messina 164
Les Amognes 199
Les Arts 204
Les Caves Augé 266
Les Caves St-Gilles 164
Les Diamantaires 191
Les Fous de l'Île 158
Les Galopins 164
Les Jumeaux 196-7
Les Quatre et Une Saveurs
    170
Les Ruchers du Roy 256
Les Sans Culottes 164
Les Vignes du Panthéon
    179
Les Vins des Pyrénées 164
L'Étoile du Berger 179
L'Étoile Verte 187
Lina's 188
Lire Entre les Vignes
    164-165
L'Os à Moëlle 201-202
L'Oulette 199
Ma Bourgogne 165
Macéo 158
Machu Picchu 180
Macis et Muscade 189
Madras Café 193
Maison Prunier 187
Marché aux Enfants Rouges
    152
Marché Bastille 152
Marché Batignolles-Clichy
    152
Marché d'Aligre 152
Mavrommatis 179
Mother Earth's 191
Mustang Café 184
New Nioullaville 197
Nicolas 264-265
Passage Brady 193-4
Perraudin 179
Piccolo Teatro 165
Pitchi Poï 158
Poilâne 261

000 map pages
000 photographs

Polidor 182
Pooja 194
P'tit Bouchon Gourmand 187
Relais Gascon 204
Robert et Louise 165
Roi du Kashmir 194
Savannah Café 179
Sawadee 202
Shalimar 194
Sinorama 200
Soprano 165
Spoon, Food & Wine 188
Stohrer 169
Swann et Vincent 165
Tana 158-9
Tao 179
Tashi Delek 180
Tea Caddy 180
Terminus Nord 193
Thai Classic 197
Thanksgiving 165
Thoumieux 186
Thuy Long 184
Ty Coz 189
Un Piano sur le Trottoir 165
Voyageurs du Monde 159
Wally le Saharien 191
Waly Fay 166
Willi's Wine Bar 159

SHOPPING

2 Mille & 1 Nuits 254
À l'Olivier 254
A Simon 253
Abbey Bookshop 258
Abou d'abi Bazar 255
Album 260
Alternatives 277
Anna Joliet 253
Antoine et Lili 266, **216**
Au Vieux Campeur 259
Bains Plus 255
Bazar de l'Hôtel de Ville 255
Bercy Village 267
Boutique 102 276
Boutique 105A 276
Boutique des 10 276
Boutique Maille 263
Boutique Paris-Musées 255
Brentano's 265
Brûlerie des Ternes 262
Cacao et Chocolat 260
Carré Rive Gauche 261
Carrousel du Louvre 81, 253
Cartier 264

Caviar Kaspia 263
Cécile et Jeanne 263-4
Citadium 274
Colette 277
Crocodisc 260
CSAO Boutique 255
Darty 266
Didier Ludot 253-4
Drouot 265
E Dehillerin 254
EOL'Modelisme 259
Espace IGN 263
Fauchon 264
Fnac Musique 255
Fromagerie Alléosse 263
Fromagerie Barthelemy 261, **48**, **261**
Galerie & Atelier Puncinello 255
Galerie Alain Carion 258
Galeries Lafayette 265, 265-8
Guerlain 263
Hédiard 264
Hermès 264, **217**
Il pour l'Homme 264
Issey Miyake 256
Jadis et Gourmande 259
Jamin Puech 266
Kenzo 277, **217**, **270**
Kiliwatch 277
Kokon To Zai 277
La Boutique des Inventions 256
La Charrue et les Étoiles 256
La Citadelle 267
La Maison de l'Astronomie 254
La Maison de la Truffe 264
La Maison de la Vanille 259
La Maison du Cerf-Volant 256
La Maison du Miel 264
La Petite Scierie 258
La Samaritaine 254
La Vallée Village 267
Le Bon Marché 261
Le Mouton à Cinq Pattes 277
Le Palais des Thés 256
Le Printemps 265, 265-268
L'Éclaireur 277
Legrand Filles & Fils 265
Les Caves Augé 266
Les Mots à la Bouche 256
Les Ruchers du Roy 256

L'Habilleur 277
Librairie de l'Hôtel de Sully 256
Librairie Gourmande 259
Librairie Ulysse 258
L'Île du Démon 260
L'Ours du Marais 256
Louvre des Antiquaires 254
Madeleine Gély 261
Madelios 264, 274
Marché aux Puces d'Aligre 267
Marché aux Puces de la Porte de Vanves 267-8
Marché aux Puces de Montreuil 268
Marché aux Puces de St-Ouen 268
Maria Luisa 278
Mariage Frères 256, 256-7
Marithé et François Girbaud 278
Mélodies Graphiques 257
Musée & Compagnie 267
Nickel 274
Nicolas 264-5
Odimex Paris 260
Onward 278
Patek Philippe 264
Poilâne 261
Printemps de l'Homme 274
Produits des Monastères 257
Réciproque 278
Red Space 276
Red Wheelbarrow Bookstore 258
Roul'tabille 258
Roxy Life Shop 254
Sennelier 262
Séphora 263
Shakespeare & Company 260, **177**, **216**
Sic Amor 258
Slip 258
Tati 267, **266**
Tea and Tattered Pages 262
Tumbleweed 258
Van Cleef & Arpels 264
Village Voice 260
Virgin Megastore 263
Voyageurs & Curieux 260
WH Smith 265
Yves Saint Laurent 265

SLEEPING

Aloha Hostel 302
Apart'hotels Citadines 282

ArtusHotel 294, **294**
Auberge de Jeunesse Jules Ferry 300
Auberge de Jeunesse Le D'Artagnan 300
Celtic Hôtel 297
Comfort Hôtel Place du Tertre 303
Comfort Inn Mouffetard 290
Delhy's Hôtel 294
Familia Hôtel 290
France Location 282-283
Grand Hôtel de Champaigne 284
Grand Hôtel de l'Univers 295
Grand Hôtel de Paris 299
Grand Hôtel du Loiret 288
Grand Hôtel du Progrès 294
Grand Hôtel Malher 286
Grand Hôtel St-Michel 290
Hostel Blue Planet 302
Hôtel Aquarelle 300
Hôtel Aulivia Opéra 300
Hôtel Aviatic 296
Hôtel Axial Beaubourg 286
Hôtel Baudelaire Bastille 286
Hôtel Baudin 288
Hôtel Beaumarchais 301
Hôtel Bel Ami St-Germain des Prés 291
Hôtel Bonséjour 304
Hôtel Brighton 284
Hôtel Britannia 298
Hôtel Caron de Beaumarchais 286, **286**
Hôtel Castex 286
Hôtel Central Bastille 286
Hôtel Central Marais 286
Hôtel Chopin 298-9
Hôtel Cluny Sorbonne 290
Hôtel Concorde St-Lazare 298
Hôtel Costes 291
Hôtel d'Angleterre 295
Hôtel Daval 286
Hôtel de Blois 297
Hôtel de Crillon 291
Hôtel de Danemark 295
Hôtel de Lutèce 290
Hôtel de Nesle 295
Hôtel de Nevers 300-1
Hôtel de Nice 287
Hôtel de Paris 296
Hôtel de St-Germain 295

Hôtel de la Bretonnerie 287
Hôtel de la Herse d'Or 288
Hôtel de la Place des
  Vosges 287
Hôtel de l'Espérance 292,
  297
Hôtel Delambre 296
Hôtel des 3 Poussins 303
Hôtel des Académies 296
Hôtel des Arts 299, 303
Hôtel des Beaux-Arts 302
Hôtel des Capucines
  Montmartre 304
Hôtel des Deux Continents
  295
Hôtel des Deux Îles 290
Hôtel des Grandes Écoles
  292
Hôtel des Marronniers 295
Hôtel du 7e Art 287
Hôtel du Bourg Tibourg 287
Hôtel du Calvados 298
Hôtel du Globe 295
Hôtel du Moulin 304
Hôtel du Panthéon 292
Hôtel du Vieux Saule 301
Hôtel Eldorado 298
Hôtel Élysée Ceramic 298
Hôtel Esmeralda 292
Hôtel Favart 298
Hôtel Français 300
Hôtel Garden Opéra 300
Hôtel Gay-Lussac 292
Hôtel Henri IV 289-90, 292

Hôtel Ibis Paris CDG
  Aéroport Gares 304
Hôtel Ibis Paris Orly
  Aéroport 304
Hôtel Ibis Sacré Cœur 303
Hôtel Jeanne d'Arc 287
Hôtel La Demeure 293
Hôtel La Vieille France 301
Hôtel Langlois 299
Hôtel Lenox St-Germain
  297
Hôtel Le Clos Médicis 295
Hôtel Le Compostelle 287
Hôtel Le Relais du Louvre
  285
Hôtel Les Sans Culottes 289
Hôtel Liberty 301
Hôtel Londres et Anvers
  301
Hôtel Luxembourg Parc 291
Hôtel Lyon Mulhouse 287
Hôtel Meurice 291
Hôtel Michelet Odéon 296
Hôtel Minerve 293
Hôtel Miramar 296
Hotel New Candide 287
Hôtel Odessa Montparnasse
  297
Hôtel Peletier Haussmann
  Opéra 299
Hôtel Pratic 287
Hôtel Relais Christine 291
Hôtel Résidence Henri
  IV 293

Hôtel Résidence Monge 293
Hôtel Ritz Paris 291, **281,
  292**
Hôtel Rivoli 289
Hôtel Royal Bastille 288
Hôtel St-André des Arts 296
Hôtel St-Christophe 293
Hôtel St-Germain des
  Prés 296
Hôtel St-Honoré 285
Hôtel St-Jacques 293
Hôtel St-Louis 290
Hôtel St-Louis Marais 288
Hôtel St-Merry 288
Hôtel Saintonge Marais 288
Hôtel Sévigné 288
Hôtel Thoumieux 297
Hôtel Utrillo 303
Hôtel Victoires Opéra 285
Hotel Victoria 299
Hôtel Vivienne 299
La Villa St-Germain des
  Prés 291
Le Village Hostel 304
Le Relais de Paris Cam-
  bronne 302
L'Hôtel 291
Maeva City Tolbiac 283,
  302
Maison Internationale
  de la Jeunesse et des
  Étudiants 289
Maison Internationale des
  Jeunes pour la Culture

et la Paix 289
Mélia Colbert Boutique
  Hotel 291
MIJE Le Fauconnier 289
MIJE Le Fourcy 289
MIJE Maubuisson 289
Nord Hôtel 300
Nord-Est Hôtel 300
Pavilion OpÉra Bourse 299
Peace & Love Hostel 301
Pension Au Palais Gour-
  mand 282
Pension Ladagnous 282
Pension Les Marroniers 282
Petit Palace Hôtel 297
Résidence Cardinal 282
Résidence des Arts 283
Résidence Le St-Germain
  283
Résidence Passage Dubail
  283
Résidence Pierre & Vacan-
  ces 283
Select Hôtel 293
Sibour Hôtel 301
Style Hotel 298
Timhôtel Montmartre 303
Timhôtel Quartier Latin 293
Timhôtel St-Georges 303
Villa Modigliani 297
Villa Opéra Drouot 299
Villa Royale Pigalle 303
Woodstock Hostel 304
Young & Happy Hostel 294

000 map pages
000 photographs

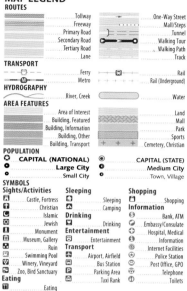

MAP LEGEND
ROUTES
Tollway
Freeway
Primary Road
Secondary Road
Tertiary Road
Lane
One-Way Street
Mall/Steps
Tunnel
Walking Tour
Walking Path
Track

TRANSPORT
Ferry
Metro
Rail
Rail (Underground)

HYDROGRAPHY
River, Creek
Water

AREA FEATURES
Area of Interest
Building, Featured
Building, Information
Building, Other
Building, Transport
Land
Mall
Park
Sports
Cemetery, Christian

POPULATION
CAPITAL (NATIONAL)
Large City
Small City
CAPITAL (STATE)
Medium City
Town, Village

SYMBOLS
Sights/Activities
Castle, Fortress
Christian
Islamic
Jewish
Monument
Museum, Gallery
Ruin
Swimming Pool
Winery, Vineyard
Zoo, Bird Sanctuary
Eating
Eating

Sleeping
Sleeping
Camping
Drinking
Drinking
Entertainment
Entertainment
Transport
Airport, Airfield
Bus Station
Parking Area
Taxi Rank

Shopping
Shopping
Information
Bank, ATM
Embassy/Consulate
Hospital, Medical
Information
Internet Facilities
Police Station
Post Office, GPO
Telephone
Toilets

Greater Paris	380
Central Paris NW	384
Central Paris NE	386
Central Paris SW	389
Central Paris SE	392
Central Paris	396
Montmartre	400
Bercy	401

Map Section

GREATER PARIS

St Ouen

A

B

C

D

Mairie de Clichy

Cimetière de Lavallois

Cimetière Parisien des Batignolles

1 See La Defense Map (p133)

Stade de Courbevoie

Pont de Levallois Bécon

Cimetière Sud

Porte de Clichy

47 Blvd Bessi

35

A14

La Défense Grande Arche

La Défense

Île de la Grande Jatte

64

Anatole France

Pablo Neoda

Louison Bobet

67

Esplanade de la Défense

Av Bineau

See Central Paris NW Map (pp384–5)

Blvd Circulaire

Pont de Neuilly

Blvd Victor Hugo

R de la République

Av Charles de Gaulle

Av du Roule

Av de Wagram

17e

Blvd Malesherbes

2 LP

Seine

Les Sablons

Blvd Maurice Barrès

Blvd Maillot

Blvd Pereire

R de Courcelles

Gare Lazai

Île de Puteaux

Mare St James

16

1

11 26 29

Arc de Triomphe

Av de Friedland

Blvd

Parc de Bagatelle

Lac Pour le Patinage

30

Avenue Foch

Av Foch

Av Victor Hugo

Av des Champs Élysées

8e

Av Marceau

Triangle d'Or

7

Av Kléber

3 Hippodrome de Longchamp

Bois de Boulogne

Lac Inférieur

20

Racing Club de France

Avenue Henri Martin

Av Henri Martin

24

Cimetière de Passy

Q d'Orsay

Q An

Garde Républicaine Cheval

Av Paul Doumer

7e

Faubourg St Germain

Étang de Boulogne

Lac Supérieur

25

La Muette

16e

Q Branly

Av de la Bourdonnais

Av Bosquet

Blvd Suchet

BoulainVilliers

Blvd Raynouard

Eiffel Tower

Blvd des Invalides

Le Bar

A13

Ranelagh

22

Jasmin

Av Mozart

R la Fontaine

Q de Grenelle

Blvd Grenelle

Av de Ségur

4 15

Michel Ange Auteuil

Église d'Auteuil

Javel

Seine

Blvd Garibald

R de Sèvres

Porte d'Auteuil

6

R Linois

Necker

Blvd

Stade Rolland Garros

18

34

Michel Ange Molitor

Chardon Lagache

63

R de la Croix Nivert

R Lecourbe

15e

Gare Montparnasse

Stade Jean Bouin

33

Exelmans

Av de Versailles

13

R Balard

R de la Convention

Parc des Princes

Ancien Cimetière

Porte de St Cloud

Boulevard Victor

Blvd Victor

41

R Lourmel

Cimetière de Vaugirard

42

68

See Central Paris SW Map (pp390–1)

5 Billancourt

Marcel Sembat

Nouveau Cimetière

Issy-Val de Seine

Héliport de Paris

Centre Sportif Suzanne Lenglen

2

Porte de Versailles

65

Blvd Lefebvre

36

Pernety

39

6

59

N10

Plaisance

Pont de Sèvres

Île St Germain

Stade Jean Bouin

Stade Voisin

Corentin Celton

Stade de la Plaine

Stade Charles Rigulot (Centre Sportif)

56

Porte de Vanves

Porte d'Orle

Cimetière de Montrouge

14e

Île Seguin

Q de Stalingrad

Jacques Henri Lartigue

Mairie d'Issy

Stade Didot

Stade Jules Noel

Île de Billancourt

Issy Ville

André Roche

Malakoff Plateau de Vanves

6 Cimetière des Longs Réages

Malakoff Rue E Dolet

Chatillon Montrouge

380

SIGHTS & ACTIVITIES (pp73–136)
AMF Bowling de Paris............................ 1 B2
Aquaboulevard...................................... 2 C5
Aquarium Tropical.................................. 3 H5
Argonaut.. 4 G1
Catacombes.. 5 E5
Centre Beaugrenelle.............................. 6 C4
Château de Bagatelle............................. 7 A3
Cimetière du Père Lachaise Conservation
  Office... 8 G3
Cinaxe... 9 G1
Cité de l'Architecture et du Patrimoine...(see 3)
Cité des Sciences et de l'Industrie.......... 10 G1
Exploradôme.. 11 B2
Grande Halle.. 12 G1
Grandes Serres..................................... 13 B4
Géode... 14 G1
Hippodrome d'Auteuil............................ 15 B4
Jardin d'Acclimation.............................. 16 B2
Jardin des Miroirs................................. 17 G1
Jardin des Serres d'Auteuil..................... 18 B4
Jardin des Vents et des Dunes................ 19 G1
Jardin Shakespeare................................ 20 B3
Lion Fountain....................................... 21 G2
Musée Atelier Henri Bouchard................ 22 B4
Musée de la Musique............................ 23 G2
Musée du Stylo et de l'Écriture............... 24 B3
Musée Marmottan-Monet....................... 25 B3
Musée National des Arts et Traditions
  Populaires... 26 B2
Parc des Princes.................................... 27 B4

Parc Zoologique de Paris........................ 28 H5
Paris Cycles.. 29 B2
Paris Cycles.. 30 B3
Piscine de la Butte aux Cailles................ 31 F5
Piscine Roger Le Gall............................. 32 H4
Pré Catalan..(see 20)
Stade Jean Bouin.................................. 33 B4
Stade Roland Garros.............................. 34 B4
Tenniseum-Musée de Roland Garros....(see 34)

EATING 🍴 (pp144–204)
À la Grande Bleue................................. 35 D1
Aquarius.. 36 D5
Chez Gladines...................................... 37 F5
Khun Akorn.. 38 G4
L'Assiette... 39 D5
L'Avant-Goût.. 40 F5
L'Os à Moëlle....................................... 41 C5
La Cagouille... 42 D5
La Fleuve de Chine................................ 43 F6
Le Jardin des Pâtes............................... 44 E5
Le Temps des Cérises............................. 45 E5
Sinorama... 46 F5

ENTERTAINMENT 🎭 (pp205–42)
Ateliers Berthier................................... 47 D1
Chez Louisette...................................... 48 E1
Cité de la Musique............................(see 23)
Cité de la Musique Box Office................. 49 G2
Conservatoire National Supérieur de
  Musique et de Danse........................... 50 G1

La Flèche d'Or Café............................... 51 H3
Le Merle Moqueur................................. 52 E5
Le Regard du Cygne.............................. 53 G2
Le Zénith... 54 G1
Théâtre de Ménilmontant....................... 55 G3

SHOPPING 🛍 (pp251–78)
Marché aux Puces de la Porte de
  Vanves.. 56 D5
Marché aux Puces de Montreuil
  Montreuil... 57 H4
Marché aux Puces de St Ouen.............(see 48)

SLEEPING 🛏 (pp279–304)
Auberge de Jeunesse Le
  D'Artagnan... 58 H3
Hôtel de Blois....................................... 59 D5
Hôtel des Beaux-Arts.............................. 60 F5
Petit Palace Hôtel.................................. 61 D5

TRANSPORT (pp332–8)
Gare Routière Internationale de Paris
  Galliéni.. 62 H3
Rent a Car Système............................... 63 B4

INFORMATION
American Hospital in Paris...................... 64 B1
Bureau des Objets Trouvès..................... 65 C5
Fusac.. 66 D5
Hertford British Hospital........................ 67 C1
Hôtel de Police..................................... 68 D5

CENTRAL PARIS – NW (pp384–5)

SIGHTS & ACTIVITIES (pp73-136)

Arc de Triomphe....1 C4
Bateaux Mouches....2 E6
Chapelle Expiatoire....3 G4
Charles De Gaulle Statue....4 F5
Cityrama....5 H6
Colonne Vendôme....6 H5
Église de la Madeleine....7 G5
Flame of Liberty Monument....8 D6
Fédération Inter-Enseignements de Hatha Yoga....9 H6
Galeries Nationales du Grand Palais....10 F6
Galleries du Panthéon Bouddhique....11 C5
Grand Palais....(see 10)
Jeanne d'Arc Statue....12 H6
Jeu de Paume....13 G6
L'Open Tour....14 H4
Ministry of Justice....15 H5
Musée Cernuschi....16 F3
Musée d'Art Moderne de la Ville de Paris....17 D6
Musée d'Ennery....18 A4
Musée Dapper....19 B5
Musée de l'Opéra....20 H4
Musée de la Contrefaçon....21 A5
Musée de la Vie Romantique....22 H3
Musée des Beaux-Arts de la Ville de Paris....23 F6
Musée du Cristal Baccarat....24 C5
Musée du Parfum Fragonard....25 H4
Musée du Parfum Fragonard Annexe....26 H5
Musée Galliera de la Mode de la Ville de Paris....27 C6
Musée Guimet des Arts Asiatiques....28 C6
Musée Jacquemart-André....29 E4
Musée Jean-Jacques Henner....30 E2
Musée Nissim de Camondo....31 F3
Obelisk....32 G6
Orangerie....33 G6
Palais de l'Élysée....34 F5
Palais de la Découverte....35 E5
Palais Garnier....(see 20)
Palais de Tokyo....36 C6
Paris Story....37 H4
Paris Vision....38 H5
Petit Palais....(see 23)
St Joseph's Catholic Church....39 D4
Winston Churchill Statue....40 F6

EATING (pp149-204)

Bistro des Dames....41 G2
Bistro Romain....42 D4
Charlot, Roi des Coquillages....43 H2
Dalloyau....44 E4
Fouquet's....45 D4
Graindorge....46 C3
L'Ardoise....47 G5
L'Étoile Verte....48 C3
La Cantine Russe....49 C6
La Chaumière en Chine....50 D5
La Gaieté Cosaque....51 G2
La Maffiosa di Termoli....52 G2
Ladurée....53 D5
Le Bouclard....54 H2
Le Man Ray....55 E5
Le Roi du Pot au Feu....56 G4
Lina's....57 G5
Macis et Muscade....58 G1
Maison Prunier....59 C4
Marché Av du Président Wilson....60 C6
Marché Batignolles-Clichy....61 G2
Marché Poncelet-Bayen....62 C3
Monoprix....63 E5
Monoprix....64 H5
P'tit Bouchon Gourmand....65 C4
Spoon, Food & Wine....66 E5
Wilson Food Market....67 C6

ENTERTAINMENT (pp205-42)

Agence Perrossier & SOS Théâtres....68 G5
Au 24....69 G2
Buddha Bar....70 G5
Bushwacker's....71 H5
Cinéma des Cinéastes....72 G2
Cinéma Gaumont Marignan....73 E5
Crazy Horse....74 D6
Cricketer....75 G4
Duplex....76 C4
Fnac Champs-Élysées....77 E5
Fnac St-Lazare....78 G4
Fnac Étoile....79 C3
Harry's New York Bar....80 H5
Hemingway Bar....(see 154)
Kiosque Théâtre....81 G5
L'Olympia....82 H5
Latina Café....83 D4
Le Lido de Paris....84 D4
Le Queen....85 D4
Le Wepler....86 G2
Lush Bar....87 G2
Montecristo Café....88 E5
Salle Pleyel....89 D3
Théâtre des Champs-Élysées....90 D6
Théâtre Mogador....91 H4

SHOPPING (pp251-78)

Barbara Bui....92 E5
Boutique Maille....93 G5
Brentano's....94 H5
Brûlerie des Ternes....95 C3
Cartier....96 H5
Caviar Kaspia....97 G5
Celine....98 E5
Chanel....99 E5
Chloe....100 F5
Christian Dior....101 E5
Christian Lacroix....102 E5
Citadium....103 H4
Colette....104 H6
Courrèges....(see 99)
Cécile et Jeanne....105 H6
Darty....106 C3
Espace IGN....107 E5
Fauchon....108 G5
Fromagerie Alléosse....109 C3
Galeries Lafayette....110 H4
Gianfranco Ferre....111 D5
Givenchy....112 D6
Gucci....113 E5
Guerlain....(see 88)
Hermès....114 G5
Hédiard....115 G5
Il Pour l'Homme....116 H6
Inès de la Fressange....117 D6
Jadis et Gourmanda....118 E5
Jean Paul Gaultier....(see 111)
La Maison de la Truffe....119 G5
La Maison du Miel....120 G4
Lafayette Maison....121 H4
Le Printemps de l'Homme....122 H4
Le Printemps de la Beauté et Maison....123 H4
Le Printemps de la Mode....124 H4
Les Caves Augé....125 F4
Lolita Lempicka....126 C4
Madelios....127 G5
Maria Luisa....128 G6
Maria Luisa Accessories....129 G5
Maria Luisa Menswear....130 H6
Mariage Frères....131 D3
Nicolas....132 G5
Nina Ricci....133 E5
Patek Philippe....134 H5
Plein Sud....135 D6
Prada....136 D6
Rue du Faubourg St Honoré....137 F4
Réciproque....138 A6
Réciproque....139 A6
Séphora....(see 77)
Valentino....140 D6
Van Cleef & Arpels....141 H5
Virgin Megastore....142 E5
WH Smith....143 G5
Yves Saint Laurent....144 G5

SLEEPING (pp279-304)

Hotel Langlois....145 H3
Hôtel Brighton....146 H6
Hôtel Britannia....147 G3
Hôtel Concorde St-Lazare....148 G4
Hôtel Costes....149 H5
Hôtel de Crillon....150 G5
Hôtel du Calvados....151 G3
Hôtel Eldorado....152 G2
Hôtel Meurice....153 H6
Hôtel Ritz Paris....154 H5
Hôtel Èlysée Ceramic....155 D3
Résidence Cardinal....156 H3
Style Hôtel....157 G2

TRANSPORT (pp332-8)

ADA Car Rental....158 G3
Air France Buses....159 C4
Batobus Stop....160 E6
Buses to Beauvais Airport....161 B3
easyCar....162 H5
Parking Pershing (Buses to Beauvais Airport)....163 B3
Roissybus....164 H4

INFORMATION

American Cathedral in Paris....165 D5
American Express....166 H4
Belgium Embassy....167 C4
Bureau de Change....168 E5
Canadian Embassy....169 E5
École de Gastronomie Française-Ritz Escoffier....170 G5
École Lenôtre....171 F5
German Embassy....172 E5
Hôtel de Police (Carte de Séjour)....173 G2
Irish Embassy....174 C4
New Zealand Embassy....175 B5
NewWorks....176 H4
NewWorks Champs Élysées Branch....177 E5
Paris Convention & Visitors Bureau....(see 166)
Paris Convention & Visitors Bureau (Main Branch)....178 H6
Pharmacie des Champs....179 D4
Pharmacie Européenne de la Place Clichy....180 H2
Spanish Embassy....181 D5
Thomas Cook....182 D4
UK Embassy....183 F5
US Consulate....184 G5
US Embassy....185 G5

OTHER

Belle Époque Toilets....186 G5
Église St-Roche....187 H6
Hôtel de la Marine....188 G5
Palais des Congrès de Paris....189 B3

R St Paul
R de Lesseps
R Voltaire
R Barbès
R Dantzig
R Aristide Briand
R Louis Rouquier
R Carnot
R Henri Barbusse
Rd President Wilson
R Gabriel Péri
R Jacques Ibert
R d'Alsace
R Maurice Ravel
R Curnonsky
Bd de Reims
Av Brunetière
Porte d'Asnières
R de Marceaux
St Marceaux

Blvd Victor Hugo
Av Bineau
R de Villiers
R Louise Michel
Louise Michel
R Vergniaud
Blvd de la Somme
Av Paul Adam
R Jean Moréas
R Stephen Mallarmé
Bd Berthier
R Jules Bourdais
R Genevé
R Pilhet Delorme
Av Verniquet
Blvd Péreire (Nord)
Blvd Péreire (Sud)
R Gustave Doré

R Borghèse
R des Dames Augustines
R Cino del Duca
Porte de Villiers
Jardin de l'Amérique Latine
Porte de Champerret
Place Stuart Merrill
Square J Bellat
R Châtelier
Place du Mal Péreire
Place du Mal Péreire Juin
R Ampère
Péreire-Lavallois
Place d'Israel

R Madeleine Michelis
R Perronet
Blvd de Dixmude
Square du Cardinal Petit de Julleville
Blvd de l'Yser
Place Renard
R Vernier
R Galvani
Blvd Goulon St Cyr
R Emile Allez
R Roger Bacon
R des Pavillons
R de Vercy
R Faraday
Villa Aublet
Place A Maillart
R Pierre Demours
R Théodore de Banville
R Gustave Flaubert
Av de Villiers
Place du Brésil
Pl Joffroy d'Abba

Av du Roule
Av du Chartres
R Armenonville
Cadet Pilot
R Sablonville
R du Midi
R Rufmonck
R de Torticelli
R Guersant
R Leborton
R Bayen
R Niel
R Laugier
R Fourcroy
R Poncelet
R Gustave Flaubert
R des Renaudes
R Théodule
Ribot
R Margueritte
R de Courcelles
Courcelle
Blvd de Courcelles

R Sablonville
Porte Maillot
Porte Péreire (Nord)
Blvd Péreire (Sud)
Belidor
R Labie
Place Tristan Bernard
Av des Ternes
Villebois Mareuil
R Villebois
Place des Ternes
Ternes
R de la Neva
R Darru
Beaucour

Blvd Maillot
Place de la Porte Maillot
R du Débarcadère
Place St Ferdinand
R St Ferdinand
R d'Armaillé
R des Acacias
R de Montenotte
R de l'Etoile
Sq du Faubourg St Honoré

Neuilly Porte Maillot Palais des Congrès
R Denis Poisson
Porte Maillot
Place du Gal Patton
Place Vet C Morandat
Argentine
Av de la Grande Armée
Av Carnot
R de Tilsitt
Charles de Gaulle-Etoile
Av Hoche
Av Bertie Albrecht
Place G Guillaumin

Square de l'Amiral Bruix
Blvd de l'Amiral Bruix
R Weber
R Berlioz
Av Alphand
R Duret
R la Sueur
R Chalgrin
R du Colonel Moll
R Brunel
R Troyon
Av de Friedland
R Argine Houssaye
R Châteaubriand

TEP Jean Pierre Wimille
Square Anna de Noailles
Blvd Marceau
R Marbeau
Villa Dupont
R Pergolèse
R Laurent Pichat
R Picot
R Piccini
Place Charles de Gaulle
Av des Champs Élysées
R de Presbourg
R Lord Byron
R Washington
R Vernet
George V

Av Foch
R St Didier
R Léonardo de Vinci
R Lauriston
Kléber
R de Saigon
R Vernet
George V
Galerie d'Anjou

Porte Dauphine
R Crevaux
R de Stax
R de Sontay
R Leroux
R Newton
R Euler
R de Bassano
R Quentin Bauchart
R Lincoln
R François Ier
R la Marr
R de la Trémoïll

La Faisanderie
R Spontini
R de Noisiel
Victor Hugo
Place Victor Hugo
R Copernic
R Paul Valéry
R La Pérouse
R Dumont d'Urville
R Auguste Vacquerie
R Keppler
R Christophe Colomb
Av Marceau

R Appert
R de Longchamp
Villa Victor Hugo
Av Victor Hugo
R Mesnil
R Boissière
R de Belloy
Place des États Unis
Av d'Iéna
Place Amiral de Grasse
R de Chaillot
R Pierre 1er de Serbie
George

R de Lota
R Thiers
R St Didier
R Léo Delibes
R Raymond Poincaré
R Cimarosa
R Hamelin
Impasse Kléber
R de Belloy
Lycée Janson de Sailly Assomption
Boissière
R Quentin

Av Henri Martin
Av de Montespan
R de la Pompe
R Herran
R Decamps
R des Sablons
R d'Eylau
Place de Mexico
R Greuze
R de Magdebourg
Place d'Iéna
Square Brignole Galliera
Place de la Reine Astrid
Alma Marceau
Place de l'Alma

Rue de la Pompe
Av Georges Mandel
R Scheffer
Trocadéro
Av du Président Wilson
R Albert de Mun
Iéna
Av de New York
Pont de l'Alma
Place de la Résistance

R de la Tour
R Cortambert
Av Paul Doumer
Cimetière de Passy
Palais de Chaillot
Jardins Chaillot
Av des Nations Unies
R Fresnel
Av de New York
Seine
Q Branly
R Cognac
Pont de l'Alma

A B C D

1 2 3 4 5 6

R Marcadet
R Darwin
R Francur
R du Mont Cenis
R du Baigneur
R Eugène Sue
Smart
Marcadet Poissonniers
R Ordener
R Marcadet
R Ernestine
R l'Olive
Marx Dormoy

R Lamarck
Place Constantin Pecqueur
Lamarck Caulaincourt
R St Vincent
R Paul Féval
R Becquerel
Lambert
Bachelet
R Nicolet
R Labat
R Pierre Budin
R d'Oran
121
R Léon
R Doudeauville
R de Panama
R de Suez
135
R de Laghouat
R Stephenson
R Jean Robert
R Philippe de Girard
217
R du Département

Av Junot
Square S Buisson
R des Saules
R Norvins
R des Saules
Lycée Maîtrise de Montmartre
Parc de la Turlure
R Custine
Château Rouge
R Myrha
R Cavé
R Richomme
Square Léon
R St Bruno
Square de Jessaint
Square Louise de Marillac

R Caulaincourt
R Lepic
R Durantin
R Tholozé
R Norvins
Place du Tertre
Montmartre
Square Nadar
Square Willette
R André del Sarte
Christiani
167
La Goutte d'Or
R de Goutte d'Or
R Polonceau
138
Place de la Chapelle
La Chapelle

Blanche
Blvd de Clichy
Place Pigalle
Pigalle
R Alfred Stevens
Anvers
Square d'Anvers
Barbès Rochechouart
Villa Garance
209
Lariboisière
Blvd de la Chapelle
R Cail
R Perdonnet

See Montmartre Map (pp400)

R Victor Massé
163
155
R Condorcet
R Pétrelle
Gare du Nord
198
Gare du Nord
R du Faubourg St Denis
199
80
35

Place G Toudouze
49
St Georges
Place St Georges
R de la Tour d'Auvergne
196
Place de Roubaix
128
216
Place Napoléon
181
Château Landon

R La Fayette
R Lamartine
Square de Montholon
Poissonnière
Gare de l'Est
Square Villemin
Square St Laurent

Blvd Haussmann
Blvd Poissonnière
Blvd de Bonne Nouvelle
Strasbourg St Denis
Blvd St Denis
Blvd St Martin
Blvd de Magenta

Bourse
Place de la Bourse
Sentier
Bonne Nouvelle
Jacques Bonsergent

Quatre Septembre
Av de l'Opéra
Pyramides
Palais Royal
Jardin du Palais Royal
Right Bank
Les Halles
Châtelet
Réaumur Sébastopol
Arts et Métiers
Square Émile Chautemps
Square du Temple
See Central Paris (L Marais M

SIGHTS & ACTIVITIES (pp73–136)
Cabinet des Monnaies, Médailles et
Antiques.................................... 1 A5
Canauxrama................................ 2 F2
Crèche..................................... 3 D4
Hammam des Grands Boulevards........... 4 C5
Les Orgues de Flandre..................... 5 F1
Louis XIV Memorial......................... 6 B6
Maison Roue Libre (Bike Rentals).......... 7 F2
Musée de l'Éventail........................ 8 C5
Musée des Arts et Métiers................. 9 C6
Musée Grévin............................. 10 B4
Musée Internationale de la
Franc-Maçonnerie....................... 11 B4
Musée National Gustave Moreau.......... 12 A3
Musée Édith Piaf.......................... 13 G5
Paris Canal Croisières..................... 14 F2
Porte St-Denis............................ 15 C5
Porte St-Martin........................... 16 C5
Tour Jean Sans Peur....................... 17 B6
Touringscope............................. 18 A4

EATING 🍴 (pp149–204)
404...................................... 19 C6
Addis Ababa.............................. 20 A3
Au Bascou................................ 21 D6
Au Trou Normand......................... 22 E6
Au Village................................ 23 F6
Aux Crus de Bourgogne................... 24 B6
Baan Boran............................... 25 A5
Bistrot Florentin.......................... 26 F6
Buffalo Grill.............................. 27 C3
Café du Théâtre.......................... 28 A6
Chartier.................................. 29 B4
Chez Jean................................ 30 A3
Chez Jenny............................... 31 E5
Chez Papa (Espace Sud-Ouest).......... 32 E2
Chez Ramona............................. 33 G5
Chez Sébastien........................... 34 E5
Chiaapas................................. 35 D3
Da Mimmo............................... 36 D4
Food Shops............................... 37 C5
Franprix Faubourg St Denis Branch....... 38 C5
Franprix Jean Pierre Timbaud Branch..... 39 E6
Franprix Jules Ferry Branch............... 40 E5
Franprix Magenta Branch................. 41 D4
Franprix Petites Écuries Branch........... 42 C4
Hard Rock Café........................... 43 B4
Haynes.................................. 44 A3
Hippopotamus (Opéra).................... 45 A5
Jewish & North African Kosher
Restaurants............................ 46 B4
Juan et Juanita........................... 47 F5
Julien.................................... 48 C5
Kastoori.................................. 49 A3
Krung Thep............................... 50 G4
Kunitoraya............................... 51 A5
L'Arbre à Cannelle........................ 52 B4
L'Ave Maria.............................. 53 F6
La 25e Image............................. 54 D4
La Marine................................ 55 E5
La Toccata............................... 56 F6
Lao Siam................................. 57 G4
Le Baratin................................ 58 G4
Le Bistro de Gala......................... 59 B4
Le Camboge.............................. 60 E4
Le Chansonnier........................... 61 E3
Le Grand Colbert......................... 62 A5
Le Grand Véfour.......................... 63 A6
Le Loup Blanc............................ 64 B6
Le Mauricien Filao........................ 65 C5
Le Monde à l'Envers...................... 66 B6
Le Paris-Dakar........................... 67 D4
Le Pavillon Puebla........................ 68 G3
Le Porokhane............................ 69 G5
Le Réveil du Xe.......................... 70 D5
Le Sporting............................... 71 D4
Le Tambour.............................. 72 B6
Le Troisième Bureau...................... 73 E6
Le Vaudeville............................. 74 A5
Le Villaret............................... 75 F6

Les Ailes................................. 76 B4
Les Diamantaires......................... 77 B4
Lina's.................................... 78 A6
Macéo................................... 79 A5
Madras Café.............................. 80 D3
Marché Belleville......................... 81 G5
Marché St-Quentin....................... 82 C3
Mother Earth's........................... 83 B4
New Nioullaville......................... 84 F5
Noodle Shops & Restaurants............. 85 D6
Passage Brady Cafés...................(see 86)
Pooja.................................... 86 C4
Roi du Kashmir........................... 87 C4
Rue Montorgueil Market.................. 88 B6
Shalimar................................. 89 C5
Stohrer.................................. 90 B6
Tana.................................... 91 B6
Terminus Nord........................... 92 C3
Thai Classic.............................. 93 G4
Ty Coz.................................. 94 A3
Voyageurs du Monde Restaurant......... 95 A5
Wally le Saharien......................... 96 B3
Willi's Wine Bar.......................... 97 A5

ENTERTAINMENT 🙂 (pp205–42)
Agence Marivaux.......................... 98 A5
Au Petit Garage.......................... 99 F5
Au Tango............................... 100 D6
Café Charbon........................... 101 F6
Café Noir............................... 102 B5
Cannibale Café.......................... 103 G5
Centre Culturel Pouya.................... 104 E5
Chez Adel.............................. 105 E4
Chez Prune............................. 106 E4
Chez Wolf Motown Bar.................. 107 D4
Cinémathèque Française................. 108 C5
Folies-Bergère.......................... 109 B4
Gibus Club.............................. 110 E5
Hôtel du Nord........................... 111 E4
L'Absinthe.............................. 112 B6
L'Apostrophe........................... 113 E4
L'Attirail............................... 114 D6
L'Autre Café............................ 115 F5
L'Opus................................. 116 E3
La Casa 128............................ 117 C3
La Champmeslé......................... 118 A5
La Favela Chic.......................... 119 E5
La Java................................. 120 F5
Lavoir Moderne Parisien................. 121 C1
Le Cithéa............................... 122 G6
Le Limonaire........................... 123 B4
Le Mécano Bar......................... 124 F6
Le Nouveau Casino...................... 125 F6
Le Pravda.............................. 126 F5
Le Pulp................................. 127 B5
Le Relais du Nord....................... 128 C3
Le Scorp............................(see 127)
Le Verre Volé........................... 129 E4
Les Abats-Jour á Coudre................ 130 G6
Les Bains.............................. 131 C6
Les Étoiles............................. 132 C4
New Morning........................... 133 C4
O'Sullivan's............................. 134 B4
Olympic Café........................... 135 C1
Opéra Comique......................... 136 A5
Rex Club............................... 137 B5
Théâtre des Bouffes du Nord............ 138 D2

SHOPPING 🛍 (pp251–78)
A Simon................................ 139 B6
Anna Joliet............................. 140 A6
Anna Moï............................... 141 B5
Antoine et Lili.......................... 142 D4
Barbara Bui............................. 143 B6
Catherine Vernoux...................... 144 A5
Darty.................................. 145 E5
Didier Ludot............................ 146 A6
Didier Parakian.......................... 147 B6
Drouot................................. 148 A4
Jamin Puech............................ 149 C4
Jean-Paul Gaultier...................... 150 A5

Jewellery Shops......................... 151 D6
Kabuki Femmes......................... 152 B6
Kenzo.................................. 153 B6
Legrand Filles & Fils..................... 154 A5
Musical Instrument Shops................ 155 A3
Passage de l'Industrie................... 156 C5
Postage Stamp Shops................... 157 B4
Roxy Life Shop.......................... 158 B6
Rue de Paradis......................... 159 C4
Rue Drouot............................. 160 A4
Rue Martel............................. 161 C4
Rue Réaumur........................... 162 D6
Rue Victor Massé........................ 163 A3
Tati.................................... 164 D5
Tati.................................... 165 C2
Thierry Mugler.......................... 166 B6
Virgin Megastore........................ 167 C2
Yohji Yamamoto........................ 168 B6

SLEEPING 🛏 (pp279–304)
Apart'hotel Citadines Opéra Drouot..... 169 A5
Auberge de Jeunesse Jules Ferry........ 170 E5
Grand Hôtel de Paris.................... 171 D4
Hôtel Aquarelle......................... 172 E6
Hôtel Aulivia Opéra...................... 173 C4
Hôtel Chopin........................... 174 B4
Hôtel de Nevers........................ 175 E6
Hôtel des 3 Poussins.................... 176 A3
Hôtel des Arts.......................... 177 B4
Hôtel Favart............................ 178 A5
Hôtel Français.......................... 179 D4
Hôtel Garden Opéra..................... 180 C4
Hôtel La Vieille France.................. 181 D3
Hôtel Liberty........................... 182 D4
Hôtel Londres et Anvers................. 183 C3
Hôtel Peletier Haussmann Opéra........ 184 A4
Hôtel Tiquetonne....................... 185 C6
Hôtel Victoria.......................... 186 B4
Hôtel Victoires Opéra................... 187 B6
Hôtel Vivienne.......................... 188 B5
Nord Hôtel............................. 189 C3
Nord-Est Hôtel......................... 190 C3
Pavilion Opéra Bourse.................. 191 B4
Peace & Love Hostel.................... 192 E2
Résidence Passage Dubail............... 193 D4
Sibour Hôtel............................ 194 D4
Villa Opéra Drouot...................... 195 B4
Woodstock Hostel....................... 196 B3

TRANSPORT (pp332–8)
ADA Car Rental......................... 197 F6
Bus Terminal........................... 198 D3
RATP Bus No 350 to Charles de Gaulle
Airport............................... 199 D3
Rent A Car Système..................... 200 C3

INFORMATION
Après la Classe......................... 201 C6
C'Clean Laverie......................... 202 E6
Club Med Gym.......................... 203 E5
Cours de Cuisine Françoise Meunier..... 204 B5
Cyber Squ@re.......................... 205 E5
Forum Voyages......................... 206 A6
Hôtel de Police......................... 207 C6
Langue Onze........................... 208 F6
Lariboisière............................. 209 C2
Laverie Libre Service.................... 210 D6
Laverie Libre Service Primus............. 211 F5
Laverie SBS............................ 212 C4
Main Post Office........................ 213 B6
Metro Jungle Web Center................ 214 E6
Nouvelles Frontières.................... 215 A6
Paris Convention & Visitor Bureau....... 216 D3
Sri Manikar Vinayakar Alayam Temple... 217 D1
St Louis................................ 218 E4
Voyageurs du Monde.................... 219 A5

OTHER
Église St Nicolas des Champs............ 220 C6

SIGHTS & ACTIVITIES (pp73-136)
AMF Bowling de Montparnasse.................1 G6
Assemblée Nationale (Palais Bourbon).....2 F1
Bateaux Parisiens.................................3 C1
Bike 'n' Roller....................................4 E2
Centaur Statue..................................5 H3
Cimetière du Montparnasse Conservation
  Office...6 G5
Club Med Gym...................................7 G4
Église du Dôme.................................8 F2
Église St Louis des Invalides................9 F2
Eiffel Tower East Pillar.......................10 C2
Eiffel Tower North Pillar.....................11 C2
Eiffel Tower South Pillar.....................12 C2
Eiffel Tower West Pillar......................13 C2
Fat Tire Bike Tours Departure Point......14 C2
Fat Tire Bike Tours Office....................15 C3
Fondation Cartier d'Art Contemporain..16 H6
Fondation Dubuffet............................17 F4
Hôtel Matignon.................................18 G2
Maison de Balzac..............................19 A2
Marionettes de Champ de Mars..........20 C2
Ministère des Affaires Étrangères........21 F1
Musée Atelier Zadkine.......................22 H5
Musée Bourdelle...............................23 F5
Musée d'Orsay..................................24 G1
Musée de l'Armée..............................25 F2
Musée de l'Homme........................(see 26)
Musée de la Marine...........................26 B1
Musée de la Poste.............................27 F5
Musée de Montparnasse.....................28 G5
Musée des Égouts de Paris..................29 D1
Musée du Quai Branly.........................30 D1
Musée du Vin....................................31 B2
Musée Ernest Hébert..........................32 G4
Musée Jean Moulin............................33 F5
Musée Maillol....................................34 G2
Musée Pasteur..................................35 E5
Musée Rodin....................................36 F2
Musée-Atelier Zadkine.......................37 H5
Observatoire Météorologique.............38 F5
Palais de Chaillot...............................39 B1
Paris Canal Croisières.........................40 G1
Patinoire de Montparnasse.................41 G5
Rucher du Luxembourg (Apiary)..........42 H4
Statue of Liberty Replica.....................43 A3
Tour Montparnasse............................44 G5
Unesco Annexe.................................45 E4
Unesco Building................................46 E3

EATING 🍴 (pp149-204)
Amorino...47 H5
Assas University Restaurant.................48 H5
Banga de Mayotte.............................49 F4
Blvd de Grenelle Market......................50 C3
Boulevard Edgar Quinet Food Market...51 G5
Brasserie Lipp...................................52 H3
Creperies...53 G5
Dietetic Shop....................................54 H5

Dix Vins...55 F5
El Fares..56 D4
Feyrouz...57 C3
Franprix...58 G5
Franprix...59 C4
Franprix Delambre.............................60 H5
Il Viaggio...61 F2
Inno..62 G5
Jean Millet.......................................63 E2
Kim Anh..64 B4
L'Atelier de Joël Robouchon...............65 H2
La Cigale..66 G3
La Coupole Brasserie.........................67 H5
La Gitane...68 D3
La Grande Épicerie de Paris.................69 G3
Lal Qila..70 B4
Le 7e Sud...71 E2
Le Caméléon.....................................72 H5
Le Dôme..73 H5
Le Tipaza...74 C4
Le Troquet.......................................75 E4
Marché Raspail.................................76 G4
Marché St-Charles.............................77 B4
Monoprix...78 D4
Mustang Café...................................79 G5
Poilâne Branch..................................80 C3
Rue Cler Market................................81 E2
Sawadee..82 B4
Thoumieux.......................................83 E1
Thuy Long..84 G5

ENTERTAINMENT 😊 (pp205-42)
Café Thomieux.............................(see 83)
Café du Musée Rodin.....................(see 36)
Cinémathèque Française.....................85 C1
Cubana Café.....................................86 H5
Fnac Montparnasse...........................87 G4
Kiosque Théâtre................................88 G5
La Coupole..................................(see 67)
Le Rosebud.......................................89 H5
Le Select..90 H5
Opus Latino......................................91 E5
Red Light..92 G5
Théâtre du Vieux Colombier................93 H3

SHOPPING 🛍 (pp251-78)
Brûlerie des Ternes Branch..................94 A2
Carré Rive Gauche.............................95 H2
Celine..96 H3
Clothes & Shoe Shops........................97 G3
Clothes & Shoe Shops........................98 G4
Fausto Santini...................................99 H3
Fromagerie Barthelemy......................100 G3
Il Bisonte...101 H3
JB Martin...102 H3
Kenzo...103 H3
Le Bon Marché.................................104 G3
Madeleine Gély................................105 H2
Marthé et François Girbaud................106 H3

Palais des Thés.................................107 G4
Poilâne..108 H3
Sennelier..109 H2
Sonia Rykiel Men..............................110 H2
Sonia Rykiel Women..........................111 H3
Tea & Tattered Pages........................112 F4

SLEEPING 🛏 (pp279-304)
Acceuil Familial des Jeunes
  Éstrangers...................................113 H3
Aloha Hostel...................................114 E5
Apart'hotel Citadines Maine
  Montparnasse...............................115 G6
Apart'hotels Citadines Tour Eiffel........116 D4
Celtic Hôtel.....................................117 G5
Hôtel Aviatic....................................118 G4
Hôtel de Danemark..........................119 H5
Hôtel de l'Espérance.........................120 H6
Hôtel de Paris..................................121 G5
Hôtel de St-Germain.........................122 H3
Hôtel Delambre...............................123 G5
Hôtel des Académies........................124 H5
Hôtel Lenox St Germain....................125 H2
Hôtel Miramar.................................126 G5
Hôtel Odessa Montparnasse..............127 G5
Hôtel Thoumioux.........................(see 83)
Le Relais de Paris Cambronne............128 D4
Paris Côté Seine..............................129 B3
Pension Au Palais Gourmand.............130 H5
Pension Ladagnous......................(see 131)
Pension Les Marroniers.....................131 H4
Villa Modigliani................................132 G5

TRANSPORT (pp332-8)
Air France Buses..............................133 G6
Air France Buses..............................134 F1
Aérogare des Invalides......................135 F1
Batobus Stop...............................(see 3)
Batobus Stop..............................(see 40)
easyCar..136 F6

INFORMATION
Adath Shalom Synagogue.................137 C3
Alliance Française............................138 H4
American Church in Paris...................139 E1
Australian Embassy..........................140 C2
Centre des Étudiants........................141 E4
Cybercafe Latin...............................142 H4
École Le Cordon Bleu.......................143 D6
Étudiants de l'Institut Catholique.......144 H4
Institut Parisien de Langue et de
  Civilisation Françaises.....................145 C3
Italian Embassy................................146 G3
Laverie SBS.....................................147 C5
Laverie Éclat...................................148 D5
Netherlands Embassy........................149 F4
Paris Convention & Visitors Bureau....(see 11)
South African Embassy......................150 E1
Swiss Embassy................................151 F2

Rue de la Pompe
A
R Greuze
Av Georges Mandel
B
Trocadéro
Av du Président Wilson
C
Place de l'Alma
Pont de l'Alma
D

R Decamps
Place du Trocadéro et du 11 Novembre
Cimetière de Passy
Av Albert de Mun
Av d'Iéna
R Fresnel
Av de New York
Pont de l'Alma
29

1
R Jules Janin
R Nicolo
Iéna
39
85
Av des Nations Unies
See pp384–5
Place de la Résistance
R Cogr

Av Paul Doumer
R Belloni
R Scheffer
R Vineuse
26
Place de Varsovie
Pont de la Bourdonnais
30
Av Franco Russe
Cité de l'Alma
R E Valentin

Place Possoz
Place de Costa Rica
Blvd Delessert
Pont d'Iéna
3
Alée Paul Deschanel
R de Monttessuy
R Rapp
Av Dupont des Loges

2
31
Square Charles Dickens
Passy
Champ de Mars Tour Eiffel
Branly
11
10
Eiffel Tower
13
12
14
20
Av Gustave Eiffel
Av Élisée Reclus
Av Émile Pouvillon
Place Jacques Rueff
Parc du Champ de Mars

19
Av de Lamballe
Place des Martyrs Juifs du Vélodrome d'Hiver
Bir Hakeim
R de la Fédération
R Jean Rey
140
Place Jacques
Allée Thomy Thierry
Anatole France
Av Pierre Loti

3
Maison de Radio France
Kennedy Radio-France
Allée des Cygnes
Nélaton
Blvd de Grenelle
R St Saëns
Desaix
Place A Carrée
80
137
15
R de Presles
Av de la Motte Picquet

43
129
de Grenelle
Place de Brazzaville
R du Docteur Finlay
R Sextius Michel
Viala
57
Place Dupleix
Dupleix
145
68
La Motte Picquet Grenelle
Square Cambronne

4
André Citroën
Javel
Road Point du Pont Mirabeau
Place de la Montagne du Goulet
Square Pablo Casals
64 82
77
70
Charles Michels
Av Émile Zola
Avenue Émile Zola
74
78 116
128
56
R Frémicourt
Cambronne

5
Square des Cévennes
Parc André Citroën
Cimetière de Grenelle
R de la Convention
Jardin Duranton
Boucicaut
Place Violet
Square Violet
Félix Faure
147
Square St Lambert
Square Gerbert
148
Place et Square Adolphe Chérioux
Vaugirard

6
Balard
Place Balard
Blvd du Général Martial Valin
Cimetière de Vaugirard
R Lecourbe
Convention
143
R de Vouill

SIGHTS & ACTIVITIES (pp73-136)
Art Deco Police Station...........................1 G5
Arènes de Lutèce..................................2 C4
Bowling Mouffetard..............................3 C5
Canauxrama Pier...................................4 E3
Carrousel...5 A4
Centre de la Mer...................................6 B4
Chapelle de la Sorbonne.........................7 B4
Children's Playground.............................8 A4
Children's Playground.............................9 E3
Colonne de Juillet................................10 E3
Direction de l'Action Sociale Building....11 E4
École de Botanique...............................12 D5
Église Notre Dame de l'Espérance..........13 F2
Église Royale du Val-de-Grâce...............14 B5
Église St-Étienne du Mont.....................15 C4
Fontaine de l'Observatoire.....................16 A5
Fontaine de la Croix..............................17 A4
Fontaine des Médicis.............................18 A4
Galerie d'Anatomie Comparée et de
   Paléontologie..................................19 D5
Galerie de Botanique............................20 D5
Galerie de Minéralogie, de Géologie et de
   Paléobotanie..................................21 D5
Gepetto & Vélos..................................22 C4
Gepetto & Vélos Branch........................23 C5
Grand Bassin.......................................24 A4
Grande Galerie de l'Évolution................25 D5
Hammam de la Mosquée de Paris.......(see 34)
Institut du Monde Arabe.......................26 D4
Jardin Alpin...27 D5
Jardin d'Hiver (Serres Tropicales)...........28 D5
Maison de Victor Hugo..........................29 E2
Manufacture des Gobelins......................30 C6
Maréchal Ney Statue.............................31 A5
Ménagerie du Jardin des
   Plantes..32 D4
Ministry of Finance...............................33 F5
Mosquée de Paris..................................34 C5
Musée de Fumeur..................................35 G2
Musée du Luxembourg...........................36 A4
Ménagerie Entrance..............................37 D4
Nomades...38 E3

Orchards...39 A4
Panthéon..40 B4
Paris á Vélo, C'est Sympa!......................41 E3
Shetland Ponies for Hire........................42 A4
Sorbonne..43 B3
Sénat...44 A4

EATING 🍽 (pp149-204)
Athanor..45 G4
Bistrot Guillaume..................................46 G1
Bistrot à Vin Jacques Mélac Brasserie..(see 121)
Blue Elephant.......................................47 F2
Bofinger...48 E3
Brasserie des Grandes Marches...............49 E3
Bullier University Restaurant.............(see 206)
Café Cannelle.......................................50 G3
Café de l'Industrie.................................51 F2
Censier University Restuarant.................52 D5
Champion...53 C4
Chez Heang...54 E3
Chez Léna et Mimille.............................55 C5
Chez Paul..56 F3
Chez Régis...57 F4
Châtelet University Restaurant...............58 C5
Coffee India...59 F3
Comme Cochons...................................60 G4
Crêperie Bretonne Fleurie.......................61 G3
Crêpes Show..62 F3
Ed l'Épicier...63 C5
Fauchon...64 B3
Food Shops...65 B4
Founti Agadir.......................................66 C5
Franprix..67 C5
Grand Apétit..68 E3
Havanita Café......................................69 F3
Indonesia..70 A4
Koutchi...71 C4
L'Encrier...72 F4
L'Étoile du Berger.................................73 C4
La Banane Ivoirienne.............................74 G3
La Grand Méricourt...............................75 F1
La Main d'Or.......................................76 F3
La Mosquée de Paris..............................77 D5

La Petit Légume...................................78 C4
La Piragua...79 G1
La Voie Lactée......................................80 C4
Lanna Store...81 G3
Le Bistrot du Dôme Bastille....................82 E3
Le Buisson Ardent................................83 C4
Le C'Amelot...84 E2
Le Clown Bar.......................................85 E1
Le Coco de Mer....................................86 D6
Le Cosi...87 B4
Le Foyer du Vietnam.............................88 C5
Le Jardin des Pâtes...............................89 C5
Le Kitch...90 E1
Le Mansouria.......................................91 G3
Le Péché Mignon..................................92 G1
Le Repaire de Cartouche........................93 E1
Le Sofa..94 E2
Le Square Trousseau.............................95 F3
Le Tournebride.....................................96 C5
Le Viaduc Café.....................................97 F4
Le Vigneron...98 C5
Les Amis de Messina.............................99 G3
Les Amognes......................................100 G3
Les Caves St Gilles..............................101 E2
Les Galopins.......................................102 F2
Les Jumeaux.......................................103 E2
Les Quatre et Une Saveurs....................104 C4
Les Sans Culottes................................105 F3
Les Vignes du Panthéon.......................106 B4
Lire Entre les Vignes............................107 F2
Machu Picchu.....................................108 B4
Marché d'Aligre.............................(see 167)
Mavrommatis......................................109 C5
Monoprix Bastille................................110 F3
Perraudin...111 B4
Place Monge Food Market.....................112 C5
Rue Mouffetard Food Market................113 C5
Savannah Café.....................................114 C4
Swann et Vincent................................115 F3
Tao...116 B5
Tashi Delek..117 B4
Waly Fay..118 G2

ENTERTAINMENT ☺ (pp205–42)
Barrio Latino....................................119 F3
Baz'art Café....................................120 E3
Bistrot à Vins Jacques Mélac.............121 H2
Boca Chica......................................122 G3
Bottle Shop.....................................123 G3
Café Aussie.....................................124 B4
Café de la Danse..............................125 F3
Café Delmas....................................126 C4
Café des Phares...............................127 C3
Café Léopard...................................128 G2
Café Universel..................................129 B5
China Club.......................................130 F3
Finnegan's Wake..............................131 C4
Fnac Musique Bastille.......................132 E3
Havanita Café...............................(see 69)
Iguana Café.....................................133 F3
Interface Bar....................................134 F2
L'Aram..135 F1
L'Armangac.....................................136 G2
L'Envol Québécois............................137 C5
L'Urgence Bar..................................138 B4
La Chapelle des Lombards..................139 F3
La Closerie des Lilas.........................140 A5
La Luciole.......................................141 C5
La Renaissance................................142 G2
Le Balajo...143 F3
Le Bataclan.....................................144 F1
Le Café du Passage..........................145 F3
Le Crocodile....................................146 B4
Le Lèche-Vin....................................147 F2
Le Petit Journal St-Michel..................148 B4
Le Piano Vache.................................149 C4
Le Réservoir....................................150 G3
Le Salon Egyptien.............................151 C4
Le Vieux Chêne................................152 C5
Le Violon Dingue..............................153 C4
Les Funambules................................154 G3
Maison de la Vanille..........................155 C4
Opéra Bastille Box Office...................156 E3
Paradis Latin....................................157 C4
Pause Café......................................158 F3
Pop In...159 E1
Sanz Sans.......................................160 F3
Satellite Café...................................161 F1
Théâtre de la Bastille........................162 F2
Théâtre du Luxembourg.....................163 A4
Wax..(see 147)

SHOPPING 🛍 (pp251–78)
Crocodisc.......................................164 B4
Jadis et Gourmande..........................165 A6
La Maison du Cerf-Volant...................166 F4
Marché aux Puces d'Aligre..................167 F4
Rue Keller.......................................168 F2

SLEEPING 🛏 (pp279–304)
Apart'hotel Citadines Bastille Nation....169 G4
Centre International BVJ Paris-Quartier
  Latin..170 C4
Comfort Inn Mouffetard.....................171 C5
Familia Hôtel...................................172 C4
Grand Hôtel St Michel.......................173 B4
Hostel Blue Planet............................174 F4
Hôtel Baudelaire Bastille....................175 F3
Hôtel Baudin....................................176 F3
Hôtel Beaumarchais..........................177 E1
Hôtel Castex....................................178 E3
Hôtel Central Bastille.........................179 F3
Hôtel Cluny Sorbonne.......................180 B4
Hôtel Daval.....................................181 F2
Hôtel de l'Espérance.........................182 C6
Hôtel de la Herse d'Or.......................183 E3
Hôtel de la Place des Vosges..............184 E2
Hôtel des Grand Écoles......................185 C4
Hôtel du Panthéon............................186 B4
Hôtel du Progrès..............................187 B5
Hôtel Gay Lussac.............................188 B5
Hôtel La Demeure.............................189 D6
Hôtel Le Clos Médecis.......................190 B4
Hôtel Les Sans Culottes.................(see 105)
Hôtel Luxembourg Parc......................191 A4
Hôtel Lyon Mulhouse........................192 E2
Hôtel Minerve..................................193 C4
Hôtel New Candide...........................194 G2
Hôtel Royal Bastille..........................195 F3
Hôtel Résidence Henri IV....................196 C4
Hôtel Résidence Monge.....................197 C5
Hôtel St-Christophe...........................198 C5
Hôtel St-Jacques..............................199 B4
Maison Internationale des Jeunes
  pour la Culture et la Paix.................200 H3
Select Hôtel....................................201 B4
Timhôtel Quartier Latin......................202 C5
Young & Happy Hostel.......................203 C5

TRANSPORT (pp332–8)
Batobus Stop...................................204 D4
Free Scoot.......................................205 G2
OTU Voyages...................................206 A5

INFORMATION
Association Maison des Femmes de
  Paris..207 G4
Centre Gai et Lesbien de Paris.............208 F3
Copy-Top Voltaire.............................209 F1
Cours de Langue et Civilisation
  Françaises de la Sorbonne...............210 B4
Cyber Ca@fé....................................211 C4
Emergencies....................................212 D6
Forum Voyages.................................213 C4
Hospital Night-Time Entrance..............214 D6
Hôpital de la Salpêtrière....................215 E5
Hôtel de Police (Carte de Séjour)......(see 207)
Laverie Libre Service.........................216 C4
Laverie Libre Service.........................217 B4
Laverie Miele Libre Service.................218 F3
Le Bateau Lavoir...............................219 C4
Luxembourg Micro............................220 A4
Paris Convention & Visitor Bureau........221 F4
SOS Dentaire...................................222 B6
Toonet Cyber Space..........................223 G3
XS Arena Luxembourg........................224 B4

OTHER
Cirque d'Hiver..................................225 E1
Église St-Médiard..............................226 C5

A   B   C   D

1   2   3   4   5   6

R des Pyramides
R St Honoré
R d'Argenteuil
R de l'Echelle
Av de l'Opéra
R Molière
R de Montpensier
R de Valois
R St Honoré

Jardin du Palais Royal
Palais Royal
Banque de France
Hôtel des Postes
Rue Montorgueil Market
R Étienne Marcel
R Française

153
152
5º Palais Royal
R du Colonel Driant
R des Petits Champs
R du Boulai
R Coquillière
R Coq Héron
R Jean Jacques Rousseau
R du Jour
223
71
205
206
204
16
126
36

Right Bank
Galerie Véro Dodat
77
287
107
275
7
62
Place René Cassin
Les Halles
R de Rambute
Forum des Halles
244

Place du Palais Royal Musée du Louvre
249
184
343
10
188
117
187
347
78
R de Marengo
R de l'Oratoire
R Bailleul
R Berger
R St Honoré
89
Place M Quentin
Châtelet les Halles

Jardin du Carrousel
Place du Carrousel
3
34
Cour Napoléon
29
Jardin de l'Oratoire
Louvre
Cour Carrée
311
Louvre Rivoli
261
336
173
Perrault
R de Rivoli
R du Roule
112
79
192
Place M de Navarre
272
26
R de la Ferronnerie
101
143
195
165
Châtelet

Q du Louvre
Jardin de l'Infante
R de l'Amiral de Coligny
Place du Louvre
240
18
241
231
R Baillet
R de la Monnaie
R Boucher
303
31
Pont Neuf
R du Pont Neuf
199
92
277
Châtelet
149
17

Seine
324
326
Q Malaquais
Place de l'Institut
6
Square du Vert Galant
66
196
Place du Pont Neuf
Pont Neuf
300
Place Dauphine
Q de l'Horloge
Palais de Justice
Île de la Cité
64
Conciergerie
Q de la Corse
Bertin Poirée
R des Déchargeurs
R Édouard Colonne
Av Victoria
150
Châtelet
Place du Châtelet
197
Q des Gesvr
Square de la Tour St Jacques

R des Beaux Arts
285
235
316
R Visconti
268
282
317
291
293
R Jacob
310
161
R Jacques Callot
108
289
198
Passage Dauphine
338
R Christine
306
273
Q des Grands Augustins
Ste Chapelle
Blvd du Palais
Cité
37
R de la Cité
R de Lutèce
351
Hôte Dieu
34

R St Benoît
119
Place St Germain des Prés
52
R Cardinale
87
81
250
R de Savoie
Q du Marché Neuf
St Michel Notre Dame
Place du Parvis Notre Dame
12
R de Rennes
146
178
17
95
342
104
R de Buci
68
R André des Arts
130
341
110
322
352
276
St Michel
Q St Michel

255
Square F Desruelles
274
80
218
278
309
333
Place St André des Arts
Place St Michel
R de la Huchette
263
298
Q de Monteb
St Germain des Prés
Gozlin
Mabillon
R du Four
128
115
R Clément
154
242
Cour du Commerce St André
R de Jardinet
R de l'Éperon
R Suger
R Danton
349
R St Séverin
166
88
St Julien le Pauvre
138
299
Square R Viviani
R des Ciseaux
267
169
116
R Guisarde
Marché St Germain
183
96
R des Quatre Vents
295
13
Odéon
Place H Mondor
348
R Serpente
R de la Harpe
202
24
247
Calande
321
R Dante
207
151
R des Anglais
Place St Sulpice
27
148
269
270
220
St Sulpice
23
R Palatine
R Lobineau
134
R de l'École de Médecine
Blvd St Germain
Cluny la Sorbonne
323
28
39
208
225
224
Maubert Mutualité
226
R de Condé
Place de l'Odéon
164
254
306
185
Place Paul Claudel
R Racine
74
Square et Place P Painlevé
167
328
214
212
226
231
R de Latran
213
Latin Quarter
Square F.A. Mariette
R des Écoles
50
R Vaugirard
Jardin du Luxembourg
R Férou
R Servandoni
R de Tournon
R Garancière

SIGHTS & ACTIVITIES (pp73-136)
16th-Century Half-Timbered Houses......1 F4
Apartment Where Jim Morrison Died......2 H5
Arc de Triomphe du Carrousel......3 A2
Archives Nationales......4 F2
Atelier Brancusi......5 E2
Bibliothèque Mazarine......6 B3
Bourse de Commerce......7 C1
Carrousel du Louvre Entrance......8 A2
Charlemagne Memorial......9 D5
Club Med Gym......10 B2
Club Quartier Latin......11 E6
Conseil d'État......(see 59)
Crypte Archéologique......12 D5
Danton Statue......13 B5
Défenseur du Temps......14 E2
Ed l'Epicier Supermarket......15 E3
Église St-Eustache......16 D1
Église St-Germain des Prés......17 A5
Église St-Germain L'Auxerrois......18 C3
Église St-Gervais-St-Protais......19 F4
Église St-Julien le Pauvre......20 D5
Église St-Louis en l'Île......21 G6
Église St-Paul-St-Louis......22 G4
Église St-Sulpice......23 A6
Église St-Séverin......24 D5
Espace Vit'Halles......25 E2
Fontaine des Innocents......26 D2
Fontaine des Quatre Evêques......27 A6
Forêt de la Licorne......28 C6
Grande Pyramide......29 A2
Guimard Synagogue......30 G4
Henri IV Statue......31 C3
Hôtel de Sully......32 H4
Hôtel de Ville Salon d'Acceuil
(Reception)......33 E3
Institut de France......(see 6)
Inverted Glass Pyramid......34 A2
La Samaritaine Rooftop Terrace......(see 241)
Maison Européenne de la Photographie....35 G4
Maison Roue Libre......36 D2
Marché aux Fleurs......37 D4
Marché aux Oiseaux......(see 37)
Mechanical Fountains......38 E3
Medieval Garden......(see 28)
Musée National du Moyen Age
(Musée de Cluny)......39 C6
Musée Carnavalet......40 H3
Musée Cognacq-Jay......41 G3
Musée d'Art et d'Histoire du Judaïsme....42 F2
Musée de l'Assistance Publique-Hôpitaux de
Paris......43 E6
Musée de l'Histoire de France......44 G2
Musée de l'Histoire de la Médecine......45 C6
Musée de la Chasse et de la Nature......46 G2
Musée de la Curiosité et de la Magie......47 G5
Musée de la Monnaie de Paris......48 B4
Musée de la Poupée......49 F2
Musée de la Préfecture de Police......50 D6
Musée de Notre Dame de Paris......51 E5
Musée National Eugène Delacroix......52 A4
Musée Picasso......53 H2
Mémorial des Martyrs de la Déportation....54 E5
Mémorial du Martyr Juif Inconnu......55 H4
Mémorial du Martyr Juif Inconnu (Under
Renovation)......56 F4
Notre Dame......57 E5
Notre Dame North Tower Entrance......58 E5
Palais Royal......59 B1
Patinoire de l'Hôtel de Ville (Winter)......60 E4
Pavillon de l'Arsenal......61 H6
Piscine Pontoise-Quartier Latin......(see 11)
Piscine Suzanne Berlioux......62 C1
Point Zéro......63 E5
Tour de l'Horloge......64 D4
Tour St-Jacques......65 D3
Vedettes du Pont Neuf......66 C3

EATING (pp149-204)
Al Dar......67 E6
Amorino......68 B5
Anahuacalli......69 E6
Au Levain du Marais......70 H3
Au Pied de Cochon......71 C1

Bel Canto......72 F4
Berthillon......73 F5
Bouillon Racine......74 C6
Brasserie de l'Isle St-Louis......75 F5
Café Beaubourg......76 E2
Café de l'Époque......77 B1
Café Marly......78 A2
Caribbean Coffee......79 C2
Champion......80 B5
Chez Albert......81 B4
Chez Hanna......82 G3
Chez Marianne......83 G3
Chez Nénesse......84 H2
Chez Omar......85 G1
Crèmerie des Carmes (Fromagerie)......(see 227)
Finkelsztajn......86 G3
Fish la Boissonnerie......87 B4
Fogon St-Julien......88 D5
Franprix......89 C2
Franprix......90 G4
Franprix Bretagne Branch......91 G1
Franprix Châtelet Branch......92 D3
Franprix Marais Branch......93 F3
Fromagerie G Millet......94 H4
Guen Maï......95 A5
Gérard Mulot......96 B5
Isami......97 F6
Jo Goldenberg......98 G4
Joe Allen......99 E1
L'Alivi......100 F4
L'Amazonial......101 D2
L'Ambassade d'Auvergne......102 F1
L'Ambroisie......103 H4
L'Arbuci......104 B5
L'As de Falafel......105 G3
L'Enoteca......106 G5
L'Épi d'Or......107 C1
La Cafetière......108 B4
La Perla......109 F4
La Soummam......110 B5
La Tour d'Argent......111 F6
La Victoire Suprême du Cœur......112 D2
Le Dôme du Marais......113 G4
Le Gai Moulin......114 F3
Le Golfe de Naples......115 A5
Le Mâchon d'Henri......116 A5
Le Petit Mâchon......117 B2
Le Petit Picard......118 F3
Le Petit Zinc......119 A4
Le Réconfort......120 G2
Le Studio......121 E3
Le Trumilou......122 F4
Le Véro Dodat......123 B1
Les Fous de l'Île......124 F5
Les Vins des Pyrénées......125 H5
Léon de Bruxelles......126 D1
Ma Bourgogne......127 H4
Mabillon University Restaurant......128 A5
Marché aux Enfants Rouges......129 H1
Mazet University Restaurant......130 B5
Monoprix......131 H4
Piccolo Teatro......132 G4
Pitchi Poï......133 H4
Place Maubert Market......(see 227)
Polidor......134 B6
Robert et Louise......135 G3
Supermarché G20......136 G4
Supermarché G20 Bastille......137 E3
Tea Caddy......138 D5
Thanksgiving......139 H5
Un Piano sur le Trottoir......140 H4

ENTERTAINMENT (pp205-42)
Amnésia......141 G3
Au Petit Fer à Cheval......142 F3
Banana Café......143 D2
Bistrot Latin......144 F3
Bliss Kfé......145 G4
Café de Flore......146 A5
Café de la Gare......147 F3
Café de la Mairie......148 A5
Café Oz......149 D3
Châtelet-Théâtre Musical de Paris......150 D3
Club Zed......151 D6

Comédie Française......152 A1
Comédie Française Discount Ticket
Window......153 A1
Comédie Française Studio Théâtre......(see 8)
Coolín......154 A5
Fnac Forum des Halles......(see 244)
Forum des Images......(see 244)
Full Metal......155 F2
Jokko Bar......156 G3
L'Apparement Café......157 H2
L'Urgence Bar......158 B6
La Chaise au Plafond......159 G3
La Charlotte en Île......160 G5
La Palette......161 B4
La Station......162 F4
La Tartine......163 G4
Le 10......164 B6
Le Baiser Salé......165 D2
Le Caveau de la Huchette......166 D5
Le Central......(see 244)
Le Champo......167 C6
Le Coffee Shop......168 F3
Le Comptoir des Cannettes......169 A5
Le Cox......170 F3
Le Duc des Lombards......171 D3
Le Dépôt......172 E1
Le Fumoir......173 C2
Le Latina......(see 144)
Le Pick Clops......174 F4
Le Quetzal......175 F3
Le Rallye......176 F6
Le Wagg......177 B4
Les Deux Magots......178 A5
Les Philosophes......179 F3
Les Scandaleuses......180 G4
Les Étages......181 G3
Mixer Bar......182 F3
Moosehead Bar......183 B5
Murphy's House......184 B2
Odéon-Théâtre de l'Europe......185 B6
Open Café......186 F3
Oratoire du Louvre......187 B2
Papou Lounge......188 B2
Point Virgule......189 F3
Pure Malt Bar......190 H4
Quiet Man......191 G2
Slow Club......192 C2
Soprano......193 H4
Stolly's......194 F4
Sunset & Sunside......195 D2
Taverne Henri IV......196 C3
Théâtre de la Ville......197 D3
Théâtre de Nesle......198 B4
Théâtre des Déchargeurs......199 D3

SHOPPING (pp251-78)
2 Mille et 1 Nuits......200 H4
A l'Olivier......201 F4
Abbey Bookshop......202 C5
Aboud'Abi Bazar......203 H4
agnès b children......204 C1
agnès b men......205 C1
agnès b women......206 D1
Album......207 D6
Album Branch......208 D6
Alternatives......209 G4
Apoc......210 G3
Au Vieux Campeur......211 D6
Au Vieux Campeur......212 D6
Au Vieux Campeur......213 D6
Au Vieux Campeur......214 D6
Blues Plus......215 D6
Bazar de l'Hôtel de Ville (BHV)......216 F3
Boutique Paris-Musées......217 G3
Cacao et Chocolat......218 B5
Cacao et Chocolat Branch......219 G3
Christian Lacroix......220 A5
Clothes Boutiques......221 H4
CSAO Boutique......222 G3
E Dehillerin......223 C1
EOL' Modelisme......224 D6
EOL' Modelisme Branch......225 D6
EOL' Modelisme Branch......226 D6
Espace Créateurs......(see 244)

SHOPPING (Continued) 📷 (pp251–78)
Food Shops.....................................227 D6
Galerie & Atelier Puncinello............228 H3
Galerie Alain Carion.......................229 F5
Issey Miyake.................................230 H4
Kenzo...231 C3
L'Eclaireur Marais Branch............(see 280)
L'Habilleur....................................232 G2
L'Ours du Marais...........................233 G4
L'Éclaireur.....................................234 G4
L'Île du Démon..............................235 A4
La Boutique des Inventions............236 G5
La Charrue et les Étoiles.................237 H4
La Maison de l'Astronomie............238 E3
La Petite Scierie.............................239 F5
La Samaritaine (Men & Sport).......240 C2
La Samaritaine Main Building.......241 C3
Le Mouton à Cinq Pattes..............242 B5
Le Palais des Thés.........................243 G3
Les Halles.....................................244 D2
Les Mots à la Bouche.....................245 F3
Les Ruchers du Roy........................246 F4
Librairie de l'Hôtel de Sully.......(see 32)
Librairie Gourmande......................247 D5
Librairie Ulysse.............................248 G5
Louvre des Antiquaires..................249 B2
Mariage Frères..............................250 C4
Mariage Frères..............................251 F3
Mélodies Graphiques.....................252 F4
Nickel...253 G3
Odimex Paris.................................254 B6
Onward...255 A5
Pleats Please.................................256 G4
Produits des Monastères................257 F4
Red Wheelbarrow Bookstore..........258 H5
Red Wheelbarrow Children's
  Bookstore...................................259 H5
Roul'tabille....................................260 F4
Rue de Rivoli.................................261 C2
Rue du Pont Louis Philippe............262 F4
Shakespeare & Company................263 D5
Sic Amor.......................................264 F4
Slip..265 F1
Tumbleweed..................................266 H4
Village Voice..................................267 A5
Virgin Megastore......................(see 8)
Voyageurs & Curieux......................268 B4
Yves Saint Laurent Rive Gauche
  Femmes......................................269 A5
Yves Saint Laurent Rive Gauche
  Hommes......................................270 A5

SLEEPING 🛏 (pp279-304)
Allô Logement Temporaire.............271 F2
Apart'hotel Citadines Les Halles.....272 D2
Apart'hotel Citadines St Germain des
  Prés..273 C4
Artushotel.....................................274 A5
Centre International de Séjour BVJ
  Paris-Louvre...............................275 C1
Delhy's Hôtel.................................276 C5
Grand Hôtel de Champagne............277 D3
Grand Hôtel de l'Univers................278 B5
Grand Hôtel du Loiret....................279 F4
Grand Hôtel Malher........................280 G4
Hôtel Axial Beaubourg...................281 E3
Hôtel Bel Ami St Germain des Prés..282 A4
Hôtel Caron de Beaumarchais........283 F4
Hôtel Central Marais......................284 F3
Hôtel d'Angleterre..........................285 A4
Hôtel de la Bretonnerie..................286 F3
Hôtel de Lille Pélican.....................287 B1
Hôtel de Lutèce.............................288 F5
Hôtel de Nesle...............................289 B4
Hôtel de Nice................................290 F4
Hôtel de Rohan..........................(see 44)
Hôtel des Deux Continents............291 A4
Hôtel des Deux Îles.......................292 F5
Hôtel des Marronniers...................293 A4
Hôtel du Bourg Tibourg.................294 F3
Hôtel du Globe..............................295 B5
Hôtel du Septième Art...................296 H5
Hôtel du Vieux Saule.....................297 H1
Hôtel Esmeralda............................298 D5
Hôtel Henri IV...............................299 D5
Hôtel Henri IV...............................300 C4
Hôtel Jeanne d'Arc........................301 H4
Hôtel Le Compostelle.....................302 F4
Hôtel Le Relais du Louvre..............303 C3
Hôtel Michelet Odéon....................304 B6
Hôtel Pratic...................................305 H4
Hôtel Relais Christine.....................306 B4
Hôtel Rivoli...................................307 F4
Hôtel Saintonge Marais..................308 H2
Hôtel St-André des Arts.................309 B5
Hôtel St-Germain des Prés.............310 A4
Hôtel St-Honoré.............................311 C2
Hôtel St-Louis...............................312 F5
Hôtel St-Louis Marais.....................313 H5
Hôtel St-Merry...............................314 E3
Hôtel Sévigné................................315 G4
L'Hôtel..316 A4
La Villa St-Germain des Prés..........317 A4

MIJE Le Fauconnier........................318 G5
MIJE Le Fourcy..............................319 G4
MIJE Maubuisson...........................320 F4
Mélia Colbert Boutique Hotel........321 D5
Résidence des Arts.........................322 C5
Résidence St-Germain....................323 C5

TRANSPORT (pp332-8)
Batobus Stop................................324 B3
Batobus Stop................................325 F4
Batobus Stop................................326 A3
Batobus Stop................................327 E5
Eurolines Office.............................328 D6
Free Scoot....................................329 E6
Noctambus (Night Bus) Stops........330 E3
Noctambus (Night Bus) Stops........331 D3
OTU Voyages.................................332 E2

INFORMATION
Access Academy.............................333 B5
Akyrion Net Center.........................334 G4
ANPE Hôtel de Ville.......................335 F3
Best Change..................................336 C2
Cyberbe@ubourg Internet C@fé......337 E2
Espace du Tourisme d'Île de France..(see 8)
Eurocentres...................................338 B4
Hôtel Dieu (Hospital)......................339 E4
Hôtel Dieu (Hospital) Emergency
  Entrance.....................................340 D4
Julice Laverie.................................341 B5
Julice Laverie.................................342 B5
Laverie Libre Service......................343 B2
Laverie Libre Service......................344 G3
Laverie Libre Service......................345 F3
Laverie Libre Service Primus...........346 G4
Nouvelles Frontières Branch...........348 C5
Pharmacie Bader...........................349 C5
Pharmacie des Halles.....................350 D3
Préfecture de Police Entrance.........351 D4
Société Touristique de Services (STS)
  Exchange Office...........................352 C5
Web 46...353 G4
XS Arena Les Halles........................354 E2

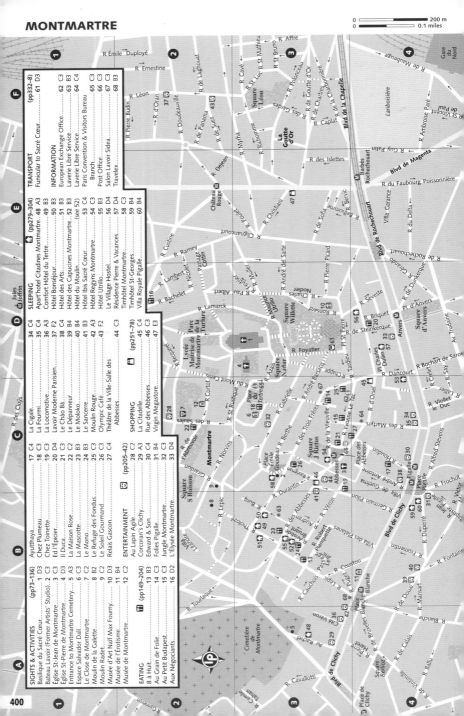

MONTMARTRE

SIGHTS & ACTIVITIES	(pp73–136)
Ayutthaya	17 C4
Basilique du Sacré Coeur	1 D3
Bateau Lavoir (Former Artists' Studio)	2 C3
Église St-Jean de Montmartre	3 C3
Édl l'Épicier	4 D3
Entrance to Montmartre Cemetery	5 A3
Espace Salvador Dali	6 C3
Le Clos de Montmartre	7 C2
Moulin de la Galette	8 B2
Moulin Radet	9 C3
Musée d'Art Naïf Max Fourny	10 D3
Musée de l'Erotisme	11 B4
Musée de Montmartre	12 C2

EATING	(pp149–204)
8 à Huit	13 B3
Au Grain de Folie	14 C3
Au Petit Budapest	15 C3
Aux Négociants	16 D2
La Cigale	17 C4
Chez Plumeau	18 C3
Chez Toinette	19 C3
La Locomotive	20 D4
Lavoir Moderne Parisien	21 C3
Le Chão Bả	22 C3
Il Duca	23 B3
La Maison Rose	24 B3
La Mascotte	25 C3
Le Mono	26 C3
Le Refuge des Fondus	27 C2

La Fourmi	35 C4
La Locomotive	36 A3
Le Chão Bả	37 F2
Le Dépanneur	38 C4
Le Moloko	39 B4
Moulin Rouge	40 B4
Le Sancerre	41 B3
Le Soleil Gourmand	42 A3
Relais Gascon	43 F2
Théâtre de la Ville-Salle des Abbesses	44 C3

SHOPPING	(pp251–78)
La Citadelle	45 C4
Rue des Abbesses	46 C3
Virgin Megastore	47 E3

ENTERTAINMENT	(pp205–42)
Au Lapin Agile	28 C2
Corcoran's Clichy	29 A3
Edward & Son	30 C4
Folies Pigalle	31 B4
Jungle Montmartre	32 C3
L'Élysée Montmartre	33 D4

SLEEPING	(pp279–304)
Apart'hotel Citadines Montmartre	48 A3
Comfort Hôtel du Tertre	49 B3
Hôtel Bonséjour	50 B3
Hôtel des Arts	51 C4
Hôtel des Capucines Montmartre	52 B3
Hôtel du Moulin	(see 52)
Hôtel Ibis Sacré Coeur	53 C4
Hôtel Regyns Montmartre	54 C3
Hôtel Utrillo	55 B3
Résidence Pierre & Vacances	56 D4
Timhôtel Montmartre	57 D4
Timhôtel St-Georges	58 C3
Le Village Hostel	59 B4
Villa Royale Pigalle	60 B4

TRANSPORT	(pp332–8)
Funicular to Sacré Coeur	61 D3

INFORMATION	
European Exchange Office	62 C3
Laverie Libre Service	63 B3
Laverie Libre Service	64 C4
Paris Convention & Visitors Bureau Branch	65 C3
Post Office	66 C3
Salon Lavoir Sidéa	67 C3
Travelex	68 B3